MW01091998

New Testament Commentary

New Testament Commentary

Exposition of the

First Epistle to the Corinthians

Simon J. Kistemaker

Baker Books

A Division of Baker Book House Co
Grand Rapids, Michigan 49516

© 1993 by Simon J. Kistemaker

Published by Baker Books
a division of Baker Book House Company
P.O. Box 6287, Grand Rapids, MI 49516-6287

ISBN: 0-8010-5260-2

Fourth printing, July 2002

12 volume set, first available 2002
ISBN 0-8010-2606-7

Printed in the United States of America

Library of Congress Cataloging-in-Publication Data

Hendriksen, William, 1900–82
    New Testament commentary.

    Accompanying Biblical text is author's translation.
    Vols. 14– by Simon J. Kistemaker.
    Includes bibliographical references and indexes.
    Contents: [1] John I-VI — [2] John VII–XII — [etc.] — [18] Exposition of 1 Corinthians.
    1. Bible. N.T.—Commentaries. I. Kistemaker, Simon. II. Bible. N.T. English.
Hendricksen. 1953.
BS2341.H4 1953   225.7'7   54-924
ISBN 0-8010-4114-7 (v. 10)

Scripture translation of the text of I Corinthians is the author's own. Unless otherwise noted, Scripture quotations are from the Holy Bible: New International Version, © copyright 1978, 1984 by the International Bible Society. Used by permission.

Contents

Abbreviations

ASV	American Standard Version
ATANT	*Abhandlungen zur Theologie des Alten und Neuen Testaments*
ATR	*Anglican Theological Review*
AusBRev	*Australian Biblical Revue*
BA	*Biblical Archaeologist*
BAR	*Biblical Archaeology Review*
Bauer	Walter Bauer, W. F. Arndt, F. W. Gingrich, F. W. Danker, *A Greek-English Lexicon of the New Testament*, 2d ed.
BDT	*Baker's Dictionary of Theology*
BEB	*Baker Encyclopedia of the Bible*
BF	British and Foreign Bible Society, *The New Testament*, 2d ed., 1958
Bib	*Biblica*
BibOr	*Bibliotheca Orientalis*
BibRev	*Biblical Review*
BibToday	*Bible Today*
BibTr	*The Bible Translator*
BibZ	*Biblische Zeitschrift*
BJRUL	*Bulletin of John Rylands University Library of Manchester*
B of T	*Banner of Truth*
BS	*Bibliotheca Sacra*
BTB	*Biblical Theological Bulletin*
Cassirer	A New Testament Translation, E. Cassirer
CBQ	*Catholic Biblical Quarterly*
ChrSchRev	*Christian Scholar's Review*
ConcJourn	*Concordia Journal*
ConcThMonth	*Concordia Theological Monthly*
CrisTheolRev	*Criswell Theological Review*
CTJ	*Calvin Theological Journal*
EDNT	*Exegetical Dictionary of the New Testament*
EDT	*Evangelical Dictionary of Theology*
EphThL	*Ephemerides théologicae lovanienses*

EvJ	*Evangelical Journal*
EvQ	*Evangelical Quarterly*
Exp	*The Expositor*
ExpT	*Expository Times*
GNB	Good News Bible
GThJ	*Grace Theological Journal*
HTR	*Harvard Theological Review*
Interp	*Interpretation*
ISBE	*International Standard Bible Encyclopedia*, rev. ed.
JB	Jerusalem Bible
JBL	*Journal of Biblical Literature*
JETS	*Journal of the Evangelical Theological Society*
JQR	*Jewish Quarterly Review*
JRH	*Journal of Religious History*
JSNT	*Journal for the Study of the New Testament*
JSOT	*Journal for the Study of the Old Testament*
JTS	*Journal of Theological Studies*
KJV	King James Version
LCL	Loeb Classical Library edition
Liddell	H. G. Liddell, R. Scott, H. S. Jones, *Greek-English Lexicon*, 9th ed.
LuthQuart	*Lutheran Quarterly*
LXX	Septuagint
Merk	Augustinus Merk, ed., *Novum Testamentum Graece et Latine*, 9th ed.
MLB	The Modern Language Bible
MM	J. H. Moulton, G. Milligan, *The Vocabulary of the Greek Testament*, 1930
Moffatt	The Bible—A New Translation, James Moffatt
MSJ	*The Master's Seminary Journal*
NAB	New American Bible
NASB	New American Standard Bible
NCV	New Century Version (The Everyday Bible)
NEB	New English Bible
NedTTS	*Nederlands theologisch tijdschrift*
Neotest	*Neotestamentica*
Nes-Al	Eberhard Nestle; Kurt Aland, rev.; *Novum Testamentum Graece*, 26th ed.
NIDNTT	*New International Dictionary of New Testament Theology*
NIV	New International Version
NJB	New Jerusalem Bible

NKJV	New King James Version
NovT	*Novum Testamentum*
NRSV	New Revised Standard Version
n. s.	new series
NTS	*New Testament Studies*
Phillips	The New Testament in Modern English, J. B. Phillips
PitPer	*Pittsburgh Perspective*
RB	*Revue biblique*
REB	Revised English Bible
ResScRel	*Recherches de Science Religieuse*
ResQ	*Restoration Quarterly*
RevExp	*Review and Expositor*
RevHistPhilRel	*Revue d'Histoire et de Philosophie Religieuses*
RSV	Revised Standard Version
RTR	*Reformed Theological Review*
RV	Revised Version
SB	H. L. Strack, P. Billerbeck, *Kommentar zum Neuen Testament aus Talmud und Midrasch*
SBL	Society for Biblical Literature
SBT	*Studies in Biblical Theology*
SEB	Simple English Bible
SJT	*Scottish Journal of Theology*
Souter	Alexander Souter, ed., *Novum Testamentum Graece*
SR	*Studies in Religion/Sciences Religieuses*
SWJourTh	*Southwestern Journal of Theology*
Talmud	The Babylonian Talmud
TDNT	*Theological Dictionary of the New Testament*
Thayer	Joseph H. Thayer, *Greek-English Lexicon of the New Testament*
ThEd	*Theological Educator* [New Orleans]
ThF	*Theologische Forschung*
ThLZ	*Theologische Literaturzeitung*
TheolZeit	*Theologische Zeitschrift*
TNT	The New Translation
TR	*The Textus Receptus: The Greek New Testament According to the Majority Text*
TrinityJ	*Trinity Journal*
TynB	*Tyndale Bulletin*
UBS	United Bible Societies *Greek New Testament,* 3d ed.
VigChr	*Vigiliae christianae*
Vogels	H. J. Vogels, ed., *Novum Testamentum Graece et Latine,* 4th ed.
VoxEv	*Vox Evangelica*

VoxRef	*Vox Reformata*
WBC	Word Biblical Commentary
WTJ	*Westminster Theological Journal*
WesThJ	*Wesleyan Theological Journal*
WUNT	*Wissenschaftliche Untersuchungen zum Neuen Testament*
ZNW	*Zeitschrift für die neutestamentliche Wissenschaft*
ZPEB	*Zondervan Pictorial Encyclopedia of the Bible*
ZTK	*Zeitschrift für Theologie und Kirche*

Preface

My predecessor, Dr. William Hendriksen, worked tirelessly on writing commentaries in the New Testament Commentary series. Even when his health began to fail, he still initiated preliminary work for a commentary on I Corinthians. He had written on all the Pauline epistles with the exception of the Corinthian correspondence. His introductory contributions to this intended commentary have been published posthumously, and I have referred to them in both text and footnotes.

Mine is the privilege of placing this volume into the hands of readers. Like the others in the series, this commentary has been composed for the benefit of the pastor and the serious Bible student. Technicalities have been placed in separate sections and footnotes to increase the readability of this book.

The translation of the Greek text is my own. Quotations from the rest of the Old and New Testament are generally taken from the New International Version. Quotations from other versions are clearly marked.

The number of scholarly articles and books that have recently been published on aspects of I Corinthians is indeed phenomenal. In this volume, I have tried to incorporate as many as possible of these current publications and cite them in either the footnotes or the bibliography. Continual research is advancing our understanding of Paul's epistle addressed to the Corinthians in the first century and to us in the last decade of the twentieth century.

Some of the explanations that I present in this volume will not meet universal consensus. This is normal for any commentator who writes on I Corinthians. Even though I differ from other writers, I pay them my genuine respect and sincerely recommend their books and articles to the readers. I trust that in my exposition, I have been faithful to the text of God's Word and have listened carefully to what God through his servant Paul is saying to us.

Simon J. Kistemaker
Easter 1993

Introduction

Outline

A. Corinth
B. Chronology
C. Message
D. Recipients
E. Theology
F. Authenticity
G. Characteristics
H. Text
I. Purpose
J. Outline

A. Corinth

1. Location

Ancient Corinth was located on a broad plain below the towering Acrocorinth, a 1,886-foot-high fortress peak on the Peloponnesian peninsula. The steep ascent of the Acrocorinth made the fortress nearly invincible, and the city itself was relatively safe. From ancient Corinth, the distance to the harbor city of Lechaeum along the Corinthian Gulf was about two miles due north. About seven miles to the east was the port city of Cenchreae along the Saronic Gulf. These two harbors brought to Corinth commerce and wealth. Ships from the west (Italy, Spain, and North Africa) brought their wares to Lechaeum; and ships from the east (Asia Minor, Phoenicia, Palestine, Egypt, and Cyrene) docked at Cenchreae.

Captains and crews were reluctant to sail the two hundred miles around the southern cape (Cape Malea) of the peninsula, where unpredictable storms made shipping extremely treacherous. Loss of ships, cargo, and lives were etched in the memories of ship-owners and sailors. Therefore, they moored in either Lechaeum or Cenchreae. From these harbors, they transported goods from larger ships across the isthmus that links the peninsula to central Greece.

Digging a canal would ease the transport of goods, as Periander (625-583 B.C.) saw; but instead he built a crossing of stone and gave it the name *diolkos*. This word means a movable platform on wheels. Small ships were placed on platforms and dragged from the Saronic Gulf on the east to the Corinthian Gulf on the west, and vice versa. The volume of goods conveyed across the isthmus contributed considerably to the amount of transit taxes Corinth collected.[1]

In antiquity, the Greek king Demetrius and the Roman emperors Julius Caesar and Gaius Caligula intended to dig a canal through the isthmus at its narrowest point (4.5 miles). Nero eventually put the plan to work but soon had to abandon the project for various reasons: finances, a belief that digging a canal was an act of sacrilege, and a theory that the water levels on the two sides of the isthmus differed.[2] Josephus records that Vespasian, the general of the Roman forces in Palestine who had enslaved countless Jews, sent some six thousand Jewish men to

---

1. Jerome Murphy-O'Connor, "The Corinth that Saint Paul Saw," *BA* 47 (1984): 147–59.

2. Suetonius *Life of Apollonius of Tyana* 4.24; Pliny *Natural History* 4.9–11; Jerome Murphy-O'Connor, *St. Paul's Corinth: Texts and Archaeology*, Good News Studies, vol. 6 (Wilmington, Del.: Glazier, 1983), pp. 53, 85.

Corinth to dig through the isthmus in 67.[3] Finally, in the latter part of the nineteenth century (1881–93), French engineers constructed and completed the Corinthian Canal.

2. History

The city of Corinth appears in Homer's *Iliad* and thus dates back to the second millennium before Christ. It influenced the entire peninsula, the isthmus, and parts of central Greece. In the seventh century B.C., Corinth reached the height of its power because of its commercial appeal. Periander boosted Corinth's commercial influence by providing the needed equipment to roll smaller ships across the isthmus. But during the next two centuries, Corinth had to face the rival power of Athens.

During the Peloponnesian War (431–404 B.C.) between Athens and Sparta, Corinth sided with Athens. This war so weakened Athens and Corinth that Philip II of Macedon subjugated Corinth in 338 B.C. His son, Alexander the Great, used Corinth as a commercial center and tourist attraction. After the death of Alexander (323 B.C.), Corinth became the leader among the Greek city-states in the Peloponnesus and the southern part of Greece.

Then in 196 B.C., the Romans conquered Greece and granted Corinth the right to be the leader of the league of cities in the province of Achaia. When the Corinthians revolted fifty years later, the Romans under Lucius Mummius destroyed their city. For a century the city was in ruins, until Julius Caesar restored Corinth in 44 B.C. and rebuilt the two harbors of Lechaeum and Cenchreae. Corinth became a Roman colony that was known as *Colonia Laus Julia Corinthiensis* (the Corinthian colony is Julian praise), that is, this colony honors Julius Caesar. The city prospered again by becoming a trading and commercial center that attracted people from numerous parts of the world.

3. People

As a Roman colony subject to Roman law, Corinth had a government similar to that of the imperial city.[4] The official language was Latin, even though Greek remained the language of the common people. Paul mentions Latin names of people living in Corinth: Tertius, Gaius, and Quartus (Rom. 16:22–23); the Jewish couple Aquila and Priscilla; Titius Justus; Crispus, the Jewish synagogue ruler; and Fortunatus (Acts 18:2, 7; I Cor. 1:14; 16:17). Roman military and civil officials, among whom was Proconsul Gallio (Acts 18:12), resided in Corinth together with a multitude of settlers who were ex-soldiers and freedmen (former slaves) from Rome. There were also merchants, craftsmen, artists, philosophers, teachers, and laborers from many countries bordering the Mediterranean Sea. The city's population included a number of Jews from Israel and elsewhere, native Greeks, displaced persons, and slaves. All these people lived and worked in Corinth or its two

---

3. Josephus *Wars* 3.10.10 [540].
4. Victor Paul Furnish, "Corinth in Paul's Time. What Can Archaeology Tell Us?" *BAR* 14 (1988): 14–27.

harbor cities. They increased the population of Corinth, added to its diversity, and strengthened its economy. The countryside contributed to Corinth's agricultural base, the city itself was a manufacturing center, and the two harbors made Corinth a hub of world trade. In short, Corinth enjoyed international recognition.

4. Religion and Culture

Greek and Roman authors in the centuries before the rise of Christianity often referred to Corinth as the city of fornication and prostitution. The Greeks had coined the term *corinthiazesthai* (literally, "to live a Corinthian life") to describe the city's immorality. Corinth had a dozen or more temples, of which the one dedicated to the goddess of love, Aphrodite, was known in antiquity for its immorality. Strabo writes about Corinth before the Romans destroyed it in 146 B.C. and notes the presence of a thousand prostitutes at the temple of Aphrodite,[5] although the accuracy of this statement has been questioned by many scholars.[6] We surmise that the city of Corinth with its two harbors accommodated a crowd of seafarers, merchants, and soldiers, and was hardly a place known for creditable morals. Paul's explicit exhortations to flee sexual immorality (5:1; 6:9, 15–20; 10:8) leave the distinct impression that promiscuity was not uncommon in that city.

The Corinthians also allowed many diverse religious groups to practice their faith. Besides worshiping Aphrodite, Corinthians worshiped Asclepius, Apollo, and Poseidon. There were also altars and temples for the Greek deities Athena, Hera, and Hermes, and shrines had been erected for the worship of the Egyptian gods Isis and Serapis.[7]

Among the diverse religious groups in Corinth were the Jews. Emperors Julius Caesar and Tiberius had given the Jews freedom to practice their religion as long as they refrained from acts of rebellion against the Roman government. And Emperor Claudius had reaffirmed this imperial edict. The Jews in Corinth had their own synagogue,[8] where they first invited Paul to preach but from which they soon expelled him. Luke relates that Jewish leaders dragged Paul before the judgment seat (*bēma*) of the proconsul Gallio[9] and charged Paul with teaching a religion contrary to the law (Acts 18:12–13). Gallio, knowing the legitimacy of

---

5. Strabo *Geography* 8.6.20.

6. Among others see H. D. Saffrey, "Aphrodite a Corinthe: Réflexions sur Une Idée Reçue," *RB* 92 (1985): 359–74.

7. Refer to Dan P. Cole, "Corinth & Ephesus. Why Did Paul Spend Half His Journeys in These Cities?" *BibRev* 4 (1988): 20–30.

8. Archaeologists have discovered a lintel with the probable inscription "Synagogue of the Hebrews." Although archaeologists ascribe a third- or fourth-century date to this lintel, the presence of a Jewish synagogue in Paul's day is not in question. Consult Richard E. Oster, Jr., "Use, Misuse and Neglect of Archaeological Evidence in Some Modern Works on 1 Corinthians (1 Cor 7,1–5; 8,10; 11,2–16; 12,14–26)," *ZNW* 83 (1992): 52–73.

9. Emperor Augustus had declared Corinth the capital of the province of Achaia, and although this province was under senatorial jurisdiction, at times the emperor appointed proconsuls to administer Roman law. Thus, Emperor Claudius sent Gallio to Corinth to serve as proconsul (presumably from July 51 to June 52).

the Jewish religion, refused to listen to the Jews because their charge had nothing to do with Roman law. For him, the matter was an internal religious issue, not a civil one, and thus he dismissed the charge.

In view of the various religious trends in Corinth, the introduction of Christianity, perceived as a variant of the Jewish faith, was not at all objectionable to the general public. Corinthian Gentiles more readily could accept the Christian faith than the Jewish religion. Paul taught that Gentiles who converted to Christianity did not need to submit to rituals of the Jewish faith that included circumcision. As a result, his teachings infuriated the local synagogue officials, who dragged Paul before Gallio. But after they lost their case at the proconsul's tribunal, Paul and the church continued to preach the gospel without fear of suffering harm (see Acts 18:10). Because the Lord had many people in that city, the church continued to increase. In contrast to the Jews, the Christians met in the homes of their members—at Corinth, in the house of Titius Justus, who lived next door to the synagogue. The Christians founded house churches that in large homes probably included at most fifty persons, in smaller homes perhaps thirty.

One of the highlights in cosmopolitan first-century Corinth was the Isthmian Games. These games were second in importance only to the Olympic Games and were conducted every two years in the spring. The games included foot races, boxing, wrestling, and chariot racing (compare 9:24–27).[10] During his eighteen months in Corinth, Paul must have been a spectator at the Isthmian Games in the spring of 51. We assume that Paul plied his trade as a tentmaker during these events and, becoming all things to all men, proclaimed the gospel of salvation (see 9:22, 27).

5. Significance

Paul chose to preach the gospel in provincial capitals, for example, Thessalonica in Macedonia and Corinth in Achaia. He considered capitals to be strategic centers where, in some cases, the traffic of the land met the traffic of the sea. From Corinth, the gospel ultimately spread to the surrounding rural villages and cities and to many parts of the Mediterranean world.

More than to any other church, Paul gave his talents, time, and tears to the Corinthian congregation. The members received three visits (II Cor. 13:1), sane counsel, lengthy letters, and perpetual prayer. They presented several practical problems that beset the fledgling Corinthian congregation. As the father of this particular church (4:15), Paul told the believers how to cope with all their difficulties. Yet his words are not limited to certain people or to a given era; Paul wrote advice for the church universal. The theological message he sets forth applies to situations that are present in countless congregations throughout the world. In fact, his teachings on marriage, divorce, separation, virgins, and wid-

---

10. Oscar Broneer, "The Apostle Paul and the Isthmian Games," *BA* 25 (1962): 2–31; and "Paul and Pagan Cults at Isthmia," *HTR* 64 (1971): 169–87.

ows (chap. 7) touch everyone. Consequently, Paul's epistle is addressed to every believer of any age or any century in all parts of the world.[11]

B. Chronology

1. Proconsul Gallio

Luke reveals that Paul spent a year and a half in Corinth during his initial visit (Acts 18:11). In context, he relates that Paul's visit to Corinth occurred during the time Gallio served as proconsul of Achaia (Acts 18:12). We know that the term limit for a proconsul was one year, from the first day of July to the last day of June. Archaeologists have discovered inscriptions near Delphi that, in one instance, mention the name *Gallio* as proconsul of Achaia in connection with Claudius; the inscription specifies the date as the twelfth year of the reign of Emperor Claudius and the twenty-sixth time that he was proclaimed emperor. Since Claudius commenced his first administrative year on the twenty-fifth of January 41, he began his twelfth year on the twenty-fifth of January 52. By that time, Gallio had served almost seven months of his proconsulship in Corinth (July 51 to June 52). After his appearance in Gallio's court, Paul remained in Corinth for many days (Acts 18:18) and then departed for Ephesus. We conclude that the date for Gallio's proconsulship is firm, so that we can say with a degree of certainty that Paul founded the Corinthian church in the years 50–52.

2. Emperor Claudius

Another reference to chronology appears in Acts 18:2, where Luke writes that Aquila and his wife, Priscilla, had recently come from Italy because Emperor Claudius (41–54) had evicted all the Jews from Rome. Roman historiographers provide further detail concerning the expulsion of the Jews. Suetonius records that Claudius "expelled the Jews because they were continually rioting at the instigation of Chrestus."[12] This historian apparently was unfamiliar with the Greek name *Christus* (the anointed one) but knew the more common name *Chrestos* (the benevolent one). Although Suetonius thought that Chrestos personally instigated the riots, we surmise that the Jews in Rome clashed with the followers of Christ. Not knowing the difference between Judaism and Christianity, Claudius ordered all the Jews banished from the imperial city. Among those who left were Aquila and Priscilla, who soon afterward arrived in Corinth.

Dio Cassius states that Emperor Claudius in his first year in office did not drive the Jews from the city but prohibited them from holding meetings.[13] This ban took place in 41. Fifth-century Christian historian Paulus Orosius writes that Josephus reports Claudius's eviction of the Jews in the ninth year of the emperor's reign, namely, 49; and he mentions that Suetonius wrote about the Jews be-

---

11. Consult Larry McGraw, "The City of Corinth," *SWJourTh* 32 (1989): 5–10.

12. *Judaeos impulsore Chresto assidue tumultuantes expulit;* Suetonius *Claudius* 25.4. Suetonius provides no date for the expulsion of the Jews.

13. Dio Cassius *Roman History* 60.6.6.

ing expelled because of the disturbances instigated by Chrestus.[14] The problem is that in all the writings of Josephus we are unable to find wording that is similar to this statement. Consequently, some scholars doubt the accuracy of Orosius's account and instead opt for the date of Dio Cassius with reference to Claudius limiting the freedom of the Jews in Rome.[15] They prefer this date to the one provided by Orosius.

Scholars who adopt Dio Cassius's earlier date raise their own set of questions relating to the chronology of Paul's visits to Corinth. For instance, if Paul first visited Corinth in 41, when Claudius issued his decree concerning the Jews in Rome, he could not have returned to Corinth until the early fifties while Gallio was there. Where did Paul go in the meantime? In an attempt to solve this chronological problem, scholars credit Luke with a vague memory and a lack of historical perception.[16] But we have difficulties accepting these suggestions. Rather, we see 49 as the date of the expulsion; it immediately precedes the first time Paul came to Corinth and fits with the sequence of Gallio's arrival in 51.[17]

3. King Aretas

Paul provides an interesting historical note in II Corinthians. He relates that the governor under King Aretas had the city of Damascus guarded to capture him, but that he escaped under cover of darkness when fellow Christians lowered him in a basket from a window in the wall (11:32–33). Aretas IV ruled as king of the Nabateans from 9 B.C. to A.D. 39 or 40. After emperor Tiberius died on 16 March 37, his successor, Gaius Caligula, granted Aretas control of Damascus as a client king. Thus Paul's escape from that city occurred after Aretas exerted his influence over Damascus in 37 and before his death two years later.[18]

4. Paul and Barnabas

On arriving in Jerusalem after an absence of three years, Paul met with Peter and James for fifteen days (Gal. 1:18–19). The believers, fearing for Paul's life, took him to Caesarea and put him aboard a ship bound for Tarsus (Acts 9:29–30). Paul founded churches in Cilicia and Syria (Acts 15:41; Gal. 1:21) and then, invited by Barnabas, went to Antioch where he taught for one year (Acts 11:25–26). During this time Paul and Barnabas traveled to Judea to provide relief for the believers suffering from the famine in 44 or 45 (Acts 11:29–30). The first missionary journey probably took place from 46 to 48, during which time Paul and Barnabas preached the gospel on the island of Cyprus and in Pisidian Antioch, Iconium,

14. Paulus Orosius, *The Seven Books of History Against the Pagans*, Fathers of the Church series, trans. Roy J. Deferrari (Washington, D.C.: Catholic University Press, 1964), p. 297.

15. E.g., Gerd Luedemann, *Paul, Apostle to the Gentiles: Studies in Chronology* (Philadelphia: Fortress, 1984), pp. 164–71; Murphy-O'Connor, *St. Paul's Corinth*, pp. 129–40.

16. Murphy-O'Connor, *St. Paul's Corinth*, p. 140; Luedemann, *Paul, Apostle to the Gentiles*, p. 170.

17. Consult Robert Jewett, *A Chronology of Paul's Life* (Philadelphia: Fortress, 1979), pp. 36–38; E. M. Smallwood, *The Jews under Roman Rule* (Leiden: Brill, 1976), pp. 210–16.

18. Jewett, *Chronology*, pp. 30–33; George Ogg, *The Chronology of the Life of Paul* (London: Epworth, 1968), pp. 22–23; see also the American title *The Odyssey of Paul* (Old Tappan, N.J.: Revell, 1968).

Lystra, and Derbe (Acts 13–14). After their return to Antioch, the church commissioned them to attend the Jerusalem Council (Acts 15). Paul writes that after fourteen years he went up to Jerusalem (Gal. 2:1). If we take this reference to mean fourteen years after his conversion in 35, we date the Jerusalem Council at 49.[19]

5. Corinthian Church

Following the meeting in Jerusalem, Paul commenced his second missionary journey by visiting the churches in Asia Minor (Acts 15:36–16:5). He crossed the Aegean Sea and traveled to Philippi, Thessalonica, Berea, and Athens (Acts 16:8–17:33). We assume that Paul arrived in Corinth in the autumn of 50 and stayed there for eighteen months (Acts 18:11).

Paul departed from Corinth in the spring of 52, sailed with Aquila and Priscilla to Ephesus, where he left them, continued his voyage to Caesarea, and traveled to Jerusalem and Antioch (Acts 18:18–22). He then journeyed through Asia Minor, strengthened the churches, and arrived in Ephesus probably in the autumn of 52 (Acts 18:23; 19:1). While teaching successively in the synagogue and the lecture hall of Tyrannus and spreading the word of the Lord, he stayed in Ephesus for three years (Acts 19:8, 20; 20:31). We are unable to pinpoint an exact time for the composition of I Corinthians, but 55 is an approximate date.[20]

In a sense, I Corinthians was a sequel to an earlier epistle Paul had written but which is no longer extant. He had sent the Corinthians a letter to tell them not to associate with immoral people (5:9). Apparently he failed to communicate his message, a fact that prompted the Corinthians to write a response (see 7:1). Paul answered the letter he had received from the church in Corinth and composed what we now call I Corinthians. After he had sent this epistle, Paul went to Corinth and paid the church a "painful visit" and followed this up with a "sorrowful letter" (II Cor. 2:1, 3–4). The visit and the sending of this letter probably took place in 55. In the ensuing year Paul composed II Corinthians.

6. Governors Felix and Festus

Having left Ephesus, strengthening the churches in Macedonia and traveling as far as Illyricum (Rom. 15:19), Paul went to Corinth to spend the winter there (I Cor. 16:6). During the winter of 57, he composed his epistle to the Romans. Following an extended journey on foot through Macedonia and a voyage to Caesarea, he arrived in Jerusalem for the celebration of Pentecost that year (Acts 20:16; 21:17). In Jerusalem Paul was arrested and sent to the Roman governor Felix in Caesarea. All indications are that Felix had been in office for a number of years when he presided over Paul's trial in Caesarea (Acts 24:2, 10). During

19. The reference "fourteen years" can either include or exclude the "three years" (Gal. 1:18) and allows for differences.
20. S. Dockx is of the opinion that Paul composed the letter in the first three months of 54. See his "Chronologie Paulinienne de l'Année de la Grande Collecte," *RB* 81 (1974): 183–95. Similarly, consult Graydon F. Snyder, *First Corinthians: A Faith Community Commentary* (Macon, Ga.: Mercer University Press, 1992), p. 8.

the last two years of his administration, he kept Paul in prison and handed him over to Porcius Festus. We have no firm date on the accession of Festus's governorship, but that of Felix probably lasted from 52 to 59. With Agrippa II, who was in the tenth year of his reign, Festus listened to Paul. Agrippa began to rule in March of the year 50, which puts the meeting with Paul in the summer of 59.[21]

The indirect references in Acts and in Paul's epistles to his life and ministry provide a chronology from the time of his conversion near Damascus to his voyage to Rome and subsequent release. Within that chronology, we can confidently date Paul's first visit to Corinth from 50 to 52 and infer that he wrote I Corinthians within three years after his departure from Corinth.

C. Message

The epistle was occasioned by a report brought to Paul by members of Chloe's household (1:11), by a letter from the Corinthians (7:1), and by the arrival of a delegation from the church in Corinth (16:17). The report from Chloe's household concerned the factions that had sprung up in Corinth and were undermining the unity of the church. Paul also had heard about incest (5:1), lawsuits (6:1–8), and immorality (6:9–20). The letter he received from Corinth asked questions about marriage (7:1), virgins (7:25), food sacrificed to idols (8:1), spiritual gifts (12:1), the collection for the saints in Jerusalem (16:1), and Apollos (16:12). The three-man delegation from the Corinthian church filled in a number of details (16:17).

1. Leadership Problems

The congregation at Corinth was near to the heart of Paul: he writes that in Christ Jesus he became their spiritual father through the gospel (4:15). Undoubtedly, Paul's relatively short period of ministry in the Corinthian church together with the variety in ethnic background and economic status of its membership gave rise to numerous problems. There were Jewish Christians who knew the Old Testament Scriptures and Gentile God-fearers who had attended the worship services in the local synagogue; affluent citizens and poverty-stricken slaves. The congregation included people of various nationalities and many languages. We can safely say that, because of its diversity, the Corinthian church did not excel in stability.

When a spirit of divisiveness entered the Corinthian church, it drove the people apart and replaced unity with discord. When Paul heard about the factions in the Corinthian congregation, he addressed the problem as the first item on his list. He was told that the church was divided into four groups, and that each followed a leader: Paul, Apollos, Cephas, or Christ. In the first verse on this subject, he appeals to the Corinthians in the name of the Lord Jesus Christ to agree with one another,

---

21. Josephus *War* 2.14.4 [284]. See also David L. Jones, "Luke's Unique Interest in Historical Chronology," in *Society of Biblical Literature 1989 Seminar Papers*, ed. David J. Lull (Atlanta: Scholars, 1989), pp. 378–87.

to avoid divisions, and to be united in mind and thought (1:10). The rhetorical question, "Is Christ divided?" (1:13), elicits a negative answer that affirms the unity of Christ's church. Who are Paul and Apollos? The answer is, mere servants to whom the Lord assigned the task of bringing people to faith in him (3:5). They are charged with the task of proclaiming and teaching God's revelation to the people, with the result that arrogance and factionalism are forbidden. Every member of the Corinthian church must learn what the Scriptures have to say and, by adopting a spirit of meekness, must prevent divisions in the church (4:6).

In view of Paul's three-year absence from the Corinthian church (52 to 55), some of its leaders had become arrogant; they opposed and challenged the leadership of Paul and his fellow workers (4:18–21; 9:1–6; 16:10–12). These leaders claimed to be wise and philosophically informed; undoubtedly they were influenced by the Greek philosophy of their day (compare 1:20–25; 2:1–5, 12–14; 3:18–22; 12:3). They were not Gnostics[22] but opponents of Paul's efforts to teach and apply Christ's gospel. Paul calls them back to God's revelation and points out that Christ is the power and wisdom of God (1:24, 30). He applies divine revelation to their daily lives that are troubled by moral and social ills.

2. Moral and Social Problems

Within the Corinthian community, a man had sexual relations with his father's wife—an evil that did not happen even among the Gentiles (5:1). Paul held the entire church at Corinth responsible for this sin and rebuked its members for not being filled with grief.[23] He instructed the Corinthians to deliver this man to Satan and to expel him from the community (5:5, 13). Paul ordered the removal of this moral decay within the church; this blot on the church would impair its effectiveness in Corinth. He expected the believers to be shining examples of moral purity within an immoral society. For this reason, Paul commanded the Corinthians not to associate with sexually immoral people but to flee sexual immorality (5:9; 6:9–11, 18).

Immorality includes the social ill of Christians bringing litigious cases before a Gentile judge (6:1). Paul repeatedly reminded the Corinthians of his earlier teachings on immorality and asked them whether they remembered his admonitions. With respect to court cases, he pointedly counseled them to find a wise man from their midst to adjudicate differences through mediation. Applying Christ's law to love one another, he asked them to choose rather to be wronged and cheated than to win a court case that inevitably was detrimental to their neighbor (6:7–8).

---

22. Walter Schmithals sees pure Christian Gnosticism in Corinth. See *Gnosticism in Corinth: An Investigation of the Letters to the Corinthians*, trans. John E. Steely (Nashville and New York: Abingdon, 1971), p. 138. However, not the middle but the end of the first century is known for an embryonic beginning of Gnosticism in the Christian church.

23. Consult Brian S. Rosner, "'οὐχὶ μᾶλλον ἐπενθήσατε': Corporate Responsibility in 1 Corinthians 5," *NTS* 38 (1992): 470–73; F. S. Malan, "The Use of the Old Testament in 1 Corinthians," *Neotest* 14 (1981): 134–66.

Other social problems in the Corinthian community were those pertaining to married couples, divorced or separated individuals, unmarried people, and widows. The church sent a letter to Paul in which the members sought his advice on marital issues. He met their request to the full by presenting an extensive discussion on a subject of universal interest (chap. 7). Indeed, in all of Scripture no one has set forth a more detailed discussion on marital issues than Paul did in I Corinthians 7. Paul based his teaching on the institution of holy matrimony in Paradise and on Jesus' pronouncement not to break marriage vows (Gen. 2:24; Matt. 19:4–6).

3. Cultural and Religious Problems

The next issue on which the Corinthians sought advice was their response to a Gentile practice: eating meat sacrificed to an idol (8:1). Those believers with strong consciences had no qualms about eating meat in an idol's temple because they regarded the idol to be nothing at all and the meat common food. They exercised Christian freedom in buying such meat at the meat market. But Paul called attention to the conscience of the weaker brother, the responsibility of the strong Christian to care for his fellow believer, and the unity of the church.

4. Church Problems

The next four chapters (11–14) relate to questions pertaining to worship services: praying and prophesying, the celebration of the Lord's Supper, spiritual gifts, the meaning of love, prophesying and speaking in tongues, and orderly worship. The problems concerning spiritual gifts were so acute that the letter the Corinthians sent to Paul asked him to explain the matter of spiritual gifts. The matter itself precedes and follows the eloquent chapter on love (13) that sets the tone for proper conduct at worship.

5. Doctrinal Problems

There are no indications that the readers asked Paul for advice on the doctrine of the resurrection. But he had heard that some members of the Corinthian church denied that there was a resurrection (15:12). In the opening remarks of his epistle, Paul wrote about the expectation of Jesus' return (1:8). This is telling because of Paul's lengthy discourse on the physical resurrection of the body in 15:12–58 and his discussion on eschatology. Paul writes that the Corinthians were in danger of being led astray by erroneous teachings on Christ's resurrection (15:12, 33–34). At the beginning and the end of his epistle, Paul encourages his readers to anticipate Christ's return.

D. Recipients

By carefully reading Paul's letter, we are able to learn something about its readers. From the historical account in Acts we know that Jews accepted the gospel and left the local synagogue. Gentile worshipers of Israel's God, known as God-fearers, also put their faith in Jesus Christ and were baptized (Acts 18:7–8).

Introduction

1. Jews and God-fearers

Paul's use of the Old Testament in his epistle reveals that he expected many readers to have a basic knowledge of the Scriptures, for he cites passages from a number of Old Testament books. He reveals his own partiality for quoting more from one book than another. To be precise, almost one-third of the total number of his direct quotations are from the prophecy of Isaiah.[24] In addition to Paul's affinity to Isaiah, he cites from Genesis, Exodus, Deuteronomy, Job, Psalms, Jeremiah, and Hosea. Concisely, for I Corinthians he relies primarily on the books of Moses and the prophecy of Isaiah.

Did the Corinthian believers readily understand the context, setting, and application of these Old Testament quotations in Paul's discourse? Jewish Christians had been taught the Scriptures from childhood on, and so were able to understand the context of particular quotes and their application. For instance, from Isaiah 22:13 Paul cites the words "Let us eat and drink, for tomorrow we die" (15:32). Jewish Christians, familiar with the history of Israel, immediately understood the historical significance of these words. They knew that Paul alluded to the nonchalant attitude of the people in Jerusalem when a foreign army was poised to devastate their country. Instead of asking God for help, these Israelites slaughtered cattle, ate the meat, drank wine, and indulged in revelry. The people in Jerusalem failed to repent, deliberately turned away from God, and spent their time carousing.

Many of the Corinthian God-fearers had gained knowledge of the Scriptures in the local synagogue and in the church. They too were able to fathom the depth of Paul's teachings and needed no further explanation.

2. Converts

Other people were converts to the faith when Paul began his ministry in Corinth. We should keep in mind that the time he spent there was only eighteen months, for Paul left in 52. When he composed I Corinthians three years later, he could not expect every member of the Corinthian church to have a thorough knowledge and understanding of the Scriptures. Many of the ecclesiastical and social problems in that church stemmed from an insufficient discernment and application of God's Word.

Paul observes that the conduct of some Corinthian believers is identical to that of worldly people, indeed to such a degree that the difference between them is negligible (3:3). He rebukes their behavior that is marked by strife, envy, immorality, and licentiousness; by their conduct they are desecrating God's temple. Paul reminds them that because God's Spirit dwells within them, their bodies are God's temple. And if anyone destroys this temple, God will destroy him (3:16–17).

With the Greek expression *pneumatikoi*, is Paul opposing people who call themselves spiritual? If this were true, we would expect that this Greek term in the mas-

---

24. This proclivity to quote from Isaiah is also evident in Romans, where Paul quotes this prophet eighteen times out of a total of sixty Old Testament passages.

culine plural would appear frequently throughout I Corinthians. This is hardly the case. Paul writes the word *spiritual* twelve times,[25] but nine of the occurrences are in the neuter gender and refer to spiritual truths, things, and bodies. When he does write the masculine form in either the singular or plural (2:15; 3:1; 14:37), he contrasts the term explicitly or implicitly with people who are either unspiritual or babes in Christ. Spiritual people are filled with the Holy Spirit, make wise judgments, are not sensual or worldly, acknowledge and obey the Lord's command.

We notice that this letter contains a number of slogans that arrogant people in Corinth used. Paul interacts with these members of the church and engages in a dialogue with them by quoting their slogans. They applied the slogan "All things are permissible to me" (6:12; 10:23) to their daily conduct. They reveled in sexual and social sins and allowed such conduct under the guise of freedom in Christ. Instead of serving their Lord and Savior, they gratified their own sinful desires. Paul takes them to task with counter statements that void the essence of their slogans. They said that all things are permissible, but Paul states that all things are not profitable. They trumpeted the lively motto, "Food is for the stomach and the stomach is for food," but Paul replies, "God will destroy both of them" (6:12–13).[26] They sought sexual gratification, but Paul points out that sexual immorality is sinning against one's own body. Once more he reminds the Corinthians that the believer's body is a temple of the Holy Spirit (6:19; see 3:16–17). Paul confronts these arrogant people who wanted to exploit Christian liberty to the fullest extent. He candidly tells them that they have become haughty in speech and need correction (4:18–21).

Many of these people were recent converts who needed nurture in the Christian faith. Of course, Jews and God-fearers were also recent converts to Christianity and had to be instructed in the gospel. The congregation at Corinth consisted of people from all levels of society and represented many nationalities. The members of the congregation demonstrated a lack of homogeneity and unity as long as they continued sinful practices that belonged to their own cultures.

3. Romans

After the reconstruction of Corinth in 44 B.C., the city became a Roman colony that was settled by innumerable people from the military or the administrative corps and by released slaves. Roman culture influenced Corinthian society and some of its customs became part of daily life.

For example, Paul writes about headcoverings of men and women at worship: a man should not have his head covered when he prays or prophesies, but a woman who prays or prophesies should cover her head (11:4–5, 13). He has in mind the custom of the Romans who in Italy and the colonies covered their heads in private and public devotions. When they offered sacrifices, prayed, or prophesied, they pulled their togas forward over their heads. Paul is trying to tell the

---

25. I Cor. 2:13, 15; 3:1; 9:11; 10:3, 4; 12:1; 14:1, 37; 15:44 [twice], 46.
26. See Roger L. Omanson, "Acknowledging Paul's Quotations," *BibTr* 43 (1992): 201–13.

Corinthian Christians that he wanted them to be distinctly separate from these Roman customs and to adopt a Christian lifestyle.[27]

4. Leaders

The Corinthian congregation was still in its developmental stage when apostles (Paul, Peter) and apostolic helpers (Apollos, Timothy, Silas, Titus) ministered to the needs of the church. Some of the leaders in the church were Stephanas and his two friends Fortunatus and Achaicus. The former rulers of the Corinthian synagogue, Crispus and Sosthenes, also were considered leaders. Paul refrains from using the term *elder*, but he asks the members to submit to those people who have dedicated themselves to the service of the church (16:15–16). Already during his first missionary journey, Paul appointed elders in every congregation he had founded (Acts 14:23). In later years, he addressed the church at Philippi "together with the overseers and deacons" (Phil. 1:1). And he instructed Titus to appoint elders in every town on the island of Crete (Titus 1:5; see also I Tim. 3:1–7). Conversely, the Corinthian congregation reveals a beginning stage of leadership positions.[28]

5. Opponents

In many places in his epistle, Paul demonstrates that he encountered opponents to his ministry and teaching. These adversaries did not necessarily present a united front, for they appear to have championed individual concerns. Paul notes that Jews demand miraculous signs and Greeks seek wisdom (1:22). He had to confront members who held incorrect views of the Christian faith, among whom were those who taught that there is no resurrection (15:12). Influenced by Greek philosophy, some denied the resurrection altogether. Others were enamored with the oratory of Greek Sophists who attracted numerous listeners. When Paul arrived in Corinth after his depressing experience at the Areopagus of Athens (Acts 17:16–34), he declared that he did not come to the Corinthians "with incomparable eloquence or surpassing wisdom" (2:1). The Sophists in Athens thought that they possessed the treasures of wisdom, and their followers attempted to imitate them. Paul did not have the gift of eloquent speech that Apollos possessed (compare II Cor. 10:10; 11:6); consequently Apollos was admired and Paul despised by some Corinthians.[29] Paul mentions Apollos seven times in this epistle, always in appreciation of his fellow worker (1:12; 3:4, 5, 6, 22; 4:6; 16:12).

E. Theology

For writers of the New Testament, the Scriptures of the Old Testament were a basic source of information. The Evangelists, especially Matthew, show that

---

27. Oster, "Use, Misuse and Neglect," pp. 67–69.
28. Compare Andrew D. Clarke, "Secular and Christian Leadership in Corinth," *TynB* 43 (1992): 395–98.
29. Consult Bruce W. Winter, "Are Philo and Paul Among the Sophists? A Hellenistic Jewish and a Christian Response to a First Century Movement," Ph.D. diss., Macquarie University, 1988.

Jesus relied exclusively on the Scriptures for his teaching. With the Old Testament in hand, the writer of the Epistle to the Hebrews teaches the superiority of Christ and the doctrine of the priesthood. Throughout his Corinthian epistles, Paul supports his teaching with quotes from the Old Testament Scriptures and even with a word of Jesus.

For instance, Paul concludes his instructions concerning the incestuous man by quoting from the Greek text of Deuteronomy 17:7, "Expel the evil man from among you" (5:13). He denounces sexual immorality with a citation from the institution of marriage in paradise (Gen. 2:24; I Cor. 6:16). His discussion on divorce begins with the teachings of Jesus that are recorded in the Gospels.[30] Jesus also refers to the institution of marriage (Gen. 2:24), to which he adds his own teaching: "What God has joined together, let no man separate" (Matt. 19:6). Paul puts this saying in his own words and writes, "A wife must not separate from her husband" (7:10). The examples taken from chapters 5–7 reveal that Paul relied on the Scriptures for instructing the readers in social and sexual morality.[31]

The Scriptures are for Paul the basis of his theology. Not only does he quote Old Testament passages but he alludes to them by presenting verbal parallels everywhere in his two Corinthian epistles. The allusions and verbal parallels are predominantly from the books of Moses,[32] the Psalms and Proverbs, and Isaiah. The Corinthian correspondence is permeated with direct and indirect references to the Old Testament Scriptures.

Paul presents God as Father, the Christ, and the Holy Spirit. He discusses the tenets of man's sin, salvation and sanctification, and God's sovereignty. Further, the doctrine of the church both at worship and in life and the teaching of the resurrection are part of Paul's theology.

1. God

Although Paul repeatedly mentions the name of Christ Jesus, he presents him in relation to God. Thus, Paul is an apostle of Christ Jesus but through the will of God (1:1); the salutation is first from God the Father and second from the Lord Jesus Christ (1:3). Paul expresses thanks to God on behalf of the Corinthians (1:4), whom God called into his fellowship (1:9). Through the message of the cross and Christ, God is the source of power and wisdom (1:18–25). God chooses the weak, the foolish, and the lowly things of the world so that they can boast in the Lord (1:26–31). God reveals his secret wisdom to his people, and he sends his Holy Spirit to make them understand and discern the deep things of God (2:10–15). God causes the increase in the church through his servants; the membership of the church is described as his field, building, and temple (3:5–17).

---

30. Matt. 5:32; 19:3–9; Mark 10:2–12; Luke 16:18.

31. Brian S. Rosner, "'Written for Our Instruction,'" *TynB* 43 (1992): 399–401.

32. Genesis, twelve occurrences; Exodus, twenty-one; Leviticus, three; Numbers, fourteen; and Deuteronomy, twenty.

For Paul, the kingdom belongs to God. He mentions the concept *kingdom* five times in his epistle (4:20; 6:9, 10; 15:24, 50). Christ Jesus delivers the kingdom to God the Father at the consummation (15:24). The reference to 4:20 speaks of the present power of God's kingdom, but the rest of the passages in this epistle relate to future blessings of the coming kingdom. God's people will inherit the coming kingdom together with Christ in glory.[33]

The Jewish creed "Hear, O Israel: The LORD our God, the LORD is one" (Deut. 6:4) appears in Paul's statement, "For us there is one God the Father" (8:6). He is both the Creator and the fulfillment of all things. Paul's designation *Father* indicates that God the Father and the Son Jesus Christ are one. Through Christ Jesus, God is also Father of his people (1:3). Moreover, in the Old Testament God is Lord, but in the New Testament Christ has that title. With other New Testament writers, Paul blurs the distinction between the lordship of God and of Christ; God accomplishes all things through his Son Jesus Christ. Here are a few examples in which Paul identifies these two Persons:

Old Testament	*New Testament*
the mind of the Lord	the mind of Christ
the day of the Lord	the day of our Lord Jesus
the name of the Lord	the name of our Lord Jesus
the will of God	the will of the Lord

Paul identifies the divinity of Jesus Christ with God the Father, because of his conversion experience near Damascus where he met the risen Christ.[34] In the church, God is at work in all the members of Christ's body: he arranges its parts, combines its members, and appoints its leaders (12:18, 24, 28 respectively). And last, God is a God of order and of peace (14:33).

2. Christ

The reader of First Corinthians is struck by the repetitious use of the full or partial phrase *our Lord Jesus Christ.* Paul stresses the truth that Christ Jesus is both Son of God and Lord of his people (1:2, 9). For Paul and the recipients of his epistle, Jesus Christ is the central figure in the entire epistle: believers are sanctified in his name, call on his name, receive his grace, and are enriched. Jesus Christ commissioned Paul to preach the gospel (1:17), revealed to him the formulary of the Lord's Supper (11:23–25), and passed on the content of the gospel (15:3–5). This gospel is expressed in various terms: the message of the cross (1:18), preaching the crucified Christ (1:23), and the testimony about God (2:1). The proclamation of Christ's resurrection is of paramount importance

---

33. Herman N. Ridderbos, *Paul: An Outline of His Theology*, trans. John Richard de Witt (Grand Rapids: Eerdmans, 1975), p. 203. Elsewhere in his epistles, Paul ascribes the kingdom to Christ and God (Eph. 5:5), and to the beloved Son of God (Col. 1:13).

34. Gordon D. Fee, "Toward a Theology of 1 Corinthians," in *Society of Biblical Literature 1989 Seminar Papers*, ed. David J. Lull (Atlanta: Scholars, 1989), p. 271.

(15:14); and believers celebrating the Holy Supper proclaim the Lord's death until he comes (11:26).[35]

Jesus Christ is the true Passover lamb that has been slain as a sacrifice for his people (5:7). As the ultimate sacrifice for the people of God he set his people free from sin and guilt (see Isa. 53:6; John 1:29; Heb. 9:26). By putting the blood of the Passover lamb on their doorposts, the Israelites in Egypt were kept safe from the destructive power of the angel of death (Exod. 12:7, 13). Similarly, through his Passover blood shed at Calvary, Christ saves his people from experiencing eternal death. Partaking of the communion cup, believers hear Jesus' words "This cup is a new covenant in my blood" (11:25) and know that he, as the supreme sacrifice, shed his blood for them. Thus, they gratefully confess the teaching of the gospel that Christ died for their sins (15:3). They are delivered from the burden of sin and death and have been granted eternal life through Jesus' death on the cross. As guests at the Lord's table they celebrate the spiritual feast of Passover.

The price Jesus paid for redeeming his people was his sacrifice on the cross. Paul writes twice to the Corinthians, "You were bought with a price" (6:20; 7:23) as a reminder that their redemption was accomplished through Christ's death. In various parts of his epistle, Paul refers to the atoning work of Christ: his death on the cross (1:23; 2:2); through the name of the Lord Jesus Christ and the Spirit of God the Corinthians have been washed, sanctified, and justified (6:11); and they ought not to destroy a brother for whom Christ died (8:11). Further, Christ is always near to his people, as Paul indicates with a reference to the spiritual presence of Christ during the forty-year journey of the Israelites in the desert (10:4). As Christ was with his people in the wilderness, so he is with the church today until the end of the age (Matt. 28:20).

The Son has been commissioned to do the will of God the Father. Through the Lord Jesus Christ all things came into being and through him his people live (8:6). Jesus Christ is their Creator and their source of life. But as we belong to Christ, Christ belongs to God (3:23). Paul writes that the head of the woman is the man, the head of every man is Christ, and the head of Christ is God (11:3). The matter of subordination also appears elsewhere (15:28). Even though all things have been placed in subjection to Christ Jesus, Christ is subject to God the Father. Hence, we observe an orderly succession: we receive everything from the Son, who in turn receives all things from God the Father, "so that God may be all in all."

Jesus' word is definitive in regard to marital separation (7:10), preachers receiving their income from the gospel (9:14), and the impossibility of serving both the Lord and demons (10:21; compare Matt. 6:24; Luke 16:13). Also, the Lord disciplines his people in the sense of judging them (11:32; and see 4:4). Last, what Paul has written to the Corinthians is the same as the Lord's command (14:37).

Paul exhorts the Corinthians to imitate him, who in Christ Jesus became their spiritual father (4:15). They are to pattern themselves after him as he is pattern-

---

35. Consult Victor P. Furnish, "Theology in 1 Corinthians: Initial Soundings," in *Society of Biblical Literature 1989 Seminar Papers*, ed. David J. Lull (Atlanta: Scholars, 1989), p. 260.

ing himself after Christ (11:1). The hearers of Christ's gospel (15:3–5) must serve their Lord because he has lavished on them spiritual gifts (1:7). On the basis of their salvation, they have been enriched in every way. Chiefly they are Christ's body and individually part of it (12:12, 20, 27). Although they eagerly await his return, they know that when he comes God will transform all those who belong to him in the twinkling of an eye (15.22–23, 51–52). Through Christ, God redeems his people, grants them the gift of immortality, and gives them victory (15:54–57). Finally, faith in Jesus Christ brings about the union of Christ and his people which guarantees their resurrection in the same sense as Christ was physically raised from the dead. "This final redemption of the body is part of the supreme triumph of the Incarnate Son."[36]

3. Holy Spirit

With his references to the Spirit of God, Paul predominantly ascribes an instrumental role to the third Person of the Trinity. More than half of these references portray the Spirit as the agent from whom, by whom, or through whom something is given, done, or revealed. The rest of the passages speak about the Holy Spirit's existence and power. Let us now examine these passages.

First, Paul stresses the work of the Spirit in chapters 2 and 12.[37] In these chapters, he discusses God's Spirit revealing deep spiritual truths and granting gifts of grace to the believers. The preaching of the gospel takes place only through the effective work of God's Spirit. Paul reports that he did not come to the Corinthians "with incomparable eloquence or surpassing wisdom" (2:1). Certainly not. He came not with persuasive words of wisdom but as a demonstration of the Spirit's power (2:4). Receiving his power from the Spirit, Paul placed the proclamation of the gospel on a higher plane than that of human wisdom.[38]

Next, God possesses secret wisdom which he reveals to his people through his Spirit (2:7, 10). Only God's Spirit is able to understand and reveal the deep things of God. These deep things are explored and interpreted by the Spirit, who knows God's thoughts (2:10, 12). The Spirit teaches the believers spiritual truths in spiritual words, which the man without the presence of the Spirit is unable to understand and therefore rejects (2:13–14).

Third, the close connection between God and the Spirit is evident, not only in identifying the Spirit as belonging to God but also as coming from him. This is evident especially in Paul's assertion that the believers' physical bodies are the temple of God's Spirit (3:16). Says Paul, "Your body is the temple of the Holy Spirit within you, whom you have from God" (6:19). That is, the sanctifying presence of the Holy Spirit within the believers indicates that their physical bodies

---

36. R. St. John Parry, *The First Epistle of Paul the Apostle to the Corinthians*, Cambridge Greek Testament for Schools and Colleges (Cambridge: Cambridge University Press, 1937), p. lvi.

37. Out of a total of eighteen references to the Spirit in this epistle, seven occur in chapter 2, seven in chapter 12, two in chapter 6, and one each in chapters 3 and 7. Note that Paul mentions the expression *Holy Spirit* only twice (6:19; 12:3), but generally speaks of the Spirit or the Spirit of God.

38. Donald Guthrie, *New Testament Theology* (Downers Grove: Inter-Varsity, 1981), p. 550.

are temples where God is pleased to dwell. Believers have been justified spiritually in the name of the Lord Jesus Christ and by the Spirit of God (6:11). Indeed, this is the only place in the New Testament that links the Holy Spirit to the work of justifying the believers. The Spirit sanctifies and also justifies God's people.

Fourth, the Spirit serves as God's agent in relation to the salvation of the people. Paul describes the activities of the Spirit with the use of a few prepositions (in italics). In his discussion of spiritual gifts (chap. 12), Paul notes that a person is able to confess the lordship of Jesus only *by* the Holy Spirit (12:3). Spiritual gifts of wisdom, knowledge, faith, and healing are given *through* and *by means of* the Spirit (12:8–9). All these gifts are the work *of* the same Spirit (12:11). And last, Paul writes that we who make up the body of Christ are all baptized *by* one Spirit (12:13).

In summary, the Holy Spirit is sent forth by God the Father to reveal to his people spiritual truths for their salvation in Jesus Christ. His task includes the work of sanctifying and justifying the saints. And he equips the believers with spiritual gifts for the edification of the body of Christ.

4. Church

Throughout all his epistles, Paul employs the word *church* most often in his Corinthian correspondence.[39] He founded many churches and stayed in Ephesus for about three years compared to eighteen months in Corinth. Nevertheless, he had a special interest in the spiritual welfare of the Corinthian church, which he counseled with letters, emissaries (Timothy and Titus), and personal visits.

a. Nature of the Church

The congregation in Corinth exhibited a disregard for the unity of the local church, and by implication the universal church. Paul compares the Corinthian church to the human body that consists of many parts that are fully dependent on one another. These parts form one body harmoniously put together to function properly. So is the spiritual body of Christ (12:12, 27).

In another place, Paul stresses the oneness of Christ's church with a reference to the celebration of Holy Communion. "The bread which we break, is it not participation in the body of Christ? Because there is one loaf, we who are many are one body, for we all partake of the one loaf" (10:16b–17).

Striving for unity in the universal church, Paul repeatedly states that his teaching and directives are meant for "every church" (4:17), "all the churches" (with variations, 7:17; 11:16; 14:33), and "the churches" (14:34). Those in Galatia expressed homogeneity with the Corinthian community by demonstrating common interest in sending a monetary gift to the saints in Jerusalem (16:1–3). And

---

39. Of the sixty-one occurrences of the term *ekklēsia* (church) in Paul's epistles, twenty-one appear in I Corinthians, nine in II Corinthians, nine in Ephesians, five in Romans, four in Colossians, three in Galatians, three in I Timothy, two each in Philippians, I Thessalonians, II Thessalonians, and one in Philemon.

the churches in the province of Asia sent their greetings to the congregation in Corinth (16:19).

b. Worship

When the members of the church regularly come together, they do so to worship their Lord. Paul devotes a number of chapters to this particular subject (chaps. 11–14). He teaches headship, prescribes decorum in dress when men and women respectively pray and prophesy at worship, discusses acceptable appearance, severely criticizes class distinctions and excessive behavior at the Lord's table, transmits the words of the institution of Communion, instructs the Corinthians to examine themselves before partaking of the holy elements, and exhorts the Corinthians to exercise restraint (11:3–34).

Paul reviews the celebration of the Lord's Supper, but he does not omit a reference to the creedal statement "Jesus is Lord" (12:3) and to baptism as an initiation into the body of Christ (12:13). In this context, baptism signifies being baptized with the Spirit of Christ.[40]

c. Gifts

In the context of three chapters (chaps. 12–14), Paul considers spiritual gifts that God has given to the church. These gifts vary from that of wisdom to that of speaking in tongues and interpreting them (12:8–10). For the benefit of the church, God appointed apostles, prophets, teachers, miracle workers, healers, helpers, administrators, speakers in tongues, and interpreters (12:28–30). After listing these spiritual gifts, Paul then discusses at length the Corinthian practice of prophesying and speaking in tongues. Of these two gifts, he values prophesying higher than speaking in tongues. Prophesying must edify, strengthen, and encourage the believers (14:3). Paul allows speaking in tongues only when it communicates intelligible truths to the church for edification and instruction and when it is orderly and done in the context of love (14:6–19). If this is not the case, the speaker must keep quiet (14:28).

d. Discipline

We detect a strained relationship between Paul and the church almost in every chapter of this epistle.[41] Recent Gentile converts attempted to bring the wisdom and the spirit of the world into the church (2:5, 12; 3:1, 3, 19). Some of the members were arrogant to such a degree that they wished to take from Paul the

---

40. Compare Guthrie, *New Testament Theology*, p. 755; Ridderbos, *Paul*, p. 373.

41. Gordon D. Fee (*The First Epistle to the Corinthians* in the New International Commentary on the New Testament series [Grand Rapids: Eerdmans, 1987], p. 8 n. 22) excludes Paul's discussion on marriage (7:1–40) and on decorum at worship (11:2–16). But even this last passage is not free from contention (see 11:16).

leadership of the church. They even questioned the validity of his apostleship (9:1–3). Hence, Paul harshly rebukes them and asks whether he should come to them with a whip or in love with a gentle spirit (4:21).

The Corinthian congregation failed to exercise corporate responsibility in expelling an incestuous man from their midst. Paul had to instruct the people to enforce discipline (5:5, 13). He also objected to the immoral behavior of some people who wanted to apply Christian liberty to sexual mores (6:12). He forbade the Corinthians from going to pagan temples for communal meals, because partaking of food offered to an idol cancels fellowship with Christ at his table (8:1–13; 10:1–22). Instead of living as Christians in a pagan society some Corinthians were living as worldly people in a Christian community.

Paul's command for orderliness at the Lord's table and his instruction for edifying worship are corrective measures that the church should implement (11:17–34; 14:1–35). As a last reproof of those people who think they are spiritually gifted, Paul notes that his words are divinely inspired because Jesus is speaking through him (14:36–37). Those who arrogantly repudiate Paul's teaching should know that God repudiates them (14:38; compare Matt. 10:33; II Tim. 2:12).

5. Resurrection

Of all Paul's writings, I Corinthians 15 stands out as the chapter on the resurrection. The redemptive fact that Christ rose from the dead is for all believers the guarantee that they too shall be raised (6:14; 15:15–16). Paul portrays Christ as the firstfruits of those who have died (15:20, 23). When the firstfruits of the ripening grain are gathered, the harvest itself is near.

Some Corinthians denied the resurrection (15:12). Whether they spiritualized their own resurrection from the dead or not, the fact remains that Paul teaches the physical resurrection of God's people.[42] He presents this doctrine with typical Semitic parallelism (15:21–22):

> by man came death
> by man came the resurrection of the dead
>
> all who are in Adam die
> all who are in Christ will be raised

Paul mentions Adam, who is the head of the human race, and Christ, who is the head of all his people. The first Adam through disobedience brought the curse of death upon the human race; the second Adam removed the curse and grants eternal life to all who believe in him. The first Adam came forth from the dust of the earth, but the second Adam came down from heaven (15:45–49). Paul states that Adam became a living being but Christ a life-giving spirit. The contrast is incomparable, because Christ has the authority to raise his people from the grave,

---

42. For a thorough discussion see Anthony C. Thiselton, "Realized Eschatology at Corinth," *NTS* 24 (1977–78): 510–26.

transform them into glorious bodies, and perform this redemptive act in the twinkling of an eye (15:52).

The conclusion of Paul's extensive discourse on eschatology sounds a note of triumph. From the prophecies of Isaiah and Hosea (Isa. 25:8; Hos. 13:14), Paul quotes verses that speak about death: "Death is swallowed up in victory" and "Where, O death, is your victory? Where, O death, is your sting?" But in these two Old Testament passages the word *victory* is absent. Isaiah's prophecy reads, "He will swallow up death forever," and Hosea has, "Where, O death, are your plagues? Where, O grave, is your destruction?" Paul freely substitutes words of Scripture with the term *victory* to climax his discourse on the resurrection.

With direct and adapted quotations from and allusions to the Old Testament Scriptures, Paul wrote his letters to the Corinthians. His writings, breathing the air of the Scriptures, demonstrate the working of the Holy Spirit, who is their primary author. The Spirit of God grants Paul apostolic authority to use and adapt Old Testament passages in presenting inspired truths to God's people. The Scriptures not only support Paul's teaching, but also indicate that his writings stand in the continued line of God's revealed Word. When Paul departs at times from the exact words of the Old Testament text, he focuses attention not on a particular word but on the context of that passage. In conclusion, for his theology Paul interprets the Old Testament text to suit the thrust of his inspired message.[43]

F. Authenticity

One of the major letters of Paul, this epistle has both internal and external credentials as being Pauline. Let us begin with the internal evidence.

1. Internal Evidence

First, this letter is self-attested, for in many places Paul refers to himself (1:1, 12, 13; 3:4, 5, 22; 16:21).

Next, the salutation, address, blessing, and thanksgiving at the beginning and the greetings and doxology at the conclusion of the letter are similar to those in Paul's other epistles.

Third, cross-references to Acts and the Pauline epistles in several places correspond with names and topics that are discussed in this letter. In both First Corinthians and Acts, the initial address is from Paul and Sosthenes (1:1), and Luke notes that Sosthenes was the synagogue ruler in Corinth who was beaten by the Jewish people in front of Gallio's court (Acts 18:17). Paul baptized Crispus (1:14), and Luke writes that Crispus was the local synagogue ruler who converted with his household (Acts 18:8). Aquila and Priscilla send greetings to the church in Corinth (16:19); a few years earlier they had been among the first members of that church (Acts 18:2–3; see also Rom. 16:3). The cross-references

---

43. See E. Earle Ellis, "How the New Testament Uses the Old," in *New Testament Interpretation: Essays on Principles and Methods*, ed. I. Howard Marshall (Grand Rapids: Eerdmans; Exeter: Paternoster, 1977), pp. 199–219.

to parallel passages in other Pauline epistles are too numerous to mention. All the evidence indisputably points to the apostle Paul.

2. External Evidence

Toward the end of the first century, Clement of Rome appeals to this epistle as "the letter of the blessed Paul, the Apostle"; the Epistle of Barnabas has verbal resemblances to 3:1, 16, 18; and the *Didache* has the Aramaic expression *Maranatha* that also occurs in 16:22.[44]

During the second century, the authenticity of Paul's epistle was well established. Justin Martyr quotes directly from 11:19 in chapter 35 of his *Dialogue with Trypho*. Marcion incorporated I Corinthians in his canon. In the last quarter of that century, the Muratorian canon ascribes the Corinthian letters to Paul and places them first in the list of Pauline epistles. In addition, Irenaeus, Clement of Alexandria, and Tertullian quote from this epistle many times.

3. Integrity

Scholars who question the unity of I Corinthians have noted the disjointed presentation of its subject matter. They see contradictions in the composition. To illustrate, Paul informs the Corinthians that he will come to them very soon (4:19) but in the concluding chapter alludes to a delay (16:5–6). Paul shows an unbending attitude toward participation in sacrifices offered to an idol (10:1–22) but is lenient in his discussion on the freedom of conscience (10:23–11:1). And for the first four chapters of his epistle Paul considers the matter of apostolicity, which he reintroduces in chapter 9. According to some scholars, these are only three examples that illustrate a lack of coherence.[45]

We do not envision that Paul with or without the help of a scribe composed the letter in one continuous segment of time. Because of his many duties in Ephesus (see Acts 19:8–10; 20:20–21, 34), Paul wrote the epistle piecemeal and this unavoidable delay contributed to breaks in its composition. Also, finding literary breaks in the other letters of Paul (see, e.g., Rom. 5:12–19 and 15:33; 16:20, 25–27), we conclude that this peculiarity is one of his characteristics. And last, Paul received information about the Corinthians from visitors (1:11; 16:17), by letter (7:1), and by oral reports (5:1; 11:18). Undoubtedly he interacted with these messengers about the problems that burdened the church in Corinth.

We are unable to trace the sequence of the epistle's composition, except by resorting to hypotheses which themselves are controlled by many variations.[46] However, the disjointed links in the letter must be viewed against the background of Paul receiving periodic information and reacting to it. The letter is a compilation of loosely connected topics. Concludes Leon Morris, "It is not a sys-

---

44. The references respectively are I Clem. 47.1; Barnabas 6.11; and *Didache* 10.6.

45. Jean Héring, *The First Epistle of Saint Paul to the Corinthians*, trans. A. W. Heathcote and P. J. Allcock (London: Epworth, 1962), p. xiii.

46. See the survey by John C. Hurd, Jr., *The Origin of I Corinthians*, 2d ed. (Macon, Ga.: Mercer University Press, 1983), pp. 43–58.

tematic theological treatise, but a genuine attempt to deal with a concrete living situation, a situation calling for an apostolic pronouncement on more than one topic. So Paul goes naturally from one subject to another, sometimes with little connecting material."[47]

G. Characteristics

We view Paul's epistle to the Romans as the charter of Christianity, in which the apostle sets forth the teachings of sin, salvation, and service. We know that the last few chapters of Romans (chaps. 12–16) are devoted to practical matters pertaining to the life of the church. By contrast, I Corinthians is from beginning to end an epistle that reveals Paul's pastoral care to the congregation in Corinth. The apostle gives practical advice not only to that particular church but also to the entire Christian church. The range of issues Paul discusses in I Corinthians is sufficiently broad so that the members of every congregation can readily turn to this epistle for guidance.

A first characteristic is that the epistle is exceptionally comprehensive in dealing with problems with which the church must cope: schisms, respect for leadership, discipline, lawsuits, broken marriages, worldly influences and practices, feminism in the church, serious problems in the worship services, misconceptions regarding the consummation, and the gathering of gifts for the poor.

Next, Paul expresses himself in a personal manner when he discusses practical problems of the Corinthians. He serves the members of the church as a pastor who has a personal interest in their spiritual welfare. The trademark of this epistle is the personal pronoun *I*, which occurs repeatedly in all its sixteen chapters.

Third, the style in which I Corinthians has been written is uncommonly good. Paul demonstrates a command of Greek that in places rivals the usage of classical authors; he uses a multitude of words that are peculiar to this letter.[48] The epistle reveals a Semitic flavor because of the author's frequent use of Old Testament passages; he even resorts to using the Aramaic words *amen* and *Maranatha*.

Last, Paul asks many rhetorical questions. Especially in the first half of his epistle, he repeats the query: "Do you not know that . . . ?"[49] He expects the Corinthians to answer positively to his questions, for they had received instruction from the apostles and apostolic associates. Therefore, by asking questions Paul refreshes the memory of the Corinthians and builds on the foundation that was laid in earlier days.

H. Text

The Greek text of I Corinthians has the support of a papyrus document (P^{46}) and major witnesses (both uncials and minuscules). The papyrus manuscript

---

47. Leon Morris, "Corinthians, First Epistle to the," *ISBE*, vol. 1, p. 775.
48. Thayer lists a total of 110 words, pp. 704–6.
49. I Cor. 3:16; 5:6; 6:2, 3, 9, 15, 16, 19; 9:13, 24.

has all the chapters but they are incomplete. The uncial manuscripts that have the complete text of all the chapters are codices ℵ, A, B, D, 06[abs], L, Ψ, 056, 0142, 0150, and 0151.[50] In short, with the addition of numerous witnesses that have a partial text, the epistle has a firmly established Greek text.

Nonetheless, the letter presents a few textual problems that all translators and commentators cannot ignore. For instance, should the reading of 2:4 be "Not in persuasive words of wisdom" or "Not with the persuasion of wisdom"? Manuscript support for the second reading is meager; for this reason translators favor the first reading.

First Corinthians 13:3 is another crucial text. Almost all translators adopt the reading "And if I give up my body to be burned." But the overwhelming manuscript support for the Greek text is "And if I hand over my body so that I may boast" (NRSV). Despite the force of external witnesses, translators are swayed by the internal evidence and choose the weaker reading, "to be burned."

Last, some Western manuscripts transpose 14:34–35 to come after 14:40. But this transposition has not met much favorable response; the reason for the change appears to derive from scribal uneasiness. Scribes were uncomfortable with the wording of Paul's directive to have women be silent in the worship service. Nevertheless, the wording remains the same after the relocation and does little if anything for the exegesis of the passage. Scholars who label these verses a gloss that was later incorporated into the text of I Corinthians need the necessary textual evidence to prove their point. This evidence is not available at present. However, it is possible to interpret the passage within the general context to show that the meaning is indeed lucid and understandable.

I. Purpose

Summarizing the content of the epistle, we can be brief in stating the purpose of I Corinthians. First, Paul sought to develop and promote a spirit of unity in the local church and at the same time to show the readers that they were part of the universal church. Next, the apostle tried to correct a number of erroneous tendencies in the Corinthian community. One of them was the apathy toward exercising discipline with respect to the incestuous man. Third, Paul answered questions that were submitted to him by letter (7:1) and delegation (16:17). And finally, Paul's epistle instructs the believers in Corinth to collect funds to aid the needy saints in Jerusalem.

J. Outline

A simple outline of I Corinthians can be committed to memory without much effort. In addition to the introductory remarks and the conclusion, the epistle consists of Paul's response to problems and concerns in the Corinthian church.

---

50. Consult Kurt Aland and Barbara Aland, *The Text of the New Testament*, trans. Erroll F. Rhodes (Grand Rapids: Eerdmans; Leiden: Brill, 1987), chart 6, endpaper.

Introduction

1:1–9	I. Introduction	
1:10–6:20	II. Response to Reported Problems	
	A. Divisions in the Church	1:10–4:21
	B. Immorality and Lawsuits	5:1–6:20
7:1–16:4	III. Response to Corinthian Concerns	
	A. Marriage Problems	7:1–40
	B. Food Offered to Idols	8:1–13
	C. Apostles and Rights	9:1–27
	D. Warnings and Freedom	10:1–11:1
	E. Worship	11:2–14:40
	F. The Resurrection	15:1–58
	G. Collection for God's People	16:1–4
16:5–24	IV. Conclusion	
	A. Paul's Requests	16:5–18
	B. Exhortations and Greetings	16:13–24

A full outline with all the headings and details is as follows:

I.	1:1–9	Introduction	
	1:1–3	A. Greetings	
	1:4–9	B. Thanksgiving	
II.	1:10–6:20	Paul's Response to Reported Problems	
	1:10–4:21	A. Divisions in the Church	
		1. Factions	1:10–17
		2. The Folly of the Cross	1:18–2:5
		3. Wisdom of the Spirit	2:6–16
		4. Workmen for God	3:1–23
		5. Servants of Christ	4:1–21
	5:1–6:20	B. Immorality and Lawsuits	
		1. Incest	5:1–8
		2. Excommunication	5:9–13
		3. Litigations	6:1–11
		4. Immorality	6:12–20
III.	7:1–16:4	Paul's Response to Corinthian Concerns	
	7:1–40	A. Marriage Problems	
		1. Proper Conduct	7:1–7
		2. Faithfulness and Marriage	7:8–11
		3. Believer and Unbeliever	7:12–16
		4. A Digression	7:17–24
		5. Virgins and Marriage	7:25–40

Commentary

1

Introduction

(1:1–9)

and
Divisions in the Church, *part 1*

(1:10–31)

Outline

1 1 Paul, called to be an apostle of Christ Jesus by the will of God, and Sosthenes our brother, 2 to the church of God which is in Corinth, to those who have been sanctified in Christ Jesus, called to be saints together with all those who in every place call on the name of our Lord Jesus Christ, their Lord and ours: 3 Grace to you and peace from God our Father and the Lord Jesus Christ.

4 I always thank my God concerning you for the grace of God which was given to you in Christ Jesus, 5 for in him you have been enriched in every way, in every utterance and all knowledge, 6 just as the testimony to Christ was confirmed in you, 7 so that you are not lacking in any spiritual gift as you are eagerly awaiting the revelation of our Lord Jesus Christ. 8 He also will confirm you to the end and keep you blameless in the day of our Lord Jesus Christ. 9 God is faithful, through whom you were called into the fellowship of his Son, Jesus Christ our Lord.

I. Introduction
1:1–9

A. Greetings
1:1–3

This is the first of the three major epistles (I Corinthians, II Corinthians, and Romans) Paul wrote. His earlier epistles were the two letters to the church in Thessalonica and his letter to the Galatians (generally accepted as the first epistle Paul composed).[1] As these earlier epistles and the extant Corinthian letters attest, controversies and questions compelled Paul to write. The necessity to write is more pronounced in I Corinthians than in any other Pauline epistle.

William Hendriksen observes, "Among all Paul's epistles there is none that covers such a wide variety of subjects and problems, stretching all the way from those relating to lawsuits, marriage and divorce, meats offered to idols, ministers' remuneration, propriety in worship, celebration of the Lord's Supper, speaking in tongues, belief in the resurrection of the body, to the exercise of Christian benevolence."[2]

1. Paul, called to be an apostle of Christ Jesus by the will of God, and Sosthenes our brother.

---

1. Some scholars date the composition of Galatians at A.D. 48/49, others in either A.D. 51/52 or 53. Paul wrote I Corinthians probably in A.D. 55 (see the Introduction to the commentary).

2. William Hendriksen, "1 Corinthians," *B of T* 280 (1987): 27.

a. *Name and calling.* "Paul, called to be an apostle of Christ Jesus." As he does in all his other epistles, Paul begins this letter by introducing himself as the writer and sender. He emphatically states that he has been called (see also Rom. 1:1; Gal. 1:15). At the time of Paul's conversion, Jesus personally called him to be an apostle to the Gentiles (Acts 9:15). He was ordained to this office when the Holy Spirit set him and Barnabas apart "for the work to which [the Spirit] called them" (Acts 13:2). Elsewhere Paul declares that as an apostle he had been sent by Jesus Christ and God the Father (Gal. 1:1). In brief, Paul was called by the Triune God: Father, Son, and Holy Spirit.

When Jesus called Paul to be an apostle, he endowed Paul with divine authority to preach the gospel and to address all the churches (4:17; 7:17; 14:33b; 16:1). Consequently, no one in the Corinthian church could legitimately question Paul's apostolicity (compare 9:1–2). Should one do so, he would be opposing the Lord. In most of his letters, Paul affirms that he is an apostle of Christ Jesus.[3] Only in the introductions of Philippians, I and II Thessalonians, and Philemon does he omit the reference to his apostleship. He uses the phrase *an apostle of Christ Jesus* as a standard introductory formula that characterizes his epistles. And he knows that an apostle functions as the representative of his sender Jesus Christ, whose message he must accurately communicate. In a sense, an apostle can be compared with an ambassador (II Cor. 5:20) who represents in another country the president or prime minister of his government.

"By the will of God." Declaring that his apostleship is based on God's will,[4] Paul effectively affirms that his calling as an apostle originates with God.

"Sosthenes our brother." The word order of this introductory verse excludes Sosthenes from the office of apostle. Paul presents him as "our brother," which means that Sosthenes is a Christian who is well known to the believers in Corinth. Yet Paul mentions him only once in all his epistles. Perhaps this Sosthenes was the ruler of the synagogue in Corinth who received a beating at the court of Proconsul Gallio (Acts 18:17). But lacking further information, we can only say that he served as a co-worker with Paul. Although Paul writes the pronoun *I* instead of *we* (e.g., vv. 4, 10, 14, 16), scholars affirm that Sosthenes supported Paul in the message communicated to the Corinthians.[5]

2. To the church of God which is in Corinth, to those who have been sanctified in Christ Jesus, called to be saints together with all those who in every place call on the name of our Lord Jesus Christ, their Lord and ours.

b. *Recipients.* Paul addresses his letter "to the church of God which is in Corinth." He writes the word *ekklēsia,* an expression that in the Hellenistic world

---

3. These are the references (with minor variations): Rom. 1:1; I Cor. 1:1; II Cor. 1:1; Gal. 1:1; Eph. 1:1; Col. 1:1; I Tim. 1:1; II Tim. 1:1; Titus 1:1.

4. See II Cor. 1:1; Eph. 1:1; Col. 1:1; II Tim. 1:1.

5. Gordon D. Fee conjectures that Sosthenes may have served as Paul's secretary (compare 16:21). *The First Epistle to the Corinthians,* New International Commentary on the New Testament series (Grand Rapids: Eerdmans, 1987), p. 31.

of the day was a time-honored technical term that generally referred to either political or guild meetings (compare Acts 19:32, 39, 41). By the middle of the first century, Christians began to refer to their own assemblies as the church (*ekklēsia*) in Christ. They used the term to distinguish themselves from the Jews, who used the word *synagogue* for their meeting places (but compare the Greek text of James 2:2). Paul carefully differentiates the gatherings of Christians from both Gentile assemblies and Jewish synagogues. Note how he does this in one of his earlier epistles: "To the church of the Thessalonians in God the Father and the Lord Jesus Christ" (I Thess. 1:1; II Thess. 1:1). He directs his two Corinthian epistles "to the church of God in Corinth" (I Cor. 1:2; II Cor. 1:1) without linking the church directly to Jesus Christ. Yet, the concept *church* can be understood only with reference to Jesus Christ, for the church of God is in him.[6]

"To those who have been sanctified in Christ Jesus." The church belongs to God, who through Christ has called his people out of the world to a life of holiness. His people do not leave the world (see 5:10) but demonstrate to the world that they have been made holy in Christ Jesus. Despite their frequent quarrels, factions, and immorality, Paul nevertheless describes the Corinthians as people who have been sanctified in Christ Jesus (compare Eph. 5:27).[7] In this epistle, Paul first states that the believers have been set aside by God to live holy lives and then paradoxically points out their sins and shortcomings. He intimates that when a believer is made holy, he is fully aware of God's gracious act, for the Christian realizes that he is constantly called to be holy (see Rom. 1:7) and to live a life of holiness.

"Called to be saints." Holiness is more than a state. For believers, sanctification is both a definitive act of God and a lifelong process.[8] God's gracious act of sanctifying believers includes their accountability to be holy. In the Greek the verb *to be* is absent from the phrase *called to be saints,* but Paul's intent is to instruct his readers to fulfill their commitment to be holy.

Paul was called to be an apostle of Christ Jesus, and thus he committed himself to be Christ's spokesman. Similarly God has called believers to a state of holiness and expects them to practice holiness. That call continued to come to both Paul and the Corinthians, so that throughout their lives they remained called.[9]

"Together with all those who in every place call on the name of our Lord Jesus Christ." With these words, Paul embraces both Gentile and Jewish Christians as equals in the church of Jesus Christ. Paul refers to the church universal, in which

6. See Lothar Coenen, *NIDNTT,* vol. 1, p. 299.

7. Consult John Calvin, *The First Epistle of Paul the Apostle to the Corinthians,* Calvin's Commentaries series, trans. John W. Fraser (reprint ed.; Grand Rapids: Eerdmans, 1976), p. 17.

8. Compare Anthony A. Hoekema, *Saved by Grace* (Grand Rapids: Eerdmans; Exeter: Paternoster, 1989), pp. 202–3. See also William W. Klein, "Paul's Use of *Kalein*: A Proposal," *JETS* 27 (1984): 56–64.

9. F. W. Grosheide, *Commentary on the First Epistle to the Corinthians: The English Text with Introduction, Exposition and Notes,* New International Commentary on the New Testament series (Grand Rapids: Eerdmans, 1953), p. 23.

all believers everywhere "call on the name of our Lord," and groups the Corinthians with all other believers. But is Paul addressing his epistle to the believers both in Corinth and in all other places? Although Paul's letters were designed to be read in the churches (Col. 4:16; I Thess. 5:27; and compare II Peter 3:15–16), this epistle is addressed specifically to the church in Corinth. The second part of verse 2 stresses the unity that believers exhibit in prayer when they call on the name of Jesus Christ. Prayer unites Christians before the throne of grace.

"Their Lord and ours." Paul wants the Corinthians to know that they belong to the body of believers. This body is worldwide, for believers everywhere acknowledge Jesus Christ as Lord. Thus Paul writes, "their Lord and ours." In the Greek text, the word *Kyrios* (Lord) is omitted; in translation it has to be supplied from the context.

3. Grace to you and peace from God our Father and the Lord Jesus Christ.

c. *Greetings.* "Grace to you and peace from God our Father and the Lord Jesus Christ." This is the common greeting that Paul employs in most of his epistles;[10] in modified form, it also appears in the letters of both Peter and John.[11] In the Hellenistic world, people commonly greeted each other with the Greek word *chairein* (translated "greetings"; e.g., Acts 15:23; 23:26; James 1:1). Its derived form *charis* signifies "grace." The Jews, however, greeted one another with the term *shalom* (peace). In the epistolary literature of the Christian church, the two expressions *grace* and *peace* appear together and have a decidedly theological meaning. R. C. H. Lenski observes that "grace is always first, peace always second. This is due to the fact that grace is the source of peace. Without grace there is and can be no peace; but when grace is ours, peace must of necessity follow."[12] Paul links both grace and peace to their ultimate source: they originate "from God our Father and the Lord Jesus Christ."

The virtues of grace and peace are God's gifts to his children, and he grants these favors as a Father. In harmony with the Lord's Prayer, in which Jesus taught his followers to say "our Father," Paul also portrays God as "our Father." Everyone who prays in the name of the Lord Jesus Christ has God as Father. Hence, all believers are God's children through Christ. And through him, they receive the blessings of grace and peace.

Greek Words, Phrases, and Constructions in 1:1–2

Verse 1

ἀπόστολος—this noun is preceded by κλητός (called) to indicate that Paul was passive and God active in Paul's appointment to apostleship.

---

10. Rom. 1:7; II Cor. 1:2; Gal. 1:3; Eph. 1:2; Phil. 1:2; II Thess. 1:2; Philem. 3; and with variations in Col. 1:2; I Thess. 1:1; Titus 1:4.
11. I Peter 1:2; II Peter 1:2; II John 3. See also the prologue of I Clem.
12. R. C. H. Lenski, *The Interpretation of St. Paul's First and Second Epistle to the Corinthians* (1935; Columbus: Wartburg, 1946), p. 28.

Verse 2

ἡγιασμένοις—the perfect passive participle in the dative plural stands in apposition to the noun *church,* which collectively is in the dative singular. In this text, the verb ἁγιάζω (I make holy) refers to a definitive act of God. The perfect tense denotes completed action with lasting result. The passive indicates that God is the agent and that he sanctifies the Corinthians in Christ. "The fundamental thought of the word is that of belonging to God; it carries the duty of being like to Him in character."[13]

B. Thanksgiving
1:4–9

For all the spiritual and material blessings that he and the recipients of his letters possess, Paul faithfully expresses thanks to God. In the opening verses of his epistles, he invariably voices words of gratitude on behalf of the people he addresses.[14]

4. I always thank my God concerning you for the grace of God which was given to you in Christ Jesus.

When Paul writes "I always thank my God concerning you,"[15] he reveals his pastoral heart. He prays for the churches he has founded and thanks God for them. He uses the adverb *always* to qualify the verb *thank.* But how is Paul able to express his gratitude to God on behalf of the Corinthian church? The members have caused him untold grief with their divisions, immorality, marital problems, and lawsuits. Can Paul accurately write the word *always?* Is he using a formula at the beginning of his epistle? No, Paul's heart is filled with gratitude because God chose to call his people out of the immoral and idolatrous environment of Corinth. Even there God established the church in fellowship with Jesus Christ (v. 9). For that reason he can continually thank God.

"For the grace of God which was given to you in Christ Jesus." This is the second time in as many verses (vv. 3 and 4) that Paul uses the expression *grace.* In the Greek, derivatives of this expression also appear in the verb *thank* (v. 4) and in the noun *gift* (v. 7). In brief, Paul stresses the concept *grace* in these verses. What is the significance of this concept? Paul is amazed at God's grace, in the form of spiritual gifts, lavished on the Corinthian Christians (see, e.g., the enumeration of gifts in 12:4–11). God's grace becomes evident in the gifts he gives to his people.

Notice that Paul uses the passive construction in the second half of this verse. Grace was given to the Corinthians by God. He is the implied agent and the Corinthians are the passive recipients (see Rom. 12:6; II Cor. 8:1). Paul gives

---

13. R. St. John Parry, *The First Epistle of Paul the Apostle to the Corinthians,* Cambridge Greek Testament for Schools and Colleges (Cambridge: Cambridge University Press, 1937), p. 30.

14. Rom. 1:8; Phil. 1:3–4; I Thess. 1:2; II Thess. 1:3; Philem. 4. Compare Eph. 5:20; Col. 1:3; I Thess. 2:13; II Thess. 1:3. See Peter T. O'Brien, *Introductory Thanksgivings in the Letters of Paul* (Leiden: Brill, 1977), pp. 108–16; and "Thanksgiving and the Gospel in Paul," *NTS* 21 (1974): 144–55.

15. Two Greek manuscripts (codices Sinaiticus and Vaticanus) omit the personal pronoun *my.*

thanks for God's faithfulness to the believers in Corinth, but he says nothing about any inherent virtues of the Corinthians. Further, Paul states that God's grace has been given in Christ Jesus. That is, in Christ the recipients of this grace have been redeemed and are now set apart from the pagan world in which they live.

5. For in him you have been enriched in every way, in every utterance and all knowledge.

a. *Translation.* This verse features variations of two crucial words. The first word in this sentence can be translated either *that* (a conjunction introducing a statement which completes the phrase *I always thank God for you*) or *for* (a causal conjunction that explains the phrase *in Christ Jesus*). Translators generally favor the second choice.

The next variation is either "in him" (NIV, RSV) or, as some translations have it, "by him" (KJV, NKJV). In apposition with the similar construction of the preceding sentence ("in Christ Jesus"), the reading *in him* is preferred. In Christ, then, the believer has received untold spiritual riches.

b. *Message.* When Paul writes "in him you have been enriched in every way," he is not specifically referring to the material possessions of the Corinthians. Some of them may be affluent (v. 26), but Paul calls attention to their spiritual treasures in Christ (see 3:21–23; in a parallel passage, Paul wishes that the Corinthians might become rich through Christ's poverty [II Cor. 8:9; 9:11]). God has untold spiritual riches which he desires to give to the redeemed through Christ.[16] According to the Scriptures, God is rich in kindness, patience, mercy, and grace (Rom. 2:4; 9:23; Eph. 1:7; 2:4). Christ possesses unsearchable riches (Eph. 3:8), for in him lie hidden all the treasures of knowledge and wisdom (Col. 2:3). God meets the believer's needs from the glorious riches that are in Christ Jesus (Phil. 4:19).

God has adorned the Corinthians with the riches that are in Christ not sparingly, but "in every way." In verse 5, Paul refrains from providing a list of spiritual gifts (see 12:4–31) but focuses attention on the number of gifts which the Corinthians have received. In this short verse, he stresses the words *every* and *all* to indicate that the recipients of God's blessings are spiritually rich beyond measure.

Paul illustrates in what respect the Corinthians have received spiritual riches: "in every utterance and all knowledge." He elucidates articulation and knowledge as two of these special gifts. The Greek term *logos* refers to the uttering of gospel knowledge (*gnosis*) which the people had. They objectively voiced the truth of the gospel which they subjectively understood. That is, with their mouths they confessed the spiritual knowledge they had in their hearts.[17] This is

---

16. Friedel Selter, *NIDNTT,* vol. 2, p. 844; Friedrich Hauck and Wilhelm Kasch, *TDNT,* vol. 6, p. 329.

17. Grosheide, *First Epistle to the Corinthians,* p. 28; Henry Alford, *Alford's Greek Testament: An Exegetical and Critical Commentary,* 7th ed., 4 vols. (1877; Grand Rapids: Guardian, 1976), vol. 2, p. 475.

the first time the word *knowledge* appears in this epistle; it occurs frequently in both letters to the Corinthians[18] and is closely related to the term *wisdom*. "Various shades of meaning appear in particular contexts, but the notion of the intellectual apprehension and application of Christian truth is constant."[19] The spiritual gifts of utterance and knowledge when appropriately used are an eloquent testimony to Christ (II Cor. 8:7). In another letter, Paul writes that he is convinced that Christians are "complete in knowledge and competent to instruct one another" (Rom. 15:14).

6. Just as the testimony to Christ was confirmed in you.

The message of verse 6 is either an afterthought that explains the preceding verse or an introduction to the following verse. I favor the first of the two choices for the following reasons: the words *just as* balance and present a comparison with the preceding verse. The verb *was confirmed* is a passive construction which implies God is the agent. This construction parallels the passive verb *have been enriched* in verse 5. Also, the gift of utterance is analogous to the witness of Christ. And last, the phrase *in you* compares with the pronoun *you* that denotes the recipients of spiritual gifts.

Some translations have the reading *the testimony of Christ*, which can be understood subjectively of the gospel itself (KJV, NKJV, MLB). In other words, God confirmed the truth of Christ's gospel in the hearts of the Corinthians. Other versions read "the testimony to (or about) Christ," which would refer objectively to the preaching of the gospel by apostles and evangelists (e.g., NIV, RSV, REB).[20] In view of the general statement *in every utterance* (v. 5), the second translation is preferred to the first.

The question ultimately is how God confirmed the testimony to Christ in the hearts of the Corinthians. Even though Paul does not explain, we venture to say that God by faith confirmed the message of the gospel in the believers through the working of the Holy Spirit.

7. So that you are not lacking in any spiritual gift as you are eagerly awaiting the revelation of our Lord Jesus Christ.

Note these two points:

a. *Result.* "So that you are not lacking in any spiritual gift." Because God conferred numerous spiritual gifts on the Corinthians, they were not lacking any of these blessings. The present tense of the verb *to lack* in this result clause indicates that they actually possessed these gifts; at this point in his epistle, however, Paul is not interested in listing the specific gifts (refer to chapters 12–14). With this verb Paul does not suggest that the Corinthians lack any gifts; rather, he means

---

18. With minor variations, in I Cor. 8:1, 7, 10, 11; 12:8; 13:2, 8; 14:6; II Cor. 2:14; 4:6; 6:6; 8:7; 10:5; 11:6.

19. O'Brien, *Introductory Thanksgivings,* p. 119; C. K. Barrett, "Christianity at Corinth," *BJRUL* 46 (1964): 269–97.

20. Refer to Bauer, p. 494; A. T. Robertson, *A Grammar of the Greek New Testament in the Light of Historical Research* (Nashville: Broadman, 1934), p. 500.

that in respect to other churches, they are not lagging behind.[21] Through God's grace they have indeed received an abundance of spiritual talents.

If we interpret verse 7 in the flow of the paragraph, we conclude that the Corinthians are not lacking in any of the spiritual gifts precisely because of the preaching of the gospel. The mention of spiritual gifts relates more to the verb *have been enriched* (v. 5) than to the verb *was confirmed* (v. 6).[22]

The word *gift* appears here for the first time in this epistle, and in this context it does not mean "miracles" (see 12:9, 28, 30). To interpret the word narrowly (i.e., as a miracle that serves to confirm the preaching of the gospel) would be restrictive and consequently unacceptable. We should not limit the term *gift* but rather interpret it in the broadest possible sense.

b. *Expectation.* "As you are eagerly awaiting the revelation of our Lord Jesus Christ." Paul links spiritual gifts to the expectation of Jesus' return. In this passage Paul twice mentions the end of time: here and in the next verse (v. 8), where he refers to the day of the Lord Jesus Christ. This emphasis is significant in view of Paul's lengthy explanation of the resurrection of the body in 15:12–58, where he explicitly discusses the eschatological moment. The Corinthians' interest in the imminent return of the Lord seems to have waned (compare 15:12, 33–34), so at the outset of his epistle, Paul wants to encourage his audience to await eagerly Christ's return.[23]

The verb *to await eagerly* is in Greek a compound that connotes intensity and earnestness in connection with Christian hope, as Paul's use of it in other epistles reveals:

> "The creation waits in eager expectation" (Rom. 8:19)
> "We wait eagerly for our adoption as sons" (Rom. 8:23)
> "We wait for it patiently" (Rom. 8:25)
> "But by faith we eagerly await through the Spirit the righteousness
>   for which we hope" (Gal. 5:5)
> "And we eagerly await a Savior from (heaven)" (Phil. 3:20)[24]

This particular verb usually occurs in the New Testament with reference to believers who express a genuine eschatological longing for the restoration of all things.

---

21. Hans Conzelmann, *1 Corinthians: A Commentary on the First Epistle to the Corinthians,* ed. George W. MacRae, trans. James W. Leitch, "Hermeneia: A Critical and Historical Commentary on the Bible" (Philadelphia: Fortress, 1975), p. 27.

22. F. W. Grosheide, *De Eerste Brief van den Apostel Paulus aan de Kerk te Korinthe,* Kommentaar op het Nieuwe Testament series (Amsterdam: Van Bottenburg, 1932), p. 48.

23. As John Albert Bengel observes, "The test of a true or false Christian is his waiting for, or dreading, the revelation of Christ." *Bengel's New Testament Commentary,* trans. Charlton T. Lewis and Marvin R. Vincent, 2 vols. (Grand Rapids: Kregel, 1981), vol. 2, p. 167.

24. See also Heb. 9:28; I Peter 3:20.

With the noun *revelation*, Paul states that at his return Jesus will remove the mystery of his being by unveiling his presence (II Thess. 1:7; I Peter 1:7, 13; 4:13). The Corinthians should eagerly look forward to the day of that revelation.

8. He also will confirm you to the end and keep you blameless in the day of our Lord Jesus Christ.

a. "He also will confirm you to the end." Who will confirm the Corinthians? God or Jesus? The person mentioned in the preceding clause is Jesus Christ. But for four reasons the flow of the paragraph (vv. 4–9) demands that not Jesus but God be the subject of verse 8. First, the paragraph begins and concludes with a reference to God (see vv. 4 and 9). Next, God enriched the Corinthians in every way and confirmed them by the preaching about Christ (vv. 5, 6). Third, the opening phrase ("God is faithful") of verse 9 denotes not a new subject but a concluding benediction in a paragraph in which God is the agent. And last, the subject of a parallel verse is God:[25] "Now He who establishes us with you in Christ and anointed us is God" (II Cor. 1:21, NASB).

In the Greek, Paul employs the verb *to confirm/to establish* twice in this paragraph (vv. 6, 8). As the preaching of the gospel confirms the believers in their faith so the promise of God's abiding power establishes them until the consummation. The phrase *will establish you* expresses not a mere wish but rather a promise which God is going to fulfill.

b. "And keep you blameless in the day of our Lord Jesus Christ." Paul is not saying that the Corinthians are blameless at the time of his writing. Instead, he looks to the future and voices his certainty that God will present them without blame at the time of the final judgment. That is, no one will be able to accuse them, for on that day they will be irreproachable. Elsewhere Paul teaches the manner in which the believers will be presented blameless before the highest court: it is through the death of Christ's physical body that God is reconciled to the sinner and declares him free from blame (Col. 1:22).

In the Old Testament, the term *the day of the Lord* is a description of the day of judgment (Joel 3:14; Amos 5:18–20). In the New Testament, the term alludes to the return of Christ (e.g., Phil. 1:6, 10; 2:16; I Thess. 5:2). Christ's return includes judgment in which both God and Christ serve as judge (see Rom. 14:10; II Cor. 5:10). In that day, believers are declared blameless "through the verdict of the judge."[26]

9. God is faithful, through whom you were called into the fellowship of his Son, Jesus Christ our Lord.

a. "God is faithful." Should anyone doubt the veracity of the preceding verses, Paul states unconditionally that God is trustworthy in fulfilling his promises. To emphasize the concept *faithful*, Paul places this word first in the Greek sentence: a literal translation is "faithful is God," who unwaveringly supports his people to

25. O'Brien, *Introductory Thanksgivings*, p. 128.
26. Conzelmann, *1 Corinthians*, p. 28.

the end (v. 8). The echo of this truth resounds throughout the Scriptures.[27] God is completely reliable.

b. "Through whom you were called into the fellowship of his Son." God the Father works out his plan of salvation through his Son, Jesus Christ; the Father originates and the Son executes this plan (compare 8:6). But is God's calling effectual for everyone? Hardly. "Many are called but few are chosen," Jesus said (Matt. 22:14). Only those who have been called into the fellowship of the Son experience the Father's enduring faithfulness. Calling is always linked to Jesus Christ, as in the case of Paul's apostleship (v. 1) and the Corinthians' call to holiness (v. 2).

Calling is real when the believer has true fellowship with Christ. This fellowship, however, demands a life of holiness in which a Christian is in body and soul conformed to the likeness of God's Son (see Rom. 8:29). As Charles Hodge puts it: "Fellowship includes union and communion."[28] Fellowship as union and communion includes both partaking of Christ's suffering and glory and belonging to the body of Christ. It means accepting the sacrament of holy communion: remembering that Christ died for us (10:16). When the believer is completely transformed in the core of his being, he has genuine fellowship with Christ. The proclamation of the gospel accepted in true faith, says John, leads to fellowship with the Father and the Son (I John 1:3).

c. "His Son, Jesus Christ our Lord." Paul acknowledges that God the Father calls the believer into fellowship, and that the believer has communion with the Son, who is Jesus Christ, namely, our Lord. Paul ends his thanksgiving with a compilation of divine names and functions. The Son, eternally begotten by the Father (Ps. 2:7), assumed human flesh and was given the name *Jesus*. The Old Testament name *Joshua* became *Jesus* in the New, with an explanation: "He will save his people from their sins" (Matt. 1:21). While the Son's given name is Jesus, his official name is Christ, that is, the Anointed One or the Messiah. The name points to his office of prophet, priest, and king. And last, when Paul calls Jesus Christ "our Lord," he alludes to his exaltation: "King of kings and Lord of lords" (I Tim. 6:15).[29]

Practical Considerations in 1:4–9

According to Luke, Paul stayed in Corinth for only a year and a half while he founded a church (Acts 18:11; presumably A.D. 50–52). In the following years, Apollos taught the Corinthians the Scriptures and continued to strengthen the believers (1:12; 3:4–6). The church was blessed with an exceptionally talented group of people (12:7–11, 27–

---

27. Deut. 7:9; Isa. 49:7; I Cor. 10:13; I Thess. 5:24; II Thess. 3:3; II Tim. 2:13; Heb. 10:23; 11:11.

28. Charles Hodge, *An Exposition of the First Epistle to the Corinthians* (1857; reprint ed., Grand Rapids: Eerdmans, 1965), p. 10. See also Hoekema, *Saved by Grace*, p. 85.

29. Compare Deut. 10:17; Ps. 136:2–3; Rev. 17:14; 19:16.

31) but was burdened by strife, divisions, moral problems, and irregularities in the worship services.

When Paul wrote I Corinthians, he pastorally approached the readers by thanking God, who had called them to a life of holiness. Many of them had lived in spiritual darkness but by God's grace now had fellowship with Jesus Christ. Paul rejoiced in their salvation. In a positive manner, he reminded the Corinthians of their commitment to Christ and urged them to ascend to a higher level of serving him in church and society. In his thanksgiving to God, he addressed the people positively in spite of their lack of love to God and their fellow men. He thus gained their confidence and interest.

Referring to the return of Christ and the end of time (vv. 7–8), Paul brings the paragraph on thanksgiving to a climax that functions as an introduction to the rest of his epistle.[30] The body of his epistle consists of admonition, rebuke, teaching, and correction. But in the longest chapter of his epistle (chap. 15), Paul discusses the doctrine of the resurrection and the eternal destiny of the believers. In short, by calling attention to the day of the Lord in this passage, Paul sets the tone for the remainder of the letter.

Greek Words, Phrases, and Constructions in 1:4, 8

Verse 4

τῷ θεῷ μου—at least two major manuscripts (codices Sinaiticus and Vaticanus) lack the possessive pronoun. The text, however, has strong support from a wide variety of Greek witnesses and versions. Many translators favor the inclusion of the pronoun *my*,[31] although others omit it.[32]

Verse 8

ἀνεγκλήτους—this is a verbal adjective that expresses a passive voice ("cannot be blamed"). The compound consists of the privative ἀ (un-), the preposition ἐν (in), and the adjective of the verb καλέω (I call).

---

10 I exhort you, brothers, in the name of our Lord Jesus Christ, that all of you agree and that there be no divisions among you, but that you be united in the same mind and thought. 11 For some of Chloe's people have told me concerning you, my brothers, that there are quarrels among you. 12 What I mean is this: that each of you says, "I am of Paul," or "I am of Apollos," or "I am of Cephas," or "I am of Christ." 13 Is Christ divided? Was Paul crucified for you? Were you baptized in the name of Paul? 14 I thank God that I baptized none of you except Crispus and Gaius, 15 that no one should say that you were baptized in my name. 16 I baptized also the household of Stephanas; beyond that I do not know if I baptized any other. 17 For Christ sent me not to baptize but to preach the gospel, not in wisdom of words that the cross of Christ may not be emptied.

---

30. J. H. Roberts, "The eschatological transitions to the Pauline letter body," *Neotest* 20 (1986): 29–35.

31. KJV, NKJV, GNB, MLB, NAB, NASB, NRSV, SEB, *Moffatt.*

32. RSV, NIV, NEB, REB, JB, NJB, *Phillips, Cassirer.*

II. Paul's Response to Reported Problems
1:10–6:20

A. Divisions in the Church
1:10–4:21

Jesus said that a kingdom divided against itself will be laid waste and a household divided against itself will fall (Matt. 12:25; Mark 3:24–25; Luke 11:17). When Paul heard about the divisions within the Corinthian church, he knew that he had to confront the readers of his letter about their factions, quarrels, and boasts before he could teach them principles of spiritual conduct.

1. Factions
1:10–17

10. I exhort you, brothers, in the name of our Lord Jesus Christ, that all of you agree and that there be no divisions among you, but that you be united in the same mind and thought.

We make these observations:

a. *Exhortation.* Paul realizes that the quarreling of the Corinthians has not yet resulted in schism, but he knows that he must call his readers back to a living relationship with the Lord and do so pastorally and positively. Thus, he addresses them as his spiritual brothers (and sisters) and exhorts them to consider the name, that is, the full revelation, of the Lord Jesus Christ. Having been called into the fellowship of God's Son Jesus Christ (v. 9), they should understand that this fellowship includes unity and harmony and excludes dissension and strife.

Paul admonishes the Corinthians through (lit.) the name of the Lord Jesus Christ. In his epistles he often exhorts his readers by calling on the mediation of God or of Christ. For instance, he exhorts the readers by the mercy of God (Rom. 12:1); "by our Lord Jesus Christ" (Rom. 15:30); "by the meekness and gentleness of Christ" (II Cor. 10:1); "in the Lord Jesus Christ" (I Thess. 4:1; II Thess. 3:12); and, finally, as in the case of Euodia and Syntyche, "to agree with one another in the Lord" (Phil. 4:2).[33] When he appeals to the name of Jesus Christ, he urges the believers to be one in the Lord.

b. *Agreement.* The reason Paul is exhorting the members of the church in Corinth is to have them agree with one another (compare Rom. 15:5). They should confess with one accord their faith in Christ. They should be at peace with each other. Paul is not pleading for uniformity of opinion but rather for a loving disposition that strives for harmony and peace (Phil. 2:1–2).

Paul forbids the Corinthians to form parties in the church. He intimates that by undermining the unity of the church, the Corinthians are becoming an af-

---

33. Consult Georg Braumann, *NIDNTT*, vol. 1, pp. 570–71; Otto Schmitz, *TDNT*, vol. 5, p. 795.

front to Jesus Christ.[34] In the same sentence, he exhorts them to be harmonious and commands them not to be schismatic ("that there be no divisions among you"). In his discourse he is not refuting heresies; rather, he seeks to prevent discord.[35] Both his positive and negative instructions form the two sides of the proverbial coin. The expression *divisions* conveys the thought of wrangling and strife that tear the church apart. In a word, Paul tells the Corinthians to desist.

c. *Unity.* The church is comparable to the human body (see 12:12–27), which is perfectly joined together and reflects unity and harmony. The Greek word *katartizein* means to make a person what God intends him or her to be, namely, perfect. It is used of those people "who have been restored to harmony."[36] They are now exhorted to work together in unity of mind and judgment. The contrast with the preceding clauses in this sentence is striking, for Paul writes, "But . . . be united in the same mind and thought." The term *mind* relates to the power of observation and the word *thought* to forming a judgment or opinion. Paul wants the Corinthians to be united in their observations and judgments and to relinquish their divisiveness. He is telling them that in respect to their mind and thought they must strive for perfect harmony and continue to live together in peace.

Although Paul desires to rid the church of divisiveness, he is not asking the Corinthians for uniformity in thought. Instead, among God's people he allows diversity in unity. As the seventeenth-century writer Rupert Meldenius put it:

> In necessary things—unity;
> In nonessential things—mutual toleration;
> And, in all things, love.

11. For some of Chloe's people have told me concerning you, my brothers, that there are quarrels among you.

a. "For some of Chloe's people." We have no information about Chloe other than her name, which occurs only once in the New Testament. Whether she lived in Ephesus, where Paul was when he wrote the letter, or in Corinth, is not known. We would expect that she resided in Corinth, for the text implies that the Corinthians knew her. Also, the news concerning the factions originated there. Another possibility is that Chloe was a businesswoman who lived in Ephesus and that her employees (either slaves, freedmen, or members of her family) regularly traveled between Corinth and Ephesus and were fully acquainted with the church. Whether Chloe was a Christian cannot be determined.[37]

---

34. Consult Thomas W. Gillespie, "A Pattern of Prophetic Speech in First Corinthians," *JBL* 97 (1978): 74–95.

35. Refer to Lawrence L. Welborn, "On the Discord in Corinth: 1 Corinthians 1–4 and Ancient Politics," *JBL* 106 (1987): 85–111.

36. Thayer, p. 336.

37. F. R. Montgomery Hitchcock is of the opinion she was either a goddess or a pagan. "Who Are 'the People of Chloe' in 1 Cor. 1:11?" *JTS* 25 (1924): 163–67.

b. "[They] have told me concerning you, my brothers." Paul mentions the source of his information and so indicates that he has not heard rumors but has received facts. He is told by people who are not sent as messengers by the church in Corinth but who come to him on their own accord. Obviously the church has not taken the initiative to inform Paul about its quarrels. Nonetheless, he deals pastorally with the members of the Corinthian church by calling them *my* brothers (and sisters). He desires good relations and thus uses the term *brothers* a second time in as many verses (vv. 10, 11).

c. "That there are quarrels[38] among you." These contentions had not yet resulted in permanent divisions but contributed to a spirit of divisiveness that hampered the spiritual welfare of the church (see James 4:2). Moreover, quarrels demonstrate a lack of love and so violate God's command to love one another.

12. What I mean is this: that each of you says, "I am of Paul," or "I am of Apollos," or "I am of Cephas," or "I am of Christ."

The clause *what I mean is this* shows that Paul is fully informed about the quarrels in Corinth. He is saying: "Let's come to the point." The issue is that the Corinthians themselves have created groups within the church and even have associated these factions with specific persons. The irony, however, is that the persons whose names have been affixed to these parties (Paul, Apollos, and Cephas) repudiate such groups and quarrels. To look at the matter from a different perspective, no leader went to Corinth to form his own party.

In the Corinthian church, one member claims that he is a follower of Paul, another declares that he belongs to Apollos, still another states that he emulates Peter, and a last one asserts that he is a disciple of Christ. We ought not to draw the conclusion that these four parties embrace all the members of the church. "No doubt there were Corinthians who joined none of the four parties."[39]

a. "'I am of Paul.'" Paul's name occurs first in the list of the four names. In an ascending order the name of Christ is last as the highest in rank; consequently, Paul's name is the least important. Paul had founded the church, but because of the existing factionalism not everyone in the church favored the apostle. Even those who were favorably disposed to Paul had gone beyond his teaching and intentions, for Paul himself had not originated a separate party. Because he preached the gospel, he had become the Corinthians' spiritual father in Christ Jesus (4:15). But Paul was not interested in receiving recognition for work he had done; rather, he was engaged in confirming the Corinthians in Christ (see v. 6). He did not want them to look at him but at the Lord.

Rejecting the divisive spirit of the Corinthians, Paul continued to uphold the integrity of Apollos. He realized that Apollos, too, repudiated the quarrels and

---

38. The Greek word for quarrels is typically Pauline. It occurs nine times in Paul's epistles and nowhere else in the New Testament. See Rom. 1:29; 13:13; I Cor. 1:11; 3:3; II Cor. 12:20; Gal. 5:20; Phil. 1:15; I Tim. 6:4; Titus 3:9.

39. Archibald Robertson and Alfred Plummer, *A Critical and Exegetical Commentary on the First Epistle of St. Paul to the Corinthians,* International Critical Commentary, 2d ed. (1911; reprint ed., Edinburgh: Clark, 1975), p. 11.

factions in the church. We know that throughout this epistle, Paul honors his co-worker Apollos and speaks appreciatively of his labors (3:4, 5, 6, 22; 4:6; 16:12).

b. "'I am of Apollos.'" We know that Apollos hailed from the renowned city of Alexandria—a university center where he was educated. He had a thorough knowledge of the Scriptures and, although he taught about Jesus, he had to learn the way of salvation more accurately from Priscilla and Aquila in Ephesus (Acts 18:24–26). He became Paul's successor in Corinth and was an eloquent speaker (Acts 18:24–28). Some people in the church were impressed by this orator, especially since they regarded Paul as a weak person whose oral presentations lacked eloquence (2:1; II Cor. 10:10; 11:6). From a human point of view, Paul faced a competitor who had bested him in the pulpit at Corinth. But both Paul and Apollos refused to see each other as competitors. They were fellow workers in proclaiming the gospel of Christ.

c. "'I am of Cephas.'" Whether in Paul's absence from Corinth Cephas (Peter) had visited the church cannot be verified. It is probable that he went there.[40] We assume that the Corinthians were acquainted with Peter, for Paul mentions that Peter was accompanied by his wife on missionary journeys (9:5). Peter, known as the head of the church and spokesman of the apostles, was highly respected. Paul identifies Peter as Cephas and seems to have a proclivity for using his Aramaic name instead of the Greek translation *Petros*. In his epistles, he refers twice to Peter (Gal. 2:7, 8) but eight times to Cephas (in the Greek—1:12; 3:22; 9:5; 15:5; Gal. 1:18; 2:9, 11, 14; see John 1:42 for the same construction). Peter and Paul had mutual respect for one another, so that we can be sure that Peter also would abhor having his name attached to a faction in Corinth.

d. "'I am of Christ.'" We encounter a number of questions when we try to interpret this saying. For example, did the Corinthians who were not associated with the other groups form a party of Christ? Were not all these Christians followers of Christ? Is Christ not in a category different from the other three persons? Did Paul set himself against the Corinthians by saying, "I am of Christ"?

We are unable to answer many of these questions because Paul provides no information other than what is given in this section of the text. The grammar of this text precludes the interpretation that Paul uttered the saying *I am of Christ*. Elsewhere he mentions the three names *Paul, Apollos,* and *Cephas* once more and then emphatically tells the Corinthians that they are of Christ (3:22–23; and II Cor. 10:7). He implies that the church universal with all its individual members belongs to Jesus Christ.

---

40. Eusebius *Ecclesiastical History* 2.25. And see C. K. Barrett, "Cephas and Corinth," in *Abraham unser Vater: Juden und Christen im Gespräch über die Bibel, Festschrift für Otto Michel zum 60,* ed. Otto Betz, Martin Hengel, and Paul Schmidt (Leiden: Brill, 1963), pp. 1–12; also his *Commentary on the First Epistle to the Corinthians,* Harper's New Testament Commentaries series (New York and Evanston: Harper and Row, 1968), p. 44.

Practical Considerations in 1:10–12

Sabine Baring-Gould wrote the magnificent hymn "Onward Christian Soldiers" and, comparing the church to a mighty army, said:

> Brothers, we are treading
> Where the saints have trod;
> We are not divided,
> All one body we,
> One in hope and doctrine,
> One in charity.

However, the countless divisions in the church make the Christian weep. Apart from geographical and linguistic conflicts, disputes within the church have been the cause of many schisms. John Calvin observes, "Where divisions are rife in religion, it is bound to happen that what is in men's minds will soon erupt in real conflict. For while nothing is more effective for joining us together, and there is nothing which does more to unite our minds, and keep them peaceful, than agreement in religion, yet if disagreement has somehow arisen in connexion with it, the inevitable result is that men are quickly stirred up to engage in fighting, and there is no other field with fiercer disputes."[41]

13. Is Christ divided? Was Paul crucified for you? Were you baptized in the name of Paul?

a. *First question.* "Is Christ divided?" Most translators understand the first three words of this verse as a question, not as a statement.[42] Because these words are followed by two interrogative sentences, scholars see a logical sequence of three questions. All three questions are rhetorical and expect a negative answer.

Paul directed the readers' attention to Christ with the query whether Christ is divided. Paul said no to this question but the Corinthians apparently said yes. These people thought that they could divide the Christ.[43] Was Christ divided up in the sense that he was torn to pieces? One commentator does not think so. G. G. Findlay comments that *to divide* "denotes *distribution*, not dismemberment."[44] But it is impossible to distribute Christ, for he is the head of the church which is his body. And the body must honor its head; from its head the members receive sustenance and direction. With the question "Is Christ divided?" Paul directed atten-

---

41. Calvin, *I Corinthians*, pp. 26–27.

42. Some translations feature an exclamatory statement: "Surely Christ has not been divided among you!" (NEB, REB) or "Christ has been divided into groups!" (GNB). Some ancient manuscripts (e.g., p46vid, 326, 1962) prefix the interrogative statement with the word *not* to conform the clause to the next two questions. And some translators have adopted the reading that includes the negative particle (see NEB, REB).

43. A few versions read "divide up" or "into" (NAB, SEB, *Cassirer*) or "parcel out" (JB, *Moffatt*).

44. G. G. Findlay, *St. Paul's First Epistle to the Corinthians*, in vol. 3 of *The Expositor's Greek Testament*, ed. W. Robertson Nicoll, 5 vols. (1910; reprint ed., Grand Rapids: Eerdmans, 1961), p. 765.

tion to the head of the body, honored Christ, and promoted the unity of the church.

b. *Second question.* "Was Paul crucified for you?" The Corinthians should immediately perceive the absurdity of this question. Not Paul but Christ was crucified for them. Some of the Corinthians may have the highest esteem for the founder of the church in Corinth, but they will have to admit that Paul did not die on a cross to deliver them from sin. They ought not to say that they belong to Paul (or even Apollos or Peter), for then they dishonor Christ.

In Paul's epistles the verb group *to crucify* occurs only eight times.[45] Here he applies to himself the term that belongs exclusively to Christ.

c. *Third question.* "Were you baptized in the name of Paul?" When the Corinthians received the sign of baptism, they were either baptized in the name of the Father, Son, and Holy Spirit (Matt. 28:19) or in the name of Jesus (Acts 2:38; 10:48; 19:5). "Baptism or faith constitutes the *belonging* to God or to the Son of God."[46] Baptism implies that one identifies completely with the person in whose name he or she has been baptized. The absurdity of claiming Paul's name (or the name of Apollos or Peter) is evident. Because of their baptism into Christ's death (Rom. 6:3), the Corinthians belonged to Jesus Christ and lived a new life. Because of the sign and seal of baptism, they were called Christians.

14. I thank God that I baptized none of you except Crispus and Gaius, 15. that no one should say that you were baptized in my name.

a. "I thank God." Editors and translators of the Greek New Testament are divided with respect to the inclusion or deletion of the word *God.* More of them favor inserting[47] the word than excluding it. Paul's usage throughout his epistles supports its inclusion, yet it is omitted from some of the major manuscripts.

b. "I baptized none of you." Paul is not offering a prayer of thanksgiving (see v. 4) but is expressing satisfaction that he has not baptized many of the believers in Corinth. He had left the task of baptizing converts to others. Similarly, not Peter and John but Philip baptized the Samaritans (Acts 8:12), and Peter instructed the six Jewish Christians from Joppa to baptize the members of Cornelius's household (Acts 10:48; 11:12).

c. "Except Crispus and Gaius." According to Luke's account, Crispus had been a synagogue ruler in Corinth, who with all the members of his household believed in Jesus (Acts 18:8). When he withdrew from the synagogue, Sosthenes succeeded him (Acts 18:17).

The name *Gaius* occurs five times in the New Testament (Acts 19:29; 20:4; Rom. 16:23; I Cor. 1:14; III John 1). When Paul spent the winter in Corinth,

---

45. I Cor. 1:13, 23; 2:2, 8; II Cor. 13:4; Gal. 3:1; 5:24; 6:14.

46. Adolf Deissmann, *Bible Studies* (reprint ed.; Winona Lake, Ind.: Alpha, 1979), p. 147; James D. G. Dunn, *Baptism in the Holy Spirit,* Studies in Biblical Theology, 2d series 15 (London: SCM, 1970), p. 117.

47. Editors of UBS, Nes-Al, Merk, Souter, and the Majority Text include it. See KJV, NKJV, NASB, NAB, NEB, REB, NRSV, SEB, GNB.

where he composed his letter to the Romans, he stayed at the house of Gaius (Rom. 16:23). We suspect that this Gaius is the same person Paul baptized when he founded the Corinthian church.

d. "No one should say that you were baptized in my name." Paul is thankful that during his ministry he did not baptize believers, so that no one could attach significance to his name. Paul certainly did not baptize people in his own name, but he wanted the people to look to Christ who redeemed them and not to the preacher who baptized them.

16. I baptized also the household of Stephanas; beyond that I do not know if I baptized any other.

Paul appears to have a lapse of memory. He fails to place Stephanas and his family with Crispus and Gaius. However, near the end of his epistle Paul reveals that Stephanas's household were the first believers in the province of Achaia (16:15). Some commentators think that Stephanas was converted in Athens, which was part of Achaia, even though his family lived in Corinth.[48] But this is nothing more than a conjecture. Stephanas himself was present when Paul wrote this epistle; he may have been the scribe who wrote the letter for Paul and refreshed his memory. Paul reveals normal human characteristics even when he is writing an inspired book of the Bible.

Stephanas and the members of his household were ardent workers in the Corinthian church who ministered to the spiritual needs of the Christians (16:15). How large was the circle of his household? The Bible teaches that the term *household* included husbands, wives, children, other relatives, slaves, and visitors. For example, Abraham had 318 trained men who had been born into his household (Gen. 14:14). Heads of families considered their households religious units in which they themselves gave leadership. Thus Luke says that when salvation came to Zacchaeus, it came to his household, too (Luke 19:9; compare John 4:53). In Acts, he reveals that households and their heads were saved and baptized: Cornelius (10:2, 48; 11:14); Lydia (16:15); the Philippian jailer (16:31–34); Crispus (18:8). Paul mentions Onesiphorus's household (II Tim. 1:16) and refers to believers who belonged to Caesar's household (Phil. 4:22). We have no information concerning the extent of Stephanas's household. As an influential person, he may have been the head of a broad family circle.

Paul writes that he cannot remember anyone else whom he baptized. He puts no value on the privilege of baptizing converts, for his calling was not to baptize believers but to preach the gospel.

17. For Christ sent me not to baptize but to preach the gospel, not in wisdom of words that the cross of Christ may not be emptied.

In this text, Paul expresses one positive element and three negative ones. The affirmative statement is that Christ sent him to preach the message of salvation. The disclaimers are that Paul was not told to baptize believers, that the procla-

---

48. Robertson and Plummer, *First Corinthians*, p. 15.

mation of this message should not become a philosophical treatise, and that Christ's cross should not lose its central position.

a. *Task.* In the preceding two verses (vv. 15, 16) Paul emphatically states that he has no interest in baptizing converts. Now he conveys the reason: Christ commissioned him to be a preacher of the gospel (Rom. 1:1; 15:15–16; Gal. 1:16). The task of preaching the gospel requires talent, education, tact, and skill. Baptizing believers is a simple act that requires no training, but preaching is a constant task of leading people to repentance, faith, new life, and growth. Baptizing is a one-time act that distinguishes a Christian from the world, but preaching takes place every Lord's Day and often on weekdays.

Paul is by no means discrediting baptism. He is following the example Jesus set during his earthly ministry: Christ proclaimed the gospel and the disciples baptized the believers (John 4:1–2). Jesus designated the apostles fishers of men (Matt. 4:19) and commissioned them to catch men through preaching. "To preach the gospel is to cast the net; it is apostolic work. To baptize is to gather the fish now taken and put them into vessels."[49] Paul had to use all his time and talent to preach the Word and hence left the matter of baptism primarily to others.

b. *Manner.* "Not in wisdom of words." Paul does not say "words of wisdom" or "wisdom to speak," but, to be precise, "in wisdom of words." This is the first time in the epistle that Paul writes the word *wisdom.* In the succeeding verses of chapters 1 and 2, he uses the word as he contrasts God's wisdom and worldly wisdom. But in this verse, the phrase *wisdom of words* describes the manner of a Greek orator who eloquently delivers a speech. In Greek rhetoric, speakers cleverly presented philosophical arguments to support a particular viewpoint. Paul separates himself from this procedure, for he proclaims the message of the cross in simple terms.

By preaching the gospel in plain terms, Paul follows the example of Jesus. Jesus proclaimed the message of salvation and the common people heard him gladly. Similarly, the apostles were commissioned to preach the gospel with simplicity and clarity. "'To tell good *news* in *wisdom* of word' is a contradiction; 'news' only needs and admits of straightforward telling. To dress out the story of Calvary in specious theorems, would have been to 'empty the cross of Christ,' to *eviscerate* the Gospel."[50]

"[So] that the cross of Christ may not be emptied." When Paul proclaimed the message of Christ's death on Calvary's cross, he was scorned in the Greco-Roman world. That world rejected the message of an ignominious death on a cross. If Paul, however, had adopted Greek practice and had delivered his message with rhetorical eloquence, the message of the cross would have been emptied of its power and glory. Then his message would have had a hollow ring and consequently no conversions and baptisms would have taken place.

---

49. Refer to Frederic Louis Godet, *Commentary on First Corinthians* (1886; reprint ed., Grand Rapids: Kregel, 1977), pp. 84–85.

50. Findlay, *First Corinthians,* p. 767.

The Corinthians knew that Paul had preached the gospel of Christ's death without resorting to oratory and human wisdom (see 2:1). In humility, he had called them to repentance and faith in Jesus Christ. He had pointed to the shameful cross of Christ by which they were saved from sin and death.

Practical Considerations in 1:16

North American culture accepts individualism as a way of life. It stimulates a desire for freedom and promotes striving for success in a competitive society. It encourages the individual to climb the social, economic, and political ladder on his or her own merits.

Statistics reveal that at least one third of the population in North America moves every year. Families are often scattered from north to south and from east to west. Adults frequently live at great distances from their parents and from their brothers and sisters. When aging parents need daily care, they are placed in retirement homes where their sons and daughters can visit them from time to time. Because of divorce, desertion, and separation, increasing numbers of families are headed by a single parent. Consequently, the family as such is a rather small unit consisting of either one or two parents and usually two to three children.

In other cultures, the family usually consists of a clan that includes grandparents, fathers and mothers, sons and daughters, uncles and aunts, nephews and nieces. Retirement homes for the elderly are nonexistent, for aging parents are cared for by their children and grandchildren. The family provides for the material, social, emotional, and spiritual needs of all its members.

When either North Americans or people of other cultures read a Scripture passage with the word *household,* the interpretation and understanding of the word invariably differ. We may safely assume that a culture which regards the family as a clan has stronger resemblance to the biblical pattern than a structure which promotes individualism and rootlessness.

Greek Words, Phrases, and Constructions in 1:10, 12, 16–17

Verse 10

ἵνα—the conjunction introduces not a pure purpose clause but an object clause following a verb that exhorts. The δέ is clearly adversative to set apart the periphrastic construction ἦτε κατηρτισμένοι (that you may be complete). The construction is in the perfect tense to show lasting effect and in the passive to imply that God is the agent.

Verse 12

μὲν . . . δέ —the contrast indicates that some are saying this and others that. The repetition of δέ points to similar speakers.

Verses 16–17

λοιπόν—this adverbial expression means "in addition to that."

οὐ—the particle literally negates the verb *send*, but the flow of the sentence definitely suggests that it limits the activity of the infinitive *to baptize*.

---

18 For the word of the cross is foolishness to those who are perishing, but to us who are being saved it is the power of God. 19 For it is written,

> "I will destroy the wisdom of the wise
> and the intelligence of the intelligent
> I will set aside."

20 Where is the wise? Where is the expert in the law? Where is the debater of this age? Has not God made foolish the wisdom of this world? 21 For since in the wisdom of God the world through its wisdom did not know God, God was pleased to save those who believe through the foolishness of the message that was preached. 22 And since Jews request signs and Greeks look for wisdom, 23 we preach Christ crucified, to the Jews a stumbling-block, and to Gentiles foolishness. 24 To those who are called, both the Jews and the Greeks, Christ is the power of God and the wisdom of God. 25 Because the foolishness of God is wiser than men and the weakness of God is stronger than men.

26 Consider your call, brothers, that there were not many wise men according to the flesh, not many powerful, not many of noble birth. 27 But God has chosen the foolish things of the world to shame the wise, and God has chosen the weak things of the world to shame the strong. 28 And God has chosen the insignificant things of the world and the despised things, the things that are not, that he might nullify the things that are, 29 that no man should boast before God. 30 But because of him you are in Christ Jesus, who has become wisdom from God for us: righteousness, and holiness, and redemption, 31 that just as it is written,

> "Let him who boasts boast in the Lord."

---

2. The Folly of the Cross
1:18–2:5

In this section, Paul teaches that what is foolishness to the world (namely, the preaching of the cross) is wisdom to God, and what is wisdom to the world (that is, philosophical systems devised by man) is foolishness to God. He delineates the effect of preaching the message of Christ's cross (v. 18), supports his teaching with an Old Testament passage (v. 19), and forces the Corinthians to draw their own conclusions by asking a series of questions (v. 20).

a. The Lost and the Saved
1:18–20

18. For the word of the cross is foolishness to those who are perishing, but to us who are being saved it is the power of God.

Every word in this text is significant, for each contributes to one powerful message. The conjunction *for* serves as a link to Paul's reference to the cross of Christ (v. 17) and makes verse 18 explanatory. When Paul writes *the word of the cross,* he separates it from the phrase *wisdom of words* (v. 17). Although the two terms translated "word" and "words" have the same original form (*logos*) in Greek, in context they have nothing in common. In fact, they are opposites. The word of the cross is the message that proclaims an event of historical and theological significance. It points to Christ who died the death of a criminal but whose death concerns the eternal destiny of man. But the wisdom of words that the orator utters is of human origin and is opposed to the message of the cross.

"The word of the cross is foolishness." For Paul's Gentile contemporaries, the account of Christ's death on a cross outside the city of Jerusalem was folly. They classified Jesus as a criminal or a degenerate slave, for only such social deviates were crucified by the Romans. Paul's message of the cross, therefore, was foolishness to the Greeks (v. 23).

"[Foolishness] to those who are perishing." The present participle *are perishing* denotes action that is in the process of occurring. This expression has both a subjective and an objective element: subjectively, the people repudiating Paul's message regard it as folly; objectively, the effect of the rejection is irrevocable doom (II Cor. 2:15; 4:3; II Thess. 2:10). They are not on the verge of perishing but in actuality are perishing.

By contrast, the Corinthians are not perishing. They have been called and sanctified (v. 2); they belong to a different class because they have accepted the "word of the cross" and believe the gospel. Therefore, Paul encourages his readers. He includes himself when he says:

"But to us who are being saved." Notice that the clause *who are being saved* serves as an explanation of the personal pronoun *us*. Paul places himself on the same level as the Corinthians and affirms that they are being saved. But were they not saved when God called them? What precisely does Paul teach concerning the time of salvation? What tense of the verb *to save* is used?[51] A few examples illuminate Paul's teaching:

> *Past:* "For in this hope we were saved" (Rom. 8:24)
>   "By grace you have been saved" (Eph. 2:5, 8)
>   "By his mercy he saved us" (Titus 3:5).
> *Present:* "Through which [gospel] you are being saved" (I Cor. 15:2)
>   "Those who are being saved" (II Cor. 2:15).
> *Future:* "How much more shall we be saved?" (Rom. 5:9)
>   "Thus all Israel will be saved" (Rom. 11:26).

Believers, then, are saved in principle during their life on earth. Throughout their earthly sojourn they cherish this blessed assurance, for they are on the way to being saved completely (compare Heb. 1:14). Complete salvation comes to them when they leave this earthly scene and enter the presence of God.

"It is the power of God." Paul confidently tells his readers: "to us belongs God's power." This language resembles what Paul uses in his epistle to the Romans: "I am not ashamed of the gospel, because it is the power of God for the salvation of everyone who believes" (1:16). God's power becomes effective when

---

51. Consult J. B. Lightfoot, *Notes on the Epistles of St. Paul from Unpublished Commentaries* (1895; reprint ed., Grand Rapids: Zondervan, 1957), pp. 157–58.

Christ's gospel is proclaimed and people accept this message in faith. "The word of the cross" has power to raise the sinner from spiritual death and to provide newness of life. In essence, God is dynamically providing salvation for his people.[52]

However, Paul's sophisticated contemporaries thought he was proclaiming utter folly by connecting God's power to the weakness of the cross.[53] Adopting Jesus' methodology of turning to the Scriptures for proof, Paul confirms his teaching by citing a passage from the Old Testament.

19. For it is written,
> **"I will destroy the wisdom of the wise**
> **and the intelligence of the intelligent**
> **I will set aside."**

This is a quotation that Paul takes almost word for word from the Septuagint, the Greek translation of the Old Testament Scriptures (Isa. 29:14; see also Ps. 33:10). The Septuagint varies from the Hebrew text, which reads, "The wisdom of the wise will perish and the intelligence of the intelligent will vanish."

The context of this Old Testament passage refers to the people of Israel who honor God with their lips but not with their hearts (Isa. 29:13; Matt. 15:8–9). God nullifies the wisdom of Israel's pundits and causes human intelligence to dissipate. He opposes wisdom that originates in a heart which is far removed from serving God. In the New Testament, James calls earthly wisdom—as opposed to heavenly wisdom—unspiritual and of the devil (James 3:15). God is not dependent on our wisdom; on the contrary, we are urged to ask God for wisdom (James 1:5), and he will liberally give it to anyone who comes to him in faith. Gordon D. Fee rightly observes: "Yet it is the folly of our human machinations that we think we can outwit God, or that lets us think that God ought to be as smart as we are."[54]

20. Where is the wise? Where is the expert in the law? Where is the debater of this age? Has not God made foolish the wisdom of this world?

a. *Allusions.* In I Corinthians, Paul appears to have a predilection for quoting from and alluding to Isaiah's prophecy.[55] Two of the questions in this verse— Where is the wise? Where is the expert in the law?—are explicitly from Isaiah, and Paul relies implicitly on Isaiah for a third question, Has not God made foolish the wisdom of the world?

In the prophet's oracle against Egypt, Isaiah queries where Pharaoh's wise men are (Isa. 19:12). Next, in the context of the misery pronounced on the Assyrians, Isaiah asks where the scribe is (Isa. 33:18, NKJV). He reflects on the siege

---

52. Compare Donald Guthrie, *New Testament Theology* (Downers Grove: Inter-Varsity, 1981), p. 592.

53. Refer to Peter Lampe, "Theological Wisdom and the 'Word About the Cross': The Rhetorical Scheme in 1 Corinthians 1–4," *Interp* 44 (1990): 120.

54. Fee, *First Corinthians*, p. 70.

55. Of the seventeen direct quotations from the Old Testament, six are from Isaiah: Isa. 29:14 in 1:19; Isa. 64:4 in 2:9; Isa. 40:13 in 2:16; Isa. 28:11–12 in 14:21; Isa. 22:13 in 15:32; Isa. 25:8 in 15:54.

of Jerusalem by the forces of Sennacherib, king of Assyria (Isa. 36–37). As the Assyrian army surrounded Jerusalem, King Hezekiah put his trust in Israel's God, who delivered him from oppression. An angel of the Lord put to death 185,000 Assyrian soldiers (Isa. 37:36). "Isaiah, reflecting on all this, pictures the people in astonishment saying: '*Where is* the scribe who (was to have *counted* the tribute (collected from the Jews)? *Where is* he who (was to have) *weighed* the tribute? *Where is* he who (was to have) counted the towers (which the Assyrians had figured on destroying)?' [Isa. 33:18]."[56] For Paul's purpose, however, the scribe is the expert in the Old Testament Scriptures.

Promising redemption for Israel, God says that he will overthrow the learning of the wise (Isa. 44:25). With a rhetorical question that expects an affirmative answer, Paul relates that God has made the wisdom of this world look foolish.

b. *Questions.* "Where is the wise?" With four questions, Paul summarizes what he stated in verse 18 and proved from Scripture in verse 19. The emphasis falls on God, who is at work in salvation and who destroys the wisdom of the wise. Should anyone with worldly wisdom intend to confront God, he would be the loser. As in Moses' time the wise men of Egypt disappeared from the scene at God's command, so likewise wisdom vanishes from the earth when teachers who are opposed to God proclaim human wisdom. Paul implies not that all the wise men have left the Corinthian scene but that their attempt to frustrate God's work is futile (see 3:19).

"Where is the expert in the law?" With the second question, Paul directs his discourse to those Jews who were trained in explaining the Old Testament Scriptures. (Incidentally, Paul himself had received this training.) These people turned to the teachings of the Old Testament law but refused to accept the message of the cross as the fulfillment of these teachings.

"Where is the debater of this age?" This third question applies to both Jewish and Greek philosophers. The phrase *this age* is the converse of *the age to come;* it contrasts the ethical values of the present world with those of Christ's kingdom.

Summarizing the preceding questions with a fourth query, Paul asks rhetorically, "Has not God made foolish the wisdom of this world?" As the world turns its wisdom against the Almighty, God turns worldly prudence into foolishness; the result is defeat for the world. Paul resorts to parallelism in the endings of the third and fourth questions. The phrases *this age* and *this world* are synonymous.[57] The Corinthians must realize that God has turned into folly the worldly wisdom of those who have rejected the message of Christ's cross, even though they themselves have not yet understood the full significance of that cross. Through it God has ushered in the age to come that transcends the present age.[58]

56. William Hendriksen, "William Hendriksen on 1 Corinthians 1.18–31," *B of T* 284 (1987): 20.

57. Barrett, *First Corinthians*, p. 53.

58. Consult James A. Davis, *Wisdom and Spirit: An Investigation of 1 Corinthians 1.18–3.20 Against the Background of Jewish Sapiential Traditions in the Greco-Roman Period* (Lanham, Md.: University Press of America, 1984), p. 74; E. McMillan, "An Aspect of Recent Wisdom Studies in the New Testament," *ResQ* 10 (1967): 201–10.

Greek Words, Phrases, and Constructions in 1:18–20

Verses 18–19

τοῖς . . . ἀπολλυμένοις—this present middle participle of the verb ἀπόλλυμι (I destroy) denotes that the process is durative and that the compound is perfective.[59]

τοῖς . . . σωζομένοις—the progressive present participle of the verb σῴζω (I save) indicates that believers are being saved.

The contrast of the particles μέν and δέ asserts that there are only two classifications: the lost and the saved.

ἀπολῶ—the verb is the future tense of ἀπόλλυμι; its close connection with the present participle of the same verb in verse 18 is interesting.

Verse 20

ἐμώρανεν—from the verb μωραίνω (I make foolish), the aorist shows completed action. See the relationship of this verb to the noun (foolishness).

κόσμου—because the manuscript evidence for including the pronoun τούτου is strong, many translators have adopted it.[60] Others suppose that the addition of the pronoun may have been influenced by the preceding expression *this age*.

---

b. Wisdom and Foolishness
1:21–25

21. For since in the wisdom of God the world through its wisdom did not know God, God was pleased to save those who believe through the foolishness of the message that was preached.

a. "For since in the wisdom of God the world through its wisdom did not know God." Both conjunctions ("for" and "since") express cause and make this verse an impassioned explanation of the manner in which God has made foolish the wisdom of the world (v. 20). Paul is specific when he says: "in the wisdom that belongs to God." The wisdom of God, not the wisdom of the world, is significant. But what does Paul mean by the phrase *the wisdom of God?* Usually two answers are given:

1. Some commentators point to the following New Testament passages: Acts 14:17, where Paul, addressing the people in Lystra, says that God did not leave himself without a witness but gave rains and fruitful seasons; Acts 17:27, in which Paul, before the Areopagus, states that men would seek God; and Romans 1:20, which declares that men are without excuse because God has made himself known in creation.[61]

2. Other commentators register objections to this line of interpretation,[62] even though they grant that the weight of these parallels is significant. One ob-

---

59. Refer to Robertson, *Grammar,* p. 827.

60. KJV, NKJV, NAB, NEB, REB, SEB, GNB, *Phillips, Cassirer.*

61. See the commentaries of Calvin, p. 39; Godet, p. 96; Hodge, p. 21; and Fee, p. 72.

62. Lightfoot, *Notes on the Epistles,* p. 161; Grosheide, *First Epistle to the Corinthians,* p. 47; W. Harold Mare, *1 Corinthians,* in vol. 10 of *The Expositor's Bible Commentary,* ed. Frank E. Gaebelein, 12 vols. (Grand Rapids: Zondervan, 1976), p. 194; Leon Morris, *1 Corinthians,* rev. ed., Tyndale New Testament Commentaries series (Leicester: Inter-Varsity; Grand Rapids: Eerdmans, 1987), p. 44.

jection is that the context of this verse relates not to God revealing himself in creation but to God saving believers through the message of Christ's cross. The basic structure of the sentence is that God in his wisdom was pleased to save those who believe the message of the cross. The main verb *was pleased* receives emphasis in the sentence and is crucial in understanding this verse.

A related objection is that the phrase *wisdom of God* stands in opposition to the phrase *the wisdom of this world*. God works out his plan of salvation in wisdom which the world calls folly. Conversely, the wisdom of the world is folly to God because it is a rejection of the message of the cross.

And a third objection is that the clause "the world through its wisdom did not know God" should not be taken logically to precede the phrase *God was pleased*. That is, God rejects the world's wisdom because of its refusal to accept divine wisdom. But it pleases God to save those who in faith accept Christ's gospel.

b. "God was pleased to save those who believe through the foolishness of the message that was preached." The verb *to please* points to the sovereignty of God as he chooses to elect believers on the basis of his decree, resolve, and purpose.[63] God's pleasure, however, is diametrically opposed to the human folly that espouses worldly wisdom. The world either purposely ignores or scathingly ridicules the preaching of the gospel because to the sinful human mind it is foolishness. But God's people continue to believe this foolish gospel and fully acclaim it as God's wisdom.

c. Finally, notice the contrast of two phrases in this verse: *the world through its wisdom* and *through the foolishness of the message that was preached*. In both instances the word *through* indicates what one trusts: the world trusts in human wisdom but the believer in the foolishness of preaching. Sunday after Sunday and even on weekdays, believers listen to the preaching of the gospel and receive instruction from the Scriptures. Preaching is not only the delivery of a sermon (although effective delivery is important in itself) but also the content of the message. Believers accept that divine content in faith and respond to God's wisdom, but unbelievers reject this wisdom and call it foolishness. The result is that while the worldly person refuses to know God and is eternally lost, the believer knows God and is forever saved.

22. And since Jews request signs and Greeks look for wisdom, 23. we preach Christ crucified, to the Jews a stumbling-block, and to Gentiles foolishness.

Paul uses the conjunction *since* a second time (see v. 21) and thus provides an additional explanation. He now becomes specific by dividing the world into two groups: the Jews and the Greeks.

a. "Jews request signs and Greeks look for wisdom." As a Jew born in a Hellenistic culture, Paul ably characterizes both Jews and Greeks. From the Gospels we know that the Jews repeatedly asked Jesus for a sign.[64] Jesus refused to give in to them, for they would not believe in him unless they saw him perform a miracle

---

63. Hans Bietenhard, *NIDNTT*, vol. 2, p. 818; Gottlob Schrenk, *TDNT*, vol. 2, p. 741.
64. Matt. 12:38–39; 16:1; Mark 8:11–12; Luke 11:16; John 2:18; 6:30.

(see John 4:48). God had entrusted to the Jews the Scriptures of the Old Testament (Rom. 3:2); they were recipients of God's covenants, the law, the promises, and worship regulations (Rom. 9:3–4). Yet when Jesus came, they refused to believe in him unless he became a miracle-worker at their command. In short, the Jews rejected the divine message of salvation that Jesus brought (John 1:11).

The expression *Greeks* is broader than a mere reference to the citizens of Corinth or even Greece as a nation; it refers to a class of people who are influenced by Greek language, philosophy, and culture. Stoic and Epicurean philosophers (Acts 17:18) sought reasons for their existence in this world. With inquisitive minds, they and their countrymen sought after wisdom. Both Jews and Greeks, however, show skepticism and stand in contrast to Paul and his helpers who preach Christ's gospel.

b. "We preach Christ crucified, to the Jews a stumbling-block, and to Gentiles foolishness." The dissimilarity is indeed striking. Paul intensifies his earlier reference to the cross (vv. 17, 18) when he intimates that in their preaching he and his colleagues are explaining the significance of Christ's crucifixion (see 2:2). Triumphantly he utters a truth that has been adopted by the Christian church as a motto: "We preach Christ crucified." But precisely what is the meaning of that saying? Paul himself provides a twofold answer.

"To the Jews a stumbling-block." From a Jewish point of view, God had cursed a crucified person forever. Even a mere reference to such a person was offensive to a religiously sensitive Jew (compare Deut. 21:23; Gal. 3:13; 5:11). Indeed, calling a crucified man the Christ, that is, the Messiah, was the height of spiritual insensitivity.

"And to Gentiles foolishness." For the Gentiles, the idea of proclaiming a message about a person who was nailed to a cross was utter foolishness. A person crucified by Roman authorities usually was a criminal slave. In the Gentiles' minds, it would be ridiculous to say anything at all regarding a man condemned so to die. Certainly, a criminal slave who died on a cross could not be Lord and Savior of mankind.

Believers accept the message of the cross and readily admit that they do not fully understand the significance of Jesus' suffering and death on the cross. Nevertheless, they know that through faith they are saved.

24. To those who are called, both the Jews and the Greeks, Christ is the power of God and the wisdom of God. 25. Because the foolishness of God is wiser than men and the weakness of God is stronger than men.

Once again Paul uses the verb *to call* (see vv. 1, 2, 9). Only those people, including Jews and Greeks, who have been effectually called by God are able to believe the message of the cross and accept it without reservations. God calls to himself a people who are beloved, holy, and separated from the world.[65] He calls

---

65. Herman N. Ridderbos, *Paul: An Outline of His Theology*, trans. John Richard de Witt (Grand Rapids: Eerdmans, 1975), p. 333; D. A. Carson, *The Cross and Christian Ministry* (Grand Rapids: Baker, 1993), pp. 22–23.

them away from those Jews for whom Christ is an offense and from those Greeks for whom Christ is folly. Coming from Jewish communities and Greek culture, these people believe the message of Christ (v. 21) and are saved. In this context the name *Christ* means the crucified and resurrected Christ.

In verses 24 and 25 Paul ascribes four qualities to God—power, wisdom, foolishness, and weakness—that we will look at individually.

a. *Power of God.* Christ is the power of God. Paul relates the word *power* not to Christ's work of creation (John 1:3; Col. 1:16–17; Heb. 1:2) but to his work of *re*-creation (see v. 18; Rom. 1:4, 16). Christ is God's power in redeeming his people. God's power is revealed in Christ's resurrection, which is the greatest miracle of all times. Indeed, the word *power* is an answer to the Jews' request for a sign.

b. *Wisdom of God.* Paul does not say that Christ personifies wisdom, but that Christ is God's reply to the Gentiles who consider the message of the cross to be foolishness. The wisdom of God contrasts with the foolishness of the Gentiles.

c. *Foolishness of God.* "Because the foolishness of God is wiser than men." Foolishness ascribed to God and compared with human wisdom is infinitely greater than the qualities ascribed to man.[66] God uses a crib in Bethlehem as a cradle for his royal Son and he selects a cruel cross as the instrument of death for his divine emissary.

d. *Weakness of God.* "And the weakness of God is stronger than men." God resorts to those things that are foolish and weak in the eyes of man to show his wisdom and strength in the work of saving God's people. Answering Paul's repeated plea to remove a thorn from his flesh, the Lord said: "My grace is adequate for you, for my power is perfected in weakness" (II Cor. 12:9; see also 13:4).

Greek Words, Phrases, and Constructions in 1:21–25

Verse 21

ἐπειδὴ γάρ—these two conjunctions ("for since") emphasize cause and explain the preceding verse.

τοῦ κηρύγματος—the noun derived from the verb κηρύσσω (I preach) refers not to the activity of preaching but to the content of the gospel.

σῶσαι τοὺς πιστεύοντας—the aorist infinitive ("to save") denotes a single action viewed in its entirety.[67] The present active participle ("they who believe") reveals continued progress.

Verse 23

ἐσταυρωμένον—from the verb σταυρόω (I crucify), the perfect tense in this passive participle shows that the deed of crucifying Jesus occurred in the past but the effect of this act is relevant for the past, present, and future.

---

66. Refer to J. M. Cooper, "The Foolishness of God versus the Wisdom of Man," *ThEd* 14 (1983): 35–40.

67. Refer to H. E. Dana and Julius R. Mantey, *A Manual Grammar of the Greek New Testament* (1927; reprint ed., New York: Macmillan, 1967), p. 196.

μὲν ... δέ—the contrast between the interests of the Jews and of the Greeks is pronounced.

Verse 25

ὅτι—this conjunction apparently introduces a coordinate clause, and so does the conjunction γάρ in the following verse (v. 26). Editors of the Greek text (Nes-Al, UBS) place a raised period (semicolon) at the end of verse 24 to show the coordinate structure of the next clause.

τῶν ἀνθρώπων—here is an implied reference to the "wisdom of men," translated "[wiser than] the wisdom of men."[68]

---

c. The Weak and the Strong
1:26–31

26. Consider your call, brothers, that there were not many wise men according to the flesh, not many powerful, not many of noble birth.

a. *Call.* When Paul presents a sensitive subject that touches his readers personally, he frequently resorts to the cordial greeting *brothers*. In the parlance of that day, this term also included women.

The verb *to consider* can in this verse be understood either as a command (the imperative mood) or as a statement of fact (the indicative mood). The verb is the first word in the Greek sentence; hence, it is emphatic. Most translators favor the imperative mood and translate it (with variations in word choice) "Consider!"[69] Others take the verb in the indicative mood and render it "you are considering."[70]

Paul tells the Corinthians to contemplate their call. But what is the significance of the expression *call* or *calling?* For one thing, God calls an individual through the preaching and teaching of the gospel. If that call is effectual through the work of the Holy Spirit, the believer enjoys intimate fellowship with Christ (vv. 2, 9, 24). Next, the believer who responds to God's call is brought into fellowship with other believers (see Eph. 4:1).[71]

Moreover, Paul reminds his readers of their spiritual calling. They are not only called, they are also holy (v. 2), and as such they are God's people. They must understand God's display of foolishness and weakness with reference to Jesus' cross. They must be willing to endure the reproach of the cross (Gal. 5:11) and show the humility of Christ. Some Corinthian Christians were of the opinion that their place in the church was superior to that of the rest of the believers (v. 12). They had no interest in advancing the spiritual welfare of fellow believers. Their divisiveness prevented them from ministering to others.[72] Paul is

---

68. C. F. D. Moule, *An Idiom-Book of New Testament Greek,* 2d ed. (Cambridge: Cambridge University Press, 1960), p. 98.

69. NEB, REB, NIV, RSV, NRSV, NASB, GNB, SEB, MLB, *Phillips,* and *Cassirer.*

70. KJV, NKJV; commentators Barrett, Bengel, Grosheide, Hodge.

71. Lothar Coenen, *NIDNTT,* vol. 1, p. 275.

72. Consult R. A. Horsley, "Wisdom of Word and Words of Wisdom in Corinth," *CBQ* 39 (1977): 224–39.

about to present teaching that relates to the educational, economic, and social status of these Corinthians: the wise, the powerful, and those of noble birth.[73]

b. *Class.* The church in Corinth consisted of ordinary people and a few leading figures who had gained educational, financial, and social prominence.[74] Among the prominent persons were Stephanas (v. 16; 16:17), the former synagogue leaders Sosthenes and Crispus (vv. 1, 14), the generous Gaius, and Erastus, the city treasurer (Rom. 16:23).

"There were not many wise men according to the flesh, not many powerful, not many of noble birth." Paul provides indirect information about the status of some church members before their conversion. By the standard of the world, that is, "according to the flesh," not many of them were counted among the wise, the ruling class, or the nobility. Although some of the Christians in Corinth were affluent, few were highborn. Jesus reveals that God hides spiritual matters from the wise and the learned but discloses them to little children who depend on others for help and guidance (Matt. 11:25; Luke 10:21).

27. But God has chosen the foolish things of the world to shame the wise, and God has chosen the weak things of the world to shame the strong. 28. And God has chosen the insignificant things of the world and the despised things, the things that are not, that he might nullify the things that are.

In these verses Paul shows God's work in redemption; he does so by the literary techniques of contrast and repetition. The adversative *but* begins a contrast, the positive side of the negative statements in the previous verse (v. 26). Antonyms in these verses are the *foolish things* and the *wise,* the *weak things* and the *strong.* The expression *many of noble birth* (v. 26) is balanced by an antonym, "the insignificant things" (v. 28). Repetition occurs in the choice of the verbs *has chosen* and *to shame,* and the phrase *of the world.*

Paul teaches two points:

a. *Sovereignty.* In these verses, Paul teaches not the doctrine of eternal election but God's sovereignty. He purposely repeats words and phrases to demonstrate that God is at work in the lives of the Corinthians (the verb *to choose* and the noun *world* each occur three times in two verses [vv. 27, 28]).

First, God rules sovereignly by choosing the foolish things of the world. These things are of no account (compare 3:18–19). For instance, according to the Roman author Seneca, God's people did a foolish thing by keeping the Sabbath; the Gentile world had no concept of a week and thus regarded resting on the Sabbath utter foolishness and a waste of time. But God uses the things which the world calls foolish to shame the men who are reputed to be wise.

73. See Gerd Theissen, *The Social Setting of Pauline Christianity: Essays on Corinth,* ed. and trans. John H. Schütz (Philadelphia: Fortress, 1982), p. 72.

74. Consult E. A. Judge, "The Social Identity of the First Christians: A Question of Method in Religious History," *JRH* 11 (1980): 201–17; Abraham J. Malherbe, *Social Aspects of Early Christianity,* 2d enl. ed. (Philadelphia: Fortress, 1983), p. 72.

Next, God chooses those things which the world considers weak to shame the strong. To illustrate, the Beatitudes teach that the meek will inherit the earth (Matt. 5:5), even though to the world meekness is the equivalent of weakness. In the parable of the great banquet (Luke 14:16–24), Jesus depicted the guests in the banquet hall not as the invited citizens but as the poor, the crippled, the blind, and the lame. Here the proverbial saying is applicable: "The last will be first and the first will be last" (Matt. 20:16).

Third, Paul states that the insignificant things and the despised things are chosen by God. For him, the noun *things* in the neuter plural "indicate[s] a mass in which the individuals have so little value that they are not counted as distinct personalities."[75] But those persons whom the world despises God chooses as his own. God works out his purpose by honoring that which is common and by abolishing things that are important.

b. *Purpose.* Paul writes three purpose clauses in verses 27 and 28. He says that God shames the wise, shames the strong, and nullifies the things that in man's eyes are important. In the sight of the world, these insignificant persons and things are of no account. They are nonexistent, as it were. The world counts only the wise, the powerful, and the people of noble birth. But God upsets the standards of the world by choosing the people who are foolish, weak, and despised by the world.[76] He nullifies (that is, he completely removes) these transitory standards to make room for eternal rules that are ushered in with the new order in Christ Jesus. God chooses that which is insignificant and despised and voids the things that are significant to the world. As Paul writes in his letter to the church in Rome, God calls "those things which do not exist as though they did" (Rom. 4:17, NKJV). God executes his plans according to his sovereign will.

29. That no man should boast before God.

Paul concludes his lengthy discussion with a negative purpose clause that excludes any human boasting in God's presence. When God reaches to the lowest level of existence to choose his own people and his own things and then exalts them, no one can ever claim credit for himself. God rules out all boasting in his presence, because not man but God himself deserves the praise and glory. As John Albert Bengel puts it, "We may glory not *before* him, but *in* him."[77]

The Corinthians apparently had not yet learned this lesson. They freely boasted in the accomplishments of men and the possession of material things. In his two epistles, Paul frequently reproves the readers for this sin of boasting.[78] In an exemplary manner, Paul teaches the people not to glory in their achievements but to praise the Lord in everything they are doing: even their eating and drinking must be done to God's glory (10:31). They must see that God has called them

---

75. Godet, *First Corinthians*, p. 112.

76. Refer to George E. Ladd, *A Theology of the New Testament* (Grand Rapids: Eerdmans, 1974), p. 398; J. I. Packer, *NIDNTT*, vol. 1, p. 73.

77. Bengel, *New Testament Commentary*, vol. 2, p. 173.

78. I Cor. 3:21; II Cor. 10:17; 11:12, 18.

out of a world of darkness into the marvelous fellowship of Christ. Whatever they receive comes to them from God the Father, who loves them through his Son Christ Jesus.

> Nothing in my hand I bring,
> Simply to Thy cross I cling;
> Naked, come to Thee for dress;
> Helpless, look to Thee for grace;
> Foul, I to the fountain fly;
> Wash me, Savior, or I die.
> —Thomas Hastings

30. But because of him you are in Christ Jesus, who has become wisdom from God for us: righteousness, and holiness, and redemption.

a. "But because of him." Paul comes to the heart of the matter by reminding the Corinthians of their salvation in Christ. They are believers, not unbelievers. For this reason, he begins the verse with an adversative particle that is translated "but." He points to God as the author of salvation. God sent his Son to save his people, to cleanse them from sin, and to bring them into his glorious fellowship. Paul can rightly say "because of him," for God is the cause of man's being in Christ Jesus.

b. "You are in Christ Jesus." The phrase *in Christ Jesus* or *in Christ* appears many times in Paul's epistles.[79] To be in Christ means to have intimate fellowship with him and with all other believers who are united with him. In other words, union with Christ is a privilege and at the same time an obligation to live a life that is dedicated to him.

c. "Who has become wisdom from God for us." Some translators, among whom are many commentators, understand the four nouns *wisdom, righteousness, holiness,* and *redemption* to be the sequence that Paul intended.[80] Another translator considers the clause a parenthetical comment, so that the main sentence reads: "From [God] you are through Christ Jesus (who has been made into wisdom for us by God) righteousness and sanctification and redemption." He places the parenthetical clause in apposition to Christ Jesus.[81] Still others assert that the concept *wisdom* is explained by the nouns *righteousness, holiness,* and *redemption.*[82]

A few remarks about these translations are in order. The grammar in the Greek text makes it difficult to coordinate the four words *wisdom, righteousness, holiness,* and *redemption.* The text seems to suggest that the word *wisdom* should be explained by the other three nouns (compare the analogous triad *washed, sanctified,* and *justified* in 6:11). Because we are in Christ, all four nouns relate first to him and then to us (see the translation of NEB and REB). This point is evident

---

79. Rom. 6:11; 8:1, 39; 16:3, 7, 9, 10; I Cor. 1:30; II Cor. 5:17; Gal. 1:22; 5:6; Eph. 1:13.

80. E.g., KJV, JB, NJB, Alford, Calvin, Godet, Hodge, Lenski.

81. W. Bender, "Bemerkungen zur Übersetzung von 1 Korinther 1:30," *ZNW* 71 (1980): 263–68.

82. See NKJV, NIV.

even when the term *wisdom* is interpreted in apposition to Christ Jesus. With respect to the four nouns, we conclude that "[wisdom] stands by itself, with the other three attached by way of definition."[83]

Wisdom has its origin in God, who causes it to dwell in Christ Jesus. In turn, through Christ Jesus we have become recipients of this wisdom. Through our union with Christ, we possess spiritual wisdom to know God and to appropriate his work for our salvation. The clause "who has become wisdom from God for us" reflects the saving work Christ has performed on our behalf: in Christ we have righteousness, holiness, and redemption. Paul writes that Christ is wisdom *for us*. He begins verse 30 with the pronoun *you,* which refers to the Corinthians. But when he mentions wisdom in respect to salvation he changes the pronoun to the first person plural *us* to include himself.

d. "Righteousness, and holiness, and redemption." In Christ we are made right with God. In another place, Paul teaches that God made Christ the One who bears our sin, so that we might become God's righteousness in Christ (II Cor. 5:21; see Rom. 10:4; Phil. 3:9). Righteousness is a single act but holiness is the result or effect of an act;[84] righteousness is an external act by which a person is declared righteous in Christ; holiness is an internal state attained through the indwelling presence of the Spirit in the believer.

Paul uses the word *redemption* in the list of the three explanatory nouns. These nouns are not presented in a doctrinal sequence, do not appear again as a triad in the same form, and are not explained in the context of the passage. Redemption perhaps appears last in the sequence because it "is the first gift of Christ to be begun in us, and the last to be brought to completion."[85] Christ Jesus offered himself on Calvary's cross for our redemption (Rom. 3:24–25).

31. That just as it is written,
     "Let him who boasts boast in the Lord."

In Christ Jesus we receive an enlightened mind (compare Eph. 1:18) to understand that, first, through his work we have been declared righteous before God; next, that God sanctifies us to make us stand in his presence without any wrinkle or spot; and, last, that God has set us free from the burden of guilt and bondage to sin. Christ Jesus is our Savior and Lord. Should there be anyone who wishes to boast, he can do so only by boasting in the Lord and by giving thanks to God the Father for the person and work of Christ.

As is his custom, Paul bases his teaching on Scripture. He quotes from Jeremiah 9:24–25 and presents a one-line summary: "Let him who boasts boast in the Lord" (author's translation; see also II Cor. 10:17). Jeremiah records a word from the Lord that instructs the people of Israel not to boast of human wisdom or earthly riches. Boasting, says the Lord, should be in understanding and knowing God, who shows kindness, justice, and righteousness to his people. Let a person

83. Findlay, *First Corinthians,* p. 773.
84. Bauer, p. 9; Thayer, p. 6.
85. Calvin, *I Corinthians,* p. 46.

boast in intimately knowing God. Paul uses this passage in summary form to tell the Corinthians to know God personally in Jesus Christ and to boast in him alone.

Practical Considerations in 1:27–29

Friedrich Wilhelm Nietzsche, born in 1844, belonged to a family of preachers. His father was a minister of the gospel and so were numerous ancestors of his mother. Studying theology, he developed a deep aversion to the Christian faith. He portrayed Jesus as a weakling who shamefully died on a cross in utter failure. Nietzsche despised not only Jesus but also all who believe Christ's gospel. According to Nietzsche, Christians favor suffering, scorn riches and learning, and prefer the weak to the strong. For him, God was dead and Jesus a fool.

Modern secularists direct similar accusations against Christ and Christianity. They contend that Christ's teachings are outdated and the Ten Commandments obsolete. They charge that Christian norms inhibit life, obstruct self-realization, and induce guilt. They teach that if we adopt human standards, we are liberated from the shackles of the Christian religion.

However, God chooses the foolish and the weak things of the world to shame the atheists, agnostics, humanists, and secularists. He abolishes their manmade standards so that they face moral bankruptcy and reap a harvest of physical violence in a decadent society. In the meantime, God chooses the foolish and the weak things of this world to advance his church and his kingdom. He honors the work of insignificant and despised people who dedicate their lives to serving God and their fellow man. He delights in those people who set their lives in harmony with his Word and who glory in their Lord and Savior Jesus Christ.

Greek Words, Phrases, and Constructions in 1:26–31

Verse 26

βλέπετε—as a first word in the sentence, this present active verb receives emphasis. It is in the imperative, not the indicative, mood. Paul frequently uses this verb in the imperative.[86]

Verses 27–28

The present tense in καταισχύνῃ (twice) indicates that God continues to shame the wise and the strong, and the aorist tense in καταργήσῃ shows that God has nullified once for all the things that are valuable to the world.

τὰ ἀγενῆ—the English translation *the insignificant things* fails to illustrate the play on words which this adjective has in respect to the substantive εὐγενεῖς (noble birth [v. 26]).

[καὶ] τὰ μὴ ὄντα—scribes probably added the conjunction καί to provide balance and harmony with the other clauses. "In adding the word, however, scribes overlooked the force of the expression τὰ μὴ ὄντα, which is not another item of the series, but is a comprehensive and climactic characterization of all the preceding items."[87] Editors of the Greek text and translators are divided on including or deleting the conjunction.

---

86. I Cor. 3:10; 8:9; 10:12, 18; 16:10; Gal. 5:15; Phil. 3:2; Col. 2:8; 4:17.
87. Bruce M. Metzger, *A Textual Commentary on the Greek New Testament*, 3d corrected ed. (London and New York: United Bible Societies, 1975), p. 545.

In these two verses, Paul resorts to the use of the neuter plural instead of the singular (e.g., v. 25, τὸ μωρόν . . . τὸ ασθενές [the foolishness . . . the weakness]). He uses the plural to refer to people.

Verse 29

μὴ καυχήσηται πᾶσα σάρξ—the syntax is Hebraic: the negative particle negates the verb *to boast* instead of the noun *flesh*. Further, the literal translation *all flesh* actually means "all people," which conveys the meaning *no one*.

Verses 30–31

ἐξ αὐτοῦ—the preposition expresses cause. For a similar use of this preposition, see John 6:66.

ἵνα—the verb γένηται (it may be) must be supplied as a subjunctive after the conjunction. The verb γέγραπται (it is written) is the perfect passive indicative and is introduced by the adverb καθώς.

Summary of Chapter 1

In the introductory part of the chapter, Paul states his name and his calling as an apostle. He addresses the members of the church in Corinth, notes that they have been sanctified and called to be holy, and greets them with an apostolic salutation. He expresses thanks to God for the grace the Corinthians had received in Christ Jesus, the confirmation of Christ's testimony, and the faithfulness of God.

Paul appeals to the people in Corinth to agree with one another. He has heard of a divisive spirit that has caused factions, namely, groups who follow Paul, Apollos, Cephas, and Christ. He reproves the Corinthians by asking them whether Christ is divided or Paul is crucified for them. He declares that Christ commissioned him to preach the gospel. For that reason, Paul says, he had baptized but few people. Moreover, he preached not with "wisdom of words," so that Christ's cross might not become meaningless.

In a discourse on the folly of the cross, Paul contrasts the wisdom of the world with the power of God. He asserts that God saves his people through the folly of preaching the gospel, which is a stumbling-block to the Jews and foolishness to the Gentiles. He observes that God's foolishness surpasses human wisdom and God's weakness excels human strength.

Paul reminds the Corinthians of their status. By human standards, few of them were wise, rich, or of noble birth. He tells them that God has chosen the insignificant and the despised things to prevent anyone from boasting. Because they are in Christ Jesus, says Paul, they should boast only in the Lord.

2

Divisions in the Church, *part 2*

(2:1–16)

Outline (continued)

2

1 When I came to you, brothers, I did not come proclaiming to you the testimony about God with incomparable eloquence or surpassing wisdom. 2 I decided to know nothing among you except Jesus Christ and him crucified. 3 I came to you in weakness and in fear and with much trembling. 4 My speech and my preaching were not in persuasive words of wisdom, but in demonstration of the Spirit and power 5 that your faith might not rest on the wisdom of men but on the power of God.

---

d. Power and Faith
2:1–5

The chapter division at this juncture is infelicitous, for Paul has not yet completed his discourse on the folly of the cross. In this last segment of the discussion he reminds his readers of his first visit to them when he came to proclaim the gospel. He came not with persuasive speech but in the power of the Holy Spirit. He brought nothing but the message of the crucified Christ to the Corinthians, so that their faith might be based on God's power.

1. When I came to you, brothers, I did not come proclaiming to you the testimony about God with incomparable eloquence or surpassing wisdom.

After Paul visited Athens during his second missionary journey, presumably in the summer of A.D. 50, he continued his travels to Corinth (Acts 18:1). As was his custom, he preferred to visit capitals from which the gospel might radiate forth to the surrounding countryside. Corinth, the capital of Achaia in southern and central Greece, had two harbors, one to the east southeast (Cenchrea) and another to the north (Lechaeum). From these harbors, mariners could take the good news to countries and cities throughout the Mediterranean basin. Indeed, Corinth was strategically located for the spread of the gospel.

a. "When I came to you, brothers." Paul arrived in Corinth in a downcast mood that resulted from his encounter with philosophers and the unfavorable response to his message in Athens (Acts 17:16–34). Soon after his arrival he found lodging in the home of Aquila and Priscilla, Jewish Christians and tentmakers who befriended Paul (Acts 18:2–3). In view of Paul's remark that the members of Stephanas's household were the first converts in the province of Achaia (16:15), we assume that Aquila and Priscilla were already Christians. Paul and his host and hostess formed the nucleus of the Christian church in Corinth. By preaching to Jews and Greeks in the local synagogue, Paul persuaded Titius

Justus, Crispus, Gaius, and Stephanas with their respective families to believe in Jesus. The Corinthian church then continued to flourish and increase numerically. When Paul left Corinth eighteen months later (Acts 18:11), Timothy and Silas continued the work of preaching the gospel.

Once again, Paul addresses the Corinthians as brothers. With this general term of affection, he appeals to all the members (male and female) of that church. In addition, he reveals his pastoral heart when he touches sensitive issues in the Corinthian church.

b. "I did not come proclaiming to you the testimony about God." Greek manuscripts have either the word *testimony* or the word *mystery*. In the Greek text, the words show some similarities in spelling that may account for the difference. The manuscript evidence for the reading *mystery* is early but limited while that for *testimony* is extensive. Numerous editors, translators, and teachers of the Greek New Testament prefer the latter term.[1] They do so on the basis of internal evidence, that is, the meaning of the context in which the term appears (compare 1:6). Paul proclaimed to the Corinthians the gospel, which is God's testimony revealed through Jesus Christ.

Some scholars understand verse 7, which has the word *mystery,* to be an explanation of verse 1. Other scholars contend that scribes were influenced by the reading of verse 7 and then introduced the word into verse 1. But when Paul came to Corinth, he presented not a mystery but the gospel of Christ, which here is embodied in the expression *testimony.*

Many translations have the reading *the testimony of God,* but others read "the testimony about God" (NIV, *Cassirer*). The difference is a matter of interpreting the genitive case. A subjective genitive means that God is the author of this testimony; the objective genitive makes Paul the proclaimer of this testimony about God. In view of a similar construction (1:6), we interpret the genitive as both subjective and objective: God is the originator of the testimony and Paul proclaims it and teaches the Corinthians about God.[2]

c. "With incomparable eloquence or surpassing wisdom." Paul openly declares that he did not come to Corinth with a message delivered in sublime eloquence and wisdom. His debates with erudite Epicurean and Stoic philosophers in Athens had been to no avail, and in Corinth he had preached the gospel neither as an orator nor as a philosopher. Instead, Paul had brought the message of salvation in simple terms that everyone in his audience could understand. This approach was unusual in a Hellenistic setting, where skillful orators were admired.

---

1. Merk, Nes-Al, Majority Text, TR, BF; JB, KJV, MLB, NKJV, NAB, NASB, NEB, NIV, RSV, *Cassirer;* G. Zuntz, *The Text of the Epistles: A Disquisition upon the Corpus Paulinum* (London: Oxford University Press, 1953), p. 101; Lothar Coenen, *NIDNTT,* vol. 3, p. 1043.
2. F. W. Grosheide, *Commentary on the First Epistle to the Corinthians: The English Text with Introduction, Exposition and Notes,* New International Commentary on the New Testament series (Grand Rapids: Eerdmans, 1953), p. 58 n. 5.

The nouns *eloquence* and *wisdom* describe the verbal skills and the mental acumen of a speaker. The two expressions refer to the words that come from a speaker's lips and the thoughts that formulate words into sentences. Of course, Paul often demonstrates in his epistle that he possesses both eloquence and wisdom. In this context, Paul refers not to a deficiency in his own abilities but to the excesses of Greek orators and philosophers. He refuses to adopt their practices; instead he plainly preaches the message of Christ's cross.[3]

In conclusion, Paul begins this verse with the personal pronoun *I* (the first word in the Greek text is in the combined form *and I*) to express intimacy with his audience. In the Greek, he ends verse 1 with the word *God* to indicate that his purpose is not to exalt himself but to point his audience to God and Jesus Christ.

2. I decided to know nothing among you except Jesus Christ and him crucified.

a. "I decided to know nothing." On the surface, Paul appears to be anti-intellectual. But that is hardly the case, for he had received lengthy and intensive training in Jerusalem. Moreover, Paul was acquainted with the Greek quest for knowledge and wisdom (Acts 17:17). But he was not interested in teaching the Corinthians methodologies which the Athenian thinkers had adopted and humanistic philosophers had espoused. Paul says that he came to preach the good news of the crucified Christ (1:23; Gal. 6:14). Jesus Christ had chosen him to carry Christ's name before Jews and Gentiles (Acts 9:15; 26:16). He did not appoint Paul to any other task. When Paul arrived in Corinth, he continued to fulfill the responsibility which Jesus had entrusted to him, namely, to preach the gospel of Christ's cross. As an ambassador in the full sense of the word, he knew no other task than to proclaim the message of his crucified Lord and Savior Jesus Christ.

b. "Among you." These words refer to the year and a half Paul spent with the Corinthians while he taught them the Word of God (Acts 18:11). In a broader sense, the expression *among you* reveals Paul's way of life as he went preaching the gospel from area to area, synagogue to synagogue, and church to church.

c. "Except Jesus Christ and him crucified." This is a more elaborate rewording of an earlier phrase, "Christ crucified" (1:23). The message of Christ's crucifixion appears to be straightforward and simple, but both Jews and Gentiles rejected Paul's appeal to believe in a crucified Christ as an offense or as foolishness. Therefore, Paul had to go beyond the historical details of the crucifixion and teach his audience the theological implications of this redemptive event in human history. He taught not only the reason for Christ's death on the cross but also the eternal benefits for every believer: forgiveness of sin, eternal life, and the resurrection of the body.

---

3. Consult Jean Héring, *The First Epistle of Saint Paul to the Corinthians,* trans. A. W. Heathcote and P. J. Allcock (London: Epworth, 1962), p. 14; Jerome Murphy-O'Connor, *1 Corinthians,* New Testament Message series (Wilmington, Del.: Glazier, 1979), p. 17.

Practical Considerations in 2:2

Ordained ministers of the gospel are expected to make proclaiming and teaching Christ's gospel their full-time calling. Ordination means that God has set them aside to preach, in the words of Paul, "in season and out of season" (II Tim. 4:2). The apostles set the example when they appointed seven men filled with the Spirit and wisdom to minister to the physical needs of the widows in Jerusalem (Acts 6:1–6). Thus, the apostles dedicated themselves to the proclamation of the Word and prayer. At times, however, Paul performed manual labor as a tentmaker to supply in his daily needs. But whenever he had sufficient material supplies, he spent all his time in the ministry of the Word.

When Christ calls someone to proclaim the gospel, this person must do so with full dedication to his call to the ministry; he must reject offers to be involved in other areas of life. He should be first and foremost a minister of God's Word. In earlier centuries, a preacher usually placed these initials after his name: V. D. M. (Verbi Domini Minister, minister of the Word of the Lord). A preacher does well to repeat and apply Paul's maxim "I . . . know nothing among you except Jesus Christ and him crucified."

---

3. I came to you in weakness and in fear and with much trembling.

What a confession from the lips of one of Christ's apostles! What honesty! What humility! Once more (see v. 1) Paul relates personal history as an example. He bares his soul and reveals his inner thoughts. He had nothing to offer except the message of Christ's death on the cross. The reception he received from the Jews in Corinth soon turned hostile, so he had to leave the local synagogue to continue his ministry in the house of Titius Justus. When discouragement overpowered Paul, Jesus appeared to him in a vision and told him not to be afraid, to keep on preaching, and not to be silent. Jesus revealed that he had many people in the city of Corinth (Acts 18:7–11).

"I came to you in weakness and in fear" (compare 4:10). From his other epistles, we learn that Paul had to cope with physical ailments; he frequently endured punishment and affliction (II Cor. 11:23–28; 12:7) and he was ill during his visit to the Galatians (Gal. 4:13–14). We assume that Paul was a rather unattractive man, perhaps small of stature (II Cor. 10:10) and plagued with poor eyesight (see Gal. 4:15; 6:11). Nevertheless, he proved to be a fearless proponent of the gospel when he preached in the synagogues and marketplaces of Damascus, Jerusalem, Antioch, Cyprus, Asia Minor, Macedonia, and Achaia.

Paul refers to his eighteen-month stay in Corinth (Acts 18:11) when he writes that he spent his time in Corinth "in fear and with much trembling." His was the arduous task of establishing a church in cosmopolitan Corinth. In the eyes of influential Corinthians, Paul was a person without strength, means, or privilege. Because of his trade, they considered him no better than a slave and had no respect for him. The Jews constantly plotted against him and eventually had him stand trial before Proconsul Gallio (Acts 18:12). The terms *fear* and *trembling* occur often in Paul's epistles as an expression of anxiety.[4] Fear is a debilitating

---

4. II Cor. 7:15; Eph. 6:5; Phil. 2:12; and see the LXX of Exod. 16:15.

force used by Satan to hinder Christ's servants and to distort their perception. Paul gives no details but confesses that during his stay in Corinth, he experienced fear and trembling. Here these terms relate to numerous social and political threats Paul had to face.

Moreover, we suggest that Paul harbored innate fear and trembling because he knew his human limitations in the tremendous task of preaching the gospel and founding a church in Corinth. He knew that while denying himself he had to trust in God to provide the necessary strength to accomplish the task.[5] This is evident from the message conveyed in the next verse.

4. My speech and my preaching were not in persuasive words of wisdom, but in demonstration of the Spirit and power.

a. *Negative.* Jesus gives the preacher the demanding task and obligation of preaching the gospel. No preacher can rely on his own insights and skills. If he does, he will be like the confident evangelist who during a worship service preached without the supporting power of the Holy Spirit. He consequently faced failure in the pulpit and humiliation before the congregation. Following the service, an elder gave him this sobering advice: "If you had entered the pulpit the way you left it, you would have left the pulpit the way you entered it." Humility ought to characterize every pastor who leads a congregation in worship.

Paul says that his speech and preaching were not in persuasive words of wisdom. He repeats what he has stated in a previous verse (v. 1) and now personalizes the words *speech* and *preaching* with the pronoun *my*. He uses these two terms to describe the message of the gospel (1:18) and the work of preaching. However, Paul refrains from identifying the speakers who persuasively speak and preach in words of wisdom.[6]

What is Paul conveying? He was able to present the gospel persuasively in carefully chosen words, as he proved in his speech before King Agrippa II (Acts 26:27–28). However, in this text Paul refuses to phrase his message in persuasive words of wisdom; he thereby implies that his wisdom originates not in man but in God.

b. *Text.* "Not in persuasive words of wisdom." The Greek text of this part of verse 4 has a few variants. In translations, these variants hardly appear except for the reading, "Not with persuasive words of *human* wisdom" (NKJV, italics added). This italicized adjective seems to be an addition that scribes have inserted to explain the concept *wisdom* and therefore is a secondary reading.

The difficulty translators face, however, is with the adjective *persuasive*. This adjective occurs nowhere else in all Greek literature. It appears that Paul himself has coined the word. This reading has support from one of the earliest manu-

---

5. John Calvin, *The First Epistle of Paul the Apostle to the Corinthians,* Calvin's Commentaries series, trans. John W. Fraser (reprint ed.; Grand Rapids: Eerdmans, 1976), p.50.

6. Timothy H. Lim suggests that these speakers are Corinthian preachers who peddled the gospel for profit. "'Not in Persuasive Words of Wisdom, but in the Demonstration of the Spirit and Power' (1 Cor. 2:4)," *NovT* (1987): 137–49.

scripts, P[46], and is the accepted text for most translators.[7] Other scholars hold that this adjective should be translated as the singular noun *persuasion*. They suggest the adoption of a shorter Greek text which deletes the term *words*, with the resultant reading *not with the persuasion of wisdom*.[8] Although strong arguments have been advanced in support of this translation, the reading *persuasion* lacks substantive manuscript support. "Not in persuasive words of wisdom" still seems to be the preferred translation. Regardless of the choice that the translator makes, difficulties remain.

c. *Positive.* "But in demonstration of the Spirit and power." Paul chooses three key words to display the spiritual power available to those who preach the Word of God. The first word is "demonstration," which is a term used in a court of law for testimony. The term signifies that no one is able to refute the proof that is presented.

The second word is "Spirit," which appears here in this epistle for the first time. The Corinthians ought to know that their spiritual birth is the work of the Holy Spirit (v. 13), that their body is a temple of the Holy Spirit (6:19), and that their spiritual gifts are the work of the Spirit (12:11). They have the evidence in themselves.

The last word is "power." In the New Testament, this word is closely associated with the Holy Spirit. For example, Jesus told the apostles that they would receive power when the Holy Spirit descended on them at Pentecost (Acts 1:8; see also Luke 24:49). In one of his epistles Paul writes, "Our gospel came to you not simply with words, but also with power, with the Holy Spirit and with deep conviction" (I Thess. 1:5). Even though the expression *power* often signifies wonders, here it has a meaning broader than miracles. The term denotes "the hand of God stretching itself out to act powerfully through the apostle in every way."[9]

Paul exhorts the Corinthians to open their spiritual eyes and observe for themselves that God is at work through his power and his Spirit. They possess visible and incontrovertible proof through the power of the gospel and the presence of the Holy Spirit.

5. That your faith might not rest on the wisdom of men but on the power of God.

In the last verse of this section, Paul states his purpose for rejecting persuasive words and superior wisdom. He has come to the Corinthians to preach the gospel. And his preaching has resulted in their personal faith in God. Paul informs them that this gift of faith neither originates in nor is supported by human wisdom. If faith were of human origin, it would utterly fail and disappear. But faith

7. Bauer, p. 639; Bruce M. Metzger, *A Textual Commentary on the Greek New Testament*, 3d corrected ed. (London and New York: United Bible Societies, 1975), p. 546.
8. Gordon D. Fee, *The Epistle to the First Corinthians*, New International Commentary on the New Testament series (Grand Rapids: Eerdmans, 1987), p. 88 n. 2; Zuntz, *The Text of the Epistles*, pp. 23–25.
9. Calvin, *I Corinthians*, p. 51.

rests on God's power that shields the believer and strengthens him to persevere (compare I Peter 1:5).

God works faith in the hearts of the Corinthians through the preaching of Christ's gospel. He not only has given them the gift of faith but also has brought them to conversion. God commissions Paul to strengthen their faith by instructing them in the truths of God's Word. In brief, the Corinthians must know that faith rests not on human wisdom but on God's power.

"Wisdom of men." Notice that Paul uses the plural noun *men* to illustrate that in Corinth many people are dispensing their own insight and wisdom. Man's discernment is temporal, faulty, and subject to change; God's wisdom is eternal, perfect, and unchangeable. When a Christian in faith asks God for wisdom (James 1:5), he experiences the working of God's power. He rejoices in the salvation God has provided for him.

Practical Considerations in 2:4

Churches that originated in the sixteenth-century Reformation have always championed the cause of an educated ministry. The origin of many universities lies in the church's desire to train future preachers. When these schools expanded and eventually became universities, theological training was and continues to be offered in affiliated divinity schools or theological seminaries. The objective has always been to equip pastoral students so that they will be able to handle the Word of God correctly (see II Tim. 2:15).

Paul himself had thoroughly studied the Scriptures. In his pastoral epistles, he exhorted Timothy to continue in what he has learned from Paul and others. He charged Timothy to preach the Word "with great patience and careful instruction," and to "do the work of an evangelist" (II Tim. 4:2, 5). Preachers should be trained to deliver sermons that are faithful expositions of the Scriptures. Moreover, sermons must be free from verbosity and from anecdotes unrelated to the biblical passage at hand. And last, preachers must be able to communicate and relate effectively to the people to whom they minister the Word of God.

Greek Words, Phrases, and Constructions in 2:1–5

Verse 1

ἦλθον . . . καταγγέλλων—the verb in the aorist active ("I came") and the participle in the present active ("proclaiming") should be taken together as a verbal unit. Paul came to Corinth with the express purpose of preaching the gospel, and after his arrival he continued to preach.

οὐ—this negative particle is placed immediately after the verb ἦλθον to show that the usual negative particle μή with the participle would mean "not proclaiming."[10] With this word order, the concept *I came proclaiming* is placed in the negative.

---

10. C. F. D. Moule, *An Idiom-Book of New Testament Greek,* 2d ed. (Cambridge: Cambridge University Press, 1960), p. 105.

Verse 2

οὐ—J. B. Lightfoot takes the negative with the verb ἔκρινα (I decided) and translates the entire clause as follows: "I had no intent, no mind to know anything."[11] The negative for the infinitive εἰδέναι (to know) should be μή. C. F. D. Moule, however, provides numerous examples of a displacement and changing of the negative particles οὐ and μή, and calls attention to the Greek text of II Corinthians 2:2, which is a similar but normal construction.[12]

Verse 4

λόγος—Paul repeatedly uses the singular and plural of λόγος in the first two chapters of this epistle (1:5, 17, 18; 2:1, 4, 13). Here the word is a synonym for the message of the gospel, especially with the twice-occurring pronoun *my* that modifies "message" and "preaching."

πειθοῖς σοφίας λόγοις—"persuasive words of wisdom." This reading is supported by codices Vaticanus, Sinaiticus, and Bezae. But textual evidence is nonexistent for the presence of the adjective πειθός (persuasive). The noun πειθώ (persuasion), which in the dative singular is πειθοῖ, occurs in other Greek literature. Its manuscript support in this verse is extremely weak, especially in the shorter reading that omits the noun λόγοις.[13]

Verse 5

ἵνα—the negative purpose clause with μή depends on the main subject κἀγώ and the verb ἐγενόμην (I came) in verse 3.

ἐν—with the dative in both occurrences, this preposition means "on."

---

6 We speak wisdom, however, among those who are mature, the wisdom not of this age or of the rulers of this age who are doomed to perish. 7 But we speak God's wisdom in a mystery—hidden wisdom, which God predestined before all time for our glory, 8 and which none of the rulers of this age understood. For if they had understood this wisdom, they would not have crucified the Lord of glory. 9 However, just as it is written,

> Things which eye has not seen and ear has not heard
> And have not entered into the heart of man,
> These things God has prepared for those who love him,

10 because God has revealed them to us through the Spirit.
Indeed, the Spirit searches all things, even the depths of God. 11 For who among men knows the things of man except the spirit of man that is within him? Thus also no one knows the things of God except the Spirit of God. 12 Now we have received not the spirit of the world but the Spirit who is from God, that we may know the things freely given to us by God. 13 And the things we speak are not words imparted by human wisdom but those imparted by the Spirit as we interpret spiritual truths in spiritual words. 14 The unspiritual man does not accept the things of the Spirit of God, for

---

11. J. B. Lightfoot, *Notes on the Epistles of St. Paul from Unpublished Commentaries* (1895; reprint ed., Grand Rapids: Zondervan, 1957), p. 171; and see Fee, *First Corinthians,* p. 92 n. 17.

12. Moule, *Idiom-Book,* pp. 156, 168.

13. Refer to Hans Conzelmann, *1 Corinthians: A Commentary on the First Epistle to the Corinthians,* ed. George W. MacRae, trans. James W. Leitch, Hermeneia: A Critical and Historical Commentary on the Bible (Philadelphia: Fortress, 1975), p. 55; Metzger, *Textual Commentary,* p. 546; R. St. John Parry, *The First Epistle of Paul the Apostle to the Corinthians,* Cambridge Greek Testament for Schools and Colleges (Cambridge: Cambridge University Press, 1937), p. 49.

they are foolishness to him and he is unable to understand them because they are spiritually discerned. 15 But the spiritual man judges all things, yet he is judged by no one. 16 For

who has known the mind of the Lord,
that he will instruct him?

But we have the mind of Christ.

---

3. Wisdom of the Spirit
2:6–16

In the second part of this chapter, Paul addresses all believers who are wise in regard to salvation. They received God's secret wisdom which he reveals to his people. Indeed, these people are led by the Holy Spirit.

a. Wisdom and the Mature
2:6–8

6. We speak wisdom, however, among those who are mature, the wisdom not of this age or of the rulers of this age who are doomed to perish.

a. "We speak wisdom, however." In the Greek sentence, the first word is "wisdom," which because of its position is emphatic. A literal translation reads, "Wisdom we speak." Paul here does not define or describe this word (see v. 7), but implies that he means God's wisdom (1:21, 24, 30). He understandably continues to build on these earlier remarks on wisdom; in subsequent verses, he unites the concepts *wisdom* and *Spirit*.

Paul contrasts divine wisdom with the wisdom of the world which has entranced some Corinthian Christians. They think that Paul's message of Christ's cross is simplistic and fails to measure up to the standards of worldly wisdom. By sharply differentiating two concepts of wisdom, Paul emphatically and confidently states that he and his fellow ministers have God's wisdom which, as he already has explained (1:18–30), is eminently superior to the wisdom of the world.

With the aid of the adversative *however*, Paul switches from the singular to the plural. In this epistle Paul frequently shifts from the singular to the plural and back again (e.g., 3:1, 2, 6, 9, 10). Here he resumes the plural of 1:23, "We preach Christ crucified." Some translators interpret the plural pronoun in verses 6 and 7 as the singular *I* (see GNB, NEB), but that is a departure from the Greek text. Paul has in mind all those who belong to the apostolic circle, among whom are his fellow workers Timothy and Silas. He wants to say that his preaching, and that of his associates, is certainly marked by wisdom. With the Greek verb *lalein* (to speak) he denotes not the content of speech but the act of speaking. But among whom do Paul and his fellow ministers speak wisdom?

b. "[We speak] wisdom . . . among those who are mature." The literature on verse 6 is indeed phenomenal; in respect to this clause, scholars raise numerous questions. For example, who are these mature people? Are there also immature Christians? Do Paul and other New Testament writers group Christians in categories? Is Paul resorting to irony when he uses the word *mature* even though he knows that the Corinthians fail to meet the standard of perfection? Are Paul and his associates speaking directly to the mature or are they with (among) the mature discussing wisdom? Is he borrowing words that belong to settings other than the Christian community of Corinth?[14] These and many other questions deserve an answer. In the interest of space, we limit ourselves to a few of them and supply the following comments:

First, New Testament writers present no evidence that distinguishes between two types of Christians: mature and immature, spiritual and natural, superior and inferior. New Testament writers do not make this distinction; instead they exhort all Christians to press on toward maturity (e.g., Heb. 6:1). Among God's people we acknowledge levels of development, for no one can claim to have reached perfection. Even the holiest men, among whom we place Job of the Old Testament and Paul of the New Testament, will have to admit that they have attained only a small beginning. Paul addresses the Corinthians as "babes in Christ" (3:1) and tells them that they think like children (14:20). Nevertheless, he regards all believers in whom the Holy Spirit effectively works as mature Christians. In other words, with the word *mature* Paul includes all the Corinthians who have received the Spirit (3:16; 12:3, 13) and who respond to Christ's gospel.

Next, in context Paul contrasts not the mature Christians and the immature Christians. Rather, he distinguishes between mature Christians who accept the message of the cross and unbelievers who consider God's wisdom foolishness. He delineates faith and unbelief, divine wisdom and worldly wisdom, the believer and the unbeliever.

Last, the Greek word that is translated "mature" or "perfect" occurs elsewhere in Paul's epistles and usually is equivalent to "adult."[15] Adults are those people who accept the gospel of Christ's cross, experience God's power in their lives, and expect the renewal of all things as a result of Jesus' resurrection. They are the recipients of divine wisdom and rejoice in it with fellow believers.

c. "The wisdom not of this age or of the rulers of this age." Paul continues to describe the meaning of wisdom in negative terms. The wisdom of this age is identical with worldly wisdom (1:20) that is characterized by a fleeting and changeable nature.

Who are these "rulers of this age"? Some scholars interpret the phrase to refer to demonic powers and allude to many New Testament passages (e.g., John 12:31; 14:30; 16:11; Eph. 6:12).[16] But this interpretation runs into difficulty in verse 8. There Paul writes that if the rulers of this world had known divine wisdom, they would not have crucified Jesus. Not demons but rulers crucified Jesus.

---

14. Consult E. Earle Ellis, *Prophecy and Hermeneutic in Early Christianity: New Testament Essays* (Grand Rapids: Eerdmans, 1978), pp. 45–62; W. Baird, "Among the Mature: The Idea of Wisdom in I Corinthians 2:6," *Interp* 13 (1959): 425–32..

15. I Cor. 14:20; Eph. 4:13; Phil. 3:15; Col. 1:28. See Gerhard Delling, *TDNT*, vol. 8, pp. 75–76; Reinier Schippers, *NIDNTT*, vol. 2, p. 62.

16. Among many others, see C. K. Barrett, *A Commentary on the First Epistle to the Corinthians,* Harper's New Testament Commentaries series (New York and Evanston: Harper and Row, 1968), p. 70.

Moreover, the demons knew Jesus, as the Gospels clearly show. The context does not allude to evil angels but rather to human beings who are considered strong (1:27). In addition, the context shows a contrast between human wisdom and divine wisdom without reference to demonic powers.[17] Other scholars, therefore, judge that the wording refers to earthly rulers who include all the political and intellectual leaders of the world. Among them are the rulers Caiaphas and Pilate, who crucified Jesus (see Acts 3:17; 4:26–27).[18]

d. "Who are doomed to perish." In the Greek, Paul uses the verb *doomed to perish*, which is the same as the translation *nullified* in 1:28 (see also 15:24, 26). He shows that God, who controls world history, causes the sudden demise of leaders, officials, teachers and their philosophies. Paul uses the present tense of the verb *doomed to perish* to indicate the continuous control that God exercises in this world. Throughout the centuries, God causes his Word to triumph and worldly wisdom and its proponents to fail.

7. But we speak God's wisdom in a mystery—hidden wisdom, which God predestined before all time for our glory, 8. and which none of the rulers of this age understood. For if they had understood this wisdom, they would not have crucified the Lord of glory.

a. *Divine wisdom.* The dissimilarity between the world's wisdom and God's wisdom is clear. In the preceding verse (v. 6), Paul mentions wisdom in negative terms; human wisdom is time-bound and leads people to frustration and eventual destruction. Here he gives a positive description: God's wisdom is eternal and limitless. It leads people from darkness to light, salvation, and glory. Paul informs the Corinthians that he and fellow preachers declare God's wisdom in a mystery. This is the first time the word *mystery* occurs in connection with wisdom. (The variant reading in verse 1 is an exception.)

b. *Mystery.* What does Paul mean by the clause, "We speak God's wisdom in a mystery"? The Greek verb *lalein* (to speak) denotes not the substance of Paul's speech but the manner of speaking (see v. 6). The genitive case of "wisdom" points to possession, origin, and character; Paul refers to God's wisdom. And "wisdom" is qualified by the expression *in a mystery*. That is, Paul does not speak a mystery; God's wisdom is mysterious.

Wisdom is a mystery and unintelligible to the unbeliever. To the believer wisdom becomes plain, for God communicates it through the gospel which the apostles preach. Paul has stated earlier that Christ is wisdom from God and thus Christ has become our wisdom (1:30). Wisdom and salvation through Christ are

---

17. Gene Miller, "ΑΡΧΟΝΤΩΝ, ΤΟΥ ΑΙΩΝΟΣ ΤΟΥΤΟΥ—A New Look at 1 Corinthians 2:6–8," *JBL* 91 (1972): 522–28; Wesley Carr, "The Rulers of This Age—1 Corinthians II.6–8," *NTS* 23 (1976–77): 20–35; see also his *Angels and Principalities* (Cambridge: Cambridge University Press, 1981), pp. 118–20. Compare Robin Scroggs, "Paul: *Sophos* and *Pneumatikos*," *NTS* 14 (1967–68): 33–55.

18. Among the commentators who espouse this view, see Calvin, p. 53; Fee, pp. 103–4; Lightfoot, p. 174; R. C. H. Lenski, *The Interpretation of St. Paul's First and Second Epistle to the Corinthians* (1935; Columbus: Wartburg, 1946), p. 96; D. A. Carson, *The Cross and Christian Ministry* (Grand Rapids: Baker, 1993), p. 47.

intimately related, for the word *wisdom* signifies "the wise acts of God in the salvation of man."[19] The process of salvation is a miracle to believers but a mystery to people who lack the Spirit of God (compare vv. 11–15). Wherever the term *mystery* appears in the New Testament, it usually is preceded by verbs meaning either "to reveal" or "to proclaim." This mystery was predestined by God before the creation of this world, but he now reveals it to his people through the preaching of the gospel (see Eph. 3:3; Col. 1:26).[20]

c. *Predestined.* Paul next refers to "hidden wisdom, which God predestined before all time for our glory." Wisdom that has been hidden until the present time is now revealed through the person and work of Christ. Peter discloses that the prophets were intently searching for the time and circumstances of Christ's coming. He says that those things eventually were revealed to the believers through the preaching of the gospel and the work of the Holy Spirit (I Peter 1:10–12). Even though this mystery of salvation is no longer hidden, it nevertheless remains something that the human mind cannot fully grasp. This mystery relates to the love of God, which is so profound that man is unable to comprehend it completely (compare Eph. 3:17–19).

God in his wisdom predestined this salvation for our glory before the human race was even created. He foreordained to save the Corinthians for their own glory, a truth Paul states in a related discourse: "What if he did this to make the riches of his glory known to the objects of his mercy, whom he prepared in advance for glory?" (Rom. 9:23).

God is sovereign and demonstrates his grace and mercy to his people, whom he predestined to glory. Paul could not have put the difference between worldly wisdom and divine wisdom in clearer terms. The contrast between the glory of believers and the glory of earthly rulers is telling. Writes J. B. Lightfoot, "Our glory increases, while their glory wanes."[21] We reflect God's virtues and glory already in this life, but in the life to come we shall shine like jewels in his crown (see, e.g., Phil. 3:21; Zech. 9:16, for the metaphor).

d. *Ignorance.* "And which none of the rulers of this age understood." Paul repeats the phrase *the rulers of this age* (v. 6). These rulers are devoid of spiritual knowledge and fail to see the significance of Christ's kingdom on earth, which comes in answer to the believer's petition: "Your kingdom come" (Matt. 6:10). They are unable to understand God's rule on earth because God has not revealed to them his divine wisdom.

Paul refrains from explaining the resistance of Jew and Gentile to God's revelation in Jesus Christ. Instead he explains the ignorance of these rulers in negative terms: "For if they had understood this wisdom, they would not have

---

19. Donald Guthrie, *New Testament Theology* (Downers Grove: Inter-Varsity, 1981), p. 95. Consult also Michael Walter, "Verborgene Weisheit und Heil Für die Traditionsgeschichte und Intention des 'Revelationsschemas,'" *ZTK* 84 (1987): 297–312.

20. Günter Finkenrath, *NIDNTT*, vol. 3, p. 504; Günther Bornkamm, *TDNT*, vol. 4, p. 820.

21. Lightfoot, *Notes on the Epistles*, p. 175.

crucified the Lord of glory." Is Paul speaking only of Caiaphas, Herod Antipas, and Pilate, or is he alluding to every leader who rules without giving God the glory? The Jewish and Gentile leaders who crucified Jesus are representative of all the rulers in the world.[22] Whoever ignores the cause of Christ takes his place with the rulers who put Jesus to death.

Jesus, the Lord of glory, is the answer to the question of the psalmist: "Who is this King of glory?" (Ps. 24:8; see also Acts 7:2). He rules not only in heaven but also on earth and makes himself known through the preaching of the gospel. If the rulers of this world submit themselves to him, he blesses them and causes them to prosper (Ps. 2:10–12).

Doctrinal Considerations in 2:7

God is sovereign in executing his plan to create the universe and to save mankind from sin. He destines his people for eternal glory. When Paul writes that before this earth was created, God already had formed a plan to save mankind for the glory of those whom he redeems, we stand in awe and wonder. Paul speaks of God's wisdom that appears in a mystery. Our human minds are unable to grasp fully the importance of God's love for sinners, because the concept *before all time* is too profound for us. And the glory which we receive partially in this life but wholly in eternity is too wonderful for us. We confess that we cannot adequately appropriate this truth in our minds.

Indeed, the doctrine of salvation, simple yet profound, can be understood only because God reveals it to us. God reveals salvation in terms of his electing grace as a truth that "must be taught wisely and carefully."[23]

Greek Words, Phrases, and Constructions in 2:6–8

Verse 6

ἐν—this preposition followed by a noun in the dative case means neither "to" nor "in," but "among."

δέ—the second δέ in the verse is sometimes translated "that is" or is replaced by a punctuation mark.

Verse 7

θεοῦ σοφίαν—the word order in this phrase is significant because it emphasizes that wisdom originates with and belongs to God.

ἐν—the preposition conveys "in the form of" or "consisting of."

ἀποκεκρυμμένην—the perfect passive participle from the verb *to hide* should be translated as a pluperfect to indicate that God's wisdom had been hidden for a long period but at present is revealed.[24]

---

22. Grosheide, *First Epistle to the Corinthians*, p. 65.

23. Westminster Confession of Faith 3.8. See also the view of J. Kenneth Grider, "Predestination as Temporal Only," *WesThJ* 22 (1987): 56–64.

24. A. T. Robertson, *A Grammar of the Greek New Testament in the Light of Historical Research* (Nashville: Broadman, 1934), p. 1117.

Verse 8

ἥν—the relative pronoun in the feminine relates not to its nearest antecedent, "glory," but to the term *wisdom*.[25]

εἰ—followed by the indicative in the protasis and with ἄν in the apodosis, this is a contrary-to-fact conditional sentence.

---

b. God and Revelation
2:9–10a

9. However, just as it is written,
   Things which eye has not seen and ear has not heard
   And have not entered into the heart of man,
   These things God has prepared for those who love him.

a. *Adversative.* As he does in many other places in this epistle, Paul substantiates his teaching with an appeal to the Scriptures. He introduces the passage with the adversative *however* followed by the formula *just as it is written*. The sentence as it stands is incomplete because it lacks a verb. We suggest the insertion of the plural verb *we understand* to balance the verb *understand* in the preceding verse (v. 8). The contrast, then, is between the "rulers of this age" (Pontius Pilate and Herod Antipas) who failed to understand God's wisdom and the Corinthians who know his wisdom. A possible translation is: "For if [these rulers] had understood this wisdom, they would not have crucified the Lord of glory. However—just as it is written—[we do understand the] things which eye has not seen and ear has not heard."[26] The contrast between verses 8 and 9 is clear. At the same time, the suggested introduction of the pronoun *we* serves both as a clarification of verses 8 and 9 and as a bridge to the pronoun *us* of the next verse (v. 10).

b. *Prophecy.* Paul loosely quotes the prophecy of Isaiah written seven centuries before Paul wrote his epistle. Yet the verb *it is written* connotes that the significance of these words remains valid even for the present.

The quotation comes from Isaiah 64:4 but differs considerably from the Hebrew text:

> Since ancient times no one has heard,
>   no ear has perceived,
> no eye has seen any God besides you,
>   who acts on behalf of those who wait for him.

Paul apparently quotes from memory, because even the Greek translation of Isaiah varies: "From eternity we have not heard, and our eyes have seen no God except you and your works which you will do for those who wait for mercy" (Isa. 64:3, LXX). In view of the divergency, some scholars think that Paul also took

---

25. Parry, *First Epistle to the Corinthians*, p. 54.
26. See B. Frid, "The Enigmatic ἀλλά in 1 Corinthians 2.9," *NTS* 31 (1985): 603–11. But Lenski (*First Corinthians*, p. 102) follows older commentators who repeat the verb *we speak* (v. 7).

words from other passages (Isa. 52:15; 65:17; Jer. 3:16). We presume that Paul relies on memory instead of having the Scriptures in front of him. He formulates a text that agrees with passages taken from the prophecies of Isaiah and Jeremiah.[27]

c. *Meaning.* What is Paul trying to say in this passage? Because he alludes to four different verses from the prophecies of Isaiah and Jeremiah, we have to interpret the passage as it stands. Paul cites three parts of the human body and presents them in negative terms: "Things which eye has not seen and ear has not heard, and have not entered into the heart [that is, the mind] of man." He concludes the quotation with a positive line: "These things God has prepared for those who love him."

We take the negative terms first. The noun *things,* omitted in some translations,[28] signifies God's wisdom that is disclosed for the purpose of man's salvation. But knowledge of salvation does not originate with man when he opens his eyes to see, or listens to what others tell him, or formulates thoughts. Paul rules out all avenues of sense perception and leaves the reader to draw the conclusion that wisdom can emanate only from God.[29] By mentioning the physical organs of eye, ear, and mind, Paul emphasizes the process of perception, analysis, and assimilation of facts. These organs by themselves cannot provide man with wisdom to understand God's divine work of salvation.

In positive terms, Paul informs the Corinthians that "God has prepared [salvation] for those who love him." In another epistle Paul writes, "God works for the good of those who love him" (Rom. 8:28).[30] Concerning God's wisdom, the author of Ecclesiasticus says, "He supplied [wisdom] to those who love him" (Sir. 1:10, RSV).

The last line of the quotation teaches two things: God is the author of our salvation, and we love him. The text teaches that God prepared the things that pertain to salvation and provides this gift regardless of our merit. Through his Word and in the fullness of time by Christ's coming, he reveals it. Consequently, when we realize this truth, we demonstrate our love to God for this marvelous gift.

10a. Because God has revealed them to us through the Spirit.

Translations differ on the first word in this clause. Some have the adversative *but,* others have the conjunction *and,* and still others favor the causal *for* or *because.* The differences stem from the reading of the Greek text and the interpretation of the preceding verse (v. 9). I prefer the causal reading for the following reasons: First, if we supply a verb in verse 9, we eliminate the need for an adversative or conjunction at the beginning of verse 10. Joining the texts with a causal

---

27. A. Feuillet, "L'énigme de 1 Cor., II,9," *RB* 70 (1963): 52–74; K. Berger, "Zur Diskussion über die Herkunft von 1 Kor. ii. 9," *NTS* 24 (1978): 270–83.

28. MLB, NAB, NIV, KJV, NKJV, SEB.

29. Walter C. Kaiser, Jr., "A Neglected Text in Bibliology Discussions: 1 Corinthians 2:6–16," *WTJ* 43 (1980–81): 301–19.

30. See also I Cor. 8:3; James 1:12; 2:5. Consult Johannes B. Bauer, "'. . . TOIS AGAPOSIN TON THEON' Rm 8:28 (I Cor. 2:9, I Cor. 8:3)," *ZNW* 50 (1959): 106–12.

conjunction clarifies the reason that we possess knowledge concerning our salvation: God revealed it to us. Next, the causal conjunction links this verse (v. 10a) to the immediately preceding quotation. And third, it does justice to the pronoun *to us* by strengthening it.[31] In the Greek, the pronoun stands first in the sentence for emphasis; that is, "To us God has revealed them." The pronoun is not limited to the apostles and their helpers but includes all believers.

Through the Holy Spirit, God makes his wisdom known to believers (Matt. 11:25; 16:17). The Spirit prepares a person to receive the truth of the gospel and leads him to Christ. God reveals his wisdom through the Spirit, so that salvation is the work of the Trinity. God originates salvation, works through his Spirit, and grants us his glory.

Greek Words, Phrases, and Constructions in 2:9–10a

Verse 9

ἐπὶ καρδίαν—the preposition ἐν might be expected, but Paul is using Septuagintal Greek that in this case literally translates the Hebrew (compare the Septuagint text of IV Kings 12:5; Jer. 3:16; 28:50; see also Luke 24:38; Acts 7:23).[32]

Verse 10a

γάρ—this conjunction is supported by P[46], Codex B, 1739, and other manuscripts. In light of the context, γάρ instead of δέ is the more difficult reading and thus is preferred; it occurs three times in as many sentences. Any scribe would be tempted to vary the sequence with the conjunction δέ.

ἀπεκάλυψεν—the verb *to reveal* relates to the word *mystery* and the perfect passive participle *hidden* (v. 7). This verb connotes special revelation in place of general revelation.[33]

---

c. The Holy Spirit and Human Wisdom
2:10b–13

Translators often differ on paragraph divisions. At this point (v. 10), many prefer to begin a new paragraph instead of breaking this verse into two parts. But we take the first part of verse 10 as a conclusion to verse 9 and the second part as the beginning of a new paragraph.[34]

10b. Indeed, the Spirit searches all things, even the depths of God.

This affirmative statement serves as an opening remark in a section on the work of the Holy Spirit. Although brief, the statement is profound in revealing to us the interpersonal relationship within the Godhead. We admit that the human

---

31. Archibald Robertson and Alfred Plummer, *A Critical and Exegetical Commentary on the First Epistle of St. Paul to the Corinthians,* International Critical Commentary, 2d ed. (1911; reprint ed., Edinburgh: Clark, 1975), p. 43.

32. Moule, *Idiom-Book,* p. 183.

33. Consult Lightfoot, *Notes on the Epistles,* p. 178.

34. E.g., the NEB, NIV, and NCV divide verse 10.

mind is unable to fathom the depth of Paul's words. In a doxology, Paul acknowledges this same inability when he asks: "Who has known the mind of the Lord? Or who has been his counselor?" (Rom. 11:34; see also Job 11:7). No human being is invited to have a share in the councils of God.[35]

The Spirit searches everything and nothing escapes his attention. Paul writes the verb *to search* in the present tense to indicate that for the Spirit the work of searching never ceases; in the presence of God all things are uncovered and open (Heb. 4:13). God knows everything and his eyes are everywhere (Prov. 15:3).

The extent of the Spirit's work reaches to the deep things of God. What are these deep things? They are the incomprehensible ways of God, which to the changeable and shallow human mind always will remain mysteries. Among these deep things are the inexhaustible richness of God's wisdom and knowledge (Rom. 11:33), God's gift of salvation to man, the spread of the gospel in every age and generation, and the coming of God's kingdom.

> God moves in a mysterious way
> His wonders to perform;
> He plants His footsteps in the sea,
> And rides upon the storm.
>
> Deep in unfathomable mines
> Of never-failing skill,
> He treasures up His bright designs
> And works His sovereign will.
> —William Cowper

11. For who among men knows the things of man except the spirit of man that is within him? Thus also no one knows the things of God except the Spirit of God.

a. *Analogy.* Employing an analogy from human life, Paul parallels the spirit of man and the Spirit of God. He asks if anyone can know what motivates a person. He answers this question by saying that only the spirit of man is able to know one's own incentives. The spirit in man is able to keep secrets from the prying eyes and ears of others.

Conversely, we must confess that even though we have been created with basic inherent knowledge about ourselves, we encounter numerous difficulties in knowing our inner motives. Our innate knowledge guides us in making decisions pertaining to the environment in which we live. We try to analyze the reasons that cause us to do and say things in an effort to know ourselves. We attempt to gain a basic understanding of our subconscious being by analyzing our mind.

b. *Difference.* Should we go beyond the basic point Paul is trying to teach, we would falter. As God told the people of Israel, "My thoughts are not your

---

35. John Calvin, *Institutes of the Christian Religion,* trans. Henry Beveridge, 8th American ed., 2 vols. (Grand Rapids: Eerdmans, 1949), vol. 1, p. 155.

thoughts, neither are your ways my ways" (Isa. 55:8). God is the creator of man's spirit (Zech. 12:1); he breathed into man's nostrils the breath of life (Gen. 2:7). But God's uncreated Spirit proceeds from the Father and the Son (John 14:26). The repetition of the expression *man* in this verse is meant to heighten the immeasurable difference between the human spirit and God's Spirit. God knows the mind of man, but man is incapable of knowing the mind of God.

In the Greek text of this verse, Paul writes two different verbs for knowing (*oida* and *ginōskō*). The first verb conveys the idea of having basic inherent knowledge—that is, the spirit within man knows his own thought. The second verb, here in the perfect tense, denotes the process of acquiring knowledge: "No man has gained an understanding of the things that belong to God, except God's own Spirit." Paul contrasts the two verbs to explain that the human mind is able to know the things concerning man but not the things concerning God. In other words, Paul is not saying that the Spirit of God is engaged in acquiring knowledge concerning the thoughts of God. The Spirit has inherent knowledge. "This change of phraseology may be regarded as a caution to us not to press the analogy."[36]

12. Now we have received not the spirit of the world but the Spirit who is from God, that we may know the things freely given to us by God.

a. "Now we have received." In the previous verse, Paul spoke in generalities that involved man's spirit. But here he specifies the Corinthians and himself by using the plural personal pronoun *we*. This pronoun takes the first place in the Greek sentence and so receives emphasis. With this inclusive pronoun, Paul has come to the heart of the paragraph on God's Spirit versus man's spirit. He offers the comforting assurance that we have received the Spirit, whom God has given us.

b. "Not the spirit of the world but the Spirit who is from God." The negative clause *not the spirit of the world* has been interpreted in various ways:

it describes the rulers of the world who crucified Jesus (v. 8);
it denotes evil that has established its own rules and objectives (see II Cor. 4:4; I John 4:4; 5:19);
it is equivalent to the wisdom of this world (1:20);
it is the spirit in man that is worldly.

We say that the spirit of the world is the spirit that makes the world secular.[37] From the time Adam and Eve fell into sin, the spirit of this world has revealed itself in opposition to God's Spirit: for example, in the lawlessness prior to the flood, in the building of the tower of Babel, and in the false teachers who sought to destroy the church in apostolic days (II Peter 2; I John 4:1–3; Jude 4–19). It is

---

36. Lightfoot, *Notes on the Epistles,* p. 179. But see Donald W. Burdick, who does press the analogy. "οἶδα and γινώσκω in the Pauline Epistles," in *New Dimensions in New Testament Study,* ed. Richard N. Longenecker and Merrill C. Tenney (Grand Rapids: Zondervan, 1974), p. 351.
37. Consult Lenski, *First Corinthians,* p. 108.

the spirit that rules a person in whom God's Spirit does not live. It is a power that determines "all the thinking and doing of men, which places itself over against the Spirit who is of God."[38]

By contrast, as Paul expresses in eloquent Greek, believers have received the Spirit that proceeds from God (see John 15:26; Gal. 4:6). God's Spirit comes to the believers from a sphere other than this world and conveys knowledge of God, creation, redemption, and restoration. Since Pentecost, God's Spirit dwells in the hearts of all believers (6:19).

c. "That we may know the things freely given to us by God." Why does God grant us the gift of his Spirit? The answer is that we may know innately the things that pertain to our salvation. The Spirit teaches us the treasures we have in Christ Jesus, whom God handed over to die on a cross so that we have eternal life (I John 5:13). If God delivered up his Son, he certainly will graciously give us in him all things (Rom. 8:32). Believers appropriate the gift of salvation through the work of the Holy Spirit. They realize through faith that in Christ sin and guilt have been removed from them, that God is reconciled to them, and that the way to heaven has been opened for them.

13. And the things we speak are not words imparted by human wisdom but those imparted by the Spirit as we interpret spiritual truths in spiritual words.

a. *Interpreter.* At this point in his discourse, Paul refers to himself and fellow preachers. He reveals that the words they proclaim are not based on human wisdom.

We make the following observations:

First, Paul uses a Greek verb that signifies the act of speaking but not the content of speech (see vv. 6, 7). Next, he purposely places the negative in the sentence before the term *words* to contrast human wisdom and divine wisdom. And third, he points out that the agent who teaches the apostles and their helpers what to preach is not a person filled with human wisdom. Instead, this person is none other than the Spirit of God. The Spirit, then, enables them to proclaim the gospel (Matt. 10:20).

Further, the gospel itself is inspired by the Spirit. This should not be understood as if the apostles were mere tools which the Holy Spirit employed to achieve his objectives. Certainly not! The authors of Scripture used their talents and skills, their training and culture, and their characteristics and peculiarities in the task of writing. Nevertheless, the Spirit taught them how to verbalize God's truths. As Paul emphatically states: "We speak . . . not *words* imparted by human wisdom but *those* imparted by the Spirit" (italics added). For Paul, then, inspiration is based not on human thinking or man's wisdom, but on the teaching which the Holy Spirit gives. Paul's style, vocabulary, diction, and syntax were the vehicles of the truth that the Spirit taught him.[39]

---

38. Herman N. Ridderbos, *Paul: An Outline of His Theology*, trans. John Richard de Witt (Grand Rapids: Eerdmans, 1975), p. 92.

39. Refer to Frederic Louis Godet, *Commentary on First Corinthians* (1886; reprint ed., Grand Rapids: Kregel, 1977), p. 154.

b. *Variation.* The translations of the last part of verse 13 differ, as a few examples illustrate:

"Expressing spiritual truths in spiritual words" (NIV)
"Interpreting spiritual truths to spiritual men" (NIV margin)
"Comparing spiritual things with spiritual" (KJV, NKJV)
"Interpreting spiritual truths to those who possess the Spirit" (RSV) or,
　　"who are spiritual" (NRSV)
"Fitting spiritual language to spiritual things" (NJB)

The exact meaning of this last part of the sentence is obscure. A literal translation of this clause does not communicate: "Interpreting spiritual in spiritual." Therefore, the reader must look to the context of this verse for guidance to choose and supply two nouns that complete the clause.

If we look at Paul's explicit references to mature Christians (v. 6) and to the spiritual man (v. 15), we can understand that the writer has in mind spiritual men. If we apply the rules of grammar, however, we face a subtle objection to this interpretation. The second adjective *spiritual* is not preceded by a definite article that designates a particular group of people (grammatically, a masculine word); hence, the possibility exists that Paul meant "spiritual words." We do not carelessly reject this interpretation[40] but we intend to give equal weight to a second interpretation, that the adjective refers to the noun *words* (grammatically, neuter). That is, Paul and his associates are interpreting spiritual truths in spiritual words (implicitly to spiritual men). Therefore, for the one adjective we supply the word *truths* and for the other the term *words;* so the clause reads: "interpreting spiritual truths in spiritual words."

c. *Explanation.* The Greek verb *synkrinō* can be translated either "combining," "comparing," or "interpreting."[41] The first of these three meanings fits the context and has been the choice of many commentators.[42] Modern translators, however, are reluctant to adopt the word *combining* because they question whether this is the meaning Paul wanted to convey.

Other scholars embrace the second choice ("comparing") and observe that the same Greek verb occurs in II Corinthians 10:12, where it means "to compare." But the respective contexts differ, which makes a similar translation for both passages difficult and unlikely.

Conclusively, then, the context seems to support the reading *to interpret.* Friedrich Büchsel notes that the translation *combine* is too weak while "compare"

---

40. Writes Donald Guthrie, "If . . . Christians who are taught by the Spirit are able to interpret spiritual truth to those who possess the Spirit, it demonstrates the Spirit's teaching ministry." *New Testament Theology,* p. 556.

41. Bauer, p. 774.

42. Among many others see Leon Morris, *1 Corinthians,* rev. ed., Tyndale New Testament Commentaries series (Leicester: Inter-Varsity; Grand Rapids: Eerdmans, 1987), p. 58.

introduces a view that is incompatible with the context. "Hence it is best to accept the meaning 'to interpret,' 'to expound,' which is predominant in the [Septuagint] 'expounding revelations of the Spirit.'"[43]

Greek Words, Phrases, and Constructions in 2:12–13

κόσμου—a number of manuscripts add the demonstrative pronoun τούτου to display contrast ("this world"), but the shorter reading has the support of earlier and stronger witnesses.

διδακτοῖς—this verbal adjective ("taught") has a passive meaning. It occurs twice and is followed both times by a subjective genitive.[44]

πνευματικοῖς πνευματικά—the first adjective lacks the definite article τοῖς, which weakens the likelihood that it is masculine (i.e., spiritual men). I prefer to keep both adjectives in the same neuter gender. The presence of λόγοις (words) in this verse suggests that Paul means that spiritual thoughts are interpreted in spiritual words.[45]

---

d. The Unspiritual and the Spiritual Man
2:14–16

Paul concludes with a last contrast in this chapter by first stating negatively what the unspiritual person fails to do. Next, he speaks positively about the spiritual man and, last, he concludes that he and the readers of his epistle "have the mind of Christ."

14. The unspiritual man does not accept the things of the Spirit of God, for they are foolishness to him and he is unable to understand them because they are spiritually discerned.

a. "The unspiritual man." The Greek word which I have translated "unspiritual" occurs here and in four other places in the New Testament.[46] The translation declares what the man is not, namely, spiritual. This is exactly what Paul means by contrasting an unspiritual person with a spiritual person. "The former is animate man, filled with soul in the sense of life-force, the natural man, in contrast to the spiritual man."[47] The natural man belongs to the world, while the spiritual man belongs to God. The one is an unbeliever and the other a believer; the one lacks the Spirit while the other has the Spirit; the one follows natural instincts (Jude 19), the other follows the Lord.

b. "[The unspiritual man] does not accept the things of the Spirit of God." Although the verb *to accept* is synonymous with *to receive* (see v. 12), the difference is

---

43. Friedrich Büchsel, *TDNT*, vol. 3, p. 954. Also see the LXX reading in Gen. 40:8, 16, 22; Dan. 5:15–17, where the verb relates to interpreting dreams.

44. Consult Moule, *Idiom-Book*, p. 40.

45. Refer to Robertson, *Grammar*, p. 654.

46. I Cor. 15:44 (twice), 46; James 3:15; Jude 19. For the translation *unspiritual*, see Bauer, p. 894, and NEB, REB, JB, MLB, RSV.

47. Günther Harder, *NIDNTT*, vol. 3, p. 684; see also Eduard Schweizer, *TDNT*, vol. 9, p. 663.

noteworthy. The first verb, which is active, refers to the object that is accepted. The second verb, which is passive, describes the manner in which the object is received. Here the translation *to not accept* is the same as *to reject*. The unspiritual man repudiates the things of the Spirit of God because he does not understand them nor does he desire them. He accepts only the things of the world.

c. "For they are foolishness to him." The spiritual things relate to sin, guilt, forgiveness, redemption, salvation, righteousness, and eternal life. To the unspiritual person, these things are meaningless, irrelevant, and even foolish. They have no place in a life that is limited to the present world.[48]

d. "And he is unable to understand them because they are spiritually discerned." Paul speaks about an inability that is caused by the absence of the Holy Spirit in the life of the unbeliever. Granted the unbeliever can excel the Christian in various ways: intellectually, educationally, philosophically, or even morally. He may be a worthy citizen and a leader in society who shuns the sensuous excesses that characterize other people. Yet, the non-Christian is unable to understand spiritual matters. He lacks the indwelling presence of the Holy Spirit to enlighten his understanding.

Paul states that the unbeliever is unable to comprehend spiritual truths "because they are spiritually discerned." The verb *discerned* is significant. First, it points to a continual process of evaluating the spiritual context in which we live. Next, the passive voice denotes that the believer guided by the Holy Spirit is able to test the spirits to ascertain whether they come from God (compare I John 4:1). Submissive to God, the Christian should judge all things spiritually.

The agnostic or atheist is unable to judge spiritually because he himself is dead in trespasses and sins (Eph. 2:1). With respect to spiritual matters, he is like a man who flips the switch during an electrical power failure and receives no light. Worse, he has no idea what caused the failure and is unable to predict the duration of the blackout. He is powerless to alter the situation but must wait until the electrical supply is restored. Similarly, unless the Spirit's power enters his life and enlightens him spiritually, he remains in spiritual darkness. The Holy Spirit enables man to see clearly the path that leads to life and to evaluate accurately the circumstances in which he finds himself.

15. But the spiritual man judges all things, yet he is judged by no one.

a. "But the spiritual man judges all things." What a delight for a spiritual person to go directly to God himself, the source of wisdom (James 1:5)! From God he receives wisdom without limitations. Consequently he is able to examine all things judiciously and give leadership in a sin-darkened world. "It is the spiritual man alone who has such a firm and sound knowledge of the mysteries of God, that he really distinguishes truth from falsehood, the teaching of God from the fabrications of men, and he is deluded very little."[49] For the believer, the Scriptures are a light on his path and a lamp before his feet (Ps. 119:105). He knows

---

48. Refer to S. D. Toussaint, "The Spiritual Man," *BS* 125 (1968): 139–46.
49. Calvin, *I Corinthians*, p. 62.

that in God's light he sees light (Ps. 36:9). In view of the spiritual person's anointing with the Holy Spirit, he has a knowledge of the truth (I John 2:20). Thus he is able to distinguish truth from error, fact from fiction, and authenticity from pretense.

Paul writes that the spiritual man judges all things. By implication, this person receives the guidance of the Holy Spirit and uses the Scriptures as his compass for the voyage of his life. The expression *all things* signifies the broad spectrum of human existence. This does not mean that the spiritual man is an expert in every area of life. Rather, with respect to the community in which God has placed him, he is able to appraise all things spiritually.

b. "Yet he is judged by no one." This is a bold statement from Paul. However, he does not wish to say that Christians are never judged (compare 14:29) but rather that the believer cannot be judged by unbelievers; they are incapable of judging a believer spiritually. The believer is judged on the basis of God's Word. The Scriptures and not manmade rules and regulations ultimately judge the spiritual man in regard to his eternal destiny.

16. For

> **who has known the mind of the Lord,**
> **that he will instruct him?**

But we have the mind of Christ.

a. *Source.* This verse is the confirmation of Paul's bold statement in the preceding passage (v. 15). In harmony with custom, Paul proves his teachings by quoting from the Scriptures, which he considers his court of appeal. He now quotes two separate lines from Isaiah 40:13 in the Greek translation of the Hebrew text (compare Jer. 23:18; Wis. 9:13). Elsewhere Paul cites the entire Old Testament passage in consecutive order (see Rom. 11:34). But now he deletes a line from the Septuagint text, namely, "Who has been his counselor?" The two lines "who has known the mind of the Lord" and "that he will instruct him" differ slightly from the Hebrew text: "Who has understood the mind of the Lord" and "Whom did the Lord consult to enlighten him?"

b. *Meaning.* In what way does the Old Testament passage prove Paul's point? The keyword in this quote is the term *mind,* which refers both to God and to Christ. Paul implies that the mind of a spiritual person must be in harmony with God's mind. When man is controlled by God's Spirit, he desires to fulfill God's law, to do God's will, and to reflect God's glory. God knows man and instructs him, but it would be absurd to think that man is able to know God and instruct him. Who has the authority to pass judgment on God's law? In his epistle, James writes that "anyone who speaks against his brother or judges him, speaks against the law and judges it" (4:11). He continues and says God is the only Lawgiver and Judge (4:12). Nevertheless, the person in whom God's Spirit resides possesses spiritual knowledge to guide and direct him in this earthly life.

Paul states that we, as believers, have the mind of Christ. In preceding verses, he gives the personal pronoun *we* an inclusive meaning. Therefore, here also the pronoun refers to Paul and fellow apostles and to the believers who heard the gospel from them. The writer of the Epistle to the Hebrews succinctly declares, "This salvation, which was first announced by the Lord, was confirmed to us by those who heard him" (2:3). The expression *mind of Christ,* then, signifies the believer's knowing Christ through the working of the Spirit and the appropriation of the gospel message.[50]

> May the mind of Christ, my Saviour,
> Live in me from day to day,
> By His love and pow'r controlling
> All I do and say.
> —Kate B. Wilkinson

Practical Considerations in 2:15–16

Does Paul mean to say that the Christian who earnestly prays for the gift of the Spirit is free from falling into error? Hardly, for many Christians can testify that because of a moment's inattentiveness, they have spent years in agonizing grief. Only Jesus' life on earth can be characterized as being without error. In all humility, his followers have to confess that their lives are far from flawless.

God's people, redeemed through the work of Jesus Christ, are called to love God with heart, soul, and mind, and to love their neighbor as themselves (Matt. 22:37–39). They should do so to express their thankfulness to God for the salvation Christ has given them. They should pray that the Holy Spirit, living within them, will lead them closer to Jesus Christ. Having fellowship with Christ means that they have the mind of Christ, and they want to serve him in thankfulness.

Greek Words, Phrases, and Constructions in 2:14–16

Verse 14

ψυχικός—this adjective is derived from the noun ψυχή (soul, life) and connotes a natural life that stands in contrast to the life of a believer who is filled with the Holy Spirit.

τοῦ θεοῦ—manuscripts that include these two words are bolstered by age, geographical distribution, and importance. Therefore, the rule that the shorter reading represents the original text cannot be maintained in this instance.[51]

μωρία . . . ἐστίν—"it is considered as folly" by the unspiritual person.[52] See also 1:18; 3:19.

ἀνακρίνεται—the verb in the present active and passive occurs three times in this verse and the next. It is a compound that signifies "looking through a series (ἀνά) of objects or particulars to distinguish (κρίνω) or search after."[53]

50. Wendell Lee Willis, "The 'Mind of Christ' in I Corinthians 2, 16," *Bib* 70 (1989): 110–22.

51. Metzger, *Textual Commentary,* p. 547. Compare Fee, *First Corinthians,* pp. 97–98 n. 5.

52. Friedrich Blass and Albert Debrunner, *A Greek Grammar of the New Testament and Other Early Christian Literature,* trans. and rev. Robert Funk (Chicago: University of Chicago Press, 1961), #190.1.

53. Thayer, p. 39.

Verses 15–16

τὰ πάντα—a number of witnesses have substituted μέν for the definite article τά to effect a balance with δέ in the next clause. It is difficult to determine the exact reading, but the possibility that μέν was substituted for τά is more likely than the reverse. Also, the question remains whether the definite article strengthens the adjective πάντα or serves to indicate the neuter plural in place of the masculine accusative singular.[54]

κυρίου—in the Old Testament, this word is another name for God. But in the New Testament, it refers to Jesus Christ. The words *Lord* and *Christ* in this context are synonymous.

ὅς—the relative pronoun in the masculine singular is used to introduce a consecutive idea, "that," or "so as to."[55]

Summary of Chapter 2

Paul reminds the Corinthians that he had not come to them as an eloquent speaker or as a philosopher. Instead he proclaimed the testimony of God, that is, the gospel of Christ which he brought not with human insight but in the power of God's Spirit. Paul declares that he preaches a message of wisdom that originates with God but which the rulers of this age had been unable to understand. He proves his teaching by quoting from a passage in the prophecy of Isaiah.

In a segment on the Spirit of God, Paul reveals that believers have received not the spirit of the world but the Spirit who comes from God. With the wisdom which the Spirit has given the believers, spiritual persons are able to judge all things spiritually.

---

54. Metzger, *Textual Commentary*, pp. 547–48.
55. Robertson, *Grammar*, p. 724.

3

Divisions in the Church, *part 3*

(3:1–23)

Outline (continued)

3 1 And I, brothers, was unable to address you as spiritual men but [address you] as men who are sensual, as babes in Christ. 2 I gave you milk to consume, not solid food, for you were not yet able to consume solid food. Indeed, you are still not able. 3 For you are still natural. For since there is jealousy and strife among you, are you not unspiritually minded and walking in the ways of man? 4 For when someone says, "I am of Paul," but someone else says, "I am of Apollos," are you not mere men?

5 What then is Apollos and what is Paul? They are servants through whom you became believers as the Lord has given a task to each one. 6 I planted, Apollos supplied the water, but God gave the increase. 7 So then neither the one who plants nor the one who supplies the water is anything, but only God causes the increase. 8 Now he that plants and he that supplies the water are one, but each one will receive his own reward according to his own labor. 9 For we are fellow workers for God; you are God's field, God's building.

10 According to the grace of God given to me, as a wise master builder I laid a foundation, and another is building on it. But let each one take care how he builds on it. 11 For no one is able to lay down a foundation other than the one that is already laid, namely, Jesus Christ. 12 Now if anyone builds upon the foundation with gold, silver, precious stones, wood, hay, or straw, 13 the work of each one will become evident; for the day will bring it to light, because with fire it will be revealed. And the fire will test what kind of work each one has performed. 14 If anyone's work which he has built is to remain, he shall receive a reward. 15 If anyone's work shall be burned up, he will suffer loss; but he himself shall be saved, and thus as through fire.

16 Do you not know that you are the temple of God and the Spirit of God lives within you? 17 If anyone destroys the temple of God, God will destroy him; for the temple of God is holy and that is what you are.

18 Let no one deceive himself. If any of you thinks that he is wise in this age, let him become foolish that he may become wise. 19 For the wisdom of this world is foolishness with God, for it is written,

"He catches the wise in their craftiness."

20 And again,

"The Lord knows the thoughts of the wise,
that they are empty."

21 So then let no one boast in men. For all things are yours, 22 whether Paul or Apollos or Cephas or the world or life or death, or things present or things to come: all things are yours. 23 And you are of Christ, and Christ is of God.

---

4. Workmen for God
3:1–23

Paul sternly addresses the Corinthians, for they prove to be babes in Christ because of their failure to grow spiritually. (The language he uses is reminiscent of words written by the author of the Epistle to the Hebrews [5:12–14].) Paul considers those Christians mature who, filled with the Holy Spirit, are able to give leadership in erecting God's building.

a. Mere Men
3:1–4

1. And I, brothers, was unable to address you as spiritual men but [address you] as men who are sensual, as babes in Christ.

a. *Address.* Whenever Paul has to rebuke his readers, he always addresses them personally and as equals. The word *brothers,* which includes the sisters in the congregation, conveys a message of solidarity. It is a pastoral address that conveys Paul's loving concern. By contrast, the Old Testament prophets never address the readers as brothers but sternly admonish them with the words *thus says the Lord.* Even though Paul's message in itself is pointed, he expresses unity with the recipients of his epistle (see, e.g., 1:10, 11, 26; 2:1).

b. *Message.* "I . . . was unable to address you as spiritual men but [address you] as men who are sensual." Notice that Paul uses the past tense to indicate when he first came to the Corinthians (2:1). At that time, many of them were Gentiles who had never heard God's revelation in the Scriptures. During his first visit to Corinth, he had approached them with the gospel which they accepted in faith. But now Paul faces people who are unspiritual and sensual in their conduct. He refers to them as "mere babes in Christ." He is describing their spiritual condition at the moment he is writing his epistle. He criticizes the Corinthians for their failure to grasp the meaning of the gospel of Christ which earlier he had proclaimed to them. Consequently, he is saying that they had failed to make progress in their spiritual growth.[1]

c. *Consequence.* Paul implies that he cannot call them spiritual men but regards them as sensual (lit. fleshy).[2] But if they are not spiritual (see 2:14), are they or are they not Christians? Yes, they are Christians, because Paul addresses the entire church at Corinth, which he describes as sanctified in Christ Jesus (1:2). Next, he declares that he and the Corinthians have received the Spirit (2:13). And last, he calls the recipients *brothers* to strengthen the bond of unity with them (3:1). Gordon D. Fee observes, "One cannot be a Christian and be devoid of [the] Spirit. On the other hand, the Corinthians are involved in a lot of unchristian behavior; in that sense they are 'unspiritual,' not because they lack the Spirit but because they are thinking and living just like those who do."[3]

Paul writes these words as a scathing rebuke. The Corinthians in general are conducting themselves as sensuous people of the world. Not only does he call them sensuous; he even uses the denigrating term *babes.* In a sense, Paul utters a

---

1. Compare James Francis, "'As Babes in Christ'—Some Proposals Regarding 1 Corinthians 3.1–3," *JSNT* 7 (1980): 41–57.

2. Compare Bauer, p. 743; Thayer, p. 569.

3. Gordon D. Fee, *The First Epistle to the Corinthians,* New International Commentary on the New Testament series (Grand Rapids: Eerdmans, 1987), p. 123; D. A. Carson, *The Cross and Christian Ministry* (Grand Rapids: Baker, 1993), pp. 70–71.

contradiction: in an earlier statement he said: "We speak wisdom, however, among those who are mature" (see the commentary on 2:6), but now he describes the Corinthians as babes, albeit babes in Christ. Maturity is not attained at the end of a probationary period. Paul indicates that maturity is reached at the time of the resurrection of the dead (refer to Phil. 3:11–15). "This means that for him, in sharp contrast to modern developmental conceptions influenced by the biological sciences, maturity is an eschatological category."[4] Mature Christians are those who are alive in Jesus Christ, are filled with the Holy Spirit, and seek to glorify God the Father.

Here, however, the word *perfect* connotes that the believer both internally and externally lives the Christian life since the time he has fully appropriated the gospel.[5] Paul differentiates mature people from babes to spur the Corinthians to action. As babes they still consume milk instead of solid food, and thus remain beginners in the faith. They may be compared with a billionaire who lives like a pauper.

2. I gave you milk to consume, not solid food, for you were not yet able to consume solid food. Indeed, you are still not able.

In spite of Paul's reference to babes, he continues to deal gently with the readers of his epistle (compare I Thess. 2:7; I Peter 2:2). He calls them babes in Christ. When a mother notices that her baby fails to grow physically, she becomes concerned and consults a physician. Likewise, Paul, who portrays himself as the father of the Corinthians "through the gospel" (4:15), is vitally interested in their spiritual growth.

The metaphor is interesting. Paul uses the same language as the writer of Hebrews, who also depicts his audience as babes who consume milk instead of solid food (Heb. 5:12–14). The author of Hebrews explains that the metaphor *milk* signifies the rudimentary doctrines of the Christian's faith. But Paul gives the figure of speech and fails to explain it. He leaves it to the reader's imagination to fill in the meaning of the metaphor.

In spiritual terms, solid food consists of advanced Christian doctrine. Paul tells his readers that they were not yet ready for solid food when he was with them. At that time, he could only teach them the elementary doctrines of salvation. But now that time has elapsed, they should have been able to comprehend the advanced teachings of the Christian faith. This does not mean that his letters to the Corinthians are devoid of doctrine. On the contrary, Paul's first epistle to the Corinthians is filled with teaching concerning morality, ecclesiology, and eschatology. Paul's comment in this verse indicates that the food he gives the Corinthians "differs in form rather than content."[6]

4. J. Stanley Glen, *Pastoral Problems in First Corinthians* (London: Epworth, 1965), p. 53.

5. Herman N. Ridderbos, *Paul: An Outline of His Theology,* trans. John Richard de Witt (Grand Rapids: Eerdmans, 1975), p. 271.

6. C. K. Barrett, *A Commentary on the First Epistle to the Corinthians,* Harper's New Testament Commentaries series (New York and Evanston: Harper and Row, 1968), p. 81; Morna D. Hooker, "Hard Sayings: I Corinthians 3:2," *Theology* 69 (1966): 19–22.

3. For you are still natural. For since there is jealousy and strife among you, are you not unspiritually minded and walking in the ways of man?

a. "For you are still natural." Without any attempt to temper his sentiments, Paul tells the Corinthians that they are natural, that is, *unspiritual* in their conduct. Other translations for this italicized word are

"worldly" (NIV)
"of the flesh" (NRSV)
"natural inclinations" (NJB)
"in a natural condition" (NAB)
"not spiritually-minded" (*Cassirer*)
"on the merely natural plane" (NEB)
"controlled by your fallen human nature" (TNT)

In the Greek, Paul uses the adjective *sarkinos* (fleshy) in verse 1 and the adjective *sarkikos* (fleshly) in verse 3. Although the difference in both the English and the Greek is only one letter, there is a distinction in meaning. Using another example, one commentator suggests the distinction between leathern and leathery.[7] An article made out of leather is leathern, but when it has the appearance or feel of leather the article is described as leathery. Thus, the expression *fleshy* (sarkinos) refers to the essence or substance of flesh while the term *fleshly* (sarkikos) describes its appearance and characteristics. The first term states an unchangeable substance; the second a characteristic that can be altered.

How does the word *natural* in this phrase differ from the word *unspiritual* in 2:14? Paul is saying that the Corinthians identify with the people in the world to such a degree that there is no observable difference between them in conduct. An unbeliever is unspiritual and, because the Spirit does not reside in him, has no spiritual insight. However, the believer who is inclined to follow the ways of the world fails to grow spiritually and subsequently must be admonished to repent.[8]

b. "For since there is jealousy and strife among you." The reason for Paul's stern rebuke lies in the fact that the Corinthians were filled with jealousy and strife (1:11; Rom. 13:13; II Cor. 12:20; Gal. 5:20). When Clement of Rome wrote his epistle to the Corinthians near the end of the first century, fully aware of their numerous congregational problems, he frequently used the terms *jealousy, envy,* and *strife.*[9] Choosing words that depict the life of the Corinthians, Clement notes the vices that for many decades have plagued them (compare James 3:14). The Corinthians quarreled among themselves, were devoid of love for one another, and behaved like unspiritual people.

---

7. G. G. Findlay, *St. Paul's First Epistle to the Corinthians,* in vol. 3 of *The Expositor's Greek Testament,* ed. W. Robertson Nicoll, 5 vols. (1910; reprint ed., Grand Rapids: Eerdmans, 1961), p. 785. See also SB, vol. 3, p. 330.
8. Consult Eduard Schweizer, *TDNT,* vol. 9, p. 663.
9. E.g., I Clem. 3:2; 4:7; 5:5; 6:4; 9:1.

c. "Are you not unspiritually minded and walking in the ways of man?" Here is a rhetorical question that Paul poses to the Corinthians, from whom he expects a positive answer. In effect they are like unspiritual people who heed the ways of the flesh, namely, the world but not the law of God. They have received the Spirit of God (2:12) but they act as if they are people of the world. They seem to indicate that the presence of the Spirit in their lives is of no account. Their daily conduct does not distinguish them from those who are without the Spirit. And their walking in the ways of man is contrary to what the life of a believer should be (see Ps. 1:3).

4. For when someone says, "I am of Paul," but someone else says, "I am of Apollos," are you not mere men?

Paul has come full circle by repeating the words he has heard from the members of the household of Chloe (1:12). After his greetings and words of thanksgiving at the beginning of his epistle, he then directly confronted the Corinthians concerning the divisiveness in the church. Now he takes only two of the slogans that the Corinthians uttered: "I am of Paul," and "I am of Apollos." The other two, "I am of Cephas" and "I am of Christ," are not repeated. Why are these names not included? Paul and Apollos had been ministers of the gospel in the Corinthian church, but not Cephas. And, surely, every believer can claim that he belongs to Christ (Rom. 14:8). Near the end of the chapter, however, Paul mentions three names: Paul, Apollos, and Cephas.

The question *Are you not mere men?* runs parallel to the phrase in the preceding verse (v. 3): "walking in the ways of man." Both phrases serve to equate the Corinthian Christians with the unspiritual people of the world. In brief, Paul compares the Christians in Corinth with their worldly counterparts.

Doctrinal Considerations in 3:1–4

The Scriptures from Genesis 1 through Revelation 22 teach that there are two classes of people: believers and unbelievers.[10] Lately, many people have introduced an extra category and speak of three divisions: the unregenerate person, the spiritual Christian, and the carnal Christian. We know that the Bible is clear on a twofold division of humanity, but can we prove that God's Word refers to a category of "born-again" believers who are carnal Christians? Often I Corinthians 3:1–4 is cited as proof.

Although Paul rebukes the Corinthians because they are mere babes in Christ and lack the maturity they should already have attained, he does not say that they are in a separate class from which they must graduate to become spiritual Christians. Paul encourages the Corinthians to grow in grace, knowledge, faith, love, and holiness.[11] In fact, Peter also stresses the need for spiritual growth in the Christian (e.g., I Peter 2:2; II Peter 3:18).

---

10. E.g., Gen. 4:1–15; Ps. 73:15–28; Hos. 2:23; Matt. 25:31–46; Eph. 2:11–13; Rev. 22:14–15.

11. J. C. Ryle, *Holiness: Its Nature, Hindrances, Difficulties, and Roots* (reprint ed.; London: Clarke, 1956), p. xv. See also Ernest C. Reisinger, *What Should We Think of "the Carnal Christian"?* (Edinburgh: Banner of Truth Trust, 1978), p. 8.

Throughout his Corinthian epistles, Paul notes that the readers are spiritual Christians. He addresses them as being sanctified in Christ Jesus (1:2); he tells them that they are in Christ Jesus who is for them wisdom, that is, righteousness, holiness, and redemption (1:30); and he informs them that they have been washed, sanctified, and justified in the name of Jesus Christ (6:11). Last, Paul calls the Corinthians new creations in Christ (II Cor. 5:17).[12]

The Christians in Corinth are spiritual people who are struggling with a behavioral problem. Paul rebukes them for their quarreling and conduct that put them on the same level as worldly people. Yet after his rebuke, he reminds them of the spiritual riches they possess in Jesus Christ (3:21–23).

Greek Words, Phrases, and Constructions in 3:1–3

Verses 1–2

ἠδυνήθην—the aorist of δύναμαι (I am able) with the negative particle οὐκ communicates that Paul desires to address the Corinthians as spiritual people but is hindered from doing so by their behavior.

σαρκίνοις—"fleshy." Adjectives ending in -ινος generally convey the meaning *made of.* Adjectives with the ending ικος (as in verse 3, σαρκικοί [fleshly]) generally mean *like.* The first category relates to material substance, the second to ethics. Paul has deliberately chosen the reading σαρκίνοις in verse 1 and σαρκικοί in verse 3.[13]

ἀλλ'—in context, the adverb is a strong adversative that signifies "yes, indeed."

Verse 3

ὅπου—this particle does not relate to place but to extent or cause and is translated "insofar as" or "since."

---

b. God's Servants
3:5–9

A pastor is not a minister of a particular church but rather a minister of Christ's gospel. It is Christ who sends him forth to minister as a servant to God's people. This is what both Paul and Apollos were doing in the church at Corinth. As Christ's servants (4:1), they waited for God to bless their labors.

5. What then is Apollos and what is Paul? They are servants through whom you became believers as the Lord has given a task to each one.

a. *Question.* "What then is Apollos and what is Paul?"[14] The office and not the person is important to Paul—not the who but the what counts. Paul lists the

---

12. Anthony A. Hoekema, *Saved by Grace* (Grand Rapids: Eerdmans; Exeter: Paternoster, 1989), p. 25. See also his contribution to *Five Views on Sanctification* (Grand Rapids: Zondervan, Academie Books, 1987), p. 189.

13. Friedrich Blass and Albert Debrunner, *A Greek Grammar of the New Testament and Other Early Christian Literature,* trans. and rev. Robert Funk (Chicago: University of Chicago Press, 1961), #113.2.

14. Many translations have the interrogative pronoun in both questions: "Who then is Apollos and who is Paul?" (KJV, NKJV, NAB, SEB, GNB, MLB, TNT, *Moffatt, Phillips*). The Majority Text reverses the order of the two names (KJV, NKJV).

names three times (vv. 4, 5, 22) but always in a different order so as to focus attention on the work which Paul and Apollos are doing and not on their personalities. The conjunction *then* links the question to the preceding verse (v. 4), where Paul rebuked his readers for the factionalism that prevailed in the Corinthian church. They ought not to focus attention on the persons but rather on the work these persons are performing on behalf of Christ.

In rhetorical style, Paul repeatedly asks questions that demand positive replies (see v. 4). He himself will even supply an answer.

b. *Answer.* "They are servants through whom you became believers." Notice that Paul calls both himself and Apollos servants to eliminate any incorrect notion that they are rival apostles who were working out their own programs; they are Christ's servants.[15] Further, W. Harold Mare observes that Paul avoids using the first person plural, "we are servants," but says only that they are servants. "The point is that no Christian worker is ever to be idolized."[16]

Next, the objective of Christ's servant is to bring people to faith in Christ. When he faithfully preaches the Word so that people believe the gospel, no one ought to extol the preacher who merely did his work (Luke 17:10). Only Christ should receive the glory and honor (compare John 3:30).

Last, Paul resorts not to using the term *slave* but *servant.* The difference is that the first term pertains to the total submission one devotes to Christ. The second term relates to the service given for Christ to his church and its members.[17] Paul is a servant of Christ's gospel (see Eph. 3:7; Col. 1:23) commissioned by the Lord himself.

c. *Task.* "As the Lord has given a task to each one." The Lord sends his servants to perform different tasks: Paul served as an exquisite teacher and Apollos as an eloquent preacher. Paul readily admits the differences in ministry, but he objects when the Corinthians show preferences that result in factions. He wants the members of the Corinthian church to avoid jealousy and strife and promote the bond of unity, love, and fellowship.

6. I planted, Apollos supplied the water, but God gave the increase.

Here is an illustration taken directly from an agricultural scene, where the farmer plants seeds or seedlings. To make the seeds germinate or the plants take root, the farmer's co-worker supplies the necessary water to the field in one way or another. The farmer is expected to do all the field work in preparation for growth. This includes plowing, fertilizing, sowing or planting, watering, weeding, cultivating, and spraying. But here the activity of man must stop, for he cannot make the plants grow. Man readily admits that he is unable to control the weather. He cannot make the sun to shine, the wind to blow, and the rain to fall. Consequently he is unable to make the plants grow and is completely dependent

---

15. See A. Dittberner, "'Who is Apollos and who is Paul?'—1 Cor. 3:5," *BibToday* 71 (1974): 1549–52.
16. W. Harold Mare, *1 Corinthians,* in vol. 10 of *The Expositor's Bible Commentary,* ed. Frank E. Gaebelein, 12 vols. (Grand Rapids: Zondervan, 1976), p. 205.
17. Klaus Hess, *NIDNTT,* vol. 3, p. 548.

on God for the harvest yield. Hence, Paul adds the adversative *but* and says that God alone gives the increase.

Similarly, Paul preached the gospel in Corinth. He planted seeds where no one had proclaimed Christ. When he left for Ephesus a year and a half later, Corinth had a fledgling church. When Apollos came to the Corinthians, he supplied the water. He helped them by demonstrating from the Scriptures that Jesus was the Christ (Acts 18:28). But all the work of both Paul and Apollos would have been in vain if God had not continued to increase the church spiritually and numerically. The Greek verbs in the text indicate that the work of Paul and Apollos was temporary but that of God is continuous. Paul and Apollos eventually left Corinth, yet God continued to enlarge the church.

7. So then neither the one who plants nor the one who supplies the water is anything, but only God causes the increase.

Verse 7 supplies the conclusion to the preceding verse (v. 6): not man but God receives the honor and glory for the work performed in the church. Paul continues to use the imagery borrowed from agriculture by referring to "the one who plants" and "the one who supplies the water." These two, however, do not receive credit, even though their labor is vital. God receives his full due. In the Greek, the word *Theos* (God) stands last in the sentence and thus receives emphasis.

Notice that in this conclusion, Paul does not mention any personal names. He is not interested in names but in results. The work of preaching and teaching the gospel that is performed everywhere can succeed only if God grants his blessing. The Corinthians must see the hand of God in the work accomplished by the ministers of the Word. The ministers are nothing in comparison to God. Should God desire to raise up a church without the aid of preachers, he could do so. But he employs ministers to effect the growth of the church (see Rom. 10:14). Paul is not deprecating the work to which preachers are called. Not at all! However, he purposely omits personal names to show the readers that not the preacher but God is important.

8. Now he that plants and he that supplies the water are one, but each one will receive his own reward according to his own labor.

a. *Unity.* "He that plants and he that supplies the water are one." Consider two agricultural workers busy in a field. One is planting seedlings and the other follows and supplies the seedlings with water. These two have one common objective: to see the plants grow and eventually mature for the harvest. Neither the two laborers nor the people who take notice of their work think of rivalry and contention but rather of unity and cooperation.

Paul and Apollos never thought of rivalry; instead as fellow servants of Christ they served the Corinthian church for God's glory. For this reason, Paul is able to say that the two of them are one. The number *one* appears in the neuter gender in Greek to indicate that both persons belong in the same category of workers in God's field.

b. *Individuality.* In the second half of this verse, Paul notes that individuality is a factor which God does not overlook: "Each one will receive his own reward according to his own labor." In the successive verses, Paul does not limit the application of the words *each one,* so that we may say that it pertains to every worker in God's kingdom. This part of the verse says that the worker toils not for his or her own glory, but for God's glory.

To illustrate from a parable, the recipients of the five and the two talents exerted themselves and with hard labor and keen insight doubled the amounts their master had entrusted to their care. When the master returned, the one with five talents gave the master ten and the one with two talents yielded four to his master. Each received individual praise and commendation for the work each had done (Matt. 25:14–23). By committing everything to their master, the two servants exhibited unwavering devotion to him. They worked for him and not for themselves. Rewards, then, are the result of faithfulness. They are not the reason for and goal of the servants' labors.

9. For we are fellow workers for God; you are God's field, God's building.

a. "For we are fellow workers for God." Does the term *fellow workers* denote the relationship between Paul and Apollos or the relationship between these two workers and God? The first interpretation would be translated "fellow workers for God" and the second "fellow workers with God."

In favor of the first interpretation is the conjunction *for* that links the preceding verse (v. 8) to the first part of this verse. Paul is saying that Apollos and he are not working for themselves but work for God.[18] They are workers in the service of God, and "are God's paid servants, rather than his colleagues."[19] From another perspective, the expression *fellow worker* is linked in other passages to nouns that convey the objective idea. For instance, Paul writes, "but we are fellow workers for your joy" (II Cor. 1:24) and "Titus is my partner and a fellow worker for you" (II Cor. 8:23; and see I Thess. 3:2).

The second interpretation is, "We also work together with God."[20] This translation is acceptable as long as the concept of equal partnership is ruled out. God and man are never equals in the proclamation of the gospel, for man is merely an instrument in God's hand and works not next to him but for him (Acts 9:15).

Many translators present the genitive case in the possessive form (we are God's fellow workers) and leave unanswered the question of interpretation. Gordon D. Fee observes that the emphatic position of the form *God's,* which occurs three times in this verse, suggests the possessive idea. He concludes that "the argument of the whole paragraph emphasizes their unity in fellow labor *under* God."[21] Nonetheless, the threefold repetition of the word *God* in verse 9 does

18. Compare these two versions with variations: "For we are partners working together for God" (GNB, RSV, *Moffatt*).

19. Barrett, *First Corinthians,* p. 86; Victor Paul Furnish, "Fellow Workers in God's Service," *JBL* 80 (1961): 364–70; Hans Conzelmann, *1 Corinthians: A Commentary on the First Epistle to the Corinthians,* ed. George W. MacRae, trans. James W. Leitch, Hermeneia: A Critical and Historical Commentary on the Bible (Philadelphia: Fortress, 1975), p. 74 n. 53; Bauer, p. 788.

20. SEB, JB, KJV, *Cassirer, Phillips.*

21. Fee, *First Corinthians,* p. 134.

not exclude the possibility that the first use is the objective ("for God"). This possibility is buttressed by two factors: the shift from the first person plural *we* to the second person plural *you* makes it probable; the preceding verses (vv. 7 and 8) make it plausible because God is the agent.

b. "You are God's field, God's building." Paul switches from the ministers to the people, from the *we* to the *you*. In the Greek, he places the pronoun *you* at the end of the sentence for emphasis. Also, he continues to use the imagery of a field.[22] Is this field to be considered active in the sense that it produces a crop? Or is it considered passive as, for instance, when it is being cultivated? The second interpretation seems to fit the context better than the first. That is, by preaching the gospel Paul and Apollos cultivated the Corinthians, whom Paul calls God's field. The Corinthians have to understand that ministers labor in the church not for themselves but for the Lord. "From this it follows that the Corinthians were wrong in yielding themselves to men, when, by right, they belong to God alone."[23]

From agricultural imagery, Paul turns to an architectural metaphor. "[You are] God's building." Just as a field is being cultivated, so a building is in the process of being erected. The builders do their work for the Lord (see Eph. 2:19–22; I Peter 2:5).

Greek Words, Phrases, and Constructions in 3:5–9

Verse 5

τί . . . τί—the Majority Text opts for the masculine τίς (who?) in both instances instead of the neuter τί (what?). Despite the early manuscript attestation for the masculine, the context demands the neuter interrogative pronoun. "Moreover, the implication of the neuter τι in ver[se] 7 is decisive for τί in ver[se] 5 (since the answer is 'Nothing' the question can scarcely have been 'Who?')."[24]

Ἀπολλῶς . . . Παῦλος—the Textus Receptus (KJV, NKJV) has reversed the order of these two names, probably to follow the sequence in the preceding verse (v. 4). The better witnesses, however, support the sequence given here.

καί—the conjunction should be understood as an explanation, in the sense of "that is to say."[25]

Verses 6–7

ηὔξανεν—the imperfect of the verb αὐξάνω (I cause to grow) differs in tense from the other two verbs (*to plant* and *to water*) in verse 6. These two verbs are in the aorist.

---

22. The editors of *EDNT*, vol. 1, p. 246, suggest that Paul was thinking of a vineyard.

23. John Calvin, *The First Epistle of Paul the Apostle to the Corinthians*, Calvin's Commentary series, trans. John W. Fraser (reprint ed.; Grand Rapids: Eerdmans, 1976), p. 72.

24. Bruce M. Metzger, *A Textual Commentary on the Greek New Testament*, 3d corrected ed. (London and New York: United Bible Societies, 1975), p. 548.

25. Blass and Debrunner, *Greek Grammar*, #442.9.

Man's work (planting and watering) is a single occurrence, but God's work (causing the increase) continues unabated.

ὥστε—this inferential particle signifies "and so, accordingly" (see v. 21).[26]

Verses 8–9

ἴδιον . . . ἴδον—the adjective depicts the particularity or individuality of the person.

θεοῦ . . , ἐσμῐεν συνεργοί—the genitive case in this particular phrase is objective ("for God" or "in the interest of God").[27]

γεώργιον—this noun refers to a field that is being tilled or cultivated.

---

c. Builders for God
3:10–15

Paul repeatedly uses the image of the building trade in his epistles. He presents Christians as God's building (vv. 9, 16) and notes that Christ is their one foundation (vv. 10–14; Eph. 2:20). He describes the spiritual life of believers as a building process (Eph. 4:29; I Thess. 5:11). And he reveals that Christians are being built together in Christ (Eph. 2:22; Col. 2:7).

10. According to the grace of God given to me, as a wise master builder I laid a foundation, and another is building on it. But let each one take care how he builds on it.

a. "According to the grace of God given to me." Before Paul continues with his building motif, he acknowledges the grace he received from God. He did not claim to belong to the closed group of the twelve apostles, and he had not received the daily teaching Jesus gave them. Paul was called sometime after Jesus' ascension and the outpouring of the Holy Spirit. He knew himself to be the last person to whom Jesus appeared, "as to one abnormally born" (15:8). Yet he was called to be an apostle. And this calling Paul considered a divine act of grace for which he repeatedly gave thanks in his epistles (see, e.g., 15:10; Rom. 15:15; Gal. 2:9; Eph. 3:2, 7–8).

In all humility, Paul attributes his position as an apostle to the grace God had given him. Hence, before he even states that he is the master builder of the Corinthian church, he precludes any hint of arrogance on his part when he calls himself wise.[28] He mentions that he is a builder by the grace of God.

b. "As a wise master builder I laid a foundation, and another is building on it." Paul employs terms which were familiar to those Corinthians who knew the building trade, especially the construction of temples. He gives himself the title *master builder,* which pertained to the contractor who supervised the work of nu-

---

26. C. F. D. Moule, *An Idiom-Book of New Testament Greek,* 2d ed. (Cambridge: Cambridge University Press, 1960), p. 144.

27. R. St. John Parry, *The First Epistle of Paul the Apostle to the Corinthians,* Cambridge Greek Testament for Schools and Colleges (Cambridge: Cambridge University Press, 1937), p. 64.

28. John Albert Bengel, *Bengel's New Testament Commentary,* trans. Charlton T. Lewis and Marvin R. Vincent, 2 vols. (Grand Rapids: Kregel, 1981), vol. 2, p. 179.

merous subcontractors. The master builder was responsible for the daily supervision of the individual builders. Likewise, Paul had the task of overseeing the work performed by his fellow laborers who were building a spiritual temple in Corinth.[29]

Paul presents himself as a wise, skillful master builder. Before his helpers Silas and Timothy arrived (see Acts 18:4–5), Paul had worked out a building plan to lay the foundation for the structure. Paul, then, is not only the architect but also the contractor who with his subcontractors builds the edifice. Further, Paul refers not to individual Christians who constitute the church but to the spiritual church itself.

The clause *and another is building on it* should not be understood negatively, as if Apollos received undue praise and approbation in Corinth. By no means! Paul laid the foundation, while the superstructure was built by others including Apollos. Indeed the term *master builder* precludes all negative criticism relative to the formation of the Corinthian church, for Paul is in charge. Paul and his fellow workers serve only one purpose, namely, the spiritual building of the church. When Paul writes the verb *to build*, he discloses the continual work of edifying the body of Christ. "The Christian community is built up together in the co-operation of all the participants (1 Cor. 3:10–15), and in the unity with apostles and prophets (Eph. 2:20), to become the one holy community of the Lord."[30]

c. "But let each one take care how he builds on it." In Romans 15:20 Paul says, "It has always been my ambition to preach the gospel where Christ was not known, so that I would not be building on someone else's foundation." In his epistle to the Romans Paul notes his own practice (not to build on someone's foundation), but here in Corinth he is the master builder who employs many people to erect a structure on the foundation he himself laid down.

In the last part of this verse, Paul exhorts the builders to produce quality craftsmanship. He wants the best performance from every worker. As he himself set the example, so he expects that all those who build on his foundation will adopt his work ethic. Their task is to edify the individual members of the church through the faithful teaching and preaching of Christ's gospel.

11. For no one is able to lay down a foundation other than the one that is already laid, namely, Jesus Christ.

a. *Proper foundation.* For emphasis the word *foundation* is first in this verse. Every house and every building needs a solid foundation. Should significant rifts and cracks occur in walls constructed on a solid base, they can never be traced to a faulty substructure. The blame then must be attributed to careless work performed by the builders of the superstructure.

What was the foundation that Paul through the grace of God laid down in Corinth? It was Christ's gospel. With divine assistance, Paul performed yeoman's

---

29. Jay Shanor, "Paul as Master Builder: Construction Terms in First Corinthians," *NTS* 34 (1988): 461–70.
30. Jürgen Goetzmann, *NIDNTT,* vol. 2, p. 253.

work when he brought the gospel to a pagan city known everywhere for its immorality. The Corinthians heard the good news of salvation through Jesus Christ: the coming in the flesh of the Son of God; the suffering, death, resurrection, and ascension of Jesus; and the reality of forgiveness and restoration for everyone who accepts Christ in true faith. The person and work of Jesus Christ revealed in the Scriptures is the true foundation on which the church is built. Paul expects the ministers of Christ's gospel to build the church and to do so faithfully in harmony with that gospel.

b. *False basis.* Paul warns the Corinthians that "no one is able to lay down a foundation other than the one that is already laid." With his warning, "let each one take care how he builds on it" (v. 10b), he alerts the builders that their work will be judged.[31] No worker in the service of the Lord can teach and preach with impunity a gospel that is contrary to Christ's gospel. No one can lay down another foundation to replace the one God himself has put in place, for he will utterly fail. No theologian can change the gospel without incurring God's wrath (compare v. 17). The apostles received this gospel from Jesus, proclaimed it to both Jew and Gentile, and then handed it down to posterity as a sacred deposit. Conclusively, the church rests on no other basis than Christ's revelation.

Paul undoubtedly was opposing some people who were actively trying to change the foundation on which the congregation in Corinth was built.

12. Now if anyone builds upon the foundation with gold, silver, precious stones, wood, hay or straw, 13. the work of each one will become evident; for the day will bring it to light, because with fire it will be revealed. And the fire will test what kind of work each one has performed.

a. "Now if anyone builds upon the foundation." Paul is not speaking of the substructure but of the superstructure, the building that is being erected by workers in God's church. The phrase *now if anyone* is sufficiently broad to include every person who is actively working on behalf of the Lord. In other words, the term *anyone* is not restricted to preachers and teachers of the gospel. Every believer ought to build a structure on the foundation of God's Word.

b. "With gold, silver, precious stones, wood, hay, or straw." Paul's figure of speech should not be either interpreted literally, understood allegorically, or applied incorrectly. With the metaphor he intends to say that the superstructure must correspond to the substructure. The materials used to build the structure must match the preciousness and durability of the foundation.

If the foundation that God has laid is his revelation in Jesus Christ, then the edifice should reflect that revelation in every phase of its construction. Paul mentions six commodities, which he presents in descending order of significance. Of the six, gold is the most precious and straw the least. Temples in the ancient world were constructed with marble and adorned with gold and silver. Ordinary houses were built with wood and bricks mixed with hay or straw. Ob-

---

31. Craig A. Evans, "How Are the Apostles Judged? A Note on 1 Corinthians 3:10–15," *JETS* 27 (1984): 149–50.

viously, no one builds an entire house of gold, silver, precious stones, wood, hay, or straw. These materials alone do not lend themselves to building a complete house.

However, Paul uses the imagery to show what people do with God's revelation in Jesus Christ. Some live by that Word, apply it to their daily lives, and develop spiritually as they seek to edify themselves and fellow believers. These people are vitally interested in sound doctrine and "the pure preaching of [God's] Word."[32] They build their spiritual houses with the precious metals and stones of the living Word. Others lead shallow lives with a veneer of Christianity; they seem to be satisfied with living in ordinary houses made of wood, hay, and straw.[33]

c. "The work of each one will become evident." Here is the conclusion to the first clause of the conditional sentence that Paul began in verse 12. He interrupts the metaphor of building to call attention not to the collective work of the church but to the work of each believer. Each person will have to give an account of what he or she has done with God's revelation in his Son. As in the parable of the talents or the pounds each servant had to appear before the master (Matt. 25:14–30; Luke 19:11–27), so everyone individually will stand before the Lord at the time of judgment (Rev. 20:11–15).

With the future tense, Paul warns the Corinthians of a time when the work of each one of them will be made visible. The books will be opened and everyone will be judged according to the works that have been recorded (Rev. 20:12). Man's work may be concealed at present but, according to Paul, the day of an open display will come soon. This display will reveal everything one has done or failed to do for Christ.

d. "For the day will bring it to light." The reference is to the day of judgment, to which Paul repeatedly alludes.[34] The direct object of the verb *to bring to light* is the noun *work* in the previous clause. The final judgment day[35] will reveal the works of everyone.

e. "Because with fire it will be revealed." The wording of this particular clause causes exegetical problems, for the verb *will be revealed* does not have a subject. In translation we supply a subject, "it," but do not indicate whether "it" alludes to either the day of judgment or the work of persons. If translators choose the first term, the text reads, "That day will make its appearance with fire" (NAB). If they choose the second term, we have this reading: "For on that Day fire will reveal everyone's work" (GNB).

---

32. Calvin, *I Corinthians*, p. 75.

33. J. M. Ford refers to the Feast of Tabernacles when people built temporary structures made of wood, hay, or straw. Even though the temporary aspect of the structure is worthy of note, the explanation that people decorated these dwellings with gold, silver, and precious stones is hardly convincing. "You Are God's 'Sukkah' (1 Cor. iii. 10–17)," *NTS* 21 (1974): 139–42.

34. See Rom. 13:12; I Cor. 1:8; 4:5; II Cor. 5:10; I Thess. 5:4; II Thess. 1:7–10; II Tim. 1:12, 18; 4:8.

35. Some translators render the word "the day of judgment" (NEB), "the Judgment Day" (SEB), "the Day of the Lord" (*Cassirer*), or "the Day of Christ" (GNB).

Both translations are appealing, but scholars favor the first choice in view of evidence from parallel texts. For instance, Paul writes about the second coming of Christ and states that "this will happen when the Lord Jesus is revealed from heaven in blazing fire" (II Thess. 1:7; see also Mal. 4:1). In addition, if the second choice is adopted, the next clause is practically identical. And last, if the term *work* is the subject, it seems incongruous to say that "fire will reveal everyone's work" and then read that "anyone's work shall be burned up" (v. 15). Revealing someone's work is not quite the same as destroying it by fire. The better choice is to regard the expression *day* as the subject and to understand the verb *to be revealed* as a reflexive: "the day will reveal itself with fire."

f. "And the fire will test what kind of work each one has performed." Paul does not necessarily equate work with a building. From a spiritual point of view, the testing by fire does not determine the eternal destiny of the Corinthians (compare v. 15); rather, it determines "whether or not they shall receive rewards *within the context of salvation.*"[36]

What are the determining factors in this testing process? They are faith in Jesus Christ (see v. 5) and the presence of the Holy Spirit in the hearts of the believers (v. 16; 6:19).[37] Rewards are based on active obedience to Christ and realized in a humble spirit of thankfulness.

14. If anyone's work which he has built is to remain, he shall receive a reward. 15. If anyone's work shall be burned up, he will suffer loss; but he himself shall be saved, and thus as through fire.

a. *First condition.* Paul concludes this part of the discourse and he does so with two conditional sentences. We begin with the first one: "If anyone's work which he has built is to remain." This part of the statement introduces the concept *permanency.* Listening carefully to Paul's discussion on building a structure, we notice that he equates the foundation of the structure to Jesus Christ (vv. 10–11). He urges the Corinthians to take care how they build on this foundation. If the foundation is priceless, so he reasons, the building also should be invaluable. The durable materials in the building (gold, silver, and precious stones) are a suitable complement to the costly foundation in Jesus Christ. The faithful worker in the church sets far-reaching goals, uses expensive materials, and takes pride in quality workmanship. The age-old anecdote of the bricklayer is fitting: A passerby saw two masons laying bricks. He asked the one what he was doing and received the curt reply, "Can't you see, I am laying bricks!" The other, when asked what he was doing, looked up and with pride in his voice exclaimed, "Sir, I am building a cathedral!"

The conclusion to the first conditional statement is that a diligent worker "shall receive a reward." Here Paul repeats what he wrote in verse 8, "each one will receive his own reward." How does Paul use the word *reward* in this epistle?

36. Charles W. Fishburne, "1 Corinthians III. 10–15 and the Testament of Abraham," *NTS* 17 (1970–71): 114.

37. Hermann Haarbeck, *NIDNTT*, vol. 3, p. 809.

Paul says that he preaches the gospel but refuses to accept remuneration for his work, even though "the Lord directed those who preach the gospel to get their living from the gospel" (9:14). Paul refuses to be obliged to anyone; he reasons that a reward must be given for something that is done on a voluntary basis.[38] Rewards are given only for work we are not obliged to do, else they are earned as payment for good works. Paul is not telling the Corinthians to earn credit for work accomplished for the Lord. On the contrary, he himself joyfully exclaims that his work is performed by "the grace of God given to [him]" (v. 10). The Christian ought not to live for recompense but for grace and mercy (compare Luke 17:10). Then the Lord will crown the toil of the believer with indispensable blessings and even praise the diligent worker (4:5). Thus the faithful Christian will receive his rewards.

b. *Second condition.* "If anyone's work shall be burned up, he will suffer loss." This is the other side of the proverbial coin. A raging fire destroys all combustible material, including wood, hay, and straw. When the fire burns out, the loss of possessions is evident. It is easy to limit the verse (v. 15) to those preachers of the gospel who are negligent in their task and see their work vanish. But the text applies to every believer and thus serves as a warning never to become negligent but to labor diligently for the cause of the Lord.[39]

"But he himself shall be saved, and thus as through fire." In spite of the loss which the neglectful believer sustains, God graciously grants him the gift of salvation. John Albert Bengel graphically describes the concept *salvation* by comparing the sinner who is saved through fire with "a shipwrecked merchant [who], at the loss of merchandise and gain, is saved through the waves."[40] This is not to say that everyone who performs the work that Christ assigns to him will be saved (Matt. 7:21–23). Salvation is God's gracious act through Christ's atoning work on the cross. No one enters heaven on the basis of good works, for the Lord says that the high priest Joshua who is accused by Satan is "a burning stick snatched from the fire" (Zech. 3:2; Jude 23).

Practical Considerations in 3:10–12

When a person who practices medicine or law opens an office in a given location, more often than not he or she will stay in that place until retirement. The doctor or lawyer serves the community and generally feels no need to move to other areas.

On the average, a pastor moves every four or five years. When he reaches retirement, he has usually served in half a dozen churches. During his earlier years in the ministry, he

---

38. Paul Christoph Böttger, *NIDNTT,* vol. 3, p. 142; Herbert Preisker, *TDNT,* vol. 4, p. 722; C. Crowther, "Works, Work and Good Works," *ExpT* 81 (1970): 166–71.

39. James E. Rosscup concludes that Paul combines the symbols that both please Christ and reward the believer: sound doctrine, activity, motives, and character. "A New Look at 1 Corinthians 3:12—'Gold, Silver, Precious Stones,'" *MSJ* 1 (1990): 33–51.

40. Bengel, *New Testament Commentary,* vol. 2, p. 181.

normally relocates once every four years and in his later ministry he usually stays a decade or more in a given congregation. Few are the pastors who fill a single pulpit for twenty-five, thirty, or even forty years. When a minister stays in one church longer than two decades, people begin to identify the congregation by his name. Then the preacher tends to become the only driving force in his congregation with the result that the congregation may splinter when the pastor retires or dies.

Some churches have flourished during long pastorates while others have enjoyed a variety of gifts and talents of pastors who served for shorter durations. All churches, however, should be built not on the name and talents of a single pastor but on the solid foundation of Jesus Christ. When this happens, the church remains strong and continues to flourish. As pastors come and pastors go, the church built on Jesus Christ endures to the end of time.

Greek Words, Phrases, and Constructions in 3:10–15

Verses 10–11

τοῦ θεοῦ—some manuscripts lack the words *of God,* which probably were eliminated because they also occur in the preceding verse (v. 9). Their absence can be explained more easily than their presence. Applying the rule that the harder reading is the more original, we accept the words as genuine.

παρά—this preposition can mean "contrary to," "other than," or "beyond" (compare Luke 13:2, 4; Rom. 14:5).[41]

Verses 12–13

εἰ—the particle introduces a simple fact condition, which has its first part in verse 12 and its concluding part in the first clause of verse 13. Paul is observing conditions in the Corinthian church and is stating fact, not probability.

ἑκάστου—Paul stresses individual responsibility by using the adjective *each* four times in six verses (vv. 8, 10, 13 [twice]).

ἀποκαλύπτεται—the present tense of the verb ἀποκαλύπτω (I reveal) can be either passive ("is revealed") or middle ("reveals itself"). Here the middle is an appropriate translation with the noun *day* as its subject.

Verses 14–15

εἴ τινος τὸ ἔργον—these two phrases in verses 14 and 15 are identical, but the verbs *will remain* and *shall be burned* are opposites. The conditional clauses express reality with their conclusions denoting reward and loss.

ζημιωθήσεται—the future passive from the verb ζημιόω (I suffer loss, forfeit) relates to someone who experiences a loss or is punished by a fine. The concept *loss* is the better of the two interpretations.

διὰ πυρός—the preposition with the genitive conveys the idea of "passing between, through."[42]

---

41. Moule, *Idiom-Book,* p. 51.
42. A. T. Robertson, *A Grammar of the Greek New Testament in the Light of Historical Research* (Nashville: Broadman, 1934), p. 582.

d. God's Temple
3:16–17

Paul continues the imagery of buildings, but now reveals that he is not speaking of an ordinary structure that serves the workmen who construct it. He calls attention to God's temple (compare v. 9), which is holy. If anyone contemplates destroying that temple, he encounters God as his enemy and will face utter destruction.

16. Do you not know that you are the temple of God and the Spirit of God lives within you?

a. "Do you not know?" The question Paul poses is a rebuke to the Corinthians. He scolds them for not knowing their own status and place in relation to God. They should have realized when they became Christians that the Holy Spirit dwelled within them and stayed with them. Elsewhere in his writings, Paul states pointedly, "We are the temple of the living God" (II Cor. 6:16), and "The whole building . . . develops into a holy temple in the Lord" (Eph. 2:21). Now he chides the Corinthians for their negligence and slothfulness in not using the knowledge they possess (1:5; 8:1).

The verb *to know* in Greek signifies inherent knowledge the believers ought to possess. They know that they are the temple of God. Yet Paul does not reveal how they came to develop this knowledge. He takes for granted that they are able to marshal this information.[43]

b. "That you are the temple of God." The wording in this clause is unique for two reasons: first, the expression *temple* is in the singular (see 6:19) and, second, in the Greek this noun is not preceded by a definite article. The Greek word for temple is *naos*, which refers to the actual temple and not to the temple complex (known in Greek as *hieron*). In his epistles, Paul nearly always writes *naos*, the word for the actual temple, to indicate that God caused the divine name to dwell there (I Kings 8:16–20).[44]

For Paul and the Corinthians, the temple of God is the church, that is, the body of believers. Even though Paul himself fulfilled a vow (Acts 18:18) and presented offerings at the temple in Jerusalem (Acts 21:23–26), for him the spiritual temple was the universal church. He also knew that when the church fails to listen to God's Word, the evil one gradually takes control and seeks to fulfill his desire to reside in that temple (II Thess. 2:4).

However, that temple belongs not to Satan but to God. Paul purposely omits the definite article before the noun *naos* to indicate the absolute use of that word. In his mind, there is no other temple than the church of Jesus Christ

---

43. Donald W. Burdick, "οἶδα and γινώσκω in the Pauline Epistles," in *New Dimensions in New Testament Study*, ed. Richard N. Longenecker and Merrill C. Tenney (Grand Rapids: Zondervan, 1974), p. 347.

44. See I Cor. 3:16, 17 [twice]; 6:19; II Cor. 6:16 [twice]; Eph. 2:21; II Thess. 2:4. He refers to the temple complex (*hieron*) only once in a discussion on material support for Christian workers (I Cor. 9:13; compare Deut. 18:1).

where the Godhead is pleased to dwell. If there is no other temple, there is no need to use the definite article.

c. "The Spirit of God lives within you." The church is holy because God's Spirit dwells in the hearts and lives of the believers. In 6:19 Paul indicates that the Holy Spirit lives in the physical bodies of the believers. But now he tells the Corinthians that the presence of the Spirit is within them and they are the temple of God.

The Corinthians should know that they have received the gift of God's Spirit. Paul had already called attention to the fact that they had not received the spirit of the world but the Spirit of God (2:12). He teaches that Christians are controlled not by sinful human nature but by the Spirit of God, who is dwelling within them (Rom. 8:9).

The behavior—strife, jealousy, immorality, and permissiveness—of the Christians in Corinth was reprehensible. By their conduct the Corinthians were desecrating God's temple and, as Paul writes in another epistle, were grieving the Holy Spirit (Eph. 4:30; compare I Thess. 5:19).

17. If anyone destroys the temple of God, God will destroy him; for the temple of God is holy and that is what you are.

a. *Condition.* "If anyone destroys the temple of God, God will destroy him." In fact, Paul is saying that the factors that can destroy God's temple are present when he is writing his epistle to the Corinthians. Without identifying them by name, he points to those who are devoid of God's Spirit. They are purposely ruining, corrupting, and destroying the church. They influence the members as they model their worldly way of life.

In the Greek, the verb *destroy* appears twice: it is the last word of the first clause and the first word of the second clause. An English translation cannot convey the emphasis of the original construction, but Paul emphasizes that the church is God's temple; whoever seeks to destroy that temple either by doctrine or by way of life will incur God's wrath. In short, God will destroy him. This is not only the law of retribution—a person gets what he deserves—but also the implied notice that the church is the apple of God's eye (compare Zech. 2:8). Whoever touches the church touches God.

b. *Reason.* "For the temple of God is holy and that is what you are." Why does God protect his church and destroy his enemies? The church belongs to God and is separated from the world (II Cor. 6:14–16). In Jesus Christ, the church is holy and as such stands before God without wrinkle or spot (Eph. 5:27). Paul becomes personal with the Corinthians and firmly states that they are indeed the holy temple of God. Despite their sins, these believers have been sanctified in Christ and have been called to be holy (1:2). The church is holy because God is holy. A seventeenth-century confession of faith declares:

> This church has existed
> from the beginning of the world
> and will last until the end.

That appears from the fact
that Christ is the eternal King,
from which it follows
that he cannot be without subjects.
And *this holy church* is preserved by God
against the rage of the whole world.
It shall never be destroyed
even though for a while
it may appear very small
and may even seem to be snuffed out.[45]

Practical Considerations in 3:16–17

When the Israelites constructed a tabernacle in the desert and in later years a temple in Jerusalem, they were the laughingstock of the nations. They were asked: "Where is your God?" They had to tell the scoffers that the structure contained no idols. In the temple dwelled the Name of God. By contrast, the temples of the Gentiles had idols that represented their gods.

When Paul taught the Corinthian believers that they were the temple of God, the unbelievers in Corinth were perplexed; they were unable to understand that a group of Christians could call themselves a temple and claim that the Spirit of God was dwelling within them. The Gentiles had difficulty perceiving a temple without a building. They were unable to comprehend how the Christian's invisible God could inhabit a visible human body.

Churches whose spiritual and historical roots are in the Reformation period of the sixteenth century have edifices for worship that are simple and seemingly empty. Apart from pulpit, pews, a baptismal font or baptistry, and a communion table, the building is empty. True, but on the pulpit in full view of any worshiper is the open Bible. The people worship God by receiving and responding to the proclamation of the Word. They worship not the Word but God who is addressing them through the Scriptures.

Greek Words, Phrases, and Constructions in 3:16–17

ναός—"the temple." The noun is without a definite article; it is the only one of its kind[46] and used in the absolute sense of the word. In verse 17, the noun appears twice with the article, but here the article has the connotation *this* or *the previously mentioned*.

φθερεῖ—the future indicative of the verb φθείρω (I destroy) has a variant reading in the present tense φθείρει, which probably became present indicative because of the same word immediately preceding it.

---

45. The Belgic Confession, article 27 (italics added).
46. Robertson, *Grammar,* pp. 794–95; Parry, *First Epistle to the Corinthians,* p. 68.

e. *Warning and Conclusion*
3:18–23

Paul has come to the conclusion of his discourse on the tension in the Corinthian church. He has reminded the believers of the spiritual riches they possess, especially those in Christ and in the Holy Spirit. Now he issues them a stern warning not to become wise in their own eyes, for that is foolishness to God. Rather, they should become fully aware of their possessions, for all things are theirs in Christ.

18. Let no one deceive himself. If any of you thinks that he is wise in this age, let him become foolish that he may become wise.

a. "Let no one deceive himself." We would have expected Paul to formulate a conclusion to the immediately preceding discussion on the foundation, building, and temple of God. Instead he warns his readers of self-deception, which Paul says is actually occurring in the Corinthian church. Paul intends to alert readers to the danger of falling away from the true teaching of God's Word. Both Paul and James repeatedly utter the admonition: "Do not be deceived."[47] Self-deception occurs when a person tries to justify his thoughts, words, and actions and refuses to admit that he is wrong. What, then, is this self-deception? Paul explains in the next sentence.

b. "If any of you thinks that he is wise in this age." First, Paul addresses everyone in the Corinthian church, teachers and learners, leaders and laity, members and adherents. Notice that he once again resorts to using the phrase *if any of you* (see vv. 12, 17) in his address to the readers.

Next, instead of referring to the imagery borrowed from agriculture and the building trade, Paul reverts to an earlier discussion on wisdom (1:20–25; 2:6; see also 4:10). Although he seems to perplex the readers by going back to earlier remarks, he makes these comments on wisdom fundamental to everything else. The Corinthians were deceiving themselves because they were enthralled by worldly wisdom.

Third, Paul specifies that the wisdom that seduces the believers has its origin *in this age*. The wisdom of the world manifests itself in people who want to be independent, govern their own lives, and manage their own affairs rather than submit to the lordship of Christ.[48]

c. "Let him become foolish that he may become wise." This statement tells the Corinthian Christians that they must take a one-hundred-eighty-degree turn. They should reject worldly wisdom and become fools in the eyes of the world. The Corinthians must see the contrast between Christianity and the world and then accept the label *fool*. Here are one or two examples of Christian foolishness. Christians obey Jesus' command to love their enemies (Matt. 5:44; Luke 6:27). The world, however, prescribes the motto *get even*. Jesus teaches his

---

47. See I Cor. 6:9; 15:33; Gal. 6:7; II Thess. 2:3; James 1:16.
48. Calvin, *I Corinthians*, p. 80.

followers to give liberally to anyone in need (Luke 6:30, 38). The world, however, suggests the implementation of the rules of individuality: "what is mine is mine." To the world, Jesus' teachings are foolish. But Paul tells his readers that if they become foolish in the eyes of the world, they will become wise in the sight of God.

Paul's objective is to have the Corinthians follow the precepts of Christ's gospel. They must be led by the Lord and be completely dependent on him for heavenly wisdom (James 1:5). The Christian who listens obediently to the voice of the Lord humbly performs deeds that emanate from a wise and understanding heart. Such a person possesses heavenly wisdom that is "pure, . . . peace-loving, considerate, submissive, full of mercy and good fruit, impartial and sincere" (James 3:17).

19. For the wisdom of this world is foolishness with God, for it is written,
   "He catches the wise in their craftiness."

20. And again,
   "The Lord knows the thoughts of the wise,
   that they are empty."

In this summary, Paul repeats the thoughts he expressed earlier when he asked: "Has not God made foolish the wisdom of this world?" (1:20). The phrase *of this world* parallels the phrase *in this age* (v. 18), and these two expressions also appear in Paul's discourse on wisdom and folly (1:20). Because the contrast between the world and the Christian community is the heart of this matter, Paul deems it necessary to reiterate his teaching on the wisdom of the world. He looks at worldly wisdom from God's point of view and declares it folly. In the words of Charles Hodge, "Even truth or true knowledge becomes folly, if employed to accomplish an end for which it is not adapted."[49]

Moreover, Paul bases his teaching on the Scriptures. Earlier he quoted from Isaiah 29:14 (1:19); now he turns first to the Book of Job and then to the psalter to show that God despises wisdom that originates in the heart of man.

The first quotation (v. 19) is Paul's literal translation from the Hebrew text of Job 5:13.[50] It is part of a lengthy speech which Eliphaz the Temanite addresses to Job. Eliphaz compares God to a hunter as he catches Job in his craftiness. In a sense, this quotation is taken out of context, but Paul has chosen it because of the keyword *wise*. Nevertheless, the text applies directly to the wise people of Paul's day who craftily scheme to further the cause of their worldly wisdom. This is a wisdom without God. But God catches the wise in their own craftiness and turns their wisdom into folly. "Man's ability to reason cannot stand up against divine sovereignty."[51]

---

49. Charles Hodge, *An Exposition of the First Epistle to the Corinthians* (1857; reprint ed., Grand Rapids: Eerdmans, 1965), p. 60.

50. This is the only direct quotation from the Book of Job in the entire New Testament. The Septuagint reading does not coincide with the Greek translation given by Paul.

51. D. A. Carson, *NIDNTT,* vol. 1, p. 413. See also Otto Bauernfeind, *TDNT,* vol 5, p. 726.

The second quotation (v. 20), taken from Psalm 94:11, is purposely adapted to the present context. A translation from Hebrew reads: "The LORD knows the thoughts of man; he knows that they are futile." Paul relies on the text of the Septuagint (Ps. 93:11, LXX), which has the plural *men*. By replacing the words *of the men* with *of the wise*, Paul alters the text and at the same time interprets it.[52] He changes the wording but not the meaning. Once more the keyword is "wise," even though Paul had to substitute it for the word *men*. Yet the context of Psalm 94 speaks of the foolish reasoning of arrogant men who oppress and kill the innocent. They boast that they are safe because the Lord neither sees nor pays attention (Ps. 94:7). These people resemble those who oppose God with worldly wisdom. Their thoughts are fully known to the Lord, for nothing is hidden from him. The Lord declares that man's thoughts are empty; that is, the opinions of the wise are futile and useless (compare Rom. 1:21).

The two citations from the Old Testament have the Lord God as subject and the wise, who are fools in the sight of God, as object. In the first quote, the wise are like a bird caught in a net; they are unable to escape. In the second, even before they are able to formulate their thoughts, God already declares their deliberations useless. Whoever seeks to oppose God with human wisdom inevitably loses.

21. So then let no one boast in men. For all things are yours, 22. whether Paul or Apollos or Cephas or the world or life or death, or things present or things to come: all things are yours.

a. "So then let no one boast in men." Paul writes a summary statement based on the preceding passage (vv. 18–20): He exhorts the Corinthians not to boast in fellow men. Because he uses the imperative of the verb, a few translators render the sentence "No more boasting about men!" (NIV; with variations, NEB, TNT).

The point of Paul's directive is to not boast in men, be they Paul, Apollos, or Cephas. In 1:31, Paul quoted from the Scriptures to bolster his argument and said: "Let him who boasts boast in the Lord" (Jer. 9:24). Now he gives the negative side of the same exhortation by telling the readers not to glory in the achievements of human beings. God grants his bountiful gifts to his people, and in their complete dependence on him they are unable to boast in themselves. They must acknowledge that God, not man, rules the world and everything in it. The psalmist professed that the earth belongs to God and everything that is in it belongs to him (Ps. 24:1). Therefore, all praise and honor are due his name.

b. "For all things are yours." Suddenly Paul shifts the focus of his concluding remarks. He turns from a negative exhortation to a positive assertion that all things belong to the Corinthians. Although the saying *All things are yours* was a Stoic proverb—"The wise man . . . is lord over all that comes to him from without"[53]—Paul removes it from its philosophical context and relates it to Jesus

---

52. Refer to Allan M. Harman, "Aspects of Paul's Use of the Psalms," *WTJ* 32 (1969): 1–23.

53. Conzelmann, *1 Corinthians,* p. 80. Consult Victor Paul Furnish, "Belonging to Christ: A Paradigm for Ethics in First Corinthians," *Interp* 44 (1990): 145–57.

Christ. God's people must see Christ's handiwork in every aspect of creation; they should glorify him for everything he has made and constantly upholds by his power. By using the expression *all things,* Paul includes the ministry of those who preach and teach the gospel. Thus he exhorts the Corinthians to see that the Lord gives them everything, both spiritual and material. God's people indeed possess all things.

c. "Whether Paul or Apollos or Cephas or the world or life or death, or things present or things to come." Now Paul begins to enumerate the categories that pertain to the expression *all things.* He repeats the names *Paul, Apollos,* and *Cephas* from his earlier discussion (1:12). These men are Christ's servants sent out to minister to the spiritual needs of God's people. In a sense, then, Paul can say to the Corinthians: "We are yours."

Rather abruptly, Paul speaks of the world, life, death, the present, and the future. Gordon D. Fee comments, "These five items . . . are the ultimate tyrannies of human existence, to which people are in lifelong bondage as slaves."[54] But Paul says that all things belong to the believers, because they are not slaves but possessors. (Incidentally, in Romans 8:38 Paul also mentions death, life, the present, and the future.)

In what respect does a believer possess the categories Paul has enumerated? The word *world* should be understood in relation to Jesus Christ, who made the world, redeemed it, upholds it, and appoints his people to be his stewards in it. Indeed, this world redeemed by Christ is the Christian's workshop. And in that workshop he glorifies his Lord, for he knows that through Christ the world belongs to him.

The next two words, "life" and "death," also refer to Jesus Christ. He is both the giver of life and the conqueror of death. The life of Christ is given to believers by the gospel (II Tim. 1:10) and by the Holy Spirit, who delivers them from death (Rom. 8:2, 6, 11). Paul eloquently writes about the defeat of death. A typical passage from one of Paul's epistles illustrates: "The death [Christ] died, he died to sin once for all; but the life he lives, he lives to God. In the same way, count yourselves dead to sin, but alive to God" (Rom. 6:10–11).[55] And last, Christians possess the present, in which God rules. Nothing happens by chance, but rather all things (e.g., health and sickness, joy and woe) come from his hand. In respect to the future, Christians place their trust and confidence in Jesus Christ, for nothing can separate them "from the love of God that is in Christ Jesus" (Rom. 8:39).

d. "All things are yours." For the second time Paul affirms that Christians possess all things. However, this statement, which in Greek consists of two words (*all yours*), is directly linked to Christ. Paul continues and says,

23. And you are of Christ, and Christ is of God.

The first part of this verse conveys the information that the Corinthians belong to Jesus Christ. He gave his life for them, sanctified them, and invited them

---

54. Fee, *First Corinthians,* p. 154.
55. See also Gal. 2:19–20; Col. 2:20; consult Walter Schmithals, *NIDNTT,* vol. 1, pp. 439–41.

to have fellowship with him. They have their life and possessions only through him. Hence they live for Christ, whose they are and whom they serve, and not for parties within the church. Let no one individually say, "I am of Christ" (1:12), for as a body they all belong to Christ. With this summary, Paul effectively puts an end to the factionalism in the church.

Sixteenth-century theologian Zacharias Ursinus posed the pertinent question, "What is your only comfort in life and death?" And he replied to his own query, "That I am not my own, but belong—body and soul, in life and death—to my faithful Savior Jesus Christ."[56] With Paul Christians are able to say, "If we live, we live to the Lord; and if we die, we die to the Lord. So, whether we live or die, we belong to the Lord" (Rom. 14:8; see Gal. 3:29).

The second part of the verse is a theological statement: "And Christ is of God." Christ has been sent forth by God to accomplish his mediatorial work in this world. Through Christ, God is the ultimate source of life for all his people. Christ is subject to God the Father, as Paul explains elsewhere in this epistle: "The Son himself shall be subjected to the one who subjected all things to him so that God may be all in all" (15:28, author's translation). Christians possess all things in Christ, who derives all things from God.

Greek Words, Phrases, and Constructions in 3:18–21

Verses 18–19

ἐξαπατάτω—the present imperative active, third person singular, from the verb ἐξαπατάω (I deceive). This verb appears only in Paul's epistles.[57] The usual verb is πλανάω, which occurs numerous times throughout the New Testament.

δοκεῖ—the impersonal form of the verb δοκέω (I think, seem), which in this instance means "think."

παρά—with the dative, the preposition metaphorically means "in the sight of God."[58]

Verse 21

ὥστε—this particle introduces the present imperative middle καυχάσθω (let no one boast). It serves as an inferential particle and means "so then" or "therefore."

ἐν—followed by the dative plural ἀνθρώποις, the preposition signifies "with reference to."

Summary of Chapter 3

Paul lists an additional reason for preaching the gospel to the Corinthians: he considers them worldly people who are only infants in Christ. Their jealousy, strife, and divisions reveal their worldliness and lack of maturity. He tells them

---

56. Heidelberg Catechism, question and answer 1.
57. Rom. 7:11; 16:18; I Cor. 3:18; II Cor. 11:3; II Thess. 2:3.
58. Moule, *Idiom-Book*, p. 52.

that Apollos and Paul are servants sent by the Lord to bring them to believe. Paul planted the seed, Apollos supplied water, but God caused growth. Everyone fulfills a task and receives a reward, but God controls workers and fields.

Switching metaphors, Paul writes that builders erect edifices for which they use gold, silver, precious stones, wood, hay, or straw. Paul likens himself to a master builder who laid a foundation, and that foundation is Jesus Christ. Upon him others are building the church. The labors of every person will be tested by fire to determine the quality of workmanship. Each one will either receive a reward or suffer a loss.

The Corinthians ought to know that they are God's temple in which his Spirit dwells. Should anyone destroy this temple, God will destroy him.

Paul concludes his discourse with an admonition not to be deceived by the standards of the world. Worldly wisdom is foolishness in God's sight, a point Paul proves by quoting from two Old Testament passages. He urges his readers not to boast in men, but to realize that in Christ they possess all things. They belong to Christ, and Christ is of God.

4

Divisions in the Church, *part 4*

(4:1–21)

Outline (continued)

4 1 So then let a man regard us as Christ's servants and stewards of God's mysteries. 2 In this connection, then, it is required of stewards that one should be found faithful. 3 But to me it is a very small thing that I should be judged by you or by a human court; however, I do not even judge myself. 4 I am not aware of anything against myself, yet not for this reason have I been justified. But the one who judges me is the Lord. 5 Therefore, do not judge anything before the end-time, until the Lord comes, who both will bring to light the hidden things of darkness and will reveal the purposes of the hearts. And then each man's praise will come from God.

6 Now these things, brothers, I have applied to myself and Apollos for your sake, that from us you might learn not to go beyond what is written, that no one of you might become arrogant, favoring the one over against the other. 7 For who makes you different from anyone else? And what do you have that you did not receive? And if indeed you received it, why do you boast as if you did not receive it? 8 You already have everything you need, you already have become rich, without us you have become kings. And I wish that you really had become kings, so that we might reign with you. 9 For I think that God has made us apostles last of all as men condemned to death, that we have become a spectacle to the world, to angels, and to men. 10 We are fools because of Christ, but you are relying on your own insight in Christ. We are weak, but you are strong; you are honored, but we are dishonored. 11 To this present time, we are hungry, thirsty, poorly clothed, beaten, and homeless. 12 We toil with our own hands; when we are scorned, we bless; when we are persecuted, we endure; 13 when we are slandered, we answer with kind words. We have become like the filth of the world, the offscouring of all things until now.

14 I write this not to make you ashamed, but to admonish you as my dear children. 15 Even if you have countless attendants in Christ, you do not have many fathers, for in Christ Jesus I became your father through the gospel.

16 Therefore I urge you to be imitators of me. 17 For this reason, I am sending Timothy to you, who is my dear and faithful child in the Lord, who will remind you of my ways that are in Christ Jesus, just as I teach everywhere in every church.

18 Now some of you have become arrogant, as if I were not coming to you. 19 But I will come to you very soon, if the Lord wills, and I will know not the word of those who are arrogant but the power they have. 20 For the kingdom of God consists not in word but in power. 21 What do you want? Shall I come to you with a rod or in love with a spirit of gentleness?

---

5. Servants of Christ
4:1–21

In this segment of his epistle, Paul relates that as a servant of Christ he is responsible to his Sender. Christ commands him to be faithful in God's service and to minister to his people. Eventually, Paul will be judged not by men but by Christ himself for the work he has performed.

a. Faithfulness
4:1–5

1. So then let a man regard us as Christ's servants and stewards of God's mysteries.

a. "So then." These two words refer to the preceding chapter, in which Paul told the Corinthians not to boast in men, whether they were Paul, Apollos, or Cephas. He instructed them instead to look to Christ, in whom they possess all things. Further, Christ's servants are fellow workers who are not in competition with one another. By using the words *so then,* Paul connects the teaching from chapter 3 to what he is about to write.

b. "Let a man regard us as Christ's servants." Notice that Paul uses the plural in this verse to refer to the apostles and their helpers, but in verse 3 he switches to the singular. With the use of the plural he reminds his readers of the preceding discussion. If all things are theirs in Christ (see 3:21–22), then let each member of the Corinthian church evaluate the apostles as Christ's servants. This word for "servant" is derived not from *diakonos* but rather from *hypēretai* (servants under their master). The word originally described the slaves who rowed below a ship's deck. In the first century, the term took on a broader meaning and signified a domestic worker. For instance, the attendant who took the scroll of Isaiah from Jesus when he preached in Nazareth was a servant in the local synagogue (Luke 4:20).[1]

Paul informs the Corinthians that the church should understand the relationship between the apostles and the church and between the apostles and Christ. The apostles are servants in the church, yet the church is not their master; the apostles have been sent by Jesus Christ to serve the church, for Jesus is their master (3:5; compare Acts 26:16). Thus, the members of the church must respect these apostles who willingly and faithfully serve them in the place of Christ and by his command.

c. "And stewards of God's mysteries." A second description of Paul and his fellow workers is conveyed by the word *stewards.* The term applies to a servant to whom his master has entrusted the oversight of the house. The steward is held responsible for his master's possessions and from time to time must give an account of his stewardship (see Matt. 25:14; Luke 16:2; 19:11–27).[2] To put it strikingly, Paul and his fellow workers were "*underlings* of Christ and *over*seers for God."[3] In this verse (v. 1), the term *stewards* does not refer to a house and its owner's personal effects; rather, the noun *mysteries* shows that it denotes stewards of God's revelation in Jesus Christ.

---

1. See Bauer, p. 842; Thayer, pp. 641–42.

2. Jürgen Goetzmann, *NIDNTT,* vol. 2, p. 255; J. D. M. Derrett, *Law in the New Testament* (London: Darton, Longman and Todd, 1970), pp. 48–77; J. Reumann, "*Oikonomia*—Terms in Paul in Comparison with Lucan *Heilsgeschichte,*" *NTS* 13 (1966–67): 147–67.

3. Jouette M. Bassler, "1 Corinthians 4:1–5," *Interp* 44 (1990): 181.

The expression *mystery* occurs frequently in the New Testament. To be precise, it appears once in Jesus' answer concerning his teaching in parables (Matt. 13:11 and the parallels Mark 4:11; Luke 8:10), twenty-one times in Paul's epistles, and four times in Revelation (1:20; 10:7; 17:5, 7).[4] But what meaning is Paul trying to convey with this expression?

We ought not simply to equate the mysteries of God with the gospel of Christ. "The mystery is not itself revelation; it is the object of revelation. . . . Revelation discloses the mystery as such. Hence the mystery of God does not disclose itself. At the appointed time it is in free grace declared by God Himself to those who are selected and blessed by Him."[5] The knowledge that God reveals to us is only a glimpse of the entire spectrum of divine knowledge. God's own knowledge will always remain a mystery to the human mind, but from the Scriptures we are able to apprehend Christ's work of redemption. The mystery of redemption is made known to us through God's Word and the working of the Holy Spirit (see the commentary on 2:7).

Paul and his co-workers are stewards of God's mysteries. As God's instruments they proclaim the gospel; they strengthen believers in their faith; and, through the working of the Holy Spirit, they build the church.

2. In this connection, then,[6] it is required of stewards that one should be found faithful.

Conclusive statements appear to proliferate in Paul's writing. The last few verses of the preceding chapter (3:21–23) were a summary, and the first verse of this chapter (4:1) also recapitulates that teaching. By saying "then," Paul once more draws a conclusion, this time from the preceding context about stewards. The inference is that if Paul and his associates are God's stewards, how do the Corinthians evaluate them? What quality should the members of the Corinthian church examine in regard to these stewards of God's mysteries? Paul's epistle seems to indicate that its recipients appreciate fluency and eloquence. But the primary requirement for a steward is faithfulness. Stewardship demands dedication that excludes all self-interest and includes sacrificial loyalty (Luke 12:42).

From the plural *stewards,* Paul turns to the singular *one.* He indicates that the requirement to be faithful applies not to the team of workers but to each individual who serves Christ (I Peter 4:10).[7] Every believer must demonstrate fidelity and dedication.

3. But to me it is a very small thing that I should be judged by you or by a human court; however, I do not even judge myself.

---

4. Of the twenty-eight occurrences in Greek, six are in the form of "mysteries of God" or "mysteries of Christ": I Cor. 2:1 (variant reading); 4:1; Eph. 3:4; Col. 2:2; 4:3; Rev. 10:7.

5. Günther Bornkamm, *TDNT,* vol. 4, pp. 820–21. See also Günter Finkenrath, *NIDNTT,* vol. 3, p. 504; Donald Guthrie, *New Testament Theology* (Downers Grove: Inter-Varsity, 1981), pp. 93–94.

6. Bauer, p. 480.

7. Some translations have the plural in the second part of the text: "that they be found trustworthy" (RSV, NRSV, TNT, *Moffatt*).

a. "But to me it is a very small thing that I should be judged by you." Paul shows no arrogance but true humility. As a trustworthy steward who checks any self-interest, Paul passes judgment on himself in a self-effacing manner. In typical Old Testament fashion (compare Judg. 6:15), Paul repeatedly expresses self-effacement before God and before the readers of his epistles (see 15:9; II Cor. 11:1; Eph. 3:8).

The superlative form of the adjective *small* serves as an introduction to the purpose clause ("that I should be judged"). The verb *to judge* in this verse signifies "to examine, interrogate." Paul frequently endured harsh judgment, first as he labored in Corinth, later when he remained imprisoned in Caesarea, and last when he was in Rome (9:3; and Acts 24:8; 28:18).[8] Paul was not afraid of being examined or interrogated, for he was willing to suffer everything for his Lord. If the Corinthians wished to interrogate him, he would count this procedure a minor matter. Or if they intended to summon him before a human court, he would also regard it as something very small in comparison to appearing before God's judgment seat. Paul was not responsible to the Corinthians but to God, who through Jesus Christ had commissioned him.

b. "Or by a human court." The Greek actually means, "a day appointed by a human court."[9] But here the expression implies a contrast to the final judgment day when every sinner has to stand before God (3:13). The term *human court* probably alludes to an ecclesiastical court that was convened to test Paul's apostleship.[10]

c. "However, I do not even judge myself." This is not a conceited statement by which Paul places himself above criticism. Not at all! Paul knows that he cannot be objective in evaluating his own thoughts, words, and deeds. Therefore, he leaves this act of judging to God, who alone can be an impartial judge. This is not to say that Paul wishes to forego any evaluation. Paul is not talking about human deeds which must be examined from time to time; he is talking about his apostleship. This kind of judging belongs to God.

Practical Considerations in 4:3

Administrators of educational institutions routinely ask students to evaluate the performance of faculty members in the classroom. Professors realize the value of this procedure, for the students quite accurately analyze both the weak and strong points of an instructor. Members of the administration are able to assist a teacher in overcoming difficulties and to express thanks for superior performance.

Pastors should be willing to subject themselves to the church's evaluation of their doctrine and life. They ought not to become hostage to fear or to loss of self-esteem. Exami-

---

8. Refer also to the Greek text of Luke 23:14; Acts 4:9; 12:19.
9. Bauer, p. 347.
10. Lawrence L. Welborn, "On the Discord in Corinth: 1 Corinthians 1–4 and Ancient Politics," *JBL* 106 (1987): 108.

nations are meant to strengthen pastors in their work and their self-worth. Conversely, if a faithful pastor is going to be examined by members of a congregation who foster evil intentions, he has every reason to object to such an examination. Paul was not afraid of critique; he told the Corinthians that he considered their judgment a small matter. "Regardless of what men think, [a pastor] ought to appeal to God."[11]

---

4. I am not aware of anything against myself, yet not for this reason have I been justified. But the one who judges me is the Lord.

a. "I am not aware of anything against myself." In the Greek, the word *nothing* is placed first for emphasis, and so Paul is saying emphatically that his conscience is clear; he is unaware of any wrongdoing (see Job 27:6). The comment should not be interpreted that he has silenced his conscience. Rather, he means that with respect to his apostleship, he has been a faithful servant who dutifully has fulfilled all his tasks. By contrast, John Albert Bengel keenly observes, "He whom conscience accuses, is held to adjudge his own cause."[12]

b. "Yet not for this reason have I been justified." The lucid wording of this clause expresses a profound truth. If Paul had been justified on the basis of his apostolic faithfulness, he would be teaching a righteousness that could be earned. Justification, however, can never rest on good works performed by man (Titus 3:5), for then the mediatorial work of Christ would have been insufficient or incomplete. On the basis of Christ's perfect work, man is fully justified.

Paul writes the verb *to justify* in the perfect tense: "I have been justified." He indicates that he has already been declared righteous, not because of his own works, but because of Jesus Christ. In his life, Paul demonstrates that he is diligent in his apostolic work, yet with his diligence he did not achieve perfection (compare Gal. 2:16; Phil. 3:12–13).

c. "But the one who judges me is the Lord." Jesus Christ is the judge, who himself has fulfilled the law (Matt. 5:17) and is the end of the law (Rom. 10:4). He has a right to judge Paul, for through the Holy Spirit Jesus commissioned him as an apostle to the Gentiles (Acts 13:1–3). Jesus judges Paul with respect to the apostolic service Paul performs in his ministry. The Lord assigns, supervises, and evaluates the work Paul must accomplish, whether in periods of frustration (see Acts 18:6–10) or in times of impending hardship (Acts 23:11). Hence, Paul tells the Corinthians, he is responsible to the Lord (compare II Cor. 5:10).

5. Therefore, do not judge anything before the end-time, until the Lord comes, who both will bring to light the hidden things of darkness and will reveal the purposes of the hearts. And then each man's praise will come from God.

Note the following points:

a. *The Lord's return.* "Do not judge anything before the end-time, until the Lord comes." Paul now closes the discussion on adverse comments that he and

---

11. John Calvin, *The First Epistle of Paul the Apostle to the Corinthians,* Calvin's Commentaries series, trans. John W. Fraser (reprint ed.; Grand Rapids: Eerdmans, 1976), p. 86.

12. John Albert Bengel, *Bengel's New Testament Commentary,* trans. Charlton T. Lewis and Marvin R. Vincent, 2 vols. (Grand Rapids: Kregel, 1981), vol. 2, p. 183.

his co-workers have received. He concludes that because Jesus himself is Paul's judge, the Corinthians should refrain from judging him. He instructs them not to judge anything but to wait until the end-time when the Lord returns. When they with Paul will stand before the judgment seat, then the time will have come to criticize the work performed by Paul (see 6:2–3). The obvious intent of this remark is to show the Corinthians that then they also will face judgment.

Notice that Paul gives the readers an emphatic command, which literally reads: "not before the end-time judge anything." Linking the consummation of the age to the return of the Lord, he tells the believers to cease uttering their judgmental comments. He is not saying that they should suspend judging altogether. Surely not! When a pastor or teacher fails to adhere to the truth of God's Word and in his teachings and life goes contrary to the Scriptures, the church must judge. But Paul forbids criticizing a person whose teaching and conduct are in harmony with Scripture. When Jesus returns—and no one knows when that will be—every believer may take part in the judging (6:2).

b. *The Lord's revelation.* "Who both will bring to light the hidden things of darkness and will reveal the purposes of the hearts." The Lord will expose both the external and the internal things that pertain to man. He will dispel the darkness and thus bring to light all kinds of things that until then remain hidden. Although the term *darkness* frequently has a sinister meaning (see, e.g., the blinding of the magician Bar-Jesus [Acts 13:11] or the command to expose unfruitful deeds of darkness [Eph. 5:11]), here the word has only a neutral connotation and refers to matters that are unknown.[13] God is the ruler of everything he has created, and that includes darkness. David notes that darkness is the same as light to God (Ps. 139:12). In the judgment day, numerous items that were unknown to the believers will come to light.

Moreover, people are able to hide thoughts and intentions in the inner recesses of their hearts. Many of these intentions never come to light during a person's earthly life. But when Jesus comes again he will expose them, so that all secrets will be disclosed (Rom. 2:16; Rev. 20:11–13).

c. *Praise from God.* "And then each man's praise will come from God." Who receives praise from God? God commends the person who possesses the inner regenerating power of the Holy Spirit and consequently listens obediently to the Word as a recipient of God's commendation (see Rom. 2:29). God will graciously apportion praise to the individual believer on the judgment day when Christ reveals all things (Rev. 22:12).

Instead of writing words of rebuke, Paul concludes this section with a positive note on praise. It serves as an exhortation to the Corinthians to desist from judging Paul and his associates and to wait for praise not from men but from God.

---

13. Bauer, p. 757.

Practical Considerations in 4:5

We should see Paul's emphasis on praise in the context of this particular verse. For example, he begins by indicating when the Christian will receive praise, namely, at the appointed time when Jesus comes. Next, he states that each person will receive praise individually. And last, this praise comes from God, not from human beings.

Scripture definitely teaches that there will be rewards in heaven for the Christian. Jesus says, "Behold, I am coming soon! My reward is with me, and I will give to everyone according to what he has done" (Rev. 22:12).[14] The Bible teaches not that a person can earn salvation, but rather that God showers his praise on the believer who faithfully does God's will. Thus, in the teaching of the parable of the talents, we hear Jesus say about both the servant with the five talents and the servant with two talents, "Well done, good and faithful servant; you were faithful over a few things, I will make you ruler over many things. Enter into the joy of your lord" (Matt. 25:21, 23, NKJV).

Greek Words, Phrases, and Constructions in 4:1–5

Verses 1–2

ἄνθρωπος—this noun is used in an indefinite and general sense that signifies "one." "This is how one (i.e., you) should regard us."[15]

ὧδε—the particle looks back to the word *stewards* in verse 1 and means "on showing that"; the adverb λοιπόν looks forward, signifying "it follows that."[16]

ζητεῖται—"it is required." Many leading manuscripts have the second person plural imperative ζητεῖτε (require!) instead. The imperative continues the series καυχάσθω (3:21), λογιζέσθω (v. 1). However, it can also be indicative ("you are requiring"). Translators prefer the impersonal, third person singular, because it balances the second part of the sentence, which has the third person singular ("be found").

Verse 3

ἐλάχιστον—this is the intensive use of the superlative adjective from μικρός and is translated "very small." The true superlative is "least" (see 15:9). The ἵνα clause follows the intensive superlative and explains its meaning: "that I should be judged."

Verses 4–5

ἐν τούτῳ—this prepositional clause means "for that reason" and expresses a causal idea.

ὁ ἀνακρίνων—the present active participle of the verb ἀνακρίνω (I examine) shows not action in the future but continued action in the present.

ὥστε—an inferential particle that signifies "and so, accordingly" (see 3:7).[17]

ὁ ἔπαινος—the noun is preceded by a definite article to emphasize that praise is given to individual Christians.

---

14. See Isa. 35:4; 40:10; 62:11; Rev. 2:23.
15. Bauer, p. 69.
16. C. F. D. Moule, *An Idiom-Book of New Testament Greek*, 2d ed. (Cambridge: Cambridge University Press, 1960), p. 161.
17. Ibid., p. 144.

b. Pride
4:6–8

6. Now these things, brothers, I have applied to myself and Apollos for your sake, that from us you might learn not to go beyond what is written, that no one of you might become arrogant, favoring the one over against the other.

a. *Application.* "Now these things, brothers, I have applied." Once more Paul addresses his readers with the salutation *brothers,* which in the parlance of that day included the sisters.[18] He uses this greeting to prepare his audience for the personal and direct message that follows. And he wants to be pastoral in his approach.

What are "these things" that Paul has applied? This question must be answered in connection with the meaning of the verb *to apply.* Other translations read

"have figuratively transferred" (NKJV)
"into this general picture" (NEB)
"to change the form of" (Bauer, p. 513)

In short, Paul is saying that he wants to use a figure of speech with "these things." In the preceding chapter Paul uses images borrowed from agriculture and the building trade; in the immediate context, he uses the imagery of stewards. Hence, the words *these things* encompass the three metaphors which Paul has written in 3:5–4:5.[19]

Paul states that what he has written to the Corinthians he has applied to himself and Apollos for the benefit of his readers. Both Paul and Apollos had served the church of Corinth for extended periods of time. But by not mentioning Peter, he indirectly calls attention to his earlier remark that Paul and Apollos are Christ's servants charged with the task of proclaiming God's mysteries (3:5; 4:1).[20] He applies the figurative language of the gardener, builder, and steward to himself and Apollos.[21] These portrayals, says Paul, are for the benefit of the Corinthians.

b. *Learning.* "That from us you might learn not to go beyond what is written." Scholars have spilled much ink in an effort to explain this part of the text. A few examples show various ways to translate this phrase:

"That you may learn in us not to think beyond what is written" (NKJV)
"May you learn from us not to go beyond what is set down" (NAB)

---

18. See, e.g., 1:10, 11, 26; 2:1; 3:1.

19. Consult Morna D. Hooker, "'Beyond the Things Which Are Written': An Examination of 1 Cor. iv.6," *NTS* 10 (1963–64): 127–32.

20. Refer to André Legault, "'Beyond the Things Which Are Written' (1 Cor. IV. 6)," *NTS* 18 (1971–72): 227–31.

21. Hooker, "'Beyond the Things Which Are Written,'" pp. 131–32.

"So that you may learn from us the meaning of the saying, 'Do not go beyond what is written'" (NIV)
"You may be taught the truth of the words, 'Nothing beyond what is written'" (*Cassirer*)

These examples reveal not so much different translations of the Greek text as differences in understanding the text itself. Some scholars are of the opinion that the words "not to go beyond what is written" are an unintelligible gloss that should be deleted.[22] But there is no textual evidence to substantiate the claim that these words are a gloss. Furthermore, omission of these words makes the verse itself incoherent. Most scholars think that these words "are evidently a proverb, or a principle in proverbial form."[23] It may have been a saying that was current in the political arena of Paul's day and served to promote unity. Paul, say these scholars, uses a maxim familiar in Corinthian circles to urge an end to the divisions in the church and to foster unity.

Nonetheless, when Paul borrows the phrase *what is written,* is he referring to the Old Testament Scriptures? Presumably, yes! The proverb itself must convey a message, which in the context of the two epistles to the Corinthians signifies the Scriptures. And in these letters, the Greek word *gegraptai* (it is written) frequently introduces quotations from the Scriptures.[24] Paul quotes repeatedly from the books of the Law, the Prophets, and the Writings. In total, there are seventeen Old Testament quotations in I Corinthians and ten in II Corinthians.

Paul's stern warning to the Corinthians not to go beyond what is written appropriates additional meaning in chapter 10. After citing a few incidents from the history of the people of Israel, he asserts: "Now these things happened to them as a warning and were written for our admonition, upon whom the ends of the ages have come" (10:11). It would indeed be too restrictive to limit Paul's warning "not to go beyond what is written" to the six Scripture passages he has quoted in the first three chapters of I Corinthians (1:19, 31; 2:9, 16; 3:19, 20). Conclusively, Paul refers to the entire Old Testament revelation.

c. *Arrogance.* "That no one of you might become arrogant, favoring the one over against the other." The last part of this verse is important, for in the succeeding verses (vv. 7–8) Paul continues to condemn pride, the basic theme of this segment.

---

22. See, e.g., Hans Conzelmann, *1 Corinthians: A Commentary on the First Epistle to the Corinthians,* ed. George W. MacRae, trans. James W. Leitch, Hermeneia: A Critical and Historical Commentary on the Bible (Philadelphia: Fortress, 1975), p. 86; Legault, "'Beyond the Things,'" p. 231. By contrast, refer to J. M. Ross, "Not Above What Is Written: A Note on 1 Cor 4:6," *ExpT* 82 (1970–71): 215–17.
23. Lawrence L. Welborn, "A Conciliatory Principle in 1 Cor. 4:6," *NovT* 19 (1987): 332; R. St. John Parry, *The First Epistle of Paul the Apostle to the Corinthians,* Cambridge Greek Testament for Schools and Colleges (Cambridge: Cambridge University Press, 1937), pp. 78–79.
24. The translation *it is written* (with variations), referring to the Scriptures, occurs in I Cor. 1:19, 31; 2:9; 3:19; 9:9, 10; 10:7, 11; 14:21; 15:45, 54; II Cor. 4:13; 8:15; 9:9.

The crux of what Paul is saying relates to the divisions in the Corinthian church: the one party favors Paul and the other party Apollos. Strutting about like ruffled roosters, members of each party arrogantly set themselves against one another. Were it not so serious, it would be comical to watch the individual members of the church parading the favorites of their parties. Paul forbids every one of the Corinthians to foster the factionalism that is rampant in the church (1:12; 3:4). Let no one trumpet his preference for one leader, whether Paul or Apollos, but let each believer strive to learn from them what the Scriptures have to say. They must learn from their leaders to listen to the teachings of God's Word.[25] In numerous places, the Scriptures warn the people against arrogance (e.g., see Job 40:12; Prov. 8:13; Gal. 6:3). The Corinthians must learn meekness and understand that everything they possess they have received from God. They hear God speaking to them from the pages of the Scriptures.

7. For who makes you different from anyone else? And what do you have that you did not receive? And if indeed you received it, why do you boast as if you did not receive it?

Paul asks the Corinthians three questions:

a. "Who makes you different from anyone else?" Paul addresses each member of the church by using the singular personal pronoun *you*. He challenges the individual who arrogantly desires to show off his superiority to state from whom he received the rank he has assumed. The question which Paul places before the puffed-up individual is rhetorical and receives a negative reply: "Of course, no one!"[26] Certainly Paul did not create a party in his name, and God did not grant any superiority to individual Corinthians. An arrogant person is unable to appeal to anyone for support.

b. "What do you have that you did not receive?" Paul again poses a rhetorical question addressed to the individual believer. This query also receives a negative reply: "Nothing!" Asked what he or she possesses, every Corinthian must acknowledge the source of everything listed. An honest answer must be that God has supplied every material and spiritual gift (see John 3:27; James 1:17). Each one is indebted to God and must praise him for these possessions and thus has no grounds for arrogance.

c. "If indeed you received it, why do you boast as if you did not receive it?" The third question follows up the second. That is, if a person has received a gift—either a spiritual or a material asset—he is obligated to express thanks. It would be the height of ingratitude not to acknowledge its source and hence to snub the donor by not expressing thanks to him. The recipient of these gifts then acts as if he had always possessed them and thus poses as their rightful owner. If God grants

---

25. Refer to F. W. Grosheide, *Commentary on the First Epistle to the Corinthians: The English Text with Introduction, Exposition and Notes,* New International Commentary on the New Testament series (Grand Rapids: Eerdmans, 1953), p. 104.

26. Conzelmann answers, "Nothing." *1 Corinthians,* p. 86. The translation of *Cassirer* also demands this reply, "Why, what is it that singles you out among men?"

grace, then his people become the recipients of untold blessings. Because they are fully dependent on God, they cannot take any credit for their acquisitions.[27]

8. You already have everything you need, you already have become rich, without us you have become kings. And I wish that you really had become kings, so that we might reign with you.

a. *Contrast.* "You already have everything you need." Paul again switches to the second person plural *you* and speaks to the church. He observes that the Corinthians think that they have filled their spiritual and material demands; they have no need of anything or anyone else. In stark contrast to reality, they considered themselves successful in church and society and, in effect, fostered the misconception that they were superior to everyone else.

"You already have become rich." Self-sufficient people delude themselves, for they believe that they are rich when they are poverty-stricken. For instance, Jesus rebukes the church of Laodicea: "You say, 'I am rich; I have indeed acquired wealth and do not need a thing.' But you do not realize that you are wretched, pitiful, poor, blind and naked" (Rev. 3:17).

"Without us you have become kings." Paul resorts to using phrases that circulated among the Stoic philosophers of that day (see the commentary on 3:21).[28] These philosophers prided themselves on being self-sufficient, and the Corinthians appeared to be influenced by their teaching. Instead of seeing themselves as citizens in God's kingdom, the Corinthian Christians act as if they are rulers in that kingdom. They claim to be kings rather than subjects of the king.

b. *Irony.* "And I wish that you really had become kings, so that we might reign with you." In this verse, Paul's tone is laced with irony. He expresses his wish that God's kingdom had indeed appeared and the Corinthian believers would be reigning with Christ (II Tim. 2:12; Rev. 3:21). If that were the case, he and Apollos would readily take a seat of royal honor next to them. But because the opposite is true, he uses sarcasm to shake the readers of his epistle. They fail to acknowledge that Christ's servants (Paul, Apollos, and others) had taught them about God's kingdom and had led them to Christ. Now they claim to be independent of these servants and deceive themselves by pretending to be rulers. The ironic comment conveys to them that they are ahead of Paul and his associates, who are still waiting for the coming of the kingdom.

Greek Words, Phrases, and Constructions in 4:6-8

Verses 6–7

In the Majority Text, the present infinitive θρονεῖν (to think) occurs after the verb γέγραπται (it is written; see KJV, NKJV). Both older and more geographically representative manuscripts, however, omit the infinitive.

---

27. Consult Calvin, *I Corinthians*, p. 91.
28. Consult Conzelmann, *1 Corinthians*, p. 87 n. 28.

ἵνα μὴ . . . φυσιοῦσθε—the verb in the second person plural middle is a present subjunctive in the context of a purpose clause (compare Gal. 4:17). The phrase εἷς ὑπὲρ τοῦ
ἑνός means "each one on behalf of one against the other (none . . . in favor of one against
the other)."[29]

The simple condition introduced by εἰ expresses reality; it features the conjunction
καί, which is intensive and is translated "indeed."

Verse 8

κεκορεσμένοι ἐστέ—the periphrastic construction with the perfect passive participle
of κορέννυμι (I satiate) and the verb *to be* in the present tense second person plural signifies that for a considerable time the Corinthians have had all the things they needed.

The verbs ἐπλουτήσατε (you have become rich) and ἐβασιλεύσατε (you have become kings) are ingressive aorists; that is, the Corinthians have become rich and from
their perspective continue to be rich.

---

c. Description
4:9–13

**9. For I think that God has made us apostles last of all as men condemned to
death, that we have become a spectacle to the world, to angels, and to men.**

If Paul expressed irony in the preceding verses (vv. 7–8), here (vv. 9–13) he realistically assesses his present condition. We assume that Paul refers to what he
had recently endured in Ephesus. He composed this epistle about the time the
riot occurred (Acts 19:23–41).

The Corinthians were acquainted with Paul's predicament as he describes the
plight of an apostle. This plight is the opposite of Paul's caustic remark that he
wished to be a king with the Corinthians and rule with them (v. 8). Instead of being at the top and reigning, he is at the bottom and faces persecution and death.

a. "For I think that God has made us apostles." Paul is not critical but observes
only that God appoints men to be apostles. He accepts this appointment as a fact,
but he has his own reflection on the significance of being an apostle. (The plural
apostles is not specific but refers to the general category *apostle*.) He has experienced that because of his apostleship he is subject to ridicule, hatred, physical
and verbal abuse, and the possibility of death. The phrase *I think* (which means
"in my opinion") is an aside and should be understood in the light of the entire
sentence.

b. "Last of all as men condemned to death." God has placed the apostles last,
as it were in a victory parade,[30] in which the conquerors appear first and the conquered last. This place marks them as victims who soon face death at either the
hand of man or the teeth of wild beasts.

---

29. Friedrich Blass and Albert Debrunner, *A Greek Grammar of the New Testament and Other Early Christian Literature,* trans. and rev. Robert Funk (Chicago: University of Chicago Press, 1961), #247.4.

30. Translators provide a dynamic equivalent at this point: "at the end of the procession" (NIV), "at
the very end of the *victory procession*" (TNT, italics in original), "at the end of his parade" (JB).

c. "We have become a spectacle to the world, to angels, and to men." Paul employs the word *theatron* (translated "spectacle"), from which we have the derivative *theater*. Note that this same Greek word appears twice in Luke's account of that riot, where Paul's associates Gaius and Aristarchus were dragged into the theater (Acts 19:29, 31) and were made a spectacle for the crowd. At amphitheaters, anyone and everyone could be present to watch the executions of slaves and criminals. Paul's statement that he is a spectacle to the world, therefore, is no exaggeration.

In apposition to the word *world,* Paul adds the two nouns *angels* and *men*. What a contrast between these two categories! Angels are sent by God to minister and be of service to his elect. Thus, when God's people endure suffering and face death, angels support and strengthen them. Angels observe everything and as messengers bring a report to God. By contrast, men are cruel and coldhearted; they take delight in seeing fellow human beings who in arenas face wild beasts that tear them to pieces.

If the Corinthians should take a moment to reflect on the life of Christ's apostles, they would have to admit that the apostles are at the opposite end of the spectrum from ruling monarchs.

10. We are fools because of Christ, but you are relying on your own insight in Christ. We are weak, but you are strong; you are honored, but we are dishonored.

a. "We are fools." Self-esteem is a basic ingredient of a balanced life, and to be called a fool is a degrading experience that can severely alter one's self-image. If a person asserts that he himself is a fool, we would suppose that irony is lacing the voice of the speaker. And that is exactly the case in the present verse.[31]

Paul states that he and his fellow apostles are fools "because of Christ" (see, e.g., Acts 14:19; 16:22–25; 17:10; 18:12). From a human perspective, Paul and the other apostles are fools to risk their lives for the sake of Christ. "Yet there is an obvious double entendre: They also thereby reflect the truth of the gospel, which is folly in the eyes of the worldly wise."[32]

b. "But you are relying on your own insight in Christ." The apostles are fools in the eyes not only of the world but also of the Corinthian believers. Paul's sarcasm is harsh when he tells the recipients of his epistle that they consider themselves to be intelligent and discerning believers in Christ. He intends to convey the contrary, because their wisdom is purely human wisdom that has nothing to do with divine wisdom in Christ.[33] We would have expected the Corinthians to be receptive to the guidance of the Holy Spirit (2:12). In their opposition to Paul, however, they are influenced by worldly wisdom (compare 3:18; II Cor. 11:19) and separated from Christ and the Holy Spirit. Instead of turning to

---

31. Consult K. A. Plank, *Paul and the Irony of Affliction,* SBL Semeia Studies (Atlanta: Scholars, 1987), pp. 44–54.

32. Gordon D. Fee, *The First Epistle to the Corinthians,* New International Commentary on the New Testament series (Grand Rapids: Eerdmans, 1987), p. 176.

33. Compare Jürgen Goetzmann, *NIDNTT,* vol. 2, p. 620.

Christ for wisdom, they rely on their own faulty insight. With his use of irony, Paul attempts to make them see their arrogance.

c. "We are weak, but you are strong; you are honored, but we are dishonored." Here is still more irony. Paul contrasts the lot of the apostles with that of the Corinthians. He readily proclaims the weakness of Christ's servants in a world in which weakness is despised and strength is praised. Then in reverse order he contrasts the honor which the Corinthians have received with the dishonor that has been ascribed to the apostles.

Elsewhere Paul contrasts his weakness (2:3; II Cor. 12:5, 9, 10; 13:4) with the virtues of power and strength. He considers his own weakness to be a mark of a true follower of Jesus Christ, for it is Christ who strengthens him (Phil. 4:13). He takes Jesus' revelation concerning Paul's weakness as an occasion of boasting; he says that Christ's power has been made perfect in him (II Cor. 12:9). The Corinthians, by contrast, claim to be strong but are weak without the close fellowship of Christ. They should be mighty in the Lord; indeed, they have been called and sanctified by him (1:2, 9).

The Corinthians profess to be honored. But because they seek to fuse the things of Christ with the things of the world, they heap nothing but shame on themselves. Conversely, the apostles are mocked, scorned, and dishonored by unbelievers; yet because of their intimate fellowship with Jesus, they are honored by God.

11. To this present time, we are hungry, thirsty, poorly clothed, beaten, and homeless. 12. We toil with our own hands; when we are scorned, we bless; when we are persecuted, we endure; 13. when we are slandered, we answer with kind words. We have become like the filth of the world, the offscouring of all things until now.

Paul employs irony in only a few remarks. He draws attention to the life the apostles live but does not want to discourage the readers. He is not asking for pity, but he desires the Corinthians to know that true servants of Christ must endure affliction and reproach.

a. "To this present time, we are hungry, thirsty, poorly clothed, beaten, and homeless." This description tallies with other passages in which Paul catalogs calamities: beatings, floggings, imprisonments, riots, shipwrecks, sleepless nights, hunger, thirst, cold, and mortal perils (II Cor. 4:8–9; 6:4–10; 11:23–27; 12:10; see Rom. 8:35; Phil. 4:12).[34] In addition, Paul must have suffered an almost fatal illness when he resided in the province of Asia, perhaps in Ephesus (II Cor. 1:8–11).

When Paul writes that he was beaten, the Greek verb indicates that he was pummeled with fists by people who rejected Christ's gospel. The verb generally refers to mistreatment Paul often had to endure.[35] The word *homeless* does not mean that Paul lacked a roof over his head. Rather, it implies that he was a wan-

---

34. R. Hodgson, "Paul the Apostle and First Century Tribulation Lists," *ZNW* 74 (1983): 59–80; William D. Spencer, "The Power in Paul's Teaching (1 Cor. 4:9–20)," *JETS* 32 (1989): 51–61.

35. Bauer, p. 441.

derer without a fixed abode.[36] During his frequent travels, he presumably used a tent which he himself had constructed.

Jesus had given his disciples the command that the worker must receive his wages (Luke 10:7). Paul clarified this command by saying that those who preach the gospel should be supported by those who hear it (9:14; and see I Tim. 5:18). Paul himself took no advantage of that ruling; he preferred to work with his own hands so as not to hinder the progress of the gospel (9:12b). As a result, Paul frequently had an inadequate supply of food, liquid, and clothing.

b. "We toil with our own hands." Every Jewish boy had to learn a trade, usually from his father, to support himself. Jesus became a carpenter, John and James fishermen, and Paul a tentmaker. Even though Paul's trade was considered menial, he was not at all ashamed of it. In both Acts and Paul's epistles, references to Paul's readiness to work with his own hands abound (see, e.g., Acts 18:3; 20:34; I Cor. 9:6; I Thess. 2:9; II Thess. 3:8). Yet in the Hellenistic culture of that day, Greeks disdained manual labor.[37] They were of the opinion that physical labor had to be performed by slaves. By working with his hands Paul lowered his status in the eyes of local citizens.

c. "When we are scorned, we bless; when we are persecuted, we endure." The world is unable to understand this attitude Paul describes. In today's rough-and-tough world, countless people live by the slogan, "I don't get mad, I get even." Scorn meets scorn and persecution encounters reaction.

The Jews observed the rule, "Eye for eye, tooth for tooth, hand for hand, foot for foot" (Exod. 21:24; Lev. 24:20; Deut. 19:21). But Jesus taught them, "Do not resist an evil person. If someone strikes you on the right cheek, turn to him the other also. . . . Love your enemies, and pray for those who persecute you" (Matt. 5:39, 44; see Luke 6:28). The apostles adopt the teaching of Jesus and demonstrate his instruction in their daily lives.

The verbs that Paul writes in this passage are in the present tense to indicate that the apostles were constantly mocked and persecuted. In response, they continued to bless their enemies and endure persecution. Paul literally says that in respect to persecution, "we are putting up with it." The apostles learned to live with oppression in a spirit of meekness consistent with the teachings of Christ (see Matt. 5:5, 9–12).

d. "When we are slandered, we answer with kind words." The verb to slander actually means "to misquote" or "to misrepresent" someone. The word conveys the idea of shading the truth so as to place someone in a bad light. The medicine which Paul prescribes is difficult to take: "We answer in a kind manner."[38] In the light of Paul's description of apostolic conduct, this translation indeed fits the

---

36. Albrecht Oepke, *TDNT*, vol. 1, p. 503.

37. Compare Grosheide, *First Epistle to the Corinthians*, p. 109.

38. Translations vary at this point: "we entreat" (KJV, NKJV), "we try to conciliate" (RSV; see NAB, *Cassirer*), "we humbly make our appeal" (NEB). Consult Bauer, p. 617.

context. Paul is saying that even when the truth is turned into a lie, he continues to love his accusers.

e. "We have become like the filth of the world, the offscouring of all things until now." The language Paul uses to depict himself and the rest of the apostles is picturesque. He refers to the scum or refuse that is wiped away in a thorough cleaning of a house or a building. Then he adds that they are "the offscouring of all things." This appears to be a synonymous expression. But in Greek literature, the word *peripsēma* (offscouring) was often used in connection with annually sacrificing criminals or deformed persons. They were the "scum of society."[39] These offerings were made for the benefit of society. Likewise, the apostles are representatives of Jesus, who was regarded as a criminal and placed on a cross for the benefit of the people (compare John 11:50).

Although Jesus gave himself as the supreme sacrifice for the sins of mankind, the apostles also suffered physically for the sake of Christ's gospel. Despised by society and considered trash, the apostles could find strength and consolation in the Lord. They knew that during their earthly life, they would have to endure the derision of the world. Hence, Paul writes the phrase *until now*. While he was writing this epistle in Ephesus, he may very well have heard some kind of ominous chant from the local people: "Christians to the lions!" (15:32).[40]

Practical Considerations in 4:11–13

Statistics reveal that the church increases numerically and spiritually in countries where persecutions, hardships, poverty, corruption, and distress are common. By comparison, church membership declines steadily in countries that exude affluence and ease. Whenever Christians are surrounded by material ease and comfort, they often tend to forget the claims of Christ. They become self-sufficient and, while maintaining a religious veneer, have lost their love for Christ and the message of salvation.

Should Christians, then, rejoice in persecution and affliction? They ought never to seek persecution for its own sake. But when they are obedient to the gospel, they will be rejected by the world and have to endure persecution. To them Jesus says, "Rejoice and be glad, because great is your reward in heaven" (Matt. 5:12). Followers of Jesus experience that worldly friends forsake them. They undergo verbal abuse that is frequently accompanied by physical and mental agony. In effect, they struggle against spiritual forces controlled by Satan (see Eph. 6:12). Yet they rejoice, for they will receive their reward.

Should Christians, then, seek poverty to be alive spiritually? Not necessarily. Abraham is known as the father of believers, yet God blessed him with numerous earthly possessions. Similarly, Job was tried, tested, and strengthened in his faith. Yet God blessed him

---

39. Consult J. I. Packer, *NIDNTT*, vol. 1, p. 479; Friedrich Hauck, *TDNT*, vol. 3, pp. 430–31; Gustav Stählin, *TDNT*, vol. 6, pp. 90–91. A. Hanson, "1 Corinthians 4:13b and Lamentations 3:45," *ExpT* 39 (1982): 214–15.

40. G. G. Findlay, *St. Paul's First Epistle to the Corinthians*, in vol. 3 of *The Expositor's Greek Testament*, ed. W. Robertson Nicoll, 5 vols. (1910; reprint ed., Grand Rapids: Eerdmans, 1961), p. 803.

with untold riches. Material wealth, however, should always be subservient to the cause of Christ and should never become the Christian's master. As Paul puts it, "Greed . . . is idolatry" (Col. 3:5). Jesus teaches that a believer should love God with heart, soul, and mind, and love his fellow man as himself (Matt. 22:37–40). Then he will be rich in Christ, even though he is considered a pauper by the world.

Henry F. Lyte gave poetic expression to his personal desire to follow Jesus and to accept the consequences:

> Jesus, I my cross have taken,
> All to leave, and follow Thee;
> Destitute, despised, forsaken,
> Thou from hence my all shalt be;
> Perish every fond ambition,
> All I've sought or hoped or known;
> Yet how rich is my condition:
> God and heaven are still my own.

Greek Words, Phrases, and Constructions in 4:9–13

Verses 9–10

δοκῶ γάρ—a parenthetical statement that means "for in my opinion"; numerous manuscripts that reflect age and wide geographic representation delete the conjunction ὅτι (that).

τῷ κόσμῳ—the noun in the dative case is explained by the indefinite nouns ἀγγέλοισ and ἀνθρώποις and means "to the world, both to angels and to men."[41]

ἡμεῖς . . . ὑμεῖς—note, first, the position of these two personal pronouns (at the beginning and the end of the three sentences, which denotes emphasis); next, their repetition; and last, their reversed order in the last sentence.

Verses 11–12

ἄχρι τῆς ἄρτι ὥρας—"until this moment." This segment (vv. 11–13) begins and ends with a time reference, ἕως ἄρτι (until now).

Except for the aorist passive ἐγενήθημεν (we have become) in verse 13, this entire segment has all the finite verbs and the participles in the present tense.

λοιδορούμενοι—the present participle of λοιδορέω (I scorn) can have a concessive meaning ("although we are scorned").

Verse 13

περικαθάρμα—this compound of περί (around) and the noun derived from the verb καθαρίζω (I cleanse) signifies the residue from scrubbing an object. The -μα ending of this noun denotes the result of the action.

περίψημα—from the preposition περί and the verb ψάω (I wipe, rub), it indicates "that which has been scraped off."

---

41. A. T. Robertson, *A Grammar of the Greek New Testament in the Light of Historical Research* (Nashville: Broadman, 1934), p. 788.

d. Admonition
4:14–17

14. I write this not to make you ashamed, but to admonish you as my dear children.

Paul has harshly rebuked the Corinthians but turns to them as a loving father who cares for his offspring (see II Cor. 6:13; Gal. 4:19; I Thess. 2:11). One thing children dread most is to be put to shame in the presence of their friends. Shame places an indelible mark on their minds, which, so it seems, they are unable to erase. The church at Corinth does not want to be disgraced in the presence of the other churches in Achaia, Macedonia, and Asia Minor (compare 6:5; II Cor. 9:4).

After a negative statement, "not to make you ashamed," Paul utters a positive remark, "to admonish you." He wants the Corinthians to listen to him for their own benefit. He admonishes them to pay attention to his words, for in Christ he is their father and they are his dear children. His words are the words of a father who in love corrects his children.[42] Paul addresses the Corinthians in genuine love; thus he writes the adjective *dear,* which in older translations is *beloved.* In the succeeding verses, he reveals the content of his admonition.[43]

15. Even if you have countless attendants in Christ, you do not have many fathers, for in Christ Jesus I became your father through the gospel.

a. "Even if you have countless attendants in Christ." With an overstatement, Paul calls attention to the concept *father.* He says to the Corinthians, "Now suppose for a moment that, in addition to Apollos and myself, you had been guarded by innumerable attendants who led you to Christ. Nevertheless, I am your spiritual father who first taught you the gospel." Paul employs the term *paidagōgos,* from which we have the derivative *pedagogue.* In Hellenistic culture, a pedagogue was either a household slave or a freedman who accompanied a child (or the children) of well-to-do parents to and from school. He was appointed to tutor the child in proper conduct, chide him whenever necessary, guard him from danger and evil influences, and to give him an interest in correct speech, grammar, and diction.[44] He helped a boy do his homework, nursed him when sick, and attended to his needs until the boy reached adolescence.

Paul purposely exaggerates when he suggests that the Corinthians would have ten thousand pedagogues to guard, chide, and correct them in respect to Christian conduct and teaching. Note that a father who employed a pedagogue always

---

42. Johannes Behm, *TDNT,* vol. 4, p. 1022.

43. For the Greek verb *nouthetein* (to warn), which is a Pauline word, see Acts 20:31; Rom. 15:14; Col. 1:28; 3:16; I Thess. 5:12, 14; II Thess. 3:15.

44. Refer to Norman H. Young, *"Paidagogos:* The Social Setting of a Pauline Metaphor," *NovT* 29 (1987): 150–76.

remained in charge of his son's education. The father was much closer to the son than the pedagogue could ever be.

b. "You do not have many fathers, for in Christ Jesus I became your father through the gospel." Each person can have countless teachers, but only one biological father. So Paul observes that the Corinthians could presumably have innumerable pedagogues to lead them to Christ, but each one could not have many spiritual fathers. For eighteen months Paul labored to plant the church at Corinth (Acts 18:11). Hence, he could truthfully say that in Christ Jesus he was the spiritual progenitor of the Corinthian church. From a Jewish perspective, a teacher who taught students the content of the Torah (the Old Testament Scriptures, other Jewish sacred literature, and oral tradition) was considered a father.[45] In that capacity, Paul asserted his apostolic authority with respect to those members of the church who questioned it.

If we look at this matter from a different perspective, we see that the church did not bring forth the apostles; rather, Jesus Christ endowed the apostles, who went forth to found the church. Although other workers, among whom were Timothy, Silas, Apollos, and Titus, came to Corinth to assist in teaching and edifying the members of the church, Paul exercised lasting authority over them.[46] Through Christ's gospel Paul is able to call himself the father of the Corinthians.

16. Therefore I urge you to be imitators of me. 17. For this reason, I am sending Timothy to you, who is my dear and faithful child in the Lord, who will remind you of my ways that are in Christ Jesus, just as I teach everywhere in every church.

a. *Imitators.* Paul brought the gospel to the Corinthians, witnessed their spiritual birth, taught them the Christian way of life, urged them to follow Christ, and demonstrated his unwavering love for them. Now he directs them to become his imitators and adopt his personal testimony of Christ.[47] By implication, Paul urges them to imitate Christ, who reveals himself in the gospel. Elsewhere in this epistle he writes, "Be imitators of me, just as I am of Christ" (11:1; see also Gal. 4:12; Phil. 3:17; II Thess. 3:7, 9). What Paul is trying to say is that one who is imitating Paul is imitating Christ.

Speaking as their spiritual father, Paul expects the Corinthians to follow his example. From the moment they are born, children are dependent on their parents for survival, care, guidance, and teaching. They copy the parents' way of life, learn elementary truths, and adopt their basic values. Children not only physically but also spiritually reflect the likeness of their father and mother. "The closer the relationship of parent and child, the more the similarities de-

---

45. SB, vol. 3, pp. 340–41.

46. Herman N. Ridderbos, *Paul: An Outline of His Theology,* trans. John Richard de Witt (Grand Rapids: Eerdmans, 1975), p. 450.

47. D. M. Stanley, "'Become imitators of me': The Pauline Conception of Apostolic Tradition," *Bib* 40 (1959): 859–77; Wilhelm Michaelis, *TDNT,* vol. 4, p. 668.

velop."[48] This close relationship, of course, is founded on love. Paul demonstrates his love toward his spiritual offspring by calling them his "beloved children" (v. 14, NKJV).

b. *Offspring.* Most translators render the Greek literally: "I have sent" or "I sent," which implies that Paul instructed Timothy to travel to Corinth. Yet we have no evidence that Timothy ever arrived in Corinth (but see 16:10–11). About this time (A.D. 55), Paul began writing the First Epistle to the Corinthians. If Timothy had been with Paul at that time, we would have expected Paul to include his name in the greetings, as in II Corinthians 1:1.

Other translators prefer the present tense of the verb: "I am sending." The reasoning is that when a writer sent a letter or a messenger, he would place himself in the position of the recipients. For the recipient the act of sending occurred in the past. But from the sender's point of view, this happened in the present.

"For this reason, I am sending Timothy to you, who is my dear and faithful child in the Lord." Along with the letter, Paul is sending Timothy to the Corinthians. Timothy became acquainted with the faith of his grandmother Lois and his mother, Eunice (II Tim. 1:5); we assume that he was converted when Paul and Barnabas came to Lystra and Derbe on their first missionary journey (Acts 14:8–21). When Timothy eventually accompanied Paul, he was heartily recommended by the Christians in Lystra (Acts 16:1–3) and presumably had been a believer for some time.

Paul called Timothy "my dear and faithful child in the Lord." This means that Paul considered himself Timothy's spiritual father. As a natural father normally loves his son, so Paul deeply loved his spiritual son (I Tim. 1:2; II Tim. 1:2; compare Philem. 10). And Timothy proved to be Paul's faithful child in working for the Lord. We learn from Acts and Paul's epistles that Timothy often completed tasks that Paul himself was hindered from doing. For example, when Paul had to leave Philippi, Thessalonica, and Berea, Timothy went there to work in his place (Acts 17:15; Phil. 2:22; I Thess. 3:1–3, 6).

c. *Instruction.* "[Timothy] will remind you of my ways that are in Christ Jesus, just as I teach everywhere in every church." As Paul's spiritual son, Timothy must refresh the memory of Paul's spiritual children in Corinth. He has to remind them of Paul's Christian conduct, mentioned here as "ways that are in Christ Jesus." These ways relate to the work Paul performed while he was with the Corinthians: teaching, preaching, counseling, shaping, nurturing, and praying. They pertain to the work Paul accomplished on behalf of Jesus Christ and the building of the church.

Paul intimates that even though he has not visited the church in Corinth for some time, let no one think that he has not been busy elsewhere. He has been teaching, chiefly in Ephesus and the province of Asia. And his teaching there is

---

48. Willis P. De Boer, *The Imitation of Paul: An Exegetical Study* (Kampen: Kok, 1962), p. 153; Eva Maria Lassen, "The Use of the Father Image in Imperial Propaganda and 1 Corinthians 4:14–21," *TynB* 42.1 (1991): 127–36.

similar to what the Corinthians received some years earlier. Furthermore, Paul believes in and contends for the unity of the church of Jesus Christ (see 7:17; 14:33). There is, therefore, no place for divisions and doctrines that are contrary to the gospel.

Doctrinal Considerations in 4:14–17

When Paul writes that he is the father of the Corinthian Christians, we immediately think of the words Jesus spoke when he pronounced his woes over the Pharisees: "And do not call anyone on earth 'father,' for you have one Father, and he is in heaven" (Matt. 23:9). Is Paul disregarding Jesus' command? Not necessarily. Jesus' words must be understood in the context in which they were spoken.

In his discourse against the Pharisees, Jesus tells the twelve disciples and the crowds to reject the title *rabbi* as a name for themselves, for they have only one Master (Matt. 23:8). Then he says that no one should call them father, because God is their Father. The term *the fathers* "became a very common way of referring to earlier teachers of the law, especially the great masters."[49] Jesus warns against the use of titles that foster pride in the persons who are so honored. In the New Testament, Paul and the other apostles are never addressed as father. When Paul uses the figure of speech of father and children, he qualifies this by saying: "In Christ Jesus I became your father through the gospel" (v. 15). Not Paul but Jesus Christ receives glory and honor.

Greek Words, Phrases, and Constructions in 4:14–17

Verse 14

οὐκ ἐντρέπων—the negative particle οὐκ precedes the present active participle of ἐντρέπω (I make ashamed). Normally the particle μή controls participles, but here the contrast of the words οὐ . . . ἀλλά calls for a departure from the rule.[50]

νουθετῶν—from the verb νουθετέω (I warn), this reading with the present participle is preferred to the finite verb νουθετῶ. Both readings have equal manuscript support, yet the use of the participle appears to be a dominant feature in Paul's writings.

Verse 15

μυρίους—this adjective in the accusative masculine plural means not "ten thousands" but rather "innumerable."[51]

ἐὰν . . . ἔχητε—with the verb in the subjunctive, the conditional sentence expresses skepticism. The adverb ἀλλ' in the apodosis signifies "at least."

ἐγὼ ὑμᾶς—notice these two personal pronouns placed next to each other to indicate the close relationship of Paul and the Corinthians.

49. K. Kohler, "Abba, Father: Title of Spiritual Leader and Saint," *JQR* 13 (1900–1901): 567–80; D. A. Carson, *Matthew,* in vol. 8 of *The Expositor's Bible Commentary,* ed. Frank E. Gaebelein, 12 vols. (Grand Rapids: Zondervan, 1984), p. 475.
50. Robert Hanna, *A Grammatical Aid to the Greek New Testament* (Grand Rapids: Baker, 1983), p. 291.
51. Bauer, p. 529.

Verse 17

ἔπεμψα—the aorist active of πέμπω (I send) is probably the epistolary aorist, "I am sending."

ὅς ὑμᾶς ἀναμνήσει—"who will remind you." This clause expresses purpose; it functions as a parallel to the preceding clause, "who is my dear and faithful child."

---

e. Approaching Visit
4:18–21

18. Now some of you have become arrogant, as if I were not coming to you. 19. But I will come to you very soon, if the Lord wills, and I will know not the word of those who are arrogant but the power they have.

a. *Arrogance.* Paul returns to a discussion of the arrogance that was exhibited by some Corinthians (see v. 6), for this sin remains a persistent evil in the congregation. It appears not only in the form of a divisive spirit but also in a lack of respect for Paul (see 9:1–3; II Cor. 10:9–10). Before he turns his attention to disciplinary matters, Paul once more urges those people who are arrogant leaders to take note (compare 1:11–12; 3:3–4).

Personified as wisdom, the Lord says: "I hate pride and arrogance, evil behavior and perverse speech" (Prov. 8:13b). These are the sins that some of the Corinthians committed (compare 5:2; 8:1). Paul wants these proud Corinthians to acknowledge their offense and to repent, so that this evil might not permeate the entire congregation.

b. *Intention.* Arrogance blinds a person to reality. The haughty leaders in Corinth thought that Paul would stay in Ephesus and not visit the Corinthians. They underestimated Paul's loving concern for the church and his intention to visit the churches in Macedonia and Achaia (Acts 19:21). Paul daily remembered the churches in prayer and continued to have a personal interest in their spiritual well-being (1:4; Phil. 1:3–4; Col. 1:3–4; I Thess. 1:2–3; II Thess. 1:3). He was determined to visit them, even if their leaders were spreading the rumor that Paul would not come to Corinth. They probably felt secure, thinking that the presence of Timothy conveyed the apostle's lack of interest in the Corinthian church. However, "they know very well that Paul is equipped with power from God."[52]

c. *Assertion.* "I will come to you very soon, if the Lord wills." Paul speaks with determination, for he is indeed going to visit the Corinthian church. He writes that he is coming very soon. After traveling through Macedonia, he intends to arrive in Corinth and spend some time, perhaps an entire winter (16:5–7). He even tells them that he will leave Ephesus after Pentecost (16:8), probably in A.D. 56.

Paul qualifies his intentions with the clause *if God wills* (see also 16:7). He knows that he serves the Lord, who sends him wherever Paul's presence is needed. He is not his own master but belongs to his Lord Jesus Christ.

---

52. Calvin, *I Corinthians*, p. 100.

d. *Purpose.* "And I will know not the word of those who are arrogant but the power they have." Paul is not interested in learning what his opponents have to say, for their accusations were uttered while he was away. He wants to know what influence these leaders have had on the church members. Should these men be filled with the Holy Spirit, they would be able to give positive leadership in the church. But if they were without the Spirit, they would lack the ability to build the church. Paul plans to spend time in Corinth to find out if these leaders have been endowed with spiritual power to advance the cause of Christ.

20. For the kingdom of God consists not in word but in power.

In the concluding remarks to this part of his letter, Paul carefully chooses his words. With the concept *kingdom,* he calls to mind God's worldwide power and influence. Paul had earlier mocked the Corinthians by calling them kings (v. 8), but now he teaches them the doctrine that Christ reigns with power throughout his kingdom.

This is the first time that Paul employs the word *kingdom* in his epistle. Although the term itself appears chiefly in the synoptic Gospels, it also occurs frequently in Paul's epistles.[53] In many passages, Paul features the present aspect of Christ's kingdom. For instance, the kingdom is a matter not of food and drink (Rom. 14:17), not of arrogant talk, but of power (I Cor. 4:20) and of lives that are worthy of God (I Thess. 2:12). In other texts, he highlights the eschatological aspect of the kingdom: wicked people do not inherit it (6:9–10; Gal. 5:19–21; Eph. 5:5).

In his references to the kingdom, Paul places appropriate emphasis on the lordship of Jesus Christ. "The exercise of lordship implies the exercise of a dominion which is closely akin to the idea of dynamic rule seen in the teaching of Jesus."[54] Even though Paul omits the name *Jesus* in this verse, the kingdom of God belongs to Christ. To him has been given all authority in heaven and on earth (Matt. 28:18). In God's kingdom, then, Jesus Christ rules supremely by exercising spiritual power (5:4; and see Mark 9:1). We enter that kingdom "only because God's saving power transforms us in a wonderful way and makes us partakers of his kingdom."[55]

21. What do you want? Shall I come to you with a rod or in love with a spirit of gentleness?

Paul ends his discourse by asking two direct questions. In his first question, he asks his readers what they want him to do; in his second he gives them a choice. Do they desire to be punished or to be loved? He puts the question not merely to those who are arrogant but to the entire Corinthian church. Everyone in the congregation shares the blame for the damage that divisiveness and arrogance

---

53. Rom. 14:17; I Cor. 4:20; 6:9, 10; 15:24, 50; Gal. 5:21; Eph. 5:5; Col. 1:13; 4:11; I Thess. 2:12; II Thess. 1:5; II Tim. 4:1, 18.
54. Guthrie, *New Testament Theology,* p. 429.
55. R. C. H. Lenski, *The Interpretation of St. Paul's First and Second Epistle to the Corinthians* (1935; Columbus: Wartburg, 1946), p. 202.

have caused. Because of their corporate responsibility, they must now respond to Paul's question.

a. "Shall I come to you with a rod?" How do we interpret the word *rod?* It can be understood literally or figuratively. Is Paul coming to Corinth as a schoolmaster or a pedagogue who applies the rod to unruly pupils?[56] This literal interpretation would suit the context in which Paul mentioned pedagogues who were given the task of correcting the behavior of children (v. 15). Yet, a figurative explanation has merit if we understand Paul to come to Corinth with "a word of power."[57] Paul offers to come to the Corinthians with a rod of spiritual power given to him by Jesus Christ. He is Christ's representative and in that capacity is able to correct the people with the authoritative Word of God. The New Testament depicts Christ endowed with absolute power that is symbolized in a rod (Heb. 1:8 [Ps. 45:6]; Rev. 2:27; 12:5; 19:15 [Ps. 2:9]). Christ uses that rod for the final overthrow of evil.[58]

b. "[Shall I come to you] in love with a spirit of gentleness?" If the choice were left to Paul, he would rather come as a loving father who speaks to repentant children. He would rather spare them than punish them, provided they repent (compare II Cor. 1:23). If he rebukes them, he does so in love. As he has demonstrated in word and deed, his love for them is genuine (see v. 14). In harmony with the teaching of Christ, he would rather come to them with gentleness.

During his earthly ministry, Jesus taught his followers to foster a spirit of gentleness (Matt. 5:5; 11:29). During his triumphal entry he himself came in to Jerusalem, gently riding on a donkey (Matt. 21:5; see Zech. 9:9). But when he approached Jerusalem, he wept over it because the inhabitants failed to recognize that in Jesus Christ God was coming to them (Luke 19:41–44). Thus, Jesus spoke words of rebuke and lamentation (Matt. 23:37–39).

Paul now is asking the Corinthians whether they want him to come and forgive them in love and gentleness or to chastise them in the event that they fail to repent. The choice is theirs.

Greek Words, Phrases, and Constructions in 4:18–21

Verse 18

ὡς—"as if." This particle introduces a subjective thought of some Corinthians, namely, "Paul is not coming."

ἐφυσιώθησαν—the aorist passive of φυσιόω (I puff up) should be translated as a perfect tense in English: "some have become arrogant."

Verses 20–21

ἐν—the preposition, which occurs twice in verse 20, controls the dative cases of the nouns *word* and *power*. It is a descriptive dative.

---

56. Carl Schneider, *TDNT*, vol. 6, p. 968.
57. Robert W. Funk, *Language, Hermeneutic, and Word of God: The Problem of Language in the New Testament and Contemporary Theology* (New York, Evanston, and London: Harper and Row, 1966), p. 303.
58. Margaret Embry, *NIDNTT*, vol. 1, pp. 163–64.

ἐν ῥάβδῳ—the preposition with the noun in the dative case denotes accompaniment ("with a rod") and should be taken with the verb ἔλθω. This verb in the aorist is a deliberative subjunctive: "Am I to come to you?"

τε—this particle is not a conjunction but rather an adjunction. It combines similar components.

Summary of Chapter 4

Paul teaches the Corinthians that he and fellow apostles are Christ's servants and stewards of God's mysteries. God expects them to be faithful, for they are responsible to him and not to men. The Corinthians should not judge the labors of these apostles; instead they ought to wait for the Lord to pass judgment, for he will uncover what is hidden in the hearts of men and he will praise them.

Paul admonishes the Corinthians not to go beyond what is written and not to be arrogant toward one another. He tells them that all their possessions have been given to them, so that they cannot boast as if they always owned them. To bring the Corinthians to their senses, Paul uses irony by asking whether they are rich and are ruling like kings. Then he reveals how apostles live in the interest of Christ and his gospel. They are weak, yet strong; they are hungry and thirsty; they lack clothing and shelter; they perform manual labor for their own support. They are abused physically and verbally, but show endurance and kindness.

The Corinthians are called Paul's dear children, for he is their spiritual father through the gospel. Paul urges them to follow his example, tells them that Timothy is sent to remind them of Paul's way of life, and says that he himself will come soon to Corinth. He concludes by asking them whether they wish to receive punishment or love and gentleness.

5

Immorality and Lawsuits, *part 1*

(5:1–13)

Outline (continued)

5 1 It is actually reported that there is immorality among you, and of such a kind that does not even happen among the Gentiles, namely, that a man has the wife of his father. 2 And you are arrogant! Should you not rather be grieved? Put the man who practiced this deed out of your midst. 3 For even though I am absent in body but present in spirit, as if I were present I have already judged the man who has so committed this. 4 When you come together and I am with you in spirit with the power of our Lord Jesus, 5 in the name of our Lord Jesus deliver this man to Satan for destruction of the flesh that his spirit may be saved in the day of our Lord.

6 Your boasting is not good. Do you not know that a small amount of yeast causes the entire batch of dough to rise? 7 Clean out the old yeast, that you may be a new batch, unleavened, just as you are. For indeed Christ has been sacrificed as our Passover lamb. 8 Therefore, let us celebrate the feast not with old yeast, namely, with the yeast of malice and wickedness, but with the unfermented bread of sincerity and truth.

B. Immorality and Lawsuits
5:1–6:20

1. Incest
5:1–8

In the conclusion of the preceding chapter, Paul gave the Corinthians a choice: he would come to them either with a rod or in a spirit of love and gentleness. He implied that if they repented he would be to them a loving father, but if not, he would have to chasten them with a rod.

This conclusion serves as a bridge to a new subject that Paul wants to discuss with the Corinthians. He has been told that someone in the church has committed the sin of incest and that this person has not been censured by the members of the church. This heinous sin in the sight of God and man must be removed. Both the man, because of his act of incest, and the church, because of its failure to act, are guilty of sin.

a. An Immoral Brother
5:1–5

1. It is actually reported that there is immorality among you, and of such a kind that does not even happen among the Gentiles, namely, that a man has the wife of his father.

a. *Report.* "It is actually reported." The first word in the Greek sentence, *holos*, is an adverb that means either "actually," "generally," or "altogether." It conveys more the concept of thoroughness than of universality[1] and signifies that the whole story has been reported. Because it stands first in the sentence, the adverb is emphatic and modifies the impersonal verb *it is reported.* Paul is not interested in revealing who the reporter is or how he has received the news. He only states the fact and does not provide details, except to say that in an earlier letter he had warned the Corinthians not to associate with immoral people (v. 9; see the commentary).

b. *Content.* "There is immorality among you . . . a man has the wife of his father." Paul relates a report on immorality that pertains to a member of the church and the wife of the man's father. We are not told if the woman is a Christian or whether the man's father is living, but Paul gives the impression the father is still alive (Gen. 35:22; Amos 2:7). In Jewish circles, the wording *wife of his father* meant "stepmother." Although the woman was not biologically related to the son, yet because of her marriage vows to his father she plunged the son into sin by having sexual relations with him. God repeatedly told the Israelites, "Do not have sexual relations with your father's wife; that would dishonor your father" (Lev. 18:8; 20:11; Deut. 22:30; 27:20). If a son purposely had sexual relations with his stepmother, the community would have to put him to death by stoning.

Would a son be free to marry his stepmother if his father had passed away? In the first two centuries of the Christian era, some Jewish rabbis condemned a marriage of a proselyte son and his pagan stepmother, but others tolerated it.[2] Is it possible that this tolerance was known to the Jewish people and proselytes in Corinth? We do not know. Regardless, Paul condemns the deed and calls attention to the conduct of the Gentiles in this matter.

"Of such a kind that does not even happen among the Gentiles."[3] When Paul mentions the word *Gentiles,* he certainly wishes to indicate the severity of the sin which the member of the church had committed. Paul alludes to the Gentiles to prod the Christian community to take action instead of allowing one member to shame the entire congregation. As one rotten apple in a box can spoil its entire contents, so one reckless sinner can make the entire Corinthian church ineffective in its witness to the Gentile community.

2. And you are arrogant! Should you not rather be grieved? Put the man who practiced this deed out of your midst.

Why were the Corinthians negligent in chastising this immoral person and expelling him? Paul's words are biting: "You are arrogant." In the preceding chapter he stated that some of the Corinthians were arrogant in their talking (4:6, 18, 19). Now he addresses all the believers in Corinth, for he knows that the leaders have led the others astray. They have been haughty for some time already and continue to be proud. They think that they are free to decide not to do anything

---

1. The SEB has, "It is being told everywhere." By contrast, JB reads, "I have been told as an undoubted fact."
2. SB, vol. 3, p. 358.
3. Cicero condemns incest: *Pro Cluentio* 5.11–14.

about this wickedness (6:12; 10:23), because they claim to possess superior knowledge (3:18; 8:1–2). Paul faces the difficulty of trying to reason with people who lack both humility and constraint.

With a rhetorical question that expects an affirmative answer Paul queries, "Should you not rather be grieved?" Now that he has alerted them to a blot on the body of the church, he is asking them to begin a period of mourning. The verb *to grieve* refers to sorrow for sin that has been committed either by oneself or by others. The Old Testament provides the example of Ezra, who mourned over the unfaithfulness of the exiles. They had returned to Jerusalem and rebuilt the temple, but had married foreign women belonging to the people around them (Ezra 10:1–6).[4] Paul tells the Corinthians to likewise enter a period of grieving and thus exhibit repentance with godly sorrow. Subsequently they will humble themselves before God and experience his loving presence.

The Corinthians must turn from their pride, show renewed obedience to God's law, and expel the evil man from the church. Paul says, "Put the man who practiced this deed out of your midst." The Greek indicates that the man has committed an act of immorality, not that he continues to practice it.

The time for church discipline has arrived. Discipline must take place, just as a surgeon must use a scalpel to remove a malignant tumor from a patient's body. If the Corinthians do not dismiss the immoral man from the church, the Christian community itself will be placed under divine condemnation (v. 13). The church of Jesus Christ is characterized by holiness and must remove the blatant and unrepentant sinner by excommunicating him. Conversely, removal accompanied by the church's repentance cleanses the body of Christ.

3. For even though I am absent in body but present in spirit, as if I were present I have already judged the man who has so committed this.

a. *Concession.* "For even though I am absent in body but present in spirit." In verses 2 and 3, Paul gives his outspoken judgment on the matter of immorality. For emphasis, he places the pronoun *you* in verse 2 over against the pronoun *I* in verse 3. He admits that geographical distance separates him from the recipients of his letter, but this does not mean that his written words can be taken lightly. On the contrary, he is with the church in spirit, and in that sense he is giving personal leadership. In spirit he takes the gavel in hand, so to speak, and chairs the meeting of the local church. He knows that he and the Corinthians have to remove the blemish from the congregation. He does this through prayer on behalf of the Corinthians and through his epistle.

b. *Judgment.* "As if I were present I have already judged the man who has so committed this." Paul tells the congregation that he has taken action with respect to the immoral man. He speaks as though he is in Corinth and in essence repeats himself when he says, "as if I were present." He writes the perfect tense, "I have already judged," to indicate that he had made a decision as soon as he heard about

---

4. Bauer, p. 642. See also Brian S. Rosner, "'οὐχὶ μᾶλλον ἐπενθήσατε': Corporate Responsibility in 1 Corinthians 5," *NTS* 38 (1992): 470–63.

the offense. "Because Paul does not speak of an action but of a judgment there is no question here of divine judgment as in the case of Ananias and Sapphira."[5]

The wording is emphatic in the clause *the man who has* so *committed this*. For the sake of style some translators delete the word *so*. A few translations, however, dutifully include it to show Paul's intended emphasis.[6] Paul writes a sequence of three concepts that serve as demonstratives (the man, so, this deed). In the Greek, he points out that the act of sinning happened in the past and has lasting effects for the church.

Let no one think that Paul is far removed from the scene and therefore powerless. Paul is not impotent; he wants the church to take action guided by his judgment. In proper assembly, the church must remove the man who has committed the crime. Paul does not list a detailed procedure for church discipline, yet we are confident that the practice of confirming the truth by two or three witnesses had to be followed (refer to Matt. 18:15–17).

4. When you come together and I am with you in spirit with the power of our Lord Jesus, 5. in the name of our Lord Jesus deliver this man to Satan for destruction of the flesh that his spirit may be saved in the day of our Lord.

a. *Meeting.* The intent of Paul's words is to move the church at Corinth to eliminate immediately this evil from its midst. He instructs the members to meet in assembly and to do so as if he himself were present. While they are gathered, they should call on Jesus' name, who himself had promised that where two or three people gather in his name he will be present (Matt. 18:20). In addition, they should know that Paul himself will be with them in spirit. They ought not to minimize his presence in spirit, as if his physical presence would be real and his spiritual presence illusory. No, not so for several reasons. First, Paul repeatedly writes, "I am with you." Next, in the Greek he uses the emphatic personal adjective *my* with the noun *spirit*. In English idiom, this adjective is deleted. Third, the phrase *in spirit* is synonymous with the phrase "the power of our Lord Jesus." Paul speaks with apostolic authority which Jesus delegated to him; as an apostle he wields divine power.

b. *Translations.* In verses 3, 4 and 5, Paul writes a lengthy sentence that lacks fluency and so reveals inner tension and agitation. The difficulty we face is the punctuation of this passage (vv. 3–5).[7] The Greek original indicates that these verses can be construed as one loosely-connected sentence: "For I verily, as absent in body, but present in spirit, have judged already, as though I were present, concerning him that hath so done this deed, in the name of our Lord Jesus Christ, when ye are gathered together, and my spirit, with the power of our Lord Jesus Christ, to deliver such an one unto Satan for the destruction of the flesh,

---

5. F. W. Grosheide, *Commentary on the First Epistle to the Corinthians: The English Text with Introduction, Exposition and Notes*, New International Commentary on the New Testament (Grand Rapids: Eerdmans, 1953), p. 121.

6. KJV, NKJV, NASB, *Cassirer*. Bauer translates the combination *so* and *this* as "so basely" (p. 597).

7. In my translation, I have made the phrase *in the name of our Lord Jesus* part of verse 5.

that the spirit may be saved in the day of the Lord Jesus" (KJV). This single sentence becomes unwieldy and fails to communicate Paul's intention.

Modern translators present shorter sentences and introduce appropriate punctuation. But even then numerous questions remain, as is evident from the following translations. How should the phrase *in the name of our Lord Jesus* be construed? This phrase can modify one of four[8] italicized clauses:

"*I have already pronounced judgment* in the name of the Lord Jesus on the man who has done such a thing. When you are assembled . . . you are to deliver this man to Satan." (RSV)

"*When you are assembled* in the name of our Lord Jesus . . . hand this man over to Satan." (NIV)

"I as one who is present have already judged *the one who has done this thing* in the name of the Lord Jesus. When you are assembled . . . such a person should be handed over to Satan."[9]

"When you and my spirit are gathered together . . . you should, in the name of the Lord Jesus, *hand over to Satan such a man* as this." (*Cassirer*)

Many translators favor the first reading because Paul, although absent from Corinth in body but present in spirit, speaks with authority in Jesus' name. His verdict, then, is not a personal opinion but is pronounced on Jesus' behalf and with his approval.

Conversely, there is wisdom in looking at a phrase in the context of the Greek text and linking it to the nearest phrase. When church officials read this epistle in Greek to the congregations, the hearers had to link the phrase in question to either the preceding or the succeeding words. If we follow this principle, we might favor either the second or the third reading.

Many scholars endorse the second reading: "When you come together in the name of our Lord Jesus and I am with you in spirit with the power of our Lord Jesus." They maintain that believers who gather in the name of Jesus know that he is the head and they are the body (Eph. 1:22–23). And these believers know that where two or three are gathered in Jesus' name, he will be in their midst (Matt. 18:20). The objection to this reading is the repetitive phrase *of our Lord Jesus*. This phrase occurs with the nouns *name* and *power* and makes them indistinguishable.

The third reading conveys the sense that the man committed sexual sin with his stepmother in the name of the Lord Jesus. But this reading meets some ob-

8. Hans Conzelmann lists six choices and Leon Morris seven. Consult Conzelmann's *1 Corinthians: A Commentary on the First Epistle to the Corinthians*, ed. George W. MacRae, trans. James W. Leitch, Hermeneia: A Critical and Historical Commentary on the Bible (Philadelphia: Fortress, 1975), p. 97; Morris's *1 Corinthians*, rev. ed., Tyndale New Testament Commentaries series (Leicester: InterVarsity; Grand Rapids: Eerdmans, 1987), pp. 84–85.

9. Jerome Murphy-O'Connor, "I Corinthians V, 3–5," *RB* 84 (1977): 245; Gerald Harris, "The Beginnings of Church Discipline: 1 Corinthians 5," *NTS* 37 (1991): 1–21.

jections. First, because of textual variants, it is difficult to decide whether the reading should be *our Lord Jesus* or *the Lord Jesus*. In view of Paul's usual wording ("our Lord Jesus") throughout the epistle—he nearly always speaks of "the Lord" without the identification *Jesus*—scholars prefer the reading with the personal pronoun *our*. Next, there appears to be an incongruity in the conduct of a Christian son who had illicit intercourse with his Gentile stepmother and invoked the name of Jesus to justify his sin. I suspect that the last name this sinner would invoke would be the name "of our Lord Jesus." Last, if this were the case, we would have expected Paul to mention the misuse of Jesus' name with scathing rebuke.

The fourth reading seems best. If we take the prepositional phrase *in the name of our Lord Jesus* with the clause *deliver this man to Satan,* the sentence conveys Paul's command to the Corinthian congregation to expel the man. Except for the phrase *in the name of our Lord Jesus,* verse 4 should be understood as a parenthetical statement. The emphasis, then, falls on Paul's command and the church's execution of it. The Corinthians must obey Paul and act on the basis of Jesus' authority. Paul says: "[I have already judged]; in the name of our Lord Jesus, deliver this man to Satan." He tells the members that when they come together they must take action, for both Paul's spirit and Jesus' power are present.[10] When the Corinthians act, they are aided by Paul's spiritual presence and Jesus' power.

c. *Destruction.* "Deliver this man to Satan." I have translated the verb *to deliver* as an imperative—the Greek has an infinitive—to show the severity of the case. Handing someone over to Satan is akin to the prescription Jesus gave his disciples: treat an unrepentant sinner as a pagan or a tax collector (Matt. 18:17). The command to deliver someone to Satan has a parallel in another epistle where Paul writes about some people shipwrecking their faith: "Among them are Hymenaeus and Alexander, whom I have handed over to Satan to be taught not to blaspheme" (I Tim. 1:20).

Paul's command to hand a person over to Satan is the act of excommunication. Excommunication purges evil from the church (compare v. 13). Believers are safe in the hand of God, from which no one, not even Satan, can snatch them (John 10:28–29). But if a sinner is delivered to the prince of this world, he faces destruction. He no longer enjoys the protection which a caring Christian community provides. When adrift and deprived of spiritual support, he will come to his senses and subsequently repent.

From the Old and New Testaments respectively we draw two examples of individuals who repented. Gomer, who as Hosea's sexually immoral wife personifies Israel, exclaims: "I will go back to my husband as at first, for then I was better off than now" (Hos. 2:7). And the prodigal son repented by confessing that he had sinned against God and against his father. He came to his senses after he herded pigs for a Gentile even on the sabbath and was physically starving. He had broken God's commands, but confessed his sin before God and of his own

---

10. Refer to G. A. Cole, "1 Cor 5:4 '. . . with my spirit,'" *ExpT* 98 (1987): 205.

volition returned to his parental home. In the words of the father, the wayward son was dead but when he returned home he was alive again (Luke 15:24, 32).

"For destruction of the flesh." What does Paul mean by the word *flesh*? For lack of pertinent detail, we are forced to resort to either of two hypotheses. The first one is an explanation that "flesh," when it pertains to the base part of man's physical life, causes him to sin.[11] In the hands of Satan, this part of a person's being perishes. We demur. Satan may destroy only that which God allows,[12] but he never leads a sinner to Christ and repentance. He is set on leading a sinner further away from God. In brief, Satan restrains rather than promotes the cause of Christ. Therefore, this explanation fails to merit favor.

We prefer the second hypothesis. In addition to the act of excommunication, God permits Satan to attack and gradually weaken man's physical body (compare Job 2:4–6; II Cor. 12:7).[13] Paul is not referring to a sudden demise (as, e.g., in Acts 5:1–10) but to a slow process of physical decline. During this process, the sinner receives ample time to reflect on his condition and repent.[14]

"That his spirit may be saved." The clause on the destruction of the flesh is grammatically subordinate to this main purpose clause. Even though the Greek word *pneuma* (spirit) in translation can refer to the Holy Spirit or man's spirit, translators understand the term to refer to not the divine but the human spirit. Nevertheless, one scholar has suggested that the Christian community had to expel the incestuous man "to avoid offense to the presence of the Holy Spirit."[15] Certainly, Scripture teaches us not to grieve or stifle the Holy Spirit of God (see Eph. 4:30; I Thess. 5:19). But that is not the point of the current passage. We reject this interpretation for at least three reasons. First, verse 5 contrasts man's flesh and spirit, not human flesh and Holy Spirit. Next, Paul states that man's spirit may be saved, not that the presence of the Holy Spirit may be kept. And last, in the preceding verses (vv. 3 and 4) the word *pneuma* occurs twice and refers to man's spirit, not to the Holy Spirit.

The destruction of the flesh serves the purpose of making the sinner's soul whole again before he dies. The gift of salvation depends on repentance, which takes place during a person's earthly life, not after his death. Scripture clearly teaches us that repentance must take place on earth, not in hell. Physical death irrevocably closes the door to a second opportunity for repentance and salvation (Luke 16:19–31).

11. N. G. Joy, "Is the Body Really to Be Destroyed? (1 Corinthians 5:5)," *BibTr* 39 (1988): 429–36; Anthony C. Thiselton, "The Meaning of *Sarx* in 1 Corinthians 5.5: A Fresh Approach in the Light of Logical and Semantic Factors," *SJT* 26 (1973): 204–28; J. Cambier, "La Chair et l'Esprit en 1 Cor. v. 5," *NTS* 15 (1969): 221–32.

12. See, however, T. C. G. Thornton, "Satan—God's agent for punishing," *ExpT* 83 (1972): 151–52.

13. Colin Brown, among others, states that "physical destruction is not envisaged" (*NIDNTT*, vol. 1, p. 466).

14. Frederic Louis Godet, *Commentary on First Corinthians* (1886; reprint ed., Grand Rapids: Kregel, 1977), p. 257; Morris, *1 Corinthians*, p. 86.

15. Adela Yarbro Collins, "The Function of 'Excommunication' in Paul," *HTR* 73 (1980): 263.

Yet Paul writes that the man's spirit may be saved on the day of the Lord, which seems to point to the judgment day. He does not imply that the man will have to wait until the end of time to be saved. Rather, Paul means that in this life the forgiven sinner receives salvation and in the day of the Lord is counted among those who are glorified. "Salvation is primarily an eschatological reality, experienced in the present to be sure, but to be realized fully at the Day of the Lord."[16] Also, the phrase *day of the Lord* can refer to more than the end of time when the judgment will take place. It can also mean a unique period during which God's people rejoice in the Lord. The Old Testament prophets understood the phrase to mean a time in which God claims victory over the world and his people triumph with him (Isa. 2:11, 17–20; Zech. 14:7).

In his infinite wisdom to bring a sinner to repentance, God uses various means and methods (see 11:32; I Peter 4:6). God is interested in the salvation of man's soul.

"In the day of our Lord Jesus." Paul hopes that even though Satan may destroy the physical body, the man's spirit may be saved at the judgment day. The question remains whether this man was restored physically and spiritually.[17]

Practical Considerations in 5:3–5

When the Israelites entered Canaan and conquered Jericho, Achan transgressed God's command by taking items devoted to God. The people stoned him and thus removed God's wrath against sin (Josh. 7:25–26). God calls his people to be a holy people.

In the Jerusalem church, Ananias and Sapphira purposely tried to deceive the Holy Spirit. Peter uncovered their deception; and God removed them from the Christian community by taking their lives (Acts 5:1–11). God wanted the followers of Jesus to honor the truth.

Paul confronted the Corinthian church with the incestuous behavior of one of its members. With a direct command, he instructed the members to expel the man from the church in the name of the Lord. The man's excommunication consists of being delivered into the hands of Satan. Paul charges the church to purge itself of wickedness and evil and to embrace the virtues of sincerity and truth (v. 8).

If Paul had not acted forcefully to exclude this man from the church, his sin would have continued to infect the entire congregation. The man's immoral conduct posed a direct threat to the existence of the church itself. Christians dwell in a glass house, so to speak, and the world is free to observe them. When the church fails to check a sin which the world condemns, the church has become ineffective.

In our culture we observe a rapid growth of sects, cults, and religions other than Christianity. The reason for this phenomenal expansion is the church's lack of credibility. Its standards of morality fail to compare with those of other faiths. For many people it has be-

---

16. Gordon D. Fee, *The First Epistle to the Corinthians,* New International Commentary on the New Testament series (Grand Rapids: Eerdmans, 1987), p. 213.

17. Consult E. Fascher, "Zu Tertullians Auslegung von 1 Kor 5, 1–5 (De Pudicitia c. 13–16)," *ThLZ* 99 (1974): 9–12; Brian S. Rosner, "Temple and Holiness in 1 Corinthians 5," *TynB* 42.1 (1991): 137–45.

come a sham: they see a church in which some leaders are corrupt, where discipline is lax, and where excommunication has become an obscure practice.

The church today must deal seriously with sin. It must attempt to bring offenders to repentance and salvation or else resort to excommunication. In word and deed, it must exhibit an intense hatred for sin and a genuine desire for holiness. Such holiness demands ardent love for Jesus Christ and total obedience to his commands.

Greek Words, Phrases, and Constructions in 5:1–5

Verse 1

ὅλως—the adverb meaning "altogether" stands first in the sentence for emphasis and modifies the verb ἀκούεται (it is reported), which in the present tense is iterative.

τοιαύτη πορνεία—the adjective denotes severity ("of such a kind"); the noun, which occurs twice, normally means "fornication" but in this context signifies "incest." The ὥστε clause is more explanatory than either a result or a purpose clause.[18]

τινα—the position of this indefinite pronoun ("someone") is unique; it is placed between γυναῖκα (wife) and τοῦ πατρός (of the father) and emphasizes both nouns.[19]

Verse 2

καὶ ὑμεῖς—the emphatic position of the pronoun with the conjunction ("and you") is balanced by the introductory phrase ἐγὼ μὲν γάρ (for I) in verse 3. The particle οὐχί is part of a rhetorical question that calls for an affirmative response.

ἵνα—although this particle usually introduces a purpose clause, here an imperative structure makes sense. Thus ἵνα is imperatival.

πράξας—the manuscript evidence for either this aorist participle or ποιήσας is about evenly divided. Both participles have the same meaning in this verse, so that the choice is difficult indeed.

Verse 3

ἐγὼ μέν—as the first word in the sentence, this personal pronoun is emphatic. The particle μέν stands by itself and is not balanced by a corresponding δέ. The present participle ἀπών (be absent) denotes concession ("although"). Its counterpart is παρὼν δέ (yet present).

Verses 4–5

ἡμῶν—manuscript evidence for this personal pronoun appears to favor inclusion instead of omission. The presence of the word Χριστοῦ following the noun Ἰησοῦ remains problematic because the external evidence of leading Greek manuscripts is strong for either inclusion or exclusion.[20] The possibility is that a scribe added the word to give extra weight to the phrase *in the name of our Lord Jesus Christ.*

18. C. F. D. Moule, *An Idiom-Book of New Testament Greek,* 2d ed. (Cambridge: Cambridge University Press, 1960), p. 140. Bauer lists it as a result clause (p. 900).

19. Friedrich Blass and Albert Debrunner, *A Greek Grammar of the New Testament and Other Early Christian Literature,* trans. and rev. by Robert Funk (Chicago: University of Chicago Press, 1961), #473.1.

20. Bruce M. Metzger, *A Textual Commentary on the Greek New Testament,* 3d corrected ed. (London and New York: United Bible Societies, 1975), p. 550.

συναχθέντων ὑμῶν—the aorist passive participle from the compound verb συνάγω (I gather) constitutes the genitive absolute construction, which extends to the next phrase (τοῦ ἐμοῦ πνεύματος, and my spirit).

παραδοῦναι—the aorist infinitive, denoting single action, takes the place of an imperative: deliver!

---

b. A Timely Illustration
5:6–8

In the preceding verses, Paul explained the basis for his judgment to exclude the sinful brother from the Christian community. He now adds a vivid illustration taken from daily life: the process of baking bread. Paul uses the example of yeast that permeates a batch of dough and can contaminate the dough if the yeast harbors harmful bacteria. But to illustrate what he has in mind, he first has to remind the Corinthians of their sinful boasting.

6. Your boasting is not good. Do you not know that a small amount of yeast causes the entire batch of dough to rise?

In a few words, Paul repeats what he had been saying earlier (see v. 2). He rebukes the Corinthians for their arrogance in not removing the sinner from their midst. He had already told them not to boast in men but in the Lord (compare 1:31; 3:21; 4:7). He wanted to humble them by showing them the reality of their situation and the seriousness of sin. Comments John Calvin, "For they were as proud as if they were living in the conditions of a Golden Age, when in reality they were surrounded by many shameful and unseemly things."[21]

If the Corinthian Christians do not act swiftly, the evil of immorality in their midst will destroy them all. Paul refers to yeast (also called leaven), which in his day consisted of dough retained from the time of the last baking. Liquid was added to a piece of this dough and was mixed with flour to start the process of fermentation. But if the yeast became infected with harmful bacteria, it would threaten the physical health of the people eating the baked bread. Hence, the cycle had to be abruptly broken by discarding the yeast. The illustration of contaminated yeast conveys the idea of its pervasiveness (see Gal. 5:9) and its potential to bring harmful results. The Christians in Corinth, and especially those of Jewish descent, knew that at the time of the Passover celebration, every bit of yeast had to be removed from homes, and for an entire week Jewish people ate unleavened bread (see Exod. 12:15). Also, from Jesus' teachings the Jewish Christians in Corinth knew that yeast often symbolized evil.[22]

The second part of verse 6 is a rhetorical question that demands an affirmative answer. Of course, the Corinthians were fully acquainted with the harmful

---

21. John Calvin, *The First Epistle of Paul the Apostle to the Corinthians,* Calvin's Commentaries series, trans. John W. Fraser (reprint ed.; Grand Rapids: Eerdmans, 1976), p. 109.
22. Matt. 16:6, 11; Mark 8:15; Luke 12:1. The parable of the yeast is an exception (Matt. 13:33; Luke 13:21).

results of infected yeast. They knew that the amount of yeast is relatively small in comparison to the batch of dough. How much more will a sexual scandal "of such a kind that does not even happen among the Gentiles" (v. 1) corrupt the entire Christian community in Corinth!

7. Clean out the old yeast, that you may be a new batch, unleavened, just as you are. For indeed Christ has been sacrificed as our Passover lamb.

a. "Clean out the old yeast." The first sentence of this verse seems to reveal an inherent contradiction. Paul commands the Corinthians to put away old yeast and at the same time states that they are "a new batch, unleavened." But yeast must be interpreted symbolically in this context. Yeast stands for evil. Just as the Jews had to remove old yeast from their homes and eat unleavened bread for an entire week, so the Corinthians must purge evil from their midst. When Paul says that they are unleavened, he means that they have been sanctified by Christ (1:2; 6:11) and are called to live holy lives. Paul stresses the positive and makes the negative subordinate to it. That is, their sanctification in Christ Jesus should prompt the Corinthians forthwith to remove the evil from their midst. Paul wants the Corinthian church to cleanse itself, much as the Jews once a year cleansed their homes of every particle of yeast.

b. "That you may be a new batch." The removal of old yeast from the homes of the Israelites in Egypt occurred in haste and symbolized their liberation from slavery (Exod. 12:33–34, 39). Purging the old yeast from the Corinthian church likewise must be done quickly; it symbolizes freedom from slavery to sin, specifically the sin of the incestuous party. Prior to celebrating the Passover feast, the Israelites had to purge every particle of yeast from their homes, because the Passover bread had to be without leaven. So the Christians in Corinth had to remove every trace of evil from their midst and demonstrate that they are "a new batch," that is, a new people in Christ.[23]

c. "For indeed Christ has been sacrificed as our Passover lamb." Paul packs a volume of theology in a rather short sentence.[24] Because he places this sentence not in a theological context but in a passage relating to discipline, he is concise. The *imagery* of the paschal lamb's slaughter on the eve of the Passover feast and Christ's death on the cross must have come quite naturally to Paul.[25] He reminds the Corinthians: The Israelites had to remove yeast from their homes before they could eat the Passover lamb. They then killed the lamb and put its blood on the sides and tops of their doorposts (Exod. 12:7, 13). But when Christ was crucified, he, as the Lamb of God, became the supreme and final sacrifice for God's people (Heb. 9:26). He removed the sin of the world (Isa. 53:5–6; John 1:29). His people are sanctified because of his death on the cross. By bringing

23. Consult Jean Héring, *The First Epistle of Saint Paul to the Corinthians*, trans. A. W. Heathcote, P. J. Allcock (London: Epworth, 1962), p. 36; SB, vol. 3, pp. 359–60.

24. Dean O. Wenthe, "An Exegetical Study of 1 Corinthians 5:7b," *Springfielder* 38 (1974): 134–40.

25. Donald Guthrie, *New Testament Theology* (Downers Grove: Inter-Varsity, 1981), p. 464.

this theological outlook to mind, Paul expects the Corinthians to make a practical application and quickly remove sin from their midst.

In a *spiritual sense,* Christians can celebrate Passover. Their sin has been purged through Christ's sacrificial death.[26] The followers of Christ are saved from eternal death by the blood of the Passover lamb slain at Golgotha. Christians are set free from the burden of guilt and have been given the gift of eternal life.

Is Paul giving a time reference in this passage that aids us in dating the epistle? No, because apart from the reference to Pentecost (16:8), this epistle is devoid of any type of chronology. From this passage we cannot deduce that Paul was about to celebrate the Jewish Passover in Ephesus. That would be putting something into the text instead of deriving something from it.

8. Therefore, let us celebrate the feast not with old yeast, namely, with the yeast of malice and wickedness, but with the unfermented bread of sincerity and truth.

a. *Negative.* "Let us celebrate the feast not with old yeast, namely, with the yeast of malice and wickedness." Paul is not requesting the Corinthian Christians to observe the Jewish celebration of Passover. If he were asking them to do so, he would be denying the significance of Christ's atonement. In addition, he would be asking Gentiles to become Jews before he could accept them as Christians. Neither is Paul saying that the Corinthians should celebrate the Lord's Supper, for in a subsequent chapter (11:17–34) he will teach them about Holy Communion. No, Paul is speaking figuratively about the joy Christians have in knowing that they are cleansed from sin. This exhortation implies celebrating our freedom in Christ Jesus, working out our own salvation (Phil. 2:12), and consecrating ourselves to do his will (Rom. 12:1–2; I Peter 2:5).

The exhortation to celebrate a life of obeying the will of Christ excludes old yeast, that is, malice and wickedness. The expressions *malice* and *wickedness* are explanations of the term *old yeast,* which itself describes one's old sinful nature. Unconverted man is characterized by the vices of ill will and evil. Ill will is the wicked disposition of a person and evil is the sinister exercise of that disposition. In Greek, Paul writes the word *ponēria* (evil), which refers to the activities of the devil.

b. *Positive.* "[Let us celebrate the feast] with the unfermented bread of sincerity and truth." The language Paul employs is unmistakably metaphorical. He urges the readers to observe the feast of consuming "unfermented bread," which means bread that is not contaminated and permeated by evil. This "bread" on which the Corinthians are to feed consists of "sincerity" or purity of mind. When Paul writes *sincerity,* he poses the opposite of the expression *ill will.* Purity of mind is an asset of the sanctified believer, whose purpose is to love the Lord and to love his neighbor as himself.

26. Refer to J. K. Howard, "'Christ Our Passover': A Study of the Passover-Exodus Theme in 1 Corinthians," *EvQ* 41 (1969): 97–108.

Further, the term *truth* is the converse of evil. Jesus calls himself "the truth" (John 14:6) but describes the devil as the evil one (Matt. 13:19) and the father of lies (John 8:44). In an earlier passage, Paul informed the Corinthian Christians that they have fellowship with Christ (1:9). Now he tells them to eat the bread of truth, which signifies that they should live a new life untarnished by the evil influences of impurity and duplicity.[27]

Instead of instructing the Corinthians to adopt exclusive standards of morality, Paul directs their attention to the truth in Christ. With that truth they are able to live in harmony with all God's precepts including moral principles.[28]

Greek Words, Phrases, and Constructions in 5:7–8

Verse 7

ἐκκαθάρατε—the aorist active imperative from the compound verb ἐκκαθαίρω (I clean out). The compound is more perfective (thorough) than directive.

νέον—in this context the adjective conveys the idea of a break with the old to be completely new. The adjective καινόν means that the new exists together with the old (e.g., the *New* Testament).

Verse 8

ὥστε ἑορτάζωμεν—here the particle does not introduce a result clause but is inferential and means "therefore." The verb in the present active subjunctive is hortatory ("let us celebrate") and denotes continued action.

μηδέ—literally, "and not." This particle should be taken as an explanation of the term *old yeast.*

---

9 I wrote you in my letter not to associate with immoral people. 10 I referred not to immoral people of this world, or greedy people and swindlers or idolaters, because then you would have to leave this world. 11 But now I am writing you not to associate with anyone who, although he calls himself a brother, is an immoral person or a greedy person or an idolater or a slanderer or a drunkard or a swindler. With such a person do not even eat! 12 For what right do I have to judge those who are outside [the church]? Do you not judge those who are inside? 13 But God will judge those who are outside.

"Expel the evil man from among you."

---

2. Excommunication
5:9–13

From the two Pauline epistles to the Corinthian church, we learn that Paul wrote two additional letters that are no longer extant. Before he penned I Corinthians, he already had sent the congregation an epistle with a message concern-

---

27. Anthony C. Thiselton, *NIDNTT*, vol. 3, p. 886.
28. Consult Ralph P. Martin, *New Testament Foundations: A Guide for Christian Students,* 2 vols. (Grand Rapids: Eerdmans, 1975), vol. 2, p. 397.

ing immorality (5:9). And before he composed II Corinthians, he sent the church an epistle which may be called "the sorrowful letter" (II Cor. 2:4) and seems to be different from I Corinthians. Altogether Paul sent four communications to Corinth (see the Introduction).

a. Miscommunication
5:9–11

9. I wrote you in my letter not to associate with immoral people. 10. I referred not to immoral people of this world, or greedy people and swindlers or idolaters, because then you would have to leave this world.

a. "I wrote you in my letter." For several reasons we cannot assume that Paul is referring to this epistle. First, other than mentioning the incestuous man, he has not yet said anything about immoral people. Next, the phrase *I wrote you in my letter* (literally, in the letter) suggests something that happened in the past; verse 11, "but now I am writing," indicates a decided contrast. And last, Paul wrote many letters that have not become part of the New Testament (16:3; II Cor. 10:10). Accordingly, we understand Paul to allude to a previous letter that has not been preserved.

b. "Not to associate with immoral people." All we have left from Paul's earlier epistle is the above-mentioned clause, which in Greek consists of only three words and in English at least four: "don't mingle with fornicators." The clause reflects Paul's concern for his readers living in the immoral city of Corinth. We lack further information on the content of the short letter of advice Paul had written, yet from his succeeding remarks we conclude that the Corinthians had misunderstood him. Now he explains what he has in mind, albeit in an awkward sentence whose meaning can best be conveyed by a paraphrase:

c. "I referred not[29] to immoral people of this world, or greedy people and swindlers or idolaters." Written communications often are open to misunderstanding. The writer means one thing but the reader understands another thing. In an oral dialogue one can ask for clarification and then receive an immediate answer. This is not the case with written correspondence, in which delays are common and anticipated. Lack of clarity, therefore, becomes a formidable hindrance to understanding. The Corinthians understood Paul's initial letter to tell them not to associate with sexually immoral people of the world—for example, those in the marketplace, the workshop, and the sports arena. The readers had laid the letter aside because they realized that Paul's order could not be implemented. In this imperfect world, Christians cannot stay away entirely from immoral people; otherwise they might as well leave this world (but see John 17:14–18).

However, Paul did not mean to say that the Corinthians should completely separate themselves from sexually immoral people. He meant to say: don't get

---

29. "I was not, of course, referring to people in general who are . . ." (REB). Bauer has "by no means" (p. 609) and Thayer "not entirely" (p. 476), but these last two translations fail to communicate.

involved with such people! (compare II Thess. 3:14). He intended that the Corinthian Christians not associate with a fellow church member who practices sexually immoral acts. He told them to expel such a person from their midst. He objects to the presence of the incestuous man in the Corinthian church and for that reason writes the phrase *sexual immorality* four times (vv. 1, 9, 10, 11). We deduce that in the previous letter he had expressed himself with a general term, "*immoral people*," but now he is direct in his use of the singular: "an immoral person" (v. 11).

The catalogue of vices (greed, swindling, idolatry) actually is an extension of Paul's prohibition not to associate with people who perpetrate sexual immorality.[30] The vices in this extended list pertain to the service of any idol instead of the living God. Greedy persons and swindlers serve not God but Money (Matt. 6:24; Luke 16:13), and Jesus reveals the impossibility of serving both at the same time. Paul pointedly calls a greedy person an idolater (Eph. 5:5; see Gal. 5:20; Col. 3:5) who will not inherit God's kingdom. Such persons are not part of the kingdom but of the world.

d. "Because then you would have to leave this world." If a Christian wanted to separate himself from worldly people, he would have to depart from human society altogether. According to Jesus' parable, the wheat and the tares grow together in the field until the harvest. Then the weeds will be cast into the fire and the wheat stored in the barn (Matt. 13:30). For the present, however, the believer has to live next door to the unbeliever.

11. But now I am writing you not to associate with anyone who, although he calls himself a brother, is an immoral person or a greedy person or an idolater or a slanderer or a drunkard or a swindler. With such a person do not even eat!

a. "But now I am writing you." The adversative *but* contrasts the first words in verse 9, where Paul alluded to an earlier letter. Paul is saying, "If any one doubted the purport of the former letter, it shall be impossible to mistake my meaning *now*."[31] I explain the adverb *now* as a reference to the present condition in the Corinthian church; it relates to time and to the matter concerning the incestuous man.[32]

b. "[Do] not . . . associate with anyone who, although he calls himself a brother, is an immoral person." In his earlier epistle Paul wrote the collective expression *immoral people*, but in the present context, the word means "an immoral person."

To describe someone who is sexually immoral as a brother is to write a contradiction. These two concepts are mutually exclusive. But Paul qualifies his statement by saying that the immoral man calls himself a brother. Yet this person, because of his sin, cannot belong to the Christian community and is exclud-

---

30. Peter S. Zaas, "Catalogues and Context: 1 Corinthians 5 and 6," *NTS* 34 (1988): 622–29.

31. G. G. Findlay, *St. Paul's First Epistle to the Corinthians*, in vol. 3 of *The Expositor's Greek Testament*, ed. W. Robertson Nicoll, 5 vols. (1910; reprint ed., Grand Rapids: Eerdmans, 1961), p. 812.

32. Bauer has *as things now stand* (p. 545).

ed from God's kingdom. His actions contradict everything the church teaches. If he remains within the Christian fellowship, the church can no longer be called Christian.

c. "A greedy person or an idolater." Paul repeats himself in this extended list of vices. Nevertheless, he wants the Corinthians to know that sexual immorality is not the only sin which the Christian community condemns. Paul's condemnation of greed and idolatry apparently addresses the social condition of ancient Corinth. Due to trade of goods, transportation of merchandise, and travelers from abroad, money ruled supreme. Love of money invariably leads to idol worship—whatever the idol may be.

Paul frequently warns the Christians not to engage in idol worship. The word *idolater* occurs four times in this epistle (5:10, 11; 6:9; 10:7) and once in Ephesians 5:5 (see also Rev. 21:8; 22:15).[33] This repeated warning reveals Paul's anxiety regarding idol worship, which he considered a blatant sin and a tribute to demonic powers.[34]

d. "A slanderer or a drunkard or a swindler." Two additional vices mentioned here are slander and drunkenness; Paul listed swindling in the preceding verse (v. 10). The list of sins he tabulates in this passage resembles some of the commandments of the Decalogue: do not practice idolatry, fornicate, steal, slander, or covet (Exod. 20:1–17; Deut. 5:6–21). Paul does not follow the sequence of the Ten Commandments; he stresses sins that were common in the culture of that day; he omits the command not to commit murder.

In respect to the consumption of wine, both the Old and the New Testaments nowhere prescribe total abstinence. Only those bound by the Nazirite vow (Num. 6:3–4) and a few others are told to abstain (Lev. 10:9; Jer. 35:6, 8, 14; Ezek. 44:21). The Scriptures, however, denounce the drunkard and warn him about the spiritual consequences of his intemperance (e.g., 6:10).

e. "With such a person do not even eat!" In an Eastern society, established norms of hospitality might not be broken. To not offer food to a relative, an acquaintance, a friend, or a guest could be interpreted as a declaration of war. The parable of the friend at midnight indicates that a host would be willing to incur his neighbor's displeasure in an effort to obtain food for his guest (Luke 11:5–8).[35] In a reversal of the established norms, Jesus often ate with tax collectors and sinners and was called their friend (Matt. 11:19; Luke 15:2)—and scandalized the religious leaders. Then, what is the point of Paul's injunction?

The matter concerns church discipline. Jesus instructed his followers that his prescribed procedure for excommunication might result in a complete separation of the Christian community and the offending sinner (Matt. 18:17). The sinner is a blot on the integrity of the church (compare II Peter 2:13; Jude 12). Such

33. The noun *idolatry* appears four times in the New Testament (I Cor. 10:14; Gal. 5:20; Col. 3:5; I Peter 4:3).
34. Friedrich Büchsel, *TDNT*, vol. 2, p. 380; Wilhelm Mundle, *NIDNTT*, vol. 2, p. 286.
35. Refer to Simon J. Kistemaker, *The Parables of Jesus* (Grand Rapids: Baker, 1980), p. 177.

a sinner must be excluded from Christian fellowship. Then he may learn to see the error of his way, repent, and return to the faith (compare II Thess. 3:14–15). By contrast, Christians could follow accepted social customs and eat with non-Christians.

Greek Words, Phrases, and Constructions in 5:9–11

Verse 9

ἔγραψα—this is not the epistolary aorist but the past tense of the verb *to write* (see Rom. 15:15).

In both verses 9 and 11, the compound present middle infinitive συναναμίγνυσθαι (to associate) is used as an imperative in an indirect command structure.

Verse 10

οὐ—this combination appears to signify "I do not mean immoral people in general."[36]

τοῦ κόσμου—the first occurrence means the secular world, the second the entire world.

καί—Greek editions including Nestle-Aland, the British and Foreign Bible Society, and Merk have the reading καί, which links the two nouns πλεονέκταις (covetous persons) and ἅρπαξιν (swindlers). The Majority Text has the reading ἤ (or), "thus mechanically conforming to the context. The reading καί is strongly supported by both Alexandrian and Western witnesses."[37]

ἐπεί—with this conjunction, the clause reveals an ellipsis of a protasis in a contrary-to-fact conditional sentence: "[if this were the case,] you would have to leave the world." The conjunction ἐπεί is not temporal but rather causal, in the sense of "for otherwise" (see 7:14).[38]

Verse 11

ἔγραψα—this is the epistolary aorist. The writer views himself to be in the place of the recipient of the letter; he writes the aorist but means the present. For a similar occurrence, see 9:15.

ὀνομαζόμενος—the present middle participle denotes concession: "although he calls himself."

μηδέ—the combination of the negative particle with the conjunction means "not even."

In two verses Paul sets forth the legitimacy of applying church discipline. He presents a clear demarcation of the lines of authority with reference to himself, to the Corinthian congregation, and to God. He concludes this section with an appeal to the congregation to let the Scriptures have the last word on this subject.

---

36. Blass and Debrunner, *Greek Grammar*, #433.2.
37. Metzger, *Textual Commentary*, p. 551.
38. Bauer, p. 284.

b. A Judgment
5:12–13

12. For what right do I have to judge those who are outside [the church]? Do you not judge those who are inside?

a. *Paul's right.* Paul comes to the end of his discourse on excommunicating willful sinners. He refers to his misunderstood letter and his subsequent explanation (vv. 9–10): he is not talking about sinners outside the Christian community. When Paul uses the expression *those who are outside,* he discloses his Jewish background. The Jewish rabbis designated people who belonged to a different religion "outsiders."[39] The "insiders" were those adhering to the Jewish faith. In this passage, Paul applies these terms respectively to the world and to the church. He openly admits that he does not have a right to judge the world. In the next chapter, Paul asks the Corinthians if they know that the saints will judge the world (6:2). But that particular verse speaks of the last judgment and not about the present time.

This is not to say that Paul condoned the sinful lives of unbelievers. On the contrary, when he walked the streets of ancient Athens, he was agitated because the city was full of idols (Acts 17:16). But Paul lacked authority to judge outside the church.

b. *The church's duty.* Within the Christian community, not Paul but the entire church must judge those cases that call for decisive separation between church and world. When a member of the church intentionally persists in sin and refuses to repent, the church must exercise discipline. Then the church regards this person no longer as one of its own but rather as one of the world. Hence, Paul asks the Corinthians a rhetorical question that demands a positive answer: "Do you not judge those who are inside?"

Anyone who claims to be a member of the church must pledge obedience to Jesus Christ. But if he or she chooses to live in disobedience to the Lord, the entire congregation must exclude this person from its ranks. If the church fails to judge, it places itself on the side of the sinner and is equally guilty before God. Not an individual church leader but the entire church is responsible for administering discipline to unruly members. Writes C. K. Barrett, "Responsibility for judgment is in the hands of the whole body of believers, not of a small group of ministerial authorities."[40]

13. But God will judge those who are outside.

"Expel the evil man from among you."

c. *God's task.* In the Greek, the difference between the present or the future tense of the verb *to judge* depends on an accent mark. But ancient manuscripts lacked accent marks, and therefore we are unable to determine whether Paul

---

39. SB, vol. 3, p. 362.
40. C. K. Barrett, *A Commentary on the First Epistle to the Corinthians,* Harper's New Testament Commentaries series (New York and Evanston: Harper and Row, 1968), p. 133.

means to say "God judges" or "God will judge." Translators are equally divided on this matter. Some favor the present tense and say that it points to competence.[41] The judging of the world we defer to God, who is both omniscient and omnipotent. And with Abraham we query, "Will not the Judge of all the earth do right?" (Gen. 18:25). He knows the lost and the saved of the people in the world. Other scholars prefer the future tense, in view of the first few verses of the next chapter (see the commentary on 6:1–4).[42] In general, however, the difference is insignificant. God judges the people and will conclude this task on the judgment day.

In this passage, Paul clearly contrasts the members of the Corinthian church, whom he emphatically addresses with the pronoun *you* (v. 12), and God (v. 13). The church administers discipline for the sake of its purity, while God judges the people of the world. God certainly judges erring church members, but the task of expelling unrepentant sinners is a duty the church must exercise.

d. *God's word.* Paul's concluding statement is a line from the Scriptures, "Expel the evil man from among you." The text with a slight variation appears repeatedly in Deuteronomy.[43] The Old Testament passage in both the Hebrew and the Greek has the imperative verb *expel* in the singular. Paul, however, uses the second person plural of the present imperative to indicate that the entire congregation must be involved in the process of purging sin to achieve purity in the church.

The passage echoes Paul's earlier directive to deliver the incestuous man to Satan (v. 5). Paul calls attention to both this man and any other person in the congregation who deliberately practices evil. Paul presumably has chosen the Greek word for "evil" that features a play on the Greek word for "fornicator."[44] The severity of expelling a sinner from the support and nurture of the church compares with the excommunication of social and moral outcasts in the Jewish society of Jesus' day. When the sinner faces total isolation, the possibility of repentance is real. Church discipline is designed to cause contrition in the heart of the sinner and to nurture a desire to return to the care of the Lord Jesus.

Greek Words, Phrases, and Constructions in 5:13

ἐξάρατε—the aorist imperative from the compound verb ἐξαίρω (I drive away) has a directive connotation (compare v. 2).

---

41. Godet, *First Corinthians*, p. 278.
42. Fee, *First Corinthians*, p. 220 n. 7.
43. Deut. 17:7; 19:19; 21:21; 22:21, 24; 24:7.
44. Consult Peter S. Zaas, "'Cast Out the Evil Man from Your Midst' (1 Cor 5:13b)," *JBL* 103 (1984): 259–61.

ἐξ ὑμῶν αὐτῶν—"away from yourselves." The Greek text of Deuteronomy 17:7 and parallels has the reflexive pronoun ἑαυτῶν. This pronoun in the second person plural is introduced by the verb ἐξαρεῖς (you must purge) in the second person singular.[45]

Summary of Chapter 5

After telling the Corinthians that he can come to them to either punish or love them (4:21), Paul reveals that he has heard about immorality within the local church. He reveals that a man has had sexual relations with his father's wife. Paul rebukes the members of the church for being arrogant; he admonishes them to grieve and to expel the sinner from their midst. He himself already has decided to exclude the man from the congregation by delivering him to Satan and then instructs the church to do so.

Using a domestic illustration, Paul notes that yeast in a small quantity permeates an entire batch of dough. But contaminated yeast—he speaks figuratively of yeast as ill will and evil—must be discarded for the unleavened bread of sincerity and truth.

Paul had written a letter to the Corinthians in which he ordered them to not associate with immoral people. Now he reveals that he had in mind not all the immoral people of the world, for then his readers would have to leave this world. Instead, he admonishes them not to associate with people in the church who are immoral, greedy, idolatrous, slanderous, drunk, or intent on swindling. He forbids them to have table fellowship with these people.

Church members must judge fellow members who engage in evil practices. Conversely, God is the judge of sinners who are outside the church. Paul concludes his discourse by quoting an appropriate verse from the Old Testament.

---

45. Blass and Debrunner, *Greek Grammar*, #288.1.

6

Immorality and Lawsuits, *part 2*

(6:1–20)

Outline (continued)

6 1 Does any one of you, when he has a lawsuit against someone, dare to go to law before the ungodly instead of the saints? 2 Or do you not know that the saints will judge the world? And if the world is judged by you, are you not competent to settle trivial cases? 3 Do you not know that we will judge angels? How much more ordinary matters? 4 If then you have cases of ordinary matters, do you appoint men who are of no account in the church? 5 I say this to your shame. Is it actually possible that there is no wise man among you who is able to be an arbitrator between his brothers? 6 However, a brother goes to law against a brother—and that before unbelievers?

7 It is, then, already an utter defeat for you that you have lawsuits against yourselves. Why not rather be treated unjustly? Why not rather be defrauded? 8 But you treat unjustly and defraud, yes, even your brothers.

9 Or do you not know that the ungodly will not inherit the kingdom of God? Do not be deceived; immoral people, idolaters, adulterers, homosexuals, sodomites, 10 thieves, greedy persons, drunkards, slanderers, swindlers—none of them will inherit the kingdom of God. 11 And that is what some of you were. However, you were washed, you were sanctified, you were justified in the name of the Lord Jesus Christ and in the Spirit of our God.

---

3. Litigations
6:1–11

For Paul, the purpose of Christianity is to permeate the world, to influence and change it according to the norms of the gospel. But Paul notices that in Corinth the opposite is taking place. The world is entering the Christian community to conform it to worldly standards. Evidence of this is the matter of court cases that are not settled within the confines of the Christian community but are taken to worldly judges. The Christian brothers who take their cases to non-Christians are causing the church to be a laughingstock in the Gentile world.

Paul interrupts his discussion on immorality to instruct the Corinthians on the course they ought to take in regard to lawsuits. The Greeks had a penchant for listening to lawyers debate cases at a court held near the marketplace in every city. The Jews in Israel and in the Dispersion had their own courts, for they were forbidden in the Talmud to go to Gentile judges.[1] Lawsuits that involved two Jews were settled in a Jewish court.

In Paul's opinion, Christians also ought to settle disputes within the confines of their own fellowship. The developing church in a Gentile world should take a leaf from the Jewish notebook on conducting lawsuits in their own circles.

---

1. SB, vol. 3, pp. 362–65.

a. The Saints Will Judge
6:1–3

1. Does any one of you, when he has a lawsuit against someone, dare to go to law before the ungodly instead of the saints?

As with the report concerning the incestuous man (5:1), we are unable to determine how Paul learned about Christians bringing lawsuits against fellow Christians to a non-Christian judge. Nor are we able to know what kind of a lawsuit Paul has in mind. We assume that Paul's discussion on judging (5:12–13) reminded him of another problem in the Corinthian church.[2] In the context of a relatively few verses, he discusses the problem in terms not of details but of principles.

a. "When [any one of you] has a lawsuit against someone." The phrase *any one of you* is purposely general, for Paul does not isolate any specific case. If even one Christian initiates a lawsuit, he has already violated a principle that Christ taught his followers, namely, to seek the good of one's fellow man even if he is an enemy (Luke 6:27).

Should a Christian ever contemplate bringing a lawsuit against anyone? Yes, if he observes and fulfills the royal law, "Love your neighbor as yourself" (James 2:8). Also note the following points: First, Paul makes no distinction between a believer and an unbeliever but merely writes "against someone." Next, he is not interested in detail but in principles. He knows that a court case often "is a fight unto death in which irreparable harm (economic, psychological, and spiritual) is done to parties."[3] The person who sues another person is bent on obtaining, under cover of law, this party's financial resources. He is intent on winning the case regardless of the damaging effect the trial may have on the defendant.

John Calvin, who studied law at two French universities before he became a theologian, keenly observed that the parties involved in lawsuits were motivated by greed, impatience, revenge, hostility, and obstinacy. He writes:

> Indeed wherever law-suits occur frequently, or the parties are obstinate in joining issue with each other with the utmost rigour of the law, it is perfectly obvious that their minds are inflamed far too much by wrongful, greedy desires, and that they are not prepared for calmness of mind and endurance of wrongs, according to the commandment of Christ.[4]

The underlying motive for civil lawsuits is often incompatible with one's Christian profession.

---

2. Peter Richardson asserts that in 6:1–8 Paul is still concerned with sexual immorality but now from a legal aspect. "Judgment in Sexual Matters in 1 Cor. 6:11," *NovT* 25 (1983): 37–58. See also V. George Shillington, "People of God in the Courts of the World: A Study of 1 Corinthians 6:1–11," *Direction* 15 (1986): 40–50; Paul S. Minear, "Christ and the Congregation: I Corinthians 5–6," *RevExp* 80 (1983): 341–50.

3. Robert D. Taylor, "Toward a Biblical Theology of Litigation: A Law Professor Looks at 1 Cor. 6:1–11," *Ex Auditu* 2 (1986): 109.

4. John Calvin, *The First Epistle of Paul the Apostle to the Corinthians,* Calvin's Commentaries series, trans. John W. Fraser (reprint ed.; Grand Rapids: Eerdmans, 1976), p. 122.

b. "Does any one of you . . . dare to go to law before the ungodly instead of the saints?" Today's secular world urges people to demand their rights and, if denied, to take a person or an agency to court. But the Bible teaches love which, when put to practice, translates into conciliation. Disputes should be settled through mediation in a spirit of promoting each other's interests. Elsewhere Paul gives additional instruction when he says, "No one should wrong his brother or take advantage of him" (I Thess. 4:6).

Paul frankly asks the Corinthians whether anyone "can bring himself to go to law."[5] He actually queries whether any Corinthian has the audacity to take a fellow Christian to court for the purpose of returning evil for evil instead of applying the Golden Rule (Luke 6:31). He wants to know if anyone is so "brazen as to seek judgement from sinners and not from God's holy people" (NJB). The Greek word *adikoi,* which I have translated "ungodly," means unbelievers; the other side of the proverbial coin is the word *hagioi,* which signifies holy ones.

The point Paul is making is that the Corinthians ought not to give the world an opportunity to ridicule Christ and to divide his church. By going to a Gentile judge, "the Corinthians are washing their dirty linen in public!"[6] If the Christians have a disagreement, let them settle it in the presence of God's own people (compare Matt. 18:17). They should fulfill the command to love their neighbor as themselves.

2. Or do you not know that the saints will judge the world? And if the world is judged by you, are you not competent to settle trivial cases?

a. *Knowledge.* "Do you not know?" At least six times in this chapter,[7] Paul reminds the readers of lessons about the end of time and morality that he taught them on earlier occasions. He engages them in a dialogue and they must respond positively to the rhetorical questions he poses. Here the question is whether the saints know that they will sit in judgment on the world (Matt. 19:28; Luke 22:30; Rev. 20:4). Of course, the Corinthians remember the lesson Paul taught them about the judgment day, when the books will be opened and everyone appears before God's throne.

b. *Authority.* "The saints will judge the world." We are confident that Paul was acquainted with the teaching of intertestamental literature that speaks of the saints judging and ruling the nations and the peoples of the world (see, e.g., Wis. 3:8). He applies this teaching to the day of judgment. At that time, the roles will be reversed, for believers will be judging the sinful world including their earthly judges. The saints not only will judge, but also will reign with Christ in the age to come (II Tim. 2:12). Incidentally, Polycarp, who quotes the words *the saints will judge the world,* comments that Paul teaches this doctrine (Epistle to the Philippians 11.3).

---

5. Bauer, p. 822.

6. Reginald H. Fuller, "First Corinthians 6:1–11: An Exegetical Paper," *Ex Auditu* 2 (1986): 99. Compare J. D. M. Derrett, "Judgement and 1 Corinthians 6," *NTS* 37 (1991): 22–36.

7. 6:2, 3, 9, 15, 16, 19. See also 3:16; 5:6; 9:13, 24.

Paul has a follow-up question: "And if the world is judged by you, are you not competent to settle trivial cases?" He employs the literary device of going from the greatest to the smallest.[8] If the believers will judge the world on the judgment day, they ought to be able to take care of common matters among themselves today. They should be able to mediate problems in the congregation and settle the matters to the satisfaction of everyone involved. Compared with their momentous duties in the life to come, they certainly are competent to take care of trivial court cases in this life. To their shame, however, they fail to do so.

Paul makes another comparison, albeit implicit: If the Corinthians receive the singular honor of judging the world, how much more do they dishonor God's name and cause when they bring insignificant court cases before a Gentile judge. By contrast, Paul teaches his readers to love (that is, to honor) God and to love their neighbor.

3. Do you not know that we will judge angels? How much more ordinary matters?

Note that Paul includes himself when he writes the first person plural. He probably had earlier spoken about the fall of the angels and that God would judge them (compare Isa. 24:21–22; II Peter 2:4; Jude 6; Rev. 20:10). We presume, however, that Paul is speaking about both the angels who left their former positions of authority and those who in purity and faithfulness continue to serve God. God's children are greater and higher in rank than the angels, for these reasons: First, man is created in God's image and has been redeemed by Christ. Next, because angels lack a physical body, they are not created in God's image and are not helped by Christ (Heb. 2:16). Third, God sends angels forth to serve man, who is about to inherit salvation (Heb. 1:14). While fallen angels receive their just punishment, holy angels continue in their glorious service.

Once again, Paul uses the familiar literary device of reasoning from the greatest to the smallest. Holy angels surround God's throne and as such are far above earthly woes and cares, while we mortals cope with ordinary matters on a daily basis. The comparison is unique, because this comparison occurs only here in Scripture. How much more, therefore, should we be able to settle commonplace concerns?

Greek Words, Phrases, and Constructions in 6:1–3

Verse 1

πρᾶγμα ἔχων πρὸς τὸν ἕτερον—this is a technical phrase current in legal circles: "having a suit against his neighbour."[9] The preposition πρός means "against." And in context, the term ἕτερον refers not to a Jew or a Gentile but to a fellow Christian with whom the plaintiff has an adversarial relation.

---

8. Lukas Vischer, *Die Auslegungsgeschichte von I. Kor. 6, 1–11, Rechtsverzicht und Schlichtung*, Beiträge zur Geschichte der Neutestamentlichen Exegese series (Tübingen: Mohr [Siebeck], 1955), p. 10.

9. C. F. D. Moule, *An Idiom-Book of New Testament Greek*, 2d ed. (Cambridge: Cambridge University Press, 1960), p. 53.

κρίνεσθαι—the middle voice of this present infinitive conveys a reciprocal idea, as if the pronoun ἀλλήλων appeared in the context: "to judge one another."[10]

ἐπί—when this preposition is followed by the genitive case, it denotes "in the presence of."

Verses 2–3

κρινοῦσιν—although ancient manuscripts lacked accent marks, the context demands not the present κρίνουσιν (they judge) but the future tense. The passive form κρίνεται with the prepositional phrase ἐν ὑμῖν features an instrumental dative, "judged by you."

κριτηρίων ἐλαχίστων—the noun signifies "lawsuits" and the adjective is an elative superlative that means "very small."

μήτι γε—here is an elliptical expression that is similar to πόσῳ γε μᾶλλον and means "not to speak of."[11]

---

b. The Wise Will Speak
6:4–6

4. If then you have cases of ordinary matters, do you appoint men who are of no account in the church?

a. *Versions.* The translations of this particular verse vary with respect to punctuation and interpretation. Is the second part of the verse a command, a statement of fact, or a question? The script in the ancient Greek manuscript was written without punctuation. Hence, editors and translators of the Greek text must determine the meaning of the text, usually by studying the context. Here are three representative versions:

"Therefore, if you have disputes about such matters, appoint as judges even men of little account in the church." (NIV)

"But when you have matters of this life to be judged, you bring them before those who are of no account in the Church." (NJB)

"If you then have judgments concerning things pertaining to this life, do you appoint those who are least esteemed by the church to judge?" (NKJV)

The first six verses of this chapter contain a number of questions. Within this sequence, the position of an imperative at the end of a sentence is uncommon (see NIV). Even a statement of fact (NJB) disrupts the flow of the interrogative sentences. It then appears logical to take verse 4 as an interrogative statement rather than a declarative or an imperatival statement. If we understand the verse to be interrogative, how should we interpret it?

---

10. Consult A. T. Robertson, *A Grammar of the Greek New Testament in the Light of Historical Research* (Nashville: Broadman, 1934), p. 811.

11. Friedrich Blass and Albert Debrunner, *A Greek Grammar of the New Testament and Other Early Christian Literature,* trans. and rev. Robert Funk (Chicago: University of Chicago Press, 1961), #427.3.

b. *Interpretation.* From the preceding verse (v. 3), the expression *ordinary matters* is repeated, as is the term *cases* from verse 2. On the basis of these two verses, Paul comes to a conclusion with a conditional clause: "If *then* you have cases of ordinary matters." He completes the sentence with a second clause, which is open to various interpretations. For instance, some translators consider the subject of the clause to be Gentile judges: "those who are of no account in the church" (NJB). Such an interpretation infers that these judges were held in contempt by the members of the Christian church (contra I Tim. 2:1–2), which seems unlikely. It also seem unlikely that the Corinthian Christians appointed Gentile judges, for these judges had already been appointed by the state.[12]

Other translators, however, understand the judges to come from the Christian community itself. But would the community appoint judges who were considered to be of little significance or who were not respected? If Paul is asking a rhetorical question, he expects a negative answer. Moreover, he indirectly rebukes the Corinthians for their arrogance in looking down on fellow Christians. A Christian of little significance, according to Paul, is at least as competent as a non-Christian judge. Thus Paul applies the principle of contrast.

c. *Conclusion.* No translation or interpretation is free from difficulties. The flow of the passage clearly depicts Paul's condemnation of the practice of Christians bringing lawsuits before Gentile judges. It seems that he prefers instead a principle used in biblical history. When Moses served God's people as judge in the Sinai desert, his father-in-law Jethro advised him to appoint assistant judges. He said,

> Select capable men from all the people—men who fear God, trustworthy men who hate dishonest gain—and appoint them as officials over thousands, hundreds, fifties and tens. Have them serve as judges for the people at all times, but have them bring every difficult case to you; the simple cases they can decide themselves. [Exod. 18:21–22]

Moses listened to Jethro and appointed capable and honorable men to serve the people as judges; these men took care of the trivial cases while Moses decided the difficult ones. Likewise, King Jehosaphat of Judah appointed judges in all the fortified cities of the land (II Chron. 19:5). When the Jews returned to Israel from Babylon, they adopted this system, which was still current in apostolic times. Indeed, in every Jewish community throughout the Dispersion, the Jews had their own court of justice, their *bêt dîn.*[13] Paul is now asking the Christians that they, too, appoint respectable and wise men from their own community to serve as judges.

5. I say this to your shame. Is it actually possible that there is no wise man among you who is able to be an arbitrator between his brothers?

---

12. A. Stein suggests that Jewish Christians, as they were accustomed, appointed a rabbi as judge in trivial cases. If this were true, the Gentile Christians would not go to a rabbi but to a Gentile judge. "Wo trugen die korinthischen Christen ihre Rechtshändel aus?" *ZNW* 59 (1968): 86–90.

13. Haim H. Cohn, "Bet Din and Judges," *Encyclopaedia Judaica*, vol. 4, col. 719–27.

The Corinthian Christians long ago should have extended the principles of Christian faith to legal matters. They should have appointed wise and capable men from their own community to settle trivial cases for fellow Christians. Accordingly, Paul rebukes his readers for their neglect and apathy. Although he earlier wrote that he would not put them to shame (4:14), now he openly tells them that his words are meant to shame them. He hopes that his rebuke will induce the readers to take immediate action to remedy the situation.

a. "Is it actually possible that there is no wise man among you?" Here is one more rhetorical question to which the Corinthians are expected to respond: "Of course there is a wise man in our community." Paul wants them to appoint a man who is able to act as mediator, that is, a person who arbitrates between two people to bring about harmony. This wise man was comparable to a Jewish rabbi who settled problems in a Jewish community either in Israel or abroad.[14]

b. "[A wise man] who is able to be an arbitrator." Paul is not suggesting that the Corinthians appoint judges to hold permanent office (see v. 7). On the contrary, this passage breathes a spirit of mediation rather than revenge. The wise man acts not as a judge who delivers a verdict, but rather as a mediator who seeks to bring two parties together for mutual understanding and agreement.

c. "Between his brothers." The Greek sentence is extremely terse in the last part of this verse: "between his brothers," which we must understand to mean two Christian brothers. I have combined the reference to the two men in the expression *brothers*.

6. However, a brother goes to law against a brother—and that before unbelievers?

This verse can be understood as either an exclamation or a question. In light of the near repetition (see v. 1), we favor an interrogative which, in the last part of this verse, emphatically expresses Paul's feelings.

The fact that a Christian brother is taking a fellow Christian to court is sufficient proof that he has set aside the command to love his neighbor. Within the Christian community this royal law (James 2:8) must function without restrictions. For Paul, this is an incredible situation that denies the fundamentals of the Christian faith. Can a plaintiff who goes to court have the spiritual, emotional, physical, and financial well-being of the Christian brother in mind? Writes Calvin,

> If a Christian therefore wants to prosecute his rights in a court of law, without going against God, he must take special care not to come into court with any desire for revenge, any bad feeling, any anger, or in a word any poisonous thing. In all this love will be the best guide.[15]

---

14. C. K. Barrett suggests the word *hakam* (wise man), which refers to a scholar with lower rank than a rabbi. *A Commentary on the First Epistle to the Corinthians*, Harper's New Testament Commentaries series (New York and Evanston: Harper and Row, 1968), p. 138. Compare L. A. Lewis, "The Law Courts in Corinth: An Experiment in the Power of Baptism," *ATR*, suppl. 11 (1990): 88–98.

15. Calvin, *I Corinthians*, pp. 122–23; see also his *Institutes of the Christian Religion*, trans. John Allen, 2 vols. (Grand Rapids: Eerdmans, 1949), vol. 2, 4.20.18.

Even though the ideal is difficult to attain, the command to love one another is a fundamental precept for the Christian. Paul returns to this point in the next few verses. But now he queries whether the Corinthians are taking fellow believers to law before a non-Christian judge. In another place (II Cor. 6:15) Paul asks: "What do believers and unbelievers have in common?" The reply is emphatically negative. Moreover, the response implies that when these two categories of people come together, the believer garners detrimental results.

Greek Words, Phrases, and Constructions in 6:4–6

Verse 4

μὲν οὖν—these inferential particles may be translated in colloquial English as "Why, I myself thought. . . ."[16]

ἐὰν ἔχητε—the particle with the verb in the present subjunctive introduces the protasis of a conditional sentence that expresses probability. The apodosis has the verb καθίζετε as the present indicative in interrogative form: "Are you appointing?"

Verses 5–6

λέγω—manuscript evidence favors this reading instead of λαλῶ (compare 15:34 and variant). The preferred reading denotes the content of speaking; the variant signifies the act of speaking.

ἔνι—this is a contraction of the form ἔνεστιν (there is), which with the negative οὐκ means "there is no." The duplication of οὐ in οὐδεὶς (no one) emphasizes the negative.

διακρῖναι—the compound verb differs in meaning from the simple verb κρίνεται (v. 6). The compound means to arbitrate, the simple connotes to judge.[17]

ἀδελφοῦ—the singular noun fails to complete the sentence. It should have been either in the plural or repeated in the singular. ". . . N[ew] T[estament] writers merely follow in the beaten track of Greek usage with proper freedom and individuality."[18]

μετά—in context, this preposition is used in an adversarial sense as "against."

---

c. The Humble Will Endure
6:7–8

7. It is, then, already an utter defeat for you that you have lawsuits against yourselves. Why not rather be treated unjustly? Why not rather be defrauded?

a. *Defeat.* From a worldly perspective, Paul turns everything upside down when he says that winning a lawsuit is a defeat for the Corinthians. Instead of telling

---

16. Moule, *Idiom-Book*, p. 163; R. St. John Parry, *The First Epistle of Paul the Apostle to the Corinthians*, Cambridge Greek Testament for Schools and Colleges (Cambridge: Cambridge University Press, 1937), p. 97.

17. Gerhard Dautzenberg, *EDNT*, vol. 1, p. 305, "*diakrinō* is used of the activity of a mediator or arbitrator in distinction to that of worldly courts." But see Bauer, p. 185; Friedrich Büchsel, *TDNT*, vol. 3, p. 947.

18. Robertson, *Grammar*, p. 409.

them that they should demand their rights, he rebukes the Corinthians for degrading fellow Christians by taking them to court.

In the preceding verse (v. 6), Paul notes a single incident of a Christian who files a lawsuit against a fellow Christian. But in this verse he addresses all the Corinthians. In other words, the practice of suing one another appeared to be not uncommon in the Christian community. Paul states that this custom is unacceptable for believers; for them a lawsuit is "an utter defeat."[19]

Usually, before a person takes someone to court, he has already spent many hours discussing his grievances in the presence of the defendant and others. Paul's use of the word *already* points to this preliminary activity during which, in his opinion, the controversy should have been settled. If the plaintiff wants to proceed and initiate a lawsuit, he faces "already an utter defeat," not only for himself but for the entire Christian community.

What is Paul trying to tell the Corinthians? Simply this: Even if a judge should rule in favor of the plaintiff, the court case already has had a detrimental effect on both the defendant and the entire Christian community. The church demonstrates a lack of love in an atmosphere of hostility and is unable to be an effective witness to the world. The plaintiff should not receive any praise for winning a lawsuit, because he does so at the expense of the Christian community. Comments John Albert Bengel, "Praise is not expressly mentioned here, but some such antithesis is intended."[20]

The word choice in the first part of this verse is unique. Paul does not say that the Corinthians had lawsuits against one another, but against themselves. The entire Christian community, so to speak, becomes a defendant before Gentile judges. The result is that these lawsuits are devastating to the morale of the Christian fellowship.

b. *Injustice.* "Why not rather be treated unjustly?" As if Paul anticipates objections to his words, he poses a question that implies a command for the Corinthians. In a subtle way, he reminds his readers of Jesus' word, "If someone wants to sue you and take your tunic, let him have your cloak as well" (Matt. 5:40; compare Luke 6:29–30). Anyone instinctively protects his possessions, but Paul, following Jesus' instruction, teaches his readers not to cling to earthly belongings. Rather, they should be willing to endure injustice.

c. *Swindled.* "Why not rather be defrauded?" If anything goes contrary to our sense of values, it is to permit ourselves to be robbed. If the Corinthians are still not convinced that material possessions have only transitory value, Paul asks them to submit to theft—and that in a court of law. By asking the Corinthians to sustain a loss of material possessions, he encourages them to pursue love for one another and reveal a forgiving spirit. A spirit of meekness and unselfishness that

---

19. Bauer, p. 349. The noun *defeat* occurs twice in the New Testament, here and in Rom. 11:12, where it means loss.

20. John Albert Bengel, *Bengel's New Testament Commentary,* trans. Charlton T. Lewis and Marvin R. Vincent, 2 vols. (Grand Rapids: Kregel, 1981), vol. 2, p. 194.

willingly endures wrong (compare I Peter 2:19–23), not a spirit of greed, gains approbation before God. He who fosters this attitude follows in the steps of Jesus.

8. But you treat unjustly and defraud, yes, even your brothers.

In this verse, Paul shows that he is fully aware of the effect litigations have had on the Corinthian community. These lawsuits have nursed an attitude of envy, anger, and hatred that now threatens the essence of the church's fellowship.

Two issues surface in this text. First, the concept of Christian fellowship is severely undermined by the litigious spirit of the Corinthians. How could a Christian still call a fellow church member a brother in the Lord if he had injured him morally, emotionally, and financially in a lawsuit? The lack of love and the presence of hatred has made true Christian fellowship impossible. When individuals attack each other, the unity of the body disintegrates (compare 12:25).

A second concern is whether a Christian may sue in court at all. If a believer ought not to initiate a lawsuit, how does justice function within the context of a Christian fellowship? A Christian should lay aside any desire to treat his brother unjustly or to defraud him. Instead he should seek the material well-being of his fellow man and thus fulfill positively the commandment not to covet the possessions of one's neighbor.

For Paul, the conduct of the Corinthians is entirely contrary to Christian principles. They ought to solve their disputes and differences through mediation, promote the welfare of the Christian community, and bear a clear witness to the world.

Practical Considerations in 6:7–8

May a Christian ever resort to court action? The Scriptures speak affirmatively to this question. To illustrate, the Book of Acts clearly shows that Paul used the Roman judicial system a number of times. Granted that he did not initiate lawsuits, he nevertheless appealed to Roman law to defend himself and the cause of Christianity (Acts 16:37; 22:25; 25:11).

Furthermore, God has instituted civil government, which includes the judiciary. Government officials and judges are appointed by God to serve the public and ensure the welfare of citizens (Rom. 13:1–5).

Should the Christian community have its own judges and lawyers? Here also the answer is affirmative. Yet Christians ought to refrain from filing lawsuits, for litigation is a blot on the community. Christians should recognize that "litigation is a manifestation of an absence of community."[21] Lawsuits contribute to the disintegration of a society and cause individualism to reign supreme. When this happens, loving concern for one's neighbor is extinguished in an atmosphere of rank egoism.

Society in general but Christians in particular ought to settle differences in a climate of mediation and reconciliation. Christian citizens should be in the forefront to foster re-

---

21. Taylor, "Toward a Biblical Theology of Litigation," p. 114.

spect for one's fellow man and thus contribute to building a stable society. They must demonstrate that esteem and love for one another are the hallmarks of decency and morality.

Greek Words, Phrases, and Constructions in 6:7

ἤδη μέν—the adverb *already* stands first in the sentence for emphasis. With it Paul points to a process that precedes court action. The particle μέν is balanced by the particle δέ that should be supplied in the rhetorical questions Paul poses.

μεθ᾽ ἑαυτῶν—the preposition has an adversarial connotation ("against"; see v. 6). The reflexive pronoun ("yourselves") is not synonymous with ἀλληλῶν (each other). The latter "would bring out the idea of diversity of interest, [while] ἑαυτῶν emphasizes that of identity of interest."[22]

ἀδικεῖσθε . . . ἀποστερεῖσθε—these two verbs in the present tense and middle voice express the idea to "let yourselves to be wronged and robbed."[23] These two middle forms express a permissive or perhaps a causative sense.

---

d. The Ungodly Will Forfeit
6:9–11

After Paul's discussion on court cases and their devastating effect on the Christian community, he broadens his discourse by mentioning sinful people who are barred from God's kingdom. In this segment, Paul distinguishes between those who deliberately sin and the Corinthians who are cleansed from sin. As he alludes to these immoral sinners, he once again lists some of the same categories of evil people (see 5:9–11).

9. Or do you not know that the ungodly will not inherit the kingdom of God? Do not be deceived; immoral people, idolaters, adulterers, homosexuals, sodomites, 10. thieves, greedy persons, drunkards, slanderers, swindlers—none of them will inherit the kingdom of God.

a. "Or do you not know?" Paul continues with the conjunction *or* that links this passage to the preceding verses (vv. 2 and 3), which feature the same rhetorical questions. Do the Corinthians know and understand the spiritual implications of lawsuits and sinful lives? The rhetorical question that Paul raises in this verse demands a positive answer.

b. "The ungodly will not inherit the kingdom of God." Paul queries whether the Corinthians are aware of basic facts that pertain to God's kingdom.

First, who will inherit this kingdom? Certainly not the ungodly, whose sexual immorality and other sins disqualify them. They are people whose desire is to do wrong.[24] They are inclined, unlike the righteous, to inflict damage on others and thus are dissimilar to the righteous. Paul does not have in mind persons who

---

22. J. B. Lightfoot, *Notes on the Epistles of St. Paul from Unpublished Commentaries* (1895; reprint ed., Grand Rapids: Zondervan, 1957), p. 212.
23. Robertson, *Grammar*, p. 808; Blass and Debrunner, *Greek Grammar*, #314.
24. Meinrad Limbeck, *EDNT*, vol. 1, p. 31.

see the error of their way and repent. He refers instead to those who willfully continue in their sins and glory in them.

Next, the word *inherit* relates to sons and daughters who share an inheritance in the kingdom and in this case are the children of God. They receive the inheritance not by works but by grace (see Eph. 2:8–9). Unrepenting sinners, however, are excluded from the kingdom.

Third, the verb *to inherit* means that there is no possibility that unrepentant sinners at some time will share God's blessing. The use of the future is definite: they will never inherit the kingdom.

And last, the concept *kingdom* occurs repeatedly in the synoptic Gospels, especially in that of Matthew. But in his first epistle to the Corinthians, Paul mentions the concept only five times (4:20; 6:9, 10; 15:24, 50). With the exception of 4:20, all these passages relate to the future blessings of the coming kingdom.[25]

c. "Do not be deceived; immoral people, idolaters, adulterers, homosexuals, sodomites." Once more Paul exhorts the readers not to be deceived (see 3:18);[26] they should be fully aware of the evil society in which they live. He enumerates sins that pertain to sexual immorality and mentions first the fornicators (see the commentary on 5:9, 10, 11). He uses this term to describe illicit intercourse either between a married and an unmarried person or between two unmarried persons. Paul affirms Jesus' doctrine that sexual immorality makes a person unclean (see v. 11; Matt. 15:19–20).

Notice that Paul places the idolaters between immoral people and adulterers. The inclusion of idolaters in this list of sexual sins seems slightly misplaced. But in the Gentile world of that day idolatry often was a source of sexual perversion (see Rom. 1:18–32).

The next three categories are adulterers, homosexuals, and sodomites. The first Greek expression, *moichoi* (adulterers), describes the sexual sin which a married person commits with someone who either is or is not married; it results in breaking the marriage bond. The next Greek word, *malakoi* (homosexuals), relates to "men and boys who allow themselves to be misused homosexually."[27] This word connotes passivity and submission. By contrast, the third Greek term, *arsenokoitai* (sodomites), represents men who initiate homosexual practices (I Tim. 1:10). They are the active partners in these pursuits.[28] From Greek and Latin prose, pottery, and sculpture, we learn that preoccupation with sexual

25. Compare George E. Ladd, *A Theology of the New Testament* (Grand Rapids: Eerdmans, 1974), p. 410; Leon Morris, *New Testament Theology* (Grand Rapids: Zondervan, Academie Books, 1986), p. 37.
26. I Cor. 15:33; Gal. 6:7; James 1:16. See also Herbert Braun, *TDNT*, vol. 6, pp. 244–45; Walther Günther, *NIDNTT*, vol. 2, p. 459.
27. Bauer, p. 488.
28. Consult David F. Wright, "Homosexuals or Prostitutes? The Meaning of *Arsenokoitai* (1 Cor. 6:9; 1 Tim. 1:10)," *VigChr* 38 (1984): 125–53; "Translating *Arsenokoitai* (1 Cor. 6:9; 1 Tim. 1:10)," *VigChr* 41 (1987): 396–98; "Homosexuality: The Relevance of the Bible," *EvQ* 61 (1989): 291–300; and William L. Petersen, "Can *Arsenokoitai* Be Translated by 'Homosexuals'? (1 Cor. 6:9; 1 Tim. 1:10)," *VigChr* 40 (1986): 187–91.

practices was prevalent among men in the first century.[29] These men wallowed in homosexual sins and rivaled even the inhabitants of ancient Sodom (Gen. 19:1–10; see also Lev. 18:22; 20:13).

d. "Thieves, greedy persons, drunkards, slanderers, swindlers." Paul now turns from sexual sins to those that pertain to material possessions, physical and verbal abuse, and robbery. He seems to echo the Decalogue, even though he does not list the ten sins he has enumerated in the order of the Ten Commandments. Except for the category *thieves,* the list is a repetition of an earlier passage (5:10–11).

e. "None of them will inherit the kingdom of God." The duplication of this solemn statement (v. 9) serves to emphasize the severity of the transgressions Paul has listed. He is not saying that a person who commits any of these sins will never inherit God's kingdom. He implies that anyone who persists in practicing these vices will be barred from entering the kingdom. But when a sinner shows genuine repentance and yields his life in faith to Christ, he is forgiven, cleansed from sin, freed from guilt, sanctified and declared righteous. The Corinthians could relate to Paul's exposé on moral sins, for some of the members had left a life of sexual and social sins.

11. And that is what some of you were. However, you were washed, you were sanctified, you were justified in the name of the Lord Jesus Christ and in the Spirit of our God.

Note the following points:

a. *Unclean.* "And that is what some of you were." Jesus says that he came to call not the righteous but sinners to repentance (Mark 2:17; Luke 5:32; I Tim. 1:15). The tax collectors and the prostitutes were the sinners in Jesus' day; they were social and moral outcasts. Jesus called them to repentance and then ate and drank with them in their homes (Matt. 11:19).

When Paul first came to Corinth, he brought the gospel of salvation to some people who lived in sexual and social sins. In his epistle, Paul now speaks not in generalities but notes that only a few Corinthians used to live a degenerate life: "some of you were [degenerates]." Because of their sinful lives they used to be unclean, but through the preaching of the gospel they have received the gift of salvation and are clean.

b. *Cleansed.* "However, you were washed, you were sanctified, you were justified." Using the strong adversative *however,* which in the Greek occurs before each one of the three verbs, Paul conveys the message of immense spiritual change. He contrasts the sinful past of the Corinthians with their new life in Christ. In addition, he writes the second person plural *you* in this particular verse in every verb form. Paul wishes to be acutely personal in his address.

"You were washed." The washing is thorough and complete. When God forgives a repentant sinner he clears the record of guilt. The verb *washed* (as trans-

---

29. Refer to Catherine Clark Kroeger, "Paul, Sex, and the Immoral Majority," *Daughters of Sarah* (May/June 1988): 26–28.

lated) and the next two verbs (*sanctified* and *justified*) are in the passive voice. The verb *to wash* appears only twice in the New Testament, here and in Acts 22:16. In the present text Paul refrains from using the verb *to baptize*, even though the act of washing away sin is linked to baptism. Here he wants to stress the effect of baptism. In Acts, Paul recounts his conversion experience in Damascus, when Ananias instructed him to be baptized and to wash his sins away (Acts 9:17–18). He underscores the act of being cleansed from sin and leaves the impression that we should understand this act figuratively.[30] As Paul himself had experienced the cleansing from his sin of persecuting Christ's church, so the Corinthians were cleansed from the sins of their former life.

"You were sanctified." Already at the beginning of his epistle, Paul told the Corinthians that they were sanctified in Christ Jesus (1:2). Now he reminds them that they were made holy. The New Testament teaches that everyone who believes in Jesus is sanctified in him (John 17:19; Acts 20:32; 26:18). Sanctification means that the believer has entered into God's fellowship (see 1:9).

"You were justified." In earlier centuries, Protestant theologians debated whether sanctification should precede justification, for elsewhere in this epistle Paul places righteousness before holiness (1:30).[31] Justification is a declarative act of God whereby the believer is pronounced righteous in Christ and is coordinated with God's act of sanctification. The three verbs (washed, sanctified, justified) are grammatically related. In the Greek, they are in the aorist tense, which describes a single instantaneous action. Paul is saying that at a given moment God declared the Corinthians both holy and righteous. In this context, he is not explaining the distinction between sanctification and justification but is writing a discourse against unrighteousness.[32]

c. *Grace.* "In the name of the Lord Jesus Christ and in the Spirit of our God." The last part of this verse reveals an implied trinitarianism, for Paul mentions Jesus Christ, the Spirit, and God. Yet this observation should not be pressed, for in this text Paul does not explicitly teach the trinitarian baptismal formula of the Great Commission (Matt. 28:19).[33] Nonetheless, the phrase *in the name of* occurs at times in connection with baptism (for instance, Acts 2:38; 8:16; 19:5).

The concluding part of the verse must be linked to every one of the preceding verbs (wash, sanctify, justify). The preposition *in* occurs twice, applies to all three verbs, and must be understood to mean "in relation to." Let us now consider how these three verbs relate to the Lord Jesus Christ and the Spirit of God.

First, the washing away of sin is the result of baptism. Believers are baptized in the name of Jesus Christ and in the power of the Spirit (e.g., see Matt. 3:11; John

30. Refer to J. K. Parratt, "The Holy Spirit and Baptism. Part 2. The Pauline Evidence," *ExpT* 82 (1971): 266–71.

31. Consult, e.g., Anthony A. Hoekema, *Saved by Grace* (Grand Rapids: Eerdmans; Exeter: Paternoster, 1989), p. 203.

32. Bengel, *New Testament Commentary,* vol. 2, p. 195.

33. Frederic Louis Godet holds that here Paul used the three divine names as a baptismal formula. *Commentary on First Corinthians* (1886; reprint ed., Grand Rapids: Kregel, 1977), p. 302.

1:33; Acts 10:48). Paul uses Jesus' full name, "the Lord Jesus Christ," but he writes "the Spirit of God," not "the Holy Spirit." The former word choice is common for Paul, especially in this epistle (2:11, 12, 14; 3:16; 7:40; 12:3).

Next, the act of sanctifying believers is based on the redeeming work of the Lord Jesus Christ and is sustained by the power of the Holy Spirit. Likewise, justification has its basis in Jesus' atoning work and becomes real to the believer through the Spirit's powerful testimony.

Last, the act of justifying the believer appears in connection with the power of the Spirit only in this text. True, in the early Christian hymn of I Timothy 3:16, Christ is vindicated by the Spirit; but nowhere else in Scripture do we find the Spirit involved in the believer's justification. The Holy Spirit takes part in the sanctification of the believer, but justification is God's work based on Christ's righteousness. Only in the present text is the Spirit linked to the believer's justification.

Practical Considerations in 6:11

God's forgiving grace offered to sinners who repent is both overwhelming and thoroughly gratifying. Jesus tells the immoral woman who entered the house of Simon the Pharisee, "Your sins are forgiven. . . . Your faith has saved you; go in peace" (Luke 7:48, 50). He addresses the woman caught in adultery by saying, "Go now and leave your life of sin" (John 8:11). To one of the criminals crucified with him he remarks, "I tell you the truth, today you will be with me in paradise" (Luke 23:43). And he calls Paul, the persecutor of the early Christians, "my chosen instrument" (Acts 9:15).

The Old Testament reveals the astonishing account of God's grace extended to Manasseh, king of Judah and son of Hezekiah. Manasseh was born into the family of Hezekiah, who loved the Lord and faithfully served him. Manasseh, however, did evil in the eyes of the Lord. He worshiped the Baals, built altars to the starry hosts in the courts of the temple, sacrificed his own son, practiced sorcery and divination, placed a carved image in God's temple, led astray the people in his kingdom, and shed innocent blood (II Kings 21:1–9, 16; II Chron. 33:1–9). Yet this king, when he came to himself in captivity, repented. God not only forgave him but restored him as king of Judah (II Chron. 33:12–13).

Reading this narrative, we are amazed at God's forgiving grace. We try to fathom the depth of God's forgiving love, and we boldly ask whether God will forgive any and every sin committed against him. Will he pardon those sins which, as Paul indicates, exclude a sinner from the kingdom of God? The answer is affirmative to every sinner who comes to God, confesses his sin, and pleads for mercy.

Here is Jesus' assurance, with one qualification:

"Every sin and blasphemy will be forgiven men, but the blasphemy against the Spirit will not be forgiven. Anyone who speaks a word against the Son of Man will be forgiven, but anyone who speaks against the Holy Spirit will not be forgiven, either in this age or in the age to come." [Matt. 12:31–32]

Greek Words, Phrases, and Constructions in 6:11

ταῦτα—the pronoun in the neuter plural is used to refer not to things but to people. A more accurate word would be τοιοῦτοι (such persons), although the neuter plural pronoun is emphatic and direct.

ἀπελούσασθε—most translators interpret this aorist middle indicative of ἀπολούω (I wash) as passive.[34] Believers are unable to wash away their own sins, for only Christ Jesus cleanses them. Yet some translators present a literal translation: "you washed yourselves clean."[35] They interpret the middle to mean that baptismal candidates submitted themselves to baptism.

ἐν—this preposition interchanges often with the preposition εἰς. "As is well known, ἐν and εἰς are really the same word. Hence the rigid distinction between the two prepositions cannot be insisted on."[36]

---

12 "All things are permissible to me," but all things are not profitable; "all things are permissible to me," but I will not be mastered by anything. 13 "Food is for the stomach and the stomach is for food," but God will destroy both of them. The body is not for immorality but for the Lord, and the Lord for the body. 14 God has not only raised the Lord but will also raise us by his power. 15 Do you not know that your bodies are members of Christ? Well, then, shall I take away the members of Christ and make them members of a prostitute? Never! 16 Or do you not know that the one who cleaves to a prostitute is one body with her? For he says,

"The two shall become one flesh."

17 But the one who cleaves to the Lord is one spirit with him.

18 Flee immorality. Every other sin a man commits is outside his body, but the immoral man sins against his own body. 19 Or do you not know that your body is a temple of the Holy Spirit within you, whom you have from God? And you do not belong to yourselves. 20 You were bought with a price; glorify God then in your body.

---

4. Immorality
6:12–20

After admonishing the Corinthians about litigations, Paul now returns to the subject of immorality. In the preceding chapter he gave instructions concerning the case of incest; now he discusses general principles pertaining to sexual immorality.

a. Permission
6:12–14

12. "All things are permissible to me," but all things are not profitable; "all things are permissible to me," but I will not be mastered by anything.

---

34. E.g., JB, KJV, NKJV, NASB, NIV, RSV, REB, SEB, TNT. Consult G. R. Beasley-Murray, *NIDNTT*, vol. 1, p. 152; *EDNT*, vol. 1, p. 137.

35. See *Cassirer; Phillips; Moffatt;* the marginal readings in RV and ASV.

36. Robertson, *Grammar,* p. 559.

In verses 12 and 13a, Paul writes two slogans that were used by the Corinthians. He lists the slogans successively and gives his appropriate response:

Slogan	*Response*
All things are permissible to me	but all things are not profitable
All things are permissible to me	but I will not be mastered by anything
Food is for the stomach and the stomach is for food	but God will destroy both of them

Let us now comment on the individual slogans and Paul's responses that follow.

a. "'All things are permissible to me.'" This slogan appears four times in Paul's first epistle to the Corinthians (6:12 [twice], 10:23 [twice]). The origin of the slogan is not of paramount importance. We cannot determine with certainty whether Paul had given his readers these words. Nor do we know whether the motto came from Greek philosophers or incipient Gnostics.[37] What is significant is that certain members of the Corinthian congregation used the slogan as an excuse to advance their understanding of Christian liberty.

Freethinking Corinthians were of the opinion that they could do whatever they pleased.[38] Their application of the motto *all things are permissible to me* exceeded the limits of acceptable Christian behavior. Instead of living as forgiven, holy, and righteous believers, they indulged in sexual and social sins. Instead of submitting to the rule of Jesus Christ, they condoned sin in the name of the freedom granted them in Christ. Instead of serving the Lord and their neighbor in genuine Christian love (Matt. 22:37–40), they served themselves.

In one of his succinct sayings, Martin Luther has shed some light on the Corinthians' faulty understanding of Christian liberty. He wrote, "A Christian is a perfectly free lord of all, subject to none. A Christian is a perfectly dutiful servant of all, subject to all."[39]

b. "But all things are not profitable" (compare Sir. 37:28). Some freethinking Corinthians seemed to apply the words *all things* to everything, including sexually immoral acts. But Paul rejects the notion that the expression must be understood to include sin; God's commandments delineate clear parameters for acceptable conduct. Although Paul agrees with the motto, he qualifies it with an adversative statement: "but not all things are helpful" (RSV). In this statement he omits the referent. That is, he does not say "helpful to me" or "helpful to you" but leaves the matter open. But our conduct, whether good or bad, always affects

---

37. Refer to Michael Parsons, "Being Precedes Act: Indicative and Imperative in Paul's Writing," *EvQ* 60 (1988): 99–127.

38. Examining the slogan of 6:12 and 10:23 in the context of chapters 8–10, James B. Hurley suggests that Paul addresses Jewish Christians. "Man and Woman in 1 Corinthians," Ph.D. diss., Cambridge University, 1973, p. 86.

39. Helmut T. Lehmann, ed., *Luther's Works*, 55 vols., *Career of the Reformer: I*, vol. 31 (Philadelphia: Muhlenberg, 1957), p. 344.

people with whom we interact. We have no right to do whatever we please without taking note of any harmful effect our behavior has on our fellow man. Selfishness is contrary to the command to love our neighbor as ourselves. Consequently, Paul writes, "But all things are not profitable."

c. "'All things are permissible to me, but I will not be mastered by anything.'"[40] Again Paul cites the motto that circulated in the Christian community at Corinth, and he once more limits its extent and thereby its impact. The expression *all things* has a counterpart in the negated pronoun *anything*.

What is Paul trying to communicate with this disclaimer? First, in the Greek Paul presents a play on words. When he says that all things are *lawful* for him, he means that he has *authority* to do all things. The play on words in Greek is reflected in the italicized terms. To have authority is to have mastery over something or someone. But, says Paul, I will not permit anything or anyone to have authority over me. Next, he becomes personal by applying the motto to himself in the first person singular. He does so quite often to provide leadership and guidance for the readers who face moral and social issues.[41] Third, by identifying himself with these issues, he notes the fact that he no longer possesses that which possesses him.

God has given us natural appetites which we may satisfy in Christian liberty. For example, we are limited by natural and moral laws: eating and drinking should be done with moderation, and sex should be kept within the bonds of holy matrimony. But if a person yields to sin, he is its slave and sin his master (compare Gen. 4:7; Rom. 6:16). A person can freely exercise Christian liberty in all things provided this takes place in communion with Christ.

13. "Food is for the stomach and the stomach is for food," but God will destroy both of them. The body is not for immorality but for the Lord, and the Lord for the body.

a. "'Food is for the stomach and the stomach is for food.'" Beginning with a general slogan, "all things are permissible to me," Paul now recites a specific proverbial saying: it pertains to food and the stomach. The composer of this saying, whoever he was, made it vivid by reversing the two nouns in its second half. Therefore, the public readily accepted the motto. But even though Paul acknowledges the truth of this proverb, he adds a comment to the motto in a manner similar to that of the preceding text (see v. 12).

God has created a world that produces a variety of foods to sustain life. If not wasted, food terminates in the stomach of the one who eats. And conversely, a stomach receives food for the benefit of the consumer. This is how God designed his great creation. But God also sets limits. Food products that are subject to perishing, and human life, which is subject to aging, in time pass away. Both food and the stomach are temporal and lack permanence.

b. "But God will destroy both of them." Here Paul addressed the temporality

---

40. See Bauer, p. 279.
41. See I Cor. 6:15; 7:7; 8:13; 10:29, 30, 33; 14:11. Consult Bengel, *New Testament Commentary*, vol. 2, p. 196.

of food and the stomach. To stress their fleeting nature, he states that God will destroy both. In this context, Paul does not elaborate on either eating foods offered to idols, Christian liberty, or eating and drinking to God's glory. Elsewhere he addresses those topics (8; 10:23–33).

c. "The body is not for immorality but for the Lord, and the Lord for the body." The message Paul delivers to the Corinthians is that they should not identify sexual appetite with an appetite for food and drink. J. B. Lightfoot notes that the Corinthians confused the prohibitions of two different categories, "meats and drinks on the one hand, and sins of sensuality on the other."[42] Food and drink should be consumed with moderation and discretion. But consumption as such is not a matter of morality, for anyone with sanctified common sense wishes to be and to remain healthy. Conversely, God's command to shun fornication and adultery relates to sexual morality.

God created the human body not for sinful pleasure but for his glory. He formed it in his image and after his likeness (Gen. 1:26), not for sexual immorality. The members of the Jerusalem Council knew that the Gentiles considered sexual immorality acceptable. Thus, to the decrees on food the council members added the moral law: "To abstain from things sacrificed to idols, from blood, from strangled animals, and from fornication" (Acts 15:29). Those Corinthians who flaunted their freedom in Christ considered themselves free to indulge in eating and in sexual gratification. But their sexual immorality violated the precepts of the Jerusalem Council and was a transgression of the Decalogue (Exod. 20:14; Deut. 5:18).

God created man's physical body for service in his creation (Gen. 1:28). He instituted marriage for the propagation of the human race and for the enrichment of the marriage partners. He sees the use of the human body for fornication to be absolutely contrary to this purpose (see I Thess. 4:3–5). Hence Paul notes that the body is to serve the Lord and, he adds, the Lord is for the body.

To the slogan of the Corinthians Paul adds his own teaching. He parallels the rhythm and style of their slogan:

Food for the stomach and the stomach for food.
The body for the Lord and the Lord for the body.

As food and the stomach are meant for each other so the physical body and the Lord serve each other. Both food and the stomach are of passing significance, but the body and the Lord have lasting significance in relation to the resurrection. The parallelism should not be pressed to its logical conclusion, for that is not Paul's purpose.[43]

---

42. Lightfoot, *Notes on the Epistles*, p. 214. See also Archibald Robertson and Alfred Plummer, *A Critical and Exegetical Commentary on the First Epistle of St. Paul to the Corinthians*, International Critical Commentary, 2d ed. (1911; reprint ed., Edinburgh: Clark, 1975), p. 123.

43. Gordon D. Fee, *The First Epistle to the Corinthians*, New International Commentary on the New Testament series (Grand Rapids: Eerdmans, 1987), p. 256.

Our physical body, created by God but stained by sin, will at death descend into the grave. It has been redeemed by Christ and will be raised as his body was raised. The Lord claims this body because it belongs to him (Rom. 14:8).

14. God has not only raised the Lord but will also raise us by his power.

Inasmuch as God destroys food and the stomach, he restores both Christ's body and ours in the resurrection. We should discern the difference in both the time and the kind between Christ's resurrection and ours. Christ is the firstfruit and we are his followers (15:15, 20). He is the author of our salvation and we are his family (Heb. 2:10–11). But this difference is not Paul's concern in the present text.

In the Gentile world of Paul's day, Greek philosophers considered man's physical body of insignificant value while they regarded his soul to be all-important. For this reason, Paul returns to the doctrine of the resurrection in chapter 15 and stresses the significance of the human body. But in the current context, he merely introduces the fact that God raised Christ from the dead; and he gives the assurance that God will also raise our bodies by his power. The understanding is that as Jesus was raised physically so our physical bodies will be raised. Note that Paul becomes personal by using the first person plural pronoun *us*, in which he himself is included.

Although committed to the grave at the time of death, our physical bodies are precious to God (compare Ps. 116:15). He has high regard for them and will raise them by his power (refer to Rom. 8:11; II Cor. 4:14; 13:4). God's power reached down to Christ's body in the tomb, and that same power will touch our dead bodies in the grave to give them life.

Greek Words, Phrases, and Constructions in 6:12–14

Verses 12–13

ἐξουσιασθήσομαι—the use of the future passive of ἐξουσιάζω (I have authority over) demonstrates a play on words, for the verb ἔξεστιν (it is permitted) denotes that the person to whom it applies has received authority (ἐξουσία).

τινος—this indefinite pronoun can be either masculine ("anyone") or neuter ("anything"). The second translation is preferred because it balances the neuter πάντα (all things).

καί . . . καί—the repetition of the conjunction signifies "both . . . and."

Verse 14

ἐξεγερεῖ—the future active ("he will raise") fits the teaching that portrays man's physical resurrection as a coming event.[44] It also balances the future tense of καταργήσει (he will destroy) in the preceding verse (v. 13). Other readings are the aorist ἐξήγειρεν, which follows the aorist of the single verb ἤγειρεν, and the present tense ἐξεγείρει, which

---

44. Refer to John 5:28–29; 11:24; Acts 24:15; I Thess. 4:16–17.

probably represents an unintentional scribal error.[45] Translators favor the first reading. The compound verb and the single verb are identical in meaning.

---

b. *Prostitute*
6:15–17

15. Do you not know that your bodies are members of Christ? Well, then, shall I take away the members of Christ and make them members of a prostitute? Never!

a. "Do you not know?" Once again, Paul asks a rhetorical question with the verb *to know* that demands an affirmative answer (see, e.g., vv. 2, 3, 9). He seems to refresh the memory of his readers by referring to earlier oral teachings.[46] He asks whether they have any knowledge concerning their own bodies.

b. "Your bodies are members of Christ." Paul continues the thought of a previous verse (v. 13) in which he stated that the body is for the Lord and the Lord for the body. Now he reveals the extent of this intimate relationship: the physical body of the believer is actually a member of Christ. In this verse Paul states the simple fact that believers are "members of Christ." In a subsequent context he extends this fact to the body of Christ, which is the church (see 12:12, 27; Rom. 12:5–6). Christ uses our physical bodies to further the cause of the gospel and to foster his fellowship. We, therefore, are Christ's hands and feet! We must obey the directives that come from Christ; he is our head and we are his limbs.

c. "Well, then, shall I take away the members of Christ and make them members of a prostitute?" Paul expects to receive a positive answer to his first question (v. 15a) and now continues with another query. Before he poses it, he wants his readers to agree with him and thus he writes, "well, then." He is saying, "If this is so, shall I take away from Christ these limbs that do his bidding and unite them with a prostitute?" Paul expects a negative answer from the Corinthians.

The Greek word *pornē* (prostitute) is an echo of the word *porneia* (fornication, sexual immorality [vv. 13, 19]; the colloquial English word *porn* derives from it). In the Greek culture of that day, prostitution and fornication were considered permissible activities. Athenaeus, a writer in the second century A.D., quotes from a speech of Demosthenes, "We keep mistresses for pleasure, concubines for daily concubinage, but wives we have in order to produce children legitimately and to have a trustworthy guardian of our domestic property."[47]

When Paul speaks of the members of Christ and the members of a prostitute, he does not intend to draw an exact parallel. Rather, he contrasts the sacred fellowship of the believer with Christ and the sinful lust of the person who has relations with a prostitute. "Christ is so joined to us, and we to Him, that we are

---

45. Bruce M. Metzger, *A Textual Commentary on the Greek New Testament*, 3d corrected ed. (London and New York: United Bible Societies, 1975), p. 552.
46. John C. Hurd, Jr., *The Origin of I Corinthians* (Macon, Ga.: Mercer University Press, 1983), p. 87.
47. Athenaeus *Deipnosophistae* 13.573b (LCL).

united in one body with Him."[48] Paul expresses justifiable indignation regarding the moral condition in Corinth, where sexual immorality occurred even among Christians. But Paul teaches that if they are united with Christ, they cannot be united with a prostitute. These two concepts are mutually exclusive. Hence, Paul answers his own rhetorical question with a sharp retort.

d. "Never!" The negative answer to Paul's question is given in one word, "never." Other versions read, "Certainly not" (NKJV), "Impossible" (GNB), or "Out of the question" (NJB). All of them stress that the matter at hand is unthinkable.

16. Or do you not know that the one who cleaves to a prostitute is one body with her? For he says,

"The two shall become one flesh."

a. "Or do you not know?" Notice the repetitive phrase *do you not know?* that occurs three times (vv. 15, 16, 19). We surmise that in his oral communications, Paul had taught the Corinthians to discontinue the sexually immoral practices of the Gentiles. They had to know that they belonged to Jesus with body and soul. Let no one say that he serves Christ in spirit but bodily is free to do as he pleases. Body and spirit are intimately connected. If a person has sexual relations with a prostitute, his act involves not merely his physical but also his spiritual being. The act affects his inner self and directs him materially, socially, and religiously. Concludes Horst Seebass, "He who unites himself to a harlot has a common existence with her. There is no purely sexual sin. The spirit of the brothel and the Spirit of Christ mutually exclude one another."[49]

b. "The one who cleaves to a prostitute is one body with her." In English the words *with her* must be supplied to make the translation of the Greek sentence complete. Scripture shows that the verb *to cleave* refers to more than a physical union; it involves a bonding relationship that has spiritual implications. Here are two illustrations: First, God commanded the Israelites to fear him, to serve him, and to cleave to him (Deut. 10:20). Next, Solomon clung to his foreign wives who induced him to worship other gods instead of the Lord God (I Kings 11:1–8).

c. "For he says, 'The two shall become one flesh.'" Paul denounces sexual sin by stating that the man "who cleaves to a prostitute is one body with her." He proves his point by alluding to the account of Eve's creation in which the verb *to cleave* occurs. "For this cause a man shall leave his father and his mother, and shall cleave to his wife; and they shall become one flesh" (Gen. 2:24, NASB). Of this verse, he cites only the last part and takes it from the Septuagint translation: "The two shall become one flesh."

This one-line quotation from the institution of marriage seems out of place, for the passage relates to the sinless state of Adam and Eve in paradise. Nevertheless, the statement holds true for every marriage (see Matt. 19:5; Eph. 5:31). Within the bonds of marriage, a Christian husband and wife become one flesh

---

48. Calvin, *I Corinthians*, p. 130.
49. Horst Seebass, *NIDNTT*, vol. 2, p. 350.

and are one in the Lord. But when the husband has illicit relations with a prostitute, he is one flesh with her and breaks his bond with the Lord. Instead of receiving God's blessing, he is under God's curse.[50] As a sexually immoral person he forfeits his share in the kingdom of God (v. 10).

17. But the one who cleaves to the Lord is one spirit with him.

This verse parallels the first part of the preceding verse: "the one who cleaves to a prostitute is one body with her" (v. 16). The verb *to cleave*, used in both verses, actually means to be glued to someone. The relationship is as close as two pieces of glass lying on top of each other; it is impossible to lift the one piece from the other because the air pressure glues them together, as it were. That is the relationship a Christian should have with the Lord.

Already Paul noted that our bodies are members of Christ (v. 15) and thus stressed the uniqueness of our physical frame. Now he mentions the close relationship of our spirit that is joined to Christ. He contrasts the bodily union of a male and a female with the spiritual union of the believer and Christ. This contrast cannot be pressed, for although a prostitute and Christ are complete opposites, body and spirit are not. For the believer, body and soul form a unit in service for the Lord. Clinging to a prostitute constitutes degradation and brings disrepute; clinging to the Lord signifies exaltation and results in esteem.

A believer becomes united with the Lord through the indwelling presence of the Holy Spirit.[51] Thus he becomes one with the Lord in spirit and enjoys an inner union with him (see, e.g., 15:45; II Cor. 3:17). In this verse (see v. 16), we also have to supply the words *with him* to complete the translation of the Greek.

Practical Considerations in 6:16–17

Striking indeed is the contrast between the person who clings to a prostitute and the one who adheres to Christ. For instance, the relationship between a man and a prostitute is momentary, without love, devoid of responsibility, mutually destructive, decidedly egocentric, and shamefully immoral. Conversely, the believer's relationship with Jesus Christ is characterized by permanence, love, trust, edification, obedience, and purity.

Prostitution makes one prone to disease and is degrading, sinful, and damaging to one's soul. However, Christ exalts a person, encourages wholesome living, instructs him or her in the law of love for God and one's fellow human being, and refreshes the believer's spirit.

An immoral person fails to enjoy matrimonial bliss, experiences failure in personal intimacy, substitutes sex for service to God, and indulges in vulgarity, obscenity, and sensuality. But a Christian builds loving and lasting companionship with his spouse, seeks

---

50. In his article, "Hard Sayings—V. 1 Cor. 6. 16," *Theology* 66 (1963): 491–93, G. R. Dunstan applies Paul's passage to a Christian who had relations with a temple prostitute.

51. Consult Donald Guthrie, *New Testament Theology* (Downers Grove: InterVarsity, 1981), p. 552; E. Earle Ellis, *Prophecy and Hermeneutic in Early Christianity: New Testament Essays* (Grand Rapids: Eerdmans, 1978), p. 67.

fulfillment in serving others, loves his Lord, joyfully worships God, cultivates wholesome speech, promotes decency, and exemplifies virtue. "Thus we can understand why the Ephesian letter [Eph. 5:21–33] emphasizes that Christ and his church, as the bridegroom and the bride, constitute the union that is normative for marriage."[52]

Greek Words, Phrases, and Constructions in 6:15–16

Verse 15

ποιήσω—this is either a future active indicative ("I shall make") or the aorist active subjunctive ("Am I to make?"). Because the sentence is interrogative, the deliberative subjunctive is preferred. It expresses doubt and incredulity.

μὴ γένοιτο—the aorist optative of γίνομαι (I am, become) in the optative with the negative particle μή expresses a negative wish in the form of a prayer: "May it not be so!"

Verse 16

κολλώμενος—Paul uses the present middle participle of the single verb instead of the compound verb in the Genesis account (2:24, LXX). Even though the compound participle προσκολλώμενος denotes direction, the difference between these two verb forms is insignificant; both in Genesis 2:24 and this verse the forms refer to the union of the sex act.[53] In addition, it has spiritual implications.

τῇ πόρνῃ—the presence of the definite article conveys the meaning that Paul refers not to a single individual but to a category.

εἰς—this preposition with the noun σάρκα (flesh) in the accusative case forms the predicate nominative construction: "the two shall become one flesh."

---

c. Purchased
6:18–20

18. Flee immorality. Every other sin a man commits is outside his body, but the immoral man sins against his own body.

a. "Flee immorality." This short command is exemplified by Joseph in the house of his Egyptian master Potiphar, whose wife tried to seduce him. Joseph left his cloak in her hand when he fled from the house (Gen. 39:12). In this command, Paul uses the verb *to flee* in the present tense, which connotes continued action. He is urging the Corinthians to shun the immorality which they daily encounter in the sexually degenerate society of Corinth (compare 10:14).

b. "Every other sin a man commits is outside his body." What is Paul saying in this succinct statement? Literature on verse 18b has been voluminous and falls into two categories: this part of the verse is either a Corinthian slogan[54] or a state-

---

52. J. Stanley Glen, *Pastoral Problems in First Corinthians* (London: Epworth, 1965), p. 93. Consult also Parry, *First Epistle to the Corinthians*, p. 105.

53. But see J. I. Miller, "A Fresh Look at I Corinthians 6. 16f.," *NTS* 27 (1980): 125–27. He suggests adhesion rather than sexual union.

54. Moule, *Idiom-Book*, p. 196; Hurley, "Man and Woman," p. 112; Jerome Murphy-O'Connor, "Corinthian Slogans in 1 Corinthians 6:12–20," *CBQ* 40 (1978): 391–96.

ment that Paul has written.[55] The first alternative is that Paul qualifies the slogan with the clause, "but the immoral man sins against his own body" (v. 18c). Scholars object to this interpretation, however, for they think that Paul's qualifying response to the Corinthian slogan is abrupt.[56] Furthermore, Paul's response is inadequate to counteract the impact of this presumed motto uttered by free-thinking Corinthians.

The second alternative is favored because in it Paul exhorts his readers to flee fornication—a sin that is detrimental to both body and soul. In that setting he utters the message of verse 18. "No other sin engages one's power of bodily personal communication in precisely so intimate a way. All other sins are in this respect by comparison 'outside' the body."[57] Most translators have supplied the word *other* to the Greek text that reads, "Every sin a man commits is outside his body." They do so because the text expresses the exception of the sin of fornication.

What about chemical dependency on drugs or alcohol? Are these also sins against the body? Granted that the craving for these substances originates within a person, the substances themselves enter the human body from the outside. But the sin of fornication which arises in the spirit seeks gratification of the physical body itself and thus is confined to the body. In a sense this sin is different from all other sins, because it stays within the body.

c. "But the immoral man sins against his own body." The adversative *but* necessitates the insertion of the word *other* in the preceding clause, "Every other sin a man commits is outside his body." Here, then, is the exception to the sins committed outside the body: fornication is the only sin directed against one's physical body (see Sir. 23:16–27). The fornicator sinfully uses his body against the Lord, who created, redeemed, and sanctified it. Thus Joseph asked Potiphar's wife, "How could I do such a wicked thing and sin against God?" (Gen. 39:9).[58] Conversely, a husband and wife who are one in the Lord communicate their love for each other in the intimacy of the sex act. And they experience mutual satisfaction instead of alienation and guilt. In short, they rejoice in God's gracious gift of marital bliss.

19. Or do you not know that your body is a temple of the Holy Spirit within you, whom you have from God? And you do not belong to yourselves.

a. "Or do you not know?" The comparative conjunction *or* provides an additional reason for fleeing sexual immorality. For the last time in this chapter, Paul rhetorically asks the Corinthians whether they have definite knowledge (see vv. 2, 3, 9, 15, and 16). They again have to give an affirmative answer to this query.

---

55. Robert H. Gundry, *Sōma in Biblical Theology: With Emphasis on Pauline Anthropology* (1976; Grand Rapids: Zondervan, Academie Books, 1987), pp. 70–75; F. W. Grosheide, *Commentary on the First Epistle to the Corinthians: The English Text with Introduction, Exposition and Notes,* New International Commentary on the New Testament series (Grand Rapids: Eerdmans, 1953) p. 151.
56. Refer to Fee, *First Corinthians,* p. 262.
57. Brendan Byrne, "Sinning against One's Own Body: Paul's Understanding of the Sexual Relationship in 1 Corinthians 6:18," *CBQ* 45 (1983): 613.
58. See SB, vol. 3, pp. 366–67.

We assume that on an earlier occasion Paul had taught them about the purpose, use, and destiny of their physical bodies.

b. "Your body is a temple of the Holy Spirit within you." Paul reminds the Corinthians of the sacredness of their bodies. He notes that the Holy Spirit makes his abode within them, so that their body is his temple. He writes the two words *body* and *temple* in the singular to apply them to the individual believer. Further, through the word order in the Greek, he places emphasis on the Holy Spirit. Paul literally writes to the Corinthians, "Your body is a temple of the one within you, namely, the Holy Spirit." That is, the physical body of the Christian belongs to the Lord and serves as the residence of the Holy Spirit.

What an honor to have God's Spirit dwelling within us! Note that Paul writes the word *temple* (see the commentary on 3:16). The Greek has two words that are translated "temple." The first one is *hieron,* which refers to the general temple complex, as in the city of Jerusalem. The second is *naos,* which denotes the temple building with the Holy Place and the Most Holy Place (see, e.g., Exod. 26:31–34; Heb. 9:1–5). *Naos* is used in the present verse. For the Jew, this was the place where God dwelled among his people until the destruction of the temple in A.D. 70. For the Christian, not a fixed geographic site but the body of the individual believer is the place where God's Spirit is pleased to dwell. In the early church, Irenaeus called individual Christians "temples of God" and described them as "stones for the Father's temple."[59] If, then, the Spirit of God dwells within us, we should avoid grieving him (Eph. 4:30) or extinguishing his fire (I Thess. 5:19).

c. "Whom you have from God." In this brief segment of the verse, Paul teaches first that the individual believers possess and continue to possess the gift of the Holy Spirit. Next, he reveals that the Spirit's origin is from God.

d. "And you do not belong to yourselves." We are not the owners of our own bodies, for God created us, Jesus redeemed us, and the Holy Spirit makes his abode within us. The triune God claims ownership, but he leaves us free to consecrate and yield our physical bodies to him. By contrast, those who commit fornication desecrate the temple of the Holy Spirit and cause untold spiritual and physical damage to themselves and others. For this reason, Paul exhorts us to flee sexual immorality (v. 18). Because God owns our body, we are its stewards and must give an account to him. Therefore, we ought to guard its sanctity and protect it from defilement and destruction. God's temple is holy and precious.

20. You were bought with a price; glorify God then in your body.

a. "You were bought with a price." These words allude to Jesus' death on Calvary's cross where he paid the price of our redemption. Jesus paid for our freedom from sin, so that as redeemed children of our heavenly Father we may share his blessings. The term *bought* calls to mind the marketplace where slaves were bought and sold.[60] If this is what Paul means, he alludes to Christians whom

---

59. Irenaeus, Ephesians 15:3 and 9:1 respectively. See also the Epistle of Barnabas 4:11; 6:15.
60. Bauer, pp. 12–13; David H. Field, *NIDNTT,* vol. 1, pp. 267–68; Fee, *First Corinthians,* pp. 264–65.

Christ has bought as slaves to serve him. Christ now owns them and is their master. In a parallel passage, Paul says the same thing: "For he who was called by the Lord while a slave is a freedman of the Lord, likewise the freedman when he was called is a slave of the Lord. You were bought with a price. Do not become slaves of men" (7:22–23; see also Gal. 4:6–7).

b. "Glorify God then in your body."[61] Here is Paul's concluding statement to a lengthy discourse on sexual immorality (6:12–20). He has skillfully turned a negative discussion to a positive exhortation. He tells the Corinthians to use their bodies, which are the Spirit's holy temple, to honor God. They can do so by listening obediently to his voice as he speaks to them through his revelation. A seventeenth-century catechism raises the question, "What is the chief end of man?" The answer is, "To glorify God, and enjoy him forever."[62]

Greek Words, Phrases, and Constructions in 6:18–20

Verse 18

ἁμάρτημα—instead of the noun ἁμαρτία (sin), which denotes the action itself, ἁμάρτημα describes the result of the action. It is a transgression.

ἐκτός—as an adverb used as an improper preposition, it signifies "*outside*" and here relates to sin. "Apart from fornication ἐ [κτὸς] τοῦ σώματος ἐστιν remains outside the body, since immorality pollutes the body itself."[63]

εἰς—this preposition indicates a goal that is set with hostile intent and means "against." The paradox is that man who cares for his own body (Eph. 5:29) turns against it by committing fornication. This particular sin, in contrast to all other sins that are outside the body, originates and stays within the body.

Verse 19

τὸ σῶμα ὑμῶν—with the plural pronoun, the singular noun is distributive. Because everyone has a physical body, the pronoun is sufficient to express the plural.

ναός—the temple, that is, the place where God dwells with his people. God has chosen the bodies of the redeemed to be the abode of his Spirit.

Verse 20

τιμῆς—"at a price." The verb ἠγοράσθητε (you were bought) controls the genitive case, is the aorist passive, and by implication has Christ as its subject. The genitive can be explained as a genitive of quantity: "you were bought for a price."[64]

δή—the shortened form of ἤδη (now, already) is a particle used with the imperative *glorify!* to show urgency, "Glorify God then in your bodies."

---

61. The Majority Text expands the last part of this verse by adding a parallel, "and in your spirit, which are God's" (KJV, NKJV). The addition lacks the support of early Greek manuscripts and, therefore, translators prefer not to accept it. See George L. Klein, "Hos. 3:1–3—Background to I Cor. 6:19b–20?" *CrisTheolRev* 3 (1989): 373–75.
62. Westminster Shorter Catechism, question and answer 1.
63. Bauer, p. 246.
64. Moule, *Idiom-Book,* p. 39.

Summary of Chapter 6

The Corinthian Christians take one another to court before Gentile judges. Paul rebukes them and inquires whether they do not have godly men who can settle their trivial disputes. He points out that the saints will judge the world and the angels. Therefore, they should appoint a wise man from their midst as mediator instead of going to law before unbelievers.

Paul teaches the readers that their disputes arise from a lack of love, tolerance, and integrity. He notes that the wicked do not inherit God's kingdom. Sex offenders, idolaters, thieves, drunkards, and slanderers also are barred from the kingdom. But the Corinthians have been washed, sanctified, and justified.

Some of the Corinthians utter slogans that everything is permissible for them, and that food is for the stomach and the stomach for food. Paul corrects the Corinthians with comments on these slogans. He teaches them that their bodies belong to the Lord; they are not meant for sexual immorality. Their bodies are members of Christ and therefore should never be united with a prostitute. Paul supports his teaching by referring to a passage from the creation account. He urges the readers to flee immorality. And he discloses that their bodies are the temple of the Holy Spirit. They have been bought with a price and are meant to glorify God.

7

Marriage Problems

(7:1–40)

Outline (continued)

7 1 Now concerning the things you wrote about: "It is good for a man not to touch a woman." 2 But on account of immorality, let each man have his own wife and each woman have her own husband. 3 Let the husband fulfill his marital duty to his wife and similarly the wife to her husband. 4 The wife does not have authority over her own body but her husband has, and likewise also the husband does not have authority over his own body but his wife has. 5 Do not deprive one another, except perhaps by mutual consent for a specified time that you may have time for prayer. Then come together again, lest Satan tempt you because of your lack of self-control. 6 But I say this as a concession, not as a command. 7 I wish that all men were as I am. However, each one has his own gift from God, one this gift and another that gift.

8 But I say to the unmarried and the widows, it is good for them if they remain as I am. 9 But if they do not exercise self-control, let them marry, for it is better to marry than to burn with sexual desire.

10 To those who are married I give this command—not I but the Lord—let a wife not separate from her husband. 11 But if she in fact leaves, let her remain unmarried or be reconciled to her husband, and let the husband not divorce his wife.

12 To the rest I say, I, not the Lord: If any brother has an unbelieving wife and she consents to live with him, let him not send her away. 13 And if any woman has an unbelieving husband, and he consents to live with her, let her not send him away. 14 For the unbelieving husband has been sanctified by his [Christian] wife and the unbelieving wife has been sanctified by the [Christian] husband; otherwise your children would be unclean, but now they are holy.

15 But if the unbeliever departs, let him leave. A [Christian] brother or sister is not bound in such matters. God has called us to peace. 16 For how do you know, wife, whether you will save your husband? Or how do you know, husband, whether you will save your wife?

17 Nevertheless, so let each one live the life the Lord has imparted to him, as God has called each one. And I am laying down this rule in all the churches. 18 Anyone who has been circumcised and called, let him not become uncircumcised. Anyone who has not been circumcised but has been called, let him not become circumcised. 19 Circumcision is nothing and uncircumcision is nothing, but the keeping of the commands is important. 20 Let each one remain in the same calling in which he was called. 21 Were you a slave when you were called, let that not bother you. But if indeed you are able to become free, make the most of it. 22 For he who was called in the Lord while a slave is a freedman of the Lord; likewise the free man when he was called is a slave of Christ. 23 You were bought with a price. Do not become slaves of men. 24 Brothers, let each one remain with God in the situation in which he was called.

25 Now concerning the virgins I have no command of the Lord, but I, as one who by the mercy of God is trustworthy, give my opinion. 26 I think, then, that on account of the present crisis it is good for a man to remain as he is. 27 If you are bound to a wife, do not seek to be released. If you are released from a wife, do not seek one. 28 But even if you should marry, you have not sinned. And if a virgin should marry, she has not sinned. Yet such people will have great affliction in this life, and I would like to spare you this trouble.

29 I say this, brothers, the time is shortened, so that from now on even those who have wives should be as though they had no wives. 30 And those who weep, let them be as though they did not weep, and those who rejoice, let them be as though they did not rejoice, and those who buy as though they

did not possess. 31 And those who use the world as though they did not fully use it. For this world in its present form is passing away.

32 I want you to be free from anxiety. The unmarried man cares for the things belonging to the Lord, how he may please the Lord. 33 But the married man cares for the things of this world, how he may please his wife, 34 and his interests are divided. Also the woman who is unmarried or the virgin cares for the things of the Lord, that she may be holy in both body and spirit. But the woman who is married cares for the things of the world, how she may please her husband. 35 I say this for your own benefit, not to restrain you but to promote decorum and devotion to the Lord without distraction.

36 But if someone thinks that he is behaving dishonorably toward his marriageable virgin—if his passions are strong and it must be so—let him do as he wishes; he does not sin. Let them marry. 37 But he who stands firm in his own heart and is under no necessity but has his desire under control and has decided in his own heart to keep his own virgin, he will do well. 38 So then he who marries his bride-to-be does well but he who does not marry her does better.

39 For a woman is bound as long as her husband lives. But if her husband dies, she is free to marry whom she pleases, only in the Lord. 40 She is happier to remain as she is, in my opinion. And I think that I also have the Spirit of God.

III. Paul's Response to Corinthian Concerns
7:1–16:4

A. Marriage Problems
7:1–40

In the preceding two chapters (5 and 6), Paul wrote concerning incest, litigations, and sexual immorality. He indignantly condemned the moral laxity of the Corinthians and urged them to live wholesome lives to glorify God. Nonetheless, he had not yet touched on the subjects of marriage, separation, virginity, and celibacy. When he received a letter from the Corinthian church, Paul was asked to give advice on marital problems in the church. In this chapter, he discusses the proper conduct of marriage partners, their abiding faithfulness in matrimony, the decorum of virgins, and continence. Apart from a few passages elsewhere in the New Testament, this chapter is unique in providing basic guidelines for those who are married, those who wish to be married or once were married, and those who want to remain single.

1. Proper Conduct
7:1–7

1. Now concerning the things you wrote about: "It is good for a man not to touch a woman."

We note the following points:

a. *Letter.* "Now concerning the things you wrote about." Paul frequently sent epistles to the Corinthian church and in turn received correspondence from them. He sent the Corinthians a letter (5:9) in which he had written about sexually immoral people in Corinth. Perhaps this letter, which is no longer extant, also referred to idolatry and other matters, but we choose to refrain from speculation.[1] The Corinthians replied to this epistle in a written communique, delivered by Stephanus, Fortunatas, and Achaicus (16:17), in which they asked counsel on a number of items. Paul responds to their request in the greater part of I Corinthians (7:1–16:12).

We are able to determine with a degree of certainty the questions they posed. One indicator is the recurring phrase *now concerning* (vv. 1, 25; 8:1; 12:1; 16:1,12; with variations).[2] Paul discusses marriage (7:1–24, 39–40), celibacy (7:25–38), meat offered to idols (8:1–11:1), worship (11:2–34), spiritual gifts (12–14), the collection for the Jerusalem Christians (16:1–4), and Apollos (16:12).[3] Because the phrase *now concerning* is lacking, we cannot determine whether in their letter the Corinthians asked him about the doctrine of the resurrection (15:12–57). It is possible that they also asked Paul concerning this teaching, because it was of current interest to the Corinthians and the Thessalonians (see, e.g., I Thess. 4:13–5:11; II Thess. 2:1–12). In their letter, the Corinthians asked Paul for advice; presumably marriage was the first item they mentioned.

b. *Chastity.* "'It is good for a man not to touch a woman.'" Is this sentence a quotation from the epistle Paul received from the Corinthians? One translation puts the statement in the interrogative, "Is it best for a man not to marry?"[4] Or is it Paul's opening statement of his discussion on marriage? In light of the context, we are inclined to give a positive reply to the first question and a negative to the second. On his own authority, Paul could not have advocated celibacy for everyone, for he would be contradicting God's utterance: "It is not good for the man to be alone" (Gen. 2:18). Then Paul would be against procreation (Gen. 1:28), God's covenant blessings from generation to generation (Gen. 17:7), and the growth of the church. But Paul is not against marriage, which he compares with the union of Christ and the church (see Eph. 5:22–33). Thus he holds a high view of matrimony.

Further, the rabbis commonly taught that marriage was man's obligation and some of them even said it was a woman's duty.[5] Whether Paul at one time was married is difficult to say (see the commentary on v. 7). In view of his keen insight into married life, the possibility that he was once married cannot be dismissed lightly.

---

1. Gordon D. Fee, *The First Epistle to the Corinthians,* New International Commentary on the New Testament series (Grand Rapids: Eerdmans, 1987), p. 7. Fee feels free to include in Paul's initial letter greedy people, robbers, and idolaters.

2. Margaret M. Mitchell, "Concerning περὶ δέ in 1 Corinthians," *NovT* 31 (1989): 229–56.

3. For a thorough discussion, see John C. Hurd, Jr., *The Origin of I Corinthians* (Macon, Ga.: Mercer University Press, 1983), pp. 61–94.

4. TNT, and see NRSV, REB. Origen notes that Paul received this epistle and kept its content intact. "Origen on 1 Corinthians, #121," ed. C. Jenkins, *JTS* 9 (1907–1908): 500. For a different view, consult W. E. Phipps, "Is Paul's Attitude toward Sexual Relations Contained in 1 Cor 7.1?" *NTS* 28 (1982): 125–31.

5. SB, vol. 3, pp. 377–78.

Paul's background and training would inhibit him from uttering a saying not to touch a woman, for it could be interpreted that he advocates celibacy for everyone. We infer that Paul is quoting a line from the letter he had received from the Corinthians. The quote, undoubtedly in greatly abbreviated form, may be considered a summary statement of the query, which Paul is now going to discuss in succeeding verses (vv. 2–7).

c. *Meaning*. What does the sentence mean? The New International Version translates the text, "It is good for a man not to marry." This translation is an interpretation of the text, but it misses the mark. The expression *to touch a woman* is a euphemistic term not for marriage but for sexual intercourse (Gen. 20:6; Prov. 6:29).[6]

Apparently, a group of believers in Corinth set themselves against the immorality prevalent in the city. They advocated celibacy and declared this state to be a norm for the rest of the local Christians. These Corinthians were saying that it is good for a man not to have sexual relations with a woman. Their statement, however, is more extensive than a mere reference to marriage. The Greek uses the general term *anthrōpos* (man) instead of the specific expression *anēr* (husband). Moreover, the Greek has the indefinite noun *gynē* (woman), which does not mean "wife." The Corinthian slogan, therefore, applied to any man and any woman.

According to Walter Bauer, the phrase *it is good* signifies that celibacy is "morally good, pleasing to God, contributing to salvation (cf. Gen. 2:18)."[7] But by quoting this statement, is Paul indicating that celibacy is preferred to marriage? No, not really. He himself alluded to the union of Adam and Eve in paradise in the knowledge that God instituted marriage (6:16; Gen. 2:24). Writes John Calvin, "For God so ordered it in the beginning that the man without a wife was half a man, as it were, and felt himself lacking in help which he particularly needed; and the wife was, as it were, the completion of the man. Therefore whatever evil or trouble there is in marriage springs from the corruption of God's institution."[8] In succeeding verses (vv. 2–5), Paul speaks favorably and knowledgeably about marriage, possibly from personal experience. He shows no indication that he discredits it in any way. In his instructions to Timothy, he writes that apostates forbid people to marry (I Tim. 4:3). Nowhere in any of his epistles does he deprecate the married state. What then is Paul trying to convey?

2. But on account of immorality, let each man have his own wife and each woman have her own husband.

a. "But on account of immorality." The first word in Paul's discourse is the adversative *but*, which qualifies the slogan in the preceding verse (v. 1b). Else-

---

6. Gordon D. Fee, "1 Corinthians 7:1 in the *NIV*," *JETS* 23 (1980): 307–14. Fee suggests the euphemism *to have relations with* as a possible translation, p. 314; *First Corinthians*, p. 275.

7. Bauer, p. 400. See also Hurd, *Origin of I Corinthians*, pp. 159–60.

8. John Calvin, *The First Epistle of Paul the Apostle to the Corinthians,* Calvin's Commentaries series, trans. John W. Fraser (reprint ed.; Grand Rapids: Eerdmans, 1976), p. 135.

where Paul exhorts his readers that they should avoid fornication (I Thess. 4:3), for it is God's will that they be sanctified. He fully realizes that the evils of sexual immorality form the fabric of Corinthian life. Paul literally says, "because of fornications." The plural illustrates the frequent occurrences of relations with prostitutes. Paul goes straight to the heart of the problem that existed in the Corinthian community. He points to illicit sexual relations some of the Christians had; they were part of a pagan society that registered no objections to fornication.

Hence, Paul endorses the slogan of those Corinthians who championed the cause of celibacy, though he knows that uttering a slogan would not keep a person from falling into sin. He is attentive to the problem which the Christians faced in Corinth. However, his approach to the problem of immorality is more realistic than that of the celibate Corinthians.

b. "Let each man have his own wife and each woman have her own husband." The inability of some people to practice continence leads them into sin. To prevent them from sinning, Paul recommends that they marry and stay together in monogamous relationships. He effectively rules out polygamy in any form. Note also that he stresses the equality of the male and the female in the state of matrimony. Each partner should have his or her own spouse, for this is how God ordained it from the beginning (see Matt. 19:8b). Paul intentionally repeats the words *each* and *own* and applies both terms equally to the husband and to the wife.

The apostle responds to the Corinthian statement (v. 1b) by using the adjective *each*. Note that their statement, "it is good for a man not to touch a woman," is followed by Paul's rejoinder "let each man have his own wife." The expressions *a man* (that is, anyone) and *each man* complement one another.

"Paul does not lay down here the *ground* of marriage, as though it were 'ordained for a remedy against sin,' but gives a special reason why those should marry at Cor[inth] who might otherwise have remained single."[9] We ought not, therefore, to accuse Paul of championing the view that marriage is merely a preventive measure against immorality.

The verb *to have* is euphemistic for the sexual act and should not be interpreted "to keep" in the sense of keeping an illicit lover. In the account regarding the incestuous man (5:1, "a man has the wife of his father"), the verb has a sexual connotation. Similarly in verse 2, Paul means that each man should have his own wife sexually and each wife should have her own husband likewise.[10] And this verse sets the tone for the next sentence in Paul's discourse.

3. Let the husband fulfill his marital duty to his wife and similarly the wife to her husband. 4. The wife does not have authority over her own body but her hus-

---

9. G. G. Findlay, *St. Paul's First Epistle to the Corinthians*, in vol. 3 of *The Expositor's Greek Testament*, ed. W. Robertson Nicoll, 5 vols. (1910; reprint ed., Grand Rapids: Eerdmans, 1961), p. 823.

10. Hurd, *Origin of I Corinthians*, p. 162.

band has, and likewise also the husband does not have authority over his own body but his wife has.

a. *Parallels*. The parallelism in verses 2 and 3 is remarkable and demonstrates Paul's interest in and concern for marriage.

Verse 2	*Verse 3*
let each man have his own wife	let the husband fulfill his marital duty to his wife
each woman have her own husband	similarly the wife to her husband

Although the next verse fails to match the rhythm of the preceding two verses, it has its own internal balance:

Verse 4

The wife does not have authority over her own body but her husband has	The husband does not have authority over his own body but his wife has

b. *Duty*. With keen insight into the intimacies of married life, Paul declares that both husband and wife should fulfill their conjugal duties toward each other. He stresses the equality of male and female in respect to marital union: "Let the husband fulfill his marital duty to his wife and similarly the wife to her husband." Further, he stresses that the husband should not demand from his wife but rather fulfill his marital obligations to her; comparably the wife should extend to her husband that which she owes him.

With the words *fulfill* and *duty*, Paul denotes the payment of a debt that each one owes the other.[11] "Marriage without sex is not only unnatural, but it is expressly forbidden."[12] He issues no command on asceticism within the bonds of marriage. Paul discourages those well-meaning but misguided Corinthian Christians who were of the opinion that married couples should abstain from sexual intercourse (see v. 5).

c. *Authority*. Verse 4 reveals that Paul has an even deeper understanding of married life than he expressed in the preceding verse (v. 3). He states that the wife has no authority over her own body, but that the husband has this power; and vice versa, the husband has no power over his own body, but his wife has this authority. John Albert Bengel correctly calls this verse "an elegant paradox."[13]

Elsewhere Paul teaches that the husband is the head of the wife (11:3; Eph. 5:23). But here he plainly declares that in respect to the sexuality of husband and wife, there is complete equality. Each partner has authority over the body of his

---

11. In place of "duty," the Majority Text has "benevolence" or "affection" (see KJV, NKJV).

12. Robert G. Gromacki, *Called to Be Saints: An Exposition of I Corinthians* (Grand Rapids: Baker, 1977), p. 88.

13. John Albert Bengel, *Bengel's New Testament Commentary*, trans. Charlton T. Lewis and Marvin R. Vincent, 2 vols. (Grand Rapids: Kregel, 1981), vol. 2, p. 199.

or her spouse, and both submit themselves to one another. Thus they experience complete mutuality.

5. Do not deprive one another, except perhaps by mutual consent for a specified time that you may have time for prayer. Then come together again, lest Satan tempt you because of your lack of self-control.

a. "Do not deprive one another." What Paul indicates in the first clause of this sentence is that some married couples in the Corinthian community are actually depriving each other of their marital rights. Out of modesty, he omits the direct object for the verb *to deprive* but expects the reader to complete the thought. The verb connotes stealing or robbing an individual of his or her possessions (compare 6:7–8), or in this instance, of one's rights (see v. 3; Exod. 21:10). Paul tells his readers to stop doing so and commands married couples (second person plural *you*) "not to defraud your spouse." Indeed, he becomes unusually personal in these intimate matters. He instructs the Corinthians that their slogan not to touch a woman (v. 1b) does not apply to married couples.

b. "Except perhaps by mutual consent for a specified time that you may have time for prayer." Paul allows abstinence from marital relations on three conditions: first, if both husband and wife agree to do so; next, if both concur that abstinence is for a limited period; and third, if both use this time for prayer. Paul permits this exception to the rule but forbids anyone to impose involuntary restrictions on his or her spouse.

The phrase *by mutual consent* stresses the equality of the sexes in respect to intimate relations. Both the husband and the wife should be fully convinced that abstinence is desirable and in their best interest. Paul immediately adds the second restriction that abstinence be temporary, because a permanent arrangement might lead to a ruined marriage and divorce. Divorce is not only contrary to the institution of marriage (Gen. 2:24; Mark 10:2–9) but it defeats the very purpose for which abstinence is intended: to lead a holy life.

Daily prayer is the hallmark of every sincere Christian. But in married life, a husband and his wife at times face crises that call for special prayer. When financial, social, spiritual, or physical problems appear to overwhelm them, they flee to God in prayer. At such times, they may voluntarily and temporarily abstain from marital intimacy.

c. "Then come together again, lest Satan tempt you because of your lack of self-control." Translators interpret the verb *to come* as a command. Paul tells the believers in Corinth that when the period of prayer has ended, married couples should resume their normal functions. Let no one say, "Temporary abstinence is good, but permanent abstinence is better." Should this be the case, it would be advisable not to marry. Paul alerts his readers to the presence of Satan, who seeks to exploit human weakness by tempting either the husband or the wife into committing adultery. To pursue permanent restraint within the bonds of matrimony is contrary to God's gracious provision of marriage and his marvelous gift of sexuality. Marriage is a protective shield that should be employed effectively against

Satan's subtleties (Eph. 5:11). Refusal to use the protection God provides is a sin for which the individual is held accountable.

Practical Considerations in 7:4–5

When God had created Adam, he declared, "It is not good that the man should be alone. I will make a helper suitable for him" (Gen. 2:18). From one of Adam's ribs he created Eve. God showed that although Adam was a perfect creation, he was incomplete until God had made Eve to be Adam's counterpart. Calvin pointedly remarks, "The man is only the half of his body, and it is the same with the woman."[14] God has made us so that in marriage the man complements the woman and the woman complements the man. In addition, both man and woman have been created with sexual needs that find true fulfillment in matrimony, which God has instituted. For that reason, Paul states that the husband has authority over his wife's body and the wife has authority over her husband's body.

If God made male and female, created them sexual beings, gave to each one power over the body of the other party, and instituted marriage, then forced and permanent abstinence within wedlock is contrary to God's design. In short, when one partner defrauds the other, he or she violates God's creational ordinance (Gen. 1:28; 2:24) and, instead of being spiritual, is sinful.

6. But I say this as a concession, not as a command.

The first word, "but," is an adversative that we understand as a qualifier of Paul's preceding comment: "Then come together again . . ." (v. 5c). That is, verse 6 should be linked to the immediately preceding verse and not to the entire context (vv. 2–5). Paul is not saying that he regards marriage as a concession. Rather, he allows temporary abstinence that has the consent of both spouses. With the demonstrative pronoun *this,* Paul refers not to marriage, which he fully endorses, but to the exception to the rule of marital rights (v. 5b).[15] Marriage in which these rights are honored is Paul's norm.

In light of the following verse (v. 7), the term *concession* alludes to the restraint which Paul allows a husband and wife to observe temporarily. But he refuses to turn this concession into a command. Although he himself had received the gift of restraint, Paul does not impose abstinence on anyone who lacked this gift.[16]

7. I wish that all men were as I am. However, each one has his own gift from God, one this gift and another that gift.

a. "I wish that all men were as I am." Paul expresses a genuine wish and not an improbable desire. But what does he have in mind? Is he advocating celibacy

---

14. Calvin, *I Corinthians,* p. 137.

15. TNT adds an interpretation of verse 6 (in italics): "Now I say this, *that I allow marriage,* as a concession, not as a command." But this addition fails to do justice to the meaning of verse 5.

16. Jean Héring, *The First Epistle of Saint Paul to the Corinthians,* trans. A. W. Heathcote and P. J. Allcock (London: Epworth, 1962), p. 50.

rather than marriage? Not at all. Paul teaches that although marriage, which God instituted, is good and commendable, not every person should be married or seek marriage. Some people have been married and are now either separated, divorced, or widowed.

The question whether Paul was married at one time is intriguing. "In order to be ordained a rabbi, the Law required that the candidate be married; and if Paul was ordained, it follows that he must have been married."[17] The rabbis taught that all Jews should be married to procreate.[18] The early church fathers debated this question at length, especially in light of Paul's thorough knowledge of marriage. If Paul was married when he lived in Jerusalem, could he have been separated from his wife when he was converted to Christianity? His wife may have remained true to Judaism. Whatever Paul's personal history may have been, we do know that he lived the life of a celibate when he wrote I Corinthians.

b. "However, each one has his own gift from God, one this gift and another that gift." Marriage has been ordained by God for the procreation of mankind and for the personal fulfillment of the marriage partners. When God removes a person's need for marriage, he will endow such a person with the gift of continence. Paul received this gift from the Lord and thus he could rejoice in his condition. But he realizes full well that not every person receives this benefaction. And thus Paul writes that God grants each person his or her own gift. The person whom God has not granted continence does well to marry (see v. 9; Matt. 19:11–12).

The Greek word *charisma* signifies spiritual gifts that range from faith, healing, miracles, prophecy, to speaking in tongues or interpreting them (12:9–11; Rom. 12:6). In this passage, Paul is not referring to any of these spiritual endowments. He is speaking about his own peculiar gift of continence. In respect to celibacy, he was given the grace to practice self-control. This does not mean that someone who is unable to do that and marries instead receives a special gift to engage in marriage.[19] Paul prescribes no law or command. Each individual should decide this matter for himself.

Finally, we may not label Paul as an ascetic who belittles marriage and glories in his celibacy. This is not the case, for he speaks eloquently about intimate matters of sexuality and marriage. He is modest in his choice of words yet candid in expressing his opinion. Paul upholds marriage, encourages people to enter matrimony, and teaches that marriage fulfills human needs that God has created. Yet he urges people who have the ability to exercise restraint to remain single as he is.

---

17. Eduardo Arens, "Was St. Paul Married?" *BibToday* 66 (1973): 1191.
18. Talmud, *Yebamoth* 63a; *Kiddushin* 29b.
19. Consult R. C. H. Lenski, *The Interpretation of St. Paul's First and Second Epistle to the Corinthians* (1935; Columbus: Wartburg, 1946), p. 282.

Greek Words, Phrases, and Constructions in 7:1–5

Verses 1–2

ἐγράψατε—the aorist active from the verb ἐγράφω (I write) lacks an indirect object. Many witnesses have the personal pronoun μοι (to me, KJV, NKJV), which the older manuscripts omit.

τὴν ἑαυτοῦ γυναῖκα—"his own wife." Notice that in distinction from verse 1b, Paul uses the definite article here and in the phrase τὸν ἴδιον ἄνδρα (her own husband). In the New Testament, the terms ἑαυτοῦ and ἴδιον show a difference: ἑαυτοῦ is followed by the noun *wife* (Eph. 5:28, 33) and ἴδιον precedes the noun *husband* (14:35; Eph. 5:22, 24; Titus 2:4–5; I Peter 3:1, 5). Nevertheless, "ἴδιος is here [v. 2] used for the sake of variety and is exactly equivalent to the ἑαυτοῦ."[20]

Verses 3–4

ὀφειλήν—this noun derives from the verb ὀφείλω (I owe) and signifies a duty or an obligation. The noun has the support of the older and better Greek manuscripts and is preferred to the reading of the Majority Text, ὀφειλομένην εὔνοιαν (the kindness that is her due).[21]

ἀποδιδότω—the compound verb, from the preposition ἀπό (back) and the verb δίδωμι (I give), in this verse denotes a distinctively personal relationship. "When a man *renders* to his wife that to which she is entitled."[22]

ἐξουσιάζει—Paul purposely chooses this word that means "to have power" and which in the passive signifies "to be mastered by" (6:12). This verb has the derived noun (authority) that in this letter occurs ten times (7:37; 8:9; 9:4, 5, 6, 12 [twice], 18; 11:10; 15:24).

Verse 5

εἰ μήτι ἄν—the presence of the particle ἄν lends a degree of expectancy to this part of the sentence.[23] The phrase means "except perhaps."

ἵνα—the first ἵνα gives an imperatival sense to the verbs in the clause. "Although that idea is not inherent within the particle itself ("do not deprive each other . . . except . . . that you may").[24]

σχολάσητε—the aorist tense of the verb *to have time* is telling because it points to single occurrence and not to continued action.

Before the word *prayer,* the Majority Text has the phrase νηστείᾳ καὶ τῇ (fasting and). The addition may have been introduced by scribes who fostered asceticism. However, the words are lacking in earlier and better manuscripts.

---

20. Adolf Deissmann, *Bible Studies* (reprint ed.; Winona Lake, Ind.: Alpha, 1979), p. 124.

21. Bruce M. Metzger, *A Textual Commentary on the Greek New Testament,* 3d corrected ed. (London and New York: United Bible Societies, 1975), p. 553.

22. Kurt Niederwimmer, *EDNT,* vol. 1, p. 128.

23. Friedrich Blass and Albert Debrunner, *A Greek Grammar of the New Testament and Other Early Christian Literature,* trans. and rev. by Robert Funk (Chicago: University of Chicago Press, 1961), #376.

24. Robert Hanna, *A Grammatical Aid to the Greek New Testament* (Grand Rapids: Baker, 1983), p. 295; see also C. F. D. Moule, *An Idiom-Book of New Testament Greek,* 2d ed. (Cambridge: Cambridge University Press, 1960), p. 145.

2. Faithfulness and Marriage
7:8–11

Paul has a systematic approach to the matter of human sexuality. After a rebuke concerning incest (5:1–5), he discusses sexual sins and exhorts the Corinthians to flee from immorality (6:12–20). Then he quotes a line in a letter he has received from the Corinthian congregation. This line reflects an opposite extreme, for it instructs everyone to avoid all sexual relationships. Paul objects to this slogan and points to God's gracious provision of matrimony.

After a discussion on a temporary exception to the full function of marriage, he turns to those who are unmarried and desire to remain single. He himself belongs to that group of people, and thus he has a word for them.

a. Unmarried and Widows
7:8–9

8. But I say to the unmarried and the widows, it is good for them if they remain as I am.

a. *Categories.* Is Paul indicating two separate categories or is the word *unmarried* a synonym for widowers? If the latter is the case, he has in mind both males and females whose spouses have died. In the Greek, Paul uses the masculine gender for the unmarried and, as may be expected, the feminine gender for the widows. However, in the context of this particular chapter, the term *unmarried* refers to a woman separated from her husband (v. 11), to men (v. 32), and to women (v. 34). "This term includes those who have never been married and those who have been married and are now unmarried."[25]

If we accept the broad interpretation given in the preceding paragraph, then the text appears to reveal redundancy. A widow is a woman who was once married but presently is unmarried and belongs to the first group. Would it not be better to group everyone into one category, or to speak of widowers and widows?[26] No, not at all. The widows were in a special class. The church supported them in their financial needs, and they were assigned particular ministries in the church (I Tim. 5:3–16). Conversely, Paul urges younger widows to remarry, to have children, and to manage their homes (I Tim. 5:14). In this way they are happy in fulfilling their natural calling.[27]

The unmarried are a class of people that includes widowers and both men and women who are single, separated, or divorced. Paul advises these people and the widows to stay unmarried as he himself is unmarried. He fortifies his advice by saying that it is good for them to stay in their unmarried condition. Nev-

---

25. Colin Brown, *NIDNTT*, vol. 3, pp. 536–37; see also Niederwimmer, *EDNT*, vol 1, p. 236.

26. Fee states a number of reasons for choosing the translation *widower, First Corinthians*, pp. 287–88; William F. Orr, "Paul's Treatment of Marriage in 1 Corinthians 7," *PitPer* 8 (1967): 5–22, see especially pp. 12–14.

27. William Hendriksen, *Exposition of I–II Timothy and Titus,* New Testament Commentary series (Grand Rapids: Baker, 1957), p. 177.

ertheless, he already has indicated that the state of matrimony is advisable (vv. 2–5). By giving counsel to those who are not married but lack the gift of continence, Paul is realistic, even descriptive. He writes,

9. But if they do not exercise self-control, let them marry, for it is better to marry than to burn with sexual desire.

b. *Passion.* "If they do not exercise self-control, let them marry." Paul fully understands human nature and gives sensible advice. Already he has spoken of incontinence (v. 5); now once more he states that some people do not exercise restraint, presumably because of their lack of self-control. To them, Paul offers the solution which God has instituted for this situation: "Let them marry!" There is no reproach, no word of disapproval for incontinence, no mention of sin. To preclude the possibility that they might fall into sin because they lack continence, Paul advises wedlock for the unmarried. Let them enter the state of matrimony and thus lead honorable and pure lives.

"For it is better to marry than to burn with sexual desire." The Greek has only the verb *pyrousthai* (to burn), but the context demands the addition of the words *with sexual desire.* Translators know that the verb by itself is incomplete and calls for an explanation. Talmudic rabbis together with scholars from the third century to the present have interpreted this verb to refer to burning in hell.[28] They perceive it as God's righteous judgment on the sinner who continues to violate sexual mores. But Paul alludes to burning with sexual desire. The common understanding of the verb *to burn* in this context is related to incontinence.

In his discussion of this sensitive subject, Paul is frank but at the same time discreet. His expressions are often incomplete so that the reader has to fill in the obvious meaning. For example, he instructed husbands and wives not to deprive each other (v. 5), but left the completion of the sentence for the reader. By saying that it is better to marry than to burn, he again invites the reader to complete the sentence. In the present verse, he teaches that incontinence has its solution within the bounds of marriage and urges the unmarried who lack self-control to seek marriage partners (v. 9). For him, marriage is the context in which husbands and wives find satisfaction for their sexual desires.[29]

With the comparative word *better* Paul is placing marriage over against burning. Paul writes that one should enter marriage as a one-time act to avoid a state of continual desire. But his advice fails to cover every situation. G. G. Findlay astutely observes, "Better to marry than to burn; but if marriage is impossible, better infinitely to burn than to *sin.*"[30]

---

28. F. F. Bruce, *1 and 2 Corinthians,* New Century Bible series (London: Oliphants, 1971), p. 68; Michael L. Barré, "To Marry or to Burn: πυροῦσθαι in 1 Cor. 7:9," *CBQ* 36 (1974): 193–202; Graydon F. Snyder, *First Corinthians: A Faith Community Commentary* (Macon, Ga.: Mercer University Press, 1992), pp. 96–97.

29. Roy Bowen Ward, "Musonius and Paul on Marriage," *NTS* 36 (1990): 281–89.

30. Findlay, *First Corinthians,* p. 825.

Practical Considerations in 7:8–9

Paul demonstrates his profound insight into human nature by candidly discussing a topic that generally causes embarrassment. He fully understands the sexual characteristics God has created in the male and the female. God created Adam and Eve and their descendants with sexual needs that are met through conjugal union in matrimony. Thus Paul counsels his readers to accept God's provision of marriage. Within the context of wedlock, both a husband and a wife fulfill each other's needs. Conversely, anyone who has not received the gift of continence but tries to exercise restraint experiences undue emotional distress. In addition, this person also faces a spiritual problem of carrying the burden of sin and guilt for his or her incontinence.

When sexual needs are met in marriage as God prescribes, a person usually lives a balanced life full of joy and happiness and is free from guilt or remorse over sexual sins. Conclusively, Paul endorses matrimony and instructs people who lack self-restraint to enjoy the sexual satisfaction that married life affords.

Greek Words, Phrases, and Constructions in 7:8–9

Verse 8

τοῖς ἀγάμοις—"the unmarried." Notice that the definite article indicates a category and sets it off from the category of widows. The substantive adjective *unmarried* applies to men and to women, yet for women the Greeks generally used the word ἄνανδρος (without a husband).[31]

ἐὰν μείνωσιν—Paul writes the present subjunctive to express duration (present tense) and uncertainty (subjunctive mood): "If perchance they remain."

Verse 9

εἰ δὲ οὐκ ἐγκρατεύονται—with the use of the particle εἰ and the present indicative of the verb, Paul states a fact. Moreover, the particle οὐκ (instead of μή) precedes the verb to underscore the negative of the verb ἐγκρατεύονται (they control themselves). This verb is in the middle with a reflexive connotation (see I Clem. 30:3).

γαμῆσαι . . . πυροῦσθαι—the first verb is the aorist active infinitive ("to marry"). The aorist denotes single action and is ingressive. By contrast, the second verb is the present passive infinitive ("to be inflamed with") to indicate continued action.

b. Married and Divorced
7:10–11

10. To those who are married I give this command—not I but the Lord—let a wife not separate from her husband.

a. "To those who are married." Here Paul addresses believers who already have married. (Incidentally, with the perfect tense in the Greek of the expres-

31. Thayer, p. 3.

sion *have married,* Paul indicates both duration and stability.) Even though he has received apostolic authority which he has demonstrated in many places (e.g., 5:5, 12; 6:18; 7:5, 8), he now appeals to the authority of the Lord Jesus Christ. Throughout his ministry, Paul repeatedly quoted words uttered by Jesus. One of these, "It is more blessed to give than to receive" (Acts 20:35), is not even found in the Gospels. In this epistle, Paul many times discloses that he has received words or commands from the Lord, which may have come to him directly by vision or indirectly through the apostles (see 9:14; 11:23; 14:37; 15:3; compare I Thess. 4:15). But now he alludes to words spoken by Jesus that were eventually recorded in the written Gospels.

Paul asserts that he has a command for married people that comes not from himself but from the Lord. He takes the words from an oral Gospel tradition. We presume that Paul heard this statement from the other apostles, probably Simon Peter (Gal. 1:18–19), and thus received it indirectly from Jesus. Paul quotes Jesus' word preserved in the Gospel tradition, which for him and the Corinthians has divine authority. In fact, the apostles and the early church accorded the same significance to the Old Testament Scriptures and the oral or written Gospel. For them, both were equally authoritative. And Paul knows that in respect to marriage and divorce, the Corinthian Christians would listen to and obey the voice of Jesus. Writing about this matter, therefore, Paul no longer exerts his authority but the Lord's. Paul steps aside and permits Jesus to speak directly to the Corinthians.

b. "I give this command—not I but the Lord." What does the Lord command? In a discussion with Pharisees who asked him about divorce, Jesus referred them to the Scriptures. Quoting from the creation account, "[God] created them male and female" (Gen. 1:27) and "For this reason a man will leave his father and mother and be united to his wife, and they will become one flesh" (Gen. 2:24), Jesus added his own comments. He said, "So they are no longer two, but one. Therefore what God has joined together, let man not separate" (Mark 10:8b–9). When subsequently the disciples desired to know more about divorce, Jesus added: "Anyone who divorces his wife and marries another woman commits adultery against her. And if she divorces her husband and marries another man, she commits adultery" (Mark 10:11–12).

c. "Let a wife not separate from her husband."[32] Paul exhibits his own authorial prerogatives by reversing the order of Jesus' statement. He begins with the wife and in the next verse (v. 11) mentions the husband. Note that in Matthew's Gospel nothing is said about the wife separating from her husband. Instead, the husband makes the decision and divorces his wife (Matt. 19:9). Matthew wrote his account for a Jewish audience, in which the husband could dismiss his wife for any reason. But his wife had no right to divorce her husband. The Gospel of

---

32. Most versions have the active voice, "to separate," or its equivalent. One translation has the middle, "separate herself" (REB); another has the passive, "be separated" (NJB); and see Jerome Murphy-O'Connor, "The Divorced Woman in 1 Cor. 7:10–11," *JBL* 100 (1981): 601–6.

Mark, however, written in a Roman context and addressed to Gentiles, reflects the Greco-Roman world. In that world, a woman had the right to take the initiative and separate from her husband, which is a circumscription for divorce. The possibility is real that influential women in the Corinthian church consulted Paul about marital relations and divorce. The apostle answers them with a word from Jesus.

The creation account teaches the unity of husband and wife, which, according to Jesus, should not be broken. The prophet Malachi also refers to the Genesis account and denounces divorce as a breach of the marriage covenant which the husband had made with his wife. He quotes the word of the Lord God, who exclaims, "I hate divorce" (Mal. 2:14–16). God's intention is that marriage vows ought not to be dissolved. Jesus allows an exception only when one of the spouses becomes unfaithful to his or her partner (Matt. 5:32; the parallel in Luke 16:18 omits the exception). The rule that dates from the beginning of human history is that a wife must not divorce her husband and, likewise, a husband must not send away his wife (v. 11).

11. But if she in fact leaves, let her remain unmarried or be reconciled to her husband, and let the husband not divorce his wife.

a. "But if she in fact leaves." The probability of divorce is all too real today. Similarly in Paul's day, divorce even among Christians was not at all inconceivable. With a conditional clause in the Greek, Paul shows that the occurrence of divorce is probable. If then Corinthian believers desired to obey the teaching of the Scriptures and Jesus, what counsel do they have for a Christian couple experiencing incompatibility that leads to divorce? Apparently, the local church was encountering a situation in which a wife initiated divorce proceedings against her husband. The question Paul must answer is how God's word in the Old Testament and Jesus' teaching apply to a specific divorce case at hand in Corinth. When divorce eventually becomes a fact, what does the church say?[33]

b. "Let her remain unmarried or be reconciled to her husband." Editors usually consider this part of verse 11 a parenthesis, so that the last part of verse 10 is completed by the last clause in the following verse. Is Paul giving his own opinion in the parenthetical clause or is this Jesus' word? And if it is Paul's own judgment, is he going beyond the exception of unfaithfulness Jesus allowed (Matt. 5:32)?

Jesus declares that God has instituted marriage, so that what he has joined together, no one should separate (Matt. 19:6). He means that the marriage partners have no right to annul the vows they have made. Neither the husband nor the wife has the "power to render a marriage invalid."[34] In other words, in the parenthesis Paul is repeating the teachings of Jesus by permitting no exceptions to the rule of marriage. When Paul writes that a wife leaves her husband, he does

---

33. Consult Stanley B. Marrow, "Marriage and Divorce in the New Testament," *ATR* 70 (1988): 3–15. Marrow even states that Jesus' teaching on divorce was impracticable in Corinth (p. 13).
34. Calvin, *I Corinthians*, p. 147.

not approve of the separation. Rather he commands her to remain unmarried or to be reconciled to her husband. By implying that the marriage bond should not be broken, Paul accepts the reality of separation. Yet he forbids remarriage and counsels the wife who initiates divorce to be reconciled to her husband. The term *reconciliation* "is never used of an innocent party. God is never said to be reconciled to us, but only we to him."[35] If the wife initiates divorce proceedings, she should be the one to exert efforts that lead to reunion.

c. "And let the husband not divorce his wife." What is true for the wife is equally true for the husband. In Greek, Paul uses a synonym for divorce, literally, "send away." Although in Jewish and Greco-Roman society the husband had the prerogative to divorce his wife and had greater freedom than his wife, Paul teaches what the Scriptures say on this subject. He refuses to follow the culture of his day but abides by God's Word. He prohibits the husband from dismissing his spouse. By implication, the husband must strive for reconciliation in case of a divorce, because marriage is for life.

Practical Considerations in 7:10–11

Paul's advice that a wife who separates from her husband should not remarry appears contrary to what he wrote earlier in this chapter. He counseled those unmarried people who had to cope with a lack of self-control to marry (v. 9). Now he writes that the woman who plans to divorce her husband must remain unmarried. But Paul links the first statement, "let her remain unmarried," to the second, "be reconciled to her husband." If the first part is not observed, the second has lost its reason for existence. As long as the woman remains unmarried, there is hope for reconciliation.

Divorce devastates the entire family. Separation affects husband, wife, children, relatives, and friends. Because it is harmful to everyone, divorce is something God hates (Mal. 2:16). In societies where the extended family is a close-knit unit, relatives exert themselves to prevent divorce if at all possible. In the church community, too, members have the corporate responsibility to help fellow members when they need counsel and advice. When difficulties arise in family life, the members of Christ's body should lend their corporate wisdom to deter permanent ruptures in family life and should facilitate healing. Describing the church, Paul writes: "If one member suffers, all the members suffer with it. If one member is honored, all the members rejoice with it" (12:26).

---

3. Believer and Unbeliever
7:12–16

12. To the rest I say—I, not the Lord: If any brother has an unbelieving wife and she consents to live with him, let him not send her away.

Observe the following points:

a. *Apostolic authority.* "To the rest I say—I, not the Lord." If we follow today's

---

35. William F. Luck, *Divorce and Remarriage: Recovering the Biblical View* (San Francisco: Harper and Row, 1987), pp. 165–66.

writing procedures, we would place the preceding passage (vv. 10–11) in quotation marks and introduce it with the phrase *Jesus said.* Verse 12 would then begin with the introduction, "To the rest I say." But Paul is writing in the style of his day. He indicates that he no longer appeals to a word spoken by Jesus but now speaks on his own authority as he does in many places throughout this chapter.[36] He faces the problem of mixed marriages in which the husband is a believer and the wife an unbeliever or vice versa. In this situation, Paul has to make a ruling on the basis of his apostolic authority.

In the first part of the chapter (vv. 2–7), Paul discusses conjugal rights in relation to the institution of marriage (Gen. 2:24). Next he addresses the unmarried and the widows in the church (vv. 8–9) and follows this with a word from the Lord for married couples who are believers (vv. 10–11). Now he encounters the problem of believers and unbelievers in the context of marriage. They are the last group of people to receive apostolic advice. Hence Paul writes, "To the rest I say." He has no word for the unbelievers.

The church now approaches the apostle to the Gentiles and seeks an answer to marital questions that relate to a Christian-Gentile husband and wife. Paul must speak on this subject with the authority Christ has given him and give advice that is in harmony with Jesus' teaching.

b. *Mixed marriage.* "If any brother has an unbelieving wife and she consents to live with him, let him not send her away." Throughout the Old Testament God forbids his people to marry Gentiles, and this is true also for the Corinthians. Elsewhere Paul tells them to marry only in the Lord (v. 39; compare II Cor. 6:14–18). But in the present situation, a Gentile husband has accepted the gospel and puts his faith in Jesus Christ. Yet his wife remains steadfast in her pagan beliefs and fails to follow her husband in his newfound faith.

Paul's advice to the Corinthians is founded on the biblical principle that marriage ought not to be dissolved. He advises the couple to stay together when the unbelieving wife is fully content to live with her believing husband. Paul calls this husband a spiritual brother (see 1:1) who gives leadership as the head of the house. If his wife is happy to stay with him and the husband is content with her, says Paul, then keep the marriage intact.

13. And if any woman has an unbelieving husband, and he consents to live with her, let her not send him away.

Paul is addressing people in the Greco-Roman world, in which the wife had the right to divorce her husband. This was not the case in Jewish society, in which only the husband could initiate a divorce.

The word *woman* in this context signifies that this person is a believer. She has become a Christian but her husband has not (yet) come to faith in Christ. However, apart from this religious issue, the couple lives together harmoniously. If

---

36. See 7:6, 8, 10, 12, 25, 32, 35, 40. Consult Peter Richardson, "'I say, not the Lord': Personal Opinion, Apostolic Authority and the Development of Early Christian Halakah," *TynB* 31 (1980): 65–86.

the husband is content to live with his believing wife, Paul's advice to her is to stay with him and entertain no thoughts about divorce.

In the case of mixed marriages, Christian spouses should do everything in their power to stay with their unbelieving partners. They should never be the first to seek divorce. Paul's counsel is: "Stay where you are."

14. For the unbelieving husband has been sanctified by his [Christian] wife and the unbelieving wife has been sanctified by the [Christian] husband; otherwise your children would be unclean, but now they are holy.

a. *Problem.* "For the unbelieving husband has been sanctified by his wife." In the Greco-Roman culture of the first century, mixed marriages as a rule meant that Christian wives had pagan husbands. A Christian husband normally would not have an unbelieving wife. The New Testament repeatedly mentions accounts of a Christian who is baptized with his entire household (e.g., Acts 16:32–34; 18:8; I Cor. 1:16). In these instances, the wife also became a Christian.[37]

Due to the harshness many Christian wives had to endure from unbelieving husbands (see I Peter 3:1–6), Paul first alludes to the believing wife who lives with a pagan husband and then the reverse. In these families, the unbelieving spouse has been sanctified by the believing partner.

What precisely is the meaning of the verb *has been sanctified?* The unbelieving husband or wife remains a Gentile and yet Paul declares that he or she has been consecrated. The incongruity of this marital relationship is striking, especially when Paul writes that a believer's body is a member of Christ himself (6:15). How can an unbelieving spouse be sanctified?

b. *Answer.* We ought to be careful about reading too much into the text. However, the gospel penetrates the world so that in a given family one spouse becomes a Christian but not the other. Then the believing spouse by conduct, word, and prayer may win his or her partner for Christ. Because of Christ's power, the influence of a believer is often stronger than the influence of an unbeliever.[38] Writes Calvin, "For the godliness of the one does more to 'sanctify' the marriage than the ungodliness of the other to make it unclean."[39] In other words, God's purpose to save his people is much more inclusive than our limited understanding of the process of salvation.

Paul is not saying that an unbelieving husband or wife has been made morally holy through his or her Christian spouse. No, man is unable to sanctify or to save a fellow human being. What the apostle means to say is that an unbelieving spouse who lives intimately with a Christian marriage partner experiences the influence of holiness.

---

37. Consult Margaret Y. MacDonald, "Early Christian Women Married to Unbelievers," *SR* 19 (1990): 221–34; "Women Holy in Body and Spirit: The Social Setting of I Corinthians 7," *NTS* 36 (1990): 161–81.

38. R. St. John Parry, *The First Epistle of Paul the Apostle to the Corinthians,* Cambridge Greek Testament for Schools and Colleges (Cambridge: Cambridge University Press, 1937), p. 112.

39. Calvin, *I Corinthians,* p. 148.

To be sanctified means that a person is influenced by the claims of Christ. The converse is equally true: anyone who is not sanctified is influenced by the claims of a world that is opposed to Christ. In the Greek, the verb *to be sanctified* is in the perfect tense, which denotes that from the moment the spouse became a Christian his or her unbelieving partner comes in contact with holiness.

c. *Sanctified.* A study of the Scriptures reveals that the Greek word *to sanctify* has at least four different meanings. It signifies, first, to set things aside for sacred functions (e.g., items relating to worship at the tabernacle [Exod. 29:37, 44]); next, to consecrate people by either baptism (I Cor. 6:11), a Christian marriage (I Cor. 7:14), or atonement for sin (Heb. 9:13); third, to reverence people, names, or things (I Peter 3:15); and last, to purify someone from evil.[40] The second meaning of the verb *to sanctify* applies to the verse at hand. The believing husband or wife sanctified the unbelieving spouse much as the temple sanctified the gold connected with it, or the altar the gift laid upon it (Matt. 23:17, 19).[41] The object was not holy in itself but was holy by association.

Paul is not saying that the Gentile spouse has a personal relationship with Christ, for then he or she would no longer be called an unbeliever. Nonetheless, this person's conduct is affected by that of the Christian partner. He or she agrees to live with a Christian in whom God's Spirit resides, fulfills the obligations that stem from the institution of marriage (Gen. 2:24), and keeps the marriage intact in obedience to Jesus' command (Matt. 19:6).[42] Both spouses live in a sanctified environment, for the home is consecrated by the reading and application of God's Word and by prayer. Paul also declares holy the children who were born either before or after the spouse's conversion to Christianity.

d. *Children.* "Otherwise your children would be unclean, but now they are holy." What about the next generation? Paul mentions the children reared in a family in which only one parent is a Christian. Although he writes two descriptive adjectives (unclean, holy) for the children of mixed parentage, he unequivocally asserts that they are holy if one parent is a believer. He implies that children are consecrated on the basis of the Christian parent's faith; they are not declared unclean on the basis of a parent's unbelief. In short, faith triumphs over unbelief in the family.

Paul declares the unbelieving spouse sanctified and the children holy. But what is the difference between the words *sanctified* and *holy* in respect to this family? Whereas the unbelieving husband or wife is sanctified by the believing spouse, the children of this spouse enjoy a covenant relationship. God made a covenant with his people and blesses it throughout the generations (Gen. 17:7). Writing about the Jewish people whom God declares holy, Paul says: "If the root is holy, so are the branches" (Rom. 11:16). When God sanctifies his people, he

---

40. Bauer, pp. 8–9.

41. Charles Hodge, *An Exposition of the First Epistle to the Corinthians* (1857; reprint ed., Grand Rapids: Eerdmans, 1965), p. 116.

42. Jerome Murphy-O'Connor, "Works Without Faith in 1 Cor., 7, 14," *RB* 84 (1977): 356.

calls them to live a life of constant holiness. A Christian mother may claim the covenant promises that her children are sanctified in God's sight and called to holiness. Timothy was the son of a Jewess and an unbelieving Greek father. His grandmother Lois and mother, Eunice, raised him in a godly home where he learned to put his faith in Jesus (II Tim. 1:5). "Covenant children are to be counted a part of God's people and should be nurtured in the Christian faith and in the fear of the Lord (Eph. 6:4)."[43]

The text fails to indicate whether Paul has in mind only the children in mixed marriages or also children of believing parents in general. If he means the latter, there is all the more reason to consider these children holy, especially when they themselves confess their faith. These children are incorporated into the life of the church through the sacrament of baptism.[44]

15. But if the unbeliever departs, let him leave. A [Christian] brother or sister is not bound in such matters. God has called us to peace.

a. "But if the unbeliever departs, let him leave." The words of Paul paint a picture of reality, because the first clause of this sentence states a simple fact. If the unbelieving husband refuses to support the faith of his wife and finds it impossible to live in a Christian atmosphere, let him go. Then he no longer can be considered sanctified through his believing wife.

The economic consequences for Christian wives forsaken by their husbands were often severe; these women experienced untold hardship. "It is likely that women who had little or no dowry for support found themselves divorced, isolated and penniless for the sake of the gospel."[45] Paul advises the Christian sister, "Do not stand in his way if he leaves the house." Paul is completely in harmony with his earlier advice that Christians ought not to divorce their spouses (vv. 10–13). But if the unbeliever decides to dismiss his wife, he, not his marriage partner, takes the full responsibility for the divorce.

b. "A [Christian] brother or sister is not bound in such matters." We have no difficulty understanding Paul's ruling to accept the voluntary departure of the unbelieving spouse. But what is the meaning of the verb *is bound*? Is he implying that the forsaken party is now no longer bound to his or her marriage vows (see Rom. 7:2)? Is he or she free to remarry and start anew?

The literal meaning of the phrase *is not bound* alludes to enslavement: "a brother or sister is not enslaved." The unbeliever is the one who breaks the marriage bond, which God had meant to be for life. Now the believer is no longer bound to that union, for his or her unbelieving spouse "has made a breach with God rather than with his or her partner."[46] In this verse Paul neither forbids nor

43. W. Harold Mare, *1 Corinthians*, in vol. 10 of *The Expositor's Bible Commentary*, ed. Frank E. Gaebelain, 12 vols. (Grand Rapids: Zondervan, 1976), p. 230.

44. See Herman N. Ridderbos, *Paul: An Outline of His Theology*, trans. John Richard de Witt (Grand Rapids: Eerdmans, 1975), p. 414.

45. MacDonald, "Early Christian Women," p. 234.

46. Calvin, *I Corinthians*, p. 150. Compare David E. Garland, "A Biblical View of Divorce," *RevExp* 84 (1987): 419–32.

advocates remarriage for the forsaken spouse and leaves this matter an open question (compare vv. 9, 11). He is interested in the Christian's witness to the world, including the unbelieving husband or wife. He urges the Christian to seek peace with the unbelieving spouse. Paul wants the Christian marriage partner to live in obedience to Christ's gospel and thus to oppose valiantly the forces of the evil one (Eph. 6;15).

c. "God has called us to peace." This is one of the fundamental principles in the New Testament.[47] In the previous chapter Paul told the Corinthians not to go to court but by mediation to settle their differences peacefully (6:1–8). Now he recommends peace in marriage by forbidding divorce and promoting reconciliation. This does not mean peace at any cost, for the Christian spouse cannot abrogate his or her faith. What Paul is saying is that the believer who endures divorce must show not hostility but conciliation toward his or her unbelieving spouse. The Christian provides the non-Christian partner opportunity to return and reestablish the marriage. Perhaps the unbelieving spouse will exclaim, "I will go back to my husband [or wife] as at first, for then I was better off than now" (Hos. 2:7). Paul forbids Christian husbands and wives to seek divorce. But, he says, if a Christian wife initiates divorce, she has to remain unmarried or be reconciled to her Christian spouse (vv. 10–11). With regard to an unbelieving partner, a Christian spouse must give him or her an opportunity to return and restore the marriage.

16. For how do you know, wife, whether you will save your husband? Or how do you know, husband, whether you will save your wife?

As long as the unbelieving partner demonstrates his or her willingness to live with the Christian spouse, he or she is sanctified. The continual Christian witness of a believing spouse may prove to be effective in aiding the unbeliever to come to faith in Christ. This witness remains in effect even for the unbelieving spouse who has left voluntarily (v. 15).

Paul's general declaration that God has called us to peace also covers family life. When in Paul's day a husband became a Christian, his wife would normally adopt the Christian faith. Peter addresses a similar marital problem: a wife who had become a believer had to live with her husband who did not embrace Christianity and showed resentment and hostility. Peter advises the Christian wife to be submissive to her husband and by her behavior to win him over to Christ (I Peter 3:1).

When Paul says that neither believing husbands nor believing wives know whether they will be instrumental in saving their pagan spouses, he points out that only God can save his people. We are unable to effect salvation, yet we are instruments in God's hand to bring it about. The believer must always hope, knowing that God will effect his plan and purpose (compare II Sam. 12:22; Esther 4:14; Joel 2:14; Jonah 3:9).

---

47. Rom. 12:18; 14:19; I Cor. 14:33; II Tim. 2:22; Heb. 12:14; I Peter 3:11.

Does Paul encourage or discourage divorce in a marriage in which the unbelieving spouse departs? In view of his emphasis on peace, albeit not at any price, he discourages divorce. Findlay keenly observes that the Corinthians, "with their lax moral notions, needed dissuasives from rather than encouragements to divorce."[48] The apostle's advice remains the same: do not break your marriage vows.

Practical Considerations in 7:15

Divorce is a soul-wrenching experience and should be avoided if possible. The cultural stipulations for marriage in ancient times demanded that the groom give the bride's father a dowry that consisted of a mutually agreed sum of money or services rendered. But a dowry could also consist of a gift which the father gave to his daughter at the time of marriage. When divorce ended marital ties, the husband departed from his wife without giving her any support. And a Christian wife could not return to her pagan family. Her father would be reluctant or would refuse to take care of a daughter whose husband had sent her away because of her religion. Her only recourse was to go to members of the church for spiritual and financial aid.

How is the Christian today to cope with a situation in which divorce has become reality? As members of the body of Christ, we feel the hurt and the harm a divorced person has to suffer. We must speak words of encouragement and provide material and spiritual help. When a Christian woman is divorced by her unbelieving husband, she should know that the Lord will provide for her in all her needs.

Greek Words, Phrases, and Constructions in 7:12–16

Verse 12

τοῖς . . . λοιποῖς—"the rest." David L. Dungan remarks that this "is Paul's customary way of referring to non-believers."[49] In a few passages (Eph. 2:3; 1 Thess. 4:13; 5:6), this expression is synonymous with τὰ ἔθνη (the Gentiles). But in the Corinthian context, Paul addresses the spouses in mixed marriages and tells the Christian partners to give leadership.

λέγω ἐγώ—this combination expresses authority: "I say." The personal pronoun shows emphatic contrast or antithesis to ὁ κύριος (see v. 10).

εἴ τις—Paul writes the conditional clause twice (vv. 12, 13) to express the fact that he is addressing reality.

αὕτη—the demonstrative pronoun in the feminine singular has its antecedent in the word *wife*. The translation should be "this one," but it is given as if the text reads αὐτή (she) that serves as the third person personal pronoun (see also οὗτος instead of αὐτός, v. 13).

Verse 13

συνευδοκεῖ—this compound verb ("she consents to") expresses both mutuality (husband and wife both agree to live together) and intensity (she or he is fully content).

---

48. Findlay, *First Corinthians*, p. 828.

49. David L. Dungan, *The Sayings of Jesus in the Churches of Paul: The Use of the Synoptic Tradition in the Regulation of Early Church Life* (Philadelphia: Fortress, 1971), p. 93.

Verse 14

γυναικί—after the word *wife*, a few Western and other manuscripts have inserted first, the adjectival expression τῇ πιστῇ (the believing) and next, the corresponding term τῷ πιστῷ after the word *brother* (see NAB). I have not adopted the Western reading, but for the sake of clarity I have added the word *Christian* in brackets (compare REB).

ἐν τῇ and ἐν τῷ—the preposition with the dative case may denote place (in the sphere of) or cause (because of).

ἀδελφῷ—instead of "brother" the Majority Text has the reading ἀνδρί (husband), which nearly every translator has adopted. Yet the better manuscripts have the reading *brother*. Bruce M. Metzger notes that although the word *husband* is a more fitting correlative to the term *wife* than the word *brother*, "the special force of ἀδελφῷ [has] not been appreciated. In order to recapture some of the nuance belonging to ἀδελφῷ, in a subsequent modification τῷ πιστῷ was added to ἀνδρί."[50]

Verses 15–16

εἰ—the particle with the present indicative tense χωρίζεται (he departs) expresses a factual statement. The present middle imperative χωριζέσθω (let him depart) is permissive.

ἐν . . . εἰρήνη—the preposition has the function of εἰς with the meaning "God has called you *into* a peace *in* which he wishes you to live."[51]

ὑμᾶς—the manuscript evidence is stronger for ἡμᾶς than for ὑμᾶς. Yet some editors of the Greek texts adopt the reading *you* even though it has the lesser support. Translators are evenly divided on the matter; some choose "you"[52] and others "us."[53]

εἰ . . . σώσεις—"whether you will save." Paul purposely leaves this direct question unanswered, for only God can respond.

---

4. A Digression
7:17–24

In the middle of his discourse on marriage, Paul digresses to emphasize a rule that he mentions three times. This is the rule he gives to the church: "remain in the place God has given you" (vv. 17, 20, 24). In support of the precept he provides two illustrations, one on circumcision and uncircumcision, and the other on the slave and the freedman. Paul uses these illustrations to provide context for the next segment of his discussion on marriage and to stress the Christian's responsibility to God.

17. Nevertheless, so let each one live the life the Lord has imparted to him, as God has called each one. And I am laying down this rule in all the churches.

a. "Nevertheless, so let each one live the life the Lord has imparted to him." The first word is an adversative that calls attention to the exception to the rule that marriage vows are binding (v. 15a, b). When the Christian spouse is di-

---

50. Metzger, *Textual Commentary*, p. 555.

51. Moule, *Idiom-Book*, p. 79. See Parry, *First Epistle to the Corinthians*, p. 114.

52. GNB, NAB, JB, NJB, NRSV, MLB, *Moffatt*. Two translations avoid making a choice and translate: "God's call is a call to live in peace" (NEB, REB).

53. KJV, NKJV, NASB, SEB, TNT, RSV, *Cassirer*, *Phillips*.

vorced by the unbelieving partner, then let it be so, says Paul. Nevertheless, when a marriage has been dissolved, life continues.

However, Paul broadens his scope to address everyone affected by the gospel. Notice that Paul uses the substantive *each one* twice in the first sentence of this verse. He knows that the gospel enters not only the relationship of husbands and wives, but also of Jew and Gentile, of slave and freedman. In whatever situation a person becomes a Christian, he or she must remain there. That is the place in life the Lord has designated for everyone. "Paul endeavoured to convince his readers that their relation to Christ was compatible with any social relation or position."[54] New converts to the Christian faith are often of the opinion that the only way to show gratitude to God for the gift of salvation is to become a minister or missionary of the gospel. This is commendable but not necessary. The Lord calls his people in all walks of life to follow him. He wants them to be Christian fathers and mothers, Christian husbands and wives, Christian employers and employees. Each one should fulfill the role the Lord has assigned to him or her and live (literally, walk) accordingly.

b. "As God has called each one."[55] In this chapter, Paul repeatedly writes that God has called the believer (vv. 15, 17, 18 [twice], 20, 21, 22 [twice], 24). God calls a person first into the fellowship of Jesus Christ (1:9) and then to a role of fulfilling the Christian life in the setting in which the Lord has placed him. This does not mean that God allows the believer no change of status, employment, or residence. The Lord often leads his people into other areas of life and gives them different roles; in whatever calling God places them, they must reflect his glory. They must live worthily in that place and environment as Christians who demonstrate the love of the Lord Jesus.

c. "And I am laying down this rule in all the churches." The rule for believers is to stay where the Lord has placed them and to live worthily in their calling. Paul repeats himself to bring the point home (vv. 20, 24). He makes this rule on the strength of his apostolic authority and applies it in all the churches (see 4:17; 14:34; 16:1).

18. Anyone who has been circumcised and called, let him not become uncircumcised. Anyone who has not been circumcised but has been called, let him not become circumcised. 19. Circumcision is nothing and uncircumcision is nothing, but the keeping of the commands is important.

Here is an example taken from a typical first-century congregation in which Jewish Christians and Gentile Christians worshiped and worked together. Such was the case in Corinth, where Christians from Jewish and Gentile backgrounds formed the church. There the ethnic differences apparently caused no discord. When God calls a person to a life of fellowship in Christ, the distinctives that separate a Jew from a Gentile are no longer valid.

---

54. Hodge, *First Epistle to the Corinthians,* p. 120.

55. The Majority Text, reflected in two translations (KJV, NKJV), has reversed the sequence of "Lord" and "God." One translator features the word *God* twice in this verse (*Cassirer*).

A Jew, who was circumcised on the eighth day after birth, should not try to undo this mark when in later life he became a Christian. As a circumcised Jew he would be able to witness effectively for Christ among fellow Jews. Such was the case of Timothy, who was circumcised to work among the Jews who knew him in Lystra and Derbe (Acts 16:3). When a Jew was called by God to follow Christ, he should not try surgically to undo his circumcision to look like a Gentile.[56] God called him to be a Jew among the Jews (see 9:20).

Similarly, when a Gentile was called by God, he should not try to become a Jew by requesting circumcision. He might envy the Jew who had received God's revelation, the covenants, and the promises (Rom. 3:2; 9:4–5). But God did not call him to be circumcised (Gal. 5:2), for in Christ Jesus the distinctions of being a Jew or a Gentile disappear.[57] God called the Gentile Christian to be a witness in the cultural setting in which God placed him.

Paul alludes to exceptional cases, for a Jew would not readily seek to efface the mark of circumcision and the Gentile normally was loath to accept that mark. Yet in Palestine, thousands of Jewish Christians were zealous for keeping the Mosaic law, including the rite of circumcision (Acts 21:20). These people at times exerted undue pressure on Gentile Christians to do likewise (see Acts 15:1–2). They continued to do so even after the Jerusalem Council ruled that those Gentiles who became Christians need not submit to circumcision (Acts 15:19–21).

Circumcision and uncircumcision have nothing to do with the Christian faith, says Paul. The Jew and the Gentile are equal in the sight of God, for in Christ Jesus he adopts both of them. Not man's external sign but his internal desire to keep God's law—that is, to do his will—is significant. Jews, however, would object to Paul's remark and point to a startling inconsistency. Although God's law stipulates circumcision as a sign of the covenant (Gen. 17:10–14), they hear Paul say that circumcision is nothing. Yet he states that keeping God's law is important (compare Sir. 32:23). Paul, however, clearly distinguishes between an external observance of the law as demonstrated by the sign of the covenant and an internal spirit that reveals obedience to God's will. The Lord wants both Jewish and Gentile Christians to fulfill the moral law. He desires obedience, not out of an erroneous belief that it is necessary to earn salvation, but out of a joyful and thankful heart for the free gift of salvation.

20. Let each one remain in the same calling in which he was called. 21. Were you a slave when you were called, let that not bother you. But if indeed you are able to become free, make the most of it.

a. "Let each one remain in the same calling in which he was called." Once more Paul states the rule which he has laid down in all the churches (see vv. 17, 24). Paul's emphasis is on the words *calling* and *called,* which relate to spiritual rebirth through God's Word and Spirit. And calling refers to one's situation in life.

---

56. Compare Josephus *Antiquities* 12.5.1 [241]; I Macc. 1:15.
57. Rom. 2:25–26; Gal. 3:28; 5:6; 6:15.

This spiritual rebirth is not merely a vertical link between God and man but also a horizontal relation that extends from a person's place in life to his or her fellow men. A calling can be understood as a position or a vocation in which a believer lives in obedience to God's precepts. Paul is saying that "everyone is to remain in the station in which he found himself when he was called."[58] For instance, a bookkeeper who converts to Christianity should not feel that he can no longer function as a bookkeeper because of his faith. Paul instructs every convert to stay where God has placed him or her in life and not to change occupation. He is saying: "Fulfill Christ's demands in the place where you were when God called you."

b. "Were you a slave when you were called, let that not bother you." Here is a concrete example taken from the social scene of Paul's day. Although many slaves acquired valuable skills, filled professional positions, and gained an education,[59] others were untrained and uneducated; these illiterate people were often despised and even abused by insensitive masters (compare I Peter 2:18–21).

We would expect Paul to condemn the institution of slavery as sinful. But he fails to address this issue. He tells the slave who has become a Christian not to worry about slavery. Paul is not interested in disturbing the existing structure of society. Christ's gospel will gradually pervade society as yeast permeates a batch of dough. He is aware of the slave's longing to be free, yet he knows that God rules supreme. Through the gospel "a higher divine ordinance is effecting itself, whereby the world is maintained."[60] The eventual change in society Paul leaves to the Lord. Now he exhorts the Christian slave not to be concerned about his lot.

c. "But if indeed you are able to become free, make the most of it."[61] The last clause in the Greek has only two words and lacks a direct object: "rather use [*it*]" (NKJV). What precisely is the meaning of the word *it*? Negatively, the word can refer to slavery; positively to freedom; and contextually to vocation. In sequence, these are three representative translations:

"Even if you have a chance of freedom, you should prefer to make full use of your condition as a slave." (NJB; see also NAB, NRSV)
"Though if a chance of freedom should come, by all means take it." (REB; see, e.g., GNB, MLB, SEB, TNT)
"But if, indeed, you become manumitted, by all means [as a freedman] live according to [God's calling]." (Bartchy, p. 183)

The first translation faces at least two objections, one grammatical and the other cultural. Grammatically the verb *use* is an imperative in the aorist tense, indicat-

---

58. Bauer, p. 436. Consult Hodge, *First Epistle to the Corinthians*, pp. 122–23.
59. S. Scott Bartchy, *ΜΑΛΛΟΝ ΧΡΗΣΑΙ: First-Century Slavery and the Interpretation of 1 Corinthians 7:21*, SBL Dissertation Series 11 (Missoula, Mont.: SBL, 1973), pp. 73–76.
60. Ridderbos, *Paul*, p. 317.
61. Refer to Bauer, p. 884.

ing a single action. It signifies a new beginning in life and not a continuation of slavery. That is, the slave when he or she is set free enters a new phase. A cultural objection is that not the slave but the master made the decision to free the servant. The master could do so for economic or social reasons, yet he determined the lot of the slave. As a rule, slaves longed to be free.[62]

Most translators prefer the second translation because they perceive the freedman to be in a better position to spread the gospel than the slave who was hampered by various restrictions. However, the slave population in the first century was numberless, so that a slave could be an effective witness among his own people.

An objection to the second translation is that the context seems to demand the interpretation of remaining in slavery. Thus, the reading "make full use of your condition as a slave" merges with the next line, "For he who was called by the Lord while a slave is a freedman of the Lord" (v. 22a). However, this objection loses its force when we take verses 21 and 22 as parallels. Verse 22b reads, "Likewise the free man when he was called is a slave of the Lord" (see the commentary on v. 22b), and serves as a counterpart of the second translation of verse 21b.

The third translation has the word *calling* as the direct object of the verb *to live* (taken from the preceding sentence). But when a Greek sentence lacks a word that is needed to complete the thought, we must supply it from the immediate context, namely, the sentence itself. Here the sentence features the concept *freedom*, not that of calling.[63] Of the three translations, therefore, the second is preferred.

The recurring theme that Paul stresses in this chapter and especially in this section (vv. 17–24) is permanence. His rule to the members of the church is to stay in the place which God has assigned to the individual (vv. 17, 20, 24). This does not mean immobility and inflexibility, however; when a slave attains freedom, for example, his human longing has been met. God created man not to be slave to his fellow man but to be free.

22. For he who was called in the Lord while a slave is a freedman of the Lord; likewise the free man when he was called is a slave of Christ.

The constituency of the Corinthian church varied from the rich and the influential to the poor and the slave. Everyone was a partaker of God's grace in Christ. As a spiritual family, the members accepted one another as brothers and sisters. Within the church, social and economic differences were overlooked. But those Christians who were slaves were fully aware of their lack of freedom. They needed a word of encouragement and exhortation.

This verse stresses the word *Lord*, which occurs twice in the sense of agent and possessor. In other words, the Lord calls his people and also owns them. The last

---

62. Consult Bartchy, *First-Century Slavery*, p. 82.

63. Compare Peter Trummer, "Die Chance der Freiheit. Zur Interpretation des *mallon chresai* in 1 Kor 7,21," *Bib* 56 (1975): 344–68.

word in the sentence, "Christ," is emphatic because of its position. Apart from an omission, the verse displays balance. The omission is in the second part of the verse, where we must supply the prepositional phrase *in the Lord.* So this part reads, "Likewise the free man when he was called in the Lord is a slave of Christ." As such, the sentence as a whole has two parallel segments.

a. "For he who was called in the Lord while a slave is a freedman of the Lord." Paul tells the Christian slave that he ought not to look at his social status but rather at the freedom he has received in Christ (John 8:36). When God called him to be part of his people, he experienced a freedom from sin and guilt. He is no longer a slave of sin but belongs to the Lord's freedmen, that is, those who are set free from slavery.

b. "The free man when he was called is a slave of Christ." When the Lord called the free man, he became a spiritual slave who obediently does the will of God (Eph. 6:6). Certainly, the slave who is a freedman in the Lord is at the same time Christ's slave, just as the free man is also Christ's freedman. Together they are brothers and sisters in the Lord (Philem. 16). Writes Frederic Louis Godet, "If in Christ slaves become free, and the free slaves, then neither slavery nor liberty is to be dreaded by the believer!"[64]

23. You were bought with a price. Do not become slaves of men.

The first part of this verse is a verbatim repetition of 6:20, but the words are placed in an entirely different context. In the preceding chapter, Paul wrote about prostitutes and instructed the Corinthians to flee sexual immorality. He reminded them that their bodies were temples of the Holy Spirit and then added that the Corinthians belonged to Christ, for they were bought with a price. Now he places the same words, "you were bought with a price," in the context of Christ freeing the slaves of sin and death. Christ set the Corinthians free from sin and paid for them with the price of his blood (see I Peter 1:18–19). Those who have been purchased by Christ should have full assurance of their salvation.

> Blessed assurance, Jesus is mine!
> Oh, what a foretaste of glory divine!
> Heir of salvation, purchase of God,
> Born of His Spirit, washed in His blood.
> —Fanny J. Crosby

Paul issues a stern warning to all the Corinthian believers not to become slaves of men. They should know that they are slaves in bondage to Christ much the same as the Israelites were to be in bondage to God (compare Lev. 25:55). Notice that Paul pastorally addresses his readers in the second person plural *you.* Because he is not specifically speaking to slaves but to the entire congregation, Paul probably has in mind human philosophies and religious systems that hold man's

64. Frederic Louis Godet, *Commentary on First Corinthians* (1886; reprint ed., Grand Rapids: Kregel, 1977), p. 362.

mind in bondage (compare 2:12). Instead of obeying the law of God, Christians entrapped by worldly thinking become slaves of men (Gal. 5:1; Col. 2:20). Consequently, Paul warns them to heed the calling in which Christ has called them.

24. Brothers, let each one remain with God in the situation in which he was called.

Paul began this segment (vv. 17–24) with a rule he gave to all the churches. He repeated the precept in the middle of the segment (v. 20), and now he ends it with that same principle (v. 24). In all three verses he specifically applies the rule to each believer. In the present verse, he adds the phrase *with God*. This means that whatever the circumstances of a believer may be, the Christian should know that God is always with him and will never forsake him (compare Deut. 31:6; Josh. 1:5; Heb. 1:5). But it also means that every believer must live worthily in the presence of God, for God's eye is always upon him. The Christian is a member of the household of faith, a citizen in the kingdom of God, and a soldier in the army of the Lord.

Why does Paul state three times the rule to stay in one's place? He has given two examples from the religious sphere (Jew and Gentile) and the social sphere (slave and free). Before and after each of these examples he stresses his rule to maintain stability. For Paul, the vocation of the individual Christian is to live before God in any circumstance. He realizes that with the entrance of the gospel into the world, society and culture need to change. Yet he calls not for a revolution but for stability. The gospel itself must effect a change. In whatever place in life the Christian finds himself, there he must live honorably before his God. "It is clear that Paul considers vocation the determining factor in a Christian's life. He issues the warning to avoid circumstances which might endanger this vocation."[65] A Christian practices the teachings of Christ, whether his or her roots were in Judaism or in paganism and whether he or she is enslaved or free.

Finally, the phrase *with God* causes the believer to look forward to the return of Christ. The early Christian longed to be with Christ and therefore set his mind not on earthly but on heavenly things (Phil. 3:19–20; Col. 3:2). The Christian lives his life on earth knowing that his eternal home is with God.

Greek Words, Phrases, and Constructions in 7:17–23

Verse 17

εἰ μή—this combination is adversative and means "but." It is equivalent to πλήν.[66] The negative protasis of this conditional sentence Paul never supplied, but we understand him to say: "In spite of the exception clause on divorce (v. 15a, b), I lay down a rule for all the churches."

---

65. F. W. Grosheide, *Commentary on the First Epistle to the Corinthians: The English Text with Introduction, Exposition and Notes,* New International Commentary on the New Testament series (Grand Rapids: Eerdmans, 1953), p. 172.

66. Blass and Debrunner, *Greek Grammar,* #376; A. T. Robertson translates it "only." *A Grammar of the Greek New Testament in the Light of Historical Research* (Nashville: Broadman, 1934), p. 1025.

περιπατείτω—the present tense in the imperative mood expresses duration: "let him keep on walking."

Verses 18–19

περιτετμημένος—the perfect passive participle of the compound verb περιτέμνω (I circumcise) shows that the action took place in the past but its effect continues in the present.

κέκληται—this perfect passive from the verb καλέω (I call) does not mean that a man was called to uncircumcision but rather he was called in that condition.

τήρησις—the noun derives from the verb τηρέω (I keep) and denotes active pursuance.

Verse 21

ἀλλ᾽ εἰ καί—these three words are at the center of the debate on translating and interpreting this particular verse. The adversative ἀλλά (however) is stronger than the particle δέ (but) and contrasts the two parts of this verse.[67] The combination εἰ καί either means "if indeed" or "although." The first translation is favored by scholars who say that the sentence means freedom from slavery; the second is advocated by those who state that slaves should remain in slavery. S. Scott Bartchy observes, "There are no examples of εἰ καί meaning 'although' or 'even if' in 1 Cor[inthians], but that in 1 Cor[inthians] 7 an emphatic καί appears before and after the usage of εἰ καί in [v. 21c]. These usages suggest that on grammatical grounds alone εἰ and καί in [v. 21c] should be translated 'if, indeed.' In view of the social and legal context, this is the translation which is required."[68]

μᾶλλον χρῆσαι—this is the aorist imperative of χράομαι (I use) that contrasts a present imperative; that is, the slave has a new beginning as a freedman. The adverb μᾶλλον either signifies "by all means" or is a comparative that excludes a social change and is translated "rather." The first translation is preferred.

Verse 22

ἐν κυρίῳ—the preposition can refer to either sphere (in the Lord) or agency (by the Lord). Most translators opt for the dative of sphere; a few have chosen agency.[69] Although the aorist passive κληθείς (twice) accommodates itself to agency, the context suggests sphere.

Verse 23

τιμῆς—see the comment on 6:20.

μὴ γίνεσθε—the present tense of the negative command implies that some Corinthians already were influenced by worldly doctrines.

---

5. Virgins and Marriage
7:25–40

After a brief interlude (vv. 17–24) in which he has provided two graphic illustrations of stability taken from the religious and the social spheres, Paul now re-

---

67. Some translations omit the adversative (e.g., NIV, NAB, NJB, NRSV, *Phillips*).

68. Bartchy, *First-Century Slavery,* p. 178.

69. See, e.g., GNB, MLB, NIV, TNT.

sumes his discussion on marriage. This subject which he introduced in verse 1 is broad and has many facets. Paul already answered questions on conjugal rights, single people, divorce, and mixed marriages. But he still faces questions that relate to virginity, marriage and serving the Lord, proper conduct toward a virgin, and the extent of wedding vows. Paul now provides counsel on these intimate and strictly personal matters.

a. Marital Status
7:25–28

25. Now concerning the virgins I have no command of the Lord, but I, as one who by the mercy of God is trustworthy, give my opinion.

a. "Now concerning the virgins." The first two words appear to refer to a question the Corinthians put to him in their letter. Paul works sequentially through the set of questions on marital problems and now answers questions about the virgins. Paul refrains from explaining the meaning of the word *virgins,* but he probably has in mind "the state of virginity itself."[70]

Virgins of marriageable age were hesitant to enter wedlock for at least two reasons: first, the "present crisis" (v. 26) of that time made marriage inadvisable and, next, some Christians in Corinth counseled them not to marry.[71] Paul discusses these matters in subsequent verses.

b. "I have no command of the Lord." Concerning the question whether celibacy is good and marriage bad, Paul could turn to Scripture and answer that God instituted marriage (6:16; Gen. 2:24). And concerning divorce, he relied on a command of the Lord, who told the Pharisees that marriage vows are lasting and should not be broken (v. 10; Mark 10:8–12). But in connection with virgins who have wedding plans, Paul has no direct command from either Scripture or the Lord.

c. "But I, as one who by the mercy of God is trustworthy, give my opinion." Paul writes his epistle by divine inspiration and not by human insight (II Peter 1:20–21). He knows that the Lord has given him apostolic authority to speak and to write for the benefit of the church. Yet he does not legislate in regard to the personal and sensitive subject of virginity. In this verse he says that he gives his opinion, and in the next verse he writes, "I think" (v. 26; and see v. 40). His approach in the second half of this chapter, therefore, differs from the first half, in which he cited a command of the Lord (v. 10). Now he speaks without a divine injunction, yet he relies on the Lord, to whom he gives credit for calling him to apostleship.

Paul notes that he was shown mercy so that he became faithful not on his own accord but by Christ's benevolence. Christ called him to be an apostle and gave him numerous gifts. Paul willingly and obediently employed these talents to

70. Calvin, *I Corinthians,* p. 155.
71. Consult Fee, *First Corinthians,* pp. 323, 327.

serve Christ's followers. Throughout his epistles, he recognized that Jesus in his mercy turned him from a persecutor of the church to its planter, builder, counselor, preacher, and teacher (see 4:1; I Thess. 2:4; I Tim. 1:13, 16). Paul became a faithful minister of the gospel in whom believers could put their confidence. He had demonstrated his faithfulness to Jesus. Further, he had earned the trust of these believers so that they would come to him for counsel. Paul gives them his opinion and he expects the Corinthians to follow his advice.

26. I think, then, that on account of the present crisis it is good for a man to remain as he is.

Paul qualifies his advice with the introductory words *I think,* and states that because of the "present crisis" celibacy is preferred to marriage. Some translators have alternate readings: "the impending distress" (MLB, RSV) or "the impending crisis" (NRSV). All others use the adjective *present* to describe the crisis. What is this crisis that afflicts the Corinthian community? Scholars usually give one of three answers: the Greek word *anangkē* (necessity, distress) either connotes a calamity that has befallen the church in Corinth, or it intimates the persecution Christians have to endure as the end of time approaches, or it refers to a famine.

The first explanation is that some misfortune had happened in the Corinthian community. Perhaps Paul's reference to the weak, sick, and dying (11:30) indicates a calamity that followed certain irregularities in celebrating the Lord's Supper. But what bearing has the celebration of Communion on postponing marriage? The distress of sickness and death in some families seems an unlikely reason for Paul to discourage marital obligations in the entire church.

The second interpretation is that Paul alludes to the end of the world in this segment (vv. 26–31). He says that the time is short (v. 29) and that this world is passing away (v. 31). Christians will bear insults and hardships because of their faith as they enter the period that leads to the end of time. Therefore, in view of this distress the unmarried person should remain single but is free to choose otherwise. If the present distress is interpreted from an eschatological perspective, no one would ever think of making wedding plans. As Leon Morris comments, however, "Paul often refers to Christ's return but he does not associate *anangkē* with it. When he uses this word it has meanings like 'compulsion' (v. 37), 'compelled' (9:16), 'hardships' (II Cor. 6:4), *etc.,* but never the events preceding the second coming."[72]

The third answer is that a famine in the Greek countryside is bringing untold misery to the citizens, especially the poor people.[73] Hence, Paul's advice to an unmarried person is appropriate, for such a person can endure the hardship of

---

72. Leon Morris, *The First Epistle of Paul to the Corinthians: An Introduction and Commentary,* Tyndale New Testament Commentaries series, 2d ed. (Leicester: Inter-Varsity; Grand Rapids: Eerdmans, 1985), pp. 112–13.

73. Refer to Bruce W. Winter, "Secular and Christian Responses to Corinthian Famines," *TynB* 40 (1989): 86–106.

a famine much better than parents who daily have to provide for their children.[74] If we consider the "present crisis" in the light of Paul's discussion on the celebration of the Lord's Supper, we see a possible indicator of a famine. In at least two passages, Paul mentions that some Corinthians are hungry when they come to the Lord's table (11:21, 34).

All three views work with hypotheses, but of these views the third one appears to give the most compelling reason for remaining unmarried. An inability to supply the daily needs of a family serves as supportive evidence for postponing marriage.

The Greek text does not run smoothly. A literal translation is: "I think then that this is good in view of the present distress, that it is good for a man to remain as he is" (NASB). We presume that Paul begins a clause but fails to complete it and then constructs a second clause. In the interest of style, most translators delete the clause *that this is good*. A last observation: Paul uses the expression *man* in the generic sense to include both men and women.

27. If you are bound to a wife, do not seek to be released. If you are released from a wife, do not seek one.

a. "If you are bound to a wife, do not seek to be released." Again Paul teaches that marriage ties should not be broken. Even if present necessities (such as a famine) make married life difficult, from the time of creation God intended that husband and wife remain together. Paul uses the perfect tense (you have been bound) to indicate an act that happened in the past with results that extend to the present. This verb can also apply to a man and a woman who were bound by betrothal vows.[75] From a Jewish perspective, a virgin was pledged to her future husband and a betrothal was tantamount to marriage (see Deut. 22:23–24; Matt. 1:18). We ought not, therefore, to restrict the interpretation of this verse to either married or engaged couples. The general context includes both married and betrothed parties. Upholding the sanctity of matrimony, Paul commands them not to seek dissolution of their marriage or engagement vows.

b. "If you are released from a wife, do not seek one." The second part of the verse parallels the first in style and syntax. Note that Paul repeats the key word *release*. Once more Paul writes a perfect tense: you have been released. But what is the meaning of the verb *to release?* Paul is advising bachelors not to contemplate marriage in the burdensome economic situation of the present time (v. 26). Says Walter Bauer, "A previous state of being 'bound' need not be assumed."[76] In addition, Paul had in mind widowers but not separated or divorced persons, for he already had expressed his thoughts about separation and divorce (vv. 10–13).

---

74. The Greek expression ἀνάγκη (distress) occurs in Epictetus 3.26.7 in respect to starvation. See also III Macc. 3:16, which notes a present difficulty when Ptolemy entered the temple in Jerusalem.

75. See especially J. K. Elliott, "Paul's Teaching on Marriage in 1 Corinthians: Some Problems Considered," *NTS* 19 (1973): 219–25.

76. Bauer, p. 483.

28. But even if you should marry, you have not sinned. And if a virgin should marry, she has not sinned. Yet such people will have great affliction in this life, and I would like to spare you this trouble.

a. *Marriage.* In the first part of this verse, Paul is not interested in discussing the moral dimension of marriage. To him, lawful marriage is not sin. Already he has made it known that if unmarried people cannot contain themselves, "let them marry" (v. 9). His counsel now pertains to the advisability of wedlock in the given circumstances. He is saying that if a man has entered the state of matrimony, he has not sinned. Similarly, if a virgin has pledged vows to her husband, she has not sinned, because her conduct is in harmony with the institution of marriage (Gen. 2:24). Paul addresses the problem of the day (namely, hardship for the Christian) and not the matter of sin.[77] He assures the Corinthians that when men or women disregard his advice concerning marriage, they have not sinned at all. They are blameless, yet they face serious difficulties.

b. *Affliction.* "Yet such people will have great affliction in this life." Paul resorts to the use of the plural to refer to a group of people who have married or are contemplating marriage. The term *affliction* is a vague expression, which in some translations occurs in the plural as "troubles."[78] Interpreters have difficulties giving an adequate explanation of this term.[79] If the word refers to a famine that is plaguing the land, it is synonymous with "the present crisis" (v. 26). Also, the literal translation, "affliction in the flesh," instead of the free version, "affliction in this life," strengthens the view that Greece experienced a famine.

c. *Wish.* "I would like to spare you this trouble." Paul becomes intimate when he addresses his readers with the personal pronoun *I.* As a pastor, he expresses the wish that he would be able to shield them from trouble. He is not against matrimony, but in the present situation he discourages marriage to spare people impending problems.

Additional Note on 7:25–28

In the second half of this chapter, Paul mentions the Greek word *parthenos* (virgin[s]) seven times (vv. 25, 28, 34 [twice], 36, 37, 38). Ascertaining the meaning of this term, however, has caused considerable debate. Here are several interpretations:

a. *Men and women.* Virgins are couples who are engaged to be married. Thus the term includes both men and women (v. 25); it also refers to a bachelor who has a marital duty to his fiancée (vv. 36–38).[80] But the context denotes female virgins, and the word does not apply to males.

---

77. Consult Lenski, *First Corinthians,* pp. 314–15.

78. RSV, SEB, GNB, JB; but REB and NJB have "hardships."

79. For instance, Grosheide thinks of pregnant women and mothers who nurse babies (Matt. 24:19). See *First Epistle to the Corinthians,* p. 177. Calvin understands the word to mean "responsibilities and difficulties" that married people face. *I Corinthians,* p. 158.

80. See Hans Conzelmann, *1 Corinthians: A Commentary on the First Epistle to the Corinthians,* ed. George W. MacRae, trans. James W. Leitch, Hermeneia: A Critical and Historical Commentary on the Bible (Philadelphia: Fortress, 1975), p. 132 n. 8.

b. *Spiritual marriage.* Virgins are couples in the Corinthian church who have decided to practice asceticism. They have a spiritual engagement that has the advantages of marriage without marital intercourse.[81] But Paul tells the Corinthians not to deprive one another of marital intimacy (v. 5).

c. *Levirate marriage.* Virgins are young widows. When a Jewish husband died, his bachelor brother was obliged to marry the young widow (Deut. 25:5–6; Matt. 22:24).[82] Although the congregation in Corinth had a number of Jewish converts, many members were Gentile Christians who were unacquainted with this Levirate practice. Further, a widow is no longer a virgin.

d. *Male celibates.* Virgins are young men who have never married. Some scholars aver that the term *virgin(s)* should be applied not to women but to men. To support this interpretation they point to the Greek text of Revelation 14:4, where the term appears with reference to men.[83] The objection to this view is that Paul in verse 28a addresses the man and in verse 28b the woman, whom he calls "*the* virgin."

e. *Marriageable virgins.* Virgins are young women who have never married. From some Corinthian believers, Paul received a question whether virgins should contemplate matrimony in respect to the pressing time in which they lived. He gives his personal advice to female virgins and their suitors and leaves the distinct impression that the term *virgin(s)* applies to young women who have not yet married. I prefer this interpretation.

Greek Words, Phrases, and Constructions in 7:25–28

Verse 25

ὡς ἠλεημένος—the particle ὡς means "as one who," which with the perfect passive participle has a causative connotation.[84] From the verb ἐλεέω (I have mercy, pity), the perfect tense of the participle reveals an act in the past that has significance for the present. The use of the passive indicates that God has shown mercy to Paul.

πιστὸς εἶναι—the infinitive is epexegetical, that is, it explains the preceding perfect participle and therefore means "pitied . . . enough to be trustworthy."[85]

Verse 26

τοῦτο καλὸν ὑπάρχειν—the two clauses of this verse disclose a repetition. Most versions, therefore, omit this phrase and translate the last part of the verse, καλὸν ἀνθρώπῳ τὸ οὕτως εἶναι, "it is good for a man to be as he is."

Verse 27

μὴ ζήτει—the present imperative conveys the prohibition: "stop seeking." Parallelism occurs in both sentences. The perfect tenses of δέδεσαι (from δέω, I bind) and λέλυσαι

---

81. Hurd, *Origin of I Corinthians*, pp. 177–80.

82. J. M. Ford, "Levirate Marriage in St. Paul: 1 Cor. 7," *NTS* 10 (1964): 362; James B. Hurley, "Man and Woman in 1 Corinthians," Ph.D. diss., Cambridge University, 1973, p. 194.

83. Matthew Black, *The Scrolls and Christian Origins: Studies in the Jewish Background of the New Testament* (New York: Nelson, 1961), p. 85; James F. Bound, "Who Are the 'Virgins' Discussed in 1 Corinthians 7:25–38?" *EvJ* 2 (1984): 3–15.

84. Robertson, *Grammar*, p. 1128; Blass and Debrunner, *Greek Grammar*, #425.3.

85. Moule, *Idiom-Book*, p. 127.

(from λύω, I loose) express an interrogative in their respective clauses. The response to these questions is expressed in two prohibitions.

Verse 28

ἐὰν δὲ καί—"if even." The particle ἐάν in both conditional sentences introduces verbs in the subjunctive γαμήσῃς (you marry) and γήμῃ (she marries). The verb forms are synonyms and identical in meaning. The first verb is in the second person singular because Paul, following the custom of that day, addresses the male. The second verb is in the third person singular and has the noun *virgin* as its subject. This noun παρθένος is preceded by the definite article ἡ to indicate the category of virgins. Three uncial manuscripts (codices B, F, and G) and one minuscule witness (429) delete the definite article.

---

b. Hardships
7:29–31

After imparting his advice to virgins and engaged couples, Paul envisions the hardships that the believers in Corinth must endure. Perhaps inadvertently, he drifts from his objective to write about marriage and ponders the immediate future. Yet he fails to state a precise eschatological perspective on the consummation of the world. He is not now interested in this subject.

29. I say this, brothers, the time is shortened, so that from now on even those who have wives should be as though they had no wives. 30. And those who weep, let them be as though they did not weep, and those who rejoice, let them be as though they did not rejoice, and those who buy as though they did not possess. 31. And those who use the world as though they did not fully use it. For this world in its present form is passing away.

a. "I say this, brothers, the time is shortened." Notice that this first part of verse 29 and the last sentence in verse 31 convey a message on the brevity of time. Between these two statements on the fleeting nature of this age, Paul places a few poetic lines. He wishes to direct the church's attention to the changing configuration of this world in which time is compressed. He wants them to realize the temporality of this age, the rapidity of events, and the brevity of life.

Paul speaks pastorally by personally addressing not only those who are married, but all the members of the Corinthian church. With the first person pronoun *I*, he addresses his readers and calls them "brothers" (including sisters) in the manner of that day. And the term *say* means solemn declaration instead of common speech.[86] The word *this* points forward and refers to Paul's time and world perspective, and backward to marriage. The phrase *the time is shortened* is intriguing because Paul is not talking about calendar time but about the era that encompasses the time in which he lives (see Matt. 24:22). Within this season, numerous events are compressed, especially those that pertain to the coming of God's kingdom through the proclamation of the gospel. Paul is telling the Corinthians to reject a

---

86. In the New Testament, the first person singular φημί (I say) occurs only in I Cor. 7:29; 10:15, 19; 15:50.

Gentile perspective on time and to adopt the view that God's kingdom has invaded this world and is transforming it (compare Matt. 11:12). For this reason, believers should have a broad outlook on life and focus on eternal essentials.

Hence, Paul instructs the Corinthians to view marriage, sorrow, joy, possessions, business, and service in the light of the new era which the Christian faith has inaugurated. Because of this faith, events are compressed and rapidly follow each other. Christians should understand that as the present form of this world passes away (v. 31), the coming of God's kingdom continues and touches all aspects of human life.[87]

b. "So that from now on even those who have wives should be as though they had no wives." Notice that Paul writes poetic lines that describe human life. We understand these lines as a composition of the apostle and not as a quotation from someone else (II Esd. 16:42–45).[88] Consider the rhythm of the poetry in its five parts with the recurring phrase italicized:

those who have wives

let them be as though

they had no wives,

and those who weep

let them be as though

they did not weep,

and those who rejoice

let them be as though

they did not rejoice,

and those who buy

let them be as though

they did not possess,

and those using the world

let them be as though

they used it not.

Paul introduces these lines of poetry with the phrase *so that from now on*. The words translated temporally as "from now on" can also mean inferentially "therefore."[89] However, the temporal use suits the context better than the inferential use, because the believers have entered a new epoch in their lives. As Christians they view the world in which they live and move from an eternal perspective (compare Acts 17:28).

---

87. Ridderbos, *Paul*, p. 312.

88. Romano Penna sees a possible parallel in Diogenes Laertius *Lives* 6.29. "San Paolo (1 Cor 7,29b–31a) e Diogene il Cinico," *Bib* 58 (1977): 237–45. Consult Wolfgang Schrade, "Die Stellung zur Welt bei Paulus, Epiktet und der Apokalyptik. Ein Beitrag zu 1 Kor 7, 29–31," *ZTK* 61 (1964): 125–54. And see Gottfried Hierzenberger, *Weltbewertung bei Paulus nach 1 Kor 7, 29–31* (Düsseldorf: Patmos, 1966), p. 30.

89. Bauer, p. 480.

What does Paul mean when he writes, "those who have wives should be as though they had no wives"? He certainly is not advocating celibacy, separation, or divorce. He does imply that Christians confine marriage to the present age.[90] In the age to come no one will be married, for everyone will be like the angels in heaven (Matt. 22:30). God himself instituted marriage at the dawn of human history; therefore, marriage does not lose its significance in the present age.

But how do we interpret the phrase *let them be as though*? In all the parts of Paul's poetic composition (wedlock, sorrow, joy, wealth, goods, and service), "we ought to be living as if we might have to leave this world at any moment."[91] That is, we should not make earthly things our ultimate objectives. Whether we are married, cast into sorrow, given to joy, or acquire possessions, Christians should not become absorbed by them. They should see the transient nature of these things and know that after having passed through this earthly vale, believers will enter eternity. In this life, then, they ought to prepare themselves for the life after death.

A Christian lives a life that in some sense is contradictory. As Paul puts it, he is sorrowful, yet he continues to rejoice; he is poor, but he makes many people rich; he has nothing, nevertheless he possesses everything (II Cor. 6:10).

c. "And those who use the world as though they did not fully use it." The last line of this poetic section appears to repeat the preceding part that pertains to buying and acquiring things. But Jesus' teaching on the stewardship of earthly possessions reverberates in this last line. Jesus taught his followers not to set their hearts on these things (Luke 6:29b–30). Jesus' followers may use the goods of this world, but they should not become engrossed in them (NIV) or misuse them (NKJV).

> Let goods and kindred go,
> This mortal life also;
> The body they may kill,
> God's truth abideth still,
> His kingdom is forever.
> —Martin Luther

d. "For this world in its present form is passing away." Paul has come full circle with his reference to the shortened time in which Christians live. He concludes his poetic contribution with a definitive declaration: this world is passing away. The world is God's creation but because of sin it is subjected to frustration and groaning (Rom. 8:20–22). For that reason, Paul writes, the present form of the world is disappearing. The expression *present form* refers to the "distinctive manifestation (or form)" of this world,[92] which one may aptly compare

---

90. Refer to Grosheide, *First Epistle to the Corinthians,* p. 177.

91. Calvin, *I Corinthians,* p. 160.

92. Johannes Schneider, *TDNT,* vol. 7, p. 958. The term occurs twice in the New Testament (I Cor. 7:31; Phil. 2:7).

with changing acts and characters in theater or film. The world itself will remain until the last day. But its appearance, because of the seasons in nature or the gradual changes in the configuration of the earth, is subject to constant change.

Acquainted with Paul's epistle, the apostle John writes almost the same words in one of his epistles. Says he, "The world and its desires pass away" (I John 2:17a). Paul means the same thing when he refers to the everyday world in which a person lives. It is the world of marrying and mourning, of exulting, expanding, and expending. And that world, says Paul, has no enduring form. Consequently, the Christian should not set his heart on that which is fleeting but on that which is lasting and eternal.

Practical Considerations in 7:29–31

Society today is characterized by instability, especially with respect to family life. Undermined by marital unfaithfulness, desertion, and divorce, family life deteriorates and in numerous cases is nonexistent. The spread of disease, famine, and poverty in large areas of the world causes untold misery, grief, and death. Bankruptcies of individuals, companies, cities, provinces or states, and even countries are commonplace. And the obsession to own, use, and abuse the world's goods or environment is thoroughly distressing.

Christ's followers are in this world, even though they are not of this world (John 17:14, 16). They are laughed to scorn when they recommend chastity to prevent immorality (Eph. 5:3–5); integrity in the workplace, store, or business to prevent greed (Prov. 11:1); and contentment with basic food and clothing to prevent envy (I Tim. 6:6).

Christians belong to the world to come and therefore are fully aware of the temporality of this earthly existence. They know that their citizenship is in heaven (Phil. 3:20) and for this reason put their trust in their eternal God. They do not live detached from this present world, but they seek to live within it in harmony with all God's commandments. To illustrate, they apply genuine love in their marriage relationship (I Cor. 13:5); they abhor exploiting their fellow man or the environment in which they live; they truly rejoice with those who rejoice, and they truly weep with those who weep (Rom. 12:15).[93]

Greek Words, Phrases, and Constructions in 7:29–31

Verse 29

συνεσταλμένος ἐστίν—the periphrastic construction consists of the perfect passive participle from συστέλλω (I shorten) and the verb *to be*. The perfect tense expresses lasting duration.

τὸ λοιπόν—this term means "finally," that is, "from now on."

ἵνα . . . ὦσιν—the present subjunctive functions as an imperative instead of the verb in a purpose clause: "let them live." The particle ὡς suggests a concessive notion, "as though."

---

93. Refer to Darrell J. Doughty, "The Presence and Future of Salvation in Corinth," *ZNW* 66 (1975): 61–90.

Verse 31

χρώμενοι . . . καταχρώμενοι—the first word is a simple and the second a compound participle from the verb χράομαι (I use). The compound participle is perfective and means "use fully." Yet because it occurs only twice in the New Testament (7:31; 9:18), there is uncertainty whether the simple and the compound forms differ at all in meaning.[94]

---

c. Marriage and Service
7:32–35

After a brief excursus in which Paul demonstrates his pastoral concern for the entire Corinthian church, he returns to the topic at hand. Once more he devotes himself to discussing the matter of marriage and celibacy, especially in connection with serving the Lord.

32. I want you to be free from anxiety. The unmarried man cares for the things belonging to the Lord, how he may please the Lord.

a. "I want you to be free from anxiety." Notice that Paul speaks to all the members of the Corinthian church by addressing them as "you" (plural). He begins and ends verses 32–35 with this personal pronoun to indicate that he addresses the entire congregation (see the commentary on v. 35).

A literal translation of the last part of the first sentence is to be "carefree," but this word conveys a negative connotation of irresponsibility. However, if we take the word in a positive sense, "free from all worries," then we understand Paul's intention (compare Matt. 6:25–34; Phil. 4:11; I Peter 5:7). This sentence, then, flows forth from the preceding section in which Paul teaches the Christians to implement the concept *let them be as though* and live in the freedom which the Lord provides.[95] This holds true for both the married and those who are single. They must leave their worries with the Lord.

b. "The unmarried man cares for the things belonging to the Lord, how he may please the Lord." Significant is Paul's purpose for placing the unmarried man before the married person. He links the sentence about the single man with his cares for the Lord to the preceding line, "I want you to be free from anxiety." Thus, he avoids placing the married man in a position that is inferior to the single person (see the commentary on v. 34a). We would have expected Paul to discuss the married man's worries first, but instead he talks about the person who is not married. He says that the unmarried man, free from worry, cares for the things pertaining to God's church.

The verb *care for* occurs five times in I Corinthians and twice in Philippians.[96] In the passages that appear outside the current chapter, Paul understands this verb positively. On that basis, we assume that Paul has in mind the positive interpretation of the verb in question.

---

94. Bauer, p. 420.
95. Jürgen Goetzmann, *NIDNTT*, vol. 1, p. 278. See also Fee, *First Corinthians*, p. 343.
96. I Cor. 7:32, 33, 34 [twice]; 12:25; Phil. 2:20; 4:6.

With the freedom Christ gives him, the unmarried man takes a positive interest in the things of the Lord. Whether he works in evangelism, missions, a pastorate, or any other place where the Lord has put him, he shows diligence and care to promote Christ's cause. He does so out of a genuine desire to please the Lord (compare I Thess. 4:1).

33. But the married man cares for the things of this world, how he may please his wife, 34a. and his interests are divided.

After mentioning the concerns of the single man, Paul next discusses those of the married man. Both the single and the married man enjoy the same freedom that Christ provides, so that the one is not inferior to the other. In fact, Paul speaks no words of disapproval concerning the married status of a worker in the church. He only remarks that the single worker has more time to devote to the cause of Christ than the other.

I take the word *to care* in a positive sense, so that there is no hint of disparagement. I understand Paul to say that the married man has a double duty, namely, to take care of the needs of his wife and children and to devote his time to work in the church. Elsewhere Paul writes, "If anyone does not provide for his relatives, and especially for his immediate family, he has denied the faith and is worse than an unbeliever" (I Tim. 5:8). Taking care of one's family is a valid and necessary concern, but it does limit the time a person can spend working for the Lord. Consequently, Paul observes, the interests of the married person are divided. Yet he does not utter any regretful disapproval of the married state; a man should please his wife. For Paul, marriage is not wrong or sinful. Gordon D. Fee pointedly concludes, "Different, yes; more involved in the present world, yes; but inferior or sinful, no."[97] Paul places both the single and the married man on the same level and views them as equal workers in the church.

34b. Also the woman who is unmarried or the virgin cares for the things of the Lord, that she may be holy in both body and spirit. But the woman who is married cares for the things of the world, how she may please her husband.

a. *Textual problem.* The differences in translating the first part of this verse become plain when we look at representative versions:

"There is a difference between a wife and a virgin. The unmarried woman cares about the things of the Lord." (NKJV; see also *Cassirer*)
"and his interests are divided. An unmarried woman or virgin is concerned about the Lord's affairs." (NIV)
"So, too, the unmarried woman, and the virgin, gives her mind to the Lord's affairs." (NJB)

Note that in the first example the Greek verb in the first sentence is translated "there is a difference." In the second, the Greek verb is translated "divided" and the clause is put with the preceding verse (v. 33). And the third example (NJB)

---

97. Fee, *First Corinthians*, p. 345.

places this clause, "and he is divided in mind," in verse 33. Note also that the third example has the added word *too* at the beginning of the sentence and has the word *and* instead of *or* between the terms *woman* and *virgin*. Last, this example unveils an incorrect grammatical structure of a compound subject (the unmarried woman and the virgin) followed by a verb in the singular.

Obviously, the Greek text of verse 34 has many variations. Editors of the Greek editions of the New Testament list them and agree on adopting one particular reading that represents the widest possible geographical area.[98] This is reflected in the reading of those Greek witnesses that extend from east to west (see the second example, NIV).

b. *Evaluation.* How do we evaluate the textual differences on which translations are based? In favor of the first example (NKJV) is that this translation maintains the balance of verses 33 and 34. Paul compares the cares of the unmarried man with those of the married man (v. 33), and he contrasts the cares of the married and the unmarried woman (v. 34).

However, the word *and* preceding the verb *is divided* in the second example (NIV) has strong textual support for being the original reading. The translators of the first example (NKJV) follow a Greek reading that deletes this conjunction. If it were added, the conjunction would impede a smooth translation of verse 34. But if we accept it as original, then the clause *and he is divided* belongs to verse 33. Next, the Greek verb *memeristai* means "is divided" in the passive voice. This verb is never used to indicate "a difference" (NKJV),[99] and it should not be translated in the active voice. And last, the first example rearranges the word order to make the expression *the unmarried woman* subject of the verb *to care* in the second sentence.

In the second example, the translators have conveniently interpreted the conjunction *and* between "unmarried woman" and "virgin" as *or*, and omit the term *too*. The third example does not do this; as a result it renders an exact translation, albeit with a compound subject that is followed by a verb in the singular. Although the textual variations in this verse are plenty, the translations featured in both the second and third examples have merit and are preferred to the first.

c. *Interpretation.* "Also the woman who is unmarried or the virgin cares for the things of the Lord." We have no certainty whether Paul writes the expression *virgin* as an explanation of the phrase *the woman who is unmarried*. Then the word which we have translated as "or" actually means "that is." Conversely, Paul may have had in mind widows, separated or divorced women, or single women.[100] Furthermore, a virgin is a person who, though single, is possibly betrothed. Hence, a comprehensive interpretation of the word *virgin* is preferred. Because

98. UBS, Nes-Al, BF, Merk. Bruce M. Metzger (*Textual Commentary*, p. 555) writes that "the least unsatisfactory reading is that supported by early representatives of the Alexandrian and the Western types of text (P[15] B 104 vg cop[sa,bo])."

99. Bauer, p. 504.

100. Refer to C. K. Barrett, *A Commentary on the First Epistle to the Corinthians*, Harper's New Testament Commentaries series (New York and Evanston: Harper and Row, 1968), p. 180.

Paul supplies no additional information, we are unable to ascertain the exact meaning of the terms in question.

What is significant is the fact that an unmarried woman is able to give herself fully to the work of the Lord (compare Rom. 16:12; Phil. 4:2–3). If she is not being courted with a view to marriage, she is completely free to devote her life to the Lord's service.

"That she may be holy in both body and spirit." Paul ascribes holiness to the entire person, to the body that is not burdened by marital and maternal duties and to the spirit which is dominated by the Holy Spirit.[101] Mind and body filled with the Spirit reflect God's holiness. This is not to say that the unmarried woman who dedicates her life to spiritual service is holier than her married sister who loves her husband and with him raises a family. Not at all. The single woman consecrates herself to the Lord because she is unrestricted in doing so.

"But the woman who is married cares for the things of the world, how she may please her husband." Here is the counterpart to Paul's comment that the married man cares for his wife (v. 33). The word *world,* here and in the previous verse, relates to the mundane cares of an ordinary household. The wife devotes herself to the care of husband and children as to the Lord (Eph. 5:22) and establishes a Christian home. As Paul stated earlier (v. 14), the holiness of the believing wife permeates her family so that even her unbelieving husband is sanctified and her children are holy.

35. I say this for your own benefit, not to restrain you but to promote decorum and devotion to the Lord without distraction.

With this verse, Paul once more shows his pastoral interest in the spiritual welfare of the people of the Corinthian community. Now he addresses all his readers, both married and unmarried, with the plural pronoun *you* (see v. 32a). Paul is concerned with the spiritual and physical welfare of all the believers in Corinth. He speaks pastorally with the first personal pronoun *I* (see, e.g., vv. 25, 29, 32) and enters the privacy of their lives only for the purpose of advancing their own interests.

In Greek, the phrase *not to restrain you* actually means "I do not put a noose on you." The expression *noose* occurs only here in the entire New Testament.[102] The phrase is derived from either war or hunting and should be understood figuratively. Paul has no desire to put the Corinthians on a leash, so to speak.

Paul has already alluded several times to the institution of marriage (see vv. 3, 5, 9) and endorses wedlock as a state ordained by God (6:16). For those who have received the gift of continence, Paul advocates a life of full-time service that is characterized by discipline and devotion to the Lord. The word which I have translated *decorum* signifies in the Greek "good order," that is, an appropriate,

---

101. Donald Guthrie, *New Testament Theology* (Downers Grove: Inter-Varsity, 1981), p. 167. Consult Margaret Y. MacDonald, "Women Holy in Body and Spirit: the Social Setting of 1 Corinthians 7," *NTS* 36 (1990): 161–81.

102. Bauer, p. 147; Thayer, p. 106.

pleasing, and attractive life. This life must depict devotion (steadfastness) to the Lord's work and, last, it must be "without distraction."[103]

Is Paul elevating the life of the unmarried above that of those who are married? Really not. In this concluding verse he says nothing about the marital status of the readers, for he addresses everybody in the Corinthian church. He is asking all the readers to serve the Lord wholeheartedly and, by implication, to permit nothing to separate them from the love of God in Christ Jesus (Rom. 8:39). He indicates that he respects the freedom of the individual Christian. Writes Calvin, "No restraint ought to be put on people's consciences, with the result that someone may be kept back from marriage."[104] In short, the Lord uses both the married and the unmarried for the advancement of his church, but all must be fully dedicated to him.

Greek Words, Phrases, and Constructions in 7:32–35

Verses 32–33

ἀμερίμνους—this compound adjective from the privative ἀ (not) and the verb μεριμνάω (I care for, am concerned) means without care, in a positive sense. The negative sense would convey the meaning *irresponsible*. The verb μεριμνᾷ in both verses should be interpreted positively.

Verse 34

καὶ μεμέρισται. καί—"and he is divided. Also . . ." The first two words form the concluding part of the previous verse (v. 33). Then the subject of the verb μεριμνᾷ (she cares) is the noun ἡ γυνή, which is corroborated by the noun ἡ παρθένος (the virgin). This reading has the strong textual support of numerous major witnesses with only the slight variation of repeating the words ὁ ἄγαμος (the unmarried). In view of manuscript support, translators favor this reading.

Verse 35

πρὸς τὸ εὔσχημον—the preposition is followed by the definite article and the compound adjective εὔσχημον, which lacks the noun *part*. The compound adjective derives from εὖ (well) and σχῆμα (behavior, deportment) and signifies "seemly" (see 12:24).

εὐπάρεδρον—from the adverb εὖ and the verb παρεδρεύω (I sit beside, attend constantly), this compound adjective connotes devotion but, as an adjective, should be translated "constant."[105] It appears once in the New Testament.

ἀπερισπάστως—an adverb that occurs once in Scripture means "without distraction." The compound stems from the privative ἀ (without) and the verb περισπάω (I am distracted).

---

103. Consult David L. Balch, "1 Cor 7:32–35 and Stoic Debates about Marriage, Anxiety, and Distraction," *JBL* 102 (1983): 429–39.

104. Calvin, *I Corinthians*, p. 164. Consult O. Larry Yarbrough, *Not Like the Gentiles: Marriage Rules in the Letters of Paul*, SBL Dissertation Series 80 (Atlanta: Scholars, 1985), p. 110.

105. Blass and Debrunner, *Greek Grammar*, #117.1.

d. Engagement and Marriage
7:36–38

Once again Paul mentions virgins in connection with marriage. He explicitly states that persons who decide to get married do not sin. Because of his gift of continence, Paul is recommending celibacy for those who also have received this gift. Others should marry, and by doing so they do not sin.

36. But if someone thinks that he is behaving dishonorably toward his marriageable virgin—if his passions are strong and it must be so—let him do as he wishes; he does not sin. Let them marry.

These verses lack clarity of expression and thus are open to a number of interpretations. For instance, who is the person described as "someone" (v. 36)? Is he the fiancé of the virgin or is he her father? If he is the father, why does Paul say "let them marry" when the fiancé has not been introduced? If we assume that Paul refers to the fiancé, why does he write, "he has decided to keep his own virgin" (v. 37)? Should the translation of verse 38 be "he who marries the virgin" (NIV) or "he who her gives in marriage" (NKJV)? And finally, do we interpret this passage from an ancient oriental point of view in which the father made the marriage arrangements for his daughter? Or do we explain the matter of engagements and marriage on the basis of today's customs? Let us study the verses of this passage line by line.

a. "But if someone thinks that he is behaving dishonorably toward his marriageable virgin." Presumably Paul has been asked to give advice in the matter that concerns a virgin of marriageable age. He begins with a conditional clause that expresses reality and continues with the word *someone*. This term must refer to a man who possesses a virgin, possibly his fiancée. The man is "behaving dishonorably" toward the unmarried woman and acting contrary to what Paul urges every believer in Corinth to do: to promote decorum (v. 35). In light of the usage of the Greek, the term *behave dishonorably* may be a euphemism for sexually indecent acts.[106] Paul advocates marriage when people, particularly those who are engaged to be married, are unable to control themselves (v. 9).

b. "If his passions are strong and it must be so." The subject of the preceding conditional clause is a man whose moral conduct has become questionable. For that reason, we maintain the same subject in this conditional clause. The intimate nature of the matter at hand causes Paul to express probability with the conditional particle *if*. In Greek, the term *hyperakmos* can mean either "past marriageable age" (with reference to the woman) or "with strong passions" (referring to the man).[107] We choose the latter. Paul adds, "and it must be so," which probably means that his sexual drive controls the man and compels him to marry.

---

106. E.g., the Greek adjective ἀσχήμονα refers to "unpresentable [private] parts" (12:23). And the noun ἀσχημοσύνη signifies indecent homosexual acts (Rom. 1:27; compare Rev. 16:15).

107. Bauer notes that when the word applies to a man, "ὑπέρ is not to be understood in the temporal sense, but expresses intensification" (p. 839). Parry, however, notes that the word "would not describe excess but rather the fading of passion." *First Epistle to the Corinthians*, p. 121.

c. "Let him do as he wishes; he does not sin. Let them marry." Earlier Paul gives the same advice: "let them marry" (v. 9) and "if you should marry, you have not sinned" (v. 28). The subject is the fiancé and his betrothed virgin for whom Paul advises wedlock.

37. But he who stands firm in his own heart and is under no necessity but has his desire under control and has decided in his own heart to keep his own virgin, he will do well.

a. "But he who stands firm in his own heart and is under no necessity but has his desire under control." Now Paul discusses the case of the man who has chosen not to marry because of financial or social pressures. This man has the inner strength to keep his desires in check and thus is like Paul, who has the gift of continence (v. 7). Other translations have the reading *control over his own will* (e.g., NIV). The Greek word *thelema* has both an objective meaning ("what one wishes to happen") and a subjective connotation ("the act of willing or desiring").[108] Here the subjective interpretation that refers to sexual desire fits the context well and is preferred (compare John 1:13).

b. "And has decided in his own heart to keep his own virgin, he will do well." First, Paul reiterates what he said in the beginning of this verse and adds, "he has decided." The man has weighed all the factors available and has arrived at a firm conclusion not to marry. Next, Paul says that this man has determined "to keep his own virgin." But what does he intend to convey with this statement? Matthew relates that Joseph, who was engaged to Mary, "had no union with her until she gave birth to a son" (Matt. 1:25). Jewish engagements were the same as marriages and ought not to be broken. According to Jewish law, a man was required to support his virgin for a year in case the engagement was dissolved.[109] The problem, however, is that the Corinthian church was not exclusively Jewish; we are not sure whether the Jewish law was enacted in Corinth. Paul commends the man who respects the virginity of his betrothed and during the present crisis (v. 26) delays wedlock.

38. So then he who marries his bride-to-be does well but he who does not marry her does better.

We hear the echo of Paul's earlier statement (vv. 8–9) in which he praises marriage and exalts celibacy. And celibacy must always be understood in connection with the special gift of continence. It is not for everyone.

Verse 38, which twice features the Greek verb *gamizō* (I give in marriage), is the cause for alternative interpretations of this section (vv. 36–38). *Gamizō* occurs with the Greek verb *gameō* (I marry) in the familiar saying, "marry and give in marriage."[110] Paul writes the verb *gameō* in verse 36 and the verb *gamizō* in verse

---

108. Bauer, p. 354.
109. Werner Georg Kümmel, "Verlobung und Heirat bei Paulus (1 Kor 7:36–38)," *ZNW* 21 (1954): 275–95; Samuel Belkin, "The Problem of Paul's Background," *JBL* 54 (1935): 49–52.
110. Matt. 22:30; 24:38; Mark 12:25; Luke 17:27; 20:35.

38. The question is whether these two verbs always differ in meaning or are at times synonymous.

Scholars state that in apostolic times the clear distinctions of classical Greek had faded, with the result that the two verbs carried the same meaning.[111] If this were not the case, the verb *gamizo* should be interpreted to mean that a father gives his daughter in marriage. The passage presents too many difficulties, however, for this interpretation. The subject of the entire passage appears to be not the father of the bride but the man who contemplates or postpones marriage. Therefore, modern translators understand the two Greek verbs as synonyms that denote "to marry."[112] Colin Brown characterizes the modern trend when he writes, "This interpretation involves no change of subject in v[erse] 36, and offers a thoroughly realistic assessment of the situation."[113] The drawback to this interpretation, however, lies in our desire to make the passage relevant to the times and culture in which we live. And this differs from the apostolic age and the culture of Corinth in which the parents were involved in the decision-making process.

Additional Note on 7:36–38

The problem of translating this passage has given rise to major divergences in interpretation. Three possibilities can be listed: father-daughter; spiritual marriage; and the engaged couple.

a. *Father-daughter.* This is the traditional explanation that still is proposed today.[114] To elucidate the word *virgin* (vv. 36, 38), translators supply the word *daughter* (NASB, NIV margin). But the subject of "let them marry" (v. 36) becomes difficult to explain when only father and daughter are mentioned. The problem can be alleviated by either accepting a variant reading, "let her marry," or stating that the plural is elliptic and means "let the daughter and her suitor marry."[115] However, in verse 36 Paul has not yet said anything about a betrothal. With respect to the present crisis (v. 26), the great affliction for married people (v. 28), and the brevity of time (v. 29), we would expect fathers to advise their unmarried daughters not to marry. And such advice would not constitute dishonorable behavior for the fathers.

Next, if Paul wished to convey the father-daughter concept, he would not need to stress that the father had determined "to keep his *own* virgin." No other virgins are mentioned in this passage.

Last, the verb *gamizō* has a causative connotation meaning: "I cause to marry." But it is questionable whether this verb is always causative. Why would a father be concerned

---

111. Consult James Hope Moulton and Wilbert Francis Howard, *A Grammar of New Testament Greek,* vol. 2, *Accidence and Word-Formation* (Edinburgh: Clark, 1929), p. 410. See also MM, p. 121.

112. Consult GNB, MLB, NAB, NIV, NCV, NRSV, REB, NJB, SEB, TNT.

113. Colin Brown, *NIDNTT,* vol. 2, p. 588.

114. Consult JB, NKJV, NASB, *Cassirer;* see also Morris, *First Epistle to the Corinthians,* pp. 116–19.

115. Archibald Robertson and Alfred Plummer, *A Critical and Exegetical Commentary on the First Epistle of St. Paul to the Corinthians,* International Critical Commentary, 2d ed. (1911; reprint ed., Edinburgh: Clark, 1975), p. 159.

about giving his virgin daughter in marriage if she is past marriageable age? That would be futile indeed. John C. Hurd, Jr., astutely observes that "the causative translation of *gamizo* would never have been questioned" if the entire passage had been free from difficulties.[116]

b. *Spiritual marriage.* A number of scholars think that a young man takes a young woman under his care and lives with her in spiritual harmony, but without physical union.[117] In case the young man has difficulty controlling himself, Paul advises him to enter a normal marriage relationship. But if the young man has the gift of continence and does not marry his virgin, he is making the better choice, says Paul.

This interpretation is based on practices at a later stage in the history of the church. There is no evidence of this practice in the middle of the first century, and this factor considerably weakens the view that the passage refers to spiritual marriage. Also, the passage itself (vv. 36–38) provides no hint at all that Paul is thinking of a spiritual marriage.[118] And last, even if the young man controls his desires, his virgin may not be able to do so, and then he is going contrary to Paul's earlier advice (see v. 9). Paul's descriptive language concerning marital duties of both the husband and the wife (vv. 2–5) must be heeded when we examine the spiritual marriage view.

c. *The engaged couple.* A young man is engaged to a young woman; because of social conditions they have decided as yet not to marry. But the physical pressures are becoming too great for the young man. Now Paul counsels the man to seek marriage as a solution to the dilemma he and his virgin are facing. Paul assures the man that in doing so he is not sinning. If the person is able to control himself and decides to postpone marriage, Paul approves of this decision.

Of the three interpretations, I favor the last one. Nevertheless, difficulties surround the third explanation, because we tend to interpret the text within our own culture and times. In respect to the numerous uncertainties that encompass this particular passage, we do well not to be dogmatic.

Greek Words, Phrases, and Constructions in 7:36–38

Verse 36

εἰ δέ τις . . . νομίζει—the particle εἰ followed by the verb in the indicative appears to show that Paul is familiar with the situation: "if someone thinks."

ἐὰν ᾖ—within the conditional sentence Paul places a second condition, but now he writes the particle ἐάν followed by the subjunctive ᾖ of the verb *to be*. The subject is the same as the preceding clause: "someone."

Verses 37–38

ἑαυτοῦ—the reflexive pronoun has lost its force and is the same as αὐτοῦ (his own).

---

116. Hurd, *Origin of I Corinthians*, p. 174. Consult David E. Garland, "The Christian's Posture; Toward Marriage and Celibacy: 1 Corinthians 7," *RevExp* 80 (1983): 351–62.

117. See, e.g., Clarence T. Craig, *The First Epistle to the Corinthians*, vol. 10 in *The Interpreter's Bible* (New York: Abingdon, 1953), p. 88; Jerome Murphy-O'Connor, *1 Corinthians*, New Testament Message series (Wilmington, Del.: Glazier, 1979), p. 75.

118. Roland H. A. Seboldt, "Spiritual Marriage in the Early Church: A Suggested Interpretation of 1 Cor. 7:36–38," *ConcThMonth* 30 (1959): 103–19; 176–89.

ὥστε—here it is an inferential particle that means "and so, accordingly."[119]

---

e. Marriage Vows
7:39–40

Paul has discussed matters of marriage, divorce, separation, virgins, and engagements. But apart from mentioning the word *widows* once (v. 8), he has not said anything about this category of people. Hence, in his concluding remarks on marriage, he devotes two brief verses to the widow.

39. For a woman is bound as long as her husband lives. But if her husband dies, she is free to marry whom she pleases, only in the Lord. 40. She is happier to remain as she is, in my opinion. And I think that I also have the Spirit of God.

a. "For a woman is bound as long as her husband lives."[120] Given in a different setting, the words of this verse nevertheless are similar to those in Romans 7:2. There Paul speaks about the law and says, "By law a married woman is bound to her husband as long as he is alive, but if her husband dies, she is released from the law of marriage." Here Paul states that the marriage bond is valid for the wife while her husband is alive; by implication, the bond is equally valid for the man as long as his wife is living. Commitment to marriage is not for the moment but for life, according to the words of Jesus (see v. 10; Matt. 19:6). Death alone properly sets the spouse free from the marital bond that keeps husband and wife together. Divorce is against the Lord's command, as Paul noted earlier (vv. 10–11). He has no need to repeat himself but instead discusses the possible remarriage of the widow.

b. "But if her husband dies, she is free to marry whom she pleases, only in the Lord." Paul resorts to the use of a euphemism by saying: "if the husband falls asleep."[121] He places no restrictions on the widow at all; in fact, elsewhere he urges the younger widows to marry again (I Tim. 5:14). Yet some widows chose not to marry, as, for instance, the prophetess Anna (Luke 2:36–37). In the second and third centuries, a prominent leader counseled widows against remarriage by calling it adultery.[122] Paul, however, asserts that the widow is free to marry, with only one stipulation: the future husband must be a believer. By adding the stipulation, Paul notes that a Christian has a way of life that is diametrically opposed to that of the unbeliever. In marriage, husband and wife should be one in the Lord.

c. "She is happier to remain as she is, in my opinion." This advice seems to suggest that the unmarried woman is in a happier frame of mind than the one who is married. But when moments of grief, loneliness, and hardship overtake the

---

119. Moule, *Idiom-Book,* p. 144.

120. The Majority Text has the addition *by law* after the verb *bound* (see KJV, NKJV). But the insertion seems to be influenced by the parallel text (Rom. 7:2). Manuscripts that are both early and geographically widespread do not have the addition.

121. Compare in Paul's epistles, I Cor. 11:30; 15:6, 18, 20, 51; I Thess. 4:13–15.

122. E.g., Tertullian; Johannes B. Bauer, "Was las Tertullian 1 Kor 7:39?" *ZNW* 77 (1986): 284–87.

widow, happiness is a fleeting dream. Conversely, a second marriage means entering another man's family, which may cause unforeseen difficulties and prevent a happy life. In Paul's opinion, the widow is well advised to stay as she is. By doing so, she will be more content than if she would marry and encounter trouble. Paul qualifies his statement with the words *in my opinion*. He repeats the wording of an earlier verse (v. 25) where he addressed the virgins. He gives his advice to the widows, but at the same time reveals that in giving his opinion he possesses the Spirit of God.

d. "And I think that I also have the Spirit of God." Paul speaks with apostolic authority, and in his epistles expresses his self-confidence because of the indwelling power of the Holy Spirit. In numerous places throughout his letters, he asserts inner confidence. Because of his poise and self-assurance, he establishes rapport with his readers and earns their respect. They acknowledge his competence and reliability and affirm his authority and credibility.[123] When Paul has a direct command from the Lord, he expects obedience from the believers. But when he offers his own opinion, even though he experiences the power of the Holy Spirit, he refrains from insisting on conformity.[124] Yet his advice is more than a personal opinion. It is backed by the influence of God's Spirit.

Summary of Chapter 7

Paul takes in hand the letter he has received from the Corinthians and quotes a particular line that advocates celibacy. He reacts by saying that because of immorality a man should have a wife and a wife a husband. In marriage, husbands and wives should not deprive each other by neglecting marital intimacy. Couples who wish to devote time to prayer may abstain from sexual activity, but after that period they should resume normal relations.

Those who are unmarried and are widows should remain in their present state, provided they have the gift of continence. If this is not the case, they should marry. With a command of the Lord, Paul speaks against divorce. Even in families where one of the spouses is a believer and the other an unbeliever, the couples should stay together and not contemplate separation. If the unbeliever leaves on his own accord, the wife is no longer bound to her marriage vows but is advised to live in peace.

Everyone should be content with the place in life to which God has called him. Paul makes this a rule for all the churches. He gives the illustrations of circumcision and uncircumcision, slavery and freedom.

Another segment of Paul's discussion on marriage concerns the virgins. He relates singleness and marriage to the present crisis and states that entering marriage is not sinful. He counsels those who marry to expect many troubles because

---

123. Stanley N. Olson, "Epistolary Uses of Expressions of Self-Confidence," *JBL* 103 (1984): 585–97.
124. Guthrie, *New Testament Theology*, p. 769.

the time in which they live is shortened. He observes that the world in the form in which they know it is passing away.

Paul notes that unmarried people have more time to devote to the Lord's service than those who are married and have to provide for the needs of their families. He urges everyone to live for the Lord without distraction. If a man is unable to control himself with regard to his virgin, Paul advises that he marry and declares that the man is not sinning. If a man can control his desire and decides not to marry, he is doing the right thing. Paul concludes his discourse on marriage by referring to marriage vows that are for life and are ended by the death of one of the spouses. He affirms that the widow is free to remarry in the Lord but advises her to stay unmarried and enjoy happiness.

8

Food Offered to Idols

(8:1–13)

Outline (continued)

8 1 Now concerning the food offered to idols, we know that "we all have knowledge." Knowledge puffs up, but love builds up. 2 If someone supposes that he knows something, he does not yet know as he ought to know. 3 But if someone loves God, he is known by God.

4 Concerning the eating of food offered to idols, then, we know that "there is really no such thing as an idol in this world"[1] and that "there is no God except one." 5 For even if there are so-called gods either in heaven or on earth, as indeed there are many gods and many lords, 6 yet,

> for us there is one God the Father,
> from whom all things are and
>   for whom we live,
> and one Lord Jesus Christ,
> through whom all things are and
>   through whom we live.

7 However, not everyone has this knowledge. Because they are accustomed to the idol even now, some people eat food as if offered to idols. And their conscience, being weak, is defiled. 8 "But food will not bring us close to God. We are neither losing anything if we do not eat nor gaining anything if we do eat." 9 But beware that this right of yours not become a hindrance to those who are weak. 10 For if someone sees you who have knowledge dining in an idol's temple, will not the conscience of someone who is weak be emboldened so that he will eat food offered to idols? 11 For the weak brother for whom Christ died is destroyed by your knowledge. 12 Thus you sin against Christ by sinning against your brothers and by wounding their weak conscience. 13 Therefore if food causes my brother to stumble into sin, I will never eat meat again that I may not cause my brother to stumble.

B. Food Offered to Idols
8:1–13

After discussing the ethical question of marriage in the previous chapter, Paul now proceeds to a topic that is both ethical and religious: may a Christian eat meat that had been offered to idols? The matter concerns the domestic and social life of numerous Christian families who have to make decisions whether or not to eat with Gentile friends.

In Paul's day, pagan sacrifices were religious acts that involved the family. Animals brought to the priest were slaughtered and sacrificed to the gods. Certain parts were burned on the altar, other parts were taken by the priest, and the rest of the consecrated meat was returned to the family that had offered the animal as

---

1. Bauer, p. 446.

a sacrifice. The family would invite friends and relatives, among whom were Christians, to a feast. At other times, consecrated meat was sold in the markets. Christians then bought the meat and consumed it in their homes.

Members of the Corinthian church faced the question whether they should eat meat that had been consecrated to an idol in a pagan temple. Were they free to go to such a feast? Could they enjoy themselves in the name of Christian liberty (see 6:12; 10:23)? The conscience of some believers was clear while that of others was burdened (8:7). The one party could say to the other party, "Do not be overrighteous," and the second party could retort, "Do not be overwicked" (Eccl. 7:16–17).

1. Knowledge
8:1–3

1. Now concerning the food offered to idols, we know that "we all have knowledge." Knowledge puffs up, but love builds up.

a. "Now concerning the food offered to idols." With the first two words of this text (see 7:1, 25; 12:1; 16:1,12), Paul turns to the next question in the letter he had received from the Corinthians. The expression *food offered to idols* is a direct reminder of the Jerusalem Council's instructions to Gentile Christians: to abstain from food that had been sacrificed to idols (Acts 15:29; 21:25; Rev. 2:14, 20). By implication, the Gentile Christians were debating whether the injunction was comprehensive or flexible.

We expect that Jewish Christians consumed only kosher food, yet they were free to eat with Gentile Christians (Gal. 2:11–14). And then there was also the brother with a weak conscience (vv. 7–13), who was at a loss to know what to do. In short, the issue of food that had been offered to idols was hotly debated in the Corinthian church. And Paul at this juncture in his epistle devotes much time and effort to the sensitive question of Christian liberty in relation to food that was eaten in a Jewish-Gentile setting (10:14–33).

b. "We know that 'we all have knowledge.'" Scholars agree that the last part of this sentence is a quotation taken from the letter which the Corinthians had sent to Paul.[2] Throughout this epistle, Paul repeatedly employs the verb *to know* in his debate with the Corinthians (see, for example, 1:16; 3:16; 6:2, 3; 8:1, 4). The Christians in Corinth had been boasting about their knowledge. Notice that they do not say: "We have knowledge." Instead, they assert that all the Christians in the Corinthian community and elsewhere possess knowledge.[3]

Even though Paul fails to explain the term *knowledge*, we deduce a few facts from the context. The Corinthians believed that idols were nothing and that God is one (v. 4). Thus, they knew that this one God is Father, and that the one

---

2. E.g., Gordon D. Fee, *The First Epistle to the Corinthians,* New International Commentary on the New Testament series (Grand Rapids: Eerdmans, 1987), p. 365; and the versions (GNB, NRSV, REB).

3. Jerome Murphy-O'Connor, "Freedom of the Ghetto (1 Cor., 8, 1–13; 10, 23–11,1)," *RB* 85 (1978): 545.

Lord is Jesus Christ (v. 6). Paul soberly reminds them that not everyone knows this (v. 7). However, if the Corinthians exalt knowledge, Paul has something to say to them.

c. "Knowledge puffs up, but love builds up." In an earlier context in which he commended the readers for having this treasure (1:5), Paul had already spoken about knowledge. But now Paul suggests that knowledge leads to arrogance, which should be absent from a Christian lifestyle (v. 11; 13:2). A Christian must begin with love. He is able to build his spiritual life only on the foundation of love. Knowledge without love puffs up. Love itself is never arrogant (13:4) but is always constructive. By implication, knowledge that is subordinate to love becomes useful.

2. If someone supposes that he knows something, he does not yet know as he ought to know. 3. But if someone loves God, he is known by God.

We observe these two points:

a. *Knowledge.* Paul continues his response to the letter he had received from the Corinthians. He reacts to the attitude of a church member who supposes that knowledge is everything. The emphasis is on the verb *suppose,* a verb that reveals the haughty stance of the Corinthian who glorifies knowledge. But elsewhere in this epistle Paul observes that knowledge passes away, because it is incomplete and imperfect (13:8–10). By itself knowledge is always limited in scope, extent, and depth.

In the first clause, Paul uses the verb *to know* in the perfect tense. With this tense, he indicates that the person who imagines he possesses knowledge has accumulated and perfected it for some time already. The result is that this person thinks he knows everything. But Paul wants to have nothing to do with this haughty attitude; he cuts the person off by saying: "he does not yet know as he ought to know." Paul already has told the Corinthians that "if any of you thinks that he is wise in this age, let him become foolish that he may become wise" (3:18; see also Gal. 6:3).

What, then, is the beginning of true knowledge? John Calvin notes that the foundation of true knowledge is personal knowledge of God.[4] We are able to recognize such knowledge when we see grace, humility, integrity, and obedience at work in a person's life. A believer recognizes his limitations when he confesses that only God has infinite knowledge and wisdom. Hence, Paul urges the Corinthians to reexamine their perspective on knowledge and to understand what they ought to know. They must realize that all knowledge is derivative and comes from God through Christ. All the treasures of God's wisdom and knowledge are stored in Christ (Col. 2:3). True knowledge therefore has a spiritual dimension that relates to God, who bases knowledge on love. Knowledge by itself is not wrong; indeed it is essential to life. But when a person fails to link knowledge to divine love, he deceives himself and fails utterly.

---

4. John Calvin, *The First Epistle of Paul the Apostle to the Corinthians,* Calvin's Commentaries series, trans. John W. Fraser (reprint ed.; Grand Rapids: Eerdmans, 1976), p. 172.

b. *Love.* "But if someone loves God, he is known by God." Human knowledge is temporal but divine love is eternal. Here Paul links the two concepts and intimates that the essential ingredient of knowledge is love. Without true love, knowledge ceases to be meaningful. But the believer, who loves God, fully comprehends that he is known by God. This does not mean that because of man's love for God he receives divine recognition. The initiator is not man but God. G. G. Findlay provides a quaint but nevertheless characteristic summary: "Paul would ascribe nothing to human acquisition; religion is a bestowment, not an achievement; our love or knowledge is the reflex of the divine love and knowledge directed toward us."[5] In fact, the Greek uses the perfect tense for the passive verb *is known* to imply that the act of knowing took place in the past but has a result that is evident in the present.

Two concluding remarks to this segment. First, the message of verse 3 with its emphasis on love contrasts the essence of verse 2 with its emphasis on knowledge. Next, the last part of verse 3 is a small digression from Paul's intention to speak about food offered to idols. Yet, Paul had to stress the biblical truth that God has shown his people (compare Exod. 33:12, 17; Gal. 4:9; I John 4:19).

Practical Considerations in 8:1–3

In the first century, when people aspired to church membership they were baptized and instructed in the truths of Christianity. These truths were the elementary teachings of Christ (Heb. 6:1–2), and in later years included both the Apostles' Creed and the Lord's Prayer. From the sixth to the sixteenth century, instruction in the Christian faith was given primarily in the family circle.

The Reformation necessitated the writing of numerous catechisms. In 1529, Martin Luther wrote his larger and shorter catechisms to instruct the people who were ignorant of the basic teachings of Christianity. John Calvin composed a catechism in 1536 and diligently educated the people in Geneva every week. The Heidelberg Catechism of 1563 became a standard instructional guide in the Reformed churches in Germany, the Netherlands, and America. In England, the Westminster theologians composed their shorter and larger catechisms in 1646 and 1647 respectively. These educational tools were designed to inculcate the Christian faith especially in the hearts and minds of the children of believers and of inquirers.

Throughout the centuries following the Reformation, teachers of the catechisms have been instrumental in imparting biblical knowledge. At times this instruction became an intellectual exercise separated from genuine faith and love. Consequently, knowledge was glorified, with ecclesiastical stagnation following as an inevitable result.

---

5. G. G. Findlay, *St. Paul's First Epistle to the Corinthians,* in vol. 3 of *The Expositor's Greek Testament,* ed. W. Robertson Nicoll, 5 vols. (1910; reprint ed., Grand Rapids: Eerdmans, 1961), p. 840. Although Fee opts for a shorter reading of the text and a different meaning, he lacks the support of the translators. *First Corinthians,* pp. 367–68.

In recent times, however, the problem which the church faces is not a lack of love but a lack of knowledge. The problem with the members of the church is not intellectual arrogance but rather biblical ignorance. The rich heritage of the past is no longer passed on from generation to generation. Apart from the Apostles' Creed, the Lord's Prayer, and the Ten Commandments, many church members know little of the Bible's content. Because of this scriptural illiteracy, the church's need of the hour is solid instruction in the truths of God's Word.

Greek Words, Phrases, and Constructions in 8:1–3

Verse 1

εἰδωλοθύτων—this substantivized verbal adjective in the neuter genitive plural derives from the noun εἴδωλον (idol) and the verb θύω (I sacrifice). It signifies meat that was sacrificed to an idol and either eaten at feasts or sold in the marketplace.[6] Its synonym ἱερόθυτόν (meat sacrificed to a divinity) appears in 10:28.

ἡ γνῶσις—in this text, the noun *knowledge* is an attribute ascribed not to God but to man. Some scholars see a link between the situation in Corinth and the Gnostic movement of the second century. However, all we are able to say with certainty is that in the middle of the first century, the beginning stages of Gnosticism were scattered here and there. As the epistles of John reflect, toward the end of that first century the Gnostic heresy entered the church. But in Paul's day Gnosticism was still in the stage of being born.[7]

Verses 2–3

ἐγνωκέναι—the perfect active infinitive of γινώσκω (I know) denotes an action in the past with lasting effect in the present.

ἔγνω—the aorist tense of this verb is ingressive ("he began to know") and is qualified by the negative *not yet*.

ἔγνωσται—the middle/passive voice of this verb in the perfect tense is not middle but passive, "he is known [by God]." The verb is synonymous with the verbs *called* and *chosen* by God (Rom. 8:28–30).

---

2. Unity
8:4–6

4. Concerning the eating of food offered to idols, then, we know that "there is really no such thing as an idol in this world" and that "there is no God except one."

---

6. Consult Gordon D. Fee, "*Eidōlothyta* Once Again: An Interpretation of 1 Corinthians 8–10," *Bib* 61 (1980): 172–97.

7. Hans Conzelmann, *1 Corinthians, A Commentary on the First Epistle to the Corinthians*, ed. George W. MacRae, trans. James W. Leitch, Hermeneia: A Critical and Historical Commentary on the Bible (Philadelphia: Fortress, 1975), pp. 15, 140. Among scholars who ascribe Gnosticism to some Corinthians, see Walter Schmithals, *Gnosticism in Corinth: An Investigation of the Letters to the Corinthians*, trans. John E. Steeley (New York: Abingdon, 1971), pp. 225–37; R. A. Horsley, "Consciousness and Freedom among the Corinthians: 1 Corinthians 8–10," *CBQ* 40 (1978): 574–89; and "Gnosis in Corinth: 1 Corinthians 8. 1–6," *NTS* 27 (1981): 32–51.

a. "Concerning the eating of food offered to idols, then." In this passage, Paul resumes the subject he introduced earlier (v. 1) and once more speaks about the matter of food offered to idols. This problem is both vexing for the readers and intricate for Paul, who had to give answers to a Christian community with a divided and varied constituency. Many of the members had roots in paganism and needed Paul's guidance to cope with the question of eating sacrificial food that had come from a pagan temple.

b. "We know that 'there is really no such thing as an idol in this world.'"[8] Once again Paul quotes from the letter which the Corinthians had sent to him. He presents the line with the same phrase used earlier (v. 1) and says, "We know." Paul repeats a spiritual truth which the Corinthians learned from the Scriptures and which now surfaces in the letter: an idol is nothing (see Isa. 44:12–20). The unknown psalmist compares Israel's God to the idols of the nations and says:

> But their idols are silver and gold,
>   made by the hands of men.
> They have mouths, but cannot speak,
>   eyes, but they cannot see;
> they have ears, but cannot hear,
>   noses, but they cannot smell;
> they have hands, but cannot feel,
>   feet, but they cannot walk;
>   nor can they utter a sound with their throats.
> Those who make them will be like them,
>   and so will all be who trust in them.
> [Ps. 115:4–8; 135:15–18]

c. "And that 'there is no God except one.'" The last part of the verse is also taken from the letter which the Corinthians addressed to Paul. It echoes the scriptural teaching that there is but one God. This is summarized in the Hebrew creed: "Hear, O Israel: the Lord our God, the Lord is one" (Deut. 6:4; see Ps. 86:10; Isa. 44:8; 45:5). The Jews recited this creed twice a day, in the morning and in the evening. The Christian church inherited this creed from the Jews, but did not recite it morning and evening.

The Corinthians confess their belief that God is one; for that reason, they say, no idol really exists. If there are no real idols but merely inanimate objects made out of wood, stone, or metal, the Corinthians argue, they are free to partake of meat which had been dedicated to such idols.[9] They regard their freedom to eat this food in the context of Christian liberty.

---

8. Literally, "An idol is nothing in the world." In the Judeo-Christian context, the word *world* would relate to "createdness" and serve as a substitute for "existence." Many versions choose a form of this substitute. Consult Murphy-O'Connor, "Freedom of the Ghetto," p. 546.

9. See Bruce W. Winter, "Theological and Ethical Responses to Religious Pluralism—1 Corinthians 8–10," *TynB* 41.2 (1990): 209–26.

5. For even if there are so-called gods either in heaven or on earth, as indeed there are many gods and many lords.

Paul writes the first part of a concessive sentence in this verse, but he fails to complete it grammatically. In verse 6 he begins a new sentence. This is due to the poetic structure of verse 6 and a lack of a smooth transition between the two verses.

What is Paul saying when he states that there are so-called gods in heaven or on earth? Is he not contradicting the preceding confession of the Corinthians that there is but one God? Not at all. He allows the Gentiles to employ their word choice when they say that there are gods in heaven and on earth. But by inserting the word *so-called,* he effectively questions the reality of these "gods." Like the psalmists, Paul repudiates the gods whom the Gentiles worship.[10] He notes that these gods exist in name only; they are devoid of authenticity. They fail to lay claim to divinity, because God rules supreme in heaven and on earth. Even though people worship Satan, whom Jesus called the prince of this world (John 12:31; 14:30; 16:11), Satan is not and never will be divine.

The Gentiles worshiped numerous gods and lords. They paid homage to gods that dwelled in heaven, were on the earth, and were in the sea.[11] The expression *lords* probably signifies spiritual beings of a lower rank who were regarded as subordinates to the gods themselves.

6. Yet,

> **for us there is one God the Father,**
> **from whom all things are and for whom we live,**
> **and one Lord Jesus Christ,**
> **through whom all things are and through whom we live.**

Scholars debate whether Paul composed this verse, because it appears here in the form of a creedal statement. Some say that Paul is the author[12] while others contend that he borrowed the statement.[13] Did Paul write these words or did he quote a confessional formula that was current in Hellenistic Jewish communities of the Christian church? The evidence is inconclusive. But in his epistles, Paul demonstrates an ability to compose doctrinal tenets, so we are unable to preclude Pauline authorship. To illustrate, Paul formulates his doctrinal tenets on the resurrection of the dead (e.g., see 15:12–18, 42–44).

a. "Yet, for us there is one God the Father." The contrast that Paul presents is between the so-called gods and the one God and Father. The Gentiles placed

---

10. See, e.g., Pss. 82:1, 6; 95:3; 96:4; 97:9; 136:2; 138:1.

11. Refer to John Albert Bengel, *Bengel's New Testament Commentary,* trans. Charlton T. Lewis and Marvin R. Vincent, 2 vols. (Grand Rapids: Kregel, 1981), vol. 2, p. 208.

12. E.g., see Fee, *First Corinthians,* p. 374; Archibald Robertson and Alfred Plummer, *A Critical and Exegetical Commentary on the First Epistle of St. Paul to the Corinthians,* International Critical Commentary, 2d ed. (1911; reprint ed., Edinburgh: Clark, 1975), p. 168.

13. For instance, Jerome Murphy-O'Connor, "1 Cor. 8, 6: Cosmology or Soteriology," *RB* 85 (1978): 253–67; R. A. Horsley, "The Background of the Confessional Formula in 1 Kor 8.6," *ZNW* 69 (1978): 130–35.

their gods in either heaven, earth, or sea. But our God, says Paul, is one God who is not confined to one location but is everywhere (compare Ps. 139:7–10).

In the Gospels and even in Acts (1:4, 7), Jesus teaches his disciples to address God as Father (Matt. 6:9). When he refers to God, he repeatedly uses that name. God and the Father are one. The apostles likewise note that God is Father of both Jesus and the believers.[14] With the term *Father,* Paul suggests the family concept and intimates that we are God's children.

b. "From whom all things are and for whom we live." When Paul addresses Gentiles in both Lystra and Athens, he teaches that God created this world (see Acts 14:15–17; 17:24–31). Paul provides instructive doctrine for the Corinthian Christians. It corresponds with his Areopagus speech, "we are his offspring" (Acts 17:28). And he emphasizes his teaching that all things come from God as we live for him (Rom. 11:36).

In Greek, the words *all things* signify the totality of things without any exclusion; God has made everything in all his creation. These two words also occur in Paul's account of Christ creating the universe (Col. 1:16; and compare John 1:3; Heb. 1:3). Thus, God the Father has created all things through his Son, the Lord Jesus Christ. We owe our existence to God the Father and therefore live for him.

c. "And one Lord Jesus Christ, through whom all things are." Notice that Paul calls Jesus Lord but not God. At the same time, he intimates that Jesus is divine through the work of creation and redemption. Here Paul treads softly, so that he will not be accused of contradicting his earlier statement that God is one. Yet, he teaches Jesus' divinity and eternity by stating that all things in creation came into being through Jesus Christ.

d. "And through whom we live." Of these lines, the last part relates to the redemption Christ has given us. Christ has created and redeemed us, so that we live through him. In a few short parallel lines, Paul teaches the doctrines of God, Christ, creation, and salvation. By inference, we conjecture that these doctrines were known to the Corinthians.

Presuming that Paul composed these lines, we have no difficulty seeing that they were easily learned, memorized, and adopted by his readers. The parallelism is striking indeed, and in their simplicity they convey deep spiritual truths that strengthen the Christian's faith.

Greek Words, Phrases, and Constructions in 8:4–6

Verses 4–5

περὶ τῆς—with the repetition of περί (see v. 1), Paul resumes his discussion prompted by the Corinthians' query on food offered to idols.

---

14. E.g., Acts 2:33; Rom. 1:7; 6:4; 8:15; 15:6; Eph. 1:2; I Peter 1:2; I John 1:2; Rev. 1:6. See also Mal. 2:10.

The Majority Text, reflected in at least three translations (KJV, NKJV, NJB), inserts the word ἕτερος (other). Stronger and more widely representative witnesses lack this word; hence most scholars do not include it.

καὶ . . . εἴπερ—"even if." The particle περ is intensive and enclitic. The clause is concessive; nevertheless, "the truth of the principal sentence is stoutly affirmed in the face of this one objection."[15] Paul puts it as an extreme case.

Verse 6

ἐξ οὗ—the preposition denotes origin but the relative pronoun refers to God, "from whom." In the combination δι᾽ οὗ (through whom), the preposition signifies agency, but the pronoun refers to Christ.

τὰ πάντα—the definite article strengthens the adjective to make the concept all-inclusive.

---

3. Conscience
8:7–8

7. However, not everyone has this knowledge. Because they are accustomed to the idol even now, some people eat food as if offered to idols. And their conscience, being weak, is defiled.

a. "However, not everyone has this knowledge." The first word is a strong adversative. It reveals that not every believer in Corinth had full knowledge of the doctrines of God, Christ, and creation which Paul had just expounded. Paul has in mind those Christians who recently had come out of paganism and whose faith in the Lord was weak because of ignorance. As a pastor and teacher, Paul is responsible for the entire membership of the church. Although he wrote that in general all of them have knowledge (v. 1), he now asserts that the weak Christians lack particular knowledge.[16] We assume that Paul learned about the lack of knowledge among some of the believers from the Corinthian delegation (Stephanas, Fortunatus, and Achaicus [16:17]). Now he addresses their need.

b. "Because they are accustomed to the idol even now, some people eat food as if offered to idols." This sentence seems almost out of place if we consider that Paul calls the Corinthians sanctified and holy (1:2). He tells them that they are God's temple and that God's Spirit lives within them (3:16; 6:19). Yet in the present verse he reveals that the weak Christians in Corinth are accustomed to idols.

The contradiction vanishes when we realize that in the Greek Paul uses the word *idols* in the singular. If he had used the plural, he would have shown that

---

15. A. T. Robertson, *A Grammar of the Greek New Testament in the Light of Historical Research* (Nashville: Broadman, 1934), p. 1026.

16. Wendell Lee Willis avers that the words *we know* in verse 1a are part of a quotation on knowledge which then contrasts the knowledge of verse 7. However, we are not persuaded that the words *we know* belong in the quotation. See *Idol Meat in Corinth: The Pauline Argument in 1 Corinthians 8 and 10*, SBL Dissertation Series 68 (Chico, Calif.: Scholars, 1985), pp. 68, 88.

some of the weak believers were still serving the gods of paganism. With the use of the singular, however, Paul refers to the pagan environment out of which the believers recently had come. The customs of their Gentile relatives, friends, and acquaintances were integrally tied to an idol. And these customs continued to have a conceptual influence on the weak Christians.[17] Even though they no longer worshiped and served idols, they were not yet released from the influence of their own past. The believers who were strong said that idols were nothing but wood and stone. Yet every time the weak Christians came in contact with something that related to an idol, they were confronted with a conflict. They were like a former addict who fights an inner battle every time he comes in contact with drugs.

With the words *even now,* Paul acknowledges the spiritual problems the weak Christians are encountering. The association they have had with the idol until their conversion remains with them to the present even after their conversion. Paul ministers to these people by showing his understanding of their plight and thus displays his love. He knows that in their associations with Gentiles, they no longer worship idols. Later in this context he exhorts them to continue their efforts to shun idolatry (10:14). But now he deals with their problem of eating food which might have been offered to idols.

c. "Eat food as if offered to idols." The spiritually strong Christians could declare that food which might have come from a temple remains ordinary food, but those who were spiritually weak were unable to say so. For them, the associations with the practices of paganism made them cringe when they ate meat that probably had come from an animal sacrificed in a temple. Any link with paganism became a stumbling block for the weak Christians. They probably were acquainted with the decree of the Jerusalem Council (Acts 15:29). Although the strong might even enter a temple and eat meat that had been sacrificed (v. 10), the weak would not even think of buying this meat at the marketplace and preparing it in their homes.[18] Beside staying away from the temples, they refused to consume sacrificial meat even in their own houses (see 10:27–28).

d. "And their conscience, being weak, is defiled." Paul is describing the subjective experience of the weak believers when he writes about their conscience being defiled. If they ate food that derived from a pagan temple, they thought that they had participated in idol worship in some way.

What is the meaning of a person's conscience being defiled? Those who are weak lack definitive principles of conduct. When they eat meat that is tainted by idolatry, they are burdened by a conscience that similarly has been stained. Their conscience is weak because knowledge of themselves is deficient in com-

---

17. A few translations reflect the Majority Text which has the reading *conscience* (KJV, NKJV, NJB, and NAB with "aware") in the place of *custom.* Of the two readings, the second is the harder to explain and therefore is preferred.

18. Consult Bruce N. Fisk, "Eating Meat Offered to Idols: Corinthian Behavior and Pauline Response in 1 Corinthians 8–10," *TrinityJ* 10 n.s. (1989): 49–70.

parison with fellow believers.[19] They lack knowledge and self-confidence. A person's conscience must be well informed to function properly. If this is not the case, he or she needlessly stumbles at various places on life's pathway (vv. 10–12).

8. "But food will not bring us close to God. We are neither losing anything if we do not eat nor gaining anything if we do eat."

a, *Text.* If we compare a few translations, we immediately notice two differences. One concerns the verb tense in the first sentence; some translations have the future, "will not bring" (e.g., RSV, NRSV, NEB, REB), and others emphasize the present, "does not bring" (see KJV, NKJV, NIV, NAB, NJB). The manuscript evidence favors the future tense, which scholars explain in relation to the judgment day. The question is whether the Corinthians are concerned about their coming to God in worship or about the effects of the final judgment.

The other difference influences the word order in the second sentence. Does the negative ("losing anything if we do not eat") precede the positive ("gaining if we do eat") or should the order be reversed? A few translators begin with the positive (KJV, NKJV, *Phillips*), whereas the others have adopted the order we prefer. Gordon D. Fee surmises that the order of the negative followed by the positive is the more difficult reading and hence the original.[20]

b. *Origin.* This particular chapter lists a few quotations from the Corinthians to which Paul responds. In this verse we also seem to have a statement that the strong Corinthians used in their conversations with the weaker members of the church. Because the next verse (v. 9) definitely is Paul's response, the present verse appears to come from the Corinthians themselves.[21]

c. *Meaning.* "'But food will not bring us close to God.'" What the strong Corinthians are saying is that food in itself has no religious significance. Paul readily agrees with that opinion. In another epistle he writes, "For the kingdom of God is not a matter of eating and drinking" (Rom. 14:17). In other words, these Corinthians are telling their weaker brothers and sisters not to worry about consequences when they eat food that may have been offered to an idol. Do not be burdened by a guilty conscience, say the strong, for God will not hold you responsible in the day of judgment.[22] The Corinthian slogan "Food is for the stomach and the stomach is for food" (6:13) expresses the same thought.

"'We are neither losing anything if we do not eat nor gaining anything if we do eat.'" The second part of the quotation from the letter written by the Corinthians emphasizes the first part. Since food by itself has no moral value, the

---

19. Consult Paul D. Gardner, "The Gifts of God and the Authentication of a Christian," Ph.D. diss., Cambridge University, 1989, p. 49; Claude A. Pierce, *Conscience in the New Testament* (London: SCM and Naperville, Ill.: Allenson, 1955), pp. 75-83; Colin Brown, *NIDNTT*, vol. 1, p. 352.

20. Fee, *First Corinthians*, p. 377 n. 6.

21. Consult the list that John C. Hurd, Jr., has compiled in *The Origin of I Corinthians* (Macon, Ga.: Mercer University Press, 1983), p. 68.

22. Jerome Murphy-O'Connor, "Food and Spiritual Gifts in 1 Cor 8:8," *CBQ* 41 (1979): 292–98.

strong believers were saying that they are not losing or gaining anything. They eat or obtain food and show their obedience to God (compare Phil. 4:12). Notice that they are not using the expression *food offered to idols;* instead they talk about ordinary food that is eaten. Perhaps by their choice of words, the Corinthians wish to indicate that even meat offered to an idol is only common food.

Paul would have to agree with those Corinthians who championed the cause of Christian liberty. But he had to take issue with them for their lack of love and compassion for weaker brothers and sisters. By calling all foods common, they refused to see the point of view of those whose conscience bothered them when they ate food that had been sacrificed to an idol.

Greek Words, Phrases, and Constructions in 8:7–8

ἀλλ᾽—note the strong adversative ("however") that follows the preceding verses but refers to the first verse (v. 1).

συνηθείᾳ—this noun features a causal connotation, "because of custom." The word has strong manuscript support, but this is equally true for the alternate reading. However, textual scholars hold that the alternate reading, συνειδήσει (conscience), "apparently arose through assimilation to the following συνείδησις."[23]

παραστήσει—in the future active tense from the verb παρίστημι (I bring before). It is a legal term and refers to court proceedings. Like the noun συνηθείᾳ (v. 7), it has the support of the stronger manuscripts and is preferred to the reading with the present tense, παρίστησι.

---

4. Sin
8:9–13

9. But beware that this right of yours not become a hindrance to those who are weak.

With an adversative, Paul indicates that although he agrees with the general sentiment of the quotation (v. 8), he rejects the context in which it is used. In preceding verses (vv. 1–2), he had told the Corinthians that knowledge and love must go hand in hand. Knowledge by itself results in arrogance, but when it is accompanied by love, it edifies. And Paul, discovering an absence of love in the conduct of some Corinthians (compare Rom. 14:15), now registers a pastoral objection.

Paul detects a dangerous attitude that will undermine the unity of the church. He commands the readers to beware of their own conduct. He drafts the phrase *this right of yours,* in which the pronoun *this* reflects a trace of his dislike for the apparent haughtiness of some Corinthians (see Luke 15:30). Moreover, this is the second time the word *weak* occurs in this chapter (see v. 7). If this expression comes not from Paul but from these spiritually strong Corinthians, a measure of

---

23. Bruce M. Metzger, *A Textual Commentary on the Greek New Testament,* 3d corrected ed. (London and New York: United Bible Societies, 1975), p. 557.

arrogance seems obvious.[24] They aggressively claim for themselves the right to Christian liberty.

However, just as knowledge without love produces pride, so freedom without love generates arrogance. The Corinthians have the right to assert their freedom to eat food, for Paul himself teaches that "no food is unclean in itself" (Rom. 14:14). Yet Christian liberty must always be observed in the context of love for one's neighbor in general and the spiritually weak brother or sister in particular.

The right that a Christian legitimately exercises should never become a hindrance to a fellow believer. Paul uses the word *stumbling block* to describe a specific obstacle a Christian can place on someone's pathway. And the hindrance here is eating sacrificial meat, which was an offense to others in the church.

The freedom which a Christian enjoys must always be asserted in the context of serving one another in love (Gal. 5:13). His attitude should not be a hindrance to the weaker members of the church. Paul is not saying that those who are weak take offense but rather that those who are strong give offense. The members who promote their right to be free are exerting undue pressure on those whose conscience restricts them from eating certain kinds of meat. Paul, therefore, alerts the freedom-loving Corinthians to demonstrate love by not offending their fellow church members.

10. For if someone sees you who have knowledge dining in an idol's temple, will not the conscience of someone who is weak be emboldened so that he will eat food offered to idols?

We make these observations:

a. *Dining.* Taking a situation from daily life, Paul envisions the possibility of a spiritually strong Corinthian who sits and eats in the temple of an idol. This believer might be asked to come to a celebration held in one of the many dining rooms of the temple. There the meat of an animal sacrificed to an idol would be consumed. He could reason that the idol was nothing more than a piece of hewn stone and the meat was ordinary food. His faith in God remained strong. Further, he would refuse to break bonds of family or friendship. He would feel obligated to attend a feast to which he was invited and would consider the meal an occasion for fellowship with relatives and friends. Because of his firm knowledge of the Christian faith, he would not see any harm in his presence at a festive meal in a temple dining room.

Although Paul provides an illustration by using the singular *you*, his intention is to portray the reality of a common occurrence. The possibility is not unreal that Erastus, for example, who was the city's director of public works in Corinth (Rom. 16:23) and a member of the local church, might attend such functions.

Maintaining Christian liberty, Paul does not reprove a person who eats in a temple dining room. He correctly observes that a spiritually strong believer is not worshiping an idol but only enjoying the company of family and friends. By

---

24. Consult Roy A. Harrisville, *I Corinthians*, Augsburg Commentary on the New Testament series (Minneapolis: Augsburg, 1987), p. 141.

contrast, in a later passage (10:19–20) Paul comments on idolatry and there delineates the sin of worshiping an idol.[25] Now he calls attention not to the eating in a dining room but to the effect this action may have on a weaker brother. This action has the potential of leading a weaker brother into idolatry.

b. *Conscience.* The weak brother is probably not a Jew, for a Jew would not think of entering a temple to eat meat that was sacrificed to an idol. Instead, the weak brother is likely a Gentile who recently converted to Christianity, whose spiritual knowledge is limited, and whose conscience is weak.[26] Paul now asks the strong Christian a question that probably conveys a touch of irony: "Does the act of eating in a temple embolden the conscience of the weaker brother?"[27]

By his conduct, the one who is strong is leading the weak one; but the fact is that he leads his brother astray. If a spiritually weak person enters the dining room and eats, his conscience is defiled instead of strengthened (see v. 7). Hence, not the weak brother but his weak conscience is emboldened. The inner voice of his conscience no longer keeps him in check.[28] At the beginning of his discussion of this subject, Paul noted that knowledge leads to pride and love leads to edification (v. 1). Paul now reiterates the same thought in different words. Conduct without love and consideration can be disastrous, especially for the spiritually weak who follow the example of the strong person to lead the way. The full responsibility for the spiritual health of the brother rests on the shoulders of the person who has knowledge. His inconsiderate conduct constitutes a sin against Christ.[29]

11. For the weak brother for whom Christ died is destroyed by your knowledge.

When the weak brother eats sacrificial meat in a pagan temple, he associates his act with idol worship. His confidence is destroyed because of his qualms of conscience. Instead of being built up he is torn down. Paul looks at the consequences of the conduct of the knowledgeable brother who intentionally overrides the objections that the weak brother raises. Paul knows that the insensitive conduct of the brother with knowledge destroys "the weak brother for whom Christ died."

What the apostle is saying in this verse concerns the spiritual life of the weak Christians. Here is a threefold explanation of Paul's point of view:

First, with the word order, Paul makes every word count in this text; he stresses especially the verbs *to destroy* and *to die.* These two verbs are key words. In this sen-

---

25. Fisk, "Eating Meat Offered to Idols," pp. 62–64.

26. Paul W. Gooch, "St. Paul on the Strong and the Weak: A Study in the Resolution of Conflict," *Crux* 13 (1975–76): 10–20.

27. Bauer, p. 558; R. St. John Parry, *The First Epistle of Paul the Apostle to the Corinthians,* Cambridge Greek Testament for Schools and Colleges (Cambridge: Cambridge University Press, 1937), p. 133.

28. F. W. Grosheide, *Commentary on the First Epistle to the Corinthians: The English Text with Introduction, Exposition and Notes,* New International Commentary on the New Testament series (Grand Rapids: Eerdmans, 1953), p. 196.

29. Consult Harold S. Songer, "Problems Arising from the Worship of Idols: 1 Corinthians 8:1–11:1," *RevExp* 80 (1983): 363–75.

tence, the verb *to destroy* is in the present tense to indicate that the action already is occurring.[30] The weaker brother "is being destroyed." With the present tense he conveys progressive action but not the thought that the weak brother "has been lost."

Next, the immediate context (v. 12) features the verb *to injure, wound* in the present tense. This verb is a synonym Paul uses to explain the meaning of "to destroy."

And last, the parallel passage in Romans 14:15 and its context shed light on the present verse. "If your brother is distressed because of what you eat, you are no longer acting in love. Do not by your eating destroy your brother for whom Christ died." If Christ paid the supreme sacrifice by dying for this weak brother, then the least a strong brother can do is to demonstrate neighborly love to fellow Christians by not eating certain foods. The intent of this verse is to depict the contrast between the death of Christ and the callousness of the strong Corinthians.

Two additional observations on this passage. First, Paul is not teaching that a strong Christian can cause a spiritually weak brother to perish, for he writes "brother" instead of "sinner" or "man." He implies that Christ continues to protect this person from harm and will enable him to stand (Rom. 14:4). In brief, loving this brother so much that he died for him, Christ will also make him withstand temptation. Second, some translators introduce the helping verb *could* (JB) or *would* (SEB) to convey the probability of experiencing ruin but not the actuality of being lost eternally. The weak brother is stunted in his spiritual growth by the lack of love from fellow Christians.[31] Nonetheless, Christ has redeemed and sanctified him (1:2) and regards him as his brother (compare Heb. 2:10–11).

Paul no longer speaks in generalities but addresses the strong Corinthians personally. He writes, "*your* knowledge," and calls attention to the loveless attitude of these Corinthians who are puffed up by knowledge (v. 1). Also, the use of the personal pronoun *you* seems to reveal that the current problem involved a number of people. By contrasting Christ's death—as an illustration of the greatest love imaginable—with the loveless knowledge of some Corinthians, Paul encourages his readers to express their love to the weaker members of the church.

12. Thus you sin against Christ by sinning against your brothers and by wounding their weak conscience.

Conclusively, the apostle comes to the heart of the matter. He writes the verb *to sin* twice in the same sentence. In the Greek, he accentuates this word by having the form *sinning* near the beginning of the sentence and the form *sin* at the very end.

Note these terms:

a. *Sin against Christ.* By writing the present tense of the verb *to sin*, Paul notes that the Corinthians are in the process of committing the sin of lovelessness

---

30. The Majority Text has the future tense ("and shall be destroyed") that is placed in an interrogative sentence (see KJV, NKJV, *Phillips;* and GNB in a declarative sentence).

31. Consult F. F. Bruce, *1 and 2 Corinthians,* New Century Bible (London: Oliphants, 1971), p. 82.

against Christ. The present tense points out the relevance and seriousness of their insult to Christ, even though their insensitivity is directed against their own brothers in Christ.

When Paul was blinded by heavenly light near Damascus, Jesus asked why he persecuted him. In bewilderment, Paul queried Jesus who he was. The reply was, "I am Jesus, whom you are persecuting" (Acts 9:5; 22:8; 26:15). Jesus and his brothers and sisters are one, so that an offense against a believer is an offense against Jesus (see Matt. 25:41–46).

b. *Against your brothers.* The strong Corinthians are sinning against their own brothers, that is, the church. They commit sin by their attitude toward fellow members in Christ. And consequently, not their fellow members but they themselves are culpable and will face judgment. Soldiers fighting a war ought not to aim their weapons at fellow soldiers. Christian brothers who sin against fellow Christians sin against God and meet him as judge "who is able to save and destroy" (James 4:12).

c. *Wounding their weak conscience.* Here is a literal translation of this phrase: "striking their conscience that is in a weakened condition." Believers who are expected to encourage and instruct fellow members repeatedly strike their weakened conscience. "What requires the tenderest handling is brutally treated, so that its sensibility is numbed."[32] From an objective point of view, the strong Corinthians continually wound the weak conscience of a brother by inducing him to eat sacrificial meat. They hit him not physically but spiritually; they strike an already weak conscience that becomes numb. From a subjective point of view the wounded conscience of the believer causes a lack of self-esteem.[33]

13. Therefore if food causes my brother to stumble into sin, I will never eat meat again that I may not cause my brother to stumble.

The conclusion to this part of the discussion is that Paul himself will provide leadership in the Corinthian church even while he is physically absent. If the spiritually strong Christians fail in their responsibility to strengthen the weak, Paul will set the example. This verse is a conditional sentence that expresses reality and certainty. The readers can be assured that Paul indeed will do that which he is telling them.

Paul writes the general word *food* instead of the term *sacrificial meat,* which was at the center of the discussion (see vv. 1, 4, 7, 10). The matter of eating food should not become a stumbling block to anyone in the church. Paul himself scolded both Peter and Barnabas for their refusal to eat with Gentile Christians in Antioch (Gal. 2:11–14). He and his associates delivered the letter of the Jerusalem Council to the Gentile Christians (Acts 15:29). Jewish Christians even refused to buy meat in a local Gentile market for fear of eating food that had been offered to an idol. They fully kept the law of Moses (compare Acts 21:20). Gentile Christians, too, were careful in dining with Gentile friends.

---

32. Robertson and Plummer, *First Corinthians,* p. 173.
33. Consult Paul W. Gooch, "'Conscience' in 1 Corinthians 8 and 10," *NTS* 33 (1987): 244–54.

For the sake of his Christian brother, Paul says, "I will never eat meat again that I may not cause my brother to stumble." In the next chapter of this epistle, he states unequivocally that "to those who are weak I became weak to win the weak. I have become all things to all men so that at least I might save some" (9:22). Paul was willing to forego eating certain foods so that he might advance the cause of Christ, the spread of the gospel, and the growth of the church.

Did Paul suggest that every Christian should become a vegetarian? No, not at all. But Paul is willing to go to any extreme to avoid hurting the conscience of anyone for whom Christ died.[34] And if that extreme means not to eat meat for some time, Paul readily adapts. He submits even his Christian liberty to the principle of love. What he is asking every believer to do is to show genuine Christian love to fulfill the summary of the Decalogue: to love God with heart, mind and soul, and to love one's neighbor as oneself (Matt. 22:37–39). Indeed, Augustine expresses a comment to this effect: "As long as you love God and your neighbor, you may do whatever you wish and you will not fall into sin."

Additional Note on 8:10

The Jerusalem Council stipulated that Gentile Christians were to abstain from food sacrificed to idols (Acts 15:29). But in Corinth, Paul allowed Christians to enter a temple and participate in feasts held in one of its dining rooms. Paul's consent in this chapter appears to be contradictory, especially because he forbade the eating of sacrificial meat in 10:14–22.

Is Paul lax in the one chapter (8:10) and strict in the other (10:18–22)? Hardly. What Paul is trying to do is walk the thin line between allowing Christian liberty and strengthening the consciences of the weak. To put it differently, in chapter 8 Paul addresses the strong but in chapter 10 the weak.

Sacrificial meat in itself is not harmful. If Christians should attend a feast where this meat was served, they were free to partake provided they did not hurt the conscience of weaker Christians. But whenever the eating of meat was directly associated with idolatry, Paul condemned this practice (10:7, 14). When a Christian became a participant in idolatry (10:18, 20), he would forge a spiritual association with an idol and thus become an idolater. Whenever Gentiles were worshiping an idol, a Christian should have nothing to do with them. He ought to know that God is a jealous God (Exod. 20:4; Deut. 5:8). In the words of James, "You adulterous people, don't you know that friendship with the world is hatred toward God? Anyone who chooses to be a friend of the world becomes an enemy of God" (James 4:4).

Practical Considerations in 8:12

In today's world, sin is taken lightly. Often it is considered something amusing, especially when it relates to sexual immorality. When the news media mention sexual esca-

---

34. John C. Brunt, "Rejected, Ignored, or Misunderstood? The Fate of Paul's Approach to the Problem of Food Offered to Idols in Early Christianity," *NTS* 31 (1985): 113–24.

pades of prominent people, the expression used is not "sin" but rather "character weakness." Indeed, the thinking seems to be that the term *sin* should not be applied to anyone because it might damage a person's reputation. Although the consequence of sin is evident, people like to pretend that there is nothing wrong.

In many parts of the world, sin is an embarrassment for the offender when his deed becomes common knowledge. Disgrace can be removed by a restorative action of presenting the offended party an appropriate gift. If the offense remains undetected, the guilty person continues to act as though nothing has happened.

In the Greco-Roman world of Paul's day, sin was a matter of frustration. Sin was compared to an archer who misses the mark and thus experiences failure. Sin, therefore, was a lack of skill that continual training could overcome. It was not something that was taken seriously.

The Scriptures, however, teach that sin is a personal affront to God and a transgression of the laws he has established. Sin is stepping over the legal boundaries within which we should live and work. Sin is an insult to God because we choose no longer to serve him but an idol. And idolatry is nothing but spiritual adultery. God loves his people like a bridegroom loves his bride. Instead of loving him as our spouse, we turn to idols and commit adultery.

Sin can be forgiven only through the shedding of blood—in the Old Testament era the blood of animals foreshadowed that of Christ. In the New Testament era, the sinner is cleansed through Christ's blood shed at Golgotha. As the writer of the Epistle to the Hebrews aptly puts it: "and without the shedding of blood there is no forgiveness" (Heb. 9:22).

Greek Words, Phrases, and Constructions in 8:9–13

Verses 9–10

ἡ ἐξουσία ὑμῶν αὕτη—the word order of this phrase is emphatic: "this right of yours." The noun ἐξουσία refers to the liberty of some Corinthians to eat sacrificial meat (also compare 9:4–6, 12, 18; 11:10).

ἐὰν γάρ τις ἴδῃ σέ—the conditional sentence with the aorist subjunctive expresses probability: "for if someone should see you." Yet the context of this passage seems to indicate that eating in a temple dining room was a frequent occurrence.

οὐχί—with this negative particle, Paul poses a rhetorical question that demands a positive answer. The clause itself discloses a shade of irony.

εἰς τὸ . . . ἐσθίειν—this present infinitive of purpose expresses the effect on the weak brother "embolden him to eat."

Verse 12

ἁμαρτάνοντες—the present tense of this participle ("sinning") with the present tense of τύπτοντες (striking) and the present tense of the verb ἁμαρτάνετε (you are sinning) all convey an impression of frequency.

καί—this conjunction is used in the explicative sense to particularize and explain that which has been said.[35]

---

35. Friedrich Blass and Albert Debrunner, *A Greek Grammar of the New Testament and Other Early Christian Literature,* trans. and rev. Robert Funk (Chicago: University of Chicago Press, 1961), #442.9.

ἀσθενοῦσαν—notice that Paul uses not the adjective ἀσθενής (weak) but the present active participle in the feminine accusative singular of the verb ἀσθενέω (to be weak). The participle depicts descriptive action.

Verse 13

διόπερ—a combination of διό (therefore) and the enclitic particle περ which adds intensive or extensive force. Here it stresses the connection of the clauses involved.[36]

εἰ βρῶμα—the particle introduces a simple-fact conditional sentence that expresses reality and certainty. The noun is purposely chosen to indicate any kind of solid food.

Summary of Chapter 8

The letter Paul had received from the Corinthians contained many questions. He answers the query concerning food offered to idols and discloses the insufficiency of declaring that an idol is nothing. The Corinthians know that there is but one God, the Father, who created all things; and they know there is one Lord Jesus Christ. Although God and Jesus Christ are known, the fact that idols are nothing is not fully known. Some people are still burdened by idolatry, idols, and foods offered to them. These people have weak consciences that become defiled. Yet food by itself has no religious value.

The freedom which some Corinthians exercise, however, may be a stumbling block to the weak. Paul warns them not to lead a brother astray when they eat food in the temple of an idol. If they crush the conscience of a weak brother, they sin against their brothers and against Christ. Paul himself is willing to abstain from eating meat to keep a weak brother from falling into sin.

---

36. C. F. D. Moule, *An Idiom-Book of New Testament Greek,* 2d ed. (Cambridge: Cambridge University Press, 1960), p. 164.

9

Apostles and Rights

(9:1–27)

Outline (continued)

9 1 Am I not free? Am I not an apostle? Have I not seen Jesus our Lord? Are you not my work in the Lord? 2 If I am not an apostle to others, at least I am to you. For you are the seal of my apostleship in the Lord.

3 My defense to those who examine me is this: 4 Do we not have the right to eat and drink? 5 Do we not have the right to take along a believing wife as also the rest of the apostles and the brothers of the Lord and Cephas do? 6 Do Barnabas and I not have the right to refrain from physical labor?

7 Who serves in the army at his own expense? Who plants a vineyard and does not eat its fruit? Or who tends a flock and does not drink from its milk? 8 I am not speaking these things according to man, am I? Or doesn't the law say these things? 9 For in the law of Moses it is written,

> "Do not muzzle the ox while it is threshing."

God is not concerned with oxen, is he? 10 Or is he actually speaking on account of us? For on account of us it is written, because the plowman ought to plow in hope and the thresher ought to thresh in hope of sharing the crop. 11 If we have sown spiritual things for you, is it a great thing if we reap a harvest of material things from you? 12 If others share in this right [of support] over you, don't we have it all the more? However, we did not use this right, but we endure all things so as not to hinder the gospel of Christ.

13 Do you not know that those who administer the holy services eat the food from the temple? And those who regularly serve at the altar share in the offerings that are on the altar? 14 Thus also the Lord directed those who preach the gospel to get their living from the gospel.

15 But I have not used any of these privileges. And I do not write these things that in this way it may turn out for my benefit. For I would rather die than. . . . No one shall render void my reason for boasting. 16 For if I preach the gospel, I have nothing to boast about. I am compelled to preach, for woe to me if I do not proclaim the gospel. 17 If I do this of my own choice, I have a reward. But if I do so under compulsion, I simply fulfill the stewardship entrusted to me. 18 What then is my reward? When I preach the gospel, I offer it free of charge so as not to make full use of my authority in the gospel.

19 For though I am free from all men, I was a slave to all to win as many people as possible. 20 To the Jews I conducted myself as a Jew to win the Jews; to those who are under the law I became as one under the law, though I myself am not under the law, to win those under the law. 21 To those who are without the law I became as one without the law, though I am not without the law of God but under Christ's law, to gain those who are without the law. 22 To those who are weak I became weak to win the weak. I have become all things to all men so that by all means I may save some. 23 And I do all things for the sake of the gospel that I may jointly share in it.

24 Do you not know that they who run in a race are all running, but only one receives the prize? So run the race that you may win. 25 And everyone who competes in the games exercises self-control in all respects. They do this to receive a perishable crown, but we an imperishable crown. 26 Indeed I run in such a way as not losing aim; I box in such a way as not beating air. 27 But I treat my body roughly and enslave it, so that after I have proclaimed the gospel to others, I myself do not become disqualified.

C. Apostles and Rights
9:1–27

Chapter 9 appears to be an interlude or a deviation from the discussion in chapter 8 and 10:14–30, but on closer examination, we observe that in 8–10 Paul develops the concept of freedom of choice or right, which he explicitly mentioned in the preceding chapter (8:9). The theme of this chapter is Christian freedom of choice, and in it Paul relates the concept to his apostleship, social life (9:4–5), and service in the church (9:12, 18). Paul possesses Christian freedom of choice, for he has apostolic rights. But for the sake of the gospel he often declines to exercise his freedom. He wants the believers in Corinth to act similarly and to live in such a way that the Lord is honored and their fellow church members are edified.

Paul also wants to prevent his readers from saying that he is detached from and fails to speak to the problems in the community. To be precise, some of the Corinthians even called his words insignificant (II Cor. 10:10).

1. Apostolic Rights
9:1–12

a. Marks of Apostleship
9:1–2

1. Am I not free? Am I not an apostle?[1] Have I not seen Jesus our Lord? Are you not my work in the Lord?

Paul poses a series of four questions that relate to his life and apostleship and that demand affirmative answers. The initial question, "Am I not free?" forms a natural bridge between the last verse of the preceding chapter (8:13) and this verse.[2] This question has nothing to do with the matter of the slave and the freedman (7:21–23). Rather, it concerns the freedom that Paul enjoyed in Jesus Christ. He defends himself against anyone who wishes to take issue with him by asking a question that requires a positive response. From Paul's associations with the Corinthians in the past, they had to acknowledge his freedom, particularly in his eating and drinking with them (compare Gal. 2:11–16).

"Am I not an apostle?" (compare 1:1). Indignantly Paul confronts criticism of his apostolic status. Since his conversion, he knew that his opponents had criticized him. They said that he could not fulfill the apostolic requirements drawn up when the apostles cast the lot to appoint Matthias as successor to Judas. An apostle had to have followed Jesus from the time of his baptism in the River Jor-

---

1. Leading Greek manuscripts read "Am I not free, am I not an apostle?" The Majority Text reverses the order (see KJV, NKJV).

2. Gordon D. Fee suggests that the context of chapter 9 is an integral part of Paul's answer to the letter written to him by the Corinthians. *The First Epistle to the Corinthians*, New International Commentary on the New Testament series (Grand Rapids: Eerdmans, 1987), p. 393.

dan to his ascension at the Mount of Olives and had to be a witness of Jesus' resurrection (Acts 1:21–26). Paul was not numbered among the Twelve and he lacked the instruction Jesus had given them. But he knew that Jesus had called him to be an apostle to the Gentiles (Acts 9:15; 22:21; 26:16–18).

"Have I not seen Jesus our Lord?" Paul defends his apostleship on the basis of his experience on the road to Damascus, an experience that confirmed Jesus' resurrection. No one in Corinth could claim ignorance of Paul's conversion experience and Jesus' personal appearance to him (15:8; Gal. 1:12, 15–16). We assume that they were thoroughly familiar with that account.

In this sentence Paul chooses his words carefully. He writes the word *Jesus*, not *Christ*, to refer to the historical Jesus of Nazareth.[3] When Paul uses the single name, he depicts the earthly Jesus (e.g., 12:3; II Cor. 4:10–14; Eph. 4:21; Phil. 2:10; I Thess. 4:14). And Paul adds the descriptive title *our Lord* to emphasize that only the Lord is able to appoint someone to apostleship. The pronoun *our* demonstrates that Paul and the Corinthians have a common bond in Jesus.

"Are you not my work in the Lord?" The Corinthians themselves had to admit that if Paul had not proclaimed Christ's gospel, they would still have been living in spiritual darkness. As Gentile Christians, they themselves were proof positive that Paul was an apostle to the Gentiles. The work of founding a church is not a human endeavor that can be executed apart from the Lord; it can be done only "in the Lord."

2. If I am not an apostle to others, at least I am to you. For you are the seal of my apostleship in the Lord.

As a former persecutor of the church, Paul realized that the Christian church would question his apostleship (see, e.g., II Cor. 10:1–11; 12:11–21; 13:1–10; Gal. 1:1, 22–23). In his absence from the Corinthian congregation, the question was raised whether he was an apostle or an imposter.

Who were these people that sowed doubt in the hearts of believers? Were they Judaizers who instigated tension among the Corinthians and refused to acknowledge Paul's apostleship?[4] We would have expected Paul to provide further details (compare, e.g., Gal. 1:6–7; 5:10), but conclusive evidence is lacking. Whoever they may have been, those whom Paul calls "others" are not members of the church in Corinth. He is not an apostle to them, but he decidedly is an apostle to the Corinthians. John Calvin paraphrases Paul's intent: "If there are some who have doubts about my apostleship, that should not be so in your case, however, for, since I planted your church by my ministry, either you are not believers, or you are bound to recognise me as an apostle."[5]

---

3. The Majority Text features the double name *Jesus Christ*, but the word *Christ* lacks manuscript support (see KJV, NKJV).

4. Consult Derk W. Oostendorp, *Another Jesus: A Gospel of Jewish-Christian Superiority in II Corinthians* (Kampen: Kok, 1967), p. 82.

5. John Calvin, *The First Epistle of Paul the Apostle to the Corinthians*, Calvin's Commentaries series, trans. John W. Fraser (reprint ed.; Grand Rapids: Eerdmans, 1976), p. 184.

Paul's certainty lies in the seal of his apostleship which he received in the Lord. With the word *seal* he identifies the Corinthian church. Its members confirm his apostolic authority and are the seal of his authentic apostolate. Indeed, they are his letters of recommendation (II Cor. 3:2).[6] Paul's credentials are valid because the Corinthian community itself certifies them. Moreover, with a conditional sentence—"If I am not an apostle to others, at least I am to you"—Paul states the reality of the situation.

Once more Paul writes the prepositional phrase *in the Lord* (see v. 1). He notes that the Corinthian believers abide in the sphere of the Lord. By implication, if the Lord appoints Paul to be an apostle, then they who are in the Lord inevitably validate his apostleship.

Greek Words, Phrases, and Constructions in 9:1–2

οὐχί—instead of the negative particle οὐκ, which he used for the first two questions, Paul now writes οὐχί to accentuate a sharper tone in the third question.

ἐν κυρίῳ—the preposition is not instrumental; it is locative and denotes relationship.

ἀλλά γε ὑμῖν εἰμι—the adversative ἀλλά and the particle γε modify the tone of the apodosis in this simple-fact conditional sentence: "to you at least I am."

---

b. Defense
9:3–6

3. My defense to those who examine me is this: 4. Do we not have the right to eat and drink?

a. *Textual division.* The word *this* may refer to either the preceding two verses (vv. 1–2) or the verses that follow (vv. 4–5). Scholars who connect verse 3 to the preceding verses apply the term *this* to Paul's apostleship that is sealed by the Corinthian church.[7] Conversely, those who see verse 3 as the beginning of a new paragraph place a colon after the term *this* and apply it to Paul's apostolic rights.[8] Of the two interpretations, the second is preferred because the general context stresses Paul's rights.

b. *Defense.* A second difficulty relates to Paul's words *my defense.* Is he writing about a court of law to which he has been called to give an account (see 4:3; Acts 22:1)? The fact that the wording is borrowed from the field of law seems to demand an affirmative answer. But in view of the geographical distance that sepa-

---

6. Reinier Schippers, *NIDNTT*, vol. 3, p. 499; Gottfried Fitzer, *TDNT*, vol. 7, pp. 948–49.

7. Among others, see Leon Morris, *The First Epistle of Paul to the Corinthians: An Introduction and Commentary*, Tyndale New Testament Commentaries series, 2d ed. (Leicester: Inter-Varsity; Grand Rapids: Eerdmans, 1985), p. 130. See TNT, *Phillips.*

8. E.g., John C. Hurd, Jr., *The Origin of I Corinthians* (Macon, Ga.: Mercer University Press, 1983), p. 109.

rated Paul from his questioners (from Ephesus to Corinth), we presume that Paul spoke figuratively.

In the context of the epistle, why does Paul speak of defense? Because Paul was a Jew and not a Gentile, the Gentile Christians in Corinth considered him to be bound to the Mosaic food laws. By stating that he would forego eating meat, he effectively precluded the possibility of consuming sacrificial meat. He defends his freedom to not exercise his rights. Succeeding verses provide the answer that Paul has the right to food, drink, companionship, and support (vv. 4–5, 12). Yet he refuses to press this right because he desires to further the cause of the gospel. He encourages table fellowship but declines to eat sacrificial meat to avoid hurting the conscience of a brother. As a Christian redeemed by Jesus Christ, he enjoys freedom from the Mosaic law but chooses not to avail himself of this freedom. He has the right to have a wife to accompany him, but he opts to remain single so that nothing may hinder him in preaching and teaching the gospel.

According to the Lord's command that a worker deserves his wages (Luke 10:7; I Tim. 5:18), the Corinthians who received Paul's teachings were obligated to support him financially. But when Paul resided in Corinth at the home of Aquila and Priscilla, he plied his tentmaking trade to support himself (Acts 18:2–3). With respect to preaching Christ's gospel, Paul unequivocally informed the Corinthians that he offered his services free of charge (v. 18).

c. *Doubts.* The fact that Paul declined to exercise his rights caused some Corinthian believers to raise questions about his conduct. Paul's response to these questions was that he figuratively faced a trial during which interrogators presented inquiries concerning his behavior. Perhaps these faultfinders were looking for an apostle whose conduct peerlessly met all their expectations. They were the vocal minority in the congregation, but they failed to intimidate Paul, who boldly presented his defense and advanced the cause of Christ.

Paul asks his opponents whether he has the right to eat and to drink. This question demands an affirmative reply. That is, the church had to provide room and board for him as recompense for the labors he performed in their midst.[9] Although there is valid reason to link this verse (v. 4) to 8:9, where the word *right* occurs in a discussion about freedom to eat meat, we are inclined to look at the succeeding rather than the preceding context. Paul speaks no longer of sacrificial food but of eating and drinking at the expense of the church in Corinth. In the following verses he informs his readers that he has refrained from using his privilege of financial support (vv. 15–18).

We lack sufficient information about specific charges Paul's opponents are leveling against him. Our explanations, then, rest not on specific evidence but on conjecture.

---

9. Refer to Wilhelm Pratscher, "Der Verzicht des Paulus auf finanziellen Unterhalt durch seine Gemeinden: Ein Aspekt seiner Missionsweise," *NTS* 25 (1979): 284–98.

5. Do we not have the right to take along a believing wife as also the rest of the apostles and the brothers of the Lord and Cephas do?

a. "Do we not have the right to take along a believing wife?" A literal translation of the Greek is "a sister (in the Lord), a wife," which in a polished translation becomes "a believing wife." Paul asks the Corinthians whether he has the right to travel with a believing wife. They will have to agree that he has the right to be married and have a wife as his travel companion.[10] Whether Paul was married at one time is difficult to determine. But in view of his knowledge of the intimacies of married life (see the commentary on 7:1–9), it is plausible to suppose he had been married.

The intimacy of husband and wife is strengthened by the common bond they possess as believers in Jesus Christ. And a missionary couple give themselves completely to the work of extending the church. If Paul had had a wife to accompany him, she would have suffered shipwreck; she would have experienced a lack of food and drink and would have had insufficient clothing (see II Cor. 11:23–28).

b. "As also the rest of the apostles and the brothers of the Lord and Cephas do?" Even though Acts is known as the Acts of the Apostles, the book relates accounts of only two apostles: Peter and Paul (John is mentioned incidentally). We know nothing from Scripture about the lives and travels of the others who belonged to the Twelve. When Paul mentions "the rest of the apostles," he implies that he was well informed about their travels and family circumstances, and so were the Corinthians. Apart from tradition, which says that Thomas journeyed as far as India, we know little about the work of the apostles. We assume that Paul is thinking of the Twelve and not about a broader circle of apostles that included Barnabas, Andronicus, and Junias (Acts 14:3, 14; Rom. 16:7; I Thess. 2:6).

The brothers of the Lord are those whom Matthew and Mark mention in their respective Gospels: James, Joseph, Simon, and Judas (Matt. 13:55; Mark 6:3). They are the half-brothers of Jesus, who, as John reports, did not believe in Jesus during his earthly ministry (John 7:5). But after his resurrection, Jesus appeared to James (I Cor. 15:7). On the day of Jesus' ascension, his brothers with their mother, Mary, and the other women met with the eleven apostles in the upper room (Acts 1:14). The Book of Acts and the epistles of James and Jude aside, we are ignorant of the work of Jesus' brothers.

The name *Cephas*, of course, is the Aramaic name for Peter (John 1:42). The Gospel writers describe Jesus healing Peter's mother-in-law in Capernaum (Matt. 8:14–15; Mark 1:29–31; Luke 4:38–39). Now Paul relates that Peter took his wife along on missionary journeys. We are unable to verify whether Peter had been in Corinth at any time. Because Paul mentions him repeatedly in this letter[11] and now even refers to his wife, we assume that Peter had visited the church in Corinth.

---

10. Johannes B. Bauer, "Uxores circumducere (1 Kor 9, 5)," *BibZ* 3 (1959): 94–102.
11. I Cor. 1:12; 3:22; 9:5; 15:5.

6. Do Barnabas and I not have the right to refrain from physical labor?

If we interpret Paul's first question concerning eating and drinking to mean that the church was obligated to supply the apostles with food and drink, then it corresponds with this third question. Here Paul asks whether Barnabas and he have the right to do exclusively spiritual work, and the answer to this query is a resounding yes. If Paul and Barnabas are thus engaged, the church will have to support them financially. But how does the second question fit in the context? Had Paul been married, the church would have been obligated to support him and his wife—an extra monetary burden for the church.

Why does Paul mention Barnabas? Paul had had a disagreement with Barnabas in Antioch of Syria (Acts 15:39–40) that caused a separation between these two co-workers. Yet Paul mentions Barnabas in his letter to the churches in Galatia (see Gal. 2:1–13). If we say that Paul wrote this epistle after the unpleasant episode in Antioch, we infer that Paul's relations with his colleague Barnabas were restored. Barnabas was Paul's companion on his first missionary journey to Cyprus and southern Asia Minor. (During Paul's second journey to Asia Minor, Macedonia, and Greece, Silas accompanied him.) We have no proof that Barnabas ever visited Corinth. But we have every reason to believe that with the healing of the breach between these two friends, they met each other again, perhaps even in Corinth.

Both Barnabas as a Levite and Paul as a Pharisee had learned a trade to support themselves. We know that Paul was a tentmaker but we have no information about the trade of Barnabas. We know that Greek culture despised physical labor, yet Paul, who had the rank of teacher, worked with his own hands to generate financial support. No wonder that the clash of cultural backgrounds caused the people in Corinth to raise questions concerning Paul's conduct. He had the right to ask for sustenance, but he refused to avail himself of this right.[12]

Practical Considerations in 9:3–6

When God instituted the priesthood in Israel, he also instituted tithing. The priests and Levites would receive no inheritance in the promised land. They had to collect a tithe from their fellow Israelites for their support and for the maintenance of the tabernacle and its services.[13] Throughout the Old Testament era, the descendants of Levi were supported by the tithes of God's people. In Jesus' day, the practice of tithing was strictly observed, especially by the Pharisees (Matt. 23:23). Even the poor widow cast her two pennies into the temple treasury (Mark 12:41–44), and thus gave all she possessed.

When Jesus sent out his disciples two by two, he instructed them not to take along any money, food, or bag (Matt. 10:5–9; Mark 6:7–11; Luke 9:3–5). He told them that the worker is worth his pay, which was their assurance that God would provide for them in all

---

12. Consult H. P. Nasuti, "The Woes of the Prophets and the Rights of the Apostle: The Internal Dynamics of 1 Corinthians 9," *CBQ* 50 (1988): 246–64.
13. See Lev. 27:30–33; Num. 18:21, 24, 26–29; Deut. 12:17–19; 14:22–29; 26:12–15.

their needs. He gave the rule that a worker in God's kingdom should receive his income from God's people (Luke 10:7).

If at all possible, ministers and missionaries should work full time in preaching and teaching God's Word. In turn, the people they serve should support them financially, so that these pastors and missionaries will be able to meet their daily needs. Although tent-making ministries have their place and purpose, God's people ought to raise the necessary funds to provide for the needs of the clergy.

Last, the members of the church express their love and gratitude to the Lord when they cheerfully give their tithes and offerings (II Cor. 9:7). From Sunday to Sunday they present their gifts to the Lord as an act of worship and expect them to be used to the glory of his name.

Greek Words, Phrases, and Constructions in 9:3–6

Verse 3

ἐμή—this possessive adjective ("of mine") is stronger and more expressive than the enclitic μου (my), especially when placed between the definite article ἡ and the noun ἀ-πολογία (defense).

αὕτη—the position of this demonstrative pronoun ("this") at the end of the verse favors the interpretation that it refers to the succeeding verses.

Verses 4–5

μή—the negative particle at the beginning of each verse introduces rhetorical questions that normally demand a negative reply. However, in both verses the main verb is negated by the particle οὐ, so that with the double negative the rhetorical questions receive affirmative answers.

ἀδελφὴν γυναῖκα—the apposition of two nouns means that the first one describes the second: "a sister (in the Lord) as a wife."

Verse 6

μόνος—in the singular, the adjective applies grammatically only to Paul. By extension, however, it also applies to Barnabas.

μὴ ἐργάζεσθαι—the particle negates the present infinitive *to work*. Nevertheless, because of the comparative particle ἤ at the beginning of the verse, the sentence depends on the negative μή of the preceding verse (v. 5) and is a rhetorical question. The two negatives cancel each other so that the query receives a positive reply.[14]

---

c. Service
9:7–12

Scholars are not unanimous in determining paragraph divisions in this part of the chapter. Some include verse 7 with the preceding segment (vv. 3–6), others

---

14. Friedrich Blass and Albert Debrunner, *A Greek Grammar of the New Testament and Other Early Christian Literature,* trans. and rev. Robert Funk (Chicago: University of Chicago Press, 1961), #431.1.

place it in a larger context (vv. 3–12), and still others have it at the beginning of a new paragraph (vv. 7–12).

The preceding section (vv. 3–6) lists three rhetorical questions that demand a positive answer. Conversely, verse 7 features three rhetorical questions that call for a negative response. We include verse 7 with verses 8–12 because it is introductory to those verses. The questions relating to agriculture are strengthened by a quotation from the law of Moses (Deut. 25:4) in verse 9, and Paul reasons from these examples to tell the Corinthians about his right to expect material support from them.

7. Who serves in the army at his own expense? Who plants a vineyard and does not eat its fruit? Or who tends a flock and does not drink from its milk?

a. "Who serves in the army at his own expense?" This is the first of the three questions in this verse that demand a negative reply. A soldier received his provisions from his superior officer, who had to supply his troops with the necessities of life—supplies taken either from government stores or from conquered nations. Should he fail in this task, his troops would revolt. No soldier would ever serve in an army at his own expense.[15] That would be unthinkable.

Paul is not asking the Corinthians for a salary, but with this example he defends his right to basic necessities. "'Wages' is unfit as a translation [in this text] because . . . no one can pay oneself wages."[16]

b. "Who plants a vineyard and does not eat its fruit?" This question also receives a negative response. An example is taken from the agricultural scene, which was familiar to the readers of this epistle. The wording is reminiscent of a proverbial saying in the Mosaic law, "Has anyone planted a vineyard and not begun to enjoy it?" (Deut. 20:6).

c. "Or who tends a flock and does not drink from its milk?" Everyone responds by saying, no one. The shepherd enjoys a daily milk supply from his animals and he can feed himself and his family with the products derived from the milk.

These three examples of the soldier, the gardener, and the shepherd pertain not only to the culture of the apostolic age; in Scripture God's people are often portrayed as an army, a vine, and a flock.[17] With these three illustrations from daily life, Paul proves the unmistakable point that he deserves financial support for his labor among the Corinthians.

8. I am not speaking these things according to man, am I? Or doesn't the law say these things? 9a. For in the law of Moses it is written,

"Do not muzzle the ox while it is threshing."

a. "I am not speaking these things according to man, am I?" Verse 8 refers to the world in which we move from day to day and reminds the readers of the ex-

---

15. Bauer, p. 602.

16. Chrys C. Caragounis, "ΟΨΩΝΙΟΝ: A Reconsideration of Its Meaning," *NovT* 16 (1974): 52. See also Oswald Becker, *NIDNTT*, vol. 3, pp. 144–45; Hans Wolfgang Heidland, *TDNT*, vol. 5, p. 592.

17. Frederic Louis Godet, *Commentary on First Corinthians* (1886; reprint ed., Grand Rapids: Kregel, 1977), p. 438.

amples Paul gave in verse 7. Examples from life are instructive, but Paul does not rest his case on self-evident observations.

b. "Or doesn't the law say these things?" As he does repeatedly in this epistle, Paul turns to the Scriptures.[18] God's Word is foundational, so when Paul teaches, he frequently quotes the Scriptures. The expression *law* is explained here as the law of Moses. Thus, from the Mosaic law Paul derives the words "Do not muzzle the ox while it is threshing" (Deut. 25:4; see I Tim. 5:18).

c. "For in the law of Moses it is written." Calvin asks why Paul did not resort to a clearer illustration from the Mosaic law, and provides the example of a hired man who lives in poverty and needs his wages. God says to the man's employer, "Pay him his wages each day before sunset" (Deut. 24:15).[19] But Paul reasons from the lesser to the greater: if God wants the farmer to take care of his ox, does he not require man to take greater care of his fellow man?

d. "Do not muzzle the ox while it is threshing." The Israelite farmer spread his grain on an outdoor threshing floor, which was hard, smooth, and level. A flat board weighed down with stones or people was drawn over the grain by a team of oxen or horses that walked in circles around a post (compare II Sam. 24:22–24). At times the farmer would have the oxen or horses tread out the grain with their feet (compare Mic. 4:12–13). The ox was permitted to eat as much grain as it desired while it was doing the heavy pulling. If a Jew muzzled the ox, he would run the risk of a scourging in the local synagogue.[20]

9b. God is not concerned with oxen, is he? 10. Or is he actually speaking on account of us? For on account of us it is written, because the plowman ought to plow in hope and the thresher ought to thresh in hope of sharing the crop.

Note these observations:

a. *Concern.* "God is not concerned with oxen, is he?" The interpretation of this question should be understood in the context of the Scriptures. As Creator of this universe, God upholds from moment to moment all that he has made. He gives food to all his creatures, both great and small. "He makes grass grow for the cattle and plants for man to cultivate. . . . The lions roar for their prey and seek their food from God" (Ps. 104:14, 21). "He provides food for the cattle and for the young ravens when they call" (Ps. 147:9). Therefore, when Paul asks whether God is concerned with oxen, he is not saying that God takes care only of people and neglects animals.

God gives man the command to permit an ox to eat grain. Man puts the animal to work for him, but God stipulates that man must care for the ox because it belongs to God's great creation (see Prov. 12:10; 27:23).[21] God is concerned

---

18. I Cor. 1:19, 31; 2:9, 16; 3:19, 20; 5:13; 6:16; 9:9; 10:7, 26; 14:21; 15:27, 32, 45, 54, 55.

19. Calvin, *I Corinthians*, p. 187.

20. SB, vol. 3, p. 382.

21. Walter C. Kaiser, Jr., "The Current Crisis in Exegesis and the Apostolic Use of Deuteronomy 25:4 in 1 Corinthians 9:8–10," *JETS* 21 (1978): 17. See G. M. Lee, "Studies in Texts: I Corinthians 9:9–10," *Theology* 71 (1968): 122–23; D. Instone Brewer, "1 Corinthians 9.9–11: A Literal Interpretation of 'Do Not Muzzle the Ox,'" *NTS* 38 (1992): 555–65.

about man's behavior toward his creation, for he wants man to be a wise steward.

b. *Address.* God is addressing men, not animals. Paul asks his readers, "Or is he actually speaking on account of us?" The answer to this question is emphatically affirmative. This does not mean that Paul disregards the intention of God's precept not to muzzle an ox while it is treading out the grain. Rather, he teaches that if man does not take proper care of his animal, one would not expect him to provide adequately for his laborer. More specifically, how does the church take care of its ministers? The expression *actually* signifies that if God commands man to care for his animals, on a higher level he instructs the members of the church to care for the ministers of the gospel.

c. *Argument.* "For on account of us it is written." With the word *for,* Paul confirms what he has been teaching in the preceding lines. He stresses that the Scriptures are written for man and addressed to him, thus he repeats the phrase *on account of us.* God speaks to man and commands him to listen obediently. However, Paul says the words *it is written* allude to the Old Testament quotation in the preceding verse (v. 9), not to the words that follow. When he writes, "because the plowman ought to plow in hope and the thresher ought to thresh in hope of sharing the crop," he no longer quotes. The Scriptures contain no such words.[22]

We presume that Paul notes a proverbial saying that originated in an agricultural community. But what is Paul trying to say? He figuratively applies these words to the Christian worker who, as a result of diligent labor, takes pleasure in sharing the produce. This worker preaches and teaches the gospel and expects rewards from a harvest. Plowing and sowing are normally followed by threshing and harvesting.

Notice the emphasis on the phrase *in hope,* which occurs twice.[23] The one who plows and sows ought to do so in hope of an eventual harvest. In this harvest both he and the one who threshes will have a share. In terms of expectant waiting, the plowman stands at the beginning of the growing season and the thresher at the end. Both of them are filled with hope that they may participate in the harvest and enjoy its rewards. In the end the farmer's hope becomes reality when he harvests the yield and rejoices. Growth in nature takes place in one season which in months usually can be counted on the fingers of one hand. Spiritual growth, however, takes longer and demands extra patience and care. The rewards are unending and satisfying beyond earthly measure.

11. If we have sown spiritual things for you, is it a great thing if we reap a harvest of material things from you?

---

22. Ecclesiasticus, referring to wisdom, says, "Come to her like a farmer who ploughs and sows; then wait for the good fruits she supplies. If you cultivate her, you will labour for a little while, but soon you will be enjoying the harvest" (Sir. 6:19, REB).

23. The Majority Text has an expanded reading in the second part of this saying: "And he who threshes in hope should be partaker of his hope" (NKJV).

At first, the words of the previous verse seem to add little to the discourse. But the present text provides the needed explanation. Paul is not talking about the plowman and the thresher as such. He has in mind the spiritual workers in God's church who may participate in the material blessings that come to the members of the church.

Paul applies the words of this text to himself and his fellow workers by using the personal pronoun *we*. Further, he writes a conditional sentence that is true to fact. He and his co-workers have indeed sown the spiritual Word of God among the Corinthians. And now they envision a spiritual and material response from the members of that church. The comparison between matters that are eternal and temporary is obvious, for the Corinthians are unmistakably recipients of the greater gifts (see Rom. 15:27). If in fact Paul sowed spiritual seed, may he not expect some material gifts in return? The question demands an affirmative response.

12. If others share in this right [of support] over you, don't we have it all the more? However, we did not use this right, but we endure all things so as not to hinder the gospel of Christ.[24]

a. "If others share in this right [of support] over you, don't we have it all the more?" The first point we notice is that Paul writes a conditional sentence to affirm the existing circumstances in Corinth. He is saying that others are exercising their right to ask for financial support. The verb *to share in* is a direct translation of the Greek (see v. 10), which idiomatically can mean "to enjoy."[25] Next, the Greek has the unadorned expression *the right*, but the context demands the added explanation *of support*. And last, the word *you* signifies not a subjective genitive ("of you") but an objective genitive ("over you").

Who are the persons to whom Paul refers indirectly? The word *others* discloses that they are people in the same category as Paul, namely, those who proclaim the gospel. We are perhaps to think of Apollos and Peter, who also minister. Paul writes that these men share in the right to expect remuneration for their daily work of preaching and teaching.

By making this comparison, Paul is asking whether he should not have the first share in the right of support. Neither Apollos nor Peter founded the church in Corinth. Paul did, and the Corinthians consider him their spiritual father (4:15). If the others exercise the right to financial support, then certainly Paul can claim it for himself.

b. "However, we did not use this right." When he arrived in Corinth on his initial visit, Paul stayed with Aquila and Priscilla. These people were tentmakers, like Paul (Acts 18:2–3), and thus were skilled in leatherwork. During the week, Paul earned enough income to pay his expenses. On the Sabbaths, however, he

---

24. Translators differ here on verse and paragraph divisions. Many follow the UBS division (GNB, NIV, NRSV, REB) and begin a new paragraph with verse 12b. But others end the current paragraph with either verse 12 (TNT) or verse 14 (NAB, NJB). I follow Nes-Al.

25. Bauer, p. 514.

preached in the local synagogue. For a period of a year and a half, Paul preached to and taught the Corinthians. He refused to avail himself of the right to gain support from the church he founded and served. Instead, he worked so he would not become a burden to the Corinthians.[26] As Paul tried to formulate a course of action that would advance the cause of the gospel, he knew that he could not escape criticism. If Paul refused to exercise his right for support, his critics would charge him with being aloof. But if he accepted support, they would call him greedy.[27]

When Silas and Timothy eventually arrived, Paul became a full-time preacher of the gospel (Acts 18:5). We know that these men brought financial gifts to Paul from the churches in Macedonia, for he himself writes: "And when I was with you and needed something, I was not a burden to anyone, for the brothers who came from Macedonia supplied what I needed. I have kept myself from being a burden to you in any way, and will continue to do so" (II Cor. 11:9). The church in Philippi supplied him again and again with monetary gifts to aid him in his work (Phil. 4:14–16). This Macedonian church set the example for others in voluntary giving. Paul was not looking for gifts but readily credited this church for the support it gave.

c. "But we endure all things so as not to hinder the gospel of Christ." The adversative *but* strengthens and explains the adversative *however* in the preceding clause.

With the pronoun *we*, Paul undoubtedly includes his fellow workers Silas and Timothy, who also may have worked at a trade to supply their physical needs. He and his co-workers endured all things, Paul writes. In the Greek, the verb *to endure* has the primary meaning of keeping silent out of love for others (compare 13:7, where the same Greek verb occurs). They put up with many inconveniences for the benefit of Christ's gospel. They themselves would do their utmost not to become stumbling blocks to anyone who wished to know Jesus Christ.

Paul and his associates would do anything for the cause of the gospel. They desired that no prospective converts to Christ might ever say that the apostles were interested in their money. Their lifestyle, then, should never become a hindrance to the Corinthians. The word *hindrance* is a military term that connotes breaking up a road to impede the advance of a pursuing enemy.[28] The word represents an interruption in a course of action, which in this case signifies the spread of the gospel of Christ (II Cor. 6:3). This gospel belongs to Christ and at the same time proclaims him.

---

26. Compare Acts 20:34–35; II Cor. 12:13; I Thess. 2:9; II Thess. 3:8.

27. William Hendriksen, *Exposition of I and II Thessalonians*, New Testament Commentary series (Grand Rapids: Baker, 1955), p. 66.

28. Thayer, p. 166. Compare Archibald Robertson and Alfred Plummer, *A Critical and Exegetical Commentary on the First Epistle of St. Paul to the Corinthians*, International Critical Commentary, 2d ed. (1911; reprint ed., Edinburgh: Clark, 1975), p. 186.

Greek Words, Phrases, and Constructions in 9:9–12

Verses 9–10

γάρ—the particle affirms the positive answer to the preceding rhetorical questions (vv. 9b–10a) in the sense of "to be sure."[29]

κημώσεις—"you shall muzzle." The manuscript evidence for this reading is weaker than for φιμώσεις (you shall muzzle), yet on transcriptural grounds scholars prefer the weaker text.[30]

ὅτι—this word can be either the conjunction *that*, the recitative, or the causal. The conjunction can be explanatory in the sense of "that is" (NEB). We can hardly take it as recitative when there is no reference to the Scriptures. Most translators give the word a causal connotation.[31]

Verse 11

εἰ—three times in three successive clauses, this particle introduces facts that are true.

ἡμεῖς ὑμῖν—note the juxtaposition of these two personal pronouns in this and the next clause (see also v. 12a). The position of ὑμῶν seems to emphasize the possessive idea ("*your* material things").

σαρκικά—this adjective describes the appearance and characteristics of flesh (see 3:3), that is, matter, and refers to material objects.

Verse 12

ἄλλοι—"others" of the same category; otherwise Paul could have used the adjective ἕτεροι (different).

ὑμῶν—the noun ἐξουσίας governs the genitive case of the pronoun with the resultant meaning "this right [of support] over you."[32] The noun itself is genitive because of the verb μετέχω (I share in).

τοῦ Χριστοῦ—the genitive is both subjective ("of Christ") and objective ("for Christ").

2. Surrender of Rights
9:13–18

a. Remuneration
9:13–14

For the apostles and their helpers, God's revelation formed a unit. True, the writer of Hebrews notes that in many ways and in many forms, God spoke to the forefathers through the prophets, and in these last days he spoke to us through

---

29. Blass and Debrunner, *Greek Grammar*, #452.2.
30. Bruce M. Metzger, *A Textual Commentary on the Greek New Testament*, 3d corrected ed. (London and New York: United Bible Societies, 1975), p. 558.
31. Among the Greek New Testament editions, only Nes-Al features verse 10b as a quotation. Yet the source of this quotation has not been located, for Sir. 6:19 is but a faint echo.
32. A. T. Robertson, *A Grammar of the Greek New Testament in the Light of Historical Research* (Nashville: Broadman, 1934), p. 500.

the Son. But it is God who through the apostles is revealing his redemptive truth to his people (Heb. 1:1–2).

When Paul writes about receiving financial support from God's people, he considers the Levitical system God had instituted in connection with the temple. He sees similarity between God's command for the support of priests and Levites and the Lord's directive concerning compensation for the messengers of the gospel.

13. Do you not know that those who administer the holy services eat the food from the temple? And those who regularly serve at the altar share in the offerings that are on the altar?

a. "Do you not know?"[33] This question—a rebuke—occurs elsewhere in Paul's first letter to the Corinthians (3:16). The readers should have known better but instead reveal a disturbing inconsistency in their religious life. Paul had given them the teachings of the Old Testament and the message of the gospel. But can we expect that Gentile Christians in Corinth were familiar with the Old Testament stipulations concerning priests and Levites?[34] In view of the comparison in the next verse (v. 14), "Thus also the Lord directed those," the answer is affirmative. The Corinthians should know from the Scriptures the divine directives that relate to the provisions for those who minister to them in God's service. And, the teaching of the Scriptures aside, the Gentile Corinthians knew that priests at the pagan temples received their income from the people who came to worship, even though this income was used for purposes other than food and clothing.

b. "That those who administer the holy services eat the food from the temple." This part of the sentence expresses a general statement about the work and ministry of all those who are connected with temple services. The tithes and offerings which the people brought to the temple in Jerusalem were for the priests and Levites. Because the tribe of Levi had no inheritance in Israel, God stipulated that the descendants of Levi should receive their income from the gifts the people brought to God's sanctuary (Deut. 18:1). The word *food* refers to the necessities of life and the expression *temple* alludes to the divine worship services, specifically in Israel. Calvin keenly observes the difference between services in pagan temples and the temple in Jerusalem: "An argument derived from the custom of the heathen, would certainly have been a poor one, for the revenues of the priests were not devoted to necessities like food and clothing, but to costly furnishings, regal splendour and extravagant luxury."[35]

c. "And those who regularly serve at the altar share in the offerings that are on the altar?" Is Paul deliberately distinguishing between those working in the temple and those serving at the altar? Hardly. As elsewhere in this epistle (e.g., 7:2–3, 21–22, 27; 8:6), Paul writes a parallel statement. He alludes to the altar in the court of the priests at the temple in Jerusalem. There the priests received a share of what was offered on the altar. The Corinthians knew about these temple reg-

---

33. See I Cor. 6:2, 3, 9, 15, 16, 19. See also 3:16; 5:6; 9:24.
34. Refer to Lev. 6:8–7:38; Num. 18:8–31; Deut. 18:1–5. See also SB, vol. 3, pp. 300–301.
35. Calvin, *I Corinthians*, p. 190.

ulations, yet they realized that Gentile Christians did not have to observe these ceremonial laws (compare Acts 15:19–21). Nonetheless, they should be able to understand that the provisions for the priests and Levites are the same for the preachers of the gospel. Not the form but the principle behind these provisions must be observed. There should not be any difference.

14. Thus also the Lord directed those who preach the gospel to get their living from the gospel.

Paul appeals to a word of the Lord which he places on a par with the stipulations in the Mosaic law. His appeal is to an authority higher than the apostles, namely, to Jesus himself. In the Gospels, Jesus told his disciples that a worker is worthy of his pay (Matt. 10:10; Luke 10:7; compare I Tim. 5:18). Paul expands Jesus' teaching by saying that those workers who devote themselves completely to the preaching and teaching of the gospel ought to be supported by the church (Gal. 6:6).

Paul writes that Jesus commanded his disciples to receive their living from the people to whom they ministered the gospel. This command calls for obedience not from the apostles but from the members of the church. Similarly God had given his instructions to support the tribe of Levi not to the priests but to the people in Israel.

This verse clearly delineates the source of support for the minister of the Word. The preacher who faithfully proclaims the gospel may expect to receive his living from the gospel. "But woe to that man who claims to live *of* the gospel without living at the same time *for* the gospel."[36]

Practical Considerations in 9:13–14

A preacher is a minister of the gospel. Although he ministers the Word to the members of the church, he is a servant not of the church but of the Word of God. True, he serves the church, which provides his annual salary; nevertheless he remains a servant of God's Word. This is a significant distinction, because the Lord sends forth his ambassador to preach that Word as a full-time minister wherever possible.

No one will dispute that a minister can be gainfully employed in the workaday world and excel with his skills. But a servant of the Word must devote his time to the preaching and teaching of the gospel. He has been called to that glorious task and has been ordained to devote himself completely to the ministry of the Word.

The Lord has instructed the beneficiaries of this ministry to supply the preacher's needs. The support which they extend to the minister, however, may go beyond the bare necessities of life. From his salary, for instance, their minister should be able to liquidate his student debts, purchase books for his ministerial library, and subscribe to theological and pastoral journals to aid him in his work. A minister should receive an adequate salary to support himself and the members of his family.

---

36. Godet, *First Corinthians*, p. 451.

Greek Words, Phrases, and Constructions in 9:13–14

Verse 13

οὐκ οἴδατε—the negative particle introduces a rhetorical question that expects a positive answer. The readers knew because Paul and his co-workers had taught them the Scriptures.

τὰ ἱερά—the adjective in the neuter plural signifies "the holy things" and pertains to everything connected with the temple.[37]

τὰ ἐκ τοῦ ἱεροῦ—the Majority Text omits the definite article τά, which in translation has to be supplied (KJV, NKJV). The evidence from textual witnesses for either omission or inclusion is strong. Paul's choice of τὸ ἱερόν (temple complex) differs from his preference for ναός (temple—the building proper). See 3:16; 6:19.

Verse 14

τοῖς—the dative expresses advantage and not the indirect object. "The command is not given *to* the missionaries, but *for* their benefit."[38]

ἐκ—followed by the genitive case, this preposition denotes either cause or source.

---

b. Reward
9:15–18

15. But I have not used any of these privileges. And I do not write these things that in this way it may turn out for my benefit. For I would rather die than. . . . No one shall render void my reason for boasting.

a. "But I have not used any of these privileges." Paul supported himself by his own trade during the three missionary journeys. His mention of Barnabas, who engaged in manual work to supply his own needs (9:6), refers to the first journey. Paul's manual labor in Thessalonica (I Thess. 2:9), Corinth (Acts 18:3), and Ephesus (Acts 20:34) took place during the second and third journeys (see also II Cor. 12:14).[39]

Paul precludes the possibility of having the Corinthians pay him for his services during a future visit. He states categorically that he has not claimed for himself the right for financial support (see 4:12). And he will continue to observe the principle of not accepting money or goods for his spiritual work. Paul is not saying that others have to follow his example in refusing to accept support from the people. And the gifts from the church in Philippi should not be understood as remuneration for services rendered but rather as tokens of love for Paul (Phil. 4:14–18).

---

37. Bauer, p. 372. Consult Gottlob Schrenk, *TDNT*, vol. 3, p. 232.
38. Fee, *First Corinthians*, p. 413 n. 95.
39. Consult Ronald F. Hock, "The Workshop as a Social Setting for Paul's Missionary Preaching," *CBQ* 41 (1979): 438–50.

b. "And I do not write these things that in this way it may turn out for my benefit." In composing his letter to the Corinthians Paul presumably relied on the services of a scribe. As he is in the process of forming his sentences, Paul realizes that some of his readers may receive the impression that he is asking the church to reimburse him for past services. He therefore makes clear that he is not asking the Corinthians for any personal benefits. On the contrary, in spite of Jesus' command that the worker be remunerated for his labors, Paul preserves the principle not to ask for any support but to rely on his own resources. He is not interested in his own advancement but in the progress of the gospel.

c. "For I would rather die than. . . ." From his epistles, we infer that Paul was readily overcome by emotion. Often he breaks off in the middle of a sentence and lets the reader fill in the gaps.[40] In this passage Paul reflects on his relationship with the Corinthians and is overcome by his emotions, so that he fails to complete the rest of the sentence. When he regains composure, he starts anew with a slightly different thought.

We can only surmise what the entire sentence may have been. Perhaps Paul was at the point of uttering a critical remark. We will never know. However, some ancient manuscripts give the sentence a semblance of continuity with a different reading in the Greek. This reading is reflected, for example, in the translation of the King James Version: "For it were better for me to die, than that any man should make my glorying void." Such a translation gives a smooth reading, but it does not convey the emotional tension that caused the break. The force of Paul's emotions resulted in a rupture in the syntax. By keeping the break in the sentence, we reflect Paul's emotional state.[41]

d. "No one shall render void my reason for boasting." What is Paul intending to say? Earlier in his epistle, he admonished the readers not to boast except in the Lord (1:31; see Gal. 6:14). Now he intimates that the Christian can never boast about himself or his own accomplishments but only about his Lord.[42] Paul can even say that his right to support from the Corinthian church is no ground for boasting. His reason for boasting, then, is that the cause of the gospel has been and is advanced free of charge. No one is able to stop him from boasting about this matter (II Cor. 11:10). Should he now receive remuneration, he would give his opponents the opportunity to make his boasting void. Even if the Corinthians should wish to pay Paul, he would refuse their aid so as not to hamper the progress of the gospel (v. 12).

16. For if I preach the gospel, I have nothing to boast about. I am compelled to preach, for woe to me if I do not proclaim the gospel.

When Jesus called Paul on the road to Damascus, he told him to preach the gospel to the Gentiles and to the people of Israel (Acts 9:15; 26:15–18). When he

---

40. Compare, e.g., Rom. 3:25; 5:12; 8:32; I Cor. 6:9; 10:32.

41. Roger L. Omanson, "Some Comments about Style and Meaning: I Corinthians 9.15 and 7.10," *BibTr* 34 (1983): 135–39.

42. Refer to Hans-Cristoph Hahn, *NIDNTT*, vol. 1, 229; Rudolf Bultmann, *TDNT*, vol. 3, pp. 651–52.

began his ministry, Paul proclaimed the good news to the Jews in the synagogues of Damascus and Jerusalem. He then taught in the church in Antioch and from there went to Cyprus and Asia Minor to acquaint Jews and Gentiles with Christ's gospel. As he reveals in his farewell address to the Ephesian elders, "I testified to both Jews and Greeks that they turn in repentance to God and faith in our Lord Jesus" (Acts 20:21). Because Paul was *appointed* to preach, he did not see that task as a reason for boasting. Instead, his commission from the Lord compelled him to preach. Paul wanted to complete the task which the Lord Jesus had given him, namely, preaching the gospel to both Jews and Greeks.

"For woe to me if I do not proclaim the gospel." Paul raises the lament which the Old Testament prophets and the New Testament apostles raised. Like Paul, these men were overcome by the urgency of uttering the message God gave them. Jeremiah said that God's Word was like a fire in his heart and in his bones (Jer. 20:9) and Amos writes that because God has spoken he must speak (Amos 3:8). Peter and John, standing before the Sanhedrin, tell this ruling body that they cannot help but speak what they have seen and heard concerning Jesus Christ (Acts 4:20).

The phrase *woe to me* describes the greatest misery imaginable for Paul. He would bring this misery upon himself if he proved disobedient to his divine mandate to preach.[43] He must preach the gospel of salvation—in his own words to Timothy, "in season and out of season" (II Tim. 4:2). If not, he would incur God's wrath and its consequences. Paul is a slave of Jesus Christ, as he often notes in his epistles (see, e.g., Rom. 1:1; Gal. 1:10; Titus 1:1), and as such he faithfully executes his task (Luke 17:10).

17. If I do this of my own choice, I have a reward. But if I do so under compulsion, I simply fulfill the stewardship entrusted to me.

This verse is obscure, and the first part fails to correspond properly to the message of the previous verse (v. 16). The second sentence fits the context, for Paul indicates that he is under divine obligation to preach the gospel. The problem, then, lies in the first part of the verse, particularly with the word *reward*. Paul seems to retrace his steps in the following verse (v. 18), where he asks and answers the question what his reward is. With his repeated use of the first person pronoun (four times), he calls attention to himself.

a. "If I do this of my own choice." If we see this verse as continuing the explanation about Paul's rights as a preacher, the difficulties remain but no longer appear insurmountable. The Corinthians cannot understand how Paul fails to defend his rights as a preacher. They view him as a preacher who has come to them of his own free will. But Paul informs them that if he had come to them of his own choice, he would have expected monetary compensation from them. Then he would have a reward.

b. "But if I do so under compulsion, I simply fulfill the stewardship entrusted to me." Paul writes the word *stewardship* to show that although he is an apostle

---

43. See Norman Hillyer, *NIDNTT*, vol. 3, p. 1054.

with rights (vv. 1–6), he serves Jesus as a steward (see 4:1). In Paul's day, stewards were slaves who were given the responsibility of managing their master's household, estate, or financial affairs.

Paul knows that he has received his stewardship from Jesus himself. Whether a steward does his task by choice or under compulsion, his responsibility remains unaltered. If such a person fulfills his task not of his own will but because his master assigned it to him, he is merely a steward. He is like the servant in the parable who plowed his master's field, prepared his master's supper, waited on him, and finally had a free moment to eat and drink. He received no expression of gratitude for his labors, because he was his master's servant. Similarly, God's servants should say, "We are unworthy servants; we have only done our duty" (Luke 17:10).

18. What then is my reward? When I preach the gospel, I offer it free of charge so as not to make full use of my authority in the gospel.

a. "What then is my reward?" Paul realizes that in his discourse he failed to explain the word *reward* in the first sentence of the preceding verse (v. 17). Now he turns his attention to it and gives his explanation. Paul's desire to be obedient to his divine commission is evident in many epistles (e.g., 15:9–10; Gal. 1:15–16; Eph. 3:8–9). He regarded his commission to preach as a privilege. As a slave of Christ he willingly obeyed his Sender and thus received a reward. This reward is not something Paul desires for himself. He proclaims the gospel free of charge (v. 18).[44]

b. "When I preach the gospel, I offer it free of charge." Jesus commanded that the worker should receive his pay (Luke 10:7). In a sense, the phrase *preach the gospel* denotes as much the preaching as the actual living in accordance with the gospel.[45] Those who preach the gospel should receive their income from the gospel (v. 14). But Paul refuses to avail himself of his apostolic right and calls his preference to preach the gospel without pay his "boast" (v. 15). He labels his action not to accept payment for his work in the ministry his "reward" (v. 18). Conversely, if he had been told to preach for a certain sum of money, he would have been thwarted in his purpose.[46] The gospel would have been proclaimed, but Paul's reason for boasting would have been taken away.

By not receiving remuneration for his services, Paul was free from obligation to anyone. No one could ever lay a claim on Paul because of some monetary accountability (see II Cor. 11:7). In this freedom, Paul could actively proclaim the good news to everyone.

The purity of Paul's motive is aptly illustrated with a parallel taken from the medical world. "A physician may attend the sick from the highest motives, though he receives a remuneration for his services. But when he attends the

---

44. See Paul Christoph Böttger, *NIDNTT*, vol. 3, p. 142.

45. Consult Richard Cook, "Paul . . . Preacher or Evangelist?" *BibTr* 32 (1981): 441–44.

46. David Prior, *The Message of 1 Corinthians: Life in the Local Church*, The Bible Speaks Today series (Leicester and Downers Grove: InterVarsity, 1985), p. 158.

poor gratuitously, though the motives may be no higher, the evidence of their purity is placed beyond question."[47] Paul preached the gospel free of charge—indisputable evidence of his pure motive.

c. "So as not to make full use of my authority in the gospel." This second part of the sentence not only further explains the first part, but also concludes the entire segment on Paul's apostolic rights. Paul knows full well that he has the apostolic right to make his living from the gospel, but he chooses to ply the trade of the tentmaker. He uses his other rights but does not receive financial recompense. The last three words of the sentence, "in the gospel," should be taken with the word *authority* and should not be understood as an abbreviated reference to preaching the gospel. Paul gratuitously offers his services in regard to the gospel.

We raise two questions. First, why did Paul choose to preach the gospel without charge? He certainly did not do it to gain higher praise than the other apostles, who did exercise their apostolic right. Even though Paul writes that he worked harder than the others, he attributes praise and thanks to God (15:10). The thought of performing work for his own advantage was repugnant to Paul. He worked for the sake of the gospel and its increasing influence in the world.

Second, is Paul asking preachers of the gospel to imitate him? The answer is a resounding no. Nowhere in Paul's epistles do we find any evidence that preachers should abrogate the command Jesus gave the workers in his kingdom. If a minister of the gospel has an independent source of income and offers his services free of charge, he is free to make that choice. But that choice is his own and he can never require it of others. In the same way, Paul made a choice to supply his financial needs by working at his trade, but he could never demand this of his fellow workers.

Greek Words, Phrases, and Constructions in 9:15–18

Verse 15

ἐγώ—the use of the personal pronoun as the first word in the sentence denotes emphasis. It is followed by the adversative δέ to indicate contrast with the preceding verse.

ἔγραψα—this is the epistolary aorist; the writer looks at his epistle from the viewpoint of the readers and uses the past tense for the present: "I am writing."

ἤ—the comparative particle *than* depends on the adverb μᾶλλον (rather) and needs another element to complete the comparison. But this necessary element is lacking, with the result that the syntax is broken. To resort to using the word ἤ (truly) as a means to circumvent the break is inadvisable. Except for a variant in Hebrews 6:14, the reading ἤ occurs nowhere else in the New Testament.

οὐδεὶς κενώσει—"no one will empty." The manuscript support for this reading is early, strong, and has broad geographic representation. By contrast, textual support for the

---

47. Charles Hodge, *An Exposition of the First Epistle to the Corinthians* (1857; Grand Rapids: Eerdmans, 1965), p. 162.

variant ἵνα τις κενώσῃ (in order that someone may empty) is weak.[48] The rule that the harder reading is more likely to be original applies here.

Verse 16

ἐὰν γὰρ εὐαγγελίζωμαι—this clause is the protasis of a conditional sentence that conveys a concessive mode: "although I preach the gospel." The apodosis affirms factual truth.

ἐπίκειται—the passive voice ("is laid [on me]"), in which Jesus is the understood agent. The present tense discloses continuing relevance.

Verses 17–18

οἰκονομίαν πεπίστευμαι—notice that the accusative case of the noun *stewardship* is retained with the perfect passive verb *has been entrusted*. The active verb πιστεύω with the dative τινί and the accusative of the noun would be expected.[49] With the passive, however, Paul indirectly refers to Jesus.

ἵνα—this appositional clause explains the preceding verse (v. 17).

εἰς τὸ καταχρήσασθαι—the prepositional phrase with the articular infinitive expresses result rather than purpose. The infinitive is perfective ("use fully").

---

3. Apostolic Freedom
9:19–27

Paul had the difficult task of working in two distinct cultures: that of Jewish Christians who lived by the Mosaic law, and that of Gentile Christians who were free from the law of Moses. He had to preach the gospel to both groups while trying to bring them together in one community of believers and serving as a faithful pastor to those Christians who had weak consciences. Paul was in the unenviable position of giving leadership by speaking to all the issues that divided the believers in Corinth. For this reason, he wanted to be free so that he could be of service to all. Having demonstrated his desire to be free as a preacher of the gospel, he discloses the strategy he employs in winning people for Christ.

a. Paul's Strategy
9:19–23

19. For though I am free from all men, I was a slave to all to win as many people as possible.

With the word *free*, Paul returns to the discussion on freedom that began this chapter (v. 1). There he implied that he was free from the dietary restrictions that the Mosaic law placed on Jews. Now he intimates that he is free from financial dependence on anyone. By not accepting compensation from the church at Corinth for his ministry, he was free from any hindrance that could obstruct his preaching.

---

48. Consult Metzger, *Textual Commentary*, pp. 558–59.

49. C. F. D. Moule, *An Idiom-Book of New Testament Greek*, 2d ed. (Cambridge: Cambridge University Press, 1960), p. 32.

Freedom is a relative concept with its own limitations. Paul does not say that he is free from all things but free from all men. He echoes the idea that began the chapter (v. 1). There he states that he is free because he has Christian liberty. Here he asserts that he is free from all men, as an objective fact, because he has not availed himself of the complete freedom he possesses.[50]

Paul could say that he was at liberty to eat or not to eat meat, and that he enjoyed financial freedom because of his tentmaking trade. Yet he was never free from God's law, for he had freedom only within the context of that law. Augustine put it succinctly: "Man is most free when controlled by God alone."

As a free man, Paul is able to relate to every believer in the Corinthian church. He has full apostolic rights to be free from human control, yet he chooses to be a servant of all the Corinthian believers. He literally fulfilled Jesus' words addressed to the disciples: "You know that the rulers of the Gentiles lord it over them, and their high officials exercise authority over them. Not so with you. Instead, whoever wants to become great among you must be your servant, and whoever wants to be first must be your slave" (Matt. 20:25–27). Paul imitates Jesus, who came not to be served but to serve.

Being a slave to all, Paul's objective is to win as many people as possible for Christ. Let it be understood that he is not vying with other apostles to bring in the most converts. Instead, he hopes to gain more adherents with the strategy of being a slave than by any other method.[51] Conclusively, Paul demonstrates that he is a servant of Jesus by being a servant to Christ's people (compare Gal. 5:13).

20. To the Jews I conducted myself as a Jew to win the Jews; to those who are under the law I became as one under the law, though I myself am not under the law, to win those under the law.

a. "To the Jews I conducted myself as a Jew to win the Jews." As one who is a slave to all, Paul begins with his own people and abides by the principle "first to the Jew and then to the Gentile."[52] Paul was born a Jew and was a Hebrew of the Hebrews (Phil. 3:5). But when he writes that he *became* a Jew to the Jews, he implies that by becoming a follower of Jesus he is a new creation (II Cor. 5:17) and thus he is no longer a Jew or a Greek.[53]

During his ministry, Paul adapted himself to Jewish customs when he tried to win the Jews to Christ. These are a few striking examples: He had Timothy circumcised "because of the Jews" (Acts 16:3); he made a Nazirite vow to express thanks to God for deliverance (Acts 18:18); he joined four Nazirites in their pu-

---

50. Compare F. W. Grosheide, *Commentary on the First Epistle to the Corinthians: The English Text with Introduction, Exposition and Notes*, New International Commentary on the New Testament series (Grand Rapids: Eerdmans, 1953), p. 211.

51. R. St. John Parry, *The First Epistle of Paul the Apostle to the Corinthians*, Cambridge Greek Testament for Schools and Colleges (Cambridge: Cambridge University Press, 1937), p. 142.

52. See, e.g., Matt. 10:5–6; Acts 13:46; Rom. 1:16; 2:9.

53. Refer to Barbara Hall, "All Things to All People: A Study of 1 Corinthians 9:19–23," in *The Conversation Continues: Studies in Paul and John. In Honor of J. Louis Martyn*, ed. Robert T. Fortna and Beverly R. Gaventa (Nashville: Abingdon, 1990), p. 146.

rification rites and paid their expenses for the sacrificial offering (Acts 21:23–24, 26).

Paul tried to promote the unity of the church by bringing Gentile Christians from Macedonia and Asia Minor (Acts 20:4) to Jerusalem. Although he was accused of not teaching the law of Moses to the Jewish people living in the Dispersion (Acts 21:20–21), he willingly appeased the Jewish Christians in Jerusalem. He wished to demonstrate that he had no objections to obeying the law of Moses.[54]

b. "To those who are under the law I became as one under the law, though I myself am not under the law." Here is a parallel to the first sentence in this verse. Both sentences apply to the Jews who are under the law of Moses and also to Christians with weak consciences.[55] But why does Paul again call attention to the Jews? The answer seems to be that he wants to make a clear distinction between those who are under the law (v. 20) and those who do not have the law (v. 21). This distinction not only applies to the Jews on the one hand and the Greeks on the other; it also seems to relate to the Christians with weak consciences who are under the law and the strong Christians who exercise their freedom from the law.[56]

The word *law* in this verse and the next (v. 21) alludes to the Mosaic law. To be precise, the civil and ceremonial part of that law proved to be a burden to the Jews (compare Acts 15:10; Gal. 5:1). Yet Paul is willing to associate with those Jews who consider obedience to the Mosaic law their duty. With fellow Jews he observes their customs that include dietary rules, washings, and Sabbath observance.

As the champion of Christian liberty (see, e.g., Gal. 2:4; 5:13), Paul will put aside his freedom in Christ and place himself in bondage to the Mosaic law. He will do so in Jewish settings for only one reason: to win the Jews to Christ. However, he adds a telling disclaimer to his willingness to observe the commandments of the law of Moses: "I myself am not under the law."[57] He remains free in Christ Jesus.

c. "To win those under the law." Paul's purpose for obeying Jewish law is to encourage Jews to convert to Christianity. He is not alluding to Jewish Christians who already know that they have freedom. He has in mind the Jews who as yet do not know Jesus and the liberating power of the gospel. He desires that "those under the law" may have the same freedom he enjoys in Christ.

Even though Paul was appointed an apostle primarily to the Gentiles (see Gal. 2:7–9), he preached the gospel of salvation to both the Jews and the Greeks (Acts

54. Consult Simon J. Kistemaker, *Exposition of the Acts of the Apostles*, New Testament Commentary series (Grand Rapids: Baker, 1990), pp. 762–64.

55. See T. L. Donaldson, "The 'Curse of the Law' and the Inclusion of the Gentiles: Galatians 3, 13–14," *NTS* 32 (1986): 94–112. Compare Stephen Westerholm, *Israel's Law and the Church's Faith: Paul and His Recent Interpreters* (Grand Rapids: Eerdmans, 1988), pp. 192–95.

56. See Hall, "All Things to All People," p. 146.

57. The Majority Text omits this clause, which may have been omitted accidentally in transcription. Consult Metzger, *Textual Commentary*, p. 559. The evidence for inclusion is overwhelming.

20:21). Thus he sought to win both "those under the law" and "those who are without the law." To both Jews and Gentiles, Paul adapted himself for the benefit of the gospel.

21. To those who are without the law I became as one without the law, though I am not without the law of God but under Christ's law, to gain those who are without the law.

a. "To those who are without the law I became as one without the law." Why does Paul not say forthrightly "Gentiles" instead of writing the lengthy circumscription "those who are without the law"? First, in this epistle he avoids alienating the Gentiles and is cautious in addressing them directly.[58] Next, he faces both the Gentiles who are ignorant of God's law and the Gentile Christians who are free from the Mosaic law. And last, "those without the law" might even refer to the strong Corinthians.

God had entrusted to the Jews the "very words of God" (Rom. 3:2) but had bypassed all the other nations (Ps. 147:19–20). The nations were people without the law. In Greek, Paul writes the term *anomos*, which has a twofold meaning: objectively, the Gentiles were without the law of God; subjectively, they were people who paid no attention to that law.[59] In the present verse the objective meaning prevails. Paul contrasts those who are without the law with those who had received the law. Yet the subjective sense is also in force, because Paul immediately adds that he himself is not without God's law. He lives in accordance with Christ's law.

Whenever Paul spent time with Gentiles, he did not observe the Jewish food laws, circumcision, and New Moon and Sabbath celebrations (see Gal. 2:11–14; Col. 2:11, 16). No wonder that in Jerusalem he was accused of teaching the Jews in Dispersion to turn away from the laws and customs of Moses (Acts 21:21). From a Jewish point of view, Paul's conduct among the Gentiles made him a Gentile. The Jews reasoned that he was not ignorant of the law; therefore he transgressed God's precepts.

b. "Though I am not without the law of God[60] but within Christ's law." With these words, Paul makes clear to both Jewish and Gentile Christians that he is not a lawless person. Notice that in three successive verses Paul emphatically informs his readers about his state:

I am free from all men (v. 19).
I myself am not under the law (v. 20).
I am not without the law of God but under the law of Christ (v. 21).

The first assertion (v. 19) should be explained in the light of the other two statements (vv. 20, 21). "Being free means being neither under law nor outside law,

---

58. The word *Gentiles* occurs only four times (I Cor. 1:23; 5:1; 10:20; 12:2).
59. Refer to Walter Gutbrod, *TDNT*, vol. 4, p. 1086.
60. Fee takes this noun as an objective genitive, "toward God." *First Corinthians*, p. 429. See also MLB.

but in Christ."[61] And the one who is in Christ Jesus is a new creation. In relation to Christ Paul is free, yet at the same time he is under Christ's law.

Engaged in a play on the term *law,* Paul is saying that he is free from the law by which the Jews sought salvation. But now that salvation has come through Jesus Christ, he subjects himself to the law of Christ. Through Christ, Paul's view of the law of God has changed. He no longer seeks salvation in relation to the law but now he wants to keep the law to show his gratitude to Christ.

What, then, is this law of Christ? The expression occurs once more in the New Testament (Gal. 6:2) and describes the implementation of love: bearing one another's burdens. Although Christ has abolished the civil and ceremonial laws, God's moral commands remain. Paul tells his reader that the keeping of these commands is important (7:19).[62] He even places the word of Jesus, that the worker is worthy of his wages (Luke 10:7), on a level with one of the Mosaic precepts (Deut. 25:4; I Cor. 9:9, 14; I Tim. 5:18). If the believer is within Christ's law, at the same time he is within God's law and obeys his will. Because Christ mediates God's law, Paul must abide by the constraints of that law in the setting of Christ's covenant. "Whatever God demands of him as a new-covenant believer, a Christian, binds him; he cannot step outside those constraints. There is a rigid limit to his flexibility as he seeks to win the lost from different cultural and religious groups; he must not do anything that is forbidden to the Christian, and he must do everything mandated of the Christian. He is not free from God's law; he is under Christ's law."[63]

c. "To gain those who are without the law." In his effort to win as many people as possible to Christ, Paul seeks to win the Gentiles to the Lord. When they put their faith in Christ, these Gentiles order their lives in accord with the law of Christ.

22. To those who are weak I became weak to win the weak. I have become all things to all men so that by all means I may save some.

We make two observations:

a. *Adaptation.* "To those who are weak I became weak to win the weak." Paul now returns to his discussion on the Christians with weak consciences (8:9–13). In a roundabout way he has come full circle by reviewing the freedom he has in Christ. Thus he discusses his relationship to the weak. We would have expected syntactical balance that included the strong. But Paul is not interested in comparing the strong with the weak. The strong were free in Christ and had no guilty conscience when they ate meat that had been sacrificed to an idol. The weak were those Corinthians who were weak in conscience; they needed Paul's counsel and his encouragement to be strengthened in their Christian faith (Rom. 14:1; 15:1).

---

61. Hall, "All Things to All People," p. 152.

62. Consult Herman N. Ridderbos, *Paul: An Outline of His Theology,* trans. John Richard de Witt (Grand Rapids: Eerdmans, 1975), pp. 284–85.

63. D. A. Carson, *The Cross and Christian Ministry* (Grand Rapids: Baker, 1993), pp. 119–20.

Verse 22 intimates that in this particular passage Paul also may have been thinking of winning the economically weak Corinthians for the Lord. Earlier in his epistle he stated that among those whom God had called there were not many who were powerful and not many of noble birth, and that God had chosen the weak and insignificant things to shame the strong (1:26–28). Now Paul resonates this same message when he writes, "I became weak to win the weak." In context, he uses the verb *to win* for both the Jews (vv. 19–20) and the Gentiles (v. 21) to lead them to a saving knowledge of Christ. But when Paul speaks about the weak—those whose consciences are weak—there is no need to write the verb *to win*. The weak already know Jesus Christ as their Savior; as weak in conscience they require help from those who are strong.

We suggest that with the phrase *I became weak to win the weak* in verse 22, Paul may have had in mind a double connotation—a connotation that refers to both the weak in conscience and the economically weak.[64] Consider the fact that during his ministry in Corinth Paul readily identified himself with the poor not only in word but also in deed. His tentmaking trade was a vivid demonstration of siding with those who were economically weak (Acts 18:1–4). Paul himself belonged to the upper class, as was reflected in the education he had received. Just the same, he voluntarily donned his apron and headband to ply his trade. The social elite of the Greco-Roman world scorned him for his demeaning trade, but the lower-class people accepted him gladly.[65] The elite considered the workshop a place not for the freeman but for the slave. Paul, however, was willing to identify with the poor to win them to Christ.

b. *Actuality.* "I have become all things to all men so that by all means I may save some." The apostle is a model for everyone who desires to win people to Christ. Paul adapted himself to different situations in every culture. With the Jews he lived as a Jew, and with the Gentiles as a Gentile (within the boundaries of Christ's command). And to the weak he became weak, so that he might become "all things to all men."

Opponents might accuse Paul of being ineffectual, unstable, and changeable. If so, they would completely misunderstand his motive. They would fail to see the driving purpose that motivated Paul in his mission endeavor: to bring the gospel to as many people as possible.

Paul was convinced that as he preached the good news of salvation, God would open the heart of every person he chose to save. If God was pleased to save Paul, who calls himself the worst of sinners (I Tim. 1:15), the Lord Jesus Christ could break into the heart of anyone who lived in spiritual darkness. Paul served

---

64. David Alan Black avers that the weak are non-Christians who were incapable of working out any righteousness for themselves. "A Note on 'the Weak' in 1 Corinthians 9, 22," *Bib* 64 (1983): 240–42. Kenneth V. Neller understands the weak to be people who lack spiritual maturity. "1 Corinthians 9:19–23. A Model for Those Who Seek to Win Souls," *ResQ* 29 (1987): 129–42.

65. Ronald F. Hock, "Paul's Tentmaking and the Problem of His Social Class," *JBL* 97 (1978): 555–64.

as God's instrument to bring sinners to God through the gospel. Paul preached, counseled, and encouraged, but the actual work of salvation belonged to God.

In a few words, Paul expresses sober realism when he writes that by being all things to all men "by all means [he] may save some." Some Greek manuscripts have the reading "I may save all," but the evidence favors the text we have adopted, "I may save some." Understandably, Paul would be the first one to say that although he worked hard to present the gospel to all people, not he but God effects salvation (Phil. 2:13). He works as if all people are to be saved but he knows that only some will respond to the gospel (see 10:33; Rom. 11:14).

23. And I do all things for the sake of the gospel that I may jointly share in it.[66]

a. "And I do all things." Notice that Paul writes the word *all* four times in verses 22 and 23. That is, he is a humble servant of the gospel who will go to any length, descend or ascend to any level of society, perform any menial task as long as the gospel is proclaimed to all people. To Paul the word *discrimination* was unknown, for he declared that in Christ there "is neither Jew nor Greek, slave nor free, male nor female" (Gal. 3:28). He knew that in Christ all believers are one.

b. "For the sake of the gospel." The clause repeats the thought of verses 15–18. Paul is a servant of the gospel, as he demonstrates by serving all classes of people. He thinks of the task which the Lord has given him and which he hopes to complete. It is the task of fully proclaiming the gospel of God's grace to all people everywhere (Acts 20:24; and see Phil. 3:7–14). Paul was ready to travel to Illyricum (modern Albania and the former Yugoslavia) and Spain to give the gospel the widest possible hearing (see Rom. 15:19, 24).

c. "That I may jointly share in it." We would expect Paul to be the loser when he announced his intention to be a servant of all those who wanted to listen to the gospel. Paul is not the loser but the beneficiary of the blessings that accompany the preaching of the good news. Whenever a person turns in faith to Christ, there is joy and happiness in the Lord. And Paul the proclaimer of the gospel participates in the joyous celebration. In addition, he receives a rich blessing from the work of preaching the good tidings of salvation.

The literal translation of this part of verse 23 is, "that I may be a co-partner in it." The word *co-partner* signifies not so much that Paul participates in the work of preaching with his associates. Rather, he is a partner in the blessings which the converts to Christ receive; that is, he rejoices with them as they claim the spiritual benefits that accrue from a life of obedience to the gospel.

Practical Considerations in 9:19–23

If Paul wanted to be all things to all men, did he not expose himself to criticism from those who would call him weak? They expected him to be a strong leader. But Paul himself shows his willingness to be a weak person among those who are weak. Remaining true

---

66. Bauer, p. 774. Instead of "all things," the Majority Text has "this" (KJV, NKJV).

to the teaching of the gospel, he was free with respect to neutral things including matters of food and drink. Paul was free from the Jews, the Gentiles, and the weak, but ministered the gospel effectively to all.

Paul follows in the footsteps of Jesus, who during his earthly ministry ate with tax collectors and prostitutes. Jesus was known as their friend (Matt. 11:19) and thus was considered to be one of them. Jesus drank water given to him by a Samaritan woman at Jacob's well, and his disciples were surprised to see him talking with a woman (John 4:9, 11, 27). Jesus told the Pharisees to pay taxes to Caesar and to give to God that which belongs to God (Matt. 22:21).[67] Jesus sets the example of accommodating himself to the culture and circumstances of the people among whom he preached the gospel. Yet the gospel itself remained unchanged.

In the interest of the gospel, missionaries, evangelists, and pastors must adapt themselves to the people and community in which they are placed. Without ever compromising the demands of the gospel, their purpose should always be to bring the people to a saving knowledge of Jesus Christ. As Jesus puts it in his high-priestly prayer to his Father, "That they may know you, the only true God, and Jesus Christ, whom you have sent" (John 17:3). And having this knowledge is life eternal.

Greek Words, Phrases, and Constructions in 9:19–23

Verse 19

ὤν—in this verse and the next two (vv. 20, 21), the present participle of εἰμί (I am) denotes concession ("although").

ἐκ πάντων πᾶσιν—the preposition with the genitive plural expresses the idea *free from*. The first adjective can be either masculine or neuter ("from all men" or "from all things"). The context favors the masculine. The second adjective refers to people ("to everyone").

τοὺς πλείονας—the adjective is comparative but in this context signifies, "as many as possible."[68]

Verse 20

τοῖς Ἰουδαίοις—the presence of the definite article before the word *Jews* indicates "those with whom I had to deal on each occasion."[69]

Verse 21

τοῖς ἀνόμοις—the definite article points to a specific group of people who are without the law, namely, the Gentiles.

θεοῦ . . . Χριστοῦ—the better Greek manuscripts have the words *God* and *Christ* in the genitive, which can be either subjective or objective. The Majority Text has the dative case for these two nouns and reads, "toward God . . . toward Christ" (NKJV). Most translators, however, take the nouns as subjective genitives ("of God . . . of Christ").

---

67. Consult Peter Richardson and Paul W. Gooch, "Accommodation Ethics," *TynB* 29 (1978): 89–142; Peter Richardson, "Pauline Inconsistency: I Corinthians 9:19–23 and Galatians 2:11–14," *NTS* 26 (1980): 347–62.

68. Compare Robertson, *Grammar*, p. 665.

69. Blass and Debrunner, *Greek Grammar*, #262.1.

Verses 22–23

ἀσθενής—some manuscripts place the particle ὡς (as) before this adjective *weak* (see KJV, NKJV, TNT, *Cassirer*). However, it is easier to explain the insertion of the particle than its deletion. Therefore, we omit this particle.

κερδήσω—the verb *to win* occurs five times in four verses (vv. 19–22). The presence of the aorist subjunctive σώσω (I save) signifies that the two verbs mean the same thing.

τοῖς πᾶσιν . . . πάντα . . . πάντως . . . πάντα—note the repeated use of the word *all* to connote Paul's exertion. The definite article refers to the individual groups mentioned in verses 20–22.[70]

αὐτοῦ—this pronoun in the genitive case refers to the gospel and is dependent on the noun συγκοινωνός (partner). Writes C. K. Barrett, "This is sometimes wrongly understood. Paul does not mean, 'a partner with the Gospel' (in the work of salvation; this would require αὐτῷ, not αὐτοῦ); nor does he mean 'one who shares in the work of (preaching) the Gospel'. His word means participation in (the benefits of) the Gospel."[71]

---

b. Paul's Illustrations
9:24–27

Every speaker knows that an apt illustration clarifies the point he is making. The risk, of course, is that the listeners often tend to forget the point but remember the illustration. Paul takes an example from the Greek sports arena and applies it more to himself than to the Corinthians. He is a model to others and expects that they will follow him.

24. Do you not know that they who run in a race are all running, but only one receives the prize? So run the race that you may win.

a. *Prize.* In the ancient world, second in importance to the Olympic Games were the Isthmian Games. Held about ten miles from Corinth, the Isthmian Games were celebrated every other year and attracted numerous athletes and spectators from many parts of the world.[72] During the year and a half that Paul spent in Corinth (A.D. 50–52), the games were held in the spring of A.D. 51. He became familiar with the contests and we assume he even witnessed some events. Paul might have plied his trade at Isthmia, where he would have an opportunity to present the gospel to numerous people who had come to participate in or to observe the games.[73]

The illustration that Paul uses speaks to the readers of his epistle, for citizens of Corinth were themselves involved in these Isthmian games. They were well informed about sprinters and long-distance runners in the arena. They knew that

---

70. Blass and Debrunner, *Greek Grammar*, #275.7.

71. C. K. Barrett, *A Commentary on the First Epistle to the Corinthians*, Harper's New Testament Commentaries series (New York and Evanston: Harper and Row, 1968), p. 216.

72. Refer to John V. A. Fine, *The Ancient Greeks: A Critical History* (Cambridge, Mass., and London: Harvard University Press, 1983), p. 118.

73. Compare Oscar Broneer, "The Apostle Paul and the Isthmian Games," *BA* 25 (1962): 2–32 (especially p. 20).

even though all the runners compete in a given race, only one person receives the prize.

b. *Exhortation.* "So run the race that you may win." Paul uses the word *race* metaphorically to indicate that all believers are participating in a spiritual race. And he is not suggesting that of all the believers who run this race only one wins the prize. Certainly not. Paul exhorts the Corinthians to take their spiritual life seriously and consider it to be a contest in which they must exert themselves to the limit.

But how does this illustration fit in the context of apostolic freedom? Paul has shown that for him the only cause that counts is the progress of the gospel. For this cause he exerts himself with all his intellectual, spiritual, and physical power. In a similar manner, the Corinthian believers must apply themselves to advance their spiritual lives as if they are engaged in a race and compete for a prize.[74]

25. And everyone who competes in the games exercises self-control in all respects.[75] They do this to receive a perishable crown, but we an imperishable crown.

a. "And everyone who competes in the games exercises self-control in all respects." Paul describes the activity of the individual with the Greek verb *agōnizomai* (I fight, struggle), from which we derive the verb *to agonize*. In the sports arena, the athlete subjects himself or herself to a severe struggle of body and mind. The contestant must practice total self-control to compete and to be victorious (II Tim. 2:5). Paul adds the words *in all respects*, which evoke images of lengthy training, arduous drills, proper diet, and sufficient rest. The athlete keeps mind and body focused on one goal: the winning of the prize.

b. "They do this to receive a perishable crown, but we an imperishable crown." The switch from the singular *everyone* to the plural *they* and *we* contrasts the objective of athletes with that of believers. The athletes in Paul's day strove for a crown that was made of either pine or parsley.[76] Imagine strenuous toil spent for a wreath of parsley that had already withered! Apart from the victory of the moment, that wreath is already worthless because it is perishing. Moreover, the spectators soon forget the feats of one victor as others win prizes.

By contrast, says Paul, we exert ourselves to win a crown that is imperishable. What is this crown that cannot perish? The New Testament teaches that it is righteousness, eternal life, and glory.[77] In other words, the crown which the believers receive has eternal value.

In the Greek, the final clause in this verse (v. 25) is extremely terse, literally, "but we an imperishable." Paul compels the reader to fill in the details from the context. He compares the two crowns by going from the lesser to the greater. He implies that if athletes exert themselves to obtain a perishable crown, Christians

---

74. Compare Gal. 2:2; 5:7; Phil. 2:16; II Tim. 4:7; Heb. 12:1.
75. Bauer, p. 216.
76. Broneer, "Apostle Paul," pp. 16–17; Colin J. Hemer, *NIDNTT*, vol. 1, p. 406.
77. See II Tim. 4:8; James 1:12; I Peter 5:4; Rev. 2:10.

should do likewise or even more to procure a crown that lasts forever. Isaac Watts put this thought in poetic lines when he asked:

> Must I be carried to the skies
> On flowery beds of ease,
> While others fought to win the prize
> And sailed through bloody seas?

26. Indeed I run in such a way as not losing aim; I box in such a way as not beating air. 27. But I treat my body roughly and enslave it, so that after I have proclaimed the gospel to others, I myself do not become disqualified.

a. *Two examples.* In the preceding verses (vv. 24–25), Paul moved from the second person plural *you* to the first person plural *we* to include himself among the recipients of the imperishable crown. From the first person plural, he now proceeds to the first person singular *I* and calls attention to his own conduct. He does so by using two illustrations borrowed from the sports arena: running and boxing.

"Indeed I run in such a way as not losing aim." Paul is coming to the conclusion of his discourse on apostolic freedom (vv. 19–27). And he applies his conclusive remarks to himself: he is the runner and the boxer. As a runner in the arena, he keeps his eye on the finish line, for he cannot afford to run aimlessly. Throughout the race, the goal is always before him, as he himself writes, "Forgetting what is behind and straining toward what is ahead, I press on toward the goal to win the prize for which God has called me heavenward in Christ Jesus" (Phil. 3:13b–14). No runner in a race loses sight of the finish line. All the other contenders are a vivid reminder of that mark. Paul is saying to the Corinthians who seemed to be lax in their spiritual pursuit, "Emulate me as you see me running toward the goal to win the prize."

"I box in such a way as not beating air." At times a boxer punches but misses his opponent and thus exposes himself to a counterpunch that can be devastating. Paul tells his readers that he is not wasting his blows on air. Instead he is a professional who boxes with purpose, precision, and skill. Paul resorts to this example only to demonstrate that in his fight for the gospel he does not miss an opportunity. The two illustrations sketch Paul's deliberate pursuit of his goal.

b. *Metaphor.* "But I treat my body roughly and enslave it." Instead of "I treat roughly," a literal translation of the Greek is "I give my body a black eye." Again the imagery is borrowed from the sport of boxing, in which boxers often appear with black and blue bruises on their faces. By borrowing this imagery, Paul is not indicating that he literally treats his physical body in a rough manner. His enemies and opponents repeatedly bruised his body when he endured floggings and beatings (II Cor. 11:23–25), but we have no reason to believe that he beat and bruised himself. With the expression *enslave*, Paul indicates that he exercises self-control and dedicates himself to his purpose.

"So that after I have proclaimed the gospel to others, I myself do not become disqualified." At first glance, this sentence does not seem to be a conclusive statement. Some translators have sensed this problem and have tried to overcome it by either expanding the sentence or changing the wording. One version has the addition given here in italics, "I myself will not be disqualified *for the prize*" (NIV). Another paraphrases, "To keep myself from being disqualified after having called others to the contest" (GNB).

Paul places himself before his readers as an example. He controls his lifestyle in such a way that no one can accuse him of preaching the gospel while contradicting it by the life he leads. Paul exerts himself physically and mentally for the benefit of the gospel; he shows his listeners that what he preaches to them is reality in his personal life.

Many scholars interpret every part of this verse to be imagery taken from the sports arena. They say that just as announcers at the games call out the names of contestants so Paul is an announcer of the gospel. They add that Paul is both an announcer and a contestant at the games.[78] But the question is whether we interpret everything in this passage figuratively or literally. For example, the word *proclaim* refers to preaching and not to announcing the names of contestants and winners at the games. Here a literal interpretation is preferred. In other parts of the passage Paul figuratively portrays himself as a contestant who strives to win the prize, namely, the crown that lasts and will not perish.

The negative in the clause "so that . . . I myself not become disqualified" relates to the content of this and the immediately preceding chapter (chap. 8). While proclaiming the good news, Paul enjoyed apostolic freedom. But he denied himself certain foods so as not to offend the weaker brothers, refused remuneration for his services, and thus became all things to all people to advance the gospel.

Doctrinal Considerations in 9:24–27

"Practice what you preach" is a caustic challenge that non-Christians frequently hurl at everyone who believes in Christ. We know that Christians are living in glass houses, so to speak, for the world is watching to see if these believers who preach and teach the gospel live up to its demands.

Paul is saying the same thing as the non-Christians, but he applies the maxim to himself. He does so intentionally to set himself as an example to those who read his epistle. By living in harmony with the gospel, he and they will be above reproach. Yet he himself intimates that he may be disqualified if he fails to practice self-control. Is Paul speaking about the possibility of falling from grace and forfeiting his salvation? Some scholars say that in the context of verse 27, Paul is speaking not of salvation but a reward for service.[79] It is true that he mentions the term *reward* in verse 18, but there it pertains to preaching the gospel free of charge and not to God's grace toward a sinner.

God elects a person in Christ and grants him or her the assurance of salvation. Conversely, God expects the believer in a test of faith to demonstrate a sincere desire to know

---

78. E.g., Robertson and Plummer, *First Corinthians*, p. 197.
79. Donald Guthrie, *New Testament Theology* (Downers Grove: InterVarsity, 1981), p. 627.

his will, to obey his commands, to be thankful for his gift of salvation, to love God and one's neighbor, to have faith in God and hope to overcome trials.[80]

If the Christian's desire is cold and his heart callous, does he run the risk of losing his salvation? Paul does not teach that God's electing love exempts the believer from all responsibility and that without a test of faith God grants him or her the crown of eternal life. Not at all, for Paul exhorts the believers to work out their own salvation with fear and trembling, because it is God who works in them to will and to work (Phil. 2:12–13).

Could Paul himself fall from grace and be disqualified? No, because he spared no effort to serve the Lord, preach the gospel, and live honorably before God and man. Elsewhere Paul warns the Corinthians to examine themselves so that they will not fail the test (see II Cor. 13:5–7). Then he adds that he and others have not failed it. Near the end of his life, Paul writes that he will receive the crown of righteousness that is in store for him (II Tim. 4:8).

Greek Words, Phrases, and Constructions in 9:24–27

Verse 24

μέν . . . δέ—in this verse and the next (v. 25), these particles show decided contrast.

τρέχετε—the present imperative, not the present indicative, as a command to the Corinthians to abandon their lax attitude and assume the role of spiritual athletes.

Verse 25

πάντα—this is an accusative plural of general reference ("in reference to all things").[81]

ἄφθαρτον—"incorruptible." This compound verbal adjective with the privative ἀ (not) denotes passive voice: it cannot be corrupted.

Verse 26

ἐγώ—at the beginning of the sentence and separated from the main verb *to run*, this personal pronoun receives emphasis.

οὐκ—the particle οὐ instead of μή is used to negate the present participle δέρων (beating). However, the position of οὐ indicates that it negates not the participle but the noun ἀέρα (air).

Verse 27

ὑπωπιάζω—"I beat black and blue." The verb is a compound of the preposition ὑπό (under) and the noun ὤψ (eye), that is, to strike under the eye. "The expr[ession] is obviously taken fr[om] the language of prize-fighting."[82]

Summary of Chapter 9

In close connection with the preceding chapter, Paul pursues the matter of apostolic rights, that is, freedom of choice. He asks whether he and fellow apos-

---

80. Compare Hermann Haarbeck, *NIDNTT*, vol. 3, p. 810.
81. Blass and Debrunner, *Greek Grammar*, #154.
82. Bauer, p. 848; Thayer, p. 646.

tles have a right to food and drink, to take a wife along on their journeys, and to be exempt from physical labor.

In a continuous series of questions he asks: Does a soldier serve at his own expense? Does a farmer not eat his own grapes? Does a shepherd refrain from consuming the milk products of his flock? Then he proves his argument by quoting the law of Moses, which forbids muzzling the ox when it is threshing. People who work in the fields share in the harvest; so Paul and his associates who sow spiritual seeds should be able to reap a material harvest from the Corinthians. Workers in the temple receive their sustenance from the temple. Likewise also the Lord commanded that preachers of the gospel should derive their living from it.

Paul refuses to avail himself of the right of material support. He wants to preach the gospel without being dependent on anyone for aid. Thus he is not obligated to anyone, is able to boast, and can freely preach the gospel. He belongs to no one, and is free to win various people to Christ: the Jews, those under the law, those without the law, and the weak. Paul is all things to all people.

With imagery borrowed from the games, he exhorts his readers to run the race to obtain the prize. He applies the illustrations to himself and says that he does not run without looking intently at the goal. He disciplines himself so as not to be disqualified.

10

Warnings and Freedom

(10:1–11:1)

Outline (continued)

10 1 For I do not want you to be ignorant, brothers, that all our fathers were under the cloud and all passed through the sea; 2 and all were baptized into Moses in the cloud and in the sea. 3 And all ate the same spiritual food, 4 and all drank the same spiritual drink. For they were drinking from the spiritual rock which followed them, and the rock was Christ. 5 However, God was not pleased with most of them, for their bodies were scattered over the desert.

6 Now these things became examples for us, so that we should not long for evil things just as those people did. 7 Do not be idolaters as some of them were. Just as it is written,

> "The people sat down to eat and drink
> and they stood up to play."

8 Nor let us practice sexual immorality as some of them practiced, when in one day twenty-three thousand fell dead. 9 And let us not test Christ as some of them did and were destroyed by snakes. 10 And do not grumble as some of them did and were destroyed by the angel that destroys. 11 Now these things happened to them as a warning and were written for our admonition, upon whom the ends of the ages have come. 12 So he who thinks he stands, let him be careful not to fall. 13 No temptation has overtaken you except that which is common to everyone. But God is faithful, who will not allow you to be tempted beyond that which you are able to bear; however, with the temptation he also will provide the way of escape that you may be able to endure it.

D. Warnings and Freedom
10:1–11:1

1. Warnings from History
10:1–13

Paul seems to introduce an entirely different subject in 10:1–13, but closer scrutiny shows continuity with the preceding passage (9:24–27). He reaches back into history to teach his readers the lesson the Israelites had to learn as they traveled from Egypt through the desert toward the promised land. In a sense, these Israelites were engaged in a contest of faith in which only two persons, Joshua and Caleb, received a blessing. The implied comparison is with the foot race (9:24) in which all the runners participate but only one receives the prize. "The one runner whom the judge of the contest crowns is the counterpart of the two faithful Israelites, to whom alone it was given to enter the Promised Land."[1]

---

1. Frederic Louis Godet, *Commentary on First Corinthians* (1886; reprint ed., Grand Rapids: Kregel, 1977), p. 478.

Why did the Israelites perish in the desert? Despite the miracles God performed to lead them out of Egypt, these Israelites lacked faith in God. They crossed the Red Sea, never lacked daily food (manna), drank water from a rock, were sheltered from the scorching sun by the cloud that accompanied them, and received numerous other blessings. Instead of worshiping God, the Israelites served idols which they had taken along from Egypt (Amos 5:26). At Mount Sinai they formed a golden calf (Exod. 32:1–6) and worshiped it. These rebellious Israelites failed the test of faith, and, Paul intimates, those Corinthians who engage in idolatry similarly fail to serve God.

a. Analogy
10:1–5

1. For I do not want you to be ignorant, brothers, that all our fathers were under the cloud and all passed through the sea; 2. and all were baptized into Moses in the cloud and in the sea.

a. "For I do not want you to be ignorant, brothers." The conjunction *for* joins this verse to the preceding context (chap. 9) and indicates a continuation of that discourse. Paul also employs the address *brothers*, which includes the sisters, and introduces new material to his discourse. He reminds the readers of events from Israel's history and uses these incidents as effective examples. Throughout his epistles, Paul expresses his desire not to see his readers ignorant of certain facts.[2] To dispel their ignorance he refers to either personal intentions and experiences or spiritual truths. These spiritual truths he will later apply to their question concerning eating meat which was offered to an idol.

b. "All our fathers were under the cloud and all passed through the sea." With this terse description, Paul mentions the exodus and the crossing of the Red Sea. God led his people by means of a cloud by day and a pillar of fire by night (Exod. 13:21). Thus, they were able to travel during either the day or the night. The cloud and the pillar of fire represented God's presence hovering over his people. Although the cloud and the pillar always attended the people (see Exod. 14:24; Num. 12:5; Deut. 31:15; Ps. 99:7), some in Israel's camp doubted God's nearness.

Paul calls the Israelites "all our fathers." He implies that the entire nation of Israel left Egypt and that this nation assumes the role of spiritual forefathers for both Jewish and Gentile Christians in Corinth. The possessive pronoun places those Gentiles who are members of the Christian community on the same level as Jewish Christians.

The phrase *all passed through the sea* alludes to Israel crossing the Red Sea on dry land while the Egyptian forces drowned in those same waters (Exod. 14). The fact that all the people safely reached the other shore demonstrates God's faithfulness toward his people in the past and assures his trustworthiness in the present.

2. Rom. 1:13; 11:25; I Cor. 12:1; II Cor. 1:8; I Thess. 4:13.

c. "And all were baptized into Moses in the cloud and in the sea." Paul's reference to baptism links past and present. He projects the Christian meaning of baptism into Christ (Rom. 6:3; Gal. 3:27) onto the exodus by saying that all the Israelites were baptized into Moses. He compares the Christians who place their faith in Jesus Christ to the Israelites who placed their trust in God, represented by his servant Moses (see Exod. 14:31). Christ redeemed his people from sin and death, while God through Moses delivered the Israelites from oppression in Egypt and the destructive waters of the Red Sea.

For the Israelites, being "baptized into Moses" signified that they were members of the covenant which God had made with his people (Exod. 24:4b–8). Moses served as mediator of that first covenant, which became obsolete, but Christ is the Mediator of the new covenant (Heb. 7:22; 8:6; 9:15). Just as God's people became a nation with Moses as its leader, so God's people today are incorporated into Christ, who is their spiritual head (Eph. 5:23).

What is the significance of the two elements, the cloud and the sea? A study of the relevant chapters in Exodus reveals that with the cloud and the sea, God separated his people from the hostile Egyptian forces. The cloud went from the front to the back of the Israelites and remained behind them to separate God's people from the armies of Pharaoh (Exod. 14:19–20). The Red Sea became a defensive barrier for the Israelites and served as a boundary between Egypt and Israel (Exod. 23:31). "The experiences of being 'under the cloud' and 'passing through the sea' both related to the *identification* of the children of Israel as a people now separated from Egypt, and under God's protection."[3] In short, by means of the cloud and the sea God separated to himself a people. The exodus must be seen from both a historical and a spiritual perspective.

As the passage through the Red Sea symbolized an end to Israel's slavery and its beginning as a new nation, so baptism for the Christian means a separation from sin and consecration to God. The experience of being under the protective cloud and passing through the waters of the Red Sea was the Israelite's prerequisite for inclusion in God's people. Similarly, the sign of being baptized into Christ is the mark of participating in his redemption. In short, being baptized into Moses represents Israel's redemption, much as being baptized into Christ entails the Christian's incorporation into his fellowship.[4]

3. And all ate the same spiritual food, 4. and all drank the same spiritual drink. For they were drinking from the spiritual rock which followed them, and the rock was Christ.

---

3. Paul D. Gardner, "The Gifts of God and the Authentication of a Christian," Ph.D. diss., Cambridge University, 1989, p. 127. Consult also William B. Badker, "Baptised into Moses—Baptised into Christ: A Study in Doctrine Development," *EvQ* 60 (1988): 23–29; Michael A. G. Haykin, "'In the Cloud and in the Sea': Basil of Caesarea and the Exegesis of I Cor. 10:2," *VigChr* 40 (1986): 135–44.

4. Consult Herman N. Ridderbos, *Paul: An Outline of His Theology*, trans. John Richard de Witt (Grand Rapids: Eerdmans, 1975), pp. 405–6; G. de Ru, "De Doop van Israël tussen Egypte en de Sinaï," *NedTTS* 21 (1967): 348–69.

a. "And all ate the same spiritual food, and all drank the same spiritual drink." Five times in five consecutive clauses, Paul writes the adjective *all.* That is, everyone who participated in the exodus was under the cloud, passed through the sea, was baptized into Moses, ate spiritual food, and drank from the spiritual rock.

God led the Israelites into the desert, away from the Egyptian granaries, and yet supplied them with "bread from heaven." The people called this bread "manna," which literally means, "what is it?" (Exod. 16:15). Every morning, except on the Sabbath, God caused manna to cover the ground (Exod. 16:2–36). This manna kept the Israelites alive until they had crossed the Jordan and ate bread baked from grain grown in Canaan. Then the daily provision of manna stopped (Josh. 5:12).

The same thing was true for Israel's need for water. During Israel's forty-year sojourn in the desert, God provided drinking water for his people and for their animals.[5] Moses struck a rock at Mount Horeb and God supplied drinking water for all the people and their cattle (Exod. 17:6). Later Moses hit a rock at Kadesh to provide water for the community and their livestock (Num. 20:11). These two recorded incidents are given as examples of God's continued care for his people. The psalmist notes that God split rocks in the desert and caused streams to come forth out of the crags (Ps. 78:15–16). In other words, God daily quenched the thirst of man and animal by giving them streams of water in the wilderness.

Rabbinic sources have recorded legendary material on the rock that supplied water for the Israelites and traveled with them during their forty-year journey.[6] We assume that Paul was acquainted with this explanation. He is interested, however, not in a legend but in God's miraculous provision of food and drink. And this supernatural act Paul describes as "spiritual."[7]

Occurring three times in verses 3 and 4, the word *spiritual* has a figurative meaning. The material substance of food, drink, and rock points to a spiritual source. Through his Spirit, God actively engages in providing for the basic needs of his people. As the elements of the Lord's Supper point to the spiritual significance of the presence of Christ, so the elements which Paul describes with the word *spiritual* ultimately point to Christ.[8]

b. "For they were drinking from the spiritual rock which followed them." God miraculously supplied for the Israelites streams in the desert. As Paul demonstrated in the preceding clause, the water indicated God's faithful provision for his people, a faithfulness that was not bound to one location, either Mount Horeb or Kadesh. It followed the Israelites continually wherever they went dur-

---

5. See Exod. 17:1–7; Num. 20:2–11; 21:16; Neh. 9:15; Ps. 78:20; Isa. 48:21.

6. Consult SB, vol. 3, pp. 406–8. See also E. Earle Ellis, "A Note on First Corinthians 10:4," *JBL* 76 (1957): 53–56; *Paul's Use of the Old Testament* (Grand Rapids: Eerdmans, 1957), pp. 66–70.

7. Some translators have adopted the expression *supernatural* in the place of "spiritual" (see NEB, REB, RSV, *Moffatt*).

8. Richard M. Davidson, *Typology in Scripture: A Study of Hermeneutical ΤΥΠΟΣ Structures*, Andrews University Seminary Doctoral Dissertation series, vol. 2 (Berrien Springs, Mich.: Andrews University Press, 1981), p. 249.

ing their wilderness travels. Yet the Israelites rebelled against God; in the Song of Moses (Deut. 32) and the Psalter, the writers delineate both God's faithfulness and Israel's rebellion.

In the Old Testament the word *rock* appears frequently as a description of God:

1. Jacob declares him "the Rock of Israel" (Gen. 49:24).
2. Moses portrays him as a rock (Deut. 32:4, 15, 18, 30, 31).
3. Psalmists call him a rock (Pss. 18:31; 62:2; 78:35; 89:26; 95:1).

c. "The rock was Christ." Although the identification of the rock with Christ is figurative, nevertheless the Old Testament alludes to a definite link. The word *rock* in the Song of Moses and the Psalter is often qualified with words that apply directly to Christ's redemptive work: the Rock is [my] salvation (Deut. 32:15; Pss. 62:2; 95:1), Savior (Ps. 89:26), Redeemer (Ps. 78:35), Begetter (Deut. 32:18).[9]

Paul seems to have made a connection between the terminology recorded in Old Testament hymnody (Song of Moses and Psalter) and Christ; thus he identifies Christ with the Rock. He thereby connects an episode from the history of Israel with the current conditions in Corinth. Christ was present in the wilderness as he is present in the church today. God's rejection of those Israelites who tested and tried him (see Ps. 95:7–11; Heb. 3:7–19) is a relevant lesson and reminder for those Corinthians who dabble in idolatry.

5. However, God was not pleased with most of them, for their bodies were scattered over the desert.

Paul wants the readers to reflect on God's boundless goodness and mercy toward his rebellious people during the exodus and the desert journey. These people distrusted God, in spite of his wonderful daily care. They longed to go back to Egypt and served idols which they made and carried with them (Amos 5:25–26; Acts 7:42–43). No wonder that God was not pleased with these Israelites. Paul writes euphemistically when he says "most of them." He actually means that only two men who were older than twenty years of age (Caleb and Joshua) pleased God and entered the promised land. The rest died in the wilderness. In graphic terms, Paul writes that the bodies of the people were scattered over the desert floor (Num. 14:16). Funerals were the order of the day, and when pestilence struck, thousands perished (Num. 16:40; 25:9). Taking the total number of men who were twenty years and older, 603,550 (Num. 1:46), and assuming that there were an equal number of women, we divide the total, 1,207,100, by 38 (the years Israel spent in the desert after the curse [Num. 14:23]). We calculate an average of about 90 deaths per day for that entire period. A grim and daily reminder of God's anger!

---

9. Gardner, "Gifts of God," p. 161; Godet, *First Corinthians*, pp. 485–86. Compare A. McEwen, "Paul's Use of the Old Testament in I Corinthians 10:1–4," *VoxRef* 47 (1986): 3–10.

Paul compares the people who died in the desert with the members of the church in Corinth. He wants the Corinthians to know that all the Israelites were recipients of God's daily provision, yet they perished because of unbelief. By analogy, he wants his readers to know that their reception of baptism and the Lord's Supper does not guarantee them eternal life. Without daily commitment to Christ, they lack eternal security and face spiritual death.

Additional Comments on 10:1–5

Paul is not interested in providing a discourse on baptism and partaking of the elements of the Lord's table. His references to the sacraments are only incidental to the objective he has in mind. He resorts to typology, which in the identification of the rock and Christ should be understood figuratively.

a. *Typology.* At first glance, Paul's identification of Christ with the rock in the wilderness which supplied the Israelites with spiritual food and drink appears to be a straightforward example of allegory. But that is not quite the case. We must take into consideration Paul's educational background. His writing often reflects a Jewish mode of interpreting Scripture. Jewish Christians read Scripture with the understanding that God's people are the same whether they belong to either the Old Testament or the New Testament era. In Paul's view the Old Testament reveals the work of the preexistent Christ on behalf of his people.

Paul's fellow Jew and contemporary, Philo of Alexandria, explains the rock in the wilderness as the wisdom and word of God. So God demonstrated his faithfulness to his people by providing for them the necessities of life from the source of his law. For Philo, manna represented God's gift in the form of his revelation. And he interpreted the Song of Moses to denote that the flinty rock (God) provided both food and drink for the Israelites (Deut. 32:13). Indeed, Philo's interpretation is distinctly allegorical.[10]

Although Paul was influenced by the educational methodology of his day with respect to interpreting Scripture, he prudently adopted scriptural terminology. And even though at times he resorted to allegory, as he himself admitted (Gal. 4:21–31; see especially v. 24), he refrained from providing correspondences at every point in his discourse. Instead, Paul presented God's inspired revelation.

b. *Responsibility.* The death of all Israelites who were twenty years and older, with the exception of Caleb and Joshua, stands in stark contrast to Paul's fivefold use of the adjective *all* in the exodus account. They all enjoyed God's favor, yet only two responded in faith. The writer of Hebrews also uses the adjective *all* when he queries, "Who were they who heard and rebelled? Were they not all those Moses led out of Egypt?" (Heb. 3:16). God revealed his trustworthiness in various ways to *all* the Israelites, yet these same people failed to put their trust in him and rebelled against God ten times (Num. 14:22). This failure should not be attributed to God, who daily revealed his faithfulness, but to the Israelites, who refused to honor him. In the first century, many Christians likewise were in danger of drifting away from the living God because of unbelief and disobedience.

---

10. Philo *The Worse Attacks the Better* 31; *Allegorical Interpretation* 2.86; *Who Is Heir* 79. Compare Andrew J. Bandstra, "Interpretation in 1 Corinthians 10:1–11," *CTJ* 6 (1971): 12–13.

Greek Words, Phrases, and Constructions in 10:1–5

Verses 1–2

οἱ πατέρες ἡμῶν πάντες—by placing the adjective *all* after the pronoun *our*, Paul stresses the noun *fathers* rather than the adjective. Otherwise he would have placed the adjective before the noun.

ἐβαπτίσθησαν—the aorist passive of the verb βαπτίζω (I baptize) enjoys substantial textual support. Yet a variant reading with the aorist middle ἐβαπτίσαντο has equal support. Nonetheless, many scholars prefer the aorist passive, which reflects the Christian mode of baptism; the middle reflects Jewish baptismal practices.[11]

Verses 3–4

ἔφαγον and ἔπιον—both verbs are aorist active and must be seen as constatives that describe the duration of the Israelites' eating and drinking in the desert. Note that the verb ἔπινον is in the imperfect tense to describe action. The aorist states the fact and the imperfect describes the manner.[12]

Verse 5

ἐν τοῖς πλείοσιν—the verb εὐδόκησεν (he was pleased) takes the preposition ἐν to complete the construction in Greek. The definite article and comparative adjective apparently mean "the majority."[13]

ἐν—the second occurrence of this preposition has a local sense as the dative of place.

---

b. Example
10:6–10

After giving the readers an analogy from Israel's forty-year experience in the wilderness, Paul lists five historical examples taken from that same period.[14] Some of the incidents overlap:

1. coveting food (Num. 11:4)
2. engaging in idolatry (Exod. 32:4, 6, 19)
3. committing immorality (Num. 25:1–9)
4. testing the Lord (Num. 21:5)
5. grumbling (Num. 14:2, 36; 16:1–35)

---

11. Consult Bruce M. Metzger, *A Textual Commentary on the Greek New Testament*, 3d corrected ed. (London and New York: United Bible Societies, 1975), p. 559. See also Friedrich Blass and Albert Debrunner, *A Greek Grammar of the New Testament and Other Early Christian Literature*, trans. and rev. Robert Funk (Chicago: University of Chicago Press, 1961), #317.

12. A. T. Robertson, *A Grammar of the Greek New Testament in the Light of Historical Research* (Nashville: Broadman, 1934), p. 883; Blass and Debrunner, *Greek Grammar*, #327.

13. C. F. D. Moule, *An Idiom-Book of New Testament Greek*, 2d ed. (Cambridge: Cambridge University Press, 1960), p. 108.

14. Consult Wayne A. Meeks, "'And Rose up to Play': Midrash and Paraenesis in 1 Corinthians 10:1–22," *JSNT* (1982): 64–78; Charles Perrot, "Les exemples du désert (I Cor. 10. 6–11)," *NTS* 29 (1983): 437–52.

Each of these five examples appears in the form of either a phrase, a sentence, or even a quotation. These brief notations seem to indicate that the readers were familiar with the historical account of Israel's experiences. Hence, the Corinthians should be able to see their own reflection in the mirror of these historical events.

6. Now these things became examples for us, so that we should not long for evil things just as those people did.

a. "Now these things became examples for us." The adverb *now* introduces a summary statement that relates to the preceding paragraph. "These things" are the historical events which Paul has mentioned previously: the cloud that guided and protected the Israelites, the passage through the Red Sea to safety, the provision of food and drink, and the sin of unbelief and disobedience. In short, all these things are the "benefits which the people received, and sins which they committed."[15]

Paul calls "these things" examples, or in Greek, *typoi*, from which we have the derivative *types*. But in the context of the first five verses of chapter 10, the literal translation *types* raises questions: For example, are most of the Corinthians going to perish as the Israelites did in the desert? That interpretation would put a predictive connotation on the word *types*. Conversely, the translation *examples* needs further elucidation. In the light of verse 5, this word conveys a sense of warning, a sense which many translators have adopted (RSV, NEB, REB, GNB, JB).[16] We do well to understand the word in question as "pictures painted by an artist, [to disclose] what sort of judgement threatens idolaters, fornicators, and others who despise God" (compare v. 11).[17]

Paul writes that the examples are "for us." By writing the first person plural, Paul clearly includes both his readers and himself. He continues his sentence with the pronoun *we*.

b. "So that we should not long for evil things just as those people did." This first reference to a historical incident calls to mind the scriptural account concerning the rabble that complained about food. Tired of their daily manna, they said, "If only we had meat to eat! We remember the fish we ate in Egypt . . . also the cucumbers, melons, leeks, onions and garlic. But now we have lost our appetite . . ." (Num. 11:4–6). These discontented Israelites tested and tried God (Ps. 106:14), who in his grace sent them an abundance of quail. Yet the Lord also punished them with a severe plague, so that they died with the meat still between their teeth (Num. 11:31–34). They were buried in a place which the Israelites called Kibroth Hattaavah (graves of craving). These people had been possessed by greed, and, as Paul states elsewhere, greed is idolatry (Col. 3:5).

15. John Albert Bengel, *Bengel's New Testament Commentary*, 2 vols., trans. Charlton T. Lewis and Marvin R. Vincent (Grand Rapids: Kregel, 1981), vol. 2, p. 216.

16. See the discussion by Bandstra, "Interpretation," pp. 14–17, and Davidson, *Typology*, pp. 250–55, 312.

17. John Calvin, *The First Epistle of Paul the Apostle to the Corinthians*, Calvin's Commentaries series, trans. John W. Fraser (reprint ed.; Grand Rapids: Eerdmans, 1976), p. 211.

Paul issues an admonition to the Corinthians and tells them what not to do. He alludes to the tenth commandment: "You shall not covet" (Exod. 20:17; Deut. 5:21). This commandment is the capstone of the Decalogue, for the sin of covetousness gives rise to all other sins (James 1:14–15).

7. Do not be idolaters as some of them were. Just as it is written,

> **"The people sat down to eat and drink**
> **and they stood up to play."**

The second reference is to the time Aaron allowed the people to make an idol in the form of a golden calf (Exod. 32:1–20). Israelites broke the second commandment, "You shall not make for yourself an idol in the form of anything in heaven above or on the earth beneath or in the waters below. You shall not bow down to them or worship them; for I, the Lord your God, am a jealous God, punishing the sin of the fathers to the third and fourth generation of those who hate me . . ." (Exod. 20:4–5; Deut. 5:8–9). In the sight of God, idolatry is a heinous sin because worshipers displace the living God with a graven image.

Paul issues a direct warning: "Do not be idolaters." He refrains from including himself in the admonition but addresses the Corinthians in the second person plural. (In verses 6, 8, and 9 he uses the first person plural.) In this verse, he specifically links the rebellious people in Israel and some of the Corinthians. The Israelites who worshiped the golden calf at Mount Sinai and the Corinthians who participated in the rites at pagan temples all transgressed the second commandment.

"The people sat down to eat and drink and they stood up to play." This quotation Paul has taken verbatim from the Septuagint translation of Exodus 32:6. The passage gives us a vignette: a feast was often followed by games of one kind or other. Such commonly accepted practices were normally above criticism. But in pagan rites, people ate and drank to honor an idol who represented a god. The dances that followed the meal often degenerated into debauchery. Hence the Greek verb *paizein*, which I have translated "to play," can have a negative connotation and mean "to sin sexually" (NCV).

Those Corinthians who entered temples at the time of pagan festivals exposed themselves to situations that might cause them to sin. Then they were in the same category as the Israelites who "got up and indulged in pagan revelry."

8. Nor let us practice sexual immorality as some of them practiced, when in one day twenty-three thousand fell dead.

The third allusion is to an event that occurred near the end of Israel's desert journey. At the instigation of Balaam, the Israelites worshiped Baal-Peor, observed Canaanite fertility rites, and indulged in sexually immoral practices (Num. 25:1–9; 31:16). This was a blot on the pages of Israel's annals and is noted a number of times in Scripture (Deut. 4:3; Ps. 106:28–29; Hos. 9:10). The Israelites now sinned against the seventh commandment: "You shall not commit adultery" (Exod. 20:14; Deut. 5:18).

One person who indulged in sexual immorality is mentioned by name and by tribe: Zimri, the son of Salu of Simeon's tribe, brought a Midianite woman into his tent and was killed by the grandson of Aaron (Num. 25:6–8, 14). God struck the Israelites with a plague as punishment for their faithlessness. Immediately after the plague, God instructed Moses and Eleazar son of Aaron to conduct the second census on the plains of Moab (Num. 26:1–2; the first census took place thirty-eight years earlier in the desert of Sinai [Num. 1:1–3]). The statistics show that the number of men twenty years and older in the tribe of Simeon during the second census (22,200) was less than half of what it was in the first census (59,300). We presume that most of the men who were killed during the plague belonged to the tribe of Simeon (see Num. 1:22; 26:14).

Paul writes that twenty-three thousand people died because of Israel's sin against God. But the historical account of Moses features a total of twenty-four thousand (Num. 25:9). The figure that Moses gives is supported by other sources (the Septuagint, Philo, and the rabbis).[18] Attempts to explain the discrepancy cover a wide range: Paul's memory failed him; the writers in Numbers and I Corinthians used round numbers; Paul followed a variant reading. John Calvin is of the opinion that "Moses gave the upper limit, Paul the lower, and so there is really no discrepancy."[19]

For lack of information all such explanations remain hypotheses. Paul, with his thorough training in the Scriptures, had available more information than we have—perhaps further details from oral tradition. For instance, the Jewish historian Josephus presents a lengthy account of this incident with speeches of Balaam, Zambrias, Moses, and others. He also writes about the slaying of those who were guilty and the destruction caused by the pestilence. However, he concludes with the remark that "there perished from the ranks no less than fourteen thousand men."[20] In short, we lack information that Paul apparently possessed.

9. And let us not test Christ as some of them did and were destroyed by snakes.

The *fourth* reference to the history of Israel is the incident of the snakes (Num. 21:4–9). Overconfident after defeating the king of Arad, the people of Israel were unwilling to travel around the kingdom of Edom. They displayed impatience, blasphemed God, denounced Moses, loathed manna, and clamored for water. In response, God sent poisonous snakes into the camp. When the people repented of their sin, Moses prayed for them, fashioned a bronze snake, and put it on a pole. The people who were bitten looked at the snake and lived (compare John 3:14–15).

---

18. Num. 25:9, LXX; Philo *Life of Moses* 1.55 [304]; for Targumim and Midrashim refer to SB, vol. 3, p. 410.

19. Calvin, *I Corinthians*, p. 209.

20. Josephus *Antiquities* 4.6.12 [155] (LCL).

Paul writes, "And let us not test Christ." A number of translators have the reading *Lord*[21] instead of "Christ."[22] The oldest Greek manuscript (P^{46}), the Western text, numerous witnesses, versions, and the church fathers have the word *Christ*. This is the primary reading that goes back to the second century, was the accepted text throughout the Mediterranean basin, and is well attested.[23] Hence, the term *Christ*, which fits the context (see v. 4), is the preferred reading. And Paul teaches that the preexistent Christ accompanied the Israelites during their desert journey.

Two additional observations. First, Paul again uses the first person plural (see v. 8) to show that the Corinthians and he are not exempt from God's judgment. They are like the Israelites in the wilderness. Israel's victorious warriors demonstrated their impatience by refusing to accept divine guidance; they received their just reward. Accordingly, believers in New Testament times (including Paul and the Corinthians) ought not to follow their own inclinations. They have to wait for answered prayer and God's providential leading.

Next, in three successive verses (see vv. 8, 9, 10), Paul specifies that only "some of [the Israelites]" fell into sin and died. With respect to the people who suffered snakebites, only some died. The rest looked at the bronze snake and lived.

10. And do not grumble as some of them did and were destroyed by the angel that destroys.

A survey of Israel's history discloses the people's habitual vice of grumbling against God, Moses, and Aaron,[24] and the frequency of their grumbling makes it difficult to determine the exact passage from which Paul takes this fifth reference. In light of this entire verse, two incidents are likely prospects. First, after hearing the reports of the spies who had returned from the promised land, the entire community grumbled against Moses and Aaron (Num. 14:2). Paul, however, declares that "some of them grumbled," and this qualified statement agrees with the account in Numbers 14:37–38. Only the ten men who spread a bad report about the promised land died instantaneously of a plague, while Joshua and Caleb lived. The other choice is the narrative that describes the insolence of Korah, Dathan, Abiram, and On, who together with 250 leaders rose up against Moses (Num. 16:1–35). Not only did all these people perish, but because of the grumbling of the entire community 14,700 persons died of a plague that God sent among them (see vv. 41, 49).

Yet even these two passages do not fully coincide with Paul's wording, for he speaks of an angel that destroys. There is no mention of an angel of destruction in Numbers, although we find references to the destroyer in a few other places

---

21. GNB, JB, NJB, MLB, NCV, NEB, NIV, REB, RSV, SEB, *Cassirer.*

22. KJV, NKJV, NRSV, TNT.

23. Consult Carroll D. Osburn, "The Text of I Corinthians 10:9," in *New Testament Textual Criticism, Its Significance for Exegesis. Essays in Honour of Bruce M. Metzger,* ed. Eldon J. Epp and Gordon D. Fee (Oxford: Clarendon, 1981), pp. 201–12.

24. See, e.g., Exod. 14:11–12; 15:24; 16:2–3, 8; 17:3; Num. 11:1; 14:2–4; 16:11, 41; Deut. 1:27; 9:28; Josh. 9:18; Ps. 106:25.

(Exod. 12:23 and Heb. 11:28; II Sam. 24:16 and I Chron. 21:15). Interestingly, in the Wisdom of Solomon 18:20–25, the writer relates the account recorded in Numbers 16:41–50. He describes Aaron the high priest stopping the destroyer from inflicting further damage on Israel. Such language meshes with Paul's usage, for he supplies a definite article and calls the angel "*the* destroyer." He thus follows the practice of the rabbis who said there was one particular angel of destruction.[25] We presume that Paul reflects the Jewish teaching of his day and has in mind the destruction of the men with Korah and the plague that struck down Israelites by the thousands (Num. 16).

Although some manuscripts have the reading *let us not grumble*, the preferred text is in the second person plural, "do not grumble." These words are addressed to the Corinthians who might be induced by some arrogant leaders to grumble against Paul. With this example taken from Israel's chronicles, the apostle adroitly points out the perils of registering complaints about God and his servants. Without threatening the Corinthians, Paul teaches them lessons from sacred history to instill within them a respect for spiritual leaders (compare Heb. 13:7, 17, 24).

Greek Words, Phrases, and Constructions in 10:6–10

Verse 6

ταῦτα—this neuter plural pronoun in the nominative is followed by the verb ἐγενήθησαν (these became) in the plural instead of the singular (compare v. 11).

τύποι ἡμῶν—the genitive can be either objective ("examples for us") or subjective ("types of us"). Many scholars prefer the objective genitive.

εἰς τὸ μὴ εἶναι—the prepositional phrase with the particle μή and the infinitive constitute a negative purpose clause which verges on a negative command. For this reason, I have included this directive with the four negative imperatives in four following verses (vv. 7, 8, 9, 10).

ἐπεθύμησαν—the verb ἐπιθυμέω (I desire, long for) occurs also in the tenth commandment of the Decalogue (Exod. 20:17; Deut. 5:21, LXX). See also James 4:2.

Verses 7–8

μηδέ—the particle appears in this verse and the next three and is followed respectively by four verbs in the present imperative.

παίζειν—"to play." However, the Hebrew equivalent, *sḥq* (Exod. 32:6), denotes licentiousness. This meaning is substantiated in three other passages (Gen. 26:8; 39:14, 17).[26]

ἐν—the Majority Text, Merk, and Souter insert the preposition ἐν to strengthen the dative of time of the phrase *in one day*. The better manuscripts lack this preposition.

---

25. SB, vol. 3, pp. 412–16. See also Ps. 105:23 (LXX; Ps. 106:23 in the Hebrew) for the compound verb *to destroy utterly*.

26. Georg Bertram, *TDNT*, vol. 5, pp. 629–30.

Verse 9

ἐκπειράζωμεν—the compound form of this verb denotes intensity and signifies "willfully put to the test" or "boldly challenge" (Ps. 77:18, LXX; Ps. 78:18 in the Hebrew). The direct object is τὸν Χριστόν.

ἀπώλλυντο—the imperfect passive of the verb ἀπόλλυμι (I destroy) denotes continued action in the past. However, in the next verse (v. 10), the same verb appears in the aorist tense, which describes a single action.

Verse 10

καθάπερ—"just as." This conjunction, which is a combination of καθά and the intensive enclitic particle -περ, occurs in the New Testament only in Paul's epistles (except for Heb. 4:2).[27]

ὀλοθρευτοῦ—the noun with the definite article appears once in the New Testament as "the destroyer." Paul takes the word from the Old Testament (Exod. 12:23, LXX; Hebrew *hammashḥit*). He employs the noun ὄλεθρον (destruction) in connection with the incestuous man whom he delivers "to Satan for destruction of his flesh that his spirit may be saved" (5:5, author's translation).

---

c. Admonition
10:11–13

In a few familiar verses (vv. 12, 13), Paul applies the historical lessons to the believers in Corinth. At the same time he discloses that God always provides help when believers face trials and temptation.

11. Now these things happened to them as a warning and were written for our admonition, upon whom the ends of the ages have come.

a. "Now these things happened to them as a warning." Numerous translations give a slightly different reading by inserting the adjective *all*, that is, "Now all these things."[28] The adjective, however, may have been added to emphasize the historical incidents mentioned in the preceding verses (vv. 6–10). Verse 11 echoes verse 6, "Now these things became examples for us."

The historical examples of idolaters, fornicators, rebels, and grumblers are pertinent reminders of God's anger toward sinners who willfully put him to the test. With the imperfect tense of the verb *to happen*, Paul depicts the recurrence of these incidents; with the phrase *to them* he clearly alludes to the Israelites on their forty-year journey through the Sinai Peninsula. God has seen fit to record these events as instructive lessons to warn his people in successive generations and in other cultures. God is a God of history who expects his people to take note of biblical history.

b. "And [these] were written for our admonition." God's Word has lasting authority for believers in every generation. Indeed, God has given us both the Old and New Testaments to admonish us to live in harmony with his precepts (see

---

27. Robertson, *Grammar*, p. 967.
28. E.g., see GNB, JB, NJB, KJV, NKJV.

9:10). The term *admonition* appears in another letter of Paul, where he instructs fathers to bring up their children "in the training and admonition of the Lord" (Eph. 6:4)—that is, they should teach their children the truths of Scripture. Likewise, God diligently admonishes his people to adhere to his written Word, and he warns that failure to obey him results in dire consequences (compare Heb. 10:31).

Let no one think that God presents himself in the Old Testament only as an avenger of evil (Ps. 139:19) and in the New Testament only as a God of love (I John 4:16). God both hates sin and loves the sinner who repents. He never changes. He loves his people; both the patriarch of Bible times and the recent convert experience the joy of God's forgiving grace. With unwavering steadfastness God fulfills his promises in the lives of the saints—every sincere believer can testify to this truth.

c. "Upon whom the ends of the ages have come." What does Paul mean when he writes "the ends of the ages"? He is not saying that God's people have come to the consummation, but instead that the end times have now begun. Other New Testament writers similarly affirm that we are now living in the last period of history (see Heb. 9:26; I John 2:18). Within the end time, which arrived with the coming of Christ, some periods in history have been completed. For example, the Old Testament era ended with the fulfillment of the messianic promises; Greek and Roman culture encountered Christ's gospel and subsequently disappeared. Writes F. W. Grosheide, "As often as a nation comes in contact with the gospel, an age finds its end."[29]

Even though Paul states that the ends of the ages have arrived, we are unable to discern the end of the period in which we live. Jesus tells us that the end comes when the gospel has been preached as a testimony to all nations (Matt. 24:14). In these end times, therefore, we must hasten the day of Christ's return by living holy and godly lives (II Peter 3:11–12) and by advancing the spread of Christ's gospel to every part of the world and every sector of society. When that task has been accomplished, the consummation of all things will come about. Together with the Corinthians, every believer must heed God's admonitions in the days that are known as the end time. The events recorded in the Old Testament Scriptures are there for the express purpose of telling Christians to avoid the pitfalls of sin and to hasten the day of the Lord.

12. So he who thinks he stands, let him be careful not to fall.

Here is an aphorism that anyone can take to heart. Indeed, we frequently choose this Scripture passage to tell someone to avoid misplaced self-reliance and inordinate pride.

With the word *so* Paul concludes his survey of Israel's history and applies its lessons to the Corinthians. He directs his application to all the readers but espe-

---

29. F. W. Grosheide, *Commentary on the First Epistle to the Corinthians: The English Text with Introduction, Exposition and Notes*, New International Commentary on the New Testament series (Grand Rapids: Eerdmans, 1953), p. 226.

cially to those people who proudly think that they have the freedom in Christ to do anything or to go anywhere. He implicitly refers to the Corinthians who visit pagan temples (8:10). These so-called strong believers should take note of the history lessons from the Old Testament, for in these lessons God is addressing them. In effect, Paul is drawing the people of Israel and the Corinthian Christian together through these Old Testament lessons.

The people of Israel took pride in their standing before God. They alone were God's people, and they thought that God would always be on their side. They felt spiritually secure because God had made a covenant with their father Abraham, a covenant he promised to keep for generations to come (Gen. 17:7). Yet the Scriptures relate that because of their disobedience to God and his Word, untold descendants of Abraham fell in the desert (see v. 5; Rom. 11:20). Says the writer of Hebrews, "See to it, brothers, that none of you has a sinful, unbelieving heart that turns away from the living God. But encourage one another daily, as long as it is called Today, so that none of you may be hardened by sin's deceitfulness" (Heb. 3:12–13).

The word *fall* points to a false security. When Paul uses this word, he refers to those Corinthians who place their trust in either church membership or baptism and communion but not in Jesus Christ. These Corinthians rely on their own insights and the "wisdom" derived from fellow men (3:18). With hearts that are not right with God, they are self-confident. Instead, Paul advises that they with childlike confidence are to trust in God from day to day. Their spiritual security should come from true faith that relies on God to fulfill his promises.

13. No temptation has overtaken you except that which is common to everyone. But God is faithful, who will not allow you to be tempted beyond that which you are able to bear; however, with the temptation he also will provide the way of escape that you may be able to endure it.

a. "No temptation has overtaken you." What an encouragement to every believer! What a relief to know that God has set limits! Paul is taking time out from his argument, so to speak, to reassure his discouraged readers with a pastoral word. As a corollary to his directive to stand firm and not to fall (v. 12), he encourages them to view their life realistically. In truth, Paul addresses every person who has come to grips with the daily problems of life.

As is true of all languages, Greek has words that have several meanings. The expression *temptation* is one of them, for it can also denote "trial." In his epistle James says, "God does not tempt anyone" (1:13). True, yet Jesus teaches his disciples the sixth petition of the Lord's Prayer, "And lead us not into temptation, but deliver us from the evil one" (Matt. 6:13). He leaves the origin of temptation an open question; a succinct distinction is that temptations are from Satan but trials are from God.

Does Paul intend to say "temptation" or "trial" in verse 13? Perhaps he wishes to convey both meanings. To illustrate, Satan appears before God in heaven, and God allows him to tempt Job, to put his faith on trial. But God uses Satan to demonstrate that Job is able to endure his trials, for in the end Job's faith triumphs (Job 1, 2, and 42).[30]

b. "No temptation has overtaken you except that which is common to everyone." The main verb in this sentence is in the perfect tense and connotes a lasting condition. It also conveys that tempting or testing takes possession of people.[31] The degree and extent of any temptation is limited by what is common to everyone. By contrast, at both the beginning and the end of his earthly ministry, Jesus withstood Satan's temptations beyond what is common to everyone. The hellish agony which Jesus withstood in Gethsemane and at Calvary no ordinary human would ever be able to endure. No believer will have to be subjected to the same experiences.

We ought not to ask to which temptations the Corinthians were subjected. Paul gives no details but only speaks a general word of encouragement that is valid for all Christians.

c. "But God is faithful, who will not allow you to be tempted beyond that which you are able to bear." God's faithfulness to his people is perfect, even though man's faithfulness to him is imperfect. Scripture proves that not God but man is a covenant breaker. Biblical writers extol the divine attribute of God's faithfulness that reaches to the sky. With variations, the theme *God is faithful* is a recurring refrain in Paul's epistles and elsewhere in Scripture.[32]

How does God demonstrate his faithfulness to believers? God promises that he will not permit anyone to be tempted beyond the point of human endurance. Even if believers knowingly place themselves in circumstances where temptations are rampant and inevitable, God demonstrates his faithfulness by coming to their rescue. Take Lot as an example. He took up residence in Sodom and had to put up with "the dirty lives of evil people," yet God helped him and rescued him from sudden destruction (II Peter 2:7, NCV).[33] In brief, as a faithful shepherd rescues his wandering sheep, so God watches his people and delivers them from predicaments which they encounter. Paul implies that God sets the limits for man's temptation in accordance with what he can bear.

d. "However, with the temptation he also will provide the way of escape that you may be able to endure it." The adversative *however* is influenced and strengthened by the word *also*. God sets limits to human temptations and he himself comes to help his people during their trials. He encourages believers to persist and eventually overcome. He becomes personally involved in the trial by opening a way of escape for those who are tempted and tried. In the Greek, Paul writes the definite article *the* in the phrase *the way of escape*. That is, for every trial God

---

30. Refer to Godet, *First Corinthians*, p. 498.

31. Bauer, p. 464.

32. I Cor. 1:9; II Cor. 1:18; I Thess. 5:24; II Thess. 3:3; Heb. 10:23; 11:11; I John 1:9; Rev. 1:5. See also Deut. 7:9; Ps. 145:13b.

33. Consult Walter Schneider and Colin Brown, *NIDNTT*, vol. 3, pp. 802–3.

prepares a way out.[34] A period of temptation and testing may be compared with a ship approaching a rocky shore and facing inevitable shipwreck. But, "suddenly and, to the inexperienced landsman, unexpectedly, [it] slips through a gap on the inhospitable coast into security and peace."[35]

The purpose for the way of escape is "that you may endure [the temptation]." The main verb which Paul uses conveys the meaning *to bear up under* the temptation. Believers' endurance prevents them from falling and makes them stand firm in the faith.[36] God's abiding faithfulness sees his people through their trials and causes them to triumph.

Doctrinal Considerations in 10:12

Jesus told Peter that he had prayed that Peter's faith might not fail (Luke 22:32). Yet, Peter declared three times in succession that he had never known Jesus. Did God fail Peter by not answering Jesus' request? Or did Peter's fear of persecution and suffering undermine and even nullify his faith? The answer is that not God's provision but only Peter's responsibility was at stake.

Faith is not a static virtue but a spiritual gift. Faith either diminishes when not exercised or increases when tried. True faith shines brightly when believers stand firm in times of testing (e.g., Gal. 5:1; II Thess. 2:15). Scripture teaches that withstanding the attacks of Satan is an enduring struggle of faith (Eph. 6:10–18; Phil. 4:12–14). In this struggle, Christians are either strong or weak; their faith can either increase or decrease (Rom. 14:1; II Cor. 10:15). True faith is firmly anchored in God. And through Christ Jesus, God gives believers necessary strength and ability to stand.

When Paul writes that "he who thinks he stands [should] be careful not to fall," he ascribes doctrinal significance to the two verbs *stand* and *fall*. Standing firm means to be fully dependent on God in Christ. David asks, "Who may stand in [God's] holy place?" And he answers, "He who has clean hands and a pure heart. . . . He will receive blessing from the Lord and vindication from God his Savior" (Ps. 24:3–5).

The verb *to fall* in the context of salvation means a loss, which translates graphically into rejecting divine grace. For example, the Israelites experienced their downfall when they defiantly challenged God. They rejected the manna which he daily supplied and the leadership which he had divinely appointed. They rejected grace by willfully disobeying God. By contrast, "if someone loves God, he is known by God" (8:3). The person who loves God demonstrates genuine evidence of possessing eternal security by believing his Word and by obeying his precepts. The believer, then, finds comfort in knowing that God will never, no never, no never forsake the soul that on Jesus has leaned for repose.

---

34. This does not mean that God cancels the testing period but that he sets a limit by showing believers the end of the trial. Compare C. F. D. Moule, "An Unsolved Problem in the Temptation-Clause in the Lord's Prayer," *RTR* 33 (1974): 65–75.

35. W. W. Gauld, "St. Paul and Nature," *ExpT* 52 (1940–41): 340.

36. Consult Gardner, "Gifts of God," p. 169.

Greek Words, Phrases, and Constructions in 10:11–13

Verse 11

τυπικῶς—this adverb, translated "a warning," occurs only here in the New Testament. Because of its strong manuscript support, many scholars prefer this reading to the one that has the word τύποι (types, examples) and its corresponding Greek verb συνέβαινον (happen) in the plural.

ἐγράφη—"it was written" is in the singular, yet ταῦτα in the preceding clause is in the plural. The preposition πρός denotes purpose: "for our admonition." And the pronoun ἡμῶν is not the subjective genitive ("of us") but the objective genitive ("for us").

Verse 12

ὥστε—this consecutive conjunction functions in a co-ordinate construction and means "therefore."

μή—after the verb *to be careful*, this particle serves as a conjunction that negatively introduces the aorist active subjunctive πέσῃ (not to fall).

Verse 13

εἴληφεν—the perfect tense of the verb λαμβάνω (I receive, take) indicates action begun in the past with lasting significance in the present.

τοῦ δύνασθαι ὑπενεγκεῖν—with the definite article in the genitive case followed by two infinitives, this construction is a purpose clause.[37] The phrase lacks the subject *you* which in some manuscripts is supplied. Note that the second infinitive is a constative aorist from ὑποφέρω, which considers the action of the verb from beginning to end.

---

14 Therefore, my dear friends, flee from idolatry. 15 I speak as to the wise: judge for yourselves what I say. 16 The cup of blessing for which we give thanks, is it not participation in the blood of Christ? The bread which we break, is it not participation in the body of Christ? 17 Because there is one loaf, we who are many are one body, for we all partake of the one loaf.

18 Consider Israel according to the flesh. Are not all who eat the sacrifices partakers at the altar? 19 What then am I saying? That food offered to an idol is anything or that an idol is anything? 20 No, however, the things they sacrifice, they sacrifice to demons and not to God. I do not wish that you become partakers of demons. 21 You cannot drink the cup of the Lord and the cup of demons, and you cannot partake of the table of the Lord and the table of demons. 22 Do we provoke the Lord to jealousy? We are not stronger than he, are we?

---

2. Warnings against Idolatry
10:14–22

In chapter 8, Paul initiated his discussion on idolatry. In that chapter, he discussed the matter of eating food that had been offered to an idol (vv. 4, 7) and dining in the temple of an idol (v. 10). Paul expressed his concern for the weaker brothers who were wounded in their conscience by the actions of the stronger Corinthians.

---

37. Robert Hanna, *A Grammatical Aid to the Greek New Testament* (Grand Rapids: Baker, 1983), p. 301.

Already in the first part of chapter 10, Paul returned to the subject of *idolatry* (vv. 6–10) and alluded to Israel's idol worship at Mount Sinai (v. 7; Exod. 32:1–20). By reflecting on the desert experiences of the Israelites, Paul suggested the basic unity of God's people through both the Old and New Testament eras. With descriptive examples of God's people in the desert, Paul admonished everyone who belongs to God's family.

Now in the second part of chapter 10 Paul addresses all the Corinthians, especially those who consider themselves strong Christians. He calls their attention to the implications of participating in sacrifices offered to idols. Although in chapter 9 he interrupted his discussion on idolatry with a discourse on apostolic rights, he implied that he had more to say. This discussion had its origin in the letter that Paul received (e.g., see 7:1), in which the Corinthians asked him about food sacrificed to idols. "In chapter 8, Paul begins as he does because of the way the Corinthians had made their points. In chapter 10, Paul works more from his own agenda."[38]

In his epistle, Paul often digresses either to clarify his message with pertinent illustrations (e.g., see 7:17–24) or to speak a word of encouragement or admonition. But now he is ready to resume his discussion on idolatry.

a. A Vivid Comparison
10:14–17

14. Therefore, my dear friends, flee from idolatry.

The first word in this verse, "therefore," joins not the preceding admonition but the allusions to Israel's idol worship (vv. 6–10) to Paul's discourse on feasting at the temple of an idol and celebrating the Lord's Supper. Paul summarizes his teaching with a command that is addressed to all the readers. Because the command is direct and forceful, he tempers it with the address *my dear friends*. At times, Paul uses an endearing term to draw his readers close to himself but at the same time he gives them a command (e.g., 4:14).

The injunction to flee from idolatry is similar to Paul's previous order: "Flee immorality" (6:18). He is addressing the Corinthians who say that they are sufficiently strong to withstand temptation when they attend feasts in pagan temples. Paul instructs them to flee from that environment as a refugee escapes from threatening external conditions. He bids them to stay as far away as possible from pagan temples and their concomitant feasts held in honor of their gods.

Does Paul's injunction to flee idolatry contradict his earlier statement, where he seems to allow the strong Corinthians to eat in a dining hall of a pagan temple (8:9)? No, not at all. First, notice that in the context of 8:9, Paul limits Christian liberty. He permits freedom as long as it does not become a hindrance to fellow believers (see also 10:24, 32). Second, in 8:10 Paul speaks about the act of eating in an idol's temple but in this verse he calls attention to idolatry itself.

---

38. Wendell Lee Willis, *Idol Meat in Corinth: The Pauline Argument in 1 Corinthians 8 and 10*, SBL Dissertation Series 68 (Chico, Calif.: Scholars, 1981), p. 112.

Even though an idol is an inanimate object of wood or stone, its environment is religious and implies worship. Here, then, is the danger of transgressing God's explicit command not to worship an idol (Exod. 20:4–6; Deut. 5:8–10), and hence Paul's imperative to flee from idolatry (compare I John 5:21). When the Corinthians enter a pagan temple and participate in festivities that are related to the worship of an idol, they sin against God. They must know that their presence in a pagan temple at the time of a feast constitutes an affront to God. With the sacrament of the Lord's Supper, God prepares his own table at which he is the host and the believers are his guests. The table in a dining room of a pagan temple and the table of the Lord belong to two diametrically opposed religious contexts.

15. I speak as to the wise: judge for yourselves what I say.

Paul says that he is addressing the wise. In another context he had ridiculed the Corinthians' wisdom (4:10), but not now. The wise are those believers who obediently fulfill the will of the Lord. But the foolish, relying on their own insight and human wisdom, come to utter ruin (compare Matt. 7:24–27). The wisdom of the prudent Corinthians lies precisely in being obedient to God's command not to worship an idol.[39] This means that they should not allow themselves even a semblance of such worship.

The Corinthians must now decide to judge wisely. They are mature Christians who should be able to discern what is central to this matter and what is peripheral. In succeeding verses, Paul gives them relevant instructions on measures they should take when they are invited to a meal in the home of unbelievers (see vv. 27–30). He wants them to be attentive to what he is saying and thus be "instructed in the school of Christ."[40]

16. The cup of blessing for which we give thanks, is it not participation in the blood of Christ? The bread which we break, is it not participation in the body of Christ?

We note the following points:

a. *Questions.* Paul now reminds his readers of celebrating the Lord's Supper, where the Lord is the host and they are guests. He puts this reminder in the form of two rhetorical questions which every believer must answer in the affirmative. When the Corinthians drink from the cup and eat of the bread during the Lord's Supper, they indeed have communion with Christ. Because they have fellowship with Jesus Christ, they ought to have nothing to do with idols. No one can serve two masters (Matt. 6:24; Luke 16:13).

b. *Setting.* The institution of the Lord's Supper took place in the upper room on the night before Jesus' death on the cross. There he articulated the purpose for this celebration by saying, "This cup is the new covenant in my blood, which is poured out for you" (Luke 22:20; see I Cor. 11:25). The term *new* in this formula calls to mind the old covenant that was ratified by the Israelites at Mount Si-

39. Compare Jürgen Goetzmann, *NIDNTT*, vol. 2, pp. 619–20.
40. Calvin, *I Corinthians*, p. 215.

nai. Moses sprinkled blood on the altar, the Book of the Covenant, and on the people. He said, "This is the blood of the covenant that the Lord has made with you in accordance with all these words" (Exod. 24:8). Immediately after the ratification of that covenant, Israel's leaders (Moses, Aaron, Nadab, Abihu, and seventy elders) went up Mount Sinai to meet God. These leaders not only saw God but also participated in a covenant meal with him (Exod. 24.9–11).

Centuries later, God announced through Jeremiah that he would make a new covenant with the houses of Israel and Judah (Jer. 31:31). This prophecy was fulfilled when Jesus, on the night of his betrayal, instituted a new covenant and participated in a covenant meal with his disciples.

c. *Sequence.* In the Gospels of Matthew and Mark, Jesus first broke the bread and then poured the wine (Matt. 26:26–28; Mark 14:22–24). But in Luke's Gospel, he takes the cup and gives it to his disciples; then he breaks the bread; and afterward he takes the cup (Luke 22:17–20). The explanation is that during the Jewish Passover meal, the participants drank at stated intervals from four cups.[41] The third cup was known as "the cup of blessing," and in time the term became a technical one. At the presentation of this third cup, Jesus instituted the Lord's Supper.

Paul writes that he himself received from Jesus the formula for celebrating the Lord's Supper (11:23–26): first breaking the bread and then drinking from the cup. But in verse 16 Paul reverses the order because he wants to use the concept *bread* as an introduction to the next verse, in which he draws a parallel between the one loaf and the one body.[42]

d. *Meaning.* "The cup of blessing for which we give thanks." In this verse Paul writes the Greek verb *eulōges* (I bless),[43] which is translated two ways. Several versions (e.g., NKJV, NRSV) give a literal translation, "the cup of blessing which we bless," while others (e.g., NCV, TNT) read, "we give thanks for the cup of blessing." Scholars who choose the latter translation interpret the verb in the light of Jewish culture and understand it as the act of giving thanks to God. This verb has a theological connotation; it must be understood in the sense of thanking God the Father for the redemptive work of his Son on our behalf. When we celebrate communion, we express our gratitude to him.

God is the bestower of blessings and we are the recipients who render thanks and praise to him. When Jesus fed the multitudes, he took the bread and gave thanks to God the Father. When he instituted the Lord's Supper, he gave thanks when he broke the bread (11:24; Luke 22:19). He set the example of giving

---

41. SB, vol. 4.1, pp. 56–61. See also William Hendriksen, *Exposition of the Gospel According to Luke,* New Testament Commentary series (Grand Rapids: Baker, 1978), pp. 959–60; Phillip Sigal, "Another Note to 1 Corinthians 10.16," *NTS* 29 (1983): 134–39.

42. In *Didache* 9:2–3, a document presumably from the end of the first century, the order is first the cup and then the bread. Consult Willy Rordorf, "The *Didache,*" in *The Eucharist of the Early Christians,* trans. Matthew J. O'Connell (New York: Pueblo, 1978), pp. 1–23.

43. Compare Joachim Jeremias, *The Eucharistic Words of Jesus,* trans. Norman Perrin from the German 3d rev. ed. (New York: Charles Scribner's Sons, 1966), p. 113.

thanks to the Father for his gifts to us. Hence, the term *eucharist*, which derives from the Greek verb *eucharisteō* (I give thanks), means gratitude or the act of giving thanks.

"[The cup] . . . is it not participation in the blood of Christ? The bread which we break, is it not participation in the body of Christ?" The word *koinonia* in this verse sometimes translated "sharing in" or "communion," is here rendered "participation in."[44] Believers participate in a vertical relationship with Jesus Christ— as Paul earlier wrote, we have fellowship with God's Son, our Lord Jesus Christ (1:9; see also I John 1:3). Believers also participate in a horizontal relationship with one another, as was evidenced by the fellowship that the early Christians experienced in the days following Pentecost (Acts 2:42). These vertical and horizontal relationships meet in the church, for the believers together form the body of which Christ is the head (see v. 17; Eph. 5:23).

In this verse, the words *cup* and *bread* signify participation in the blood and body of Christ. By their participation believers receive God's favor in the form of untold spiritual and material blessings. But this participation also entails the Christian's responsibility of reverential obedience to Jesus Christ.

When they celebrate the Lord's Supper, believers also affirm a covenant relationship. "This cup is the new covenant in my blood" are the words Paul received from the Lord (11:25; Luke 22:20). The same thing holds true for his reference to Jesus' body (11:24; Luke 22:19). We see a striking parallelism in the way the two words *cup* and *bread* are explained:[45]

cup = participation in the blood of Christ (10:16)	bread = participation in the body of Christ (10:16)
the new covenant in my blood (11:25)	my body which is for you (11:24)

e. *Conclusion.* Paul uses the personal pronoun *we* in this verse and the next: "We give thanks . . . for we all partake." This pronoun does not apply only to Paul and fellow apostles who administer the sacrament of communion. It is not restricted to the clergy who serve at the table of the Lord. No, all believers who come to the table are the Lord's guests and he is the host. This interpretation becomes evident from a study of the next verse.

17. Because there is one loaf, we who are many are one body, for we all partake of the one loaf.

a. *Translations.* The Greek text itself is rather simple, with a limited and even repetitive vocabulary. But simplicity is not always the equivalent of clarity. The first part of this verse can be translated in two different ways: "For we, being

---

44. Literature on this subject is extensive. As a representative example, I mention only Willis, *Idol Meat*, pp. 167–222.

45. Gardner, "Gifts of God," p. 177; Willis, *Idol Meat*, p. 206; Stuart D. Currie, "Koinonia in Christian Literature to 200 A.D.," Ph.D. diss., Emory University, 1962, pp. 42–44; Elmer Prout, "'One Loaf . . . One Body,'" *ResQ* 25 (1982): 78–81.

many, are one bread and one body" (NKJV) or "Because there is one loaf, we, though many, are one body" (REB). What then is the difference?

In the first translation, the conjunction *and* has to be supplied because it is lacking in the Greek text. This absence should serve as a caution to the translator not to treat the terms *bread* and *body* as synonyms. If believers are described as bread, how then can they partake of bread? Accordingly, the second translation is preferred because it avoids tautology.[46]

b. *Links.* The causative conjunction *because* links verse 17 to the preceding verse, where Paul discussed believers' participation in the breaking of communion bread. The apostle emphasizes that every believer partakes of the one bread. (The translation in this commentary uses the idiom of "one loaf" rather than the generic, "one bread.") Eating bread together at a meal links the participants and forms a bond of unity.

c. *Unity.* The church in Corinth consisted of Gentiles who had become believers and Jews who had converted to the Christian faith. Yet these two groups formed one body, so that Paul could say, "we who are many are one body." Indifferent to racial barriers, they were all one in Christ. Together they all partook of the bread when they celebrated the communion service. When contemporary believers partake of the one bread, they too show that they are one body and belong to the fellowship. This text, then, reveals the unity that prevails on the horizontal level.

d. *Partaking.* In this verse, Paul twice uses causal conjunctions: "because" and "for." The two causal clauses, "because there is one loaf . . ." and "for we all partake of the one loaf," reinforce one another; both stress the significance of the one loaf. The body of believers partakes of the one substance, bread. Partaking of the elements of the Lord's Supper rules out that any member of the church may go to a pagan festival in the temple of an idol or that any pagan may come to the Lord's table.[47] Here, then, is Paul's purpose for stressing the fact that believers partake of the one loaf: Christianity and paganism are mutually exclusive (see v. 21 for his explicit statement).

Practical Considerations in 10:16–17

Some Greek words have crept into our vocabulary and are quite often used in descriptive names for churches. I mention only two: *agapē* and *koinonia*. So we have the "agape church" and the "koinonia fellowship." The first title means the church that practices love. The second one is redundant because "koinonia" means fellowship. Why resort to the use of foreign words, when we have lucid expressions in our own language?

Nevertheless, the meaning of the term *koinonia* should not be minimized, for it is profoundly spiritual. When the pastor pronounces the benediction at the conclusion of a worship service, he asks God that the fellowship of the Holy Spirit may be with the depart-

---

46. Godet, *First Corinthians*, p. 512.
47. Johannes Eichler, *NIDNTT*, vol. 1, p. 639.

ing congregation (see II Cor. 13:14). During communion, the believers are guests at the table of the Lord, eat the bread and drink from the cup, and thus experience fellowship with Jesus as host (Matt. 26:26–28; I Cor. 10:16; 11:23–25).

Christ's fellowship is a vital element in the life of the congregation that comes to expression in unanimity and unity through the working of the Holy Spirit. In this fellowship, the individual is never alone but is always upheld and supported by all the other believers. In the early church, believers came together for apostolic instruction and fellowship, for communion and prayers (Acts 2:42). In fact, Luke candidly writes about the economic conditions of the church members: "For there was no needy person among them" (Acts 4:34). The word *fellowship*, therefore, connotes untold spiritual and material blessings for God's people.

Greek Words, Phrases, and Constructions in 10:14–17

Verse 14

διόπερ—"for this very reason." This particle probably is similar to διό and logically connects the preceding passage to the present sentence.[48]

φεύγετε ἀπό—the verb φεύγω (I flee) is frequently followed by the preposition ἀπό (from). Here it is in the present imperative as a command to keep on doing so.

εἰδωλολατρίας—this noun is preceded by the definite article ("*the* idolatry") as a reference to the "worship of idols which you [Corinthians] know so well."[49]

Verse 15

κρίνατε—the aorist active imperative of the verb κρίνω (I judge) signifies that the Corinthians themselves (ὑμεῖς) must evaluate this particular matter. They must approve Paul's injunction.

φημί—although this verb is a synomym of λέγω (I say), here it conveys the thought *I mean* (compare v. 19).

Verse 16

τῆς εὐλογίας—"of blessing." Some manuscripts have the reading *of thanksgiving*, but they lack basic support. The genitive is descriptive.

εὐλογοῦμεν—the present tense of this verb and that of κλῶμεν (we break) shows repeated occurrence. In the context of celebrating the Lord's Supper, the verb εὐλογέω (I bless) is synonymous with εὐχαριστέω (I give thanks).

οὐχί—this negative particle introduces rhetorical questions that demand a positive response.

Verse 17

ὅτι and γάρ—these two causative conjunctions support each other with two separate clauses.

μετέχομεν—in the current context, this verb ("we partake") means approximately the same as the verb κοινωνέω (I share).[50]

---

48. Refer to Moule, *Idiom-Book*, p. 164; Hanna, *Grammatical Aid*, p. 310.

49. Nigel Turner, *A Grammar of New Testament Greek* (Edinburgh: Clark, 1963), vol. 3, p. 173.

50. But see W. A. Sebothoma, "Koinonia in I Corinthians 10:16," *Neotest* 24 (1990): 63–69.

b. An Example of Symmetry
10:18–22

A comparison of the preceding section (vv. 14–17) and this one reveals repetition of phrases and, on closer inspection, symmetry.[51] Indeed, we can place sentences from these two sections in an order that reflects this symmetry, the progression of Paul's thought, and the contrasts within it:

A		Fleeing from idolatry, judging for yourselves		14–15
	B	Cup of blessing, partaking of the bread		16–17
		C	Sacrifices at the altar	18
			D Idols and food offered to them are meaningless	19
		C′	Sacrifices to demons, not to God	20
	B′	Cup of the Lord, cup of demons		21
A′		Provoking the Lord to jealousy		22

Interpreting this passage (specifically vv. 18–22), I closely follow its symmetrical arrangement and elucidate its words, phrases, and clauses. In the context, Paul weaves in explicit and implicit references to Israel and stresses the contrast between participation at the Lord's table and participation in rites at the altar of an idol.

18. Consider Israel according to the flesh. Are not all who eat the sacrifices partakers at the altar?

a. "Consider Israel according to the flesh."[52] This literal translation sounds stilted but expresses Paul's intent. Other versions have "people of Israel" (e.g., NIV) or "those of Israelite descent" (MLB). But when Paul elsewhere discusses the two states of mind—the one of the sinful nature and the other of the Spirit—he writes the phrase *according to the flesh* (Rom. 8:5a). With this phrase he points to Israel that lacked spirituality.

When Paul exhorts the Corinthians to look at sinful Israel, he implicitly reminds them of the examples he gave from Israel's history (vv. 6–10). They must now receive the application of these examples that were recorded as a warning for them (v. 11) and judge for themselves (v. 15). They would have to evaluate the decisive difference between festivities held in the dining room of a pagan temple and the celebration of the Lord's Supper.

b. "Are not all who eat the sacrifices partakers at the altar?" For people of Jewish descent, this is self-evident. The question Paul poses is rhetorical and receives an affirmative answer. It refers to the priests and Levites of Israel who served at

---

51. I am indebted to Xavier Léon-Dufour for prompting me to construct this symmetrical arrangement. See his *Sharing the Eucharistic Bread: The Witness of the New Testament*, trans. Matthew J. O'Connell (New York and Mahwah, N.J.: Paulist, 1982), p. 207.
52. Compare NAB, and KJV, NKJV.

the altar and even to the people who presented offerings to the Lord.[53] Indeed, the persons who eat of the sacrifices offered to God have fellowship with him. This is the positive aspect that Paul is expounding.

But this rhetorical question also has a negative emphasis. The question is preceded by the phrase *Israel according to the flesh,* which in the larger context points to the incident of Israel worshiping the golden calf. Aaron built an altar and announced a festival for the following day. "So the next day the people rose early and sacrificed burnt offerings and presented fellowship offerings. Afterward they sat down to eat and drink and got up to indulge in revelry" (Exod. 32:6). The Israelites partook of sacrifices made not to God but to an idol, the golden calf. When they ate the sacrifice, they broke their covenant vow (Exod. 24:3, 7), forsook the Lord God, and participated in the sin of worshiping an idol. If Moses had not pleaded for mercy, God would have destroyed them. This historical event was recorded to caution every reader in subsequent generations, including the Corinthians, not to follow their example of idolatry.

19. What then am I saying? That food offered to an idol is anything or that an idol is anything?

This verse flows forth from the preceding verse, which negatively disclosed Israel's sinful sacrifice to an idol. If Paul had intended to give a positive sense to the question in verse 18, there would have been an awkward transition to the next verse.[54] But this is not the case, for Paul is indirectly asking his readers to consider a sordid episode from Israel's history.

True, Paul's cryptic statement in the preceding verse can be misunderstood and needs to be expanded in verse 19, where he asks his readers to grasp the significance of his message. He queries whether they understand that offering food to an idol is in vain or that an idol as such is without value (compare 8:4). The answer to both parts of the question is negative. Of course, the food of the sacrifice in itself is meaningless and so is the idol made of wood or stone. The difficulty, however, lies in the sin of worshiping an idol and in subscribing to the beliefs that are "implied in the act of joining in such worship."[55]

20. No; however, the things they sacrifice, they sacrifice to demons and not to God. I do not wish that you become partakers of demons.

a. *Difference.* Many translators supply a subject for the verb *to sacrifice* in the first clause of this sentence. They add "the Gentiles" (NKJV) or "pagans" (e.g., NIV). Because of the reference to demons, translators interpret this verse in terms of pagan sacrifices.

The question is, however, was Paul thinking of the Gentiles of his day, who

---

53. Lev. 7:6, 15; Deut. 18:1, 4; Philo *Special Laws* 1.40 [221]. See Sverre Aalen, "Das Abendmahl als Opfermahl im Neuen Testament," *NovT* 6 (1963): 128–52.

54. Consult Gardner, "Gifts of God," p. 183.

55. R. St. John Parry, *The First Epistle of Paul the Apostle to the Corinthians,* Cambridge Greek Testament for Schools and Colleges (Cambridge: Cambridge University Press, 1937), p. 152; Willis, *Idol Meat,* p. 192; Gordon D. Fee, "*Eidōlothyta* Once Again: An Interpretation of 1 Corinthians 8–10," *Bib* 61 (1980): 172–97.

place their sacrifices on the altars of their gods? In all likelihood, Paul intends to continue the example of Israel's worship of the golden calf when the people turned from serving God to serving demons. In fact, he proves his point by quoting from the Song of Moses, which describes Israel's unfaithfulness at that time:

> Israel grew fat and kicked.
>> They were fat and full and firm.
> They left the God who made them.
>> They rejected the Rock who saved them.
> They made God jealous with foreign gods.
>> They made him angry with hated idols.
> *They made sacrifices to demons, not God.*
>> They were gods they had never known.
> They were new gods from nearby.
>> Your ancestors did not fear them.
> You left God who is the Rock, your Father.
>> You forgot the God who gave you birth.
>> [Deut. 32:15–18, NCV]

In the examples from Israel's history (vv. 1–10), Paul often alluded to the Song of Moses. The Rock as Israel's Savior and the Rock that bore them (Deut. 32:15, 18) is reflected in verse 4. And verses 6–10 describe how the Israelites made God jealous and provoked him (Deut. 32:16).

Because Paul alludes to the Song of Moses in the current verse (v. 20), we assume that the Corinthians probably had memorized it and sang it in their worship services. A fragment of this song, then, would be sufficient to make the Corinthians think of Israel's forty-year desert journey. Briefly put, Paul's wording, "the things they sacrifice, they sacrifice to demons and not to God" relates to Israel's entire desert experience and particularly to the worship of the golden calf.

b. *Demons.* "I do not wish that you become partakers of demons." The word *demons* occurs twice in this verse and twice in the next (v. 21), which indicates that Paul wishes to stress the incompatibility of worshiping both God and demons. Paul teaches that the worship of idols is vain and empty. But he also sees behind the idols the presence of Satan and his cohorts.

For Paul, there is no neutral middle ground between God and Satan, good and evil, virtue and vice. If this were the case, the second half of this verse would be not only pointless but even contradictory. In earlier statements, Paul declared that idols are nothing and thus meaningless (8:4; 10:19). However, the emphasis now is not on the wooden or stone object that the pagans revere as their idol but on the concept *idolatry.* And that concept is much broader, because it embodies the worship of demons that are represented by an idol.[56] Although an idol in itself is nothing, the demons that induce people to worship an idol are powerful.

---

56. I. Howard Marshall correctly dismisses contradiction in Paul's reference to the unknown god (Acts 17:23). See his *Last Supper and Lord's Supper* (Grand Rapids: Eerdmans, 1980), pp. 122, 173 n. 31.

In the Greek text, Paul instructs the Corinthians not "to become partakers of *the* demons." The definite article, which is omitted in English for stylistic reasons, denotes demons as an entire class.

The Greek translation of the Old Testament was undoubtedly used by the Corinthians, and it describes unfaithful Israel worshiping demons. This description appears in the Law, the Prophets, the Writings, and elsewhere.[57] From the Scriptures and from pagan literature, the Corinthians knew about demon worship. And the phrase *become partakers* vividly recalls Paul's earlier remark in verse 18, that the Israelites were partakers of the altar when they presented sacrifices to their idol (Exod. 32:6). Now he elaborates and declares that they actually worshiped demons. The implication for the Corinthians is clear. When the strong Corinthians participate in a festival that honors an idol at a pagan temple, they actually worship demons.

21. You cannot drink the cup of the Lord and the cup of demons, and you cannot partake of the table of the Lord and the table of demons.

Once again Paul follows the symmetrical sequence in verses 14–22 (see the commentary preceding verse 18). That is, this verse parallels verses 16 and 17. There he spoke about the cup of blessing which pertains to the celebration of the Lord's Supper. Here he uses the phrases *cup of the Lord* and *table of the Lord.*

The message is plain. When a believer is the guest at the Lord's table and drinks from the Lord's cup and eats the bread, he or she is one with Christ. As Jesus told his listeners on two different occasions, "You cannot serve both God and Money" (Matt. 6:24; Luke 16:13), so Paul clearly states the impossibility of serving both the Lord and demons.

The strong Corinthians face a dilemma: Should they partake of the cup of the Lord and eat at his table or dine with idolators in the temple of an idol? They cannot do both. The Lord and demons stand diametrically opposed to each other. The believers who say that they are strong spiritually should see this dilemma in proper perspective. They must choose between Christ or Satan. They must flee from idolatry (v. 14).

22. Do we provoke the Lord to jealousy? We are not stronger than he, are we?

a. "Do we provoke the Lord to jealousy?" This sentence completes the symmetrical structure. In verse 14, Paul instructed his readers to flee from idolatry; idolatry is an affront to God, for God is a jealous God, as the Decalogue teaches (Exod. 20:5; Deut. 5:9). Now, with another allusion to the Song of Moses—"they made God jealous with foreign gods" (Deut. 32:16, NCV)—he speaks of the jealousy of the Lord. The Corinthians must never provoke the Lord to jealousy. They should take note of the lesson Israel had to learn in the wilderness and not commit the sin of idolatry—that is, by "partak[ing] of . . . the table of demons" (v.21). Paul uses the word *Lord* to point to Jesus Christ in the preceding verse (v. 21) and alludes to God in this verse. He thus affirms Jesus' divinity.

---

57. See the LXX of Deut. 32:17; Isa. 65:11; Ps. 95:5 (96:5, Hebrew); Ps. 105:36–37 (106:36–37); Bar. 4:7; and see Rev. 9:20.

b. "We are not stronger than he, are we?" To ask the question is to answer it. No one should entertain the thought of standing above God. In his general epistle, James takes to task the person who speaks against a brother or judges him. James says that such a person speaks against the law; and he who criticizes the law places himself above the Lawgiver and Judge (4:11–12). Similarly, in a pastoral manner Paul includes himself in the question. He wants everyone to be submissive to God and in obedience to serve the Lord Jesus Christ. If a Corinthian asserts that he is strong, he should "ask himself whether he thinks he is 'stronger' than God himself, that is, by willing and doing what God does not will (v. 22).[58]

Practical Considerations in 10:22

Jealousy can turn a friend into an enemy, a gentle person into a monster, and a virtue into a vice. A jealous person breaks the tenth commandment of the Decalogue, where we are told not to covet. God instructs his people to be content. "Godliness with content-ment is great gain" (I Tim. 6:6), says Paul, who himself knew what it was to be in need or to have plenty (Phil. 4:12).

Scripture reveals the dire effects of sinful jealousy. In Old Testament times, Joseph's brothers were jealous and sold him to Midianite merchants on their way to Egypt (Gen. 37:4, 28). The ten tribes in the northern kingdom were jealous of the tribes of Judah and Benjamin and frequently fought them (Judg. 12:4; II Sam. 3:1). In the New Testament era, Jewish leaders were jealous of the apostles whom they jailed and flogged (Acts 5:17–18, 40).

Jealousy is also ascribed to God, but his jealousy is a sinless, righteous sentiment by which he vigilantly protects his holiness. This type of jealousy must be understood in the context of Israel's status as God's special people. They owed him faithful obedience, for he alone is God, but instead they worshiped idols and provoked God to jealousy (e.g., see Hos. 2:2). When he is provoked, he expresses his wrath; when his people have sinned but repent, God's love is unbounded. In Jesus Christ, divine love is unfathomable in depth (John 3:16).

Greek Words, Phrases, and Constructions in 10:18–22

Verses 18, 20

θυσιαστηρίου—"altar." Notice the play on words: the altar has θυσίας (sacrifices) which the worshipers θύουσιν (sacrifice).

Majority Text, Textus Receptus, and Souter have inserted τὰ ἔθνη (the Gentiles) as the subject of the verb *to sacrifice*. Inclusion of the plural neuter subject violates the rule that a neuter plural subject needs a verb in the singular. But lesser manuscripts that have the neuter plural also have provided the singular verb θύει to maintain this rule. These varia-tions appear to be scribal efforts to make the text intelligible. On the basis of stronger wit-

---

58. Ridderbos, *Paul*, p. 304.

nesses, other editions (BF, Merk, Nes-Al, and UBS) delete the subject. "[τὰ ἔθνη] could not be absent from so many outstanding witnesses if it had been in the text originally."[59]

Verse 21

οὐ ... καί—these two Greek words feature a decided contrast in the sentence even though the conjunction means "and."

τραπέζης—"table." The presence of a definite article is expected and its absence stresses the characteristic quality of the table of the Lord against the table of the demons.[60]

μετέχειν—the present infinitive of the verb *to share* is introduced by the auxilary verb δύνασθε (you are able). A verb of sharing takes the partitive genitive and in this instance controls the noun *table.*

Verse 22

παραζηλοῦμεν—"we provoke to jealousy." The present indicative states the fact and the interrogative form the element of surprise.[61] This compound form appears in the aorist indicative in Deuteronomy 32:21 (LXX).

23 "All things are permissible," but not all things are profitable. "All things are permissible," but all things do not edify. 24 Let no one seek his own interest but that of another. 25 Eat anything that is sold in the meat market without asking questions for conscience' sake. 26 For,

"The earth is the Lord's and everything in it."

27 If any of the unbelievers invites you and you wish to go, eat whatever is set before you without asking questions for conscience' sake. 28 But if anyone says to you, "This is meat offered to an idol," do not eat it, for the sake of the man who informed you and for conscience' sake. 29 I am speaking not of your own conscience but of that of the other man. For why should my freedom be judged by the conscience of another? 30 If I partake with thanksgiving, why am I denounced for something for which I express thanks?

31 Therefore, whether you eat or drink or whatever you do, do all things to the glory of God. 32 Give no offense either to the Jews, or to the Greeks, or to the church of God, 33 just as I also please all men in all things, seeking not my own profit but the profit of many, so that they may be saved. 11. 1 Be imitators of me, just as I am of Christ.

3. Freedom of Conscience
10:23–11:1

Some Corinthians who had observed Paul could now argue that he contradicted himself. They could say that he exercised Christian liberty by eating in Gentile homes but restricted them from doing so—that is, eating at a Gentile's house. He had given his word not to eat meat again to avoid causing his brother to fall into sin (8:13). Paul needed to explain himself to avoid teaching conflicting precepts. He had to make a distinction between what is essential and what is nonessential. His most important teaching was that the Corinthians should live

59. G. Zuntz, *The Text of the Epistles: A Disquisition upon the Corpus Paulinum* (London: Oxford University Press, 1953), p. 102.

60. Blass and Debrunner, *Greek Grammar*, #259.3.

61. Robertson, *Grammar*, p. 923.

in a way that promoted the interest of their fellow men (v. 24) and glorified God (v. 30). All other things were expendable. In a sentence, eating sacrificial meat in a temple dining hall is idolatry but eating meat bought in the meat market is permitted. On the other hand, if a Christian dines as a guest in a Gentile home and learns that the meat has come from an idol temple, he should abstain from eating it for the sake of someone else's conscience.

a. Freedom and Scripture
10:23–26

23. "All things are permissible," but not all things are profitable. "All things are permissible," but all things do not edify. 24. Let no one seek his own interest but that of another.

a. "'All things are permissible,' but all things are not profitable." This Corinthian slogan appeared earlier (6:12) but in a context that concerned sexual immorality: some Christians in Corinth took liberties in respect to their social life. In this verse Paul again quotes the slogan, but he will apply it in the matter of eating meat that was sold in the meat market (v. 25).

The brevity of the slogan *all things are permissible* obscures Paul's intent. The personal pronoun *for me* is lacking (compare 6:12; see Sir. 37:26–28), and so it seems unlikely that he speaks only about himself. The context suggests a wider application: Even philosophers in Hellenistic circles raised similar questions on freedom, and the Jews were prone to ask questions on what was permissible and what was not. For this reason, they had received from their clergy hundreds of manmade rules and stipulations. Yet they believed that a good man, because he acted blamelessly, was free indeed.[62] Nonetheless, within the membership of the Corinthian church Jewish Christians apparently were challenging Paul on Christian liberty. In respect to the question of idolatry in chapter 10, Paul seems to address Jewish Christians.[63] However, not only believers of Jewish origin but also those of Gentile stock could challenge Paul.

Paul has a rejoinder to the Corinthian slogan: "But not all things are profitable." With an implied allusion to self-seeking interests, Paul points out that a person's selfishness cancels the possibility of receiving rewards.

b. "'All things are permissible,' but all things do not edify." Paul repeats the slogan but this time he gives a different response, the negated verb *to edify*. The work of edifying is always action performed for the benefit of someone else.[64] It is, therefore, the opposite of that which is profitable (i.e., benefits oneself). Paul taught the Corinthians that love and pursuit of peace lead to mutual edification (8:1; Rom. 14:19).

---

62. Philo *Every Good Man Is Free* 3 [21.22]; 6 [41]; 9 [59–61]. See also R. A. Horsley, "Consciousness and Freedom among the Corinthians: 1 Corinthians 8–10," *CBQ* 40 (1978): 574–89.

63. See James B. Hurley, "Man and Woman in 1 Corinthians," Ph.D. diss., Cambridge University, 1973, p. 86.

64. Bengel, *Bengel's New Testament Commentary*, vol. 2, p. 220.

c. "Let no one seek his own interest but that of another." Continuing his pastoral advice to the believers in Corinth, Paul adds a sentence that is reminiscent of exhortations in his other epistles: "Each of us should please his neighbor for his good, to build him up" (Rom. 15:2) and "Each of you should look not only to your own interests, but also to the interests of others" (Phil. 2:4). The content of all these injunctions echoes the teaching of Jesus when he summarized the Decalogue: "'Love your neighbor as you love yourself'" (Matt. 22:39, NCV). Paul notes that this summary is the fulfillment of the law (Rom. 13:10) and James calls it the royal law.

Seeking the interests of someone else is not easy. By nature we are inclined to look after our own interests first, and afterward, if time and resources permit, we think of others. Jesus taught the parable of the good Samaritan to show the expert in Old Testament law how to love his fellow men (Luke 10:25–37). Paul's injunction to seek the good of another strengthens the rejoinder *but all things do not edify*. Edifying and seeking someone else's good are the same.

25. Eat anything that is sold in the meat market without asking questions for conscience' sake.

a. "Eat anything that is sold in the meat market." The transition between this verse and the preceding context seems abrupt. Indeed, editors of the Greek New Testament display a break to indicate that Paul introduces a new subject.[65] Perhaps Paul should have introduced his practical examples (vv. 25–27) with an appropriate sentence, but he does continue with the same subject. He intertwines the principle of exercising Christian freedom with application to circumstances his readers would encounter.

One of these circumstances was buying food in the meat market (see also the commentary on chap. 8). The meat market in ancient Corinth was known as the *makellon,* a term that also occurred in Latin (*macellum*).[66] Rabbis permitted Jews in the Dispersion to buy meat in the *makellon,* but they stipulated that their compatriots could not purchase meat that had been sacrificed to an idol. Also, the shopkeeper had to declare that he did not keep in his store any nonkosher meat, which was forbidden to Jews.[67] But what about the Gentile Christians who belonged to the Corinthian church? They encountered hardly any problems. The ordinary citizen in Corinth bought meat products that often had no connection at all with idolatry. Comments C. K. Barrett, "The problem of *eidōlothyta* [food sacrificed to an idol] would seldom arise, and possibly would never have arisen in a Gentile Church like that of Corinth if Jewish Christians (the Cephas group, perhaps) had not raised it."[68]

---

65. Nes-Al, BF.

66. H. J. Cadbury, "The Macellum of Corinth," *JBL* 53 (1934): 134. See also Johannes Schneider, *TDNT*, vol. 4, pp. 370–72.

67. SB, vol. 3, p. 420.

68. C. K. Barrett, "Things Sacrificed to Idols," *NTS* 11 (1965): 146. It is also published in his *Essays on Paul* (Philadelphia: Westminster, 1982), p. 49.

b. "[Eat anything] without asking questions for conscience' sake." When Paul advises his readers to eat meat without questioning its origin, he addresses Jewish Christians who would insist on buying and consuming only kosher food. He also deliberately opposes Jewish teaching. He believes that when sacrificial meat is sold to the public, it has lost its religious significance.

Paul is hardly encouraging the strong Corinthians to eat, for they are the ones who cause others to stumble (see v. 32). And it is unlikely that he suddenly wants to persuade the weak (8:1) to eat sacrificial meat.[69] Instead, Paul appears to speak to his fellow countrymen. Their conscience bothers them when they eat food that may not meet Jewish standards. They turn to Paul and ask him what the Scriptures say on this point.

26. For,

"The earth is the Lord's and everything in it."

When Paul imparts pastoral advice, he frequently anticipates opposition and therefore turns to the Scriptures to establish his teaching.[70] He now quotes the familiar words of Psalm 24:1, which has a message similar to that of other psalm quotations (Pss. 50:12; 89:11).

We know from Jewish literature that this particular psalm citation was used in prayers said at mealtime.[71] "The principal content and purpose of these benedictions is to give praise and thanks to God for the abundant goodness which he has bestowed upon his creatures and, at the same time, to obtain permission from him to enjoy the fruits of this world; for 'the earth is the Lord's, and the fullness thereof' [Ps. 24:1]."[72] The fact that Paul is thinking of mealtime prayers is evident from his later remarks about taking part in a meal and giving thanks to God (v. 30).

In contrast to the rabbis who employed the words of Psalm 24:1 in their mealtime prayers, Paul provides an additional interpretation by accepting and giving thanks for all kinds of food. We hear an echo of the heavenly voice that told Peter not to "consider unclean what God has made clean" (Acts 10:15; see vv. 9–16). By implication, Jewish Christians could buy meat at the meat market and should not ask questions about the origin of such meat when they consumed it. When Paul cites Psalm 24:1 to strengthen his argument, he fails to write a conclusion. Yet his intent is clear. Even if food had been offered to an idol, it should not be a matter of conscience for the Corinthians, because God is the Lord of creation.[73] The sense of Psalm 24:1 is reflected in Paul's comment on creation: all things come through God the Father and the Lord Jesus

69. Gardner, "Gifts of God," p. 190; see also Willis, *Idol Meat*, pp. 230–34.

70. See, e.g., 3:19, 20; 6:16; 9:9; 14:21.

71. Refer to *Berakhôth* 35a–b.

72. Joseph Heinemann, *Prayer in the Talmud: Forms and Patterns*, Studia Judaica, ed. E. L. Ehrlich (Berlin and New York: Walter de Gruyter, 1977), vol. 9, p. 18.

73. Compare Duane F. Watson, "1 Corinthians 10:23–11:1 in the Light of Greco-Roman Rhetoric: The Role of Rhetorical Questions," *JBL* 108 (1989): 301–18.

Christ (8:6). If the Lord, who has created all things, sanctifies the food, then Christians may take it from his hand in answer to the petition, "Give us today our daily bread" (Matt. 6:11).

Greek Words, Phrases, and Constructions in 10:24

τοῦ ἑτέρου—the adjective means "another" in the sense of someone different from oneself. The same word occurs in verse 29 with a similar meaning.

To express more clearly the message of this verse, some translators have adopted the extra word ἕκαστος (each) that is inserted in some Greek texts: "Let no one be concerned about his own well-being, but each about the well-being of the other" (*Cassirer*, see also NJB, NKJV). The textual support for the word *each*, however, is insignificant and secondary.

---

b. Freedom and Conscience
10:27–30

27. If any of the unbelievers invites you and you wish to go, eat whatever is set before you without asking questions for conscience' sake.

a. *Practical concerns.* Christians in Corinth faced the question whether they might accept invitations from unbelievers and be guests at their tables. The Greek text indicates that these invitations were commonplace: "If, as in fact happens, any of the unbelievers invites you, go and eat." The scene is not now a dining room in a temple (see Paul's prohibition in v. 20) but the home of a Gentile.

How does a Christian witness effectively when he is invited to dine with an unbeliever? Paul himself becomes all things to all men, including the Gentiles, to win them for Christ (9:20–22). To decline invitations for fear of eating meat offered to an idol would rule out the possibility of presenting the claims of Christ. And to ask questions about the food that is served and then to refuse to eat it would be an unnecessary affront to the host.

Paul's advice is simple and direct: "If you want to go, go and eat what is placed before you." He puts the choice before every individual. He neither commands nor encourages, but wants the individual to decide. He realizes that the Christians in Corinth have family obligations and social commitments which ought not to be broken. Through these bonds with family and community, they may be able to advance Christ's cause. With an open mind they should consider an invitation to a Gentile home.

b. *Conscience.* Paul repeats the wording of verse 25. He believes that a person's conscience is burdened not by things but by individuals, as is evident from the illustration in the next verse (v. 28). Therefore, the Corinthians should not raise questions that are based on misgivings about the origin of food. They should not erect an unnecessary barrier between themselves and a Gentile host. If that is the case, they display the attitude of legalistic Pharisees who obey the letter but not the spirit of the law.[74]

"For conscience' sake." This phrase can be taken with either the verb *to eat* or the participle *asking*. If we take the wording in the sequence in which it is presented, we construe the words *for conscience' sake* with the participial phrase *without asking questions* instead of with the verb *to eat*. Both the syntax and the context seem to indicate that the matter of asking is of primary concern to a believer. We understand the clause to signify that a guest should eat what is presented and live in ignorance about the origin of the food. Guests, then, would be wise not to ask questions so that their consciences remain free.

28. But if anyone says to you, "This is meat offered to an idol," do not eat it, for the sake of the man who informed you and for conscience' sake. 29a. I am speaking not of your own conscience but that of the other man.

a. "But if anyone says to you, 'This is meat offered to an idol.'" The Greek text here does not express certainty and fact as did the conditional clause in the preceding verse (v. 27a). Instead, Paul cites a circumstance that may present itself to a Christian guest in the private dining room of a Gentile host. This is a likely scene: Other guests are present and all are engaged in animated conversation. When the matter of the Christian religion is broached, someone reveals that the meat has come via the meat market from the temple of an idol. Then the Christian faces a test and must respond in harmony with his religious beliefs.

The informant appears to be a scrupulous Christian, the Gentile host, or an unbeliever. Many scholars favor the first choice because in verse 29a Paul explicitly mentions the other man's conscience.[75] Thus, they understand the informant to be a weak Christian and the man who receives the information, a strong Christian. But would a Christian first inquire about the food and then stay for dinner? Of course not. Would he purposely follow the example of a strong Christian but afterward have a guilty conscience? No. Conversely, could the Christian's response affect the conscience of a Gentile? Yes, as is clear from Paul's comprehensive remark in verse 32, where he includes Jews, Greeks, and members of the church.[76] Although the details of this scene are sketchy, we believe that either the Gentile host or another unbeliever posed the question.

Paul places on the lips of the Gentile the Greek word *hierothyton*, which refers to meat that had been slaughtered in a pagan rite.[77] Paul apparently quotes this

74. Compare Hans Conzelmann, *1 Corinthians: A Commentary on the First Epistle to the Corinthians*, ed. George W. MacRae, trans. James W. Leitch, Hermeneia: A Critical and Historical Commentary on the Bible (Philadelphia: Fortress, 1975), p. 177 n. 15.

75. E.g., C. K. Barrett, *A Commentary on the First Epistle to the Corinthians*, Harper's New Testament Commentaries series (New York and Evanston: Harper and Row, 1968), p. 242; Margaret E. Thrall, "The Pauline Use of ΣΥΝΕΙΔΗΣΙΣ," *NTS* 14 (1967): 118–25.

76. Refer to Gordon D. Fee, *The First Epistle to the Corinthians*, New International Commentary on the New Testament series (Grand Rapids: Eerdmans, 1987), p. 484.

77. The term literally means "sacrificed in a temple." See F. F. Bruce, *1 and 2 Corinthians*, New Century Bible series (London: Oliphants, 1971), p. 100; Horst Seebass, *NIDNTT*, vol. 2, p. 235; Gottlob Schrenk, *TDNT*, vol. 3, p. 252.

word to show that it was the exact term used by a Gentile. He himself favors the Greek expression *eidōlothyton*, which even in transliteration discloses that he refers to food that has been sacrificed to idols. This term, used in a derogatory manner with reference to the Gentiles, was current among both Jews and Christians.[78]

b. "Do not eat it for the sake of the man who informed you and for conscience' sake. I am speaking not of your own conscience but of that of the other man." In Greek the command is direct and applies to a prevailing situation: Stop doing what you are doing! The cause of Christ is at stake in this case, so that the Christian ought not to utter the slogan, "All things are permissible" (v. 23). Rather, he should ask why the informant has brought the matter of sacrificial meat to his attention. If the Christian is put to the test, he does well to realize that the unbeliever is observing to see whether he abides by Christian principles of conduct. He has a duty to honor his Lord and to further the spread of the gospel. If by eating food sacrificed to an idol he discredits the Christian faith in the eyes of the unbeliever, then instead of drawing the unbeliever to Christ he drives him away.

Most versions place a dash at the end of verse 28 to point out an abrupt break. In that verse Paul fails to explain whose conscience he means. However, a close look at the next verse (v. 29a) is enlightening, for here he contrasts the conscience of the Christian with that of the informant. Paul uses a Greek word that may be interpreted "different." He is saying, therefore, "I am not referring to your own conscience that gives you freedom, but to a conscience that differs from yours and belongs to the informant." He reminds a Christian who wishes to exercise his freedom to be sensitive to the conscience of the unbeliever.

29b. For why should my freedom be judged by the conscience of another? 30. If I partake with thanksgiving, why am I denounced for something for which I express thanks?

a. "For why should my freedom be judged?" Who is the speaker in this verse? From the answers that scholars present, I select two.[79] Paul may be repeating a remark from a strong Christian, or the personal pronouns *my* and *I* may refer to Paul himself. If Paul were recording the words of a strong Christian, we would have expected an introductory phrase: "For why should you say, 'My freedom is judged by the conscience of another'?" This is not the case; instead, the personal pronouns refer to Paul himself.

What is Paul trying to communicate with this question? In the light of the two preceding chapters (8 and 9), in which he explains at length his liberty, he is saying that Christian freedom must function in the context of love for God and for neighbors. The verb *to judge* can be interpreted in the unfavorable sense of "condemn," an interpretation reinforced by the presence of the verb *to denounce* in the next verse (v. 30). Thus, Calvin is of the opinion that others will condemn us if we wrongly exercise Christian liberty. "If we use our freedom just as we like, and thereby cause offence to our neighbours, the result will be that they will con-

---

78. Bauer, p. 221. Refer also to I Cor. 8:1, 4, 7, 10; 10:19; Rev. 2:14, 20; and *Didache* 6:3.

79. For details, consult Fee, *First Corinthians*, p. 486 n. 52.

demn our freedom. Therefore, because of our fault and lack of consideration, the outcome will be that this matchless gift of God will be condemned."[80]

The Christian freedom that Paul advocates in his epistles means that we "serve one another in love" (Gal. 5:13). This freedom should never elicit scorn and contempt from either fellow Christians or unbelievers, for then it has lost its objective.[81]

b. "By the conscience of another." A literal translation of this phrase is to take the adjective *another* with the noun *conscience*, as in "by another conscience" (ASV, RV). The sense of the verse, however, is that the adjective *another* refers to a person, which is the translation in all other versions. Paul does not specify whose conscience that may be.

c. "If I partake with thanksgiving, why am I denounced for something for which I express thanks?" This second question follows up the preceding one (29b). Paul is saying that if he utters a prayer but knows that others (either a weak believer, a host, or a Gentile) take issue with his decision to eat sacrificial food, his prayer is ineffective. The Gentiles especially will ask, "What sort of religion is that?"[82] They will regard the conduct of a Christian to be nothing more than pretense and hypocrisy. Consequently, no one should give someone else a reason to slander the Christian religion. Paul presents his counsel in the form of questions that are designed not to allow anyone to doubt his Christian sincerity, and in verses 29b and 30, he is telling the Corinthians that they ought to act prudently.

Even in translation a play on the words *thanks* and *thanksgiving* is evident. Thanksgiving, part of a prayer that both Jews and Christians offer to God at mealtime for the daily provisions of food and drink (see the commentary on v. 26), recognizes God as the giver of the food. But if a Christian cannot pray sincerely because of adverse criticism, he ought to abstain from eating sacrificial meat and thereby avoid bringing the cause of Christ into possible disrepute (compare Rom. 14:6). Nonetheless, a Christian remains free to eat whatever is set before him, even if he decides to abstain.[83]

Greek Words, Phrases, and Constructions in 10:27–29

εἰ—the particle introduces a simple-fact conditional clause that is followed by the apodosis with a present imperative ἐσθίετε (eat!).

---

80. Calvin, *I Corinthians*, p. 224.

81. Refer to Nelson D. Kloosterman, *Scandalum Infirmorum et Communio Sanctorum: The Relation between Christian Liberty and Neighbor Love in the Church* (Neerlandia, Alberta: Inheritance Publications, 1991), p. 30.

82. Godet, *First Corinthians*, p. 527. See also G. G. Findlay, *St. Paul's First Epistle to the Corinthians*, in vol. 3 of *The Expositor's Greek Testament*, ed. W. Robertson Nicoll, 5 vols. (1910; reprint ed., Grand Rapids: Eerdmans, 1961), p. 869.

83. Barrett, *First Corinthians*, p. 244.

ἐὰν δέ τις ὑμῖν εἴπῃ—this clause conveys probability with the verb in the subjunctive mood. The conditional sentence is completed with the negative command *do not eat* in the present imperative.

ἄλλης συνειδήσεως—the adjective in the feminine singular ("other") modifies the noun *conscience*. The genitive describes the means with the preposition ὑπό (by). Translators supply the word *someone* or something similar to indicate the possessor.

---

c. Conclusion
10:31–11:1

31. Therefore, whether you eat or drink or whatever you do, do all things to the glory of God.

In these concluding remarks, Paul utters the same sentiments he writes more expansively in one of his prison Epistles, "And whatever you do, whether in word or deed, do it all in the name of the Lord Jesus, giving thanks to God the Father through him" (Col. 3:17). Paul exhorts the Corinthians to live their lives for God's glory; to be positive without being offensive; and even in the daily activity of eating and drinking to exalt God's goodness and grace.

We are unable to glorify God unless our lives are in harmony with him and his precepts. Nothing in our conduct should obstruct God's glory from being reflected in us. That is, in everything we do and say, no matter how insignificant, the world should be able to see that we are God's people. Exalting God's glory ought to be our chief purpose in this earthly life (compare 1 Peter 4:11).

32. Give no offense either to the Jews, or to the Greeks, or to the church of God, 33. just as I also please all men in all things, seeking not my own profit but the profit of many, so that they may be saved.

a. "Give no offense." In this summary, Paul reiterates in positive terms what he implied in his questions in preceding verses (vv. 27–30). A Christian must seek to live blamelessly wherever he finds himself. Earlier Paul wrote that he conducted himself as a Jew to the Jew, as a Gentile to the Gentile, and as a weak person to the weak for the purpose of winning them for Christ (see 9:19–23). So once more he mentions the categories of Jews, Gentiles (here: Greeks), and the comprehensive term *church of God*.

We should not think that Paul failed to press the claims of Christ out of fear of being offensive. On the contrary, he boldly told both the Jews and the Greeks to turn to God in repentance and to put their faith in Jesus Christ (Acts 20:21). However, presenting Christ's gospel effectively also requires tact, courtesy, and persistence. Paul strove to be all things to all men, and in his concluding remarks he invites his readers to do likewise.

Notice that Paul includes the members of the church. They as individual believers have the corporate responsibility of caring for one another. If a weaker member of the church is offended, the entire congregation is offended and should respond. "If one member suffers, all the members suffer with it," writes Paul in a succeeding chapter (12:26).

b. "Just as I also please all men in all things, seeking not my own profit but the profit of many." Throughout this epistle and elsewhere, Paul sets himself up as an example of Christian conduct, even to the point of instructing the Corinthians to become his imitators.[84]

What kind of an example is Paul? He tries to please all men in all things. At first glance, he appears to ingratiate himself to others. But on closer inspection, he is consistent in his teaching of loving his neighbor as himself to show that neighbor the path of salvation in Christ. Paul never asked anything for himself, even though he was entitled to financial support for his labors (9:12–18). Instead he labored as a tentmaker to support himself in his daily needs. As a workaday craftsman, he identified with those people who were economically weak (see the commentary on 9:22). He stood ready to aid anyone, whether Jew, Gentile, or Christian, who asked for help. But in everything he did, he sought to glorify his God by pointing the people to Jesus Christ. Accordingly, he could write that he did nothing for his own profit but worked for the benefit of others.

c. "So that they may be saved." This is Paul's objective in life: to bring people to a saving knowledge of Christ. The main verb in this purpose clause is in the passive voice, and has Jesus as the implied agent. An apostle, Paul serves his Sender as a faithful ambassador who proclaims the gospel and explains the way of salvation. God expects his emissaries to be faithful to his Word as they call men, women, and children to conversion. Nevertheless, Paul is unable to save humanity, for this is not man's prerogative but God's initiative. Through the atoning work of Jesus Christ and the working of the Holy Spirit, God grants salvation to his people.

11:1. Be imitators of me, just as I am of Christ.

When the New Testament was divided into chapters, this verse unfortunately became the first verse of chapter 11. The context clearly shows that it serves as the concluding line of chapter 10.

Paul sets the example and implores his readers to follow him. He himself emulates Christ, in whose footsteps every believer must walk (I Peter 2:21). We follow Christ not in the sense of enduring agony and pain in Gethsemane and at Calvary. Rather, we obediently walk in his footsteps by showing our love and thankfulness to him and by keeping his precepts.

Practical Considerations in 10:27–33

We have a tendency to relegate the message of this passage to the first century. At that time, the gospel entered the world to displace a pagan culture with a Christian lifestyle. The conflict between Christianity and paganism raged throughout the ancient world. But today the battle has not subsided, nor has a truce been signed. Although cultures have changed and environments differ, the strife itself continues.

---

84. I Cor. 4:16; 11:1; Phil. 3:17; 4:9; I Thess. 1:6; II Thess. 3:7, 9.

Christians must be sincere, honest, trustworthy, dependable, prudent, and efficient in this strife. But the constant pressures on Christians in today's world test them. Closely watched by the world, Christians are expected to honor their word, maintain their moral integrity, and avoid even the appearance of evil. In business deals, at social gatherings, on special assignments, Christians must make decisions that often call for compromise. Should they ever shade the truth in either advertising, accounting, or reporting? Should all Christians steadfastly refuse intoxicants regardless of the circumstances? And should Christians always observe the sanctity of the Lord's Day no matter where and with whom they are?

Paul answers to these dilemmas by giving the basic principle of doing all things, even the common activities of eating and drinking, for the glory of God. Christians who love the Lord with heart, soul, and mind and love their neighbors as themselves will do everything to please their Lord. For them, as it was in the case of Paul, God is central in every aspect of life. Paul's conscience was free in the presence of his Lord.

Summary of Chapter 10

Paul asserts that all the Israelites who left Egypt under the cloud passed through the sea and were baptized into Moses. All these people ate the same spiritual food and drank the same spiritual drink from the spiritual rock that accompanied them, namely, Christ. Yet, because he was displeased with them, God scattered their bodies across the desert floor.

The historical events that Paul relates serve to alert the Corinthians to the dangers of idolatry. He recalls the incident of the Israelites eating and drinking when they worshiped the golden calf, a festivity that degenerated into pagan revelry. During their journey through the wilderness, they tested God's patience. As punishment, some were bitten by poisonous snakes and others were killed by an angel. The Corinthians are instructed to take note so that they do not succumb to idolatry. Yet, Paul says, God is faithful and will not permit a temptation greater than they can bear.

After issuing a direct command to flee idolatry, Paul instructs the readers to observe the significance of the Lord's Supper. They must know that partaking of the cup and of the bread demonstrates unity. Eating food offered to idols makes one a participant with demons. Paul shows the utter inconsistency of drinking from the cup of demons and from the cup of the Lord. This is testing the Lord.

The slogan *All things are permissible* is interpreted and applied to eating meat bought at the meat market. Specific instances of eating in a private home of an unbeliever are considered. Paul advises the Christians to do everything for God's glory and to avoid giving offense to either Jews, Greeks, or members of God's church.

11

Worship, *part 1*

(11:2–34)

Outline (continued)

11

2 I praise you because you remember me in all things, and you guard the traditions just as I delivered them to you. 3 But I want you to understand that Christ is the head of every man, and the man is the head of a woman, and God is the head of Christ. 4 Every man who prays or prophesies with something on his head dishonors his head. 5 But every woman who prays or prophesies with her head uncovered dishonors her head. For she is one and the same as a woman whose head is shaved. 6 For if a woman does not cover her head, let her also have her hair cut off. But if it is disgraceful for a woman to have her hair cut off or shaven, let her cover her head.

7 For a man ought not to cover his head, because he is the image and glory of God. But the woman is the glory of man. 8 For man does not come from woman but woman from man. 9 Indeed, man was not created for the sake of the woman but woman for the sake of the man. 10 For this reason the woman ought to have authority on her head because of the angels. 11 However, in the Lord, woman is nothing apart from man, and man is nothing apart from woman. 12 For as the woman is from the man, even so is the man through the woman, and all things are from God.

13 Judge for yourselves: Is it proper for a woman to pray to God with her head uncovered? 14 Does not nature itself teach you that it is a disgrace to a man if he lets his hair grow long, 15 but if a woman lets her hair grow long, it is her glory? Because her long hair has been given to her as a covering. 16 But if anyone is inclined to be contentious, we do not have such a custom, nor do the churches of God.

E. Worship
11:2–14:40

1. Man and Woman in Worship
11:2–16

In the next four chapters (chaps. 11–14), Paul instructs the Corinthians in the matter of worship. He begins with worshipers, both male and female, who pray or prophesy, and then explains proper conduct at the Lord's table. Between a lengthy discussion on the gifts of the Spirit and speaking in tongues, he places his letter of love. He concludes with an exhortation to prophesy, a command not to forbid tongue speaking, and a rule to maintain order.

a. The Man and the Woman
11:2–6

Paul fully understands his people and approaches them as a seasoned pastor. He knows that they are still babes in their spiritual lives and need much corrective advice. But before he admonishes them, Paul praises them for their efforts to follow his teachings.

2. I praise you because you remember me in all things, and you guard the traditions just as I delivered them to you.

a. "I praise you." No other passage in this epistle has words of praise for the Corinthians (contrast vv. 17, 22), except for the introductory section in which Paul gives thanks to God for the grace extended to them (1:4–9). Immediately following this introduction, he reproves the readers for their factionalism in the church (1:10–12). Similarly, in the current chapter Paul praises the Corinthians for their remembrance of him and the traditions he had entrusted to them. But subsequent to these commendations, he instructs them in the proper conduct of men and women, especially in public worship.

b. "Because you remember me in all things." Why does Paul praise the Corinthians? Because they have remembered (the Greek verb has the perfect tense) and continue to remember him in all things. This means that numerous Christians in Corinth have fond memories of Paul and follow his instructions. But many of the Corinthians did not keep Paul's teachings, as is evident from the succeeding context. For that reason, some translators prefer the temporal adverb *always* or its equivalent[1] for the phrase *in all things*. With this translation, they eliminate possible disharmony between this verse (v. 2) and the rest of the chapter. In the Greek, however, Paul is consistent in writing the phrase *in all things* (he also used it in two preceding verses, 9:25 and 10:33). Because of Paul's earlier usage, we hold to this translation.

c. "And you guard the traditions just as I delivered them to you." The second part of verse 2 explains the phrase in question. "All things" are those apostolic teachings that Paul had delivered to the Corinthians in earlier times; they are the traditions that the apostles had received and subsequently transmitted to others. For instance, Paul writes that he received information from the Lord and passed it on to the Corinthians (v. 23; 15:3; II Tim. 2:2).

At this juncture in the epistle, we have no definite indication that Paul is trying to answer a question which the Corinthians had raised in their letter. Chapter 11 does not have the formula "Now concerning the things you wrote about" that in both full and abbreviated form occurs elsewhere (7:1, 25; 8:1; 12:1; 16:1,12). Probably the letter contained a question regarding Christian conduct in the multicultural society of Corinth. And Paul addresses that problem in the following verses (vv. 3–16).

3. But I want you to understand that Christ is the head of every man, and the man is the head of a woman, and God is the head of Christ.

a. *Construction.* After verse 2, Paul begins a subject he has not mentioned elsewhere. He teaches his readers about the relationships of Christ to man, man to woman, and God to Christ in a sequence of three clauses:

---

1. NEB, REB, TNT, NAB, JB, NJB, *Moffatt.*

Christ is the head of every man
the man is the head of a woman
God is the head of Christ

Note that Paul begins and ends with the word *Christ* and that the first and third clauses are balanced. Also note that the sequence of the first two clauses is smooth. But the progression of these three clauses with the repetitive word *head* raises questions that center on the meaning of that single word.

b. *Meaning.* Commentators are divided on the meaning of the Greek word *kephalē* (head). Some interpret it to mean "source,"[2] while others maintain that it signifies "authority."[3]

Some scholars have examined the evidence and discovered that the Septuagint, the Greek translation of the Hebrew Bible, records a number of places where the term *head* figuratively means "chief" or "ruler." Two examples are, "You have preserved me as the head of nations. People I did not know are subject to me" (II Sam. 22:44), and, "'For the head of Aram is Damascus, and the head of Damascus is only Rezin. . . . The head of Ephraim is Samaria, and the head of Samaria is only Remaliah's son'" (Isa. 7:8, 9). The accumulated evidence from the Septuagint, Philo, and Josephus is impressive. Still other scholars question whether the Hebrew word *rosh* (head) metaphorically denotes "chief" or "ruler." They state instead that *kephalē* means "source" in Greek literature,[4] and that the expression *head* derives from Greek usage that connotes "source." In fact, one writer asserts that "there is simply no basis for the assumption that a Hellenized Jew would instinctively give *kephalē* the meaning 'one having authority over someone.'"[5]

The question scholars face is whether Paul addressed the Corinthians from a Jewish perspective (that head means authority) or a Hellenistic point of view (that head means source). Did Paul speak from his own background or did he accommodate himself to the Hellenistic culture? One scholar who examined the debate on this matter concludes, "The upshot of this discussion is that a Hellenistic Jewish writer such as Paul of Tarsus could well have intended that *kephalē* in 1 Cor[inthians] 11.3 be understood as 'head' in the sense of authority or supremacy over someone else."[6]

---

2. Among many others, Colin Brown, *NIDNTT*, vol. 2, p. 160.

3. E.g., Heinrich Schlier, *TDNT*, vol. 3, p. 679; Bauer, p. 430.

4. Consult, e.g., C. K. Barrett, *A Commentary on the First Epistle to the Corinthians,* Harper's New Testament Commentaries series (New York and Evanston: Harper and Row, 1968), p. 248.

5. Jerome Murphy-O'Connor, "Sex and Logic in 1 Corinthians 11:2–16," *CBQ* 42 (1980): 492. Refer also to his article, "1 Corinthians 11:2–16 Once Again," *CBQ* 50 (1988): 265–74; see John P. Meier, "On the Veiling of Hermeneutics (1 Cor. 11:2–16)," *CBQ* 40 (1978): 212–26.

6. Joseph A. Fitzmyer, "Another Look at ΚΕΦΑΛΗ in 1 Corinthians 11:3," *NTS* 35 (1989): 510. Consult also Wayne Grudem, "Does ΚΕΦΑΛΗ ('Head') Mean 'Source' or 'Authority Over' in Greek Literature? A Survey of 2,336 Examples," *TrinityJ* 6 n.s. (1985): 38–59.

c. *Interpretation.* One interpretation of this passage—that "head" means "source" or "source of life"—is based primarily on three passages in Paul's epistles (Col. 1:18; 2:19; Eph. 4:15). As Christ is the source of man's being, so man is the source of woman. The interpretation that man is the source of woman is strengthened by Paul's assertion that the woman came from man (vv. 8, 12). The conclusion is drawn that Paul teaches not a doctrine of subordination but of "the unique relationships that are predicated on one's being the source of the other's existence."[7] Further, the creation account teaches that God made Eve out of one of Adam's ribs (Gen. 2:21–23), so that Adam is the source of Eve. But if we view verse 3 in terms of strict parallelism, difficulties arise. We certainly reject the thought that God created Christ, for Christ is eternal and uncreated. Even though Scripture reveals that God became his Father (Ps. 2:7; Heb. 1:5; 5:5), and "it is from God the Father that Christ, as Son, derives his eternal being,"[8] Christ was not "physically created from a piece taken out of God."[9] Nor is man physically taken out of Christ. Conclusively, if we seek to interpret the expression *head* as "source," the parallels to other Scripture passages and those within verse 3 itself break down.

When we understand the expression *head* to mean "authority," however, the parallels hold true. Christ has authority over man, man over woman, and God over Christ. Yet this authority does not necessarily imply the superiority of one party and the inferiority of the other. Even though God has authority over Christ (see 15:24–28), Christ is not inferior to God the Father. In a similar manner, "the authority of man over woman does not imply the inferiority of woman or the superiority of men."[10] On the contrary. Just as Christ in his essence is equal to God the Father, so woman in her being and worth is equal to man.

And, last, the Greek is unclear whether Paul has in view the husband-wife relationship or that of man and woman. On the basis of the parallel, "For the husband is the head of the wife as Christ is the head of the church" (Eph. 5:23), we opt for the first interpretation.

Doctrinal Considerations in 11:3

In a discussion on the word *head* in the current text, we ought to look at the other places where Paul uses this term. In his epistles it occurs seventeen times, of which seven instances have the literal meaning of the word and ten the figurative connotation.[11]

---

7. Gordon D. Fee, *The First Epistle to the Corinthians*, New International Commentary on the New Testament series (Grand Rapids: Eerdmans, 1987), p. 503.

8. F. F. Bruce, *1 and 2 Corinthians*, New Century Bible series (London: Oliphants, 1971), p. 103. See also Stephen Bedale, "The Meaning of *kephalē* in the Pauline Epistles," *JTS* n.s. 5 (1954): 211–15.

9. James B. Hurley, *Man and Woman in Biblical Perspective* (Grand Rapids: Zondervan, 1981), p. 166. Compare Noel Weeks, "Of Silence and Head Covering," *WTJ* 35 (1972): 21–27.

10. Thomas R. Schreiner, "Head Coverings, Prophecies and the Trinity," in *Recovering Biblical Manhood and Womanhood: A Response to Evangelical Feminism*, ed. John Piper and Wayne Grudem (Westchester, Ill.: Crossway, 1991), p. 130.

11. Literal: I Cor. 11:4 (twice), 5 (twice), 7, 10; 12:21. Figurative: I Cor. 11:3 (three times); Eph. 1:22; 4:15; 5:23 (twice); Col. 1:18; 2:10, 19.

When Paul develops his teaching of Christ's authority over the church and all creation, he expounds the headship of Christ. In Ephesians 1:22, Paul introduces Christ's headship with a reference to his heavenly exaltation far above all "*rule and authority, power and dominion.*" The text itself speaks of the execution of Christ's divine authority: "And God placed all things under his feet and appointed him head over everything for the church." The theme that Christ is the head of the church also occurs in Ephesians 4:15; 5:23; and Colossians 1:18; 2:19. Christ is called the head over all things (Col. 2:10).

In one passage, Paul parallels the headship of Christ and the church with the husband as the head of the wife. In this particular text we have a parallel that is instructive for interpreting I Corinthians 11:3. This is the reading: "Wives, submit to your husbands as to the Lord. For the husband is the head of the wife as Christ is the head of the church, his body, of which he is the Savior" (Eph. 5:22–23). The analogy of husband and wife to Christ and the church is clear. The wife submits to the husband as the church submits to Christ. But headship has its own unique quality, as the text indicates: Christ is the Savior of the church, which is his body. The church, then, has its existence in him. Likewise, on the basis of the account of Eve's creation (Gen. 2:21–23), the husband acknowledges that the woman is from man and is dependent on him. Thus, headship signifies authority but it also includes a reference to origin that affects a continued relationship.[12]

We infer from the parallel of I Corinthians 11:3 and Ephesians 5:22–23 that Paul presents Christ's headship as a model. Just as Christ is the head of every man and of the church, so the husband is the head of the wife. As Christ submits to God the Father, so the wife submits to her husband.[13]

---

4. Every man who prays or prophesies with something on his head dishonors his head.

a. *Qualification.* Before we begin the explanation of this verse, we should realize that dress codes vary from culture to culture and from age to age. The city of Corinth had a mixed population of Greeks, Romans, Jews, and a number of people of other nationalities. When Paul discusses hairstyles and head coverings, we have to keep in mind that he was telling his readers to adopt Christian practices in a pagan world. Paul objected to blurring the genders but wanted the Corinthians to demonstrate visually the clear distinction between men and women.

b. *Interpretation.* The translation of this text is simple; its interpretation is not. For example, does the man pray and prophesy at home or in church, in private or in public? How do we explain the verb *prophesy*? What does "something on his head" mean? And, do the two occurrences of "head" mean the same thing or does the second instance refer to Christ (see v. 3)?

First, the praying and prophesying appear to take place in a public worship service. Why should Paul write about someone praying in the privacy of his home? And in respect to prophesying, in another context Paul says that the person who prophesies edifies the church (14:4). This verse, therefore, refers to public worship.

---

12. Refer to Herman N. Ridderbos, *Paul: An Outline of His Theology*, trans. John Richard de Witt (Grand Rapids: Eerdmans, 1975), p. 382.

13. Compare Hurley, *Man and Woman*, p. 145.

Next, when Paul writes "every man who prays or prophesies," he alludes to audible prayer uttered in a worship service. He links the verbs *pray* and *prophesy* with the particle *or*, and in a later chapter discloses that the gift of prophecy should be eagerly desired (14:1, 39). He leaves the impression that prayer is common, but prophecy occasional. But what is the meaning of the verb *to prophesy*? This word signifies preaching, teaching, or explaining God's revelation. In effect, this is what Priscilla and Aquila did when they invited Apollos to their home to explain to him God's Word more accurately (Acts 18:26). Similarly, both Simeon and Anna the prophetess spent their time in the temple courts worshiping God with prayer and praise and explaining God's revelation in Jesus as the salvation and redemption of his people (Luke 2:25–38).

Third, what does "something on his head" mean? Paul literally says, "having [something] hanging down from the head." If he had written the word *something*, which is supplied, the text would have been clearer. The supplied word is needed to understand Paul's phrase. The words that Paul uses occur in the writings of the Greek author Plutarch (b. A.D. 46 or 47 some forty miles from Corinth) and refer to something that is resting on the head. "Greek literature contemporary with the New Testament demonstrates that the phrase *kata kephalē* can clearly mean 'on the head.'"[14]

In their native land and in their colonies the Romans covered their heads during private and public devotions. Offering sacrifices, praying or prophesying, they would pull their toga forward over their heads. This devotional practice may have penetrated society in Corinth, which was a Roman colony. "So when Paul reminds Christian men to pray and prophesy with head uncovered, the recommendation fits the context of shunning the worship of idols."[15] Paul wanted the Corinthians to separate themselves from pagan customs and be distinct in their Christian practice.

Last, does the second occurrence of "head" have the same meaning as the first (the physical head) or does it allude to Christ (the spiritual head)? Commentators are divided on this point. The preceding verse (v. 3) teaches that Christ is the head of man and the husband is the head of the wife. By extension, then, the man with a covered head dishonors Christ and the wife with an uncovered head dishonors her husband. However, if we take the second occurrence to refer to Christ, then the message of verse 7 seems to be redundant. The succeeding context, moreover, seems to indicate that the woman who prays or prophesies with an uncovered head dishonors not only her husband but also her own head. If

---

14. Richard Oster, "When Men Wore Veils to Worship: The Historical Context of I Corinthians 11:4," *NTS* 34 (1988): 486. He lists many references to both Josephus and Plutarch. For different views, see James B. Hurley, "Did Paul Require Veils or the Silence of Women? A Consideration of 1 Cor. 11:2–16 and 1 Cor. 14:33b–36," *WTJ* 35 (1973): 193–204; Jerome Murphy-O'Connor, "The Non-Pauline Character of I Corinthians 11:2–16?" *JBL* 95 (1976): 615–21.

15. Cynthia L. Thompson, "Hairstyles, Head-coverings, and St. Paul: Portraits from Roman Corinth," *BA* 51 (1988): 104. Consult David W. J. Gill, "The Importance of Roman Portraiture for Head-Coverings in 1 Corinthians 11:2–16," *TynB* 41.2 (1990): 245–60.

this is so, a literal interpretation for verse 4 is not altogether out of place.[16] We do well, therefore, to accept both the literal and figurative explanations.

Paul wishes to maintain a clear distinction between the sexes, so that no man and no woman will bring dishonor to the church. He does not want a man to cover his head at a public worship service, for that act reflects pagan practice and implicitly rejects the creation order (see the commentary on vv. 5–6, 13–15). Correspondingly, he does not want a woman to come to the worship services without a head covering.

5. But every woman who prays or prophesies with her head uncovered dishonors her head. For she is one and the same as a woman whose head is shaved. 6. For if a woman does not cover her head, let her also have her hair cut off. But if it is disgraceful for a woman to have her hair cut off or shaven, let her cover her head.

a. "But every woman who prays or prophesies." Verses 4 and 5 are parallel and reveal the equality of men and women in the church. In the Old Testament era, not the woman but the man received the sign of the covenant (e.g., Gen. 17). He served as representative for the woman. But in the New Testament era, male and female are one in Christ Jesus (Gal. 3:28). That is, both man and woman are equal before the Lord. This becomes evident when Paul ascribes the religious functions of praying and prophesying to both man and woman. Both men and women know that their prophesying consists of teaching and preaching God's revelation or exhorting and counseling others from the Scriptures (see Acts 18:26).

b. "With her head uncovered dishonors her head." The interpretation of this verse depends on verse 3, where Paul says that the man is the head of woman, which in the family circle means that the husband is the wife's head. If the Corinthian woman puts aside her head covering in public, she thereby renounces the subordination to her husband that God intended her to show. She appropriates to herself authority that belongs to her husband.[17] When in the Corinthian church a woman goes against the structure of creation, she dishonors her husband.

In Paul's day, a woman should cover her head. If she failed to do this, she dishonored not only her own head but also showed disrespect to her husband. She ought to have respected her husband by wearing a head covering in public. But, we ask, does she have to have her head covered when she neither prays nor prophesies? In the privacy of her home no; in public, yes.

c. "For she is one and the same as a woman whose head is shaved." At first glance, this remark appears to be tactless and harsh. But we must consider these words in the cultural context of first-century Corinth. Paul explains himself in

---

16. Compare Murphy-O'Connor, "Sex and Logic," p. 499.

17. Consult Werner Neuer, *Man and Woman in Christian Perspective*, trans. Gordon J. Wenham (Westchester, Ill.: Crossway, 1991), p. 113; H. Wayne House, "Should a Woman Prophesy or Preach before Men?" *BS* 145 (1988): 154.

succeeding verses, where he notes that nature itself teaches that long hair is the glory of a woman (v. 15). For a woman to have her head shaved was and still is a mark of disgrace and humiliation. Whether Paul is thinking of the practice of humiliating an adulterous woman by cropping her hair is difficult to say. First-century Roman author Dio Chrysostom mentions that, on the island of Cyprus, a woman who had committed adultery was shorn by the authorities to identify her as a prostitute.[18] The message Paul conveys to the Corinthian women is that they should honor their husbands by observing the cultural standards of their day. Writes David W. J. Gill,

> What Paul may be saying is that if women in the church will not wear a veil, then they will be seen as dishonouring their husbands which might affect their place in society. If the wife insists on being unveiled then she might as well wear a sign of humiliation by having her hair cut. If she does not wish to bring such shame to her husband, herself and her family then she should be veiled.[19]

The principle was for the wife to honor her husband; the application of this principle was to wear a veil in public. To not wear a veil was a sign of rebellion on the part of a wife.

d. "For if a woman does not cover her head, let her also have her hair cut off." Paul presents a logical approach to the whole matter by saying that a wife who is unveiled in public is as much a shame to her husband as a shorn and shaven head is to herself.

e. "But if it is disgraceful for a woman to have her hair cut off or shaven, let her cover her head." The emphasis in the last part of this verse is on the word *disgraceful*. Paul puts the wife in the uncomfortable position of having to make a choice: if she wants to go without a veil in public, let her be shaved and consort with disreputable women; if she objects to being shorn and shaved, let her wear a veil and associate with respectable women. Notice that not the husband but the wife must make the decision. And the decision is a matter of her willingness to have a submissive relationship with her husband "by the ordinance of creation."[20]

Practical Considerations in 11:4–6

Cultural standards differ from country to country and change in the course of time. When we consider hairstyles and head coverings, the variations are especially striking. Hair can be either long or short, and in many cultures the covering of the head relates to religious observances (e.g., Judaism, Islam, and branches of Christianity).

---

18. Dio Chrysostom *Discourses* 64.2–3.
19. Gill, "Head-coverings," p. 256.
20. Bruce, *1 and 2 Corinthians*, p. 104.

In the Christian church, head coverings were considered a necessity in colder climates. During the Reformation, John Calvin and his colleagues wore skullcaps to ward off the cold. But would they wear these caps during a worship service or follow Paul's prescription not to pray or prophesy with a covered head? Writes Calvin,

> For we should not be so hide-bound by conscientious principles as to think a teacher is doing anything wrong in wearing a skull-cap on his head, when he is speaking to the people from the pulpit. But all that Paul is after is that it may be made clear that the man is in authority, and that the woman is in subjection to him, and that is done when the man uncovers his head in the sight of the congregation, even if he puts his skull-cap on again afterwards so as not to catch cold.[21]

Two centuries later, in 1741, the German New Testament commentator John Albert Bengel had to face a different cultural development: What to think of wigs? He remarks that wigs are substitutes for hair that is too thin. "Therefore the head of a man is scarcely more dishonored by them, while he prays, than while he does not pray."[22] Yet Bengel is of the opinion that if he would be able to ask Paul, the apostle would persuade people not to wear wigs because they are "unbecoming to men, especially those who pray."

During the first half of the twentieth century, women adhered to the custom of wearing hats in church. But in the second half of this century, those ladies who adorn their heads with hats in Christian churches are few indeed.

How do we apply Paul's words on head coverings, or the lack of them, today? Is Paul reflecting cultural patterns of his day in the Corinthian church and elsewhere (v. 16), patterns which are no longer in vogue? And are cultural patterns that are subject to change actually indicators of basic and abiding principles?

Paul proclaims Christ's gospel that sets people free from the Jewish civil and ceremonial laws. He rejects the idea of asking Gentiles to adopt Jewish customs as a step in becoming Christians (Gal. 5:1–6). Similarly, Paul does not intend to tell believers everywhere throughout the centuries to adopt the customs he wants the Corinthian Christians to follow. What he does stress in this segment is that in the marriage relationship the wife honors and respects her husband and the husband loves and leads the wife. This is the basic principle that may be applied in diverse ways in the varying cultures throughout the world. The principle remains the same, even though its application varies.

If Paul allows women to pray or prophesy in a worship service, is he not contradicting himself with respect to the wife submitting to the authority of her husband? No, not necessarily. Within the marriage relationship the wife must honor her husband by being submissive to him. But in the church, the Holy Spirit filled both the men and the women and thus both prayed and prophesied. Before the Lord, both men and women were recipients of the gifts of the Spirit. However, Paul is not abrogating the distinctive roles of each gender. Although men and women are new creatures in Christ, the husband-wife relationship remains intact.[23]

---

21. John Calvin, *The First Epistle of Paul the Apostle to the Corinthians*, Calvin's Commentaries series, trans. John W. Fraser (reprint ed.; Grand Rapids: Eerdmans, 1976), pp. 230–31.

22. John Albert Bengel, *Bengel's New Testament Commentary*, trans. Charlton T. Lewis and Marvin R. Vincent, 2 vols. (Grand Rapids: Kregel, 1981), vol. 2, p. 223.

23. Consult Hurley, "Veil," p. 204.

Greek Words, Phrases, and Constructions in 11:2–6

Verses 2–3

The Majority Text includes the term ἀδελφοί (brothers) after the introductory words *I praise you.* Bruce M. Metzger observes: "If the word were present originally (as at 10.1 and 12.1, where no witness omits it), its absence from [early and other major manuscripts] would be inexplicable."[24]

μέμνημαι—this perfect middle from μιμνήσκω (I remember) functions as a continuative present.

πάντα—the neuter plural is an accusative of respect, "in all respects."

ἡ κεφαλὴ ὁ Χριστός—"Christ is the head." The definite article appears with both the subject and the predicate nominative. This means that the nouns are interchangeable and identical. By contrast, the clause κεφαλὴ γυναικὸς ὁ ἀνήρ has one definite article to indicate that "man is not affirmed to be woman's head in quite the same sense that Christ is man's head."[25]

Verses 4–5

κατὰ κεφαλῆς ἔχων—the literal translation is "having down from the head" but the participle needs an object, "a covering." Hence, the suggested version is, "with a [covering?] on the head (i.e. down upon)."[26]

τὸ αὐτό—the neuter pronoun refers to an unveiled woman as an example but not as a particular person: "she is one and the same as a woman whose head is shaved."

Verse 6

εἰ—this particle twice introduces conditional sentences with the indicative mood to show reality with the logical deduction of Paul's argument.[27]

κείρασθαι, ξυρᾶσθαι—"to be cut, to be shaven." The first infinitive is the aorist middle and the second the present middle. In the middle voice, the infinitives denote permission: "a woman allowed her hair to be cut or shaven."

---

b. Image and Glory
11:7–12

The Gospels, especially that of Matthew, portray Jesus as a teacher who repeatedly appeals to the Old Testament and at times asks his audience whether they

---

24. Bruce M. Metzger, *A Textual Commentary on the Greek New Testament*, 3d corrected ed. (London and New York: United Bible Societies, 1975), pp. 561–62.

25. Robert Hanna, *A Grammatical Aid to the Greek New Testament* (Grand Rapids: Baker, 1983), p. 302.

26. C. F. D. Moule, *An Idiom-Book of New Testament Greek*, 2d ed. (Cambridge: Cambridge University Press, 1960), p. 60. See also R. St. John Parry, *The First Epistle of Paul the Apostle to the Corinthians*, Cambridge Greek Testament for Schools and Colleges (Cambridge: Cambridge University Press, 1937), p. 158.

27. Friedrich Blass and Albert Debrunner, *A Greek Grammar of the New Testament and Other Early Christian Literature*, trans. and rev. Robert Funk (Chicago: University of Chicago Press, 1961), #372.2.

have read the Scriptures (see Matt. 12:3; Mark 2:25; Luke 6:3). He proves his teaching from God's Word.

Writing to the Corinthians, Paul follows Jesus' example and bases his instruction on the Old Testament Scriptures. We would expect the Jewish Christians to be familiar with the content of the Old Testament, and that those Christians who came out of paganism would lack a firm grasp of the Scriptures (see the Introduction). Paul, however, is the teacher who opens God's Word and takes his instruction from the first two chapters of Genesis in the next few verses.

7. For a man ought not to cover his head, because he is the image and glory of God. But the woman is the glory of man.

a. "For a man ought not to cover his head." The first word, the causal conjunction *for*, connotes that the entire present passage is an explanation of the preceding verses (vv. 5–6) that alludes to the creation account (Gen. 1:26–27; 2:18–24). Paul writes a general principle that applies to prayer and prophesying when he says that a man ought not to cover his head. (This does not mean that a person may not protect himself against inclement weather and wear a hat or a cap). Paul calls attention to the key concept that man is God's image and glory.

b. "Because he is the image and glory of God." We only have the word *image*, but not "likeness," which we would have expected to find in an allusion to the first chapter of Genesis (v. 26; see also Gen. 5:1; 6:9). An image is the exact representation of someone or something: a statue of a famous leader, the head of a ruler on a coin, or a picture on a television screen. "Man in his authority relation to creation and to his wife, images the dominion of God over the creation and the headship of Christ over his church."[28]

We would also expect Paul to state that both the woman and the man are created in the image of God (Gen. 1:26–28); instead, with the word *glory* Paul provides not a parallel but a comparison. Man is the image and glory of God, while a woman is the glory of man but not the image of man.[29] Paul has stated that God is the head of Christ, Christ the head of man, and man the head of woman (v. 3). Because of his teaching on man's headship, he is not now interested in discussing Eve being created in God's image.

Instead of "likeness," Paul writes the word *glory*, which some versions translate with the supplied verb *reflect* or the noun *reflection*.[30] In fact, one translation even omits the expression *glory* altogether, "since [man] is the image and reflection of God, but woman is the reflection of man."[31] It is true that man reflects God's glory. This is evident from Psalm 8:5, where man is described as crowned with glory and honor. But from another point of view, man ascribes and brings glory to

28. Hurley, *Man and Woman*, p. 173.

29. F. W. Grosheide, *Commentary on the First Epistle to the Corinthians: The English Text with Introduction, Exposition and Notes*, New International Commentary on the New Testament series (Grand Rapids: Eerdmans, 1953), p. 255.

30. Compare GNB, NAB, JB, NJB, NEB, REB, *Cassirer*.

31. NRSV; Bauer, p. 204.

God.[32] Persons were created for God's glory. The chief purpose of man is to glorify God and to enjoy him forever, as a well-known seventeenth-century catechism puts it.[33] Man attributes honor to God.

The phrase *glory of God* can be interpreted subjectively, objectively, or both. Subjectively, God confers his glory on man; objectively, man renders glory to God. Likewise, subjectively, the husband loves and protects his wife and, objectively, the wife brings glory to her husband by being his helper (Gen. 2:18, 20).

c. "But the woman is the glory of man." The last part of verse 7 begins with the adversative *but* to set this clause off against the preceding sentence. The woman is the glory not of God but of man, that is, her husband. Created to assist her husband, she seeks to honor him by recognizing his headship. The word *glory* appears once more in this context when Paul appeals to nature and remarks that long hair is the woman's glory (v. 15). Why should the woman bring glory to her husband? Paul answers this question in the next two verses.

8. For man does not come from woman but woman from man. 9. Indeed, man was not created for the sake of the woman but woman for the sake of the man.

Paul supports his teaching with facts taken from the creation account (Gen. 2:18–24):

> God created both Adam and Eve.
> Adam did not create Eve.
> God first made Adam and then Eve.
> God made Eve out of Adam.
> God created Eve because of Adam.

As God simultaneously created animals male and female, so in one creative act he could have made Adam and Eve from the dust of the earth. But he did not do so. God first made Adam and then, declaring that it was not good for man to be alone (Gen. 2:18), supplied him with a helper suitable to his needs. From one of Adam's ribs he fashioned Eve to be Adam's wife. God presented her to Adam, and Adam sang his wedding song:

> "This is now bone of my bones
> and flesh of my flesh;
> she shall be called 'woman,'
> for she was taken out of man."
>
> [Gen. 2:23]

Many people today seem to think that the creation of Adam and Eve is a story from the dawn of human history and has little, if any, present significance. However, at creation Adam was formed first, then Eve (I Tim. 2:13). God made this

---

32. Fee, *First Corinthians*, p. 516.
33. Westminster Shorter Catechism, answer 1.

distinction for all times, and with it he reveals his design and purpose for the sexes. Although man and woman are equal before God and in Christ (Gal. 3:28), they have been given different roles. The husband takes primary responsibility in his headship, and the wife fulfills her role as helper. This relationship cannot be reversed, because the creation story teaches "a non-reversible orientation of the woman towards the man as the reference point for her life."[34] The fact that Eve was created to assist Adam suggests that she is subject to him. When God created Eve as Adam's helper, he assigned to her a supportive and submissive role (Gen. 2:18). By appealing to the creation account, Paul is able to write that man was not created for woman but woman for man.

10. For this reason the woman ought to have authority on her head because of the angels.

a. "For this reason." Paul continues his discourse, tightly connecting this verse to the preceding ones (vv. 7–9). The conjunction *for* (v. 8) explains verse 7, and the word *indeed* (v. 9) shows that verse 9 gives additional support to verse 8. The conjunction in verse 10 serves to bind the verse to the larger argument.

b. "The woman ought to have authority on her head because of the angels." The translation of this part of the text is problematic, as is evident from these representative versions:

"a sign of authority" (NIV)
"the sign of her authority" (REB)
"a sign of submission" (NAB)
"a covering over her head to show that she is under her husband's authority" (GNB).

It is obvious that translators are forced to interpret the Greek text. The wording in the original is terse and obscure. At the head of this section, I present a literal translation, which I readily admit lacks elegance and clarity. My version omits the phrase *a sign of* and fails to indicate whether the expression *authority* means the woman's authority or that of her husband.

When we try to clarify this passage, we must consider the preceding and the succeeding context. Thus far Paul has stated the principle that man is the head of woman just as Christ is the head of man and God the head of Christ. He has given directions on how men and women should conduct themselves while praying or prophesying. Paul has told women to cover their heads so they do not shame their "heads," namely, their husbands. And he has defended his words by appealing to the creation account in the first two chapters of Genesis. Now Paul concludes this segment of his discussion by saying that "the woman ought to have authority on her head because of the angels."

This verse has been the subject of study by numerous scholars, yet every writer has to admit that his or her explanation of the text displays weaknesses. In spite

---

34. Neuer, *Man and Woman*, p. 73.

of all the suggestions that have been offered, the text remains enigmatic and fails to communicate. These are some of the proposed interpretations:

1. When a woman in public worship prays or prophesies, she displays the new freedom she has in Christ. The woman derives her authority from God, and with her headcovering she is able to demonstrate that power.[35] The weakness of this suggestion is that a discussion on equality fits Galatians 3:28 but in the current passage Paul says nothing about freedom.

2. "A sign of authority." Many translations have enhanced the reading by adding the phrase *sign of* or simply *veil*.[36] Numerous commentators assert that the word *authority* relates not to the authority of the woman but to that of her husband. The context speaks of the husband being the wife's head, and this interpretation leaves the impression that the term *authority* is equivalent to submission. In Greek, however, the term *exousia* never has an objective or a passive sense, that is, being under someone else's authority. It always has a subjective or an active sense relating to one's own authority. And last, with this interpretation the Greek preposition *epi*, which means "on," now has the meaning *over*. The husband has authority over his wife. Paul has said as much earlier (v. 3), but he is not saying this in verse 10.

3. The expression *authority* has been linked to the creation account of Adam and Eve in Genesis 1:26–28. This passage states that both male and female received the mandate to rule (have authority over) the fish, birds, and every living creature on this earth.[37] This ingenious explanation makes the woman an active participant with man in exercising authority, but the text itself gives the explanation insufficient support.

4. While praying or prophesying in a worship service, a woman receives spiritual authority. Instead, she ought to accept the position assigned to her since creation, to recognize her husband as head. She is unable to pray in the Spirit when rebelling "against the order of creation hallowed by God's Spirit."[38] Here is a plausible explanation that does justice to the concept *authority*. Nonetheless, this concept must relate to the last phrase in the text, "because of the angels."

5. Could it be that Paul with his rabbinical training is asking women to be covered with a veil because of the angels? With the evidence gleaned from Qumran, we know that an unveiled woman in a sacred assembly "is like a bodily defect which should be excluded."[39] The reason for this exclusion is that holy angels who are present at worship services are offended by defects. This approach may

---

35. Consult Morna D. Hooker, "Authority on Her Head: An Examination of I Cor. XI.10," *NTS* 10 (1963–64): 415–16.

36. SB, vol. 3, pp. 435–36; Werner Foerster, *TDNT*, vol. 2, pp. 573–74.

37. Refer to Hurley, "Veils," pp. 211–12.

38. Neuer, *Man and Woman*, p. 115.

39. Joseph A. Fitzmyer, "A Feature of Qumran Angelology and the Angels of I Cor. XI.10," *NTS* 4 (1957–58): 48–58.

shed some light on the reference to the angels, but it does nothing for interpreting the meaning of "authority."

All these suggestions are helpful in understanding aspects of the problems we encounter in verse 10, yet all show weaknesses. Scholars must conclude that a satisfactory explanation is not available. In all humility, I confess that I really do not know what Paul intended to say in this verse.

c. "Because of the angels." This short verse has two causal expressions: the first one is translated "for this reason" and the second one "because." Some translators combine these two causal expressions with the word *and* or *also*. Whether we supply a connection or follow the Greek word order, the fact remains that scholars simply do not know what the reference to angels means. In I Corinthians, the word *angels* occurs four times (4:9; 6:3; 11:10; 13:1). But a study of this word in the context of these passages fails to give us an idea what Paul has in mind. Interpreters must admit that, all the research aside, they have no acceptable explanation for this particular clause.

Although translators encounter a mystery in verse 10, we nevertheless must see it in the light of the preceding and succeeding context. Paul writes that "man was not created for the sake of the woman but woman for the sake of the man" (v. 9) and "for this reason, the woman ought to have authority on her head because of the angels" (v. 10). In verse 11, which begins with the adversative *however*, Paul changes the discussion to emphasize an important point: "In the Lord neither is woman [anything] apart from man, nor man [anything] apart from woman." This verse is a continuation of verse 9, where Paul speaks of the creation account. In verse 11, Paul implies spiritual *re*creation and says that man and woman depend on each other "in the Lord." Between these two verses, Paul places the enigmatic words of verse 10 that ascribe authority to a woman. She may pray or prophesy provided her head is covered (vv. 5, 13). Thus, a woman possesses authority as she shows respect in the presence of God's angels.[40]

11. However, in the Lord, woman is nothing apart from man, and man is nothing apart from woman. 12. For as the woman is from the man, even so is the man through the woman, and all things are from God.

a. *Structure.* These two verses balance two earlier verses (vv. 8–9) and reveal an almost perfect parallelism, provided we view verse 10 as a parenthetical comment. Thus we see the crosswise structure in the subjects of verses 8 and 12.

Verse 8a, b
For man does not come
from woman but
woman from
man.

Verse 12a, b
For as the woman is
from the man, even so
is the man through
the woman.

---

40. Compare Annie Jaubert, "Le Voile des Femmes (I Cor. XI.2–16)," *NTS* 18 (1971–72): 419–30.

Similarly, verses 9 and 11 show contrast, especially with the adversative *however*. They also have a crosswise structure.

Verse 9a, b	*Verse 11a, b*
Indeed, man was not created	However, . . . woman is nothing
for the sake of the woman	apart from man,
but woman for the sake	and man is nothing
of the man.	apart from woman.

b. *Intention.* What is Paul trying to communicate with the literary structure of this passage? First, verse 8a contrasts verse 12b, while verses 8b and 12a correspond. Paul asserts that through natural birth man (and for that matter also woman) has his biological origin through a woman. Only Adam can say that God gave him life; all other men and women receive their life through birth. With this remark, Paul does not undermine the creation order. Indeed not, for in verse 12a he repeats what he says in 8b (woman is from man). With these two verses, he conveys the thought that in respect to natural birth men and women share equality.

Next, the content of verses 9a and 11b, strengthened by the adversative *however*, is a forceful reminder of reality. And, verse 11 has a significant statement, "in the Lord," which I have placed at the beginning of that text. With these two qualifiers in mind, let us look carefully at these verses.

Paul is saying, "Indeed, man was not created for the sake of the woman" (v. 9a), which is in accord with the creation order. "However," he continues, "in the Lord, . . . man is nothing apart from woman" (v. 11b). This is a candid statement, to be sure! The second part is equally revealing: "Woman [was created] for the sake of the man" (v. 9b), which is followed by the rejoinder, "However, in the Lord, woman is nothing apart from man" (v. 11a).

Paul points out the interdependence of both the husband and the wife, who in the Lord wonderfully complement each other. Even though the husband is the head of his wife, he is dependent on her in numerous ways. In turn, a wife needs her husband just as much as he needs her. When death or divorce separates the couple, they experience a tearing apart of the fabric of marriage that bound them together. As long as the Lord grants them life, let husband and wife be bound in mutual love and service to one another.[41]

Paul is not in the least diminishing the force of God's creation order. He adds a second qualifying statement to these two verses: "and all things are from God." He means to say that the husband has no advantage over the wife because Adam was created before Eve. In the Lord, both parties show reciprocity and complementary dependence and assistance, for all these things have been designed by God himself. Man and woman, everything that pertains to birth, relationships, and married life—all come from God.

---

41. Calvin, *I Corinthians*, p. 233.

Practical Considerations in 11:11–12

Christianity has been and remains a force that liberates women from oppression and servitude. In many other religions, women are owned from birth by their fathers and on marriage by their husbands. They lack freedom, are in bondage, and never acquire equality. Even in ancient Israel, a female was secondary to any male. In a particular line of the eighteen-petition prayer, a man renders thanks to God for making him neither a slave, a Gentile, nor a woman. Women were not considered worthy of studying the Scriptures and were denied an education.

The New Testament teaches especially the basic equality of the sexes. For instance, in both his Gospel and Acts, Luke mentions men and women in the same breath: Zachariah and Elizabeth, Joseph and Mary, Simeon and Anna, Ananias and Sapphira, Aquila and Priscilla. Paul states unequivocally that in Christ Jesus male and female are one (Gal. 3:28). He commends female workers in the cause of the gospel, among whom are Phoebe, Priscilla, Mary, Tryphena, Tryphosa, Persis, and Julia (Rom. 16:1–15).

History books record the missionary endeavors of numerous women and sing their praises for extending Christ's church. On the home front godly women are a quiet force to make the church strong and productive. A godly mother leads her little ones to Jesus and trains them in the fear of the Lord. Although women fill roles and functions that differ from those of men, both in the Christian home and church they enjoy equality with men. Both depend on each other (11:11), for both men and women realize that they in turn must depend on God for everything (11:12).

Greek Words, Phrases, and Constructions in 11:7–12

Verse 7

μέν . . . δέ—these two particles disclose a definitive contrast between the man and the woman. Note that the word ἀνήρ (man) lacks the definite article but the word γυνή (woman, wife) has it.

ὀφείλει—"ought." Here the verb is negated and has "man" as its subject; in verse 10 the same verb is positive and refers to woman. Paul's choice of words and his sentence structure may be nothing more than coincidental.

Verse 10

ἐξουσίαν ἔχειν—"to have authority." The four Evangelists frequently use this phrase to portray the authority of Jesus or of God the Father. In I Corinthians, however, Paul applies the word ἐξουσία to either Christ, himself, fellow apostles, or other Christians.[42] A few ancient versions and patristic witnesses have the variant reading κάλυμμα (veil), which is meant to explain the text but is of doubtful authenticity.

Verses 11–12

πλήν—the adversative particle *however* appears at the conclusion of an argument to summarize a main point.[43]

---

42. I Cor. 7:37; 8:9; 9:4, 5, 6, 12, 18; 11:10; 15:24.
43. A. T. Robertson, *A Grammar of the Greek New Testament in the Light of Historical Research* (Nashville: Broadman, 1934), p. 1187; Bauer, p. 669.

ἐκ ... διά—the first preposition denotes source ("from") and the second agency ("through").

τὰ πάντα—the definite article expresses the totality of all things under God's control.

---

c. Man and Woman Again
11:13–16

A careful study of verses 13–15 discloses that Paul uses some phraseology that is identical to that of verses 4–7. These are the words that occur in both sections: woman, uncovered, to pray, man, glory. As the first two verses (vv. 2–3) form an introduction to this entire segment of the chapter so verse 16 serves as a conclusion.[44] In short, this segment is a beautifully constructed piece of literature that teaches an orderly development as Paul expounds the relationship of man and woman at worship.

13. Judge for yourselves: Is it proper for a woman to pray to God with her head uncovered?

a. *Command.* Paul now makes his concluding remarks and wants to involve his readers in thinking through the matter he has discussed. He tells them to look at the facts, use their minds, and judge for themselves. In another discourse, Paul said the same thing (see 10:15).

b. *Question.* With two rhetorical questions, Paul challenges his readers to respond.[45] He expects a negative reply to the first one (v. 13) and a positive response to the second (vv. 14–15a). Following the sequence within the text, we now discuss the first query: "Is it proper for a woman to pray to God with uncovered head?" On the basis of Paul's earlier remark that a woman who prays or prophesies with an uncovered head dishonors her head (v. 5a), the reader immediately answers the question in the negative. Note that Paul omits the verb *to prophesy* in this question, for the emphasis here is not so much on function in the worship service as on manner.

Paul asks a question on propriety ("Is is proper?"). Attendance at and participation in a service dedicated to worshiping God requires proper decorum. When we worship the Lord, we approach God in his holiness. The angels covered their faces in God's presence and called to one another, "Holy, holy, holy is the Lord Almighty; the whole earth is full of his glory" (Isa. 6:2–3). So Paul asks whether it is proper for a woman to pray to God with her head uncovered. She was expected to follow the cultural practices of that day, come to church in acceptable and appropriate dress, and participate in the worship service.

What does Paul mean with the expression *uncovered head?* It tells a woman that she ought to uphold her feminine honor and dignity in public by wearing a head

---

44. Thomas P. Shoemaker, "Unveiling of Equality: 1 Corinthians 11:2–16," *BTB* 17 (1987): 60–63. Compare Murphy-O'Connor, "1 Corinthians 11:2–16 Once Again," p. 274.

45. Alan Padgett ("Paul on Women in the Church: The Contradictions of Coiffure in 1 Corinthians 11:2–16," *JSNT* 20 [1984]: 69–86) translates the questions in verses 13–15a as declarative sentences. But he lacks support from editors and translators.

covering. In his time and culture, women wore veils to be in marked distinction from men. God has created a distinct difference between men and women and he desires that his people mark this dissimilarity with appropriate dress. If a woman refuses to abide by these codes, she purposely negates the differentiation which God has designed.

In the next two verses (vv. 14–15), Paul appeals to nature itself and demonstrates that the difference between male and female is based on regular natural order that originates in creation. In other words, Paul does not say that because Christian women are free in Jesus Christ they may abandon cultural mores. No, Paul wants them to live in harmony with the creation order and abide by the mores of their day. Is it proper for a Corinthian woman to worship God with an uncovered head? The answer is no.

14. Does not nature itself teach you that it is a disgrace to a man if he lets his hair grow long, 15. but if a woman lets her hair grow long, it is her glory? Because her long hair has been given to her as a covering.

a. "Does not nature itself teach you?" With the word *nature*, Paul is thinking of the natural order that God has created. When God created male and female, he gave the male shorter hair than the female. "*Nature* (i.e., God) has made men and women different from each other, and has provided a visible indication of the difference between them in the quantity of hair he has assigned to each."[46] Even the pagan philosopher Epictetus, a Stoic who taught in the second half of the first century, speaks of the difference in hair of men and women respectively. He concludes, "Wherefore, we ought to preserve the signs which God has given; we ought not to throw them away; we ought not, so far as in us lies, to confuse the sexes which have been distinguished in this fashion."[47] Even a pagan writer acknowledges the difference God has created and made part of a creation order.

b. "[Does not nature teach] that it is a disgrace to a man if he lets his hair grow long?" Paul poses a rhetorical question that demands a positive reply. In the cultural context in which Paul moved, long hair was a disgrace for a man but glory for a woman. Jewish men cut their hair. Occasionally they permitted their hair to grow for a stipulated period because they had made a vow (see Acts 18:18; 21:24), but afterward they shortened it.

From coins, statues, and paintings that depict men in the Greco-Roman world of the first century, we know that men trimmed their hair. A few centuries earlier, the Spartans on the Peloponnesian peninsula wore long hair—a fact duly noted by Greek authors, who comment that in Greece men usually cut their hair while women let it grow.[48] In Paul's day, the Corinthians followed the cultural trends of the Greeks and Romans and had their hair cropped. To have long hair, except for religious purposes or periods of mourning, was shameful to them.

---

46. Barrett, *First Corinthians*, p. 256.
47. Epictetus 1.16.9–14.
48. Herodotus 1.82.7; Plutarch *Moralia* 267B.

c. "But if a woman lets her hair grow long, it is her glory." The cultural contrast concerning hair lies in the words *disgrace* for men and *glory* for women. In this part of the text, Paul balances a negative expression with a positive.

The counterpart of the rhetorical question that expects an affirmative answer concerns the woman. Paul already has stated that it is a disgrace for a woman to have her hair cut or shaved off (v. 6). Now he gives the positive evaluation and asserts that long hair is a woman's glory. He wisely omits details regarding length of hair and hairstyles, for these are often subject to fads and fashions and involve personal choices. The cultural pattern in Israel, for example, was that a woman would not unloose her hair in public. Any woman who appeared in public with loose hair identified herself as a prostitute. It is not surprising, therefore, that Simon the Pharisee was horrified when a prostitute entered his home and wiped Jesus' feet with her hair (Luke 7:36–50). But Paul is not talking about bound or loose hair; he states the objective fact that a woman's long hair is beautiful. Long hair is her husband's joy.

d. "Because her long hair has been given to her as a covering." The last part of verse 15, due to its brevity, presents problems for correctly understanding the text. What is the meaning of the words *as* and *covering?*

If we take the Greek in the order in which Paul presents it, this causal clause serves as a supportive answer to the preceding rhetorical question. Paul states the reason for a woman's long hair: it has been given to her as a covering. For the passive verb *has been given* we supply the subject *God*, who as Creator endows women with a natural covering. However, a difficulty in this clause lies in the Greek word *anti*, which I have translated "as." *Anti* can signify "instead of." This interpretation says that one thing is replaced by another, namely, long hair replaces a veil or a covering. The clause, then, is translated "Her long hair is given her instead of a veil."[49] My translation of this Greek word indicates that one thing is equivalent to another. Then it means "for, as"[50] (e.g., "An eye for an eye and a tooth for a tooth" [Matt. 5:38]). Because of the entire context of Paul's discussion on proper decorum, scholars prefer this second reading.

But in verses 5b and 6, which are the counterpart of verse 15b, Paul tells the Corinthian women to cover their heads in public. He implies that they use a head covering in the form of a scarf or a veil. If the women refuse to do so, they renounce the authority of their husbands and repudiate the divine principle of headship (v. 3). The word *covering* in the last clause of verse 15 alludes to an article of clothing, that is, something made out of cloth.

The second clause of verse 15 summarizes, as a general statement, Paul's contention that the Corinthians should exhibit the creational differences of the sexes in their dress code. Not men but women have long hair that serves as a covering. Women show this created difference with the hair that nature has provided. Paul urges the Corinthian women to wear a head covering in addition to

---

49. Hurley, *Man and Woman*, p. 163.
50. Bauer, p. 73.

long hair as a symbol of honoring their husbands and showing submission to them.

In today's culture, the presence of a hat does not signify subordination of a wife to her spouse. And Paul is not asking a woman to wear a headpiece or to put up her hair. Rather, he wants a woman to be distinctively feminine in respect to hair and dress and thus fulfill the role that God has intended since creation. He wants her to be submissive to her husband in her femininity. "The unique beauty of a woman is gloriously manifest in the distinctive femininity portrayed by her hair and her attendance to feminine customs."[51]

16. But if anyone is inclined to be contentious, we do not have such a custom, nor do the churches of God.

This is the conclusion to Paul's discussion on women's proper conduct. In a discourse on matters that affect personal predilections, a speaker or writer can expect to receive reaction from his audience or readers. Paul indicates as much with a conditional sentence that states a simple fact. Yes, there are people who wish to assert their individual rights. They probably use their slogan, "All things are permissible" (6:12; 10:23), and clamor for personal freedom. Even though Paul promotes Christian liberty, he teaches obedience to God's ordinances and precepts. He desires that all things be done decently and in order.

a. "But if anyone is inclined to be contentious." By using the term *anyone,* Paul speaks in generalities. He addresses neither the men, the women, nor a group of people. If anyone, even with good intentions, wants to argue about this matter, he will not receive a hearing from Paul. He has no time for someone whose mind is set on debating an issue for the sake of argument. The term that Paul has chosen to describe this person is "one who loves to argue." This person could be either a woman who asserts herself with respect to accepted norms and wants to be free or a man who comes to her defense to debate Paul. We are not given any details in this summary statement.

b. "We do not have such a custom, nor do the churches of God." Paul refuses to be challenged on his teachings that are based on the Old Testament Scriptures. He knows that the rest of the apostles support him, and therefore he confidently writes the personal pronoun *we.* This is not the so-called editorial we, but an inclusive pronoun that embraces other leaders in the churches.

What does the word *custom* connote in this setting? Calvin was of the opinion that Paul objected to the habit of arguing and disputing everything.[52] Among Jewish and Gentile Christians, such conduct may have been evident especially in regard to matters of personal conduct. However, the passage itself conveys the sense that Paul has in mind the cultural practice of that day: that women wear head coverings during public worship services. He is saying that he, his fellow apostles, and the rest of the churches abide by the rule of being properly attired

---

51. John MacArthur, Jr., *1 Corinthians,* MacArthur New Testament Commentary series (Chicago: Moody, 1984), p. 262.

52. Calvin, *I Corinthians,* p. 235.

at worship. In brief, Paul appeals to the witness of the entire Christian church. Quite often in his writings he refers to all the churches.[53] He brings the unity of the church to bear on the issue at hand. And he states implicitly that the contentious person, standing alone in this dispute, will have to face the whole church.

Greek Words, Phrases, and Constructions in 11:13–16

Verse 13

ὑμῖν αὐτοῖς—this combination is used in place of the reflexive pronoun σεαυτοῖς (for yourselves).[54]

πρέπον—the neuter participle connotes that which is culturally acceptable and suitable.

Verses 14–15

ἤ—the Majority Text has the particle *or* at the beginning of verse 14, but it lacks wide geographical support from textual witnesses.

ἐάν—in both verses denotes probability: "in case it happens that . . ."

Verse 16

εἰ—this particle introduces a simple-fact condition. Note that in the two clauses, Paul contrasts the indefinite pronoun τις (anyone) with the personal pronoun ἡμεῖς (we) with emphasis.

---

17 But in giving these instructions I do not praise you, because when you come together it is not for the better but for the worse. 18 For in the first place when you come together in the church, I hear that there are factions among you and in part I believe it. 19 For there must be dissensions among you, so that those who are proven [believers] may become evident among you. 20 Therefore, when you come together in the same place, it is not to eat the Lord's Supper. 21 For as you eat, each one takes his supper before others; one remains hungry and another is drunk. 22 For do you not have houses for the purpose of eating and drinking? Or do you despise the church of God and put to shame those who have nothing? What shall I say to you? Shall I praise you? In this I do not praise you.

23 For I have received from the Lord that which I also delivered to you, that the Lord Jesus, in the night in which he was betrayed, took bread, 24 and when he had given thanks, he broke it and said: "This is my body, which is for you. Do this in remembrance of me." 25 In the same way, also taking the cup after supper he said: "This cup is the new covenant in my blood; do this as often as you drink it in remembrance of me." 26 For as often as you eat this bread and drink this cup, you proclaim the death of the Lord until he comes.

27 Therefore, whoever eats the bread or drinks the cup of the Lord unworthily shall be guilty of [profaning] the body and blood of the Lord. 28 But let a man examine himself and thus let him eat of the bread and drink of the cup. 29 For he who eats and drinks eats and drinks judgment to himself, if he does not discern the body. 30 Because of this, many among you are weak and ill and many have died. 31 But if we judged ourselves correctly, we would not be judged. 32 When we are judged, we are disciplined by the Lord so that we may not be condemned with the world.

---

53. Compare Rom. 16:4, 16; I Cor. 7:17; 14:33; 16:1, 19; II Cor. 8:1, 18, 19, 23, 24; 12:13; Gal. 1:2, 22; I Thess. 2:14; II Thess. 1:4.
54. Robertson, *Grammar*, p. 303.

33 Therefore, my brothers, when you come together to eat, wait for one another. 34 If anyone is hungry, let him eat at home that you may not encounter judgment. And the rest of the things I will arrange when I come.

---

2. The Lord's Supper
11:17–34

From a discussion on headship, propriety, and acceptable practice in worship, Paul now turns to the celebration of the Lord's Supper. He first examines the excesses at the meetings of the Corinthians (vv. 17–22), then the institution and formulary of the Lord's Supper (vv. 23–26), and last the preparation for worthily eating of the bread and drinking of the cup (vv. 27–32). Paul concludes this section with an exhortation to exercise restraint (vv. 33–34).

a. Excesses
11:17–22

17. But in giving these instructions I do not praise you, because when you come together it is not for the better but for the worse.

a. "But in giving these instructions I do not praise you." Paul begins with the adversative *but* to separate this verse from the preceding discourse. Is the break with the previous verses complete or partial? The answer depends on the interpretation of the term *these instructions*. This term might look forward to what Paul is going to say about the conduct of the Corinthians when they celebrate the Lord's Supper. Then the break is complete. Or the term looks back, so that these instructions relate to what Paul had been saying earlier. Accordingly, the break is partial.

The fact that the Greek text has the pronoun *this* in the singular, not the plural (which most translations show), gives it a general connotation. Some scholars aver that this pronoun normally refers not to succeeding but to preceding material (compare 7:6).[55] They understand the pronoun to refer to Paul's instructions on the proper conduct of men and women in public worship services. They add that Paul's instructions for the correct observance of the Lord's Supper (vv. 28–34) are far removed from the current passage. They, therefore, opt for a partial break in the context.

Considerations for a complete break predominate, however. First, the content of the passage itself reveals that Paul introduces a new subject: the Lord's Supper. Paul places the verb *I praise* in the negative to contrast his positive statement at the beginning of the chapter (v. 2) and to repeat the negative in verse 22. In verse 2, he praised the Corinthians for guarding the traditions; here he censures them for unruly conduct which he must correct with pertinent instructions. Paul writes two distinct sections (vv. 2–16 and 17–34), which he begins with

---

55. See the respective commentaries of Barrett, p. 260; Bruce, p. 108; Grosheide, p. 264; Robertson and Plummer, p. 238.

praise and censure respectively. And the second half of this verse (v. 17) is a causal clause that refers to the Corinthians' meetings which, as the rest of the chapter shows, were unruly. In short, the forward look is preferred.

b. "Because when you come together it is not for the better but for the worse." In these few words, Paul compresses what he has heard concerning his readers' unseemly behavior. He has become aware of the disorder by which the church is despised and the poor are humiliated (v. 22). Furthermore, the unworthy manner in which the Lord's Supper is celebrated is a sin against the body and blood of the Lord (v. 27). Christians failed to observe basic rules of courteous conduct. Paul mentions two extreme examples: some people remain hungry while others become drunk (v. 21). He had to rebuke the Corinthians by saying that their meetings did more harm than good.

18. For in the first place when you come together in the church, I hear that there are factions among you and in part I believe it.

a. "For in the first place." When a speaker says or writes *first*, he is expected to proceed to the next point. A logical presentation that begins with the phrase *in the first place* must be followed with succeeding points. But Paul does not always give an orderly sequence of his thoughts. Elsewhere Paul also begins to enumerate his points but never lists a single one beyond his "first of all" (Rom. 3:2). Nonetheless, with this phrase Paul wants to emphasize the importance of his instruction. He wants his readers to pay close attention to what he is going to say.

b. "When you come together in the church." In context, the phrase *when you come together* alludes to worship services, because Paul uses the phrase repeatedly in this chapter (vv. 17, 18, 20, 33, 34; and see 14:23, 26). We assume that worship services were generally held in private homes or at times, to accommodate the entire congregation, outdoors. From other New Testament passages we learn that Christians used to meet for worship not in large buildings but in private homes known as house churches.[56] This means that the Corinthian church met in subgroups in the homes of prosperous members.

The words *in the church* should be understood as a general term that does not signify a building. Here the term should be interpreted in the sense of the body of Christ at worship services held at various places.

During the worship services, Paul's letters were read to the members of the church. Paul himself instructed the churches to exchange his letters and cause them to be read (see Col. 4:16; I Thess. 5:27; see also Rev. 1:3). These letters were placed on the same level as the Old Testament Scriptures and thus received canonical status (compare II Peter 3:15–16).

c. "I hear that there are factions among you." We have no information on how Paul heard about these irregularities. But members of Chloe's household (1:10–12) had told him about factions in the church, and a delegation from Corinth had given him an oral report (16:17). He elaborates not on personalities or theo-

---

56. See Rom. 16:5; I Cor. 16:19; Col. 4:15; Philem. 2.

logical matters but on social and economic issues evident at Corinthian worship services (vv. 20–22).

The factious spirit in the congregation probably originated for several reasons. Not only was there a desire to associate with either Paul, Apollos, Peter, or Christ (1:12); members of the church also came from different cultural, social, and economic backgrounds. These believers were either Jews, Greeks, Romans, or nationals from other countries. Some were merchants, government officials, and professionals who belonged to the educated class. They were prosperous and lived in spacious homes. By contrast, laborers and dock workers were poor and usually lived in rented quarters.

d. "And in part I believe it." With the last clause in this verse, Paul expresses himself cautiously. Relying only on hearsay, he guards himself so that no one can accuse him of speaking rashly. Not everyone in Corinth is guilty of arrogance. Yet Paul wishes to call attention to the excesses that are prevalent in the Corinthian community, and he is fully aware that cultural and social differences remain facts of life.

19. For there must be dissensions among you, so that those who are proven [believers] may become evident among you.

a. *Difficulties.* This verse is perplexing for both translators and commentators. First, some versions put the text in parentheses to indicate that it is an explanatory note which could have been relegated to a footnote.[57] Others introduce the first clause of the verse with translations that reflect concession or consent: "I admit," or "indeed."[58] Next, the text itself features the term *dissensions* as a variant of the word *factions* in verse 18. The text has the adjective *proven*, which must be supplemented with the noun *believers*. And, last, it has the phrase *among you* twice. This verse is difficult to translate.

b. *Explanations.* Although this text digresses slightly from the discourse proper, we do not need to put it in parentheses. In fact, the word *therefore* in verse 20 draws a conclusion based on the text in verse 19.

Paul is realistic and notes that separations occur because of Christ's gospel. He does not condone the schisms within the church but signifies that true believers should be cut off from societies inimical to that gospel. He urges that believers separate themselves from unbelievers (refer to II Cor. 6:14–18).

In one verse (v. 18) the writer counsels against factions but in the next verse allows dissension (v. 19). Still these two verses do not contradict each other; factions occur within the church while dissensions, in the good sense of the word, are voluntary separations from those who do not teach the doctrine of Christ. This interpretation of the term *dissensions* is strengthened by the rest of the verse, "so that those who are proven [believers] may become evident among you."[59]

---

57. See NCV, GNB.

58. *Cassirer*, NRSV.

59. Consult Henning Paulsen, "Schisma und Häresie. Untersuchungen zu 1 Kor 11,18.19," *ZTK* 79 (1982): 180–211.

The proven believers are Christians who have been approved by God because they stood the tests he gave them. Tested in spiritual warfare, they are recognized among God's people as genuine Christians.[60] These believers shun things that pertain to worldliness. They love and obey God, adhere to Christ in faith, and demonstrate their loyalty to him in church and society.

In this verse the phrase *among you* occurs twice: first in regard to dissensions, and next with respect to believers. Some Greek manuscripts delete one or both of these occurrences. Yet the textual support is strong for accepting both as genuine readings. Paul is saying that among the believers in the Corinthian church, unbelievers will infiltrate and with their teaching and lifestyle cause disruptions. Writes Frederic Louis Godet, "The Second Epistle to the Corinthians shows in how brief a period this anticipation of the apostle was realized."[61] True followers of Christ will oppose the unbelievers in their midst.

c. *Necessity.* The verse in Greek begins with the word *dei*, which denotes not obligation but necessity. Paul tells the readers that dissensions among them are a necessity to bring out the best in true believers. God works out his own purposes to strengthen Christians in times of testing and to punish unbelievers for their wicked deeds.

Practical Considerations in 11:18–19

Factors relating to language, culture, and geographic boundaries cause separation within the church. Early in church history linguistic differences among widows in Jerusalem caused neglect of one group (Acts 6:1). The fact that in the early church the New Testament Scriptures were translated into various languages (e.g., Latin, Coptic, Syriac) reflects the development of various churches along linguistic and often geographic lines.

During the Middle Ages, many distinctive groups arose in the Roman Catholic Church. And from the time of the Reformation, Protestant denominations have experienced untold fragmentation. The church today compares with a tree of numerous branches and twigs that form one unit. The imagery of a tree is helpful in explaining the origin and roots of denominations; nevertheless, unity appears to be elusive. Even if we say that unity does not imply uniformity, we know that Jesus' prayer calls us to strive for oneness in the Christian church (see John 17:21).

Unity and truth should be the two sides of the proverbial coin. Unity overcomes linguistic, cultural, and geographic barriers when believers confess and uphold the truth of Scripture. Conversely, unity and harmony should never be achieved at the expense of truth.

Christians must separate themselves from the forces of unbelief and disobedience. They have the duty, on the basis of numerous admonitions, to depart from these forces (II Cor. 6:14–18). On the other hand, believers should strive to maintain, defend, and

---

60. Consult Gerd Schunack, *EDNT*, vol. 1, pp. 341–42; Walter Grundmann, *TDNT*, vol. 2, p. 259.
61. Frederic Louis Godet, *Commentary on First Corinthians* (1886; reprint ed., Grand Rapids: Kregel, 1977), p. 569.

promote the unity of the body of Christ. Church leaders can split a church without much effort but have an extremely difficult time mending breaches.

Paul briefly describes some deplorable conditions and voices his disapproval of the Corinthians' lack of loving consideration for their poor brothers and sisters in Christ. He rebukes them for their ill-mannered behavior and informs them that he cannot praise them (v. 22). He teaches them how to observe Communion and counsels them to wait for one another when they come together for a fellowship meal (vv. 27–33). Paul's exquisite "letter of love" (chap. 13), although given in a different context, contains explicit instructions for how the well-to-do in Corinth can practice brotherly love.

20. Therefore, when you come together in the same place, it is not to eat the Lord's Supper.

With the word *therefore*, Paul summarizes the preceding context (vv. 17–19) and with the first clause he repeats what he has said earlier in verse 18. In that verse he mentions the church. Here he calls it "the same place." Whether he means the church being assembled in one particular place (compare 14:23) or gathered in private homes is not particularly relevant in this verse. What Paul desires in the entire church is unity that can be achieved only in the context of love. He knows that the factions in the Corinthian church seriously undermine genuine love among God's people.

The text of verse 20 is grammatically awkward, for it lacks balance. We would expect literary balance with the personal subjects *you* in both clauses. But such is not the case; the second clause has an impersonal *it* instead of a personal subject *you*. This switch causes confusion and leads to a possible misunderstanding. Does Paul mean not to eat the Lord's Supper at all? Or is he saying that it is no longer appropriate for the Corinthians to do so? In light of the factionalism in the church, we presume that Paul's contention is that partaking of Communion is inappropriate for the Corinthians. When believers come together in assembly, they cannot properly celebrate the Lord's Supper, because their loveless acts and unseemly behavior make true observance inconceivable. The Corinthians no longer honor the Lord when they come together for either a meal or Holy Communion.

In his history of the early church, Luke refers to the celebration of Communion as "the breaking of bread" (Acts 2:42; 20:7, 11). By contrast, Paul calls the sacrament "the Supper of the Lord." The expression *of the Lord* occurs only once more in the New Testament, in Revelation 1:10, where John speaks of "the Day of the Lord." That is, both the Supper and the Day belong to our Lord Jesus Christ. We surmise that the term *Lord's Supper* became current about the time of Paul's correspondence with the Corinthian church and that the expression *Lord's Day* was well established by the end of the first century.

21. For as you eat, each one takes his supper before others; one remains hungry and another is drunk.

Even though the information Paul provides is scanty, we infer that the Corinthians had displayed inconsistent behavior at their love feasts. What precisely do we know about love feasts? Luke tells us that after Pentecost the early Christians came together in their homes and shared their food as they enjoyed common meals (Acts 2:46). The practice of sharing food with one another became the hallmark of the Christian church. Christians came together to eat a meal for nourishment and to partake of the elements of the Lord's Supper (Acts 20:7, 11). At these gatherings they demonstrated the love of Christ for one another in word and deed. In a relatively short time, however, discrimination against the underprivileged became a common occurrence (see Jude 12; compare II Peter 2:13).

In all probability, the Corinthians observed class distinctions in worship services and at the love feasts: prominent members received preferential treatment. The rich people consumed choice food from their own larders and left the remainder for the poor.[62] They had no patience to wait until everyone had arrived.[63] Instead they ate without waiting for the day laborers and slaves. We conjecture that some of the poor who were unable to come earlier saw that all the food had been consumed. They are the ones whom Paul describes as being hungry. The affluent, by contrast, had used their time to eat their fill and drink excessively. The word *each* in the text applies to the rich, not the poor.

22. For do you not have houses for the purpose of eating and drinking? Or do you despise the church of God and put to shame those who have nothing? What shall I say to you? Shall I praise you? In this I do not praise you.

a. "For do you not have houses for the purpose of eating and drinking?" Paul now raises a number of questions. The first one is rhetorical and calls for a positive reply. This is not a query addressed to every reader. Not at all. Paul boldly confronts the prosperous homeowners and tells them to eat and drink at home. He implies that they should not even attend love feasts if they have neither regard nor love for the poor.

b. "Or do you despise the church of God and put to shame those who have nothing?" In Acts, Luke records that some prominent people became members of Christ's church. For instance, Luke mentions the Roman proconsul Sergius Paulus in Cyprus (13:6–12), the merchant Lydia from Thyatira (16:14), and Titius Justus at Corinth (18:7). The rich, however, were a minority while the poor were in the majority. Are the rich in Corinth looking down on those who are poor? Humble people may be materially poor but spiritually rich; the reverse is often true of the rich. Indeed, from a spiritual perspective the poor should take pride in their high position (James 1:9).

---

62. Gerd Theissen, *The Social Setting of Pauline Christianity: Essays on Corinth*, ed. and trans. John H. Schütz (Philadelphia: Fortress, 1982), pp. 145–74.

63. Excavations at ancient Corinth have given us insight into the sizes of homes. Dining rooms in these homes could accommodate only a limited number of people. Some twenty to thirty people sat down to eat while the rest of the guests had to stand. Consult Jerome Murphy-O'Connor, *St. Paul's Corinth: Texts and Archaeology*, Good News Studies, vol. 6 (Wilmington, Del.: Glazier, 1983), p. 159.

Paul rebukes the rich for looking down on the poor who are their spiritual brothers and sisters. The rich are despising the church, which is the very body to which they belong. They should realize that Jesus, the head of that body, loves and cherishes every member. Moreover, no part of the body can afford to disregard another part (see 12:14–27). With a rhetorical question, Paul approaches the rich and asks them if they realize that they are despising the church by humiliating the poor. To their shame they have to admit that this is the case.

c. "What shall I say to you? Shall I praise you? In this I do not praise you." With two successive questions, Paul indicates that he is at a loss to express himself effectively. He puts the matter before his readers and asks them, as it were, to assist him in finding the correct words. "What am I to say to you? Am I to praise you?" They know the answer to the second query. They themselves have to admit that they are unworthy of praise. To underscore his disapproval, Paul repeats his earlier remark: "I do not praise you" (v. 17).

Greek Words, Phrases, and Constructions in 11:17–22

Verse 17

παραγγέλλων—the present participle from παραγγέλλω (I command, instruct) denotes the mode in which Paul emphasizes his reason for being unable to praise the Corinthians.

κρεῖσσον, ἧσσον—these two comparative adverbs are positive in meaning: "in a good . . . bad way."[64]

Verse 18

μέν—this particle has no counterpart in the next verse (v. 19) but has an implied contrast in verses 20–22 without the expected particle δέ. Friedrich Blass and Albert Debrunner interpret πρῶτον (in the first place) and its lack of sequel to mean "from the very outset."[65]

ἐν ἐκκλησίᾳ—this phrase without the definite article (in [the] church) is synonymous with ἐπὶ τὸ αὐτό (in the same place) in verse 20.

ἀκούω—the verb *I hear* actually means "I am told."

Verse 19

γὰρ καί—this combination is the reverse of the usual καὶ γάρ (indeed) and signifies "for also, for precisely."[66]

δόκιμοι—an adjective meaning "approved" from the verb δοκιμάζω (I test, examine [v. 28]). See Rom. 14:18; 16:10; II Cor. 10:18; 13:7; II Tim. 2:15; James 1:12.

Verses 20–21

συνερχομένων ὑμῶν—this is the genitive absolute construction with the present participle and personal pronoun in the genitive case: "when you come together." The sub-

---

64. Blass and Debrunner, *Greek Grammar*, #244.2.
65. Ibid., #447.4.
66. Bauer, p. 151.

ject of the main verb ἔστιν is impersonal, however, and causes a more or less awkward construction.

προλαμβάνω—"I take beforehand." First, this is the iterative or customary present, which shows that the action happened frequently in Corinth.[67] Next, the preposition πρό (before) has not lost its temporal meaning in the context in which Paul uses it.[68]

Verse 22

μή—the negative particle in a rhetorical question expects a positive reply. The particle οὐκ negates the verb *to have*.

ἐσθίειν—"to eat." The present infinite is used to indicate repeated occurrence. The two preceding verses (vv. 20–21) feature the aorist infinitive φαγεῖν (to eat) which is constative.

εἴπω—this is the aorist subjunctive of the verb *to say*, just as ἐπαινέσω is the aorist subjunctive of the verb *to praise*. In two successive questions, Paul uses deliberate subjunctives. The future indicative ἐπαινῶ appears in the following declarative sentence.

b. Institution
11:23–26

When churches celebrate Holy Communion, they hear the words Paul received from the Lord and which he has passed on to believers. The words of this particular passage are the formulary used for the observance of the Lord's Supper. That is, we use the words Paul gave to the Corinthians and not the words recorded by the Gospel writers. The wording in the Gospel accounts, and even the sequence, differs from that given by Paul in this chapter. The commentary on the following verses (vv. 23–26) will discuss the dissimilarity of the various accounts.

23. For I have received from the Lord that which I also delivered to you, that the Lord Jesus, in the night in which he was betrayed, took bread, 24. and when he had given thanks, he broke it and said: "This is my body, which is for you. Do this in remembrance of me."

a. "For I have received from the Lord that which I also delivered to you." When Paul expressed his perplexity in not knowing what to say to the Corinthians (v. 22), he did not mean to convey to them that he was speechless. On the contrary, as the father of the Corinthian church he teaches its members the significance and proper manner of celebrating the Lord's Supper. Believers must understand that when they eat the bread and drink from the cup of the Lord, they are guests at his table. If Christians partake without loving their fellow church members, they are dishonoring the Lord himself. For that reason, they must learn the words spoken by the Lord when he instituted his Supper.

---

67. Consult Robertson, *Grammar*, p. 880.
68. Refer to Liddell, p. 1488; Burghard Siede, *NIDNTT*, vol. 3, p. 750; Gerhard Delling, *TDNT*, vol. 4, p. 14. By contrast, see the careful study of Bruce W. Winter, "The Lord's Supper at Corinth: An Alternative Reconstruction," *RTR* 37 (1978): 73–82.

Paul says that he has received the Communion formulary from the Lord. Does he mean that Jesus communicated this formulary at the time of Paul's conversion or during a subsequent vision? Either is possible. But the Lord Jesus also communicated his word indirectly to Paul, as he did through the agency of Ananias in Damascus (Acts 9:17). Thus, Paul may mean that some of the apostles taught him the words of the institution of the Lord's Supper. In fact, Paul spent fifteen days in the company of Peter (Gal. 1:18). We conjecture that Paul received the information through the agency of other apostles. Nonetheless, the revelation came first from Jesus, who is the Lord of this tradition and personally directs the development of the church.[69]

The words *received* and *delivered* are technical terms that denote the individual links in the chain of tradition. (Elsewhere Paul alludes to this handing on of divine revelation [see 15:3]. A perfect example is Paul's preaching in Thessalonica, where he orally transmitted the gospel to the Thessalonians. They in turn passed it on by word of mouth to people throughout Macedonia and Achaia [I Thess. 1:5, 6–8].) The words of the institution originated not with Paul but with Jesus. Hence, these words are divine and must be honored, kept, and transmitted. Paul is saying that he received the words of the Lord's Supper from the Lord through the apostles and now passes them on to the Corinthians. He expects these people to accept this sacred trust and tradition which they must in turn pass on to others.

b. "That the Lord Jesus, in the night in which he was betrayed." We are confident that the account of the events regarding Jesus' betrayal and arrest were familiar to the readers. By adding the name *Jesus* to the title *Lord*, Paul directs the attention of the readers to the earthly life of Jesus and the humiliation which the Lord experienced. But see the contrast: while Jesus' adversaries were laying their plans to arrest and murder him, the Lord instituted the sacrament of Holy Communion.

Paul describes the act of betrayal with a Greek verb in the imperfect tense to indicate a deed that was in progress. Only Paul gives this information as an introduction to the very words Jesus uttered. The Evangelists place the institution in the immediate context of the Passover feast and the broader context of Jesus' impending agony in Gethsemane and subsequent suffering and death at Calvary, thus placing the Lord's Supper in the context of history. But Paul discloses that Communion also is the repeated act of receiving and delivering the sacrament until the Lord returns (v. 26).

c. "[Jesus] took bread, and when he had given thanks, he broke it." In the Greek, we see the same wording in Luke 22:19. The accounts of Matthew 26:26 and Mark 14:22 are nearly identical in translation except for a different verb form for "gave thanks." And the Gospel accounts specify that Jesus gave the bread to his disciples. Paul, however, omits this detail; he probably wanted to provide a general context applicable to everyone who partakes of the bread.

---

69. Compare Robert Paul Roth, "Paradosis and Apokalupsis in I Corinthians 11:23," *LuthQuart* 12 (1960): 64–67.

The words of the formulary echo other traditions or events. For example, at the feeding of the five thousand, Jesus took the bread, looked up to heaven, gave thanks, and broke it.[70] Jewish fathers followed the same ritual at a meal or at a Passover feast. Near the conclusion of the Passover celebration, Jesus instituted the Lord's Supper when he took bread—a reference to his own body that was about to be subjected to suffering and death.

d. "[He] said: 'This is my body, which is for you. Do this in remembrance of me.'" The Gospel writers also record this saying of Jesus; and we can compare their wording with that of Paul:

Matt. 26:26	Mark 14:22	Luke 22:19	I Cor. 1:24
Take and eat;	Take it;		
this is	this is	This is	This is
my body.	my body.	my body given for you; do this in remembrance of me.	my body, which is for you. Do this in remembrance of me.

We see that the accounts of Matthew and Mark are almost identical, as are those of Luke and Paul. A dissimilarity between Matthew and Mark is the addition of the imperative *eat* in Matthew's narrative. Likewise, Luke has the verb *given*, which Paul omits. Luke and Paul do not record the command *take and eat* at the beginning of Jesus' saying; conversely, Luke and Paul alone feature Jesus' command to "do this in remembrance of me." All four writers have the words *this is my body* in common.

Since the time of the Reformation theologians have discussed the interpretation of the words *this is my body*. A commentary is not the place to present a lengthy theological discourse. But I will make a few remarks. The morsel of bread which Jesus held in his hand did not become his physical body; the bread remained bread. It was a symbol that stood for the reality of his body. Much as the dove descending on Jesus at the time of his baptism represents the Holy Spirit, so the bread represents Christ's body.[71]

Jesus said to his disciples, "This is my body, which is for you." On the eve of his death, he spoke prophetically about his physical body that would be nailed to a cross as an atonement for sin. His body would be delivered for all who believe in Christ and at Communion partake of the bread. Jesus indicated that he would die in their place (compare Rom. 5:7–8).

---

70. Matt. 14:19; Mark 6:41; Luke 9:16; and see John 6:11.
71. Calvin, *I Corinthians*, p. 245.

What shall we say about the exalted and invisible body of the ascended Christ? The bread which the believer eats is a sign of that glorified body which is now in heaven. Through the Holy Spirit, partakers of the bread are brought together by faith into fellowship with Christ and experience his sacred presence and power.

The command to "do this in remembrance of me" can be understood in both an objective and a subjective sense. Objectively, it refers to our prayer to God that he will graciously remember the Messiah and cause his kingdom to come at his appearing.[72] Subjectively, it means that we as partakers at the Lord's table remember his death on the cross. Of these two interpretations, the second one appears to be more relevant in the context. Within the Corinthian church, the people failed to observe the Lord's Supper properly (vv. 20–21). They needed to remember Jesus' death and reflect on its implication for them. Hence, Paul repeats the words of Jesus as a reminder to the Corinthians that the Lord's Supper is an act of remembrance.[73]

By eating the bread and drinking from the cup, Paul says, we proclaim the Lord's death (v. 26). We must do this repeatedly, as Jesus' command indicates, to remember his death. But there is much more to the Lord's Supper than a remembrance of his death. We also call to mind Christ's redemptive work, his resurrection and ascension, his promise to be with his people always, and his eventual return.[74]

Practical Considerations in 11:23–24

What is the meaning of the Lord's Supper when a Christian partakes of the holy elements? I remember the first time that I was given the privilege to participate. For weeks I had looked forward to the celebration of the Lord's Supper, but this anticipation was restrained when I ate and drank with the other worshipers. I had expected a supernatural influx of divine power, but nothing miraculous happened during that worship service. I thought about Christ's death on the cross of Calvary, the remission of sin, and the presence of the Lord. In a sense, that first experience for me was sobering and devoid of magic.

As time went by, I matured spiritually and began to experience Christ's presence at the Communion services. As the host, he invited me to be his guest at the table. As the Mediator of the new covenant that God had made, he considered me a covenant partner. As the Lamb of God slain at Golgotha, he cleansed me from my sins. As my brother and

---

72. Joachim Jeremias, *The Eucharistic Words of Jesus*, trans. Norman Perrin from the German 3d rev. ed. (New York: Charles Scribner's Sons, 1966), p. 252; Richard J. Ginn, *The Present and the Past: A Study of Anamnesis* (Allison Park, Penn.: Pickwick Publications, 1989), p. 20.

73. Fee, *First Corinthians*, p. 553. Consult also Fritz Chenderlin, *"Do This as My Memorial." The Semantic and Conceptual Background and Value of Anamnēsis in 1 Corinthians 11:24–25*, Analecta Biblica 99 (Rome: Biblical Institute Press, 1982); M. H. Sykes, "The Eucharist as 'Anamnesis,'" *ExpT* 71 (1960): 115–18.

74. Consult Otfried Hofius, "Herrenmahl und Herrenmahlsparadosis. Erwägungen zu I Kor 11,23b–25," *ZTK* 85 (1988): 371-408; "To sōma to hyper hymōn I Kor 11,24," *ZNW* 80 (1989): 80–88.

friend, he showed me how to live to God's glory and express my thankfulness to him. As the source of bliss, he filled me not with grief and sadness for his death but with joy and gladness for his presence.

What is the meaning of the Lord's Supper? It is a time of reflecting, rejoicing, and thanksgiving. As we experience the spiritual presence of the Lord at the table, we with the church of all ages and all places fervently pray *Maranatha*, "Come, O Lord" (16:22; see also Rev. 22:20).[75]

---

25. In the same way, also taking the cup after supper, he said: "This cup is the new covenant in my blood; do this as often as you drink it in remembrance of me."

a. *Variations.* The wording of this verse is almost identical to that of Luke's account. In the Greek text of the three synoptic Gospels, only Luke has the expression *in the same way*, and only he omits the verb *to take* (22:20; compare Matt. 26:27; Mark 14:23). For the sake of clarity the word *taking* has to be supplied in verse 25.

Matthew writes that Jesus takes the cup and commands his disciples, "Drink from it, all of you" (26:27). Mark has a declarative sentence that states, "they all drank from it" (14:23). But Luke records Jesus' comment: "This cup is the new covenant in my blood, which is poured out for you" (Luke 22:20b). Paul relates the first part of Luke's sentence but not the second. And of all Last Supper accounts, only that of Paul has the words, "Do this as often as you drink it in remembrance of me." Conversely, the three synoptic Evangelists show balance in respect to the beneficiaries of the bread and the cup when they write, "poured out for many/you" (Matt. and Mark/Luke).

Both Matthew and Mark write, "my blood of the covenant." But Luke records Jesus' words as "the new covenant in my blood." Did Jesus say "*new* covenant" in fulfillment of Jeremiah's prophecy (Jer. 31:31) and Luke recorded the adjective *new*? Did both Matthew and Mark delete this adjective? Regardless of the question concerning variations, Luke's and Paul's accounts show remarkable similarities in wording.

b. *Meaning.* "In the same way, also taking the cup after supper, he said." Paul uses the phrase *in the same way* to parallel with a minimum of words the taking of the bread and the taking of the cup. The conjunction *also* affirms that Jesus adopted the same procedure with the cup as with the bread. When Paul writes "after supper," he intimates that after the bread was distributed and eaten, the cup had to be filled for the third time, according to custom.[76] Then it was passed on to the disciples. At a Jewish Passover meal, the participants drank at intervals from four cups (see the commentary at 10:16). When Jesus took the cup, it was

---

75. *Didache* 10:6. See also I. Howard Marshall, *Last Supper and Lord's Supper* (Grand Rapids: Eerdmans, 1980), p. 152.

76. Compare S. K. Finlayson, "I Corinthians xi.25," *ExpT* 71 (1960): 243.

the third cup known as "the cup of blessing."[77] At this moment he instituted the second part of the Lord's Supper. Conversely, the partaking of the bread and of the cup in the Corinthian church may have been separated by some interval, in view of the phrase *after supper* (v. 25).

"'This cup is the new covenant in my blood.'" According to Paul and Luke, Jesus does not say that the liquid in the cup is his blood and thus he fails to compose a direct parallel with his words *this is my body*. Although Matthew and Mark balance the terms *body* and *blood* in their Gospels, in the accounts of Luke and Paul the parallel fails because the expression *new covenant* is central. This expression gives the word *blood* a deeper spiritual meaning. The cup represents the new covenant that Jesus ratifies with his blood. When Moses confirmed the first covenant at Mount Sinai, he sprinkled blood on the people and said, "This is the blood of the covenant that the Lord has made with you" (Exod. 24:8; see also Zech. 9:11). Animal blood was sprinkled for the first covenant, Christ's blood for the new covenant.

What is a covenant? "The word 'covenant' points to a unilateral disposition made by God in favour of man, and is not to be understood in terms of a mutual agreement made between two parties of equal standing."[78] God instituted the first covenant in the days of Moses (Exod. 24:4b–8); he gave the Israelites promises which he fulfilled; as their part of the covenant obligations, the Israelites were asked to keep God's law, which they failed to do. By making a new covenant with his people, God made the old one obsolete (Heb. 8:13). He ratified this new covenant with Christ's blood shed once for all (Heb. 9:26; 10:10). God appointed Jesus as the mediator of this covenant (Heb. 7:22; 8:6), and Jesus fulfilled it by giving up his body and blood. Concisely, in the word *covenant* lies the implicit parallel of Jesus' body that was slain for the benefit of his people and Jesus' sprinkled blood that confirms this new covenant with them (compare Rom. 3:25).

Every believer who drinks from the cup at the Lord's table is a member of the covenant that Christ has ratified in his blood. This also holds true for eating the bread. All those who partake of the one loaf signify that they participate in the one body of Christ (10:17). Together they form a covenant community.[79]

c. *Command.* "'Do this as often as you drink it in remembrance of me.'" For a second time, Jesus issues a command to observe the sacrament of Communion. But he is more specific in giving this command. He instructs his people to celebrate and, whenever they do, to remember him in connection with his shed blood for the remission of sin.

In Old Testament times, the Israelites were commanded to observe Passover on the fourteenth of the Hebrew month Nisan. By contrast, Jesus commands his people to both eat the bread and drink of the cup regularly, but refrains from giving

77. SB, vol. 4, pp. 630–31; Leonhard Goppelt, *TDNT*, vol. 6, pp. 154–55.
78. Geoffrey B. Wilson, *I Corinthians: A Digest of Reformed Comment* (London: Banner of Truth Trust, 1971), pp. 168–69.
79. Barrett, *First Corinthians*, p. 269.

his followers a fixed schedule. Some churches have Communion once every three months, others celebrate it monthly, and still others weekly. Although the Lord's Supper is observed in numerous churches on Maundy Thursday or Good Friday, its celebration is not limited to a stated time. Instead Jesus says, "As often as you observe Communion, you must remember that I offered myself on your behalf."

26. For as often as you eat this bread and drink this cup, you proclaim the death of the Lord until he comes.

a. "For as often as you eat this bread and drink this cup." Of all the New Testament writers who record the words of the institution of the Lord's Supper, only Paul has Jesus' command: "Do this as often as you drink it in remembrance of me." Paul adds his own summary of and insight into the Lord's Supper. With the conjunction *for*, he summarizes Jesus' formulary. He repeats the words *as often as* and links them to both the eating of the bread and the drinking of the cup. These two actions must always be equal elements of this sacrament. At the Corinthian love feasts and Communion services, irregularities occurred which Paul now seeks to rectify.

b. "You proclaim the death of the Lord." Paul teaches that all those who eat the bread and drink from the cup symbolically proclaim Jesus' death.[80] By his death, Jesus has made them partners of the new covenant that God established with his people and of which Christ is the mediator. Paul reminds them of the spiritual benefits that accrue from Jesus' sacrifice on the cross, and they by partaking of the bread and the cup acknowledge unity one with another in Christ.

When the church celebrates the Lord's Supper in the setting of a worship service, ministers of the Word ought to proclaim the significance of Christ's death. Whenever they expound the Word verbally, the worshipers proclaim it silently by partaking of the sacramental elements.

c. "Until he comes." The members of the church proclaim both Jesus' death and his return. They look forward to the day when Christ shall return and they shall be forever with the Lord. In the church of the second half of the first century, believers celebrated Communion and then prayed *Maranatha* (Come, O Lord).[81]

Christians cannot suppress their desire to be with Jesus; they must proclaim his death, resurrection, and return. In a similar vein, the prophet Isaiah notes his inability to suppress this desire:[82]

> For Zion's sake I will not keep silent,
> > for Jerusalem's sake I will not remain quiet,
> till her righteousness shines out like the dawn,
> > her salvation like a blazing torch.
> > > > > > > > [Isa. 62:1]

---

80. Beverly R. Gaventa, "'You Proclaim the Lord's Death': I Corinthians 11:26 and Paul's Understanding of Worship," *RevExp* 80 (1983): 377–87.

81. See *Didache* 10:6; Jeremias, *Eucharistic Words*, p. 253.

82. Otfried Hofius, "'Bis dass er kommt': I Kor. xi. 26," *NTS* 14 (1968): 439–41.

Greek Words, Phrases, and Constructions in 11:23–26

Verse 23

ἐγώ . . . ὑμῖν—note that these two personal pronouns occupy key positions for emphasis: the first one at the beginning of the first clause and the other at the end of the main sentence.

ἀπὸ τοῦ κυρίου—"from the Lord." The difference between ἀπό and παρά after the verb παραλαμβάνω (I receive) is negligible.

παρεδίδετο—the imperfect denotes the act of betraying or delivering ("he was delivered"). The passive is a Semitic construction to avoid using the name of God. According to Peter at Pentecost, the Father delivered Jesus over to sinful men (Acts 2:23).[83]

Verse 24

The Majority Text, reflected in two translations (KJV, NKJV), has expanded the text by incorporating the words *take and eat.* Early and major manuscripts would not omit these words, however, if they were part of the text. For this reason, editors of the Greek New Testament regard them as an insertion influenced by the text of Matthew 26:26. Similarly, the Majority Text inserts the expression *which is broken* between "this is my body" and "for you." The verb *broken* is an echo of the same verb used for the breaking of bread.[84]

τοῦτο μού ἐστιν τὸ σῶμα—"The gender of the demonstrative pronoun is natural, being attracted into the gender of the predicate nominative, τὸ σῶμα μου; the reference may very well be to ἄρτος [bread] although it is masculine."[85] In the present clause, the predicate nominative probably receives emphasis: "This is my *body*" instead of "*This* is my body" or "This *is* my body."

τοῦτο ποιεῖτε—the demonstrative pronoun *this* includes all the parts of the ceremony (see also v. 25). The present imperative of the verb *to do* calls for repeated action.

εἰς—this preposition controls the accusative case and connotes purpose: "to remember me."

τὴν ἐμὴν ἀνάμνησιν—the presence of the possessive adjective *my* between the definite article and the noun expresses emphasis. It is the act of remembering Jesus' person and work.

Verses 25–26

ἐμῷ and ἐμήν—both possessive adjectives are placed between a definite article and a noun to indicate emphasis.

ὁσάκις—this adverb expresses the idea of indefinite repetition ("whenever"). It occurs in both verses (vv. 25, 26) with the present subjunctive ἐσθίητε (you eat).[86]

ἄχρι οὗ ἔλθῃ— "until he comes." "This clause is not a simple time reference but ἔλθῃ is a prospective subjunctive which . . . may therefore be freely translated 'until (matters have developed to the point at which) he comes.'"[87]

---

83. Jeremias, *Eucharistic Words,* p. 107; P. Coleman, "The Translation of *paredideto* in 1 Co 11.23," *ExpT* 87 (1976): 375.

84. Refer to Metzger, *Textual Commentary,* p. 562.

85. Robert G. Hoerber, *Studies in the New Testament* (Cleveland: Biblion, 1991), p. 7.

86. Robertson, *Grammar,* p. 974.

87. Jeremias, *Eucharistic Words,* p. 253.

c. Preparation
11:27–34

Merely reciting Jesus' words while properly celebrating the Lord's Supper is insufficient to rectify the deplorable conditions at the Corinthian love feasts and Communion ceremonies. Paul wanted the Christians at Corinth to examine their spiritual and social lives. After repenting of their sins, they are to come freely to the Lord's table in the knowledge that they will not be condemned. They must realize the sacredness of the sacrament and the necessity of coming to the Holy Supper with profound reverence. Celebrating Communion calls for joy and happiness but never for superficiality and carelessness.

27. Therefore, whoever eats the bread or drinks the cup of the Lord unworthily shall be guilty of [profaning] the body and blood of the Lord.

a. *Translation.* First, translators and editors of the Greek text differ on the division of this text. Should the verse be the conclusion of the preceding paragraph or the beginning of a new one? Most scholars think that Paul commences another aspect of his teaching about the Lord's Supper and therefore opt for a new paragraph.

Next, the sentence is clear in Greek but not in English. The word *profaning* or its equivalent should be supplied to clarify that the nonchalant partaker of Communion is sinning against the Lord himself. If we provide a literal translation, it means that the partaker of the Lord's Supper is guilty of murdering Jesus.

b. *Incompatibility.* "Therefore, whoever eats the bread or drinks the cup of the Lord unworthily." Both bread and cup belong to the Lord, so that anyone who partakes of both these elements without observing Christ's holiness sins against him. Paul writes the little word *or* to emphasize the fact that when the eating or drinking is profaned, the partaker stands guilty. In light of the parallel sentences in the preceding and succeeding verses (vv. 26, 28), the connective *or* appears to mean the same thing as *and*.

Explanations of the adverb *unworthily* are numerous and diverse because the adverb by itself can be understood in various ways. To illustrate the options: persons are of the opinion that they are not worthy of such holy food and drink; partakers come without repentance of sin and thus without self-examination; affluent Corinthians reveal contempt for the poor; communicants fail to express gratitude to Christ by turning the sacrament into a frivolous feast.[88]

Perhaps Paul intended that the adverb *unworthily* be interpreted as broadly as possible. True, some of the Corinthians demonstrated a lack of love, while others failed to make a distinction between the love feast and the observance of Communion. Both were wrong, and Paul confronts them. But the text has a message for the universal church, too. Christians should never regard the celebration as a mere ritual. Rather, sincere believers ought to anticipate the Lord's Supper.

---

88. For additional interpretations, see William Ellis, "On the Text of the Account of the Lord's Supper in I Corinthians xi.23–32 with Some Further Comment," *AusBRev* 12 (1964): 43–51.

Christians should confess their unworthiness because of sin but their worthiness because of Christ. Paul is not demanding perfection before believers are allowed to come to Communion. He advocates a lifestyle that is governed by the claims of Christ's gospel and which attributes the highest praise to God.

c. *Guilt.* "[He] shall be guilty of [profaning] the body and blood of the Lord." The words *unworthily* and *guilty* are juxtaposed in the Greek and explain each other, as a contemporary illustration helps us understand. A person who burns the flag of his native country testifies that he has no respect for his homeland. Granted that a flag is a mere piece of cloth, we nevertheless know that it is a symbol of a nation; disrespect for a flag is understood as contempt for the country it represents.

Likewise, partaking unworthily of the Communion elements signifies sacrilege. Persons who profane the bread and the cup of the Lord offend the Lord himself. Purposely they have chosen not to proclaim Christ's death but to set themselves against the Lord and take their place with those who killed him. These people are guilty of the body and blood of the Lord, because they put the Son of God to open shame and treat him with insolence (compare Acts 7:52; Heb. 6:6; 10:29).

28. But let a man examine himself and thus let him eat of the bread and drink of the cup.

Is Paul counseling the Corinthians to conduct self-examination before coming to the Lord's table? Should a pastor exhort the parishioners to examine themselves before they celebrate Communion? The answer to these two queries is a resounding yes. Here are the reasons:

First, with the adversative *but* Paul prescribes self-examination for everyone who desires to partake of the bread and the cup of the Lord. He understands the word *man* generically to exclude no one.

Next, the meaning of the verb *to examine* is applicable both to the original readers of this epistle and to the members of the church universal. The present tense of the imperative verb *to examine* indicates that anyone who partakes of the Lord's Supper must examine himself regularly. The Corinthians should know that they cannot partake of Communion with hearts filled with either contempt or frivolity. After due self-examination they must approach the Lord's table with genuine love for both the Lord and their fellow man. This holds true for all Christians everywhere. They are to come to the Communion table with hearts attuned to God and the Scriptures (compare II Cor. 13:5–6). That table truly symbolizes the holiness of the Lord and his sacred presence. Into this holiness God's people may enter when they have sought and obtained remission of sin. In brief, the table of the Lord tolerates neither unbelief nor disobedience.[89] It is for those people who express true faith in Jesus Christ and proclaim his death in expectation of his return.

---

89. Contra Norman M. Pritchard, who advances the hypothesis that unbelievers were present at the Lord's table in Corinth. See his "Profession of Faith and Admission to Communion in the Light of I Corinthians 11 and Other Passages," *SJT* 33 (1980): 55–70.

29. For he who eats and drinks eats and drinks judgment to himself, if he does not discern the body.

a. *Text.* This passage explains and supports the preceding verse (v. 28). Some Greek manuscripts have an expanded reading of this text. They add the adverb *unworthily* after the clause *he who eats and drinks* and the words *of the Lord* following the term *body*—that is, "For he who eats and drinks in an unworthy manner eats and drinks judgment to himself, not discerning the Lord's body" (NKJV). A few translations feature both additions,[90] others embrace only the second expansion.[91] The longer reading, however, appears to be a well-meant attempt to explain the text with the help of verse 27. In ancient times, a scribe usually would not condense but rather enlarge a text. The more difficult text is the shorter reading, and because omission of the words in question is hard to explain, we accept the shorter reading.[92]

b. *Meaning.* "For he who eats and drinks eats and drinks judgment to himself, if he does not discern the body." The first part of the verse is repetitious and is explained in the second clause. The causal conjunction *for* links this verse to the preceding context that speaks of self-examination prior to partaking of the Communion elements. Anyone who eats and drinks without such introspection, receives God's judgment but not God's condemnation if he or she repents and properly differentiates. A person's failure to submit to self-examination results in God's subsequent judgment. This is as inevitable as night follows day.

What is Paul's advice? He says that judgment happens only if a person discerns not the body. That is, the partakers must make a clear distinction between the bread that they eat at the love feast for nourishing their physical bodies and the bread of the Lord's Supper for the benefit of the body of believers.[93] We eat bread to nourish our bodies, but that same bread is holy when it is set apart for Communion. The act of differentiating relates to the eating of bread, which harmonizes with the immediate context.

Does the term *body* (v. 29) refer to the body of the Lord, as in some translations? Is it an abbreviation for "the body and blood of the Lord" (v. 27)? Or is it a reference to the body of believers (10:16)?[94] Almost all commentators understand this verse (v. 29) in the light of its immediate context that speaks of the body of the Lord; they see a close connection between verses 27 and 29. Commentators understand that the better manuscripts omit the words *of the Lord* as modifiers of the term *body*. Yet they understand that this particular term is a shortened form of the full clause "the body and blood of the Lord" in verse 27.

---

90. KJV, NKJV, *Phillips.*

91. NIV, GNB, TNT, *Cassirer.* Two versions have "body *of Christ*" (MLB, SEB), but without textual support.

92. Consult Metzger, *Textual Commentary*, pp. 562–63.

93. Compare Gerhard Dautzenburg, *EDNT*, vol. 1, p. 305. See also Siegfried Wibbing, *NIDNTT*, vol. 1, pp. 503–4.

94. For a detailed discussion, consult Fee, *First Corinthians*, pp. 563–64; see also Bruce, *1 and 2 Corinthians*, p. 115.

And last they doubt that Paul expects the reader to perceive that he means "the body of believers" (10:16). Paul is referring to the body of the Lord which the Communion bread and cup represent.

Practical Considerations in 11:27–29

The psalmist asks the Lord who of all people may be admitted to God's sanctuary (Ps. 15:1). To put it differently, who may be a guest at your table, Lord? The answer is: a person who is blameless, righteous, truthful, morally upright, and obedient to God's law. Does this mean that only those who are perfect can enter the sanctuary and sit at the Lord's table? No, but even in ancient Israel the people had to prepare themselves before they entered the tabernacle or temple grounds. They had to submit themselves to self-examination before they entered the courts of the Lord for the three feasts of Passover, Firstfruits, and Booths.[95] Similarly, in the New Testament, Christians are asked to examine themselves before they come to the table of the Lord.

But who may be admitted to the Communion table? German theologian Zacharius Ursinus struggled with the same question. In 1563, he formulated a biblical answer that is thorough and to the point:

> Those who are displeased with themselves
>   because of their sins,
> but who nevertheless trust
> that their sins are pardoned
> and that their continuing weakness is covered
>   by the suffering and death of Christ,
> and who also desire more and more
> to strengthen their faith
> and to lead a better life.
> Hypocrites and those who are unrepentant, however,
> eat and drink judgment on themselves.[96]

---

30. Because of this, many among you are weak and ill and many have died. 31. But if we judged ourselves correctly,[97] we would not be judged. 32. When we are judged, we are disciplined by the Lord so that we may not be condemned with the world.

a. "Because of this." The result of the Corinthian neglect is evident in the Christian community. At the conclusion of his discourse on the Lord's Supper, Paul courageously points out the sad effect of the abuses.

b. "Many among you are weak and ill and many have died." As the Corinthians' first pastor, Paul probably received detailed oral information about the physical health of the church members from the three-man delegation (16:17).

---

95. Willem A. VanGemeren, *Psalms*, in *The Expositor's Bible Commentary*, 12 vols. (Grand Rapids: Zondervan, 1991), vol. 5, p. 148.
96. Heidelberg Catechism, answer 81.
97. Bauer, p. 185.

He heard that many of the members were indisposed, others were sick, and still others had passed away. Those who were indisposed were inflicted with temporary illnesses; the sick were failing in health and many of them had no hope of recovery; those who died are euphemistically described as "they who are asleep."

With prophetic insight, Paul draws his conclusions from the news he has received. He deems it necessary to inform the Corinthians that their illnesses and deaths are related to the verdict that God has handed down to them. This verdict stems from their improper observance of the Lord's Supper. Hence, he once more calls attention to their self-examination.

Paul gives no one a license to become a self-appointed judge of someone else's afflictions. Instead, he urges everyone to conduct a true self-examination of one's moral and spiritual life.

c. "But if we judged ourselves correctly, we would not be judged." The English translation is unable to match the Greek text, which has a double reflexive, one in the verb *to judge ourselves* and the other in the pronoun *ourselves*. Paul wants to avoid giving the Corinthians the idea that others may judge them. He wants everyone correctly to examine his or her own life.

Verse 31 is actually a conditional sentence that conveys a contrary-to-fact meaning. Paul is saying that if we subject ourselves to thorough self-examination (which we are not now doing), we would not be judged (but we are receiving God's judgment). With the first person plural, Paul includes himself even though the conditional sentence clearly relates to the Corinthians alone. They are at fault; nevertheless God wants them to repent and change their attitude.

d. "When we are judged, we are disciplined by the Lord." Paul himself interprets for us the meaning of the verb *judged*. He says not that God punishes us but that he disciplines us. God punished his Son who bore our sins on the cross and with his death removed them. If God should punish us, Christ would not have borne all our sins. But God will not punish both Christ and us. God disciplines us, so that we may turn to him in full penitence. By repenting of our sinful ways, we experience God's forgiveness, grace, mercy, and love (II Cor. 7:10). We should understand that afflictions are God's instruments to bring us closer to him. He chastises us because we are his children (compare I Peter 4:17; Heb. 12:5–7, 10). Often sickness lingers because sin persists—in his epistle James advises the sinner to confess his sin so that he may be healed (5:16a).

e. "So that we may not be condemned with the world." In two preceding verses (vv. 27, 29), Paul stated that anyone who eats and drinks without discerning the difference between love feasts and Communion is under judgment. But judgment is not the same as condemnation; the one is a timely warning, the other an irrevocable sentence. If we fail to heed God's warning which he graciously sends us, we shall face damnation and perish with the world of hardened unbelievers. God does not delight in the death of either the righteous who willfully go astray or the wicked. Rather, God urges everyone to repent and, as a result, live (Ezek. 18:32).

33. Therefore, my brothers, when you come together to eat, wait for one another. 34a. If anyone is hungry, let him eat at home that you may not encounter judgment.

With the adverb *therefore*, Paul now summarizes his discourse on the Lord's Supper. He addresses his readers once more with the tender greeting *my brothers*, which includes the sisters (see 1:11; 14:39; 15:58). With this greeting, he conveys both his love and concern. As a faithful pastor, he provides practical advice that will help them to correct the practices at their love feasts and the celebration of Communion.

The counsel Paul gives is to convert thoughts and words into deeds. If the Corinthians duly examine themselves with respect to their conduct at communal gatherings and then repent, they ought to make visible amends at future meetings. When they come together for their common meal to nourish their physical bodies and for the Lord's Supper, they ought to exercise patience and wait for one another. The Greek verb *ekdechomai* (I wait for) occurs six times in the New Testament and always has the same meaning.[98] It describes Paul waiting for Silas and Timothy in Athens and the farmer patiently waiting for the spring and autumn rains. It supports the intent of verse 21, where Paul decries the lack of patience on the part of those Corinthians who failed to wait for fellow Christians.[99] Here he wants them to express genuine love for one another: the rich for the poor, and the poor for the rich.

When they come together for Communion, the Corinthians must realize that the intent is to receive spiritual rather than physical nourishment. Paul exhorts them to differentiate between spiritual and physical needs. He says, "If anyone is hungry, let him eat at home." With the word *anyone*, he addresses all the members of the Corinthian church, both the rich and the poor. And he implies a clear separation of the love feasts and the celebration of the Lord's Supper. He tells the Corinthians to eat and drink at home and thus reinforces his earlier remark about their private homes (v. 22). They ought to know that partaking of the bread and the cup at Communion is meant to satisfy not physical hunger but a spiritual desire for fellowship with Christ and his people. If the Corinthians correctly make this distinction, Paul says they will not encounter God's judgment.

34b. And the rest of the things I will arrange when I come.

In this chapter, Paul has discussed proper conduct for the worshiper at both the worship services and the observance of Communion. These subjects probably were not mentioned in the letter Paul had received, but he was fully aware of the situation in Corinth. He saw the advantage of giving his instructions in writing to have them recorded for the Corinthian community and all the churches.

---

98. Acts 17:16; I Cor. 11:33; 16:11; Heb. 10:13; 11:10; James 5:7; see also the variant reading of John 5:3.

99. Bruce W. Winter interprets the Greek verb *ekdechomai* as "'receive one another' in the sense of sharing [food]." See "The Lord's Supper," pp. 79–80. Consult also Fee, *First Corinthians*, pp. 567–69.

We have no details on what Paul means with the phrase *the rest of the things*. We assume that the phrase refers to other irregularities in the Corinthian church, but these need not be disclosed. These can wait until he arrives. Then he will give further instructions when he meets them face to face (compare II John 12; III John 13–14). After visiting the churches in Macedonia, Paul hopes to come to Corinth and spend the winter there (16:5–8).

Greek Words, Phrases, and Constructions in 11:27–34

Verse 27

ὥστε—this is an inferential particle that introduces an independent clause (followed by the indicative) or introduces a clause with an imperative (see v. 33). In both instances it means "therefore."

ἀναξίως—this adverb occurs only here in the New Testament. It consists of the particle ἀ (un) and the adverb ἀξίως (worthily) and signifies "in an unworthy or careless manner."

Verse 28

Note that all the verbs in this verse are in the present tense of the imperative mood—*to examine, to eat*, and *to drink*—to convey repeated and habitual action.

ἄνθρωπος—this is the generic use of the term *man*, which Paul purposely places between the verb *to examine* and the reflexive pronoun *himself* for the sake of emphasis.

Verse 29

κρίμα—here is the first word of an extended family of the root κρι- (separate), sprinkled throughout verses 29–34; each one has its own nuance: κρίμα, διακρίνων, διεκρίνομεν, ἐκρινόμεθα, κρινόμενοι, κατακριθῶμεν.[100] The noun κρίμα, also in verse 34, means "judgment" in the sense of verdict.

ἑαυτῷ—in the context of this verse, the reflexive pronoun ("for himself") is a dative of disadvantage.

διακρίνων—the present active participle denotes condition: "if he is not discerning."

Verses 33–34

ὥστε—an inferential particle that is similar to οὖν (therefore). See verse 27.

εἴ τις πεινᾷ—the better manuscripts lack the postpositive conjunction δέ of the Majority Text. The particle εἰ (if) denotes a fact expressed with the indefinite pronoun *anyone* and the present indicative of the verb *to be hungry*.

ὡς ἄν—followed by the aorist subjunctive ἔλθω (I come), this combination is equivalent to ὅταν (whenever) and the subjunctive.[101]

διατάξομαι—"I will arrange." This verb in the future middle reveals that Paul is thinking not of external but of doctrinal matters.

---

100. Blass and Debrunner, *Greek Grammar*, #488.1b.
101. Ibid., #455.2.

Summary of Chapter 11

After praising the Corinthians for remembering him and his teachings, Paul discusses the authority of Christ, man, and God. From this discussion he draws some principles about proper conduct in worship. He mentions the impropriety of a man praying and prophesying with covered head and a woman with uncovered head. He teaches that a woman should have her head covered. Otherwise she should have her hair cut off, which would be a disgrace to her. He also teaches that man is the glory of God and woman is the glory of man. Woman is taken from man and man is born from woman, but all things are from God. Long hair is a disgrace to a man but it is a woman's glory.

Paul does not praise the Corinthians for their meetings, which are detrimental rather than beneficial. He remarks that when they come together for the Lord's Supper, some remain hungry but others are drunk. Their humiliation of the poor and deviation from the norms are blots on the church of God. Paul, therefore, teaches them the institution of Communion as he received it from the Lord. He instructs them to regularly eat the bread and drink the cup as a proclamation of the Lord's death, in expectation of his return.

Indifferent observance of Communion is a sin against the Lord himself. Paul urges the Corinthians to examine themselves before they eat and drink from the Lord's table. Lack of self-examination results in divine judgment, as is witnessed by sickness and death among the Corinthians. Self-examination that leads to repentance precludes God's judgment.

Paul concludes his discourse with an admonition to satisfy hunger pangs at home, so that the Lord's Supper can be observed properly. He informs his readers that he will give further instructions when he comes to visit them.

12

Worship, *part 2*

(12:1–31)

Outline (continued)

12 1 Now concerning the spiritual gifts, brothers, I do not want you to be ignorant. 2 You know that when you were Gentiles, you were led astray to the mute idols, in whatever way you were led. 3 Therefore, I make known to you that no one speaking by the Spirit of God says, "Jesus is cursed," and no one is able to say, "Jesus is Lord," except by the Holy Spirit.

4 There are varieties of gifts, but the same Spirit. 5 And there are varieties of ministries, but the same Lord. 6 And there are varieties of activities, but the same God is working all things in all [people]. 7 But to each one is given the manifestation of the Spirit for the common good. 8 To the one is given a word of wisdom through the Spirit and to another a word of knowledge according to the same Spirit. 9 To another is given faith by the same Spirit and to another gifts of healing by the one Spirit. 10 And to another are given activities that elicit miracles, to another prophecy, and to another distinguishing of spirits, to another different kinds of tongues, to another interpretation of tongues. 11 The one and the same Spirit works all these things, apportioning them to each one individually as he desires.

12 For as the body is one and has many members, and all the members of the body, though they are many, are one body, thus also is Christ. 13 For indeed by one Spirit all of us were baptized into one body, whether Jews or Greeks, whether slaves or free, and all were made to drink of one Spirit.

14 For indeed the body is not one member but many. 15 If the foot should say, "Because I am not a hand, I am not of the body," for this reason it ceases not to belong to the body. 16 And if the ear should say, "Because I am not an eye, I am not of the body," for this reason it ceases not to belong to the body. 17 If the whole body were an eye, where would the hearing be? If the whole body were hearing, where would the sense of smell be? 18 But now God has placed the members, each one of them, in the body just as he desired. 19 And if everything were one member, where would the body be? 20 But now there are many members but one body.

21 The eye is not able to say to the hand, "I have no need of you." Or again, the head to the feet, "I have no need of you." 22 By contrast, the members of the body that appear to be weaker are even more indispensable. 23 And whatever members of the body we deem less honorable, on these we place greater honor, and our unpresentable parts are treated with greater modesty. 24 And our respectable parts have no need of this. However, God has combined the members of the body by giving greater honor to those that lack it, 25 that there may be no division in the body but that the members may have the same care for one another. 26 And if one member suffers, all the members suffer with it. If one member is honored, all the members rejoice with it.

27 You are the body of Christ and individually members of it. 28 And God has appointed in the church, first apostles, next prophets, third teachers, then miracles, then gifts of healing, helpful deeds, administrations, kinds of tongues. 29 Are all apostles? Are all prophets? Are all teachers? Are all [workers of] miracles? 30 Do all have gifts of healing? Do all speak in tongues? Do all interpret? 31 But eagerly desire the greater gifts.

And I will show you an even more excellent way.

3. Spiritual Gifts
12:1–31

a. The Holy Spirit
12:1–11

Paul moves from a discussion on the proper celebration of the Lord's Supper to other aspects of worship. Chief among them is the matter of spiritual gifts that the church members have received for the benefit of the Christian community. The Holy Spirit has endowed these members with gifts that enhance and promote the life of the church. He works through individual believers and uses them as instruments to fulfill God's purpose.

The first segment of this chapter reveals more about the work of the Holy Spirit than does any other passage in I Corinthians.[1] Since the explicit references to the Holy Spirit in an earlier chapter (2:4–14), Paul has not yet broached the subject of the Spirit's gifts. Now he teaches the doctrine of the Trinity in which the Holy Spirit fills the prominent role of endowing believers with extraordinary gifts.

(1) The Christian's Confession
12:1–3

1. Now concerning the spiritual gifts, brothers, I do not want you to be ignorant.

a. "Now concerning." We immediately recognize these introductory words. They often signal Paul's response to issues raised in the letter he had received from the Corinthian church. In their epistle, the people had raised a number of issues, among them marriage and virgins (7:1, 25), food offered to idols (8:1), spiritual gifts (12:1), and the collection for God's people (16:1).

Paul fails to give us a quotation from this letter, as he did at earlier occasions (7:1; 8:1), so we have no knowledge of the precise wording in the Corinthian request for information. All we know is that the Corinthians wanted him to comment on spiritual gifts. He now discusses the gifts which the Spirit has given to the members of the congregation.

b. "The spiritual gifts, brothers." In this epistle, Paul often writes the term *brothers* when he discusses a sensitive topic with the Corinthians (for instance, 1:10). This address implicitly includes the female members of the Christian community, so that Paul speaks to the entire church.

The topic that Paul expounds in this chapter is spiritual gifts. The Greek adjective *pneumatikōn* (spiritual) appears alone in the original text, so that we are compelled to add a word. We complete the thought not with the noun referring to persons (2:15; 3:1; 14:37), which some scholars prefer,[2] but with the word *gifts* (compare 14:1). The Holy Spirit is the giver of these gifts, so that the translation

---

1. The Greek word *pneuma* appears twelve times in eight verses: 12:3 [twice], 4, 7, 8 [twice], 9 [twice], 10, 11, 13 [twice].

2. Among others, see F. F. Bruce, *1 and 2 Corinthians*, New Century Bible series (London: Oliphants, 1971), p. 116.

gifts from the Holy Spirit[3] is not only plausible but attractive. The Holy Spirit continues to provide believers with these gifts.

In a previous passage (see 1:7), Paul used a synonym for spiritual gifts when he wrote the Greek term *charisma* (gift; that is, gift of grace). We have the English derivative *charisma*, which refers to personal leadership ability. But in the present chapter the word *charisma* points to the activities of the Holy Spirit. This is evident when Paul enumerates, among others, the gifts of wisdom, knowledge, healing, working of miracles, prophecy, speaking in tongues and interpreting them (vv. 4, 9, 28, 30, 31).

c. "I do not want you to be ignorant." This clause recurs in Paul's epistles.[4] For this verse, we must ask the question, "Ignorant of what?" and supply the answer. Paul does not want the Corinthians to be ignorant of the proper use of spiritual gifts. Instead of using them for the benefit of fellow believers, some Corinthians displayed these gifts as badges of superiority. Of these gifts, they considered the gift of speaking in tongues unique and of great importance.[5] In the next three chapters (12–14), Paul shows the Corinthians how to evaluate and use spiritual gifts.

2. You know that when you were Gentiles, you were led astray to the mute idols, in whatever way you were led.

a. *Grammar.* We begin with three grammatical observations. First, the sentence in the Greek is syntactically incomplete because the verb *were* is missing in the second clause. This clause literally reads, "you being led astray." But by supplying the verb *were*, we achieve correct syntax. Next, for the clause *when you were Gentiles*, some scholars conjecture that the Greek word *hote* (when) should be *pote* (once): "once you were Gentiles." Conjectures, however, are permissible only when all acceptable explanations fail. And that is not the case here, for there is no available textual evidence to support the conjecture. Last, another translation for the clause *in whatever way you were led* is "as impulse drove you" (NAB; see *Moffatt*). But this reading does not merit favor, because it is admittedly quite free, and it hardly improves our understanding of the text.

b. *Intent.* "You know that when you were Gentiles." How does this verse follow in sequence? The answer lies in the verb *to know*. Paul states that he does not want the readers to be ignorant (v. 1). Then he asserts that they know their religious past (v. 2). And finally he declares that he makes known to them how to profess that Jesus is Lord (v. 3).

The term *Gentiles* relates to the preconversion days of those church members who had left paganism. Paul refers to their former days as he now addresses them as Gentile Christians. He had directed his earlier discourses to both Jewish and Gentile believers, but here he speaks to those Christians who formerly were pagans and worshiped idols.

---

3. GNB; see also NEB, REB, NJB.

4. Rom. 1:13; 11:25; I Cor. 10:1; 12:1; II Cor. 1:8; I Thess. 4:13.

5. Compare John C. Hurd, Jr., *The Origin of I Corinthians* (Macon, Ga.: Mercer University Press, 1983), pp. 71–72.

"You were led astray to the mute idols." Is it possible that Paul has in mind the excesses that marked pagan religious festivals of that time? Were the Corinthians led astray by a demon who caused them to experience ecstatic frenzies?[6] Scholars point out that on the basis of vocabulary and context the evidence for religious frenzies is lacking in this passage.[7] The verb *to lead astray* relates more to movement than to religious ecstasy. Nonetheless, the passive form of this verb calls for an implied agent. In opposition to the Holy Spirit, the agent is Satan or one of his representatives (compare 10:20–21).

Paul uses the Hebraic term *mute idols* (Ps. 115:5; Hab. 2:18–19; III Macc. 4:16). He intimates not merely that icons made of wood, stone, or metal are voiceless but that the gods whom they represent have nothing to say.

"In whatever way you were led." The Greek verb *led* in the imperfect tense reveals repeated occurrences. From time to time, pagans went to their temples and were being led there by an evil power. These former pagans were stumbling around in darkness. They remained in the grip of the devil until they were set free by God's Spirit and confessed Jesus as their Lord.

3. Therefore, I make known to you that no one speaking by the Spirit of God says, "Jesus is cursed," and no one is able to say, "Jesus is Lord," except by the Holy Spirit.

a. "Therefore, I make known to you." Some scholars consider verses 2 and 3 and their content as an aside and place them in parentheses.[8] But the force of the conclusive adverb *therefore* goes back to verse 2 and the entire preceding passage (vv. 1–2). If we understand the present verse (v. 3) as a conclusive statement, then we see that Paul describes the spiritual condition of the Gentile Christians in Corinth. This does not mean that we have an explanation for this verse that is completely satisfactory. It means that in the Corinthian context we are able to separate the past (v. 2) from the present (v. 3). Paul is now speaking about the spiritual life of the believers in Corinth. He says that he is going to make something known to them (compare 15:1; II Cor. 8:1; Gal. 1:1).

b. "No one speaking by the Spirit of God says, 'Jesus is cursed.'" Paul balances this assertion with the statement, "And no one is able to say, 'Jesus is Lord,' except by the Holy Spirit." If Paul had given only the second declaration, we would not have to face difficulties. But because he has written both, the question is whether Paul describes actual occurrences of cursing Jesus within the local Christian community.

---

6. Bruce, *1 and 2 Corinthians*, p. 117; compare H. Wayne House, "Tongues and the Mystery Religions of Corinth," *BS* 140 (1983): 134–50.

7. Wayne A. Grudem, *The Gift of Prophecy in 1 Corinthians* (Washington, D.C.: University Press of America, 1982), pp. 162–64. See also D. A. Carson, *Showing the Spirit: A Theological Exposition of 1 Corinthians 12–14* (Grand Rapids: Baker, 1987), pp. 25–26; Karl Maly, "1 Kor 12:1–3, eine Regel zur Unterscheidung der Geister?" *BibZ* 10 (1966): 82–95; André Mehat, "L'Enseignement sur 'les Choses de l'Esprit' (1 Corinthiens 12, 1–3)," *RevHistPhilRel* 63 (1983): 395–415.

8. See the translation of *Moffatt*.

Who are the people that place a curse on Jesus? The answers to this question are numerous and varied. I will list those that are most commonly given:

1. *Jewish leaders.* Those who curse Jesus are the Jews who, knowing that he died on a cross, applied the Scriptures to the crucified Christ: "Anyone who is hung on a tree is under God's curse" (Deut. 21:23). By hanging Jesus on a cross, the Jewish people had handed him over to God and expected that the curse would forever annihilate him. But when the Christians proclaimed Jesus' name, the Jews continued to call forth a divine curse on Jesus.

In reaction to the Christian witness, Jewish leaders attempted to keep their kinsmen from becoming converts to Christianity. Thus, in their local synagogues they instructed the Jewish people to curse Jesus. Anyone associated with a Christian confessing Jesus as Lord was considered to be a sinner. In times of persecution, Christians were compelled to renounce Jesus as Lord and reject him as Savior by cursing him.[9] But why would Paul indirectly allude to leaders in Jewish synagogues? And why would he suddenly address Christians of Jewish descent, when he is instructing believers who at one time had been pagans (v. 2)?

2. *Gnostic teachers.* Other scholars have suggested that Paul is opposing Gnostic teachers who taught a dualism of the material and the spiritual.[10] The physical body of Jesus belonging to the material world had to be cursed; only the spiritual Christ was confessed as the exalted Lord. This proposal assumes that Gnosticism was firmly rooted in the Christian community of Corinth during the middle of the first century. But Paul's epistles to the Corinthians hardly support the suggestion that Gnosticism was rampant in Corinth. This assumption would gain credibility if it applied to events near the end of that century, not in Paul's day. Also, the Gnostics would ascribe lordship not to Jesus but only to Christ.

3. *Paul's formulation.* Another suggestion is that with the phrase *Jesus is cursed* Paul formulates a counterpart to the genuine confession *Jesus is Lord.* The objection to this suggestion is that in the syntax of the present verse (v. 3) Paul uses the declarative mood and describes not probability but reality.

4. *Holy Spirit.* A final suggestion is that Paul wishes to make known the meaning of the concept *by the Holy Spirit,* which occurs twice, once in relation with cursing Jesus and the other with respect to confessing him as Lord. The person, whether Jew or Gentile, who blasphemes Jesus' name will not be uttering his curse through God's Spirit. The person, whether Jew or Gentile, who confesses Jesus' lordship is filled with the Holy Spirit.[11] In view of Paul's emphasis on the Spirit, we are confident that he is not speaking about a specific location or a particular

---

9. J. D. M. Derrett, "Cursing Jesus (1 Cor. XII.3): The Jews as Religious 'Persecutors,'" *NTS* 21 (1974–75): 544–54. Jouette M. Bassler contends that Paul recalls his own past history of cursing Jesus. "1 Cor. 12:3—Curse and Confession in Context," *JBL* 101 (1982): 415–18.

10. Walter Schmithals, *Gnosticism in Corinth: An Investigation of the Letters to the Corinthians,* trans. John E. Steely (New York: Abingdon, 1971), pp. 124–30; Norbert Brox, "Anathema Iēsous (1 Kor 12,3)," *BibZ* 12 (1968): 103–11.

11. Refer to Carson, *Showing the Spirit,* p. 31. Consult also Traugott Holtz, "Das Kennzeichen des Geistes (I Kor xii.1–3)," *NTS* 18 (1972): 365–76.

group of people. He is stressing the absence or the presence of the Holy Spirit by which people speak about Jesus. For that reason, we favor this fourth explanation.

c. "And no one is able to say, 'Jesus is Lord,' except by the Holy Spirit." Paul teaches that the believer in whom God's Spirit dwells joyfully confesses his loyalty to Jesus by acknowledging him as Lord.

The confession *Jesus is Lord* is one of the oldest creeds, or perhaps *the* oldest creed, in Christendom (compare John 13:13; Phil. 2:11). Jews who converted to Christianity on the day of Pentecost believed that God made Jesus both Lord and Christ (Acts 2:36). Converted Gentiles forsook their pagan past and pledged allegiance to Jesus as their Lord and Savior (Acts 16:31; see also Rom. 10:9). Christians of both Jewish and Gentile origin accepted Jesus as ruler of the world, as King of kings and Lord of lords (I Tim. 6:15; Rev. 1:5; 17:14; 19:16).

Some people may call Jesus Lord and even perform valuable tasks in his service. But if they are not filled with God's Spirit and therefore fail to do the Father's will, Jesus dismisses them by saying: "'I never knew you. Away from me, you evildoers'" (Matt. 7:23). Jesus exercises his sovereign will in this world. He recognizes only those people who, led by the Holy Spirit, acknowledge his true divinity and obediently bow to his authority.

Greek Words, Phrases, and Constructions in 12:1–3

Verse 1

περί—this preposition is used in an absolute sense: "as for" or "now about."[12]

δέ—although the particle can mean either "but," "and," or "now," the translation *now* is preferred.

τῶν πνευματικῶν—the adjective with the definite article can be interpreted either in the masculine gender, "the spiritual men," or the neuter gender, "the spiritual matters." This verse does not depend on the preceding chapter, so that it should be regarded as a heading for a different subject. In a heading, the neuter serves a better purpose than the masculine.

Verse 2

ἦτε . . . ἀπαγόμενοι—the context demands that we add the second person plural ἦτε (you were) in the imperfect tense with the present passive participle (led astray) to form a periphrastic construction.

ὡς ἂν ἤγεσθε—the imperfect indicative verb of ἄγω (I lead) with the particle ἂν signifies repetition: "as you would be led [from day to day]."[13]

Verse 3

λαλῶν—present participle denoting activity of speaking, and λέγει, the present indic-

---

12. C. F. D. Moule, *An Idiom-Book of New Testament Greek*, 2d ed. (Cambridge: Cambridge University Press, 1960), p. 63.

13. A. T. Robertson, *A Grammar of the Greek New Testament in the Light of Historical Research* (Nashville: Broadman, 1934), p. 974; Robert Hanna, *A Grammatical Aid to the Greek New Testament* (Grand Rapids: Baker, 1983), p. 304.

ative denoting the content of that which is spoken. See also the synonym presented in the form of the aorist infinitive εἰπεῖν (to say).

ἀνάθεμα Ἰησοῦς—the verb *to be* is lacking and when supplied can be in either the subjunctive or the indicative ("let Jesus be cursed," or "Jesus is cursed"). The indicative is favored because of the parallelism of the confession *Jesus is Lord*. The neuter noun ἀνάθεμα derives from the neuter perfect participle τὸ ἀνατεθειμέ νον (that which has been set up). It refers to a votive offering to a deity for the purpose of consecration or damnation. Here the word refers to damnation, with the intention of requesting God to place a curse on Jesus.

κύριος—this word relates to the Hebrew term *Yahweh* and signifies "sovereign ruler."

---

(2) Different but Divinely Derived Gifts
12:4–6

If we understand the first three verses of this chapter to be Paul's introduction to teaching about spiritual gifts and the Holy Spirit, then the following paragraph is the beginning of a detailed elaboration of this theme. Paul notes the varieties of gifts and asserts that they originated from the Triune God: the Holy Spirit, the Lord Jesus Christ, and God the Father. These gifts are diverse, and God is the giver of every one of them.

4. There are varieties of gifts, but the same Spirit. 5. And there are varieties of ministries, but the same Lord. 6. And there are varieties of activities, but the same God is working all things in all [people].

If we momentarily suspend the repetition of the expressions *there are varieties of* and *but the same* in order to focus attention on the nouns in these verses, we see the following arrangement:

> There are varieties of *gifts*,
> > *ministries*,
> > *activities*,
> but the same [Holy] *Spirit*,
> > *Lord* [Jesus],
> > *God* [the Father]
> > is working all things
> > in all [people].

We can then make three pairings: gifts and Spirit, ministries and Lord, activities and God; all things and all people together form the conclusion. To put it differently, with respect to the Spirit there are the varieties of gifts; in relation to the Lord, those gifts are ministries; and with reference to God, they are activities. Now let us look at the passage verse by verse.

a. "There are varieties of gifts, but the same Spirit." The term *varieties* is in the plural to reveal the comprehensive spread of God's grace to his people. It suggests that these gifts were different in function and widely distributed among the Christian community, so that every believer has some gift or gifts but never all of them (see I Peter 4:10). The word *varieties* signifies that the church of

Christ reveals unity in diversity. Think, for example, of a well-shaped tree. That tree produces a multitude of leaves, yet no two leaves are alike. Similarly, the church reflects unity in its totality but not uniformity in its parts. The church has been blessed with varieties of gifts that reflect diversity and contribute to unity.

What are these gifts? In the introductory verse (v. 1), Paul mentioned *pneumatikōn* (spiritual gifts), but now writes *charismata* (gifts of grace). In this chapter, Paul notes examples of nine gifts: wisdom, knowledge, prophecy, faith, healings, miracles, spiritual discernment, speaking in tongues, interpretation of tongues (vv. 8–10, 28; compare Rom. 12:6–8). Yet Paul does not intend to be exhaustive and complete. In fact, the number of gifts that are noted in New Testament books totals about twenty.[14]

The clause *there are varieties of gifts* is adjoined to the clause *but the same Spirit.* Notice that Paul does not say *of the same Spirit* and thus imply that the Spirit is the only one who gives these gifts. The fact is that all three persons in the Trinity (Father, Son, and Holy Spirit) present gifts to God's people (e.g., see Eph. 4:8). Paul uses the adversative *but* in the second clause of this verse (v. 4) to contrast the variety of gifts and the sameness of the Spirit. The Spirit enables the members of Christ's church to receive, develop, and apply these gifts in unity. Whatever the gift may be, the same Spirit is at work in the life of the believer. Because the Holy Spirit stands behind every gift distributed to the people, there ought not to be any pride or division among the Corinthians. The Spirit does not initiate separation. Rather, he promotes unity.

b. "And there are varieties of ministries, but the same Lord." In this verse (v. 5), Paul teaches that the Lord Jesus Christ is responsible for the diversity of spiritual ministries in the Christian community. The Greek word *diakoniōn* actually means services that are performed within the context of the church. Derivatives in the English language, diaconate and deacon, breathe the spirit of service to the body of Christ. The services rendered are without limit. To mention only three ministries from an incalculable multitude: one person preaches the morning or evening sermon, another teaches a Sunday school class, and still another sings in the choir. Christ equips each person to serve him in worship, outreach, teaching, counseling, encouraging, administration, and governing—to say no more.

No one should boast of having received a greater gift or a higher position in the church than other members, because all gifts and positions derive from the Lord. On the night of his arrest, Jesus washed the feet of his disciples and said, "I have set you an example that you should do as I have done for you. I tell you the truth, no servant is greater than his master, nor is a messenger greater than the one who sent him" (John 13:15–16). Service in church and community ought to be rendered in the spirit of Jesus, who endows and empowers his people with tal-

---

14. Ralph P. Martin, *The Spirit and the Congregation: Studies in 1 Corinthians 12–15* (Grand Rapids: Eerdmans, 1984), p. 11. See Klaas Runia, "The 'Gifts of the Spirit'" *RTR* 29 (1970): 82–94.

ents and abilities. Jesus is the same for every believer and shows no favoritism. He fully acknowledges the service of each individual, whatever it may be, when it is humbly performed for him (Matt. 25:34–40).

c. "And there are varieties of activities." What are these varieties of activities? The Greek word *energēmata*, which I translate "activities," occurs twice in the New Testament (vv. 6 and 10). In verse 6, the word is closely connected with the concept *gifts*, while in verse 10 it signifies miraculous powers. The word, which has derivatives in English (energy, energetic, and energize), means action as the result of God's energizing power. To illustrate, when a pastor preaches on a given Sunday he may have a well-prepared sermon. But he can communicate effectively only when God grants him the power to preach. Completely dependent on his Sender for strength, he realizes that he serves as God's mouthpiece during the worship service.

d. "But the same God is working all things in all [people]." God sends forth his people into countless situations to be his servants. God's kingdom is without borders and his citizens dwell wherever he has placed them. In his service, they speak at his command whenever he tells them to do so. God places his people in every sector and segment of society, so that they make known his truth everywhere. He wants his people to minister to all hurting people—men, women, and children. He gives them his power to heal a broken world that needs help physically, emotionally, spiritually, and materially.

Practical Considerations in 12:4–6

The variety of gifts and the number of talents within the Christian community are astounding indeed. For example, some people have the gifts of public speaking, singing or playing musical instruments, teaching, counseling, developing creative art, or composing poetry or music. In an unobtrusive way, Christians often contribute greatly to the well-being of society. Because of their talents and skills, they are able to give leadership in many areas of public and private life.

Jesus has placed his people at strategic positions throughout the world. He calls them to use their talents for the coming of his kingdom and the extension of his church. He desires that his people use their gifts for the common good of humanity. Through this worldwide ministry of his servants, Jesus makes known his name to all nations, races, and peoples, in all the languages of the world. The name that is known more than any other name in all the world is Jesus.

God's people should never use their gifts and talents for personal interests and satisfaction, even though the recipients themselves may greatly benefit from them. However, they blatantly sin against God by their disobedience, if they allow such selfishness ever to occur. God asks his servants to go forth in his name and serve him wherever he places them. Many times this involves leaving behind relatives, friends, and possessions. God's promise to them is that he will give them a hundred times as much in this life and eternal life as their inheritance (Matt. 19:29).

---

(3) Gifts for the Common Good
12:7–11

7. But to each one is given the manifestation of the Spirit for the common good.

Too often, ministers of the gospel, evangelists, and missionaries are considered to be the only recipients of special gifts. Too often, a distinction is made between sacred and secular occupations. Kingdom service is frequently understood to be performed by those people who have been ordained to serve the Lord in special ministries.

Paul writes that the manifestation of the Spirit is given to each believer. That is, the Holy Spirit dwells in every believer (6:19) and thus makes his presence known with some indication of gifts. In the life of every Christian, the Holy Spirit reveals himself in one way or another. This does not mean that every believer is limited to one gift. For instance, Paul himself had received the gifts of continence and of speaking in tongues (7:7; 14:18).

The phrase *the manifestation of the Spirit* can be either objective or subjective. In an objective sense, it signifies an action that reveals the presence of the Spirit. Subjectively it means an action which the Spirit generates. Perhaps we should accept the objective interpretation of this phrase in view of the passive verb *is given*, which implies that God is the one who gives the various gifts.[15]

The evidence of the Spirit's presence in the life of the believer serves the common good of the entire community. The Spirit uses the gifts of the individual Christian for the edification of the church (compare Eph. 4:12), a theme that Paul later applies in his discussion about the use of speaking in tongues (14:4). The intent here is to promote the common good and to prohibit anyone from using a gift for personal profit. Paul does not rule out that the gift itself may benefit the individual,[16] but God confers his gifts on his people so that all may be edified (14:26).

8. To the one is given a word of wisdom through the Spirit and to another a word of knowledge according to the same Spirit.

How does the Holy Spirit manifest himself? In the gifts that God bestows on his people. Paul lists a total of nine representative gifts (vv. 8–10), a list that is not meant to be exhaustive. Whether he intended to categorize them is difficult to ascertain. Scholars attempt to make a distinction between gifts that are either temporal or permanent, verbal or nonverbal, and important or less important. An attractive threefold division of these gifts follows:

1. Pedagogical: wisdom and knowledge
2. Supernatural: faith, healings, miracles

---

15. Gordon D. Fee, *The First Epistle to the Corinthians*, New International Commentary on the New Testament series (Grand Rapids: Eerdmans, 1987), p. 589 n. 30. See also John Calvin, *The First Epistle of Paul the Apostle to the Corinthians*, Calvin's Commentaries series, trans. John W. Fraser (reprint ed.; Grand Rapids: Eerdmans, 1976), p. 261.

16. Carson, *Showing the Spirit*, p. 35.

3. Communicative: prophecy, spirit discernment, tongues, interpretation of tongues[17]

Paul uses a variety of words in the Greek text of verses 8–10. Apparently he is interested only in stylistic diversity, not in making distinctions. For instance, referring to the Spirit he employs the prepositions *through, according to,* and *by* merely for the sake of change.

In addition, here are nine gifts, but the only one that is specifically called a gift is the one of healing (v. 9). Indeed, we assume that Paul exercises authorial freedom in the choice of vocabulary.

a. "To the one is given a word of wisdom through the Spirit." Wisdom is the first of the two pedagogical gifts. God who gives this gift of wisdom conveys its content through the agency of the Holy Spirit. A literal translation of the Greek is "word of wisdom"; other translators render it "utterance of wisdom" (e.g., NRSV, *Cassirer*). The gift is the ability to speak divine wisdom which believers receive through the Holy Spirit (compare 2:6–7). Divine wisdom is contrasted with human wisdom (1:17, 20, 25).

Isaiah's prophecy that the Spirit of wisdom would rest on the Messiah (11:2) was fulfilled in Jesus, who increased in wisdom (Luke 2:52). Jesus' promise to give divine wisdom to his disciples was exemplified in the case of Stephen, who was filled with wisdom and the Spirit (Acts 6:10). And last, James tells his readers that if anyone lacks wisdom he or she should ask God, who gives generously without finding fault (James 1:5). Believers, then, may ask in faith for wisdom and God will honor their requests.

b. "And to another a word of knowledge according to the same Spirit." Knowledge, the second pedagogical gift, "is essentially the intimate personal knowledge of God which depends, not upon intellect but on love, and on God's knowledge of or acquaintance with . . . man."[18] The term denotes affinity and signifies a personal relationship that exists between God and the redeemed person in Christ. This knowledge, given by God through his Spirit, must be put to use within the Christian community for the benefit of all the members. It comes to expression in knowing, understanding, and explaining to his people God's revelation in the Scriptures and in creation.

Wisdom and knowledge overlap,[19] and in this verse Paul places them together and alludes to an earlier discussion on these two themes (2:6–16). Through-

---

17. Refer to William Baird, *The Corinthian Church, A Biblical Approach to Urban Culture* (New York: Abingdon, 1964), p. 139. R. C. H. Lenski presents similar categories: intellect, faith, and tongues. See his *Interpretation of St. Paul's First and Second Epistle to the Corinthians* (1935; Columbus: Wartburg, 1946), p. 499.

18. R. St. John Parry, *The First Epistle of Paul the Apostle to the Corinthians*, Cambridge Greek Testament for Schools and Colleges (Cambridge: Cambridge University Press, 1937), p. 180.

19. Consult Carson, *Showing the Spirit*, p. 8.

out I Corinthians Paul repeatedly uses the expression *knowledge*,[20] though the
meaning varies in context.

**9. To another is given faith by the same Spirit and to another gifts of healing
by the one Spirit.**

a. "To another is given faith by the same Spirit." The third gift is faith. Together with miracles and healings, it is part of the category of supernatural gifts.
Because every true believer has faith in Jesus Christ, Paul is not thinking of saving faith. He has in mind complete and unshakable trust that God will perform
miracles.

Jesus told his disciples that faith as small as a mustard seed can move mountains (Matt. 17:20; I Cor. 13:2). The apostles demonstrated that faith in post-Pen-
tecost times. For instance, Peter and John courageously opposed the members of
the Sanhedrin, preached the gospel, and healed a cripple in the name of Jesus
(Acts 3:1–4:2). Paul accepted Jesus' word to testify for him in Rome (Acts 23:11).
During the storm on the Mediterranean Sea, when all aboard the ship despaired
of their lives and gave up hope, Paul's faith wavered not. He encouraged the
crew and passengers by saying that he trusted in God; everyone would be safe
and land on some island (Acts 27:23–26, 34).

Countless believers have demonstrated their trust in God and have seen their
faith rewarded in miraculous ways. The writer of Hebrews presents a list of Old
Testament heroes of faith (Heb. 11), which has an unwritten counterpart in New
Testament times. This writer overlooks the faith of Elijah, but James mentions
his name and says that he was a man just like us (James 5:17–18). The special gift
of faith, therefore, is not limited to an Old Testament prophet and a New Testament apostle.

b. "And to another gifts of healing by the one Spirit." Faith and the gifts of
healing are closely related. James writes that the prayer offered in faith by the
church elders will make the sick person well (James 5:14–15). When these people claim the words written by James and trust that God will hear and answer
their earnest prayer, the miracle of healing frequently occurs. We make two cau-
tionary remarks, however: first, these elders should not expect that they have received a permanent gift to heal every member of the church who is ill; next, in
spite of fervent prayer offered in faith, God may choose not to restore someone
to normal health and strength.

Not only apostles but also deacons received the ability to perform miracles
of healing in the early years of the Christian church. At that time, all the sick
who came to the apostles were healed (Acts 5:16b). Peter healed people even
by having his shadow fall on them (Acts 5:15–16). Both Stephen and Philip performed miracles of healing in Jerusalem and Samaria (Acts 6:8; 8:6–7). At
Lystra in Asia Minor, Paul healed a man who was crippled in his feet (Acts 14:8–
10). But he himself was afflicted with an ailment which he called a thorn in his
flesh. Although Paul pleaded with the Lord to heal him, Jesus answered him:

---

20. I Cor. 1:5; 8:1, 7, 10, 11; 12:8; 13:2, 8; 14:6.

"My grace is sufficient for you, for my power is made perfect in weakness" (II Cor. 12:9).

Moreover, in his epistles Paul indirectly admits that he lacked the ability to heal either Epaphroditus (Phil. 2:27), Timothy (I Tim. 5:23), or Trophimus (II Tim. 4:20). Why did God not provide Paul the ability to heal his friends? Perhaps we should look for an answer in the purpose of restoring the sick. The New Testament teaches that miracles of healing were generally performed to strengthen faith and broaden the circle of believers. In some circumstances, God might not heal a patient merely to further his or her physical well-being.

Believers today lack the gift of healing that the apostles possessed at the time the New Testament church was in its infancy. Presently when believers pray in faith and wait for a divine answer, they frequently learn that no healing is taking place. God may choose either to heal a person through medicines and physical care or not to heal at all. Those believers who pray for the sick and see restoration through prayer ought not to boast about possessing the gift of healing. Christians have no claim to a permanent gift but must give God all the glory and honor for healing the sick. When there is no immediate answer, believers should continue to pray and not stop asking for help in time of need (Heb. 4:16).[21] Healing happens because God responds to prayer believers offer in faith. Believers acknowledge that God performs the miracle of healing the sick in answer to prayer. They exercise the power of prayer knowing that "the prayer of a righteous man is powerful and effective" (James 5:16b).

10. And to another are given activities that elicit miracles, to another prophecy, and to another distinguishing of spirits, to another different kinds of tongues, to another interpretation of tongues.

a. "And to another are given activities that elicit miracles." This is the third gift in the sequence of supernatural gifts. If the healing of the sick is a temporary gift, so is the gift to perform miracles. Throughout the Scriptures, miracles are supernatural acts that occur contrary to the laws of nature. God temporarily intervenes in nature by performing the miracle. Man is the instrument and God the agent.

The Old Testament teaches that God through Moses performed miracles prior to and during the exodus from Egypt.[22] After the exodus, the sun stood still when the Israelites conquered Canaan (Josh. 10:13). When Elijah and Elisha served God as prophets, many miracles happened.[23] Daniel's three friends walked unharmed out of the blazing furnace, and Daniel himself was safe in the den of lions (Dan. 3:19–27; 6:16–23).

In New Testament times, Jesus' earthly ministry was delineated by numerous miracles which ranged from healings, exorcisms, and raising the dead, to feed-

---

21. Consult Edward N. Gross, *Miracles, Demons, and Spiritual Warfare: An Urgent Call for Discernment* (Grand Rapids: Baker, 1990), pp. 66–67; B. B. Warfield, *Counterfeit Miracles* (reprint ed.; Edinburgh: Banner of Truth, 1986), p. 169.
22. See Exod. 4:1–9; 7:8–13:16; 14:21; 17:1–6; Num. 11:31; 20:2–13.
23. I Kings 17:8–24; 18:30–39; II Kings 2:13–25; 5:8–14.

ing multitudes. More miracles took place during Jesus' ministry than at any other time in biblical history. The supreme miracle of Jesus' resurrection was followed by his ascension. Apart from narrating the occurrences of healings, temporary blindness, exorcism, and raising the dead, in his history of the early church Luke records only the miracles of releasing apostles from imprisonment (Acts 5:19; 12:6–10; 16:22–28).

We make four observations. First, when Paul writes that miracles are among the supernatural gifts (see also vv. 28–29), he does not intimate that every believer receives the power to work miracles. Instead he notes that the gift of miracles was a distinctive mark of an apostle (II Cor. 12:12). Next, the New Testament teaches that in the apostolic church, God worked miracles only to confirm the message of the gospel (Acts 6:8; 8:7; 13:6–12; Heb. 2:4). Third, miracles of healing and miraculous powers seem to overlap now and then in the New Testament,[24] although a distinction should be made between miracles in nature and those that relate to the human body. Last, at the conclusion of the apostolic era, the miracles in nature appear to have come to an end.

b. "To another prophecy." Among the communicative gifts, prophecy is the first, followed by spirit discernment, tongues, and interpretation of tongues. How significant was prophecy in the early Christian church, especially in Corinth? In a preceding chapter (11:4–5), Paul declared that a man who prays and prophesies should not do so with covered head; a woman, however, should have her head covered when she prays and prophesies in the worship service. Paul seems to imply that praying and prophesying go together (I Thess. 5:17–20), but he does not list prayer among the spiritual gifts. In the context of gifts, to be sure, he adds prophecy and speaking in tongues which, in a sense, is prayer (compare 14:13–17). "Prophecy and prayer are not the same, but they belong very closely together."[25]

The current passage indicates not that every believer receives the prophetic gift but that God grants it distributively to his people. God governs that person who occasionally serves as his mouthpiece either to utter predictions (e.g., Agabus, Acts 11:28; 21:11) or more often to interpret God's will to the church (Eph. 4:11).[26] Paul writes that some people in Corinth receive a revelation from God to instruct and encourage the believers (see 14:30). Yet the prophetic utterances of those people, says Paul, are subject to close examination by others (14:32). He reveals that prophets do not stand above the church but are members of that Christian community and are subject to it. The church must examine prophetic utterances in the light of the Scriptures, much as the Bereans carefully examined Paul's teachings to determine if these utterances were true (Acts 17:11). For the prophets and the church, the Scriptures are the standard.

---

24. Refer to Richard B. Gaffin, Jr., *Perspectives on Pentecost: Studies in New Testament Teaching on the Gifts of the Holy Spirit* (Phillipsburg, N.J.: Presbyterian and Reformed, 1979), p. 51.

25. Gerhard Friedrich, *TDNT*, vol. 6, p. 853.

26. Calvin, *I Corinthians*, p. 263; *Institutes of the Christian Religion*, 2 vols., trans. John Allen, 8th American ed. (Grand Rapids: Eerdmans, 1949), vol. 1, 4.3.4.

With the last book of the New Testament, God completed the canon of Scripture (Rev. 22:18–19) and gave no additional canonical revelation. Before the closing of the canon, predictive prophecies had temporal significance (see Acts 11:28; 21:11). The nonpredictive prophets explained and taught the Scriptures as they exhorted the members in the churches.[27]

c. "And to another distinguishing of spirits." This short clause introduces the second gift in the communicative category, and that gift is linked to the preceding gift of prophecy. Paul is saying that some believers have received the gift to distinguish spirits. In another passage (14:29), he asserts that prophetic utterances should be examined and evaluated. But these two passages do not convey the same message and should not be used to explain each other.[28]

The power and influence of spirits can be discerned by their word, deed, and appearance. First, the devil communicates false information. Appearing as an angel of light (II Cor. 11:14), Satan deceived Eve with a message that differed from that which God had given to her husband (Gen. 2:16–17; 3:1, 4–5). The prophet Micaiah revealed to the kings of Israel and Judah that a lying spirit spoke through the mouths of all the prophets in Israel (I Kings 22:21–23; II Chron. 18:20–22). Jesus discerned the voice of Satan when Peter rebuked Jesus for saying that he would die (Matt. 16:23). Paul recognized Bar-Jesus as the son of the devil (Acts 13:10) and the fortune-telling of the slave girl as words spoken by an evil spirit (Acts 16:18). And last, John told his readers to test the spirits because of the message uttered by false prophets (I John 4:1–3).

Next, Satan and his cohorts are able to work miracles. Thus, Satan performs "all kinds of counterfeit miracles, signs and wonders" through the man of lawlessness to deceive the people (II Thess. 2:9–10). Jesus predicts that in the last days great miracles will occur through false Christs and prophets to deceive the elect— if possible (Matt. 24:24). And the beast that comes forth out of the earth speaks like Satan, exercises all authority, performs miracles, causes fire to descend from heaven, and deceives the people dwelling on the earth (Rev. 13:11–14).

Last, the devil enters the Christian community with counterfeit teachers (Jude 4; see also II Peter 2:1–2). When the conduct of some people differs from the norms prescribed in Scripture, those who have the gift of discernment ought to take action to expose the truth from the lie. An analogy is a bank teller, who is able to detect counterfeit money by indelibly pressing on his memory the appearance of genuine currency. When a counterfeit bill or coin surfaces, the teller immediately recognizes it. Similarly, persons with the gift of discernment are filled with the Holy Spirit and instantly recognize a spirit of falsehood. As the tell-

---

27. Consult E. Earle Ellis, *Prophecy and Hermeneutic in Early Christianity: New Testament Essays* (Grand Rapids: Eerdmans, 1978), p. 130; John MacArthur, Jr., *1 Corinthians*, MacArthur New Testament Commentary series (Chicago: Moody, 1984), p. 303.

28. Wayne A. Grudem, *The Gift of Prophecy in the New Testament and Today* (Westchester, Ill.: Crossway, 1988), p. 70; see also his article, "A Response to Gerhard Dautzenberg on 1 Corinthians 12.10," *BibZ* 22 (1978): 253–70.

er uses his gift for the financial well-being of the bank, so the spiritual man uses his for protecting fellow believers.

d. "To another different kinds of tongues, to another interpretation of tongues." The last two gifts of communication, together with that of prophecy, seem to have caused considerable controversy in the Corinthian church. Paul lists the gifts once more in the concluding section of the current chapter (vv. 28, 30) and then devotes an entire chapter (14) to them.

The word *tongue* can mean either a known language (Acts 2:6, 8, 11) or tongue-speech (I Cor. 14:2, 4, 28); in the present epistle, the word can signify either—the meaning depends on the context. In the commercial city of Corinth, where international visitors and temporary residents were numerous and where various languages were spoken, translators were in great demand. On the other hand, the Corinthian congregation also experienced the phenomenon of tongue-speaking. Tongue-speech alludes to an act of worship directed to God; but when other believers were present in Corinth, the message had to be interpreted for the benefit of the audience. To promote reverence in the worship service, Paul demanded that tongue-speech be edifying, intelligible, orderly, and controlled.

Notice that Paul writes the expression *kinds of tongues*. This points to both varieties of known languages (14:9–10) and tongue-speech. He attributes all these tongues and their interpretation to the work of the Holy Spirit (vv. 7, 11). Thus, he indicates that the Spirit gives the interpreter of tongue-speech ability to understand and convey the meaning of the spoken message.[29]

11. The one and the same Spirit works all these things, apportioning them to each one individually as he desires.

a. "The one and the same Spirit." Throughout the first eleven verses of this chapter, Paul stresses the work of the Holy Spirit. He states that a genuine confession of Jesus' lordship can come only by the Holy Spirit (v. 3). Although all three persons in the Trinity give spiritual gifts, Paul now intimates that these gifts are channeled through the Spirit. Thus, he notes that the Spirit is the agent (v. 4). He often uses the expression *the same* before the noun *Spirit* (vv. 4, 8, 9), and now in the concluding verse is even more descriptive by saying "one and the same Spirit." Paul emphasizes that every one of the nine gifts has its origin in the Holy Spirit. He implies that the Spirit prohibits the recipients of these gifts from boasting about rank or recognition.

b. "The same Spirit works all these things." Both the gifts and the power to energize believers originate with the Holy Spirit. He stands back of the gifts and enables the recipients to use them effectively for the benefit of the community (I Peter 4:10).

c. "Apportioning them to each one individually." No one in the Christian community receives all the gifts and no one is without a gift. Paul clearly asserts

29. Consult Arnold Bittlinger, *Gifts and Graces: A Commentary on 1 Corinthians 12–14*, trans. Herbert Klassen and Michael Harper (Grand Rapids: Eerdmans, 1967), p. 52. Compare Vern S. Poythress, "The Nature of Corinthians Glossolalia: Possible Options," *WTJ* 40 (1977): 130–35.

that the Holy Spirit allocates them to each person in the church, to the one this gift and to another that gift. The Spirit neglects no one, so that the totality of talents in the church constitutes a rich reservoir of ability and proficiency.

d. "As he desires." With this last clause, Paul teaches that the Holy Spirit is not merely an impersonal power but a person with divine identity. The Spirit exercises his prerogative to determine and distribute individual gifts to the believers, even though the Christian has the privilege to ask for them in prayer. The Spirit of God knows what the church needs and thus distributes gifts wisely and effectively.

Practical Considerations in 12:8–11

When individual Christians claim to have received either a word of wisdom, a word of knowledge, or a prophecy from the Lord, fellow believers are not always convinced. If someone declares that the Lord has told him or her what to do or what to say, this person can use a word from the Lord to silence a challenger and sway an audience. We acknowledge that the assertion of having received a word of either wisdom or knowledge is highly subjective. The reception of a word of wisdom or knowledge always occurs in the privacy of the human heart and cannot be examined objectively by others. In addition, personal messages often are influenced by human emotions.

When Paul lists the spiritual gifts, he ascribes no supernatural value to the terms *word of wisdom* and *word of knowledge*. He writes common words to convey the obvious meaning that someone is able to speak wisely and knowledgeably.[30] Scripture teaches that in answer to a believer's prayer for wisdom, God grants this particular gift without finding fault (James 1:5). God guides the believer to speak discerningly and informatively about a matter at hand. Thereupon fellow Christians listen and carefully evaluate the spoken word. When this happens, believers attest to the fact that God has granted to the speaker the gift of heavenly wisdom.

Greek Words, Phrases, and Constructions in 12:7–11

Verse 7

ἑκάστῳ—"each one." When the term ἕκαστος occurs as a substantive, as in this passage, it refers to each individual. Paul addresses each believer individually in the universal church. For a strengthened form, see verse 18.[31]

πρὸς τὸ συμφέρον—the preposition πρός with the accusative connotes "leading to [the common good]."[32] The substantive is a present participle which signifies "that which is beneficial."

Verse 8

μὲν . . . δέ—these two particles portray balance in a series of entries in verses 8–10.

---

30. Compare Grudem, *Prophecy in the New Testament*, p. 320.
31. Bauer, p. 236; Franz Georg Untergassmair, *EDNT*, vol. 1, p. 404.
32. Moule, *Idiom-Book*, p. 53.

διὰ... κατά—Paul employs these prepositions and ἐν in the next verse (v. 9) to describe the action of the Holy Spirit. He uses different prepositions only for the sake of variation.

δίδοται—note that Paul writes the present passive indicative ("is being given") to convey the meaning that God continues to give these special gifts to his people.

ἄλλῳ... ἑτέρῳ—these two forms in verses 8–10 occur only for variety in writing style.

Verse 9

All the qualitative nouns (e.g., faith, gifts, prophecy) that occur in this verse and the next are without the article. The article is omitted for nouns that express abstract qualities.[33]

ἑνί—this is the dative singular of the neuter numeral one. Some manuscripts have the reading αὐτῷ (the same) but the textual support favors the numeral.[34]

Verse 10

ἄλλῳ and ἑτέρῳ—"other." These two adjectives are interchanged only for stylistic reasons.

γένη—this plural noun, "kinds," must be supplemented with the adjective *different*.

Verse 11

τὸ ἓν καὶ τὸ αὐτό πνεῦμα—notice the use of the two definite articles before the noun *Spirit*. They are part of an idiom and show emphasis.

ἰδίᾳ ἑκάστῳ—"each his own." The adjective ἰδίᾳ conveys the classical sense: "his own private gift."[35]

---

b. The Body
12:12–31

For the first part of this chapter, Paul wrote about the Holy Spirit and the spiritual gifts he distributes to the believers. In the second part, he speaks about the church not as individuals but as a unit. He portrays the church in terms of the human body, which in itself is among the most marvelous of God's creations. For Paul, the illustration of the human body serves to display diversity in the interest of unity.

(1) The Body and the Spirit
12:12–13

12. For as the body is one and has many members, and all the members of the body, though they are many, are one body, thus also is Christ.

a. "For as the body is one and has many members." With the conjunction *for*, Paul bridges a break between the present passage and the preceding verses and elaborates on his teaching. In the previous part, Paul noted that individual members of the church received a variety of spiritual gifts. He looked at the proverbial

---

33. Robertson, *Grammar*, p. 758.
34. Bruce M. Metzger, *A Textual Commentary on the Greek New Testament*, 3d corrected ed. (London and New York: United Bible Societies, 1975), p. 563.
35. Nigel Turner, *A Grammar of New Testament Greek*, vol. 3 (Edinburgh: Clark, 1963), p. 191.

trees but failed to call attention to the forest. Now he takes in the totality of the individual members, refers to the body, and demonstrates its basic unity.

Paul compares the body, that is, the human body (see vv. 14–26), with Christ. We would expect Paul to compare the body and the church, not the body and Christ, but for him the church is the body of Christ (v. 27). Elsewhere Paul writes that Christ is the head of the church, which is his body (Eph. 1:22–23). In short, with the word *Christ* Paul presents a compressed theological thought of bringing body and head together. Paul uses a figure of speech, called metonymy, in which a part represents the whole unit. In other words, Christ represents the entire church. He identifies himself completely with the church, as is evident from Jesus' question to Paul on the way to Damascus: "Saul, Saul, why do you persecute me?" (Acts 9:4). Jesus taught that he and his people are one (Matt. 10:40; 25:45).

b. "And all the members of the body, though they are many, are one body, thus also is Christ." The human body is a highly diversified organism. Each member has its own distinct function but also contributes to the working of the entire body. So it is with the body of Christ, in which every member has received some spiritual gift. In this body, the employment of each gift is designed to serve not the individual member but the entire church.[36]

13. For indeed by one Spirit all of us were baptized into one body, whether Jews or Greeks, whether slaves or free, and all were made to drink of one Spirit.

This text presents a number of difficulties that stem from the expressions *by one Spirit, baptized, into one body,* and *all were made to drink.* The combination of these terms is unique. What did Paul have in mind when he wrote that all of us are baptized by one Spirit? And what is the significance of making everyone to drink of one Spirit? We comment on the italicized terms but admit that problems remain.

a. *By one Spirit.* The Greek text has the preposition *en* that can be translated either "by" or "in." Most translators have adopted the reading *by* to reveal means or agency.[37] They think that this interpretation is the better of the two, for it avoids the awkwardness of having two quite similar prepositional phrases in the same clause: "*in* one Spirit . . . *into* one body." I prefer the translation *by.*

Conversely, other translators believe that the Greek preposition *en* denotes sphere or place and thus translate it "in."[38] They point out that in the New Testament, the Holy Spirit is never described as the baptizer. Rather, the Spirit is the sphere into which the baptismal candidate enters. The Gospels declare that Jesus baptizes his followers with the Holy Spirit (Matt. 3:11; Mark 1:8).

---

36. Refer to Calvin, *I Corinthians*, p. 264; Leonard Sweetman, Jr., "The Gifts of the Spirit: A Study of Calvin's Comments on I Corinthians 12:8–10, 28; Romans 12:6–8; Ephesians 4:1," in *Exploring the Heritage of John Calvin*, ed. David E. Holwerda (Grand Rapids: Baker, 1976), p. 275.

37. GNB, KJV, NKJV, MLB, NASB, NCV, NIV, RSV, SEB, TNT, *Cassirer, Moffatt, Phillips.*

38. JB, NJB, NAB, NEB, NRSV, REB.

b. *Baptized*. When Paul writes, "all of us were baptized," is he referring to a literal or a figurative baptism? If taken literally, Paul is talking about water baptism. However, the verb *to baptize* often conveys a metaphorical sense. For instance, Jesus asks James and John whether they are able to be baptized with a baptism similar to his own (Mark 10:38). Jesus is alluding not to his baptism in the Jordan but to his death on the cross (see also Luke 12:50; Acts 1:5; and I Cor. 10:2). It is preferable to state that Paul has in mind a figurative use of baptism.[39]

Paul writes, "all of us were baptized," and "all were made to drink of one Spirit." These words extend to a circle that is far broader than the Corinthian community and includes all believers. This means that all true believers in Jesus Christ have been baptized by the Holy Spirit. The text teaches that regenerated Christians are incorporated into one body by the Holy Spirit but it says nothing about a subsequent baptism of the Spirit.[40]

Some scholars interpret the text as a reference to the sacraments of baptism and the Lord's Supper.[41] But this is difficult to maintain. First, in the present context Paul gives no indication of introducing a discussion on the sacraments. Next, the text simply does not allude to water baptism. Third, the assertion that the verb *to make to drink* refers to the drinking of the Communion cup cannot be sustained. And last, the Greek verb tense calls for a single occurrence of drinking, which is incongruent with the repeated observance of the Lord's Supper.

The flow of this verse intimates that to be baptized means to become a living member of the church upon conversion. When spiritual regeneration takes place in individuals, they enter the body of Christ, that is, the church. Not the external observance of water baptism but the internal transformation by the Holy Spirit brings people into a living relationship with Christ.[42]

c. *Into one body*. Here Paul stresses the unity of the church in its diverse forms. He notes the racial, cultural, and social differences that existed in the Corinthian church: there were Jews and Greeks, slaves and free. Regardless of their status and position in life, these people came together to worship God in one church. If the church should practice discrimination, it would be in direct conflict with the law of love. All people who are spiritually renewed in Christ are equal to one another.

The preposition *into* denotes movement from the outside to the inside. Persons who have been regenerated by the Holy Spirit leave the world when they become living members of the church. "For Paul to become a Christian and to become a member of the Body of Christ are synonymous."[43]

39. Consult J. D. G. Dunn, *Baptism in the Holy Spirit*, Studies in Biblical Theology, 2d series 15 (London: SCM, 1970), p. 129; Ronald E. Cottle, "All Were Baptized," *JETS* 17 (1974): 75–80.
40. Refer to Anthony A. Hoekema's discussion in *Tongues and Spirit-Baptism: A Biblical and Theological Evaluation* (reprint ed.; Grand Rapids: Baker, 1981), pp. 61–62.
41. Among others, see Bittlinger, *Gifts and Graces*, pp. 57–58.
42. Consult Gaffin, *Perspectives on Pentecost*, p. 29.
43. Dunn, *Baptism in the Holy Spirit*, p. 129.

d. *All were made to drink.* In verse 13, the adjective *all* appears twice not to indicate two distinct stages of the Christian experience but to reinforce the new status. In fact, the verse itself "rules out any interpretation of baptism which requires it to be complemented by a later rite for the impartation of the Spirit."[44] For this reason, Paul once more writes the expression *one Spirit* and says that all believers were made to drink of this Spirit. We sense that the two verbs *baptize* and *drink* have much in common. By looking for a parallel, we see similar wording in one of Paul's epistles: "For all of you who were baptized into Christ have clothed yourselves with Christ. There is neither Jew nor Greek, slave nor free, male nor female, for you are all one in Christ Jesus" (Gal. 3:27–28).

In the Corinthian and Galatian passages, Paul stresses the unity in Christ Jesus regardless of racial, cultural, social, and sexual differences. He states that all were baptized by one Spirit into Christ. And he adds that the believers have been made to drink of the Spirit (v. 13) and have clothed themselves with Christ (Gal. 3:27). Just as Christians are clothed with Christ, so they are saturated with the Holy Spirit. The Greek verb *potizō* can mean either "I give to drink" (Matt. 25:35) or "I irrigate" (I Cor. 3:6–8).[45] The second meaning is appropriate, for Jesus also connects the Holy Spirit to the concept *living water* flowing from the believer (John 4:10; 7:38–39). When this spiritual saturation occurs, the individual believer enjoys a bountiful harvest, namely, the fruit of the Spirit (Gal. 5:22–23).

Greek Words, Phrases, and Constructions in 12:12–13

καθάπερ . . . οὕτως—the adverbs denote balance: "just as" and "so." The first adverb occurs seventeen times in the New Testament, all but once in Paul's epistles.

πάντα τὰ μέλη—the adjective πάντα (all) is emphatic: "all the members."

καὶ γάρ—"for indeed." Both words keep their own individual meaning.[46]

ἐποτίσθημεν—the aorist passive of ποτίζω (I give to drink; irrigate) demands a direct object in the form of ἓν πνεῦμα (one Spirit). The Majority Text features the preposition εἰς (into) before the accusative case, but the manuscript support is weak (KJV, NKJV).

---

(2) The Physical Body
12:14–20

From Paul's point of view in the middle of the first century, the human body with its numerous members was a descriptive parallel of the church universal. The body with its many members has been created to function effectively as a unit, and the church with its gifted members also forms an effective entity. Yet the world-

---

44. G. R. Beasley-Murray, *Baptism in the New Testament* (Grand Rapids: Eerdmans, 1962), p. 171.

45. Refer to G. J. Cuming, "*Epotisthēmen* (I Corinthians 12:13)," *NTS* 27 (1981): 283–85; E. R. Rogers, "*Epotisthēmen* Again," *NTS* 29 (1983): 139–42.

46. Friedrich Blass and Albert Debrunner, *A Greek Grammar of the New Testament and Other Early Christian Literature*, trans. and rev. Robert Funk (Chicago: University of Chicago Press, 1961), #452.3.

wide church today is so diverse in language, culture, race, boundaries, tradition, history, and theology that a comparison with the human body seems simplistic. Nonetheless, in the local church especially Paul's illustration is apt. It points out that as the body functions harmoniously, so must the church of Jesus Christ.

14. For indeed the body is not one member but many.

With the introductory words *for indeed,* Paul resumes the thought he began to develop in verse 12, where he spoke of many members and one body. He repeats the same words to illustrate that unity and diversity characterize not only the human body but all created bodies. For any living organism to exert itself productively, it must coordinate all its varied parts, function compatibly, and in its diversity show unity in purpose.

Paul is thinking of the church of Jesus Christ and especially of the Christian community in Corinth. Aside from all its problems, this community has been blessed with numerous gifts and talents (see vv. 28–31). The analogy is clear, for as the human body with its numerous members has been created to function smoothly, so the Corinthian church with its many gifted people ought to perform harmoniously. "As the beauty of the human body is brought out by the variety of its parts, so the glory of the body of Christ appears in the diversity of its members."[47]

15. If the foot should say, "Because I am not a hand, I am not of the body," for this reason it ceases not to belong to the body. 16. And if the ear should say, "Because I am not an eye, I am not of the body," for this reason it ceases not to belong to the body.

With these hypothetical illustrations, Paul imagines parts of the human body talking to each other. Because the foot is not as skillful as the hand, it may look up to the hand and declare, "Because I am not a hand, I am not of the body." But such talk is nonsense. Feet are part of the body and make it complete. Paul's implied application for the Corinthians is to eradicate all envy with respect to a particular spiritual gift that a member has not received. This one church member ought not to feel inadequate because of a lack of some spiritual gift. And no one should separate himself from the body of believers out of envy or spite.[48]

There is also a difference between the respective functions of the ear and the eye. A person who is deaf is nonetheless able to see everything, but every blind person lives in perpetual darkness. The ear may think that the function of seeing is more important to the human body than the function of hearing. Thus the ear may feel less important than the eye. For this reason, the ear may argue: "Because I am not an eye, I am not of the body." But such talk is idle and useless. To function properly, the body needs all its members. Likewise, no one in the Corinthian congregation may separate himself from the church, because every member is important for the wholesome functioning of the entire body.

---

47. R. B. Kuiper, *The Glorious Body of Christ* (Grand Rapids: Eerdmans, n.d.), p. 288.
48. Calvin, *I Corinthians,* p. 267. Compare the view of Fee, *First Corinthians,* p. 610.

17. If the whole body were an eye, where would the hearing be? If the whole body were hearing, where would the sense of smell be?

With the help of a ludicrous illustration, Paul drives home the point of unity and mutual dependence. The human body which consists of many parts can never be only an eye. If this were the case, says Paul, it would see but not hear. The body would be unable to function properly. Moreover, if the whole body had have only the component of hearing, it would not be able to detect any odors, whether good or bad. Indeed, without the variety of body parts that fill their assigned roles, the body itself would rapidly deteriorate and die.

Paul portrays the absurdity of nurturing jealousy because of the spiritual gifts which the individual members of the Corinthian congregation had received. He not only teaches but also strives to attain the unity of the Christian church. The members of the Corinthian church need each other. Each has received some spiritual gift on which the rest of the congregation depends. The recipient of any gift must understand that all the members of the church depend on him or her to exercise that spiritual gift. When all the members employ the talents the Holy Spirit has distributed to God's people, then the entire church functions efficiently for the benefit of all.

18. But now God has placed the members, each one of them, in the body just as he desired.

Answering his own direct questions (v. 17), Paul gives a brief conclusion which he introduces with the words *but now,* that is, "as a matter of fact."[49] Momentarily he leaves the world of hypothetical illustrations and returns to reality.

God is the subject of this verse, for he is the Creator of the body (Gen. 2:7). At creation, God made a human body that was free from any flaw or weakness. He designed the body to make all its members function properly and display unity. Even though marred by the effect of sin, the human body still remains a marvelous creation. Its design reveals the hand of the Creator, who gave each individual member a unique place in the body (see also 15:38; Rev. 4:11).

By implication, the spiritual gifts which God has distributed are given according to his design. Through his Spirit, God works out his plan and purpose in the people he has redeemed. Two examples, one from the Old Testament and the other from the New, demonstrate the employment of gifts. First, when God instructed Moses to build the tabernacle in the desert, he filled Bezalel, Oholiab, and other craftsmen with the Spirit of God and skill to build the Tent of Meeting (Exod. 31:1–6). Next, when the church in Jerusalem increased in number so that the apostles could no longer perform all their tasks, God raised up seven men filled with the Spirit and wisdom. These seven deacons served with their gifts and talents to meet the needs of the church (Acts 6:1–6). Does this mean that God endows only a few leaders with special gifts? Not at all, for Paul has already noted that every believer receives a spiritual gift (v. 11). Therefore, within

---

49. Bauer, p. 546.

the church no one ought to be idle—each one must use the talent God has given him or her for the edification of the body of Christ.

19. And if everything were one member, where would the body be?

If all the members of the church would think, act, speak, and dress alike while displaying one and the same talent, we would see not a body but only one member. Paul literally asks, "And if all the parts altogether were one member, where would the body be?" To ask the question is to answer it.

At the beginning of this discussion (v. 14), Paul looked at the totality of the body that consists of many parts (v. 14). Now he looks at the parts that become alike and queries where the body may be. A single entity that lacks diversity may be a unit but it is unable to function as an organic body. An entity without any differentiating parts can be as useless as a lump of discarded clay.

20. But now there are many members but one body.

On the contrary, says Paul, the church includes many members who together constitute one body. And this body expresses harmony and unity, much as choir members singing their assigned parts create musical harmony. Paul concludes this part of the discussion with the same wording he wrote earlier in verse 12. In that verse he mentioned one body and many parts, but here he presents the reverse of that statement.

Practical Considerations in 12:14–20

Numerous churches, especially the ones that have existed for many years, are coping with a measure of indolence. A few faithful saints appear to do all the work in the congregation: they serve as members of the council or board; they teach Sunday school classes; they visit the sick and welcome new members; they are involved in youth work. Most of the members, except for attending the Sunday worship services, are idle. Even though people receive spiritual food, they are weak from lack of exercise. Because of their inactivity, they are spiritually atrophied. Their atrophy results in spiritual heart failure.

Other members observe the activity of those who are faithful. But instead of emulating their example, these members are filled with discontent. Many criticize the leadership in the church, display envy, nurture grudges, and cause friction. When disgruntled members do not receive the attention they desire, they leave for another church. There the cycle of discontent and envy often begins anew after the initial welcome is over.

Every member of the body of Christ ought to realize that God has bypassed no one in the distribution of gifts and talents. He or she may not bury these talents through idleness, for there will eventually be a day of reckoning when God demands an accounting. In that day, God will commend and reward those who have been faithful by employing and developing their gifts. But he will condemn and punish those unbelievers who neglected their talents by criticizing the church and by ultimately deserting her.

Greek Words, Phrases, and Constructions in 12:15–18

Verses 15–16

Some Greek New Testaments (Nes-Al, UBS, TR) and translations (KJV, NKJV, NAB, JB, TNT) present the last clauses in these two verses as interrogatives. However, if these clauses were to be rhetorical questions expecting a negative reply, the particle μή, not οὐ, would have to be the reading. Here Paul uses the negative οὐ in both verses. The verses, therefore, should be read as statements.

The repetition of the negative particle οὐ in both verse 15 and verse 16 should not be understood as a double negative. Rather, the repetitive occurrence of this particle strengthens the negation.

παρὰ τοῦτο—this combination is an idiom that means "on that score," "for that reason."[50]

Verse 18

νυνὶ δέ—the particle δέ is adversative ("but"); the adverb νυνί (now) has lost its reference to time and relates merely factual information.

ἔθετο—the aorist middle of the verb τίθημι (I place, put) is deponent and signifies "he arranged."[51]

---

(3) The Honorable and the Unpresentable Parts
12:21–26

Editors of the Greek New Testament do not see the need for a new paragraph at this juncture. But there is need, for Paul slightly changes the subject matter by introducing the element of superiority expressed by certain members of the body. This claim reflects the social and spiritual conditions in the Corinthian church. With continued illustrations, Paul tries to convince those members that their arrogance hampers the unity of the church.

21. The eye is not able to say to the hand, "I have no need of you." Or again, the head to the feet, "I have no need of you."

Once more Paul personifies members of the human body. The eye is speaking to the hand and the head addresses the feet. The message is that the eye and the head respectively want to be independent of the other parts of the body. They do not want to admit that their existence is based on the interdependent relations with other physical members. What would the eye achieve without the use of the hand? And what would the head do for lack of mobility? The picture that Paul draws portrays the absurdity of independence. The individual parts of the body all aid each other in the total functioning of the whole.

Notice that Paul uses the singular term *eye* not to call attention to the physical part of the human anatomy but to a person's competence to see. The word *hand* also appears in the singular to express a person's ability of touching, taking, holding, and giving objects. We always refer to dexerity by using the singular, for instance, sleight of hand. The word *head* must be understood as the collective part of the body that incorporates all the senses and the working of the mind.

What is Paul trying to say to his readers? This is the lesson: A member in the Corinthian church who had received the gift of healing, for example, should not

---

50. Moule, *Idiom-Book*, p. 51.
51. Bauer, p. 816; Blass and Debrunner, *Greek Grammar*, #316.1.

feel self-sufficient and say to the other members, "I have no need of you." This air of superiority flies in the face of Paul's teaching on servanthood (9:19; II Cor. 4:5; Gal. 5:13). The person who has the gift of healing needs the supportive ministry of those who have received the rest of the spiritual gifts. In brief, within the church all the members need one another with all their expertise and ability for mutual edification. The revered Augustine aptly said:

> God is not greater if you reverence him,
> but you are greater if you serve him.

22. By contrast, the members of the body that appear to be weaker are even more indispensable.

Paul stresses the contrast between the stronger and the weaker members of the human body. The stronger are hands and feet (v. 21). But those parts that we tend to call weaker—Paul does not specify them—are actually indispensable. To illustrate, internal physical organs appear to be weak because they cannot be seen, yet everyone realizes that the body cannot function without them. A physician surgically removes an internal organ from his patient, but in many cases the patient afterward needs to take medication for the rest of his or her life to counteract the loss of this organ.

A person who is quiet by nature may be disregarded by those who are more aggressive and in the public eye. Yet this subdued person often proves to be mighty in prayer and a hero of faith. He or she is an indispensable member of the Christian community and has turned apparent weakness into strength. The prophetess Anna was such a prayer warrior and spiritual giant (Luke 2:36–38). Let no one in the Corinthian church despise any of the members by calling them weak, for these very people are essential to the well-being of the congregation. Jesus himself told Paul: "My grace is sufficient for you, for my power is made perfect in weakness" (II Cor. 12:9).

23. And whatever members of the body we deem less honorable, on these we place greater honor, and our unpresentable parts are treated with greater modesty. 24a. And our respectable parts have no need of this.

Paul first mentions the weaker members of the human body (v. 22), then in descending order he cites the less honorable ones, and last, the unpresentable parts. Then he alludes to the body's presentable members.

a. "And whatever members of the body we deem less honorable, on these we place greater honor." The key word in the first main clause of verse 23 is the verb *to place*. This verb in the Greek literally means "to put or place around" someone articles of clothing. In other words, it means to dress. We clothe the less honorable parts of the human body more carefully than the nobler parts. Fashionable shoes hide unsightly feet, shoulderpads add stature to a sagging physique, and an attractive dress or an elegant suit gives charm to an extended figure.

b. "And our unpresentable parts are treated with greater modesty." When we refer to the unmentionable parts of the body, we express ourselves with modesty. Paul has no need to be specific, because every reader knows what he is trying to say. The parts to which Paul alludes are those whose exposure is indecent and creates shame and embarrassment. These parts are not merely accorded a measure of modesty: they receive even greater care. The English translation is unable to convey the play on words in the Greek *aschēmona* and *euschēmona*. Some versions have translated these terms as "unseemly" and "seemliness" or "uncomely" and "comely" (NASB, *Cassirer*). I suggest that we approximate the assonance of the Greek words by saying "our unrespectable parts are treated with even more respect."

Decency and modesty should ever be striking characteristics of a Christian community in a dissolute and immoral world. In the pagan culture of the first century, nudity was commonplace and perfectly acceptable, especially in the sports arenas. We as Christians, Paul observes, think that certain parts of our anatomy are less honorable and, therefore, must be clothed properly.

c. "And our respectable parts have no need of this." Paul refrains from delineating what these parts of the body may be, but he may be referring to a person's face, which needs no covering. Although one's face needs daily care, it generally causes no shame or embarrassment.

24b. However, God has combined the members of the body by giving greater honor to those that lack it, 25. that there may be no division in the body but that the members may have the same care for one another.

The paragraph division in most translations is unfortunate, because this verse has two functions. The first part of verse 24 concludes the preceding segment. Verse 24b serves as the opening statement of the conclusion of the matter Paul is illustrating.

a. "However, God has combined the members of the body." The adversative *however* marks the transition from the main argument to Paul's concluding remarks. Paul repeats an earlier statement (v. 18) when he says, "God has combined the members," but here he uses a different verb in the past tense. This tense signifies an action that took place in the past but still has effect today. To be sure, Paul has in mind the creation of Adam at the dawn of human history (Gen. 2:7). Adam's descendants have the same kind of body that God created for their progenitor.

b. "By giving greater honor to those that lack it." God sovereignly creates a human body without consulting anyone. This means that man has no power to determine the composition of his own body. Jesus says, "You cannot make even one hair white or black" (Matt. 5:36). God has absolute authority in composing the human body. In the same way, he intermingles the individual components within the church so the weaker instead of the stronger receive special attention. By blending the various parts of the body, God creates perfect harmony. The stronger elements compensate for the weaker, so that the latter receive even greater recognition than the former. And by blending the many parts of the church, God creates strength and beauty. The creation of the church is God's work.

c. "That there may be no division in the body." With the word *division*, Paul is speaking more about the church than the human body (see 1:10–12). The physical body created by God cannot cause a division within itself. But within the church, the members are able to cause a split and the possibility of a schism is real. Hence, Paul asserts that within the church of Christ no division should occur.[52] He applies the imagery of the physical body to the church, even though the implied metaphor loses some of its effect. Nonetheless, Paul strives for the unity of the body of Christ (Rom. 12:5) not only in the Corinthian congregation but also in the broader context of relationships of Jewish Christians in Jerusalem with Gentile Christians abroad (see especially Acts 21:17–21).

d. "But that the members may have the same care for one another." The members of the church need each other to do the Lord's work effectively. The person who has received the gift of teaching is in great demand for instructing children, youth, and adults. The preacher must heed the spiritual needs of everyone in the congregation. Persons who have the qualifications to govern the church in its various ministries are indispensable. And the deacons who can minister to the needy perform a essential task. All these people express a genuine concern for the other members in the church.

No one should ever be neglected within the church. Concern for one another ought to be the hallmark of the Christian community, for in this context concern has a positive connotation. It refers to the care that God accords his people and the care that God expects them to show to one another.[53] Paul echoes the second part of the summary of the Decalogue, "Love your neighbor as yourself" (Lev. 19:18; Matt. 22:39).

26. And if one member suffers, all the members suffer with it. If one member is honored, all the members rejoice with it.

This is one of the most beautiful texts in Paul's first epistle to the Corinthians. It describes the effect genuine care can have on the members in the Christian church. When love prevails, we see the church as a live physical body. A stubbed toe impairs one's ability to walk and thus affects the entire body. Filling one's stomach with delicious food satisfies all the parts of the body, but the pain of a stomach ulcer has an opposite effect. Similarly, when a member in the congregation mourns the death of a loved one, the entire congregation grieves with the mourner. When one member receives recognition for either an accomplishment or an anniversary, the rest of the members surround the recipient with joyful adulation. The Christian community mourns with those who hurt and rejoices with those who celebrate.

---

52. Murray J. Harris, *NIDNTT*, vol. 3, p. 544.
53. Compare Jürgen Goetzmann, *NIDNTT*, vol. 1, p. 278.

Practical Considerations in 12:25–26

The church of Jesus Christ is an organism, not a society; a communion, not a guild; a fellowship, not an association.[54] Membership in a society, guild, or association means paying annual dues and required or voluntary attendance at meetings. Failure to remit dues results in cancellation of membership. A society consists of officials and members who join in common effort to achieve a set goal. A society normally functions administratively in a specific area, for instance in business or politics. But we can never say that a society is a living entity. By contrast we use the term *organism* when we describe a body with a number of parts that perform various functions for the well-being of the whole. Thus an organism is alive and belongs to the world of either humans, animals, or plants. That is, God creates an organism.

Church members belong to the living body of Christ, receive spiritual food, mature in faith, and express Christian love in tangible ways to their neighbor. Within the context of the church, the members need one another as they love, nurture, teach, train, equip, and support fellow members. They do so with the spiritual gifts and talents God has given them.

Life within the church is unique. Each member with his or her gift depends on others with their gifts to advance the cause of Christ. Without support a believer fails, but together with fellow believers he succeeds. In effect, the church is alive and will remain so until the end of time. It is a living body whose head is Christ.

Greek Words, Phrases, and Constructions in 12:22–25

Verses 22–24

πολλῷ μᾶλλον—"how much more." The construction is the dative of comparison in which the positive adjective is used for the comparative.

περισσοτέραν—this comparative adjective modifies both nouns (τιμήν, honor; and εὐσχημοσύνην, modesty) and is translated "more abundant" or "greater."

συνεκέρασεν—this compound verb is more emphatic than the simple verb κεράννυμι (I mix). Here the verb connotes "to mix together, blend, unite." The aorist is constative.[55]

ὑστερουμένῳ—the present passive participle means "to come short of, be lacking, be inferior."[56]

Verse 25

ἵνα μή—these words begin a negative purpose clause with the verb ᾖ (is). The construction is continued with the adversative ἀλλά (but on the contrary) as a positive purpose clause with the verb μεριμνῶσιν (they cared).

---

54. Donald Guthrie observes, "The [early] churches were living organisms rather than organizations." *New Testament Theology* (Downers Grove: Inter-Varsity, 1981), p. 741.

55. Robertson, *Grammar*, p. 832.

56. Consult William L. Lane, *NIDNTT*, vol. 3, p. 952–56.

(4) Members and Gifts
12:27–31

Paul now returns to a discussion on membership in the church and on the gifts that God grants to the members. In verses 8–10, he enumerated nine gifts that the Holy Spirit distributes to the members of the church. In the next few verses (vv. 28–30), he ranks these spiritual gifts by priority. The gifts of speaking in tongues and interpreting them are the last on the list. These gifts are discussed later in great detail (chap. 14).

Paul prefaces his discussion on spiritual gifts with a comprehensive statement about membership in the church of Jesus Christ. His affirmation summarizes what he has been saying in the preceding segment of this chapter (vv. 12–26).

27. You are the body of Christ and individually members of it.

a. "You are the body of Christ." Paul addresses the members of the Corinthian church with the personal pronoun *you*. They are the people who have been made holy in Christ Jesus and are called to be holy (1:2). Yet these people quarreled, caused divisions, failed to expel an immoral brother, brought lawsuits against fellow brothers, criticized the apostles, and did not properly observe the Lord's Supper. In spite of all these shortcomings, Paul tells the Corinthians that they are the body of Christ.

In the Greek text, Paul uses the noun *body* in the absolute sense of the word. That is, the word appears without the definite article which, for the sake of acceptable English, we have supplied. Paul does not say "a body" or "the body," but merely "body" to indicate that this is the one and only, for there is no other body of Christ. He is not referring to Christ's physical body but rather speaks figuratively about the church as Christ's body (e.g., Eph. 1:23; Col. 1:24). To say it differently, Paul states that the church to which the Corinthians belong is one entity without division.

The church as Christ's figurative body exists in him and belongs to him. It is genuinely united with Christ, for every individual member is by faith included in him.[57] Each local congregation is a microcosm of the entire church, so that everyone who observes the congregation's various functions knows that this body is the church in action. Here Paul states the principle of unity in multiplicity. In the next clause he notes multiplicity in unity.

b. "And individually members of it." We have no information about the size of the Corinthian church, but Paul avers that every individual member is part of Christ's body. By saying this, Paul underscores the individuality of the members, for each has received a different gift from the Lord. With these gifts and functions at their disposal, all the members together contribute to the well-being of the Christian community.

---

57. Herman Ridderbos, *Paul: An Outline of His Theology*, trans. John Richard de Witt (Grand Rapids: Eerdmans, 1975), pp. 375–76.

28. And God has appointed in the church, first apostles, next prophets, third teachers, then miracles, then gifts of healing, helpful deeds, administrations, kinds of tongues.

In earlier verses, Paul taught that God arranges the parts of the human body (v. 18) and combines its various members (v. 24). This is true not only for a person's physical body but also for the church. God distributes to the members in the church a variety of gifts designed to serve its membership. The appointment to an office or the giving of a function comes from God himself. He calls individuals to an official position within the church, even though church members call, ordain, or install them in the position. As the writer of the epistle to the Hebrews says, "No one takes this honor upon himself; he must be called by God" (Heb. 5:4). So, for instance, Paul and Barnabas were called by the Holy Spirit and ordained by the church in Antioch (Acts 13:1–3). They functioned in the church as apostles, prophets, and teachers.[58] Conclusively, the phrase *in the church* applies to the church universal and not merely to the Corinthian congregation.

In descending order, Paul enumerates three groups of persons who have received spiritual gifts. They are apostles, prophets, and teachers. In another epistle, he lists four groups: "It was [Christ] who gave some to be apostles, some to be prophets, some to be evangelists, and some to be pastors and teachers" (Eph. 4:11; compare Rom. 12:6–8). He also lists five gifts, though by implication persons are given and exercise these gifts.

a. "First apostles." Jesus directly commissioned twelve people to be apostles, including Matthias, who succeeded Judas (respectively, Luke 6:13–16; Acts 1:23–26). The apostolic circle extended beyond the Twelve, however, for Paul was an apostle (Rom. 1:1) and so was Barnabas (Acts 14:14). Paul writes that Andronicus and Junias were highly regarded among the apostles but probably did not function as such (Rom. 16:7). This text apparently means that the apostles had great respect for these two people.[59] The apostles served as Christ's ambassadors to proclaim, teach, and record the good news.

Paul is not saying that every individual congregation had its own apostles. Certainly not. The apostles served the entire church in its formative years. The apostolic office was temporary and ceased with the death of the last apostle, John, who died probably in A.D. 98. Indeed, the stipulations laid down for apostleship made it impossible to have successors. First, the apostles were to have followed the Lord Jesus from his baptism to his ascension and, second, they were to be a witness of his resurrection (Acts 1:21–22). Although Paul did not accompany Jesus, he had seen the Lord and thus was able to testify of his resurrection (9:1; Rom. 1:1–4). This is the reason that Paul calls himself "one abnormally born" (15:8).

58. Refer to Ellis, *Prophecy and Hermeneutic in Early Christianity*, p. 139.
59. See also the Greek text of II Cor. 8:23; Phil. 2:25, I Thess. 2:6.

b. "Next prophets." Unlike the apostles, who served the entire church, the prophets often served local congregations (e.g., Acts 13:1). Even though an apostle (e.g., John in the Book of Revelation) could utter prophecies, a prophet never functioned as an apostle. In a few passages Paul lists the apostles and prophets together (Eph. 2:20; 3:5), but he does not equate the two; they remain distinctly separate, for apostles are apostles and prophets are prophets.[60] We cannot equate the office of apostle and prophet in the current text and other passages (Eph. 4:11; Rev. 18:20; *Didache* 11:3).

Apostles spoke and wrote with the same authority God had entrusted to the Old Testament prophets. They were witnesses to Jesus' life, death, and resurrection.Prophets in the New Testament era also spoke with the authority of the Holy Spirit. They stood next to the apostles in the work of laying the church's foundation (Eph. 2:20) and, in rank, they were second to the apostles. Furthermore, the statements of the prophets had to be evaluated (14:29) to guard against the utterances of false prophets whose influence undermined the well being of the church.

The early church had predictive prophets, among whom was Agabus (Acts 11:28; 21:10); John on the island of Patmos also filled that role (Rev. 1:3; 22:9, 18). At Antioch, the church was instructed by teachers and prophets, namely, Barnabas, Simeon Niger, Lucius of Cyrene, Manaen, and Paul (Acts 13:1); in Jerusalem were Judas and Silas (Acts 15:32); and in Caesarea resided the four daughters of Philip the Evangelist (Acts 21:8–9). Prophets were engaged in teaching the members of local churches.They gave instruction on Christian conduct,[61] and they stood next to those people who had received the gift of teaching the content of the Scriptures.

Although prophets received the gift of prophecy, we have no evidence that they filled a permanent office in the early Christian communities. Their gift was an ability to prophesy, that is, to receive God's revelation and to preach his Word. "In the sub-apostolic period the prophet could still take precedence over the local minister, but the day was not far off when this gift of prophecy passed to the local ministers who preached the word to edify the members of the Christian fellowship."[62]

The early church had a number of prophets, among whom were Agabus (Acts 11:28; 21:10) and Judas and Silas (Acts 15:32). The influence of prophecy came to an end in the second century, however, when Montanus, claiming to be a prophet with new revelation concerning Christ's return, arose in Asia Minor. For

---

60. F. David Farnell, "Does the New Testament Teach Two Prophetic Gifts," *BS* 150 (1993): 62–88. By contrast see Grudem, *Prophecy in the New Testament and Today*, p. 62.

61. *Phillips* interprets the term *prophets* as "preachers of power." Consult David Hill, "Christian Prophets as Teachers or Instructors in the Church," in *Prophetic Vocation in The New Testament and Today*, ed. J. Panagopoulos, *Supplements to Novum Testamentum*, vol. 45 (Leiden: Brill, 1977), pp. 122–23.

62. James G. S. S. Thomson, "Spiritual Gifts," *BDT*, p. 499. Compare David E. Aune, *Prophecy in Early Christianity and the Ancient Mediterranean World* (Grand Rapids: Eerdmans, 1983), p. 204; Hermann Sasse, "Apostles, Prophets, Teachers," *RTR* 27 (1968): 11–21.

some time Montanism became influential but soon was condemned as spurious.[63] Because of its fraud, Montanism was held in low esteem. Prophets no longer enjoyed prominence when the church relied more on the Scriptures than on prophecy.

c. "Third teachers." If Paul distinguishes between prophets and teachers, what then is the difference between them?

First, the teacher in Paul's day received respect for his ability to instruct others. For instance, the people addressed Jesus with the Hebrew term *rabbi*, which literally means "my great [teacher]." In contrast to teachers, prophets were not always accorded high esteem, for the tactics of false prophets gave prophecy a bad name. Indeed Paul admonishes the Christians, "Do not treat prophecies with contempt" (I Thess. 5:20).

Next, while the true prophet waited with his message until he received a revelation (14:30), the teacher possessed the Scriptures as the revealed Word of God. Students had to learn sound doctrine and the traditions which the instructors taught them. (Books were so costly that only the rich could afford them. Thus, the teacher usually resorted to the pedagogical method of repetition to aid the students in committing his instruction to memory.) Paul relates that he was an apostle and a teacher of Christ's gospel (II Tim. 1:11).

And last, according to Paul the work of the teacher is closely related to that of the pastor (Eph. 4:11). Much of the pastor's time is devoted to teaching his people.

d. "Then miracles." Paul calls attention to miracles and not to miracle workers. The literal translation is "miracles," which by implication refers to those who perform them. Because miraculous deeds seldom occur, the gift of doing wonders is not permanent (read the explanation of verse 10).

e. "Then gifts of healing." Gifts of healing also lack permanency (see the commentary on verse 9). The Greek word for "gifts" is *charismata*, which appears at the beginning of the list of spiritual gifts in verse 4 and at the end of the chapter in verse 30. Of all the gifts, Paul characterizes only healings (plural in the Greek text) as *charismata*.

f. "Helpful deeds." The Greek word *antilēmpseis* occurs only once in the entire New Testament and is variously translated "assistants" (NAB), "forms of assistance" (NRSV), or "works of mercy" (*Cassirer*). The verb from which it derives appears three times in the New Testament. In Luke 1:54 the verb means to help Israel, as it also does in the Septuagint text of Isaiah 41:9; in Acts 20:35 it refers to helping the weak; and the verb form in I Timothy 6:2 means to benefit.[64]

In the current passage the noun signifies the helping hand of love and mercy both within and beyond the Christian community. One commentator asserts that the term conveys "the definite suggestion of assistance given by governing

---

63. Gerhard Friedrich, *TDNT*, vol. 6, pp. 859–60; David Hill, *New Testament Prophecy* (Atlanta: John Knox, 1979), pp. 186–92.
64. Consult Gerhard Delling, *TDNT*, vol. 1, p. 375.

authorities to any who are in need or oppressed."[65] But it is more likely that members of the Christian community and not the government received the spiritual gift of helping one another.

g. "Administrations." The Greek term *kybernēseis* also occurs but once in the New Testament. A related noun which appears twice (Acts 27:11; Rev. 18:17) means "pilot" or "sea captain." The English verb *to govern* derives from the Latin *gubernare* and the Greek *kybernan*, which means "to hold the helm, to steer." Paul seems to intimate that the spiritual gift *kybernēseis* is the ability to hold the helm of the church.

In the Pastoral Epistles, Paul writes that the elders who rule the church effectively, especially the ones who are engaged in preaching and teaching (I Tim. 5:17), are worthy of double honor. That is, Paul refers to ruling elders and to teaching elders.[66] The person who possesses the gift to be a statesman in the church is indeed worthy of great respect.

h. "Kinds of tongues." This is the last of the nine gifts. Since Paul had in mind to list them by rank, the last one is the least important. We assume that some believers in the Corinthian church had excessively valued tongues, so that this gift became a controversial issue. Consequently, Paul corrected the misconception of these believers by placing the gift of tongues last in the list, writing an entire chapter on love, and then instructing the believers to communicate in intelligible speech.

The expression *kinds of tongues* is identical to the words in verse 10 (consult the commentary). Paul is not alluding to one particular language, intelligible or unintelligible, but to a variety of languages which were spoken in the metropolitan area of Corinth. Yet the speaking of unfamiliar languages or the practice of tongue-speech often causes alienation and estrangement, so that translators or interpreters are needed to overcome linguistic barriers. However, note that in this particular list Paul fails to include the spiritual gift of interpreting tongues, but see verse 30.

29. Are all apostles? Are all prophets? Are all teachers? Are all [workers of] miracles? 30. Do all have gifts of healing? Do all speak in tongues? Do all interpret?

Paul is asking seven rhetorical questions, all of which receive a negative answer. These negative responses clearly demonstrate both the diversity and the universality of the church. The church is not limited to a local congregation. The first question ("Are all apostles?") is addressed to the Corinthians and implies that the apostles did not originate in Corinth.

Prophets are present in the Corinthian community (14:29), but certainly not every believer has received prophetic gifts. The same thing can be said of teachers, of those who perform miracles, of the believers who have the gifts of healing,

---

65. Parry, *First Epistle to the Corinthians*, p. 187.

66. Churches of Reformed persuasion maintain the distinction of teaching elders (pastors) and ruling elders. Consult Calvin, *I Corinthians*, p. 272.

and of the ones who speak in tongues. Not everyone receives these same gifts. Notice that Paul overlooks both the "helpful deeds" and the "administrations." Instead he adds the gift of interpreting tongues (see v. 10).

No one in the church can claim to possess all the gifts that Paul mentions. The members of the church individually and collectively depend on one another for the talents and abilities which each one possesses. Conversely, the distribution of gifts among the members of the church discloses both diversity and unity.

31. But eagerly desire the greater gifts.
And I will show you an even more excellent way.

The conclusion to this chapter is relatively short, but its interpretation presents many problems. Does Paul exhort his readers to seek the first three positions in his list: apostle, prophet, and teacher? The requirements for the apostolic office—having followed Jesus from his baptism to his ascension, and being a witness of his resurrection (Acts 1:21–22)—prevented nearly everyone from seeking it. Paul encourages especially the gifts of prophecy and, by implication, teaching (chap. 14). The current passage should be understood as a summary statement in the form of an introduction to Paul's chapter on love. Yet this summary offers a number of difficulties.

a. *Text.* How do we understand the verb *to desire?* Is it in the indicative or the imperative mood? Some scholars are of the opinion that the first line of verse 31 should be read in the indicative mood: "You are striving after the greater gifts."[67] Most Bible translations, however, present the verse in the imperative mood: "But eagerly desire the greater gifts."[68] This reading is supported by two parallel texts that use the same verb in the imperative: After the interlude of Paul's epistle of love (chap. 13), he resumes his discussion on spiritual gifts and writes, "Strive eagerly for the spiritual gifts" (14:1).[69] And Paul concludes by saying, "Eagerly desire to prophesy" (14:39).

Next, what is meant by the adjective that modifies the word *gifts?* Almost every translation reads either "greater" or "higher" gifts. A textual variant allows an alternative, "the best gifts" (KJV, NKJV).[70] Not only on the basis of the Greek text but also because of the context itself, commentators favor the translation *greater* or *higher.*

b. *Meaning.* Why does Paul instruct the Corinthians to strive eagerly for greater gifts when in an earlier verse (v. 11) he writes that the Holy Spirit distributes them according to his design (see also v. 18)? When Paul writes, "But eagerly de-

---

67. Gerhard Iber, "Zum Verständnis von I Cor. 12, 31," *ZNW* 54 (1963): 43–52; Bittlinger, *Gifts and Graces*, pp. 73–75; Max-Alain Chevallier, *Esprit de Dieu, Paroles d'Hommes* (Neuchâtel: Delachaux, 1966), pp. 158–63; Martin, *The Spirit and the Congregation*, pp. 34–37.

68. E.g., NIV, NRSV, NJB.

69. David L. Baker calls this "a catch-phrase in the Corinthian Church." See his article, "The Interpretation of 1 Cor. 12–14," *EvQ* 46 (1974): 224–34.

70. This reading finds support in both the Western witnesses and the Majority Text, but is limited by a lack of older and Alexandrian manuscripts.

sire the greater gifts," he uses the Greek verb *zēloō* (I strive after something), which in this context conveys a positive meaning. Paul exhorts the believers in Corinth to attain the goal of receiving and developing their spiritual gifts for the edification of the Christian community.[71] The sense of the Greek noun *zēlōtēs*, from which we have the derivative *zealot*, is to do eagerly that which is good (Titus 2:14; I Peter 3:13).

We assume that some Corinthians had given prominence to the gift of tongue-speaking, but Paul puts it last in his list at both the beginning and the end of the chapter (vv. 10, 28, 30). Although he does not discount the value of the gift, he nevertheless regards it as "the lowest of God's spiritual blessings."[72] Thus, he urges the readers of this epistle to strive for the greater gifts.

c. *Interlude.* "And I will show you an even more excellent way." At this point, scholars differ on paragraph division. Some include verse 31b with the preceding, some with succeeding, verses. Others make the two sentences of verse 31 a separate paragraph. I suggest that the second half of this verse forms a bridge between chapters 12 and 13 and thus should stand by itself.

Paul presents his exposition of love as an interlude in his discussion on gifts. He says that love is not spiritual gifts but rather a way of life.[73] He shows that without the context of love, a spiritual gift cannot function and is worthless. Love is the most important fruit of the Spirit; it is the first one mentioned in the list of nine virtues (Gal. 5:22–23).

Paul tries to define the meaning of love, but he can only describe it in positive and negative clauses. Upon concluding the interlude, he returns to his discussion on spiritual gifts.

Practical Considerations in 12:29–31

We stand amazed when someone develops talents we never knew he or she had. When we see this unfolding, we express our appreciation and speak of hidden talents. For instance, we are able to detect hereditary traits and know that God is the giver of these talents. In similar fashion, Paul speaks of the Holy Spirit distributing spiritual gifts to the individual believers (see vv. 11, 18). But if God grants us choice gifts, how can we strive after even greater gifts? It seems preposterous to ask God for additional gifts when we already have received the talents he has distributed.

Paul tells the Corinthians that in their zeal for spiritual gifts, they must "seek to excel in the work of edifying the church" (14:12). In the word *seek* we hear an echo of Jesus' word: "Ask and it will be given to you; seek and you shall find; knock and the door will be opened to you" (Matt. 7:7; Luke 11:9). God is sovereign and wants us to come to him. He desires that we ask him so that he may freely give us his gifts.

---

71. Albrecht Stumpff, *TDNT*, vol. 2, p. 888; Hans-Christoph Hahn, *NIDNTT*, vol. 3, p. 1167.

72. Hurd, *Origin of I Corinthians*, p. 192. By contrast, Fee argues that tongue-speaking "is listed last not because it is 'least,' but because it is the problem." *First Corinthians*, p. 572.

73. Carson, *Showing the Spirit*, p. 57.

As recipients of these spiritual gifts, however, we ought never to be filled with envy, to boast, or to be proud (13:4). These vices stifle love and deny the purpose for employing spiritual gifts, namely, to edify the church.

Greek Words, Phrases, and Constructions in 12:27–28

Verse 27

ὑμεῖς—the plural personal pronoun receives emphasis as the first word in the sentence. It serves Paul's purpose to apply his discourse directly to the Corinthian believers.

Notice that this verse features four nouns (σῶμα, Χριστοῦ, μέλη, μέρους) but no definite articles. The absence in each case varies; for example, the name *Christ* may or may not have a definite article. The word σῶμα (body) must be understood as an absolute—that is, there is only one body, the church. And that body is the possession of Jesus Christ. Therefore the genitive case in Χριστοῦ is neither subjective or objective but possessive.[74]

Verse 28

οὓς μέν—the relative pronoun has its antecedent in μέλη (v. 27) and thus elucidates the concept *body*. The particle μέν lacks its counterpart δέ because of the ordinal numbers *first, second,* and *third*. After these three, Paul continues with ἔπειτα (then), which is used twice.

ἔθετο—the context demands the translation *he appointed* but in verse 18 "he placed." See the grammatical comment at verse 18.

Summary of Chapter 12

Paul tells the Corinthians of the spiritual gifts they had received and reminds them of their pagan backgrounds in which they were often led astray to the mute idols. But as believers they should know that only through the power of the Holy Spirit are they able to say, "Jesus is Lord."

The same Spirit, the same Lord, and the same God provide spiritual gifts for the common good of the church. Nine of these gifts are listed: wisdom, knowledge, faith, healing, miracles, prophecy, spirit discernment, tongues, and interpreting tongues. These gifts are the work of the Holy Spirit, who apportions them to each believer according to his divine will.

To describe the church, Paul uses the analogy of man's physical body that consists of many parts yet expresses harmonious unity. Because the body has numerous parts, not a single one of them can of its own accord separate itself; every part continues to be connected with the body: the foot, the hand, the ear, and the eye. God arranges all the parts of the body in the places where he wants them to be. The individual parts of the body need each other, for even weaker members are indispensable. God even gives greater honor to those parts that lack it.

---

74. C. K. Barrett, *A Commentary on the First Epistle to the Corinthians*, Harper's New Testament Commentaries series (New York and Evanston: Harper and Row, 1968), p. 292.

The body itself demonstrates unity in purpose: it suffers when one part suffers and it rejoices when one of its parts is honored.

Within the church are apostles, prophets, and teachers. Paul enumerates the gifts of miracles, healing, helpful deeds, administrations, and tongues. He queries whether everyone has received all the gifts, and then urges all the believers to strive eagerly for the greater gifts. He concludes by saying that he is showing them a more excellent way of life.

13

Worship, *part 3*

(13:1–13)

Outline (continued)

13 1 If I speak in the tongues of men, even those of angels, but have not love, I am only echoing bronze or a clanging cymbal. 2 And if I have [the gift of] prophecy and understand all mysteries and all knowledge, and if I have all faith so as to remove mountains, but have not love, I am nothing. 3 And if I give away all my possessions to feed the poor, and if I give up my body to be burned, but have not love, it profits me nothing.

4 Love is patient and is kind, love is not jealous, love does not brag, is not arrogant. 5 Love does not behave indecently, does not seek its own things, does not become irritated, does not keep a record of wrongs, 6 does not rejoice in evil, but rejoices in the truth, 7 covers all things, believes all things, hopes all things, endures all things.

8 Love never fails. But if there are prophecies, they shall be set aside; if there are tongues, they shall cease; if there is knowledge, it shall be set aside. 9 For we know in part and we prophesy in part. 10 But when perfection comes, that which is in part shall be set aside. 11 When I was a child, I used to talk as a child, think as a child, reason as a child. But when I became a man, I set aside childish things. 12 For now we see in a mirror an indistinct reflection, but then we shall see face to face. Now I know in part, but then I shall know fully, even as I have been fully known.

13 Now remain faith, hope, love, these three; and the greatest of these is love.

---

4. Letter of Love
13:1–13

Inspired by the Holy Spirit, Paul gave the world a love letter without equal. Here is Paul's writing at its best on a subject that awakens everyone's interest, love. His presentation of love, however, is without sentimentality, devoid of sensuality, and free from sexuality.

The world has poured a sensual meaning into the word *love* that centers on sex and the sex act. Another use of this word is to equate it with a degree of fondness for either an action or an object, as in "I love to do it," or "I love it." By contrast, the love that Paul has in mind is divine in origin and transcends earthly meanings. It is expressed in the well-known verse, "For God so loved the world" (John 3:16). The human mind cannot fully grasp the depth of that divine love. God commands us to love him with heart, soul, and mind, and to love our neighbor as ourselves (Matt. 22:37–39). This love is embodied in the Greek term *agapē*, which means either God's love for man or man's love for God. Also, we are to love our neighbor, even if the neighbor is our enemy. In brief, *agapē* originates with God, who communicates his divine love which he expects us to reflect and return to him.

Paul wants his readers to live within the context of divine love and day by day demonstrate this love. He shows them that this love indeed is the more excellent way of life. He wants them to receive and employ their spiritual gifts in the setting of that love. He knows, for instance, that when a Christian prophesies or speaks in a tongue within the framework of divine love, the church will be edified and strengthened. Without this love, the believers are unable to share the benefits of these spiritual gifts. Paul looks at the six gifts of speech, prophecy, mysteries, knowledge, faith, and charity. He concludes that outside the context of love, these gifts are meaningless.

In the first three verses of the chapter, Paul introduces conditional clauses that are contrasted with statements on the absence of love. And to each of these clauses, he adds conclusions of descriptive reality. The next section (vv. 4–7) is a description of love in both positive and negative terms. Paul follows this section with a discussion on the permanency of love. When prophecies cease, tongues are silenced, and knowledge disappears, perfection comes at the consummation (vv. 8–12). And last, the concluding verse profiles the triad of faith, hope, and love. The greatest of these three is love (v. 13).

a. Prerequisite of Love
13:1–3

1. If I speak in the tongues of men, even those of angels, but have not love, I am only echoing bronze or a clanging cymbal.

In addition to the majestic rhythm in this verse, a number of items are noteworthy. First, Paul speaks hypothetically of a possible mastery of both human and angelic speech; he resorts to the use of a conditional clause. Next, in this verse, as in verses 2, 3, 11, and 12, he refers to himself in the first person singular. Throughout the entire chapter the Corinthian Christians and their problems are never mentioned, although he includes his readers with the plural pronoun *we* in verse 12a. And third, in the Greek Paul places the verb *to speak* between the words *of men* and *even those of angels*. The position of this verb undoubtedly is meant to stress the reference to angelic speech.[1] The verb itself signifies more the ability to speak than the content of speech.

a. "If I speak in the tongues of men, even those of angels." With this conditional statement, Paul indicates that he himself does not engage in tongue-speaking in public worship (14:19). He appears to be saying, "Suppose that I as the Lord's apostle have the highest possible gift of tongues, those that men use, and those even that angels use—how you Corinthians would admire, even envy me and desire to have an equal gift!"[2]

The word *tongues* can be understood to mean known languages; but in context it appears to mean tongue-speech, which some Corinthians regarded as

1. This construction is unique and occurs only here in the Greek text of the New Testament. See D. A. Carson, *Showing the Spirit: A Theological Exposition of 1 Corinthians 12–14* (Grand Rapids: Baker, 1987), p. 58 n. 20.
2. R. C. H. Lenski, *The Interpretation of St. Paul's First and Second Epistle to the Corinthians* (1935; Columbus: Wartburg, 1946), p. 545.

heavenly speech. We do not know what supernatural language angels speak (compare II Cor. 12:4; Rev. 14:1–3) or whether angels are able to understand human speech.[3] Conversely, angels communicate with people in human terms that are frequently recorded in both the Old and New Testaments.

b. "But have not love, I am only echoing bronze or a clanging cymbal." The point at issue is not the speaking of tongues, whether human or angelic, but the practice of love. Within the context of the Christian church, be it in Corinth or anywhere else, lack of love and its deplorable consequences are often painfully evident.

True love reveals itself in loving the unlovable, for this is what God does. He shows us his love in the death of his Son while we were still in sin (Rom. 5:8). God always comes to us first in love before we come to him in repentance and faith. "This is love: not that we loved God, but that he loved us and sent his Son as an atoning sacrifice for our sins" (I John 4:10). The apostle John tells his readers to show love to one another as God has shown his love to them.

Paul now teaches that love ought to permeate the entire context of Christian living. No one can boast of having the gift of speech, whether human or heavenly, and at the same time show a lack of love. If this happens, says Paul, the noise you hear is comparable to that of echoing bronze or a clanging cymbal. The sounds of a gong and a cymbal are monotones; when these sounds are prolonged, they eventually become annoying to the human ear. We have learned that when something is said without love, even if it is expressed most eloquently, the spoken words are empty and meaningless. They are comparable to a bronze vase that echoes when struck or to a cymbal that clangs in worship (Ps. 150:5, LXX).[4] Paul applies his words not to the Corinthians but to himself. He literally says, "I have become echoing brass. . . ." The common Greek spoken by Paul often used the perfect tense ("have become") for the present tense ("I am").

2. And if I have [the gift of] prophecy and understand all mysteries and all knowledge, and if I have all faith so as to remove mountains but have not love, I am nothing.

a. *Prophecy.* The next gift that is mentioned in verses 1–3 is prophecy, or as a literal translation would read, "I have prophecy." This means more than "to prophesy," for it signifies that a person has become a prophet.[5] In the preceding list of gifts (12:28), prophecy is second and tongues last. But here Paul begins with tongue-speaking and then introduces prophecy.

Paul exalts the gift of prophecy, because a prophet, in contrast with the tongue-speaker, strengthens and edifies the church (14:1–5). The prophet can

3. SB, vol. 3, p. 449. See Testament of Job 48–50.
4. Consult William Harris, "'Sounding Brass' and Hellenistic Technology," *BAR* 8 (1982): 38–41; William W. Klein, "Noisy Gong or Acoustic Vase? A Note on 1 Corinthians 13.1," *NTS* 32 (1986): 286–89; Ivor H. Jones, "Musical Instruments in the Bible, Part I," *BibTr* 37 (1986): 101–16.
5. E. Earle Ellis, *Prophecy and Hermeneutic in Early Christianity: New Testament Essays* (Grand Rapids: Eerdmans, 1978), p. 25 n. 15.

be effective in his ministry as long as his prophecies are true. But, says Paul, a prophecy spoken outside the context of love amounts to nothing.

The Old Testament provides striking examples of prophets who in love brought God's message to the people of Israel. Moses was God's prophet par excellence, for he regularly stood between God and his people to convey God's word to them (see Deut. 5:5). Considered a very humble man as he served the people, Moses received God's revelation in visions and dreams; God spoke to him face to face. Moses demonstrated his faithfulness in God's house, that is, among the people (Num. 12:3, 6–7; Heb. 3:5–6). He watched over God's people, loved them, and prayed for them.[6]

However, a false prophet speaks words not out of love for God's people but for personal gain. A prophet who speaks presumptuously in God's name or in the name of other gods must be put to death, says the Lord God.[7]

b. *Mysteries and knowledge.* Once again Paul speaks hypothetically by saying that even if he understood all mysteries and all knowledge, but had no love, it would be of no avail to him. Some scholars take this saying as an explanation of the word *prophecy.* They read, "If I have prophecy, that is, know all mysteries and all knowledge . . . but do not have love I am nothing."[8]

This interpretation has merit, because both the terms *mysteries* and *knowledge* depend on the verb *to understand* and are thus intimately connected. And another passage links prophecy and mystery (Rev. 10:7). Moreover, mysteries are truths which God has hidden from his people. If God's people want to understand these mysteries, they need divine wisdom. A true prophet receives insight into God's mysteries and explains them to the people.[9]

In an earlier passage about knowledge Paul says, "We speak God's wisdom in a mystery" (2:7), for he and his co-workers are "stewards of God's mysteries" (4:1). In the present passage, Paul refers to all mysteries; the term *all mysteries* may be a synonym for wisdom that receives a place next to knowledge (see 12:8). But even if Paul should possess the ability to understand all mysteries and all knowledge, without love everything would be in vain.

c. *Faith.* "And if I have all faith so as to remove mountains but have not love, I am nothing." Faith is God's gift to man, a gift which the recipient must constantly exercise, strengthen, and amplify (see 12:9). When faith lies dormant, it disappears, while unbelief and disobedience take its place. For example, Jesus' disciples were unable to cast out a demon from a boy who suffered from epileptic fits. But when Jesus came, he told the demon to come out of the boy and nev-

---

6. Willem A. VanGemeren, *Interpreting the Prophetic Word* (Grand Rapids: Zondervan, Academie Books, 1990), p. 33.

7. Deut. 18:20. See also Jer. 14:14; 23:16, 26; Ezek. 13:2–3, 17.

8. Ellis, *Prophecy and Hermeneutic in Early Christianity*, p. 52; John Calvin, *The First Epistle of Paul the Apostle to the Corinthians*, Calvin's Commentaries series, trans. John W. Fraser (reprint ed.; Grand Rapids: Eerdmans, 1976), p. 275.

9. Herman Ridderbos, *Paul: An Outline of His Theology*, trans. John Richard de Witt (Grand Rapids: Eerdmans, 1975), p. 451.

er to enter him again (Mark 9:25). In private the disciples asked Jesus why they had failed. Jesus said, "Because you have so little faith. I tell you the truth, if you have faith as small as a mustard seed, you can say to this mountain, 'Move from here to there' and it will move. Nothing will be impossible for you" (Matt. 17:20; compare 21:21).

The remark on moving mountains is a Jewish proverbial saying that conveyed the idea of making the impossible possible.[10] It attests to the intensity of exercising one's faith to remove insurmountable barriers. Both Jesus and Paul, in their respective contexts, allude to this proverb.

Whenever a person is able in faith to do the impossible, he or she is highly respected and greatly admired within the Christian community. But faith ought to be exerted in harmony with love. Otherwise it is useless. The brevity of Paul's conclusion, "I am nothing," is forthright and to the point, for indeed, faith without love is ineffectual.

3. And if I give away all my possessions to feed the poor, and if I give up my body to be burned, but have not love, it profits me nothing.

a. *Charity.* After enumerating the gifts of tongues, prophecy, knowledge, and faith, Paul refers to his charitable willingness to part with earthly possessions. He literally says, "If I dole out all my goods to feed [the poor]." We supply the object, "the poor." The Greek verb *psōmizō* (I give out or away, dole out) in this text is revealing. It differs from Jesus' command to the rich young ruler to give all his money to the poor in a single action (Matt. 19:21). Rather, Paul says that he would give away all his possessions piecemeal over a lengthy period. The obvious implication is that he would receive the praises of his fellow men. But Paul adds that if he would perform deeds of charity without love for the recipients of his gifts, those deeds would not mean anything at all. Then his motives would be self-centered and self-serving. His deed would fail to fulfill the royal law, "Love your neighbor as yourself" (James 2:8), and would be condemned in God's sight.

b. *Self-sacrifice.* "If I give up my body to be burned, but have not love, it profits me nothing." The better Greek manuscripts support an alternate reading, "If I give up my body that I may glory," and at least one translation has adopted it.[11]

Translators have to consider the contextual evidence in addition to the testimony of manuscripts before they can make a choice. For instance, Paul repeatedly uses the verb *to glory* in his epistles (thirty-five times). The verb *to glory* can be understood either negatively or positively. When viewed negatively—that is, as boasting—the word hardly suits the present context, in which Paul is enumerating spiritual feats. "The motive of self-glorification makes the addition of [the clause *have not love*] unnecessary as it is obvious that [love] is not the guiding principle behind such a motive."[12]

---

10. SB, vol. 1, p. 759.
11. NRSV; SEB tries to combine both readings and has "[I could] sacrifice my body, so that I could brag about it."
12. J. K. Elliott, "In Favour of καυθήσομαι at I Corinthians 13.3," *ZNW* 62 (1971): 298.

When understood positively, the verb means that Paul renders glory to God through physical suffering (II Cor. 11:23–29; 12:10).[13] If we adopt this positive explanation of the verb *to glory*, we encounter at least three detractions. First, attractive though the explanation may be, it still is obscured by the clause *but have not love*. Paul knows that glorifying God without love is useless; for this reason he says, "It profits me nothing." Next, why would Paul speak hypothetically if he has in mind his own physical sufferings? And last, this explanation attempts to fill in an incomplete sentence. The introductory words, "if I give my body," need a predicate to give meaning to the sentence.

By comparison, the reading *if I give my body to be burned* is explicit and presents a complete thought. When we adopt this translation, we readily admit to difficulties that remain. Why would Paul voluntarily offer his physical body to the flames, while the three young men were forcefully thrown into the fire (Dan. 3:19–20)? And the reference cannot be to the Neronian persecution, during which Christians were burned at the stake, because that persecution had not yet commenced.

What then is the meaning of this intriguing clause? If Paul intends his remark on moving mountains to be taken figuratively, we may expect that the clause on surrendering his body to the flames also is a metaphor. And this may well have been his intention provided the words *if I give my body to be burned* are the original text.

Additional Comments on 13:1–3

The first lines in each of the three verses reveal difficult but attainable feats. The three goals of speaking other human languages (v. 1a), prophesying and understanding all mysteries and all knowledge (v. 2a), and distributing one's material possessions (v. 3a) can be achieved. Two additional goals can be reached: a person can possess faith to remove mountains, figuratively speaking (v. 2b); and, in an extreme case, he can choose to deliver his body to the flames (v. 3b). These two are attainable feats, albeit that the second implies self-glorification through suicide. (Should we adopt the alternate reading for the second part of verse 3, "if I hand over my body so that I may boast" [NRSV], the matter of attainability becomes irrelevant.) The one unattainable goal for human beings is to speak in the tongues of angels (v. 1a).

In fact, we lack certainty as to Paul's intention in verse 3b. The suggestion has been made that he attempts to match the words of Jesus, who during the institution of the Lord's Supper said that he gave up his body: "This is my body which is for you" (11:24; Luke 22:19).[14] But this suggestion is a hypothesis that faces at least one significant objection: the readers of Paul's epistle would be hard pressed to understand that the cryptic clause *if I hand over my body* refers to the communion formula that Paul discussed in 11:24.

---

13. Gordon D. Fee, *The First Epistle to the Corinthians*, New International Commentary on the New Testament series (Grand Rapids: Eerdmans, 1987), p. 635.
14. J. H. Petzer, "Contextual Evidence in Favour of ΚΑΥΧΗΣΩΜΑΙ in 1 Corinthians 13:3," *NTS* 35 (1989): 242–43.

Surely Paul would have augmented this clause with an allusion to the Lord's Supper to make himself understood.

Even though the translation *if I give my body to be burned* has its own difficulties,[15] it is a complete thought and in a sense flows smoothly. This reading "is attested from all other parts of the ancient Christian world and from the earliest times onwards (Tertullian, Aphraates)."[16] Admittedly, the reading *if I give my body so that I may boast* is equally attested. We conclude that this textual problem is so complex that it is imprudent to be dogmatic.

Greek Words, Phrases, and Constructions in 13:1–3

Verses 1–2

ἐάν—Paul uses five conditional clauses in verses 1–3 with this particle to indicate an uncertain or hypothetical statement. The forms καὶ ἐάν and κἄν (v. 3) are mere variations.

ἀγάπην—abstract nouns (e.g., faith, hope, love; see v. 13) often do not need the definite article to express their qualities.

ἠχῶν—"echoing." This descriptive present participle modifies the noun χαλκός (brass). The adjective ἀλαλάζον (clanging) is onomatopoeic.

ὥστε—the particle ("so that") with the present infinitive μεθιστά ναι (to remove) introduces an ellipsis. The auxiliary infinitive δύνασθαι (to be able) should have been added.[17]

Verse 3

καυχήσωμαι—"I may boast." This reading has the best manuscript support—P[46], ℵ, A, B, 048, 33, 1739—and on external grounds is the preferred Greek text of the three editions of the United Bible Society, and Nestle-Aland (26th ed.).

καυθήσωμαι—"I may burn." The future subjunctive, supported by K Ψ, is a grammatical monstrosity.[18] It is the text of the Textus Receptus, Majority Text, and Souter.

καυθήσομαι—"I may burn." The future passive with ἵνα instead of the subjunctive occurs frequently in Koine Greek. With the textual support of C, D, F, G, L, a number of uncials, and some church fathers, this is the adopted Greek text of the British and Foreign Bible Society (2d ed.), Nestle-Aland (25th ed.), Merk, and Vogels. It is also the choice of nearly all translators.

On the basis of internal evidence, translators and numerous commentators favor the weaker reading to the stronger reading. This occurs more often in the New Testament and is not at all uncommon.[19]

---

15. A literal translation is "If I give my body that I may be burned." Grammatically, the last part should be "that it [the body] may be burned."

16. G. Zuntz, *The Text of the Epistles: A Disquisition upon the Corpus Paulinum* (London: Oxford University Press, 1953), pp. 35–36. Consult René Kieffer, "'Afin que je sois brûlé' ou bien 'Afin que j'en tire orgueil'? (1 Cor. XIII.3)," *NTS* 22 (1975): 95–97.

17. C. F. D. Moule, *An Idiom-Book of New Testament Greek*, 2d ed. (Cambridge: Cambridge University Press, 1960), p. 144.

18. G. G. Findlay, *St. Paul's First Epistle to the Corinthians*, in vol. 3 of *The Expositor's Greek Testament*, ed. W. Robertson Nicoll (1910; reprint ed.; Grand Rapids: Eerdmans, 1961), p. 898; Bruce M. Metzger, *A Textual Commentary on the Greek New Testament*, 3d corrected ed. (London and New York: United Bible Societies, 1975), p. 564.

19. E.g., refer to II Cor. 4:6, where λάμψει (light shall shine) has the better manuscript evidence, but translators prefer the weaker reading λάμψαι (let light shine) because of internal testimony.

Unquestionably, the concept *love* can more easily be explained in terms of what it is not than what it is. The first line of Paul's description is positive, the succeeding lines are negative, and the concluding statement is positive. Paul describes the concept *love* in a poetically arranged paragraph (vv. 4–6).

> Love is patient and is kind.
> Love is not jealous, does not brag, is not arrogant.
> Love does not behave indecently,
> > does not seek its own things,
> > does not become irritated,
> > does not keep a record of evil,
> > does not rejoice in unrighteousness,
> but rejoices in the truth
> > covers all things,
> > believes all things,
> > hopes all things,
> > endures all things.

In sequence we count two affirmative descriptions, eight negative, and five positive attributes. We now discuss them one by one.

---

b. Portrayal of Love
13:4–7

4. Love is patient and is kind, love is not jealous, love does not brag, is not arrogant.

Many translators punctuate the sentence differently by dividing the first clause and making the noun *love* the subject of the second clause: "Love is patient; love is kind and envies no one" (NEB). Punctuation in verse 4, however, has no bearing on its meaning.

a. "Love is patient." The Greek verb which we have translated "is patient" actually means to be forbearing in respect to actual offenses and injuries one receives from others. It signifies that one is slow in avenging and slow in becoming angry.[20] It demonstrates a willingness to take someone's unpleasant character traits in stride and to exhibit enduring patience. As God is forbearing with us, so we must tolerate our fellow man (compare Matt. 18:26, 29).

b. "[Love] is kind." In the New Testament the verb *to be kind* appears only here. Clement of Rome wrote an epistle to the Corinthian church in which he quotes a saying of Jesus that has the same Greek verb: "As you are kind, so will you be shown kindness."[21] The noun *kindness* occurs repeatedly in Paul's epistles. For instance, after placing love as the first fruit of the Spirit, Paul lists the fruits of patience and kindness (Gal. 5:22).

---

20. Thayer, p. 387.
21. I Clem. 13:3.

c. "Love is not jealous." Jealousy is a vice for which we even have selected a color: green. We know that when a person is green with envy the probability for trouble is real. The Bible is filled with illustrations that portray the disastrous effect jealousy has on personal relationships. To mention but a few: Cain envied Abel and killed him (Gen. 4:3–8); Jacob's sons were jealous of Joseph and sold him into slavery (Gen. 37:11, 28); the high priest and his associates were filled with jealousy and jailed the apostles (Acts 5:17–18); and the Jews were jealous of Paul and Barnabas and expelled them from Pisidian Antioch (Acts 13:45–50).

Jealousy can have a positive connotation in the sense of guarding one's honor. For instance, God is a jealous God who commands his people to worship him only (Exod. 20:5; Deut. 5:9). But in the current verse, jealousy is a vice that is the exact opposite of love. Love, however, is free from envy.

d. "Love does not brag." Paul uses a verb that depicts a person as a braggart or windbag.[22] Such a person parades his embellished rhetoric to gain recognition. His behavior is marked by egotism, subservience toward superiors, and condescension toward subordinates. A braggart exhibits pride in himself and his accomplishments. But such bragging is devoid of love to God and to one's fellow man, and is a blatant sin. Further, bragging and arrogance go hand in hand.

e. "[Love] is not arrogant." In an earlier context, Paul told the Corinthians "not to go beyond what is written, that no one of you might become arrogant, favoring the one over against the other" (4:6). He instructed them to obey the teaching of the Scriptures, for then they would avoid arrogance. Some of the Corinthians were arrogant indeed and, while undermining Paul's authority, they thought that he would not return to Corinth (4:18–19; 5:2). Many of them prided themselves in possessing knowledge. Paul, however, set them straight by saying: "Knowledge puffs up, but love builds up" (8:1). Without love knowledge degenerates into obnoxious arrogance; with love it is a valuable asset. Arrogance is inflated selfishness, while love is genuine humility. Arrogance is devoid of love and love is devoid of arrogance; indeed both are mutually exclusive.

5. Love does not behave indecently, does not seek its own things, does not become irritated, does not keep a record of wrongs.

Paul continues his description of love by presenting still more clauses that depict love from a negative perspective.

a. "Love does not behave indecently." We perceive the echo of Paul's advice to a man who thinks that he is acting dishonorably toward the virgin to whom he is engaged (7:36). Likewise here, Paul has in mind unbecoming, improper, and inappropriate behavior in any situation. The Greek text indicates that such conduct is not in harmony with the established norm of decency.

A person who demonstrates love always strives for proper decorum in relation to others. Whether the people whom he meets occupy a high or a low position in society, whether they are friend or foe, the virtue of love is evident in his con-

---

22. Bauer, p. 653.

duct. The royal law, "Love your neighbor as yourself" (James 2:8), demands nothing less than proper behavior that characterizes gentility.

Decent behavior does not stop with words and attitude. It also pertains to one's apparel and appearance. Proper dress and a groomed look commend a person who desires to please others, for love extends to all aspects of one's demeanor.

b. "[Love] does not seek its own things." Translators differ on the meaning of this clause. The one says that love "does not insist on its own way" (NRSV), another that "it never seeks its own advantage" (NJB), and still another that it "does not claim its rights" (*Cassirer*). Even though their emphases differ, all these versions convey the same message. In shortened form the clause simply connotes, "[Love] is not selfish" (NCV).

Paul himself had shown the Corinthians the example of selfless love when he served them as their pastor for a year and a half. He labored faithfully without any financial support from them (9:18). Repeatedly he instructed them to seek the welfare of others, not their own (10:24, 33). Paul showed the Corinthians that personal advantage pertains not only to financial gain. It also pertains to demanding that others fulfill one's own wishes. By contrast, love flourishes in an atmosphere where two people trust each other and know that they will promote the welfare of the other (compare Prov. 3:29; Zech. 8:17).

c. "[Love] does not become irritated." No one is immune to irritation caused by others, not even those who possess poise and grace. After leading the Israelites through the desert for nearly forty years, Moses lost his temper when the people quarreled with him for lack of water (Num. 20:2–11). He was considered to be a very humble person (Num. 12:3); nevertheless, he was unable to control his anger in the face of a grumbling population.

Righteous anger is permissible and in certain instances even necessary. Thus, Jesus expressed anger at the money changers and sellers of cattle, sheep, and doves in the temple area of Jerusalem (John 2:13–17). The psalmist, however, warns the reader not to sin in anger (Ps. 4:4). And Paul expands the advice by saying not to let anger spill over into the next day (Eph. 4:26).

The Greek verb *paroxynein* means to stir someone to anger. This was what Paul felt when he was provoked by the idolatry of the people in Athens (Acts 17:16). Similarly, members in the Corinthian community had to endure tensions that resulted in untold provocation.[23] They had to deal with factions, immorality, lawsuits, friction in or disputes about marriage, and eating food offered to an idol. Disagreements were common and disrupted relationships. Paul himself knew from experience that the break between Barnabas and himself resulted from a sharp disagreement (Acts 15:36–41). He notes that love has no room for irritation.

d. "[Love] does not keep a record of wrongs." Here is a verbal portrait of a bookkeeper who flips the pages of his ledger to reveal what has been received

---

23. Heinrich Seesemann, *TDNT*, vol. 5, p. 857; Hans-Christoph Hahn, *NIDNTT*, vol. 1, p. 110.

and spent. He is able to give an exact account and provide an itemized list. Some people are keeping a similar list of wrongs that they have experienced. But love is extremely forgetful when it comes to remembering injury and injustice. When wrongs have been forgiven, they ought to be forgotten and never be mentioned again.

6. [Love] does not rejoice in evil, but rejoices in the truth.

The sentence is perfectly balanced with two clauses that feature the same verb but have direct objects that are opposites: wrongdoing and truth (compare Rom. 1:18; I John 1:6). As love characterizes God, so evil describes the devil. Love takes notice of the evil in this world but never gloats over it. Instead it grieves over the sins that human beings commit against one another. These wrongdoings may appear in numerous forms: intentional and unintentional evils, sins of commission and omission, harsh persecution and mild neglect, and last, national conflicts and personal controversies.

On the other hand, one of the characteristics of love is the constant attempt to discover good and praiseworthy words, thoughts, and deeds in a person. Love searches out the truth and rejoices when that truth is triumphing over wrong. Love and truth are inseparable partners residing in God himself. God shares these characteristics with his people. He endowed them with love and truth, which, though tainted by sin, are renewed in Christ Jesus through the indwelling of the Holy Spirit.

7. [Love] covers all things, believes all things, hopes all things, endures all things.

Paul concludes this poetic section with a fourfold summary of the positive force of love. Love is always active, never passive, as the verbs make evident:

a. Love "covers all things." The translations of the first clause in this verse (v. 7) are numerous and varied: love "patiently accepts all things" (NCV), "always supports" (TNT), "bears all things" (NRSV), and "never gives up" (GNB). The Greek verb in question, *stegein*, can mean "to endure" (see 9:12; I Thess. 3:1, 5). But the verb also signifies "to cover." Peter writes that love covers a multitude of sins (I Peter 4:8; see Prov. 10:12; 17:9). Love is the virtue "that throws a cloak of silence over what is displeasing in another person."[24] Hence "the idea of covering things with the cloak of love" is fitting.[25] Moreover, the translation *covers* eliminates redundancy, for the last clause in this verse "endures all things."

b. Love "believes all things." This does not mean that a Christian filled with love lacks the qualities of wisdom and discernment and thus becomes the gullible dupe of every falsifier. On the contrary, love is always wise and discerning.[26]

The clause signifies that a Christian has faith in God, who will work out his divine plans even when all the indicators seem to point in different directions.

---

24. Bauer, p. 766. Adolf von Harnack, "The Apostle Paul's Hymn of Love (1 Cor. XIII) and Its Religious-Historical Significance," *Exp* 8.3 (1912): 385–408, 481–503.

25. Wilhelm Kasch, *TDNT*, vol. 7, p. 587; SB, vol. 3, p. 766.

26. Calvin, *I Corinthians*, p. 278.

Filled with love for God and neighbor, a believer trusts that God indeed will make his or her paths straight (Prov. 3:5–6).

c. Love "hopes all things." With this clause, Paul introduces hope, the second member in the triad of faith, hope, and love (see v. 13). He shows that love gives rise to both faith and hope, so that indeed love is the greatest virtue in this triad. Of these three virtues, hope is often the neglected member overshadowed by faith. Nevertheless, when a tripod loses one of its legs, its fall is inevitable. When a Christian nurtures love and faith but neglects hope, he fails and falters in his spiritual life.

Paul frequently writes the verb *to hope*, which appears in his epistles nineteen times out of a total of thirty-one occurrences in the New Testament.[27] Hope is patient, waiting for positive results that eventually may be realized. Hope is the converse of pessimism and the essence of healthy optimism. Hope is never focused on oneself but always on God in Christ Jesus.

d. Love "endures all things." The verb *to endure* connotes perseverance and tenacity in all circumstances. It means to endure in times of pain, suffering, deprivation, hatred, loss, and loneliness. New Testament writers repeatedly exhort us to persevere: Paul tells us that if we endure with Christ, we will also reign with him (II Tim. 2:12); Peter urges slaves to endure the pain of unjust suffering for the Lord's sake (I Peter 2:19–20); and John on the island Patmos endures exile for the sake of God's Word (Rev. 1:9). The suffering which the apostles and early Christians had to endure for the sake of the gospel is eloquent testimony of fervent love for God.

Greek Words, Phrases, and Constructions in 13:4–7

Verse 4

ἡ ἀγάπη—the definite article preceding abstract nouns is not translated in English.[28]
περπερεύεται—this verb means to "conduct oneself like a πέρπερος" (i.e., a "braggart, windbag").[29]

Verses 5–6

τὰ ἑαυτῆς—"its own things." However, the definite article in the neuter plural may denote "its own way."

χαίρει, συγχαίρει—the compound in this text has the same meaning as the simple verb: "rejoice."[30]

---

27. Refer to Ernst Hoffmann, *NIDNTT*, vol. 2, p. 241.

28. A. T. Robertson, *A Grammar of the Greek New Testament in the Light of Historical Research* (Nashville: Broadman, 1934), p. 794.

29. Friedrich Blass and Albert Debrunner, *A Greek Grammar of the New Testament and Other Early Christian Literature*, trans. and rev. Robert Funk (Chicago: University of Chicago Press, 1961), #108.5; Robert Hanna, *A Grammatical Aid to the Greek New Testament* (Grand Rapids: Baker, 1983), p. 306.

30. Bauer, p. 775.

Verse 7

πάντα—this adjective occurs four times in succession with four different verbs. It can be translated as "all things," but can also serve adverbially and signify "always."[31]

The enduring character of love stands in contrast to the gifts of prophecies, tongues, and knowledge, which are temporary and will eventually disappear. However, perfection will ultimately terminate these imperfect faculties and give human beings complete maturity. When partial knowledge fades, perfect perception and full comprehension take its place. But faith, hope, and love will remain forever, and of these three, love is the greatest.

---

c. Permanence and Perfection of Love
13:8–13

8. Love never fails. But if there are prophecies, they shall be set aside; if there are tongues, they shall cease; if there is knowledge, it shall be set aside.

a. "Love never fails." This clause supports the message of the preceding verse and forms a concise summary of the previous passage (vv. 4–7). At the same time the clause is introductory to the verses that ensue (vv. 9–13). Notice that the word *love* occurs at the beginning of this verse and reappears twice in verse 13. Between these two occurrences, Paul describes the temporary character of the spiritual gifts (vv. 8–10) and gives three illustrations to illustrate that which is immature and imperfect—a child, a reflection, and knowledge (vv. 11–12). In this segment, Paul stresses immaturity, imperfection, and temporality.

Love, however, is endless and never loses its validity. As God's Word never "falls to the ground," so his love never fails.[32] Love is eternal because it is one of God's attributes (I John 4:8, 16). It emanates from God to all his people throughout time and eternity. While everything else in God's creation comes to an end, love continues to be an active and lasting influence.

b. "But if there are prophecies, they shall be set aside." Whereas love is timeless, predictive prophecies are temporal. Love remains active, but prophecies have only partial significance; as Paul explains in verse 9, "We prophesy in part" (compare v. 12b). Because of their partial nature, they shall be put aside. Paul says nothing about the content of these prophecies, except that they have passing relevance.

The Greek verb *katargein* that Paul uses four times in verses 8, 10, and 11 is the one which we translate "to set aside," or "to pass away, to cease." It is related to the adjective *argos* (idle, inactive, unproductive; see, e.g., Matt. 12:36); the verb means that something is put aside or has become ineffective. Prophecies and knowledge are overtaken by fulfillment and thus are put aside, much as an adult

---

31. Robertson, *Grammar*, p. 487; consult Oda Wischmeyer, *Der Höchste Weg. Das 13 Kapitel des 1. Korintherbriefes* (Gütersloh: Gütersloher Verlagshaus Gerd Mohn, 1981), p. 105.
32. Wolfgang Bauder, *NIDNTT*, vol. 1, p. 609.

discards things belonging to his childhood days.[33] We discard prophecies and knowledge, because we prophesy and we know in part (v. 9).

c. "If there are tongues, they shall cease." Paul only mentions the term *tongues* but does not explain it. He reserves that discussion for the next chapter (chap. 14; consult the commentary). The verb *to cease* in the second clause is a synonym and a variant of the verb *to be set aside* (vv. 8, 10, 11). There is virtually no distinction between the two Greek verbs that describe the termination of both prophecies and tongues. True, the verb with prophecies is in the passive voice (believers are the implied agents), while the verb with tongues is interpreted as the active voice. The difference is only a stylistic change and nothing more.[34]

d. "If there is knowledge, it shall be set aside." Paul refrains from elucidating the meaning of the term *knowledge* at this point. He mentioned the gift of knowledge in the preceding chapter (12:8), where it relates to an affinity between God and his people. We assume that he refers to the Christian's ability to discern, understand, and explain God's revelation. He states that it shall be set aside in the future.

9. For we know in part and we prophesy in part. 10. But when perfection comes, that which is in part shall be set aside.

a. "For we know in part and we prophesy in part." These two verses form one sentence in the Greek, but this sentence in two parts raises a few questions. What specifically does Paul wish to say? If indeed knowledge is imparted for the benefit of fellow believers and so is prophecy, are these verses a circumlocution for the preaching, teaching, and explaining of God's will revealed in the Scriptures? We know God's truth only partially and proclaim it in segments, so Paul applies the words *in part* to both verbs *to know* and *to prophesy*. He appears to indicate that the activity of knowing God's truth and prophesying it occurs only in fragmentary form. That is, our knowledge and our prophesying are incomplete.

Two matters stand out: Paul writes the personal pronoun *we* and the present tense of the verbs *to know* and *to prophesy*. Does the pronoun refer to Paul and his associates or does he include the readers of his epistle? Is the present tense limited to his age or is it still valid today? Paul employs the personal pronoun *we* only in verses 9 and 12, obviously in a general sense. And the present tense of the verbs does not appear to be limited to his own time. Notice that he contrasts verses 9 and 10 by saying that when perfection comes the partial shall be set aside.

If knowledge pertains to our aptitude to comprehend and interpret God's revelation, what is the meaning of prophesying? Persons who filled the office of prophet in Old or New Testament times received divine revelation and proclaimed it to God's people. Prophets in these two eras were instrumental in writing the Scriptures. But in addition to developing and completing the canon, prophets interpreted God's Word to his people. When the books of the Old Testament were complete, the office of prophet ended. Similarly, when the New

---

33. J. I. Packer, *NIDNTT*, vol. 1, p. 73; Gerhard Delling, *TDNT*, vol. 1, p. 453.
34. Consult Carson, *Showing the Spirit*, pp. 66–67; Fee, *First Corinthians*, p. 644.

Testament canon was perfected, the number of prophets dwindled and they eventually disappeared.[35]

We distinguish between revelatory prophecy that terminated when the canon was complete and declaratory prophecy that continues even today.[36] Scholars dispute this distinction by saying that "preaching is essentially a merging of the gifts of teaching and exhortation, prophecy has the primary elements of prediction and revelation."[37] This observation is correct but describes only the revelatory aspect of the prophet's task and not his declaratory role. Interpreting Scripture is a prophetic function that has its roots in the postexilic period. At the Jerusalem Council, James reveals the continuity of preaching in Old and New Testament times: "For Moses has been preached in every city from the earliest times and is read in the synagogues on every Sabbath" (Acts 15:21). The rabbis could not imagine that Israel was ever without local synagogues and schools.[38]

In Old Testament times, there were countless prophets in Israel, so that no city was ever without them. These people were interpreters of the Law and spoke with the authority of the Holy Spirit. They differed from the revelatory prophets only in degree by serving God as his spokesmen. Indeed, when the Old Testament canon was complete, the rabbis in effect took the place of the prophets. In the rabbinic tradition, the prophets of the classical period were "no more than interpreters of the Law speaking with the authority of the Spirit and charged to unfold only what the Law contains."[39] If in the Old Testament era numerous prophets expounded God's Word, so also in New Testament times prophets interpreted Scripture. From the Book of Acts we know that prophets had a ministry that was not merely restricted to receiving divine revelation. Both Barnabas and Paul, called prophets and teachers (13:1), proclaimed the Word of God (13:5; 14:21). And the prophets Judas and Silas were sent to the churches to encourage and strengthen the believers (15:27, 32). Concludes E. Earle Ellis: "The prophet is the Lord's instrument, one among several means by which Jesus leads his church. As one who makes known the meaning of Scripture, exhorts, and strengthens the congregation, and instructs the community by revelations of the future, the Christian prophet manifests in the power of the Spirit the character of his Lord, who is the Prophet of the end-time (3:22)."[40]

---

35. Gerhard Friedrich, *TDNT*, vol. 6, p. 859; David Hill, *New Testament Prophecy* (Atlanta: John Knox, 1979), p. 187.

36. Refer to John MacArthur, Jr., *1 Corinthians*, MacArthur New Testament Commentary series (Chicago: Moody, 1984), p. 303; and *Charismatic Chaos* (Grand Rapids: Zondervan, 1992), p. 69.

37. F. David Farnell, "When Will the Gift of Prophecy Cease?" *BS* 150 (1993): 184. See also Ernest Best, "Prophets and Preachers," *SJT* 12 (1959): 145; Robert L. Thomas, "The Spiritual Gift of Prophecy in Rev 22:18," *JETS* 32 (1989): 204; Gerhard Friedrich, *TDNT*, vol. 6, p. 853.

38. SB, vol. 4, pp. 115–16.

39. Rudolf Meyer, *TDNT*, vol. 6, p. 818; see also E. Earle Ellis, *Prophecy and Hermeneutic in Early Christianity: New Testament Essays* (Grand Rapids: Eerdmans, 1978), pp. 132–34; Colin Brown, *NIDNTT*, vol. 3, p. 87; and SB, vol. 2, p. 128.

40. Ellis, *Prophecy and Hermeneutic*, p. 144.

Paul's frequent use of the verb *to prophesy* in his discussion on spiritual gifts points to preaching the Scriptures and encouraging the believers. The New Testament reveals that the work of a prophet consisted of encouraging and strengthening the believers (Acts 15:32; I Cor. 14:3), and predicting immediate events (Acts 11:28; 21:10–11). Hence, the verb *to prophesy* includes the work of those who preach and teach the message of God's revelation recorded in the Scriptures. As Paul notes, the gifts of knowing and prophesying belong to the time between Christ's ascension and the consummation of this age.

A study of the verb *to prophesy* in the Greek text of I Corinthians shows that this particular verb always appears in the present tense. Whether it is in the indicative or the subjunctive mood, whether it is a participle or an infinitive, the verb conveys present continuous action.[41] The use of the present tense signifies that Paul has in mind not only revelatory prophecy that came to an end with the close of the canon, but also consistent preaching and teaching of the Word. Among the list of spiritual gifts (12:8–10, 28–30), the ability to preach is absent. This fact is telling, for it implies that the gift of prophecy includes preaching and interpreting God's Word to his people.

The Greek verbs *euaggelizomai* and *kērussō* (I preach) do not appear in chapters 12–14, and only a few times elsewhere in this epistle. Paul writes either verb always with reference to himself and his apostolic helpers (1:17, 23; 9:16–18, 27; 15:1–2, 11–12), but not to others. His use of the verb *to prophesy* in the chapters on spiritual gifts alludes to those prophets who interpret the revealed Word of God.

Even though a first-century prophet exhorted and taught the believers, this does not mean that every Christian functions as a prophet.[42] Paul himself is asking the rhetorical question that expects a negative answer, "Are all prophets?" (12:29). In I Corinthians, prophesying embodies both receiving God's revelation and explaining it for the benefit of the believers. When the foundational period of the Scriptures ended, direct revelation ceased and the task of interpreting the Scriptures continued.

As in the past, so today; God uses preachers as his mouthpieces to proclaim his will. Swiss theologian Heinrich Bullinger composed an influential confession of faith in 1566. In this confession he clearly delineates the preaching of God's Word by the ministers:

> We believe that the very Word of God is proclaimed, and received by the faithful; and that neither any other Word of God is to be invented nor is to be expected from heaven: and that now the Word itself which is preached is to be regarded, not the minister that preaches.

Further, the confession describes the role of prophets: "In former times the

---

41. I Cor. 11:4, 5; 13:9; 14: 1, 3, 4, 5, 24, 31, 39.
42. Compare Max Turner, "Spiritual Gifts Then and Now," *VoxEv* 15 (1985): 13.

prophets were seers, knowing the future; but they also interpreted the Scriptures. Such men are also found still today."[43]

God of the prophets! Bless the prophets' sons;
Elijah's mantle o'er Elisha cast;
Each age its solemn task may claim but once;
Make each one nobler, stronger than the last.

Anoint them prophets! Make their ears attent
To Thy divinest speech, their hearts awake
To human need; their lips make eloquent
To gird the right and every evil break.

—Denis Wortman

b. "But when perfection comes, that which is in part shall be set aside." Paul contrasts the word *perfection* with the twice-used term *in part* of the preceding verse (v. 9). When has the time for perfection arrived or when will it come? Three interpretations are given:

1. Paul wrote at a time when the canon of the New Testament was still incomplete. With the clause *when perfection comes*, he looked forward to God's completed revelation in the Scriptures.[44] When the last verse of the New Testament was written, the canon was complete and God gave no further revelation. One of the objections to this view is that we cannot expect the Corinthians in A.D. 55 to link perfection to the closing of the canon in the last decade of the first century.

2. The literature of the New Testament usually equates the Greek expression *teleion* with maturity. Indeed, of its eight occurrences in Paul's epistles, six are translated "mature," while the seventh, adjectivally, describes the perfect will of God (Rom. 12:2).[45] That leaves only the eighth occurrence (13:10), which some scholars see as the completed stage in the maturing process of the believer.[46] Paul's illustration of a child becoming a man lends credence to interpreting the current text in the context of maturity. However, the conclusion to this illustration rules out the believer's maturity, for no one is able to claim full knowledge (v. 12b). Therefore, we argue that the verse instead points to the consummation.

3. When believers depart from this earthly life, they leave everything behind that is imperfect and incomplete. They enter heaven and experience the joy and peace of a sinless state. But their perfection will not be complete until Christ's return, the resurrection, and the final judgment day.[47] At the end of cosmic time, the spiritual gifts which believers now possess in part will cease. Their imperfect

---

43. Second Helvetic Confession, chapters 1 and 18 respectively.
44. Among others see, Kenneth L. Gentry, Jr., *The Charismatic Gift of Prophecy*, 2d ed. (Memphis: Footstool, 1989), pp. 53–56.
45. I Cor. 2:6; 14:20; Eph. 4:13; Phil. 3:15; Col. 1:28; 4:12.
46. E.g., Robert L. Thomas, *Understanding Spiritual Gifts: The Christian's Special Gifts in the Light of 1 Corinthians 12–14* (Chicago: Moody, 1978), pp. 106–8.
47. Calvin, *I Corinthians*, pp. 280–81.

spiritual gifts on earth will be superseded by their perfect state of knowledge at the consummation.[48]

11. When I was a child, I used to talk as a child, think as a child, reason as a child. But when I became a man, I set aside childish things.

The present verse is a comparison of the believer's earthly life and his subsequent perfection in the presence of the Lord. The analogy (v. 11) that Paul uses is that of a child and an adult. Notice that Paul writes the first person singular *I*, and depicts himself as a child who talks, thinks, and reasons. A child normally has a limited but developing vocabulary with which he or she communicates. The thought patterns of a child are immature and incomplete, and that is exactly what an adult expects from a child.

Paul employs the past tense when he refers to his childhood and to his entering the state of manhood. He compares the two periods of his life and then draws the conclusion that the things that interested him as a child had no attraction for him when he became a man. He does not belittle the talking, thinking, and acting of a child—these are characteristic of childhood. But when the child enters adulthood, everything takes on proper dimensions. To illustrate, the primary-school building which a child attends appears big and formidable. But when he or she visits these premises in later years, the school appears to have shrunk in size.

Similarly, at present we have received God's revelation which is sufficient for our salvation. Yet we realize that our knowledge remains partial until we personally see Christ face to face. At that time we will clearly understand God's design and purpose.

12. For now we see in a mirror an indistinct reflection, but then we shall see face to face. Now I know in part, but then I shall know fully, even as I have been fully known.

a. "For now we see in a mirror an indistinct reflection." Realizing that the analogy conveys his message partially, Paul adds an illustration taken from daily life: looking into a mirror.[49] He is saying that our present life is similar to persons who see a vague image of themselves in the mirror. We must understand that a mirror in Paul's day was a piece of polished metal that was often laid flat on a table. The reflection in this metal plate cannot be compared with reality—mirrors, then, remain imperfect instruments. However, a person is unable to see himself or herself without the use of a mirror.

Conversely, the saying "to see in a mirror a vague reflection" may have been a common metaphor used by philosophers to refer to something that is puzzling.[50]

---

48. Consult Richard B. Gaffin, Jr., *Perspectives on Pentecost: New Testament Teaching on the Gifts of the Holy Spirit* (Phillipsburg, N.J.: Presbyterian and Reformed, 1979), pp. 110–12; R. Fowler White, "Richard Gaffin and Wayne Grudem on 1 Cor 13:10: A Comparison of Cessationist and Noncessationist Argumentation," *JETS* 35 (1992): 173–81.

49. Job 37:18; II Cor. 3:18; James 1:23; Wis. 7:26; Sir. 12:11.

50. "We see only puzzling reflections in a mirror" (REB). Consult Gerald Downing, "Reflecting the First Century: I Corinthians 13:12," *ExpT* 95 (1984): 176–77; see also Richard Seaford, "I Corinthians XIII. 12," *JTS* 35 (1984): 117–20.

b. "But then we shall see face to face." The city of Corinth was known for its mirrors. There, the expression *looking into a mirror* was well known to its citizens. Paul contrasts this phrase with the words *face to face* that appear repeatedly in the Old Testament. God uses the locution *face to face* when he tells Aaron and Miriam that he addresses Moses personally (Num. 12:8; see Exod. 33:11; Deut. 5:4; 34:10). To other people God often revealed his truth in oracles and prophecies, but to Moses God spoke clearly and directly.

Paul conveys the comparison that with our human minds we are unable to grasp the full meaning of God's truth today. But in the future God will grant us the gift of perfect knowledge to understand his revelation.

c. "Now I know in part, but then I shall know fully, even as I have been fully known." The first clause is a repetition of the first part of verse 9, except that currently Paul continues to write about himself in the first person singular (see v. 11). With the two adverbs *now* and *then,* he accentuates a stark contrast; the present age is placed over against the coming age. Even though Paul fails to state a specific time reference for the second adverb *then,* he obviously has in mind life after death. In short, the parallel with verses 9 and 10a is clear.

The verb *to know fully* occurs twice in the last clause of verse 12, once as an active in the future tense ("I shall fully know") and once as a passive in the past tense with an implied agent ("I have been fully known [by God]"). These two verbs are linked by the adverb *as,* which means that as God knows Paul so Paul will know God. This is not to say that Paul will have knowledge that is divine, for Jesus explicitly states that no one knows the Father except the Son (Matt. 11:27). We always remain creatures who are finite, while God is infinite in light that is unapproachable (I Tim. 6:16). The term *knowledge* signifies that as God knows Paul as his adopted son, so Paul will fully know God as his Father when he sees him face to face.

The present verse should be seen in the light of the theme of this passage (vv. 8–12), namely, love. Paul began by saying "love never fails." Full knowledge must be understood in the framework of divine love, for to be known by God "means the same as to have been chosen by him and loved by him."[51]

Additional Comments on 13:8–12

A few unanswered questions remain to be discussed. Why does Paul list prophecies, tongues, and knowledge in verse 8, but only knowing and prophesying in verse 9? Have tongues come to an end before the other two gifts cease? Will knowledge and prophecy continue until Jesus returns?

First, Paul writes the nouns *prophecies* and *knowledge* in verse 8 and the verbs *know* and *prophesy* in verse 9. He not only shifts from the noun to the verb but also reverses the sequence of prophecies and knowledge. It is clear that he displays variation in style and word choice. Moreover, he probably failed to repeat the word *tongues* (v. 9), because he

---

51. Ridderbos, *Paul,* p. 294.

would have broken the cadence: "For we know in part and we prophesy in part." An additional remark on tongues would have been superfluous.

Next, Paul states that tongues will cease, but he does not reveal when this will be. The New Testament shows that the matter of tongues pertained to the earlier part of the apostolic period (Acts 2, 10, 19), that it was a concern in Corinth (I Cor. 12, 13, 14), and that it disappeared in later years. When in A.D. 96 Clement of Rome wrote his letter (I Clement) to the Corinthian church, he nowhere mentions tongues in all the sixty-five chapters of that letter. The speaking of tongues is discussed in the commentary on the next chapter.

Third, knowledge and prophecy will continue until the final consummation. No specific time in history is listed to reveal when the individual gifts will cease.[52] Throughout this present age, believers will expand their knowledge of God's revelation, but always "in part." Likewise, the task of preaching, teaching, and explaining God's Word will extend to the end of time. When the believer's knowledge of God is eventually perfected, both knowledge and prophecy in their imperfect state will be discarded as obsolete and useless.

Then in God's presence we shall know fully his revelation.

---

13. Now remain faith, hope, love, these three; and the greatest of these is love.

Paul returns to the word *love* that was mentioned last in verse 8a but which remained in the background all along. Next to this term he places faith and hope, so that these three virtues form a well-known triad that occurs frequently in the New Testament.[53]

The first word in this verse, "now," can mean either "for the moment" or "therefore." The first explanation relates to time and the second to logic. The preceding verse features adverbs of time, "now" and "then," so that the temporal aspect fits the context of verse 13. But in the light of Paul's discourse, he differentiates the triad of faith, hope, and love from the gifts of prophecy, tongues, and knowledge. These gifts are set aside and cease, but the three virtues remain. Hence it is apparent that Paul wrote a logical conclusion to this chapter and not merely a temporal description of the present age.

However, the verb in the first clause of verse 13 is difficult to interpret: "So faith, hope, love abide." Does the verb signify that this triad of Christian virtues extends from the present into eternity? The Scriptures teach that faith and hope pertain to the present age, but they cease when faith becomes sight (II Cor. 5:7) and hope becomes reality (Rom. 8:24). Saving faith in Jesus Christ comes to an end, but another aspect of faith, namely, trust in him, remains forever; similarly, hope in Jesus Christ is timeless (see 15:19). Faith and hope are intimately linked, so that where there is faith there is hope.[54] We interpret the three virtues of faith, hope, and love to endure without end, for they are present in both time

---

52. Compare Thomas R. Edgar, *Miraculous Gifts: Are They for Today?* (Neptune, N.J.: Loizeaux, 1983), p. 344.

53. Rom. 5:2–5; Gal. 5:5–6; Eph. 4:2–5; Col. 1:4–5; I Thess. 1:3; 5:8; Heb. 6:10–12; 10:22–24; I Peter 1:3–8, 21–22.

54. Ernst Hoffman, *NIDNTT*, vol. 2, p. 242; Rudolf Bultmann, *TDNT*, vol. 2, p. 532.

and eternity.[55] Accordingly, it is impossible not to recognize a temporal element in the word *now* of verse 13, yet the logical connotation predominates.

Why is love the greatest virtue in the triad? We note that in this entire chapter Paul extols the characteristics of love but makes faith and hope subservient to love (v. 7). We presume that the triad was well known in the early Christian church. Indeed, Paul twice alludes to these three virtues in this chapter (vv. 7, 13).

Paul singles out love but sees no need to explain the attributes of the other two virtues. For him, love is basic because of God's eternal love for his Son and through him for his people (Eph. 1:5–6). In both his Gospel and first epistle John echoes the same truth: God is love (e.g., John 3:16; I John 4:7–8, 16). In time and eternity the concept *love* remains foundational in divine-human relationships.

Will the saints in glory extend the virtues of faith, hope, and love? Scripture is silent on the life hereafter, which in itself contains a warning not to speculate. Yet we know that God does not set aside the three virtues he has given the individual believer. Love for God and trust in Christ continue to endure in eternity.

Greek Words, Phrases, and Constructions in 13:8–13

Verse 8

παύσονται—the future tense in the middle voice of the verb παύω (I stop) has the active meaning. Throughout the New Testament, this verb is always in the middle as a deponent. On the other hand, the passive voice of καταργηθήσεται (it shall be set aside) is a true passive.

Verses 9–10

ἐκ μέρους—these two words translated "in part" are used adverbially twice in verse 9, once in verse 10, and once in verse 12a. They contrast the imperfect with the perfect.

Verse 11

Notice that the imperfect tense is used four times in verse 11a to describe the activities of a child. The perfect tense γέγονα (I became) expresses a continued state and is equivalent to the present tense.

Verse 12

ἐν αἰνίγματι—in Greek the noun signifies "riddle" but adverbially the phrase means "indistinctly."[56] From this noun, we have derived the word *enigma*.

ἐπιγνώσομαι—this compound verb consisting of the preposition ἐπί and the verb γινώσκω (I know) expresses the perfective idea, that is, "I shall know thoroughly." The middle voice is deponent.

---

55. Marc-François Lacan, "Les trois qui demeurent: I Cor. 13:13," *ResScRel* 46 (1958): 321–43; F. Neirynck, "De grote drie bij een nieuwe vertaling van I Cor. XIII,13," *EphThL* 39 (1963): 595–615.
56. David H. Gill, "Through a Glass Darkly: A Note on I Corinthians 13:12," *CBQ* 25 (1963): 427–28.

καί—the conjunction is ascensive and is translated "even."

Verse 13

νυνὶ δέ—the combination can mean either "and now" (time) or "and so" (inference).

μένει—this verb in the singular has a compound subject. The neuter plural ταῦτα is an appositive subject that demands a verb in the singular.

μείζων—the comparative adjective serves as a superlative: "the greatest."[57]

ἡ ἀγάπη—the use of the definite article calls the reader's attention to the same noun without the article in verse 13, that is, the aforementioned love.

Summary of Chapter 13

In the midst of a discussion on spiritual gifts (chaps. 12–14), Paul devotes an entire chapter to the subject *love*. He fulfills a promise that he will show his readers the most excellent way (12:31). Love is the most important gift that the Christian must acquire and apply. In conditional sentences, Paul lists the gifts of tongues, prophecy, knowledge, faith, giving money to the poor and a physical body to the flames. But without love these gifts are nothing.

Paul describes love positively as patient and kind but then resorts to saying what it is not. It cannot be jealous and does not brag. It is not proud, rude, selfish, or easily provoked; it bears no ill, and takes no delight in wrongdoing. It protects, trusts, hopes, and endures. It never fails.

Although love is eternal, the gifts of prophecy, tongues, and knowledge are temporal and are set aside. Paul uses examples drawn from daily life: the words, thoughts, and reasons of a child are compared to an adult; and one's reflective image in a mirror is juxtaposed with seeing each other face to face. Paul concludes with the three virtues of faith, hope, and love; but he extols love as the greatest of these three.

---

57. Blass and Debrunner, *Greek Grammar*, #244. Ralph P. Martin interprets the adjective as a comparative: "Greater than these (three) is the love [of God]." See his article, "A Suggested Exegesis of 1 Corinthians 13:13," *ExpT* 82 (1971): 119–20.

14

Worship, *part 4*

(14:1–40)

Outline (continued)

14 1 Pursue love, strive eagerly for the spiritual gifts, especially that you may prophesy. 2 For the one who speaks in a tongue does not speak to men [and women] but to God. For no one understands him, but in the Spirit he speaks mysteries. 3 But he who prophesies speaks to men [and women] for their edification, encouragement, and consolation. 4 He who speaks in a tongue edifies himself. He who prophesies edifies the church. 5 Now I wish that all of you speak in tongues, especially that you may prophesy. And greater is the one who prophesies than the one who speaks in a tongue, unless he interprets, so that the church may be edified.

6 But now, brothers, suppose I come to you speaking in tongues, what shall I profit you unless I speak to you by revelation or by knowledge or by prophecy or by teaching? 7 In the same way, lifeless things, whether flute or harp, make a sound; if they do not produce distinct notes, how will anyone know what is being played on the flute or the harp? 8 For if the trumpet produces an indistinct sound, who will prepare himself for battle? 9 So also you, unless you utter a distinct message with your tongue, how will anyone know what is being said? For you will be speaking into the air. 10 There are undoubtedly ever so many languages in the world and none without meaning. 11 If then I do not know the meaning of the language, I shall be a foreigner to the one who is speaking and the one who is speaking in my presence is a foreigner. 12 So even you, since you are eager for spiritual gifts, seek to excel in those that edify the church.

13 Therefore, let the one who speaks in a tongue pray so that he may interpret. 14 For if I pray in a tongue, my spirit prays, but my mind is unfruitful. 15 What then is the result? I shall pray with my spirit, and I shall pray also with my mind. I shall sing with my spirit and I shall sing also with my mind. 16 Otherwise if you bless [only] with the spirit, how shall the one who fills up the place of the uninformed say amen to your thanksgiving? Because what you utter he does not understand. 17 For you are giving thanks well enough; however, the other man is not edified.

18 I thank God that I speak in tongues more than all of you. 19 However, in the church I would rather speak five words with my mind so that I may even teach others than ten thousand words in a tongue.

20 Brothers, do not be children in your thinking, but be babes in regard to evil. Be mature in your thinking. 21 In the Law it is written,

> "With strange tongues and with the lips of strangers
> I will speak to this people,
> Even so they will not obey me, says the Lord."

22 Therefore, tongues are a sign not for the believers but for the unbelievers. And prophecy is not for unbelievers but for believers. 23 So if the whole church comes together in one place and everyone speaks in tongues, and the novices or unbelievers enter, will they not say that you are out of your mind? 24 But if all prophesy and a certain unbeliever or novice enters, he is convicted by all and judged by all. 25 The hidden things of his heart become evident, and thus falling on his face he will worship God, declaring,

> "God is truly among you."

5. Prophecy and Tongues
14:1–25

The previous chapter served as an interlude that stresses the abiding value of love. This virtue is basic to the well-being of the church and becomes the instrument through which the spiritual gifts listed in 12:8–11, 28–30 function properly and effectively. Indeed the last verse in chapter 12, "But eagerly desire the greater gifts" (v. 31), and the first verse of chapter 14, "Pursue love, strive eagerly for the spiritual gifts, especially that you may prophesy," set the stage for Paul's discourse on prophesying and tongue-speaking.

Between the apostles and the teachers Paul placed the prophets as second in rank; he lists the gift of tongues last (12:28). But now he lists prophecy first and tongues second (vv. 1–2), and as he begins this chapter so he concludes it. He writes, "Eagerly desire to prophesy and do not forbid speaking in tongues" (v. 39; compare I Thess. 5:20).

a. Eager Pursuit
14:1–5

1. Pursue love, strive eagerly for the spiritual gifts, especially that you may prophesy.

The three verbs in this verse are directives: the first two are imperatives (pursue love! strive eagerly!), and the third is an indirect command (that you may prophesy). All of them are in the present tense to indicate that the readers should always seek to obey these injunctions.

a. "Pursue love." This brief exhortation serves as a fitting conclusion to the entire discourse on love in chapter 13. Paul uses the verb *to pursue* elsewhere in connection with righteousness, hospitality, and peace (Rom. 9:30; 12:13; 14:19).[1] The verb denotes that pursuing something must be done with intensity and determination. That is, we must pursue love with all our heart, soul, mind, and strength (compare Mark 12:30). In short, Paul exhorts the readers to put the message of his letter of love (13) into practice.

b. "Strive eagerly for the spiritual gifts." The second command is closely tied to the first one, so that the two imperatives in the present tense are nearly synonyms. The connection, however, depends less on these two successive verbs than on the nouns *love* and *spiritual gifts*. With the phrase *an even more excellent way* (12:31), Paul shows that love dominates the greater gifts. Paul now calls these gifts spiritual (see 12:1) and strongly urges the Corinthians to desire them. Perhaps the emphasis falls more on the concept *spiritual* than on that of *gifts*.

c. "Especially that you may prophesy." Among the spiritual gifts is prophecy, which Paul now selects for special attention. Earlier he recorded this gift be-

---

1. See Phil. 3:12; I Thess. 5:15; I Tim. 6:11; II Tim. 2:22.

tween those of doing miracles and discerning spirits (12:10; and compare 12:28–29). But in the context of chapter 14, he compares it with the gift of tongues and says that he prefers prophesying to tongue-speaking (v. 5).

Should everyone eagerly desire the ability to prophesy? Obtaining this gift depends first on the giver and second on the petitioner. God's sovereignty to give or to withhold does not cancel man's responsibility to pray.[2] Paul can urge the Corinthians to pray earnestly for the gift of prophecy but he is unable to assure them that God will grant the same gift to everyone (12:11). Whatever gift the Holy Spirit confers on a believer must be employed in love for the benefit of the church. In addition, we observe that without the Holy Spirit a person is unable to prophesy. While God is calling forth today preachers, teachers, and exhorters of his revelation, Paul is urging them to respond to that call.

2. For the one who speaks in a tongue does not speak to men [and women] but to God. For no one understands him, but in the Spirit he speaks mysteries. 3. But he who prophesies speaks to men [and women] for their edification, encouragement, and consolation.

a. "For the one who speaks in a tongue does not speak to men [and women] but to God." Of the two gifts, prophecy and tongues, Paul takes the latter first and points out that speaking in a tongue is private worship directed to God (see v. 4). Speaking to God in a tongue is comparable to personal prayer: The one who prays speaks to himself and to God (v. 28) and does so within the context of love. Accordingly, speaking in a tongue without interpretation does not communicate anything meaningful, because the people are unable to understand the words that are spoken. Granted that God knows every spoken word, his people are unable to understand these words and thus are not edified.

b. "For no one understands him, but in the Spirit he speaks mysteries." Speaking and hearing are the two sides of the proverbial coin. When language is not understood, people cannot communicate. And a failure to communicate results in alienation for the people involved. According to the account in Acts 2:4–11, everyone present in the temple courts was able to understand the messages proclaimed in many known languages by those filled with the Holy Spirit. But in the current text, Paul refrains from writing about interpreters. Instead he notes that the message spoken in a tongue without interpretation is directed not to people but to God.

The Greek word *pneuma* can be translated either "spirit" or "Spirit," and translators are divided on this point. The term refers to either the human spirit or the Holy Spirit. In the setting of this chapter, Paul mentions the human spirit twice more: "For if I pray in a tongue, my spirit prays" (v. 14) and "The spirits of prophets are subject to the prophets" (v. 32). This provides support for the interpretation that Paul has in mind the spirit within man.

---

2. Max Turner, "Spiritual Gifts Then and Now," *VoxEv* 15 (1985): 32. Compare also Wayne A. Grudem, *The Gift of Prophecy in the New Testament and Today* (Westchester, Ill.: Crossway, 1988), p. 213.

However, the word *spirit*, both with and without the capital letter, must be studied in relation to the term *mysteries*. That term is the content of this last clause in verse 2. We find a parallel in 13:2, where Paul also speaks about mysteries that are closely linked to prophecy. Through the Holy Spirit, God originates both in prophecies and in tongues mysteries that are incomprehensible (compare 2:6–16; I Peter 1:10–12). Nonetheless, the Holy Spirit reveals these mysteries and employs his people to express them.[3] The Holy Spirit, then, is the agent who works within a person and relates mysteries.

Paul and his associates were stewards of God's mysteries (2:7) who had been entrusted with the mysteries God reveals in Christ (4:1). Through the preaching of the gospel, they explained these mysteries to God's people. But in the current passage, Paul says that anyone who utters mysteries in the Spirit does not address himself to the people. Thus he must address himself to God, but he is unable to do so because God is the giver. The way out of this dilemma is to make these mysteries known to the believers and to explain them for their edification.

c. "But he who prophesies speaks to men [and women] for their edification, encouragement, and consolation." The contrast between tongue-speaking and prophecy is obvious: the tongue-speaker fails to communicate, but the person who prophesies addresses people with a message.[4] This message has a threefold purpose: it must be instructive, encouraging, and comforting for the believers (compare I Thess. 2:12). It builds people in their faith, points them to Christ, and teaches them to live holy lives. Moreover, the prophetic message heartens and inspires the hearers to be able to face the burdens of their daily lives. And the spoken words comfort, nurture, and sustain God's people in periods of depression, sorrow, and heartache. According to New Testament usage, the recipients of comfort are those who grieve, who are imprisoned, and who are poverty-stricken widows.[5]

Within the setting of chapters 12–14, this passage provides a helpful description of prophecy. It delineates the functions of the prophetic word without any reference to a predictive role or permanent validity.

Doctrinal Considerations in 14:1–3

The emphasis in this segment is on edification and intelligibility. This applies to the person who speaks in a tongue and the one who prophesies. If tongue-speech does not convey a message to the hearers, the church receives no benefit at all. Persons who speak in a tongue and afterward serve as their own interpreters run the risk of being asked why they do not utter intelligible words from the start (but see v. 13).[6] Paul declares that he

---

3. Refer to Richard B. Gaffin, Jr., *Perspectives on Pentecost: Studies in New Testament Teaching on the Gifts of the Holy Spirit* (Phillipsburg, N.J.: Presbyterian and Reformed, 1979), pp. 79–80.

4. *Phillips* translates "he who prophesies" as "he who preaches the Word of God." And GNB has the reading *the one who proclaims God's message*.

5. Consult Gustav Stählin, *TDNT*, vol. 5, p. 822; Georg Braumann, *NIDNTT*, vol. 1, p. 329.

6. Compare Thomas R. Edgar, *Miraculous Gifts: Are They for Today?* (Neptune, N.J.: Loizeaux, 1983), p. 212.

himself would rather speak five understandable words to instruct the church than ten thousand and not be understood (v. 19).

The Old Testament prophet was an Israelite who was called by God, empowered by the Holy Spirit, and given a divine message which he proclaimed with authority.[7] He foretold God's revelation, often pertaining to the birth and coming of the Messiah. His message embodied the hope that God would fulfill the promise of the Messiah's coming.

The New Testament prophet proclaimed a message that could be either predictive or nonpredictive. For the New Testament prophet, the task of predicting the Messiah's coming had ended and that of proclaiming the gospel had begun.

In I Corinthians, Paul stresses nonpredictive prophecy when he indicates that the work of prophesying consists of edifying, encouraging, and consoling the believers. Anyone who prophesies ministers to the church, proclaims God's revelation, interprets the plan of salvation, and applies the truth of the gospel. Prophesying "aims to bring God's truth to bear on human lives with a view to their understanding and growth."[8] In effect, the work of prophesying and of teaching overlap (see the commentary on 12:28). Both the first-century prophet and the modern-day preacher and teacher aspire to edify the Christian community (vv. 5, 12).

The church must constantly test the words of prophecy to see if they are authentic. Thus, Paul charges the Corinthian church with the duty of discerning the gift of prophecy, whether predictive or nonpredictive, and to shield prophecy from abuse and misuse (v. 29). For that reason, he begins and ends this chapter by encouraging his readers to strive eagerly for the gift of prophecy (vv. 1, 39).

Specifically, then, the significance of prophecy in the New Testament constitutes at least three different aspects of prophecy exemplified in the four Gospels, Acts, the epistolary literature, and Revelation.

First, we mention the predictive feature of prophecies by Agabus, Paul, and John. Agabus predicts a severe famine in the entire Roman world during the reign of Emperor Claudius, and many years later he foretells Paul's arrest (Acts 11:28; 21:11). We ought not to push the exact details of Agabus's words to their logical extreme, because that is not the intention of his predictions. In another instance, aboard ship on the stormy Mediterranean Sea, an angel conveys the message to Paul that the lives of all 276 people will be saved, although the ship itself will be shipwrecked on an island (Acts 27:23–26). Paul reports the news to the sailors, soldiers, passengers, and prisoners. Within a day or two, all of them are able to testify to the fulfillment of Paul's prophecy. Further, in the last book of the New Testament, John is portrayed as a prophet (Rev. 22:9). He writes a prophecy of the things that must soon take place, and thus he both predicts and proclaims God's Word (Rev. 1:3).

Next, in the first century some people filled the office of prophet, which had a rank following that of the apostle (Eph. 4:11). The Holy Spirit gave the gift of this particular office to the early church. But when the work of the apostles and the prophets was completed at the close of the church's foundational period (see Eph. 2:20), there were no successors to fill these two official positions.[9] When the Old Testament canon was com-

---

7. Consult Willem A. VanGemeren, *Interpreting the Prophetic Word* (Grand Rapids: Zondervan, Academie Books, 1990), pp. 32–33.

8. Ralph P. Martin, *The Spirit and the Congregation: Studies in 1 Corinthians 12–15* (Grand Rapids: Eerdmans, 1984), p. 66.

9. Compare Gerhard Friedrich, *TDNT*, vol. 6, pp. 859–60; Edgar, *Miraculous Gifts*, p. 83; George W. Knight III, *Prophecy in the New Testament* (Dallas: Presbyterian Heritage, 1988), pp. 19–20.

pleted, the prophetic office ceased to exist. Similarly, upon the completion of the New Testament, the number of prophets dwindled and disappeared.

First-century prophets had a preaching and teaching ministry to strengthen, encourage, and instruct the people (12:28–29; 14:3; Acts 13:1; 15:32). They were called prophets and teachers, yet with the difference that a prophet was a teacher but a teacher was not necessarily a prophet. Both the prophet and the teacher sought to edify the church.

Last, only when a person becomes the mouthpiece of the Holy Spirit can prophecy be uttered. Jesus told the twelve disciples (apostles) that in case they were arrested and had to speak, the Spirit of the Father would speak through them (Matt. 10:19–20). The apostles did appear before the Sanhedrin, where Peter, filled with the Holy Spirit, spoke eloquently about obeying God rather than man (Acts 4:8–12, 19–20; 5:29–32). Stephen, who was not an apostle but a deacon known to be full of the Holy Spirit, also addressed the Sanhedrin (Acts 6:5; 7:2–53).

Every believer may ask God to give him or her the right words to speak when the need arises, and God will hear and answer these petitions. Especially preachers and teachers are able to testify that, in response to their prayers, the Holy Spirit has given them the ability to utter fitting words that reflect God's revealed Word. Yet no one should ascribe infallibility to either the speakers as persons or their messages, for they proclaim nothing that can be added to the Scriptures. Such preaching and teaching of Scripture has been and always will continue to be prophecy. "Prophecy has been and remains a reality whenever and wherever Bible truth is genuinely *preached.*"[10]

---

4. He who speaks in a tongue edifies himself. He who prophesies edifies the church.

a. "He who speaks in a tongue edifies himself." Paul already indicated that the person who speaks in a tongue addresses not the people but God (v. 2). Now he states that the tongue-speaker edifies himself. Paul says nothing about interpreters, for he knows that without interpretation the congregation will not benefit from the spoken words. Without an interpreter the message is unintelligible.

How does a person who speaks in a tongue edify himself? Some scholars interpret the verb *to edify* negatively, because they think that a person ought to use his gifts for the benefit of the church. They suppose that Paul resorts to sarcasm in the first part of this verse and marshal at least two arguments to prove their case. First, Paul teaches that the gifts which the Spirit gives are for the common good of the church (12:7); next, in his letter of love he intimates that gifts should never serve self-centered ambition.[11]

However, Paul seems to speak positively here, for he encourages all his readers to speak in tongues (v. 5). He also notes that private prayer to God, even when spoken in a tongue, is a matter between the believer and God (II Cor. 12:2–4; see also v. 2 and the commentary on it). Hence, no one is free to invade an-

---

10. J. I. Packer, *Keep in Step with the Spirit* (Old Tappan, N.J.: Revell, 1984), p. 217.
11. Robert L. Thomas, *Understanding Spiritual Gifts: The Christian's Special Gifts in the Light of 1 Corinthians 12–14* (Chicago: Moody, 1978), pp. 207–8; John MacArthur, Jr., *1 Corinthians,* MacArthur New Testament Commentary series (Chicago: Moody, 1984), p. 372; H. Wayne House, "Tongues and the Mystery Religions of Corinth," *BS* 140 (1983): 143–44.

other's religious privacy; prayer, whether spoken or unspoken, is a two-way street. God receives praise and thanks from the speaker and at the same time grants him or her comfort and encouragement.

In this chapter Paul emphasizes the concept *edification*, as the repeated use of the verb *edify* and the noun *edification* attest.[12] Elsewhere Paul tells the recipients of his letter: "seek to excel in [the work of] edifying the church" (v. 12b).

b. "He who prophesies edifies the church." Paul once more stresses the fact that with respect to either tongues or prophecy, the latter is greatly preferred. The fundamental principle of loving one's neighbor as oneself, clarified in Paul's discourse on love (13), comes to expression in the voice of prophecy. The setting for prophecy is a public worship service where the members have come together for praise, prayer, and instruction. The setting can also be a small gathering of two or three in the name of the Lord (see Matt. 18:20). Prophecy must always be spoken against the backdrop of love for one's neighbor.

Paul notes that the person who prophesies edifies the church. In this text, he means not the universal church but the local congregation. When someone speaks to God in a tongue, the worshiper follows a vertical path; but when this person prophesies to the members of the church, he or she reaches out to fellow believers on a horizontal level.

5. Now I wish that all of you speak in tongues, especially that you may prophesy. And greater is the one who prophesies than the one who speaks in a tongue, unless he interprets, so that the church may be edified.

a. *Wish.* When Paul asserts that he would like to have all the Corinthians speak in tongues, he is not promoting tongue-speaking itself. Rather, he contrasts this sentence with the next one, in which he exalts the gift of prophecy. The allusion is definitely to the words of Moses when he was told that Eldad and Medad were prophesying in the camp of Israel. When Joshua perceived a threat to Moses' leadership, he urged Moses to stop the rivals. Then Moses asked: "Are you jealous for my sake? I wish that all the Lord's people were prophets and that the Lord would put his Spirit on them!" (Num. 11:29). Following in the footsteps of Moses, Paul earnestly desired that the Holy Spirit might come upon God's people in full measure.

Paul expresses the wish that all the Corinthians speak in tongues, yet he is not contradicting himself. Earlier he wrote that not everyone receives the same spiritual gifts (12:30). Now he wants the readers to view everything in proper perspective. Of the two gifts, tongue-speaking and prophesying, he deems prophecy the greater of the two. Paul repeats the clause he wrote at the beginning of this chapter, "especially that you may prophesy" (vv. 1 and 5). The repetition itself indicates that he values prophecy far above tongues, yet he considers both gifts to have edifying features.

b. *Differences.* Although Paul judges the gift of prophecy to be superior in value to the gift of tongues, he moderates his own assessment with the qualifying con-

---

12. The Greek verb occurs three times (14:4 [twice], 17) and the noun four times (14:3, 5, 12, 26).

junction *unless*. Paul writes, "unless he interprets, so that the church may be edified." He says that tongue-speaking is acceptable provided the speaker interprets his message. He is not saying that the prophets are the interpreters.[13] In fact, from the chapter itself we are unable to know who these interpreters are. In an earlier chapter Paul mentioned both the gift of tongues and the gift of interpretation and stated that God grants these gifts to various groups of people (12:28–31). The point Paul is making is that tongue-speaking when interpreted becomes valuable because it serves to edify the members of the church.

Paul compares the prophet with the tongue-speaker and considers the prophet to be the greater of these two. But what is the meaning of the adjective *greater*? The same adjective appears in 12:31, where Paul writes, "But eagerly desire the greater gifts." In the last verse in chapter 12, however, the apostle fails to indicate what these greater gifts are. And in the current text, Paul employs the adjective *greater* only to compare tongue-speaking with prophesying. The text itself appears to communicate nothing more than a mere comparison. With respect to effective communication that is beneficial to God's people, not the prophet but the words of the prophet are greater because they edify the Christian community. And when the congregation is edified, then the basic principle of love prevails.

Is Paul placing interpreted tongue-speaking on the same level as the words of a prophet? At Pentecost (Acts 2:1–12), tongue-speaking and preaching the gospel were identical. But in Acts, we nowhere read that interpreters were needed to translate the messages. We assume that in cosmopolitan Corinth, where people had come from many countries, numerous languages were spoken. In addition, some Corinthians spoke in tongues and followed a practice that may have had its origin in the pagan circles from which the Corinthians had come. After their conversion to Christianity, they did not see a difference between their ecstatic experience in pagan circles and the power of the Holy Spirit working within the Christian community.[14] Paul does not forbid them to speak in tongues (v. 39); he wants them to be receptive to this gift coming from the Holy Spirit and to use it for edifying the church in the context of love.

Greek Words, Phrases, and Constructions in 14:1–5

Verse 1

τὴν ἀγάπην—the definite article points to the same noun in the preceding chapter and verse (13:13).

ἵνα—this particle introduces the verb *to prophesy* in the present subjunctive as an indirect command. The particle and verb give content to the present imperative ζηλοῦτε (strive eagerly).

---

13. Terrance Callan, "Prophecy and Ecstasy in Greco-Roman Religion and 1 Corinthians," *NovT* 27 (1985): 138.

14. House, "Tongues," p. 147.

Verses 2–3

ὁ λαλῶν—the present active participle of the verb λαλέω (I speak) expresses the activity of speaking but not its content.

ἀνθρώποις—the dative as the indirect object does not differ much from the dative of advantage.[15] However, in these two verses we prefer the indirect object.

δέ—this adversative particle stresses the difference between the one who speaks in a tongue and the other who prophesies. The verb λαλεῖ (v. 3) is followed by three nouns—edification, encouragement, and comfort—that in English syntax call for a preposition and a possessive pronoun ("for their") to make the sentence complete.

Verses 4–5

ἐκκλησίαν—without the definite article, this noun could refer to the universal church. Here, however, it signifies the local congregation.

θέλω—this verb controls two verbal objects, the indirect discourse construction ὑμᾶς λαλεῖν (that you speak) and the indirect command ἵνα προφητεύητε (that you may prophesy).

ἐκτὸς εἰ μή—a literal translation shows redundancy ("except except"), "but it may be presumed that, without the εἰ μή, ἐκτός would have been virtually a preposition."[16] See 15:2.

---

b. Fitting Analogies
14:6–12

After the introductory verses (vv. 1–5) of a discussion on tongues and prophecy, Paul now explains that if tongues are to be valuable assets in the church, they must be beneficial to the entire membership. To make his point, he uses pertinent examples from the areas of music and languages.

6. But now, brothers, suppose I come to you speaking in tongues, what shall I profit you unless I speak to you by revelation or by knowledge or by prophecy or by teaching?

a. "But now, brothers." *Now* transmits not a temporal connotation but a logical one: "but because things are so." On the basis of practices in the congregation, Paul is challenged to give his own view on tongues. He addresses the Corinthians with the word *brothers*, which in the parlance of that day included the sisters in the church. With the use of that term, Paul places himself on the same level as any one of them. Because the matter of tongue-speaking is a sensitive issue, Paul has to correct the thinking and the actions of the people at Corinth, and has to do so pastorally and tenderly.

b. "Suppose I come to you speaking in tongues." For the first part of a conditional sentence Paul writes a clause that expresses supposition or probability. By

---

15. A. T. Robertson, *A Grammar of the Greek New Testament in the Light of Historical Research* (Nashville: Broadman, 1934), p. 538.

16. C. F. D. Moule, *An Idiom-Book of New Testament Greek*, 2d ed. (Cambridge: Cambridge University Press, 1960), p. 83.

saying "suppose," he invites the readers to give him their reaction should he ever appear in their midst speaking in tongues. He has every intention of paying them a visit (16:5), but not for the purpose of speaking in tongues.

Paul writes the expression *tongues* in the plural instead of the singular. Somewhat later he testifies that he has the ability to speak in tongues more than any of the Corinthians (v. 18), and again he uses the plural. The phrase *speaking in tongues* is an abbreviated form of the original clause, "to speak in other tongues" (Acts 2:4).[17] Paul refuses to address the Corinthians in tongues, for he wants to communicate his message intelligibly (see v. 19). A lack of communication means a lack of love, yet love should be the hallmark of all personal relationships in the church. Moreover, Paul never refers to tongue-speaking "without pointing out its inferior value, and comparing it unfavorably with speech that is intelligible."[18]

c. "What shall I profit you unless I speak to you by revelation or by knowledge or by prophecy or by teaching?" The answer Paul expects from the Corinthians is negative, unless, of course, he edifies them with his spiritual gifts. The gifts that the Holy Spirit distributes are meant to serve the church so that all the members may benefit from them. Consequently, when Paul eventually arrives in Corinth, he comes to edify the people with intelligible messages from God.

Paul delivers his messages in the form of either revelation, knowledge, prophecy, or teaching. We do well to take these four categories as two pairs that reinforce each other:

revelation and knowledge
prophecy and teaching

In the first pair, *revelation* can be taken to mean, first, the additions to the developing New Testament at that time. Next, it can refer to insights into God's Word revealed to the apostles and prophets (Eph. 3:5; Phil. 3:15). And last, it may signify a divine message to Paul (e.g., going to Jerusalem to see if the gospel he preached was in harmony with that of the apostles [Gal. 2:2; compare also II Cor. 12:1, 7]). Paul now states that he divulges revelation for the benefit of God's people. Likewise, he shares with the Corinthians knowledge that presumably pertains to God and his Word.

The second pair enhances the preceding one. Prophecy runs parallel with revelation, and teaching finds its counterpart in knowledge.[19] A prophet is unable to prophesy without a revelation and a teacher cannot impart instruction without knowledge. A person who receives revelation and then prophesies is a

---

17. Friedrich Blass and Albert Debrunner, *A Greek Grammar of the New Testament and Other Early Christian Literature*, trans. and rev. Robert Funk (Chicago: University of Chicago Press, 1961), #480.3.

18. Frank W. Beare, "Speaking with Tongues: A Critical Survey of the New Testament Evidence," in *Speaking in Tongues: A Guide to Research on Glossolalia*, ed. Watson E. Mills (Grand Rapids: Eerdmans, 1986), p. 124; reprint from *JBL* 83 (1964): 229–46.

19. Refer to Thomas L. Wilkinson, "Tongues and Prophecy in Acts and 1 Corinthians," *VoxRef* 31 (1978): 16.

mouthpiece of the Holy Spirit; and someone who has knowledge and teaches the members of the church experiences the help of the Spirit (12:8). Last of all, revelation and knowledge relate to a person's internal possessions, while prophecy and teaching allude to a person's external activities.[20]

7. In the same way, lifeless things, whether flute or harp, make a sound; if they do not produce distinct notes, how will anyone know what is being played on the flute or the harp?

Paul resorts to analogies to prove that in the church a lack of communication is pointless. He bypasses the animal world and takes an example from the world of music. Paul could have chosen the horn, the trumpet, the cymbals, or the gong. Instead, from the woodwind instruments he selects the flute and from the string instruments the harp. Flute playing was common at both funerals and weddings (Matt. 9:23; 11:17). The psalmists mention the harp a number of times (Pss. 33:2; 137:2; 149:3; 150:3) and leave the impression that this instrument was used in worship services at the temple and elsewhere.[21]

Music must be agreeable to the ear to be acceptable to the audience. The musician must skillfully produce pleasing sounds that disclose the distinct characteristics of the instrument that is played, whether the flute or the harp. Thus a relationship is formed between the player and the listener. But if the player produces a cacophony of sounds, everyone will depart from his presence.

8. For if the trumpet produces an indistinct sound, who will prepare himself for battle?

To ask the question is to answer it. Paul takes an example from warfare in which the bugler on the city wall alerts the citizens to an impending onslaught by an approaching army. The sound of the trumpet is a warning call to every able person to prepare himself for battle. But if the trumpeter plays in such a way that the notes cannot be heard, the citizens continue either their daily labors or their nightly sleep. In either case, inaction spells disaster.

With these examples taken from daily life, Paul seeks to show the Corinthians the utter futility of speaking in tongues that do not communicate a spiritual message. Because comprehension is lacking, people turn away from the tongue-speaker and leave the church.

9. So also you, unless you utter a distinct message with your tongue, how will anyone know what is being said? For you will be speaking into the air.

a. "So also you." This phrase introduces the direct application of the analogy. Paul uses this saying twice (see v. 12) to emphasize his point. The Corinthians emit sounds that listeners are unable to appreciate and understand, much as musical instruments that are incorrectly handled convey nothing significant.

b. "Unless you utter a distinct message with your tongue." The responsibility to speak clearly and understandably is now laid before the Corinthians. Paul

---

20. Henry Alford, *Alford's Greek Testament: An Exegetical and Critical Commentary*, 7th ed., 4 vols. (1877; Grand Rapids: Guardian, 1976), vol. 2, p. 591.

21. Consult Daniel A. Foxvog and Anne D. Kilmer, "Music," *ISBE*, vol. 3, pp. 436–49.

waits for them to conform to his direct reproof. He wants them to speak intelligibly. Note that he uses the adjective *distinct* as the converse of the adjective *indistinct* that describes the trumpet (v. 8). Further, the phrase *with your tongue* can mean either the physical speech organ, a known language, or ecstatic speech. Of these three, the first explanation appears to be the best. First, the noun *tongue* is rather personal, as it is modified by the pronoun *your*. Next, the noun serves as the counterpart of the musical instruments mentioned earlier (vv. 7–8). And last, the preposition *with* signifies instrumentality that applies more to the organ of speech than to a language as a whole.

c. "How will anyone know what is being said?" The wording of this question repeats the wording in verse 7. There the question was asked how anyone would know what is being played, and here of what is being said. The parallels are striking and aptly underline the comparison. The answer to the question that Paul raises is the unequivocal "no one."

d. "For you will be speaking into the air." Here is the reason that no one is able to understand a word of what is said. The speaker faces the wind, so to speak, and loses all the qualities of effective communication. His voice cannot be heard, his words are lost, and his efforts are wasted (compare 9:26).

10. There are undoubtedly ever so many languages in the world and none without meaning.

Now Paul is ready to present another analogy; this time he takes it from the area of voices. This covers a broad range that includes the calls and the cries in the animal world. Paul's first analogy relates to inanimate objects in the area of music; his second example pertains to voices of living beings. John Calvin notes that voices include even the barking of a dog, the neighing of a horse, the roar of a lion, and the braying of a donkey. In addition, there are the songs, calls, and chirps of countless birds.[22] But in this verse Paul distinctly suggests human languages. If he should even try to survey the multitude of languages and dialects in the world of his day, Paul certainly would have to say "undoubtedly." To express this thought, he uses a well-known Greek formula *ei tychoi* (if it should turn out that way).

Languages that cannot be understood create formidable barriers in society. A case in point is those countries that cope with multiple languages and ethnic divisions within their borders. These divisions usually stem from the fact that when people do not understand a language spoken to them, they are frustrated. "Speech without meaning is a contradiction in terms."[23] Thus, in the Corinthian church uninterpreted tongue-speaking created barriers that could result in divisions.

---

22. John Calvin, *The First Epistle of Paul the Apostle to the Corinthians*, Calvin's Commentaries series, trans. John W. Fraser (reprint ed.; Grand Rapids: Eerdmans, 1976), p. 289.

23. Archibald Robertson and Alfred Plummer, *A Critical and Exegetical Commentary on the First Epistle of St. Paul to the Corinthians*, International Critical Commentary, 2d ed. (1911; reprint ed., Edinburgh: Clark, 1975), p. 310.

11. If then I do not know the meaning of the language, I shall be a foreigner to the one who is speaking and the one who is speaking in my presence is a foreigner.

Paul writes a conditional sentence that expresses probability. Although he was able to converse in a number of languages, Paul himself did not understand the Lycaonian dialect of the people in Lystra (see Acts 14:11–14). He personally experienced that his presence among people who could not understand his speech made him a foreigner to them and, similarly, his inability to understand the language made the speakers foreigners to him. The Greek word *barbaros*, from which we derived the term *barbarian*, denotes any person whose native tongue differs from Greek. Originally the expression conveyed nothing negative and was used to distinguish Greek-speaking people from those who spoke another language.

A spoken language must convey meaning; otherwise it is ineffective and impotent. If it fails to communicate, language alienates speakers and hearers. A literal translation of the phrase *the meaning of the language* is "the power of the language." The Greek term *dynamis* (power) can also be translated "force," which makes good sense in this text.[24] From the setting of this word we may deduce that the force of unintelligible speech creates a sense of fear and insecurity in the heart of the hearer. But in the church fear and insecurity ought to have no place. "Where God's love is, there is no fear, because God's perfect love takes away fear" (I John 4:18, NCV).

12. So even you, since you are eager for spiritual gifts, seek to excel in those that edify the church.

a. "So even you." At the conclusion of his second analogy, Paul repeats the phrase he used at the end of the first analogy (v. 9). The Christian community, aware of the many nationalities and languages represented in the city of Corinth, should understand the frustration someone experiences by not being able to understand a certain spoken language. This means that Paul's illustration is apt, because it can be applied to the matter of tongue-speaking in the local church.

b. "Since you are eager for spiritual gifts." After his discussion on prophecy and tongues, Paul has come full circle. At the beginning of this chapter, he urged the readers to strive eagerly for spiritual gifts (v. 1; compare 12:31). Paul actually writes, "since you are zealots for spirits" (compare 12:10). He uses two nouns in this clause, "zealots" and "spirits," that call for closer scrutiny.

First, Paul tells the Corinthians to become zealots, which is a word that has either a negative or a positive connotation. He himself had been a zealot by keeping the traditions of Judaism and, as a consequence, tried to destroy the church (Acts 22:3; Gal. 1:14). But in this verse, the word signifies a positive striving after the gifts of the Spirit (compare Titus 2:14; I Peter 3:13).[25]

---

24. Bauer, p. 207. See Gordon D. Fee, *The First Epistle to the Corinthians*, New International Commentary on the New Testament series (Grand Rapids: Eerdmans, 1987), p. 665 n. 39.

25. Consult Wolfgang Bauder, *NIDNTT*, vol. 3, p. 1167; Albrecht Stumpff, *TDNT*, vol. 2, pp. 887–88.

Next, Paul's intent is not to ask the Corinthians to pursue the spirits. Rather, he exhorts them to become recipients of spiritual gifts. Some commentators understand the term *spirits* to mean "various breathings of inspirations in the assemblies of the Church."[26] This undoubtedly is true, but we come closer to Paul's intention if we say that the Holy Spirit reveals himself in distributing a multitude of spiritual gifts to his people. As Paul stated earlier: "The one and the same Spirit works in all these things, apportioning them to each one individually as he desires" (12:11). In brief, the plural noun *spirits* refers to the Holy Spirit distributing many of his spiritual gifts to his people.[27]

c. "Seek to excel in those that edify the church." The emphasis in this clause is on the concept *edification*, which is one of Paul's important themes in this chapter (see the commentary on v. 4). The Holy Spirit endows his people with spiritual gifts for the purpose of edifying the church of the Lord Jesus Christ. Paul does not specify which gifts the members are to use for their mutual edification. Instead, he exhorts them to excel. The words *in those* following the imperative *seek to excel* are not in the Greek text, yet the flow of the sentence suggests that they be included. The message Paul leaves with the Corinthians is that they excel in edifying the church with the spiritual gifts they have received.

Doctrinal Considerations in 14:6–12

Any pastor or teacher will attest to the fact that sermons or lessons are soon forgotten but apt illustrations last a lifetime. A wise speaker, however, uses verbal pictures sparingly. He knows that although a presentation saturated with stories may be entertaining, it often lacks substance or coherence. And an incoherent sermon or lecture is unintelligible. Jesus taught numerous parables, but all of them have a ringing message that is instantly understandable to every listener.

The analogies Paul presents are taken from daily life and support the main point of the argument. A flute and a harp are meant to convey pleasing melodies, and a bugle ought to emit clear tones to warn the citizenry. These two illustrations enhance, clarify, and strengthen the point Paul tries to make.

Paul lays down four principles that the Corinthians had to observe: first, tongues should be interpreted; next, they must edify the members of the church; third, they ought to be intelligible in the context of love (see v. 1a); and last, orderliness must be characteristic of believers at worship (see especially v. 33a).

Within the Christian community of Corinth, tongue-speakers were voicing meaningless utterances. Paul shows that when he is with the believers he will bring them some revelation, knowledge, prophecy, and teaching. He informs them that his task is to preach the crucified Christ and his gospel (1:23; 15:1). This gospel is intelligible and edifying

---

26. Frederic Louis Godet, *Commentary on First Corinthians* (1886; reprint ed., Grand Rapids: Kregel, 1977), p. 704. Fee avers that for the Corinthians it is "the Spirit manifesting himself through their individual 'spirits'" (*First Corinthians*, p. 666).

27. Bauer, p. 677. See Gaffin, *Perspectives on Pentecost*, pp. 76–77.

only when the Holy Spirit is associated with it. Comments J. Stanley Glen, "The Spirit of God signifies an ultimate intelligibility."[28] Word and Spirit go together when a preacher or a teacher clearly communicates God's revelation, for the Holy Spirit is inseparably connected with the Word of God. In short, the Spirit explains the word intelligibly.

Greek Words, Phrases, and Constructions in 14:6–12

Verse 6

ἐν—this preposition followed by the dative case in four nouns is descriptive and actually means "consisting of."[29]

διδαχῇ—the noun can signify either the act of teaching or the body of doctrine (KJV). Scholars favor the first interpretation.

Verses 7–8

ὅμως—the usual translation is "nevertheless," "yet." However, the setting of the adverb demands that it introduces a comparison and, therefore, should be translated "likewise" or "just as" (see Gal. 3:15).[30]

πῶς γνωσθήσεται—literally, the Greek reads "how will it be known?" In an acceptable English translation, we use the active voice and add the word *anyone*: "how will anyone know?"

παρασκευάσεται—a verb in the middle voice and future tense has a direct bearing on the person involved: "who will prepare himself?"

Verse 10

εἰ τύχοι—the particle introduces a conditional clause with the present optative of the verb τυγχάνω (I obtain). The clause appears as a formula signifying "perhaps" or "if it should turn out that way" (see also 15:37). The formula as a protasis is not followed by a corresponding apodosis. In the current text, it probably tries to limit the impact of the adjective τοσαῦτα (so many) in the sentence: "there are probably ever so many different languages."[31]

Verses 11–12

ἐὰν οὖν μὴ εἰδῶ—the conditional clause, expressing probability with the verb οἶδα (I understand; see v. 16), is followed by the future tense of the verb *to be* and τῷ λαλοῦντι (the one speaking) as a dative of respect: "I shall be, in the eyes of the speaker, a barbarian."[32]

ζητεῖτε—the present imperative ("seek!") is located in the middle of the second part of verse 12. The word order is striking, because the emphasis falls on the church's edification of its members. Paul wants the Corinthians to pursue wholehearted edification.

28. J. Stanley Glen, *Pastoral Problems in First Corinthians* (London: Epworth, 1965), p. 184.
29. Moule, *Idiom-Book*, p. 79.
30. Joachim Jeremias, "*Homōs* (1 Cor. 14, 7; Gal. 3, 15)," *ZNW* 52 (1961): 127–28; R. Keydell, "Homos," *ZNW* 54 (1963): 145–46.
31. Bauer, p. 829; Blass and Debrunner, *Greek Grammar*, #385.2.
32. Moule, *Idiom-Book*, p. 46.

c. Praying and Praising
14:13–17

Throughout this chapter Paul questions the usefulness of religious activity that is devoid of edification. In this section he writes that intelligibility requires the use of the believer's mind in praying, singing, praising, and giving thanks to God. A believer who does not employ the mind and practices tongue-speaking without interpretation utters a series of meaningless syllables. The gift of speaking in tongues can be validated only when there is interpretation (v. 5).

13. Therefore, let the one who speaks in a tongue pray so that he may interpret.

The adverb *therefore* links the present verse to the preceding passage (vv. 6–12) and especially to verse 12. There Paul stresses both edification and intelligibility. On the basis of these principles he exhorts the Corinthians that the person who engages in tongue-speaking should pray for interpretation.

The wording of the text is clear, yet its interpretation presents a few questions. Does Paul mean that the same person may possess the gift of speaking in a tongue and afterward, in answer to prayer, receive the gift of interpretation? Can a person possess these two gifts at the same time or is the first one coming to an end when the second one is received? Is Paul telling the tongue-speaker to pray that someone may be found who is able to translate the spoken words?

Finding satisfactory answers to these questions is difficult because the wording of the text is compact and measured. However, we should realize the setting that Paul describes is not the privacy of one's house but a public worship service. In this setting, the spoken word must always be lucid and instructive; otherwise the speaker ought to remain silent (vv. 5, 28). The tongue-speaker usually has full control of his senses and thus is able to either begin or stop at any time.[33] Neither the speaker nor the listener is edified by unintelligible speech. Moreover, tongue-speaking and the interpretation of tongues should be linked, for they are gifts of the Holy Spirit that are meant to edify the church.

Further, if a person speaks a foreign language, someone should be found to translate his words.[34] Paul wants everyone in the audience to receive the benefit of the message. In a subsequent context, he says that someone else should be found to interpret the spoken words (vv. 27–28). If an interpreter is not present, the speaker must remain silent.

14. For if I pray in a tongue, my spirit prays, but my mind is unfruitful. 15. What then is the result? I shall pray with my spirit, and I shall pray also with my mind. I shall sing with my spirit and I shall sing also with my mind.

The first clause is conditional, and in it Paul is not saying that he himself prays in a tongue (compare vv. 18–19). He only states what would happen if he should

---

33. Turner, "Spiritual Gifts," p. 44.
34. Robert H. Gundry, "'Ecstatic Utterance' (N.E.B.)?" *JTS* 17 (1966): 302–3.

do so: his spirit would be praying without the use of his mind. Paul himself sets the example by praying in distinct words that everyone is able to understand.[35]

a. "For if I pray in a tongue, my spirit[36] prays, but my mind is unfruitful." This text explains the preceding verse (v. 13), being connected by the introductory word *for*.[37] That is, Paul uses his personal life as an example for the Corinthians. In an earlier passage, he stated that speaking to God in a tongue is a private matter without benefit to the church (vv. 2–4). In private prayer, only the human spirit communicates with God. But Paul rejects such praying in public worship. He says that the mind is unproductive, because it does not edify others. Although the exact words in Jesus' command to love God with heart, soul, and mind (Matt. 22:37) differ from those found in this text (vv. 14–15), the exercise of prayer should employ the same faculties.

How do the spirit and the mind function? The human mind, which has the capacity to think and understand, is intimately linked to the human spirit. When the Holy Spirit controls both the spirit and the mind, a person usually flourishes and prospers. But when the human spirit is not governed by the Holy Spirit, the mind remains spiritually idle and the result is sterility.[38]

It is possible for the spirit and the mind to function separately, but Paul intimates that a person's spirit and mind must be equally engaged to be productive.[39] Accordingly, Calvin makes this pointed observation concerning the Corinthian situation: "But if someone endowed with the gift of tongues spoke sensibly and intelligently, it would have been pointless for Paul to say that 'the spirit prays but the understanding is unfruitful', for the understanding must have been acting together with the spirit."[40]

b. "What then is the result? I shall pray with my spirit, and I shall pray also with my mind." The spirit and the mind must work together in the exercise of prayer to utter intelligible words. They must edify the church members who listen to these words. Thus, Paul urges the Corinthians to pray in a language that is known to everyone present in the worship service. He tells the Corinthians that both the spirit and the mind must pray effectively for the benefit of the church.

---

35. Consult Anthony A. Hoekema, *Tongues and Spirit-Baptism: A Biblical and Theological Evaluation* (reprint ed.; Grand Rapids: Baker, 1981), p. 92.

36. The possessive pronoun *my* before the noun *spirit* does not refer to the Holy Spirit, for in Scripture the Spirit is never identified as "my spirit." One translation has "the Spirit in me" (NEB), but its successor gives the exact wording of the text, "my spirit" (REB).

37. Textual support for this reading is ample; the conjunction γάρ (for) is included in Greek New Testaments and so translated in most versions. Jean Héring advocates ignoring the conjunction. *The First Epistle of Saint Paul to the Corinthians*, trans. A. W. Heathcote and P. J. Allcock (London: Epworth, 1962), p. 150.

38. By contrast see William G. MacDonald, "The Place of Glossolalia in Neo-Pentecostalism," in *Speaking in Tongues: Let's Talk about It*, ed. Watson E. Mills (Waco: Word, 1973), pp. 81–93; Tony Campolo, *How to Be Pentecostal without Speaking in Tongues* (Dallas: Word, 1991), pp. 32–33.

39. Compare Donald Guthrie, *New Testament Theology* (Downers Grove: InterVarsity, 1981), p. 170; Gaffin, *Perspectives on Pentecost*, p. 77.

40. Calvin, *I Corinthians*, pp. 291–92.

Indeed, praying calls for an intense concentration of the mind: we praise God, confess our sins, thank him for blessings received, and humbly petition him to fill our needs. To pray without engaging one's mind is useless, says Paul. Hence, speaking in tongues without the use of the mind results in a failure to communicate with those who listen. In verse 14, Paul clearly states that if the mind is unfruitful, there is no intelligibility, no understanding, and no edification.[41]

By writing the future tense in verse 15, Paul expresses his own will and determination, that is, "I shall certainly pray with my mind, and I shall indeed sing with my mind." Among the aspects of worship (see v. 26) are both prayer and praise. The first one usually consists of petitions and the second one is the joyful response to blessings received. Seventeenth-century English bishop Thomas Ken gave poetic expression to the thought of praising the Triune God for such blessings in the familiar doxology:

> Praise God, from whom all blessings flow;
> Praise Him, all creatures here below;
> Praise Him above, ye heavenly host;
> Praise Father, Son, and Holy Ghost.

c. "I shall sing with my spirit and I shall sing also with my mind." Paul deliberately places praise next to prayer. He reasons that for his spirit to pray effectively, he must use his mind. And when his spirit wants to sing joyful praises to God, Paul must do so with full understanding of the words and music. The Gentiles, says Jesus, engage in meaningless babbling when they pray (Matt. 6:7). He warns his listeners not to be like them but to pray intelligently the words of the Lord's Prayer (Matt. 6:9–13). Similarly, singing ought to be expressed in meaningful words with appropriate melodies. Both the one who prays and the one who sings gain a spiritual blessing when their hearers obtain a celestial benefit.

The setting obviously is a worship service during which the members of the congregation participate in prayer and in singing psalms, hymns, and spiritual songs (see Eph. 5:19; Col. 3:16). When one sings praises to God, he or she should pay close attention to the words and the tune, or one's singing may result in nonsense and dissonance. As the spirit and the mind work together in praying, so they ought to be in tandem when singing.

16. Otherwise, if you bless [only] with the spirit, how shall the one who fills up the place of the uninformed say amen to your thanksgiving? Because what you utter he does not understand.

a. *Result.* "Otherwise, if you bless [only] with the spirit." Paul is saying that if the Corinthians do not speak and sing intelligibly, they will offend those who are unable to understand the words of the one who is praying. To be precise, in the Greek Paul uses the second person singular *you* as if he addresses a person who is

---

41. Edgar, *Miraculous Gifts*, p. 181 n. 11.

challenging his discourse. Hence, once more he stresses the consequence of praying and giving thanks with the spirit but not with the mind.

The verb *to bless* should be taken together with the noun *thanksgiving*, for both terms explain the worshipful acts of praying and singing. In this context, to bless means to offer praise to God in worship. Because of Old Testament teaching, the verb was used in everyday life especially before and after a meal.[42] Blessing is the act of praising, whereas thanksgiving is the content of that praise. Blessing may be the most worthy part of prayer, but unless it is uttered in understandable language, it is useless to everyone who participates in the worship service.

b. *Response.* "How shall the one who fills up the place of the uninformed say amen to your thanksgiving?" Paul asks a question that is contextual and can be understood only when we are familiar with worship services in the ancient synagogue and church. At the conclusion of a prayer in a synagogue, it was customary for the audience to utter a responsive amen—a Hebrew term that means "So let it be!"—as a sign of wholehearted approval of what was said.[43] This custom continued in the worship service of the early church, as is evident from Paul's writings and those of church fathers.[44] The members of the church voiced their consent to a prayer that one of them had uttered. If they had not understood a prayer expressed in a language unknown to them, they would be unable to say amen.

The clause *one who fills up the place of the uninformed* is difficult to interpret. The Greek word *idiōtēs* (uninformed) occurs again in verse 23 (there, with the term *unbelievers;* see the commentary); in the current text we perhaps do well to understand "the uninformed" to be one who fills the role of disciple, an inquirer whose status is between an unbeliever and a full-fledged Christian (compare also the commentary on vv. 23–24).[45] Just as the synagogues had God-fearers whose status was between those of unbelievers and proselytes, so in its evangelistic outreach the early church had disciples or inquirers. Moreover, the use of the singular in this verse and the next should not be overlooked. With the singular, Paul uses a Hebrew idiom that actually means to play a part, or fill a role.[46]

In this passage, however, the inability to understand a spoken language, not an inability to understand the Christian faith, is at issue. For that reason, most commentators apply the Greek term *idiōtēs* to a person who lacks the gift of either tongues or interpretation yet is a full member of the church. Such a person is untrained and unskilled in understanding the language that is spoken and thus is deprived of spiritual blessings. Paul focuses attention on a particular individual who evidently is a tongue-speaker and another person who is not.

---

42. Hans-Georg Link, *NIDNTT*, vol. 1, pp. 212–13; Hermann W. Beyer, *TDNT*, vol. 2, pp. 759–63.
43. See Ps. 106:48; I Chron. 16:36; Neh. 5:13; 8:6. See also SB, vol. 3, pp. 456–61.
44. II Cor. 1:20; Justin Martyr *Apology* 1.65; Tertullian *Public Shows* 25.
45. Bauer, p. 370.
46. Consult Josephus *War* 5.2.5 [88]; Epictetus *Diss.* 2.4.5.

c. *Reason.* "Because what you utter he does not understand." The sense of the current passage is that someone who fails to understand the prayer is not edified at all and thus is unable to say amen in confirmation to the spoken words. Paul reproves anyone who speaks in a tongue without the benefit of an interpreter, and thus he implicitly reiterates that tongue-speaking is not a high-ranking gift.

17. For you are giving thanks well enough; however, the other man is not edified.

Paul emphatically addresses the individual who speaks in a tongue during a worship service. He says to him, "You, in fact, you are giving thanks." He praises this person for thanking God and commends him: well done! Paul does not find fault with this person's expressions of gratitude but rather with the manner in which he expresses them. He reproves him for the total disregard for "the other man," because the uninformed person receives no benefit from the prayer that was uttered in a language that was not understood. Paul's last clause in this verse is a ringing rebuke for the tongue-speaker who failed to edify the uninformed person. In short, anyone who gives leadership in a worship service must speak intelligibly to enlighten and instruct his fellow man.

Practical Considerations in 14:15–17

The New Testament church emerged from local Jewish synagogues in both Israel and the Dispersion. When Christians founded churches in distinction from Jewish synagogues, the liturgical structure of worship in these two assemblies remained quite similar. Both the Jew and the Christian sang the psalms and hymns recorded in the Old Testament, yet in time the Christians added songs from the New Testament—for instance, the songs of Mary, Zechariah, and the angels (Luke 1:46–55; 68–79; 2:14).[47]

Leaders in both gatherings read portions from the Scriptures (selections from the Law and the Prophets), but in the church they also read the Gospels, Acts, and epistolary literature. The sacred writings were kept safe in the custody of local officials, who encouraged the people to memorize the Scriptures. Worshipers learned by heart the psalms, hymns, songs, and numerous parts of Holy Writ. And at every worship, these parts were repeated and augmented.

When the writer of Hebrews wrote his epistle, he quoted primarily from psalms, hymns, and messianic prophecies sung and recited by the people at worship. Thus he was able to communicate clearly and effectively, because everyone in the audience was familiar with the Old Testament quotations and Christ's gospel.

In addition, the people confessed their faith in accord with their respective creeds. The Jew recited the Shema (Deut. 6:4) and the Christian declared his faith in Jesus Christ as Lord and Savior (I Cor. 12:3; Phil. 2:6–11; I Tim. 3:16). Preaching in the local churches was in the form of teaching, exhortation, and edification. Apart from administering baptism and celebrating the Lord's Supper, church leaders and members offered congregational prayers to which the people expressed their concurrence with the customary amen.

---

47. Other hymns of the church are recorded in Paul's epistles (Rom. 11:33–36; Eph. 5:14; Phil. 2:6–11; Col. 1:15–20; I Tim. 3:16; II Tim. 2:11–13).

The church as a body not only heard the sermons and prayers but also tested them.[48] Sermons and prayers were to be understood and had to edify everyone present in the worship service.

From the information provided in Acts and the epistles, we are not aware of any church other than the one in Corinth that practiced tongue-speaking in the first century. No other New Testament writer, with the exception of Luke in Acts 2, 10, and 19, mentions tongue-speaking. Furthermore, aside from I Corinthians 12–14, the other New Testament passages that list spiritual gifts refrain from recording the gift of tongues. And in his First Epistle to the Corinthians, Paul discourages the practice of uninterpreted tongue-speaking. Although he urges the Corinthians to strive for the gift of prophecy (vv. 1, 5), he does not exhort them to seek the gift of speaking in tongues. Paul shows that of all the spiritual gifts the one of tongues is the least. He encourages the readers of his epistle to desire the greater gifts (12:31). On the other hand, he does instruct the Corinthians not to forbid anyone from speaking in a tongue (v. 39). Tongue-speaking is a gift of the Holy Spirit.

Greek Words, Phrases, and Constructions in 14:13–17

Verse 13

διό—"and so." This combination of the preposition διά (because of) and the neuter singular relative pronoun ὅ (which) summarizes the message of the preceding verse (v. 12).

Verse 15

ψαλῶ—the context indicates that the future tense expresses purpose: "I shall sing . . . and I shall sing with my mind."

Verses 16–17

ἐπεί, ἐπειδή—the words translated "for otherwise" allude to an ellipsis that means "if it were different."[49]

μὲν . . . ἀλλ'—these two words signal a sharp contrast between the tongue-speaker and the uninformed worshiper.

---

d. Thanksgiving
14:18–19

18. I thank God that I speak in tongues more than all of you. 19. However, in the church I would rather speak five words with my mind so that I may even teach others than ten thousand words in a tongue.

a. *Admission.* At least one translation reads "speaking in different kinds of languages" (NCV), and indeed Paul was able to converse in Semitic and in Indo-European languages and thus serve Jesus Christ as a cosmopolitan missionary.

---

48. Refer to Ralph P. Martin, *The Worship of God: Some Theological, Pastoral, and Practical Reflections* (Grand Rapids: Eerdmans, 1982), pp. 35–36.

49. Bauer, p. 284.

The Greek text, however, has the plural form *tongues*, not the singular, and does not say "different kinds of tongues" (12:10, 28) but "tongues." It appears that Paul focuses attention more on speaking in tongues than on his ability to speak different known languages.

Paul gives thanks to God[50] for granting him the ability to speak in tongues—more than people in the Corinthian community. His comparison relates not so much to frequency of occurrences as to the quality of his speaking in tongues.[51] We presume that Paul's admission of possessing this gift most likely came as a surprise to the believers, especially to the tongue-speakers. Although we know that both Peter and Paul at times fell into a trance (Acts 10:10; 22:17; compare II Cor. 12:1–6), we have no record in the New Testament that they ever spoke in tongues.

Why does Paul reveal this personal information? I venture to say that he urges the Corinthians to follow his example of using his gifts only for edifying the Christian community. Paul's objective in relating a personal experience is to show that he would not use the gift in public unless others would benefit from it.

b. *Use.* Paul immediately qualifies his statement that he has the ability to speak in tongues. He clearly indicates what his conduct would be in the setting of a worship service: "In the church I would rather speak five words with my mind." The words *in the church* state the location and make clear that Paul is not referring to the privacy of one's home (see the commentary on v. 4). The church is the place where God's people worship, where they praise God communally, and where they hear the gospel. In church, they are edified through the teaching and preaching of God's Word and are subsequently strengthened in their faith. Speaking in uninterpreted tongues does not contribute to the edification of the people and so Paul discourages the practice.

The numeral *five* in the expression *five words* is idiomatic, much as we use the numeral *six* in the saying "six of the one and half a dozen of the other." In the New Testament, five occurs as a round number with such nouns as sparrows (Luke 12:6), family (Luke 12:52), yoke of oxen (Luke 14:19), brothers (Luke 16:28), talents (Matt. 25:15), and the foolish and wise virgins (Matt. 25:2).[52]

"With my mind" denotes speaking intelligibly and reminds readers of Paul's earlier insistence on praying and singing with the mind (vv. 14–15). The phrase *with my mind* also evokes a contrast between speaking words that are intelligible or unintelligible: that is, the difference between prophecy or tongue-speaking.[53]

"So that I may even teach others." The Greek verb *katecheō* (I teach) actually means that a teacher utters words that are directed to listeners who are seated at his feet. In the early church, the verb connoted a question-and-answer method

50. Compare Rom. 1:8; 7:25; I Cor. 1:4; Phil. 1:3; Col. 1:3; 3:17; I Thess. 1:2; 2:13; II Thess. 1:3; 2:13; Philem. 4; Rev. 11:17.

51. F. W. Grosheide, *De Eerste Brief van den Apostel Paulus aan de Kerk te Korinthe*, Kommentaar op het Nieuwe Testament series (Amsterdam: Van Bottenburg, 1932), p. 466.

52. SB, vol. 3, p. 461; Colin J. Hemer, *NIDNTT*, vol. 2, p. 689.

53. James D. G. Dunn, *Jesus and the Spirit: A Study of the Religious and Charismatic Experience of Jesus and the First Christians as Reflected in the New Testament* (Philadelphia: Westminster, 1975), p. 229.

that we associate with the term *catechism*.[54] Paul would rather speak five words teaching others the gospel of Christ than ten thousand words that are unintelligible to the Corinthians. In effect, Paul rules out the possibility that he will ever publicly speak in a tongue, especially in a worship service.[55] He implicitly encourages the Corinthians to adopt his model. If they want to exercise the gift of tongue-speaking, let them do so in private. And if they wish to do so in public, let them use an interpreter (v. 27).

Greek Words, Phrases, and Constructions in 14:18–19

λαλῶ—there are two variants, λαλῶν (speaking) and λαλεῖν (to speak), which appear to be improvements of the verb λαλῶ (I speak) but lack the introductory conjunction ὅτι (that).

ἐν ἐκκλησίᾳ—this construction is idiomatic and means "at church." It refers not to a building but to the gathering of people at worship.

ἤ—the comparative particle takes the place of the adverb μᾶλλον (rather).

μυρίους—literally, "tens of thousands." See 4:15.

---

e. Tongues and Scripture
14:20–25

At this juncture in the discourse on tongues, Paul reminds his readers of the virtue of love. He wants them to practice the rule of love, overcome evil, and present themselves as mature Christians. He points them to the Scriptures so that they may be guided in their thinking by God's revelation.

20. Brothers, do not be children in your thinking, but be babes in regard to evil. Be mature in your thinking.

The term *brothers*, which includes sisters, generally means that Paul introduces and discusses a sensitive topic (see vv. 6, 26, 39). With this word, he places himself on the level of the readers and expresses fellowship with them. Paul gives leadership and expects the Corinthians to follow him. Thus he issues two commands, one negative and the other positive.

"Do not be children in your thinking, but be babes in regard to evil." The negative command comes first, which in the Greek shows that the Corinthians persistently demonstrated childish ways in their thinking. Some of them possibly flaunted their gift of tongues and demeaned others who lacked this gift. Paul now tells them to stop doing so and to act like adults. He undoubtedly has in mind the words God conveyed to Jeremiah, who wrote about the people of his day:

---

54. II Clem. 17:1. Hermann W. Beyer, *TDNT*, vol. 3, pp. 638–40. Consult C. H. Dodd, "The Primitive Catechism and the Sayings of Jesus," in *New Testament Essays: Studies in Memory of Thomas Walter Manson*, ed. A. J. B. Higgins (Manchester: Manchester University Press, 1959), pp. 106–18.

55. Compare D. A. Carson, *Showing the Spirit: A Theological Exposition of 1 Corinthians 12–14* (Grand Rapids: Baker, 1987), p. 105.

> "My people are fools;
>   they do not know me.
> They are senseless children;
>   they have no understanding.
> They are skilled in doing evil;
>   they know not how to do good."
>   [Jer. 4:22]

The Corinthians were more interested in entertainment than in education. They preferred the spectacular of tongue-speaking to the specifics of doctrinal issues. Spiritually, they pretended to be adults but in performance they were children.

As the spiritual father of the Corinthian believers (4:15), Paul exhorts them to be adults in their intellectual and spiritual perceptions.[56] He contrasts his negative exhortation with a positive one ("be babes in regard to evil"), yet these two exhortations are not truly parallel. We might have expected him to write "Do not be children in your thinking, but be mature in your thinking." Nonetheless, he urges the Corinthians to be mature people of God and to employ their inner being (heart, soul, and mind) in pursuing that which is good (compare Rom. 16:19). And with respect to doing evil, he wants adults to be as naive as infants. Paul vaguely echoes the words which Jesus spoke to his disciples before they began their missionary journey: "Therefore be as shrewd as snakes and as innocent as doves" (Matt. 10:16).

21. In the Law it is written,

> **"With strange tongues and with the lips of foreigners**
> **I will speak to this people,**
> **Even so they will not obey me, says the Lord."**

Paul quotes from one of his favorite books in the Old Testament, the prophecy of Isaiah. Of the seventeen quotations from the Old Testament Scriptures in I Corinthians, Paul has six from Isaiah.[57] Here he introduces the quotation with the phrase *in the Law*. Following Jewish practice, he applies the word *law* to the entire Old Testament (Rom. 3:19; and see John 10:34; 12:34; 15:25).[58] In addition, the wording is not an exact quotation from either the Hebrew or the Septuagint text but appears to be Paul's weaving the Old Testament text into his discourse. Incidentally, the wording is similar to the translation of Aquila.

In translation, the Hebrew text has this reading:

> Very well then, with foreign lips and strange tongues
> God will speak to this people,

---

56. Refer to Georg Bertram, *TDNT*, vol. 9, pp. 220–35.

57. I Cor. 1:19 (Isa. 29:14); 2:9 (Isa. 64:4); 2:16 (Isa. 40:13); 14:21 (Isa. 28:11–12); 15:32 (Isa. 22:13); 15:54 (Isa. 25:8).

58. SB, vol. 3, pp. 462–63.

to whom he said,
"This is the resting place, let the weary rest";
and "This is the place of repose"—
but they would not listen.

[Isa. 28:11–12]

Paul has reversed the two parts of the first line, "foreign lips" and "strange tongues." In the second line he substitutes "I" for "God"—in other words, God speaks directly to the people. He deletes the third and fourth lines and half of the fifth. And last, he adds "even so" and "says the Lord" to the second half of line five.

a. *Historical setting.* Paul takes the words from Isaiah's prophecy from the middle of a section that depicts Isaiah being ridiculed by intoxicated priests and prophets. These drunken clerics mock him by asking whether he is trying to explain his message to small children. They say that Isaiah's message is, "Do and do, do and do, rule on rule, rule on rule" (Isa. 28:10, 13). In Hebrew, these lines sound like baby talk:

*sav lasav sav lasav
kav lakav kav lakav.*

Their simplicity approaches unintelligibility. The Israelites scorned Isaiah, who came to them with God's word expressed in simple and clear Hebrew. Now God would come to them with Assyrian armed forces, whose soldiers would speak to them in a foreign language (contrast II Kings 18:26, where Assyrian officials addressed the people of Jerusalem in the Hebrew tongue). God pronounced a curse on them because of their unbelief.[59] He told them that they would be exiled to Assyria, where they would hear unintelligible speech (compare Deut. 28:49; see also Isa. 33:19; Jer. 5:15). Nevertheless, they refused to believe his word—"they would not listen."

b. *Current setting.* With the expression *even so* Paul stresses the hearers' unwillingness to listen to God and obey him. He interprets this attitude as disobedience: "Even so they will not obey me, says the Lord." But to whom does Paul apply this quotation? Who are these people who do not obey the Lord? They are not the Corinthians, because they are the ones who speak in tongues.

In the next three verses Paul repeatedly writes the term *unbelievers* (three times in the plural and once in the singular, vv. 22–24); moreover, the New Testament frequently lists the expression *apistoi* (unbelievers) and applies it to people whose background could be either Judaism or paganism.[60] God gave both the Jew and the Gentile the choice of either obeying or disobeying him. The Jews who refused to accept Christ's gospel were acquainted with the prophecy of Isa-

---

59. Consult O. Palmer Robertson, "Tongues: Sign of Covenantal Curse and Blessing," *WTJ* 38 (1975–76): 43–53; MacArthur, *1 Corinthians*, p. 382.
60. Matt. 17:17; Mark 9:19; Luke 9:41; 12:46; John 20:27; I Cor. 6:6; 7:12, 13, 14, 15; 10:27; 14:22, 23, 24; II Cor. 4:4; 6:14, 15; I Tim. 5:8; Titus 1:15.

iah. Because they rejected the message of Scripture, they were indeed unbeliev-ers. For them, this passage from Isaiah was a sign. For unbelieving Gentiles likewise, the phenomenon of tongue-speaking was a sign. Admittedly, the scene that Isaiah depicts and the Corinthian setting differ considerably. And the ques-tion about the identity of unbelievers remains.

22. Therefore, tongues are a sign not for the believers but for the unbelievers. And prophecy is not for unbelievers but for believers.

The first sentence in this text has been problematic for every interpreter. The conclusive *therefore* marks the beginning of the crux. What is Paul trying to con-clude after he quotes Isaiah's prophecy? He is applying the quotation in its mod-ified form to the people in Corinth and says, "for this reason tongues are a sign not for the believers but for the unbelievers." In Corinth, speaking in uninter-preted tongues resulted inescapably in confusion and unintelligibility. Thus, Paul indicates that tongue-speaking is a sign from God for unbelievers who ei-ther notice God's sacred presence at the worship service or turn away from God by hardening their hearts.

Nevertheless, the first sentence of verse 22 would be relieved significantly of one problem if the reading could be "a sign not for unbelievers but for believ-ers." The interchange of the two words *believers* and *unbelievers* would be help-ful.[61] But this substitution is ruled out for lack of Greek manuscript support.

Another approach is to interpret verse 22 as a rhetorical question instead of a declarative statement. The assumption, then, is that an imaginary opponent had raised the rhetorical question which Paul now incorporates in his dis-course. Paul tries to answer him in verses 23–25.[62] Certainly this is an ingenious solution to the problem in verse 22. But whenever Paul introduces quotations that come to him from Corinthian sources, these quotes reveal three basic char-acteristics:

> brevity,
> Paul's sustained qualification, and
> his unambiguous response.[63]

Because these characteristics are not present in verses 22–25, we hesitate to view verse 22 as a rhetorical question.

A more satisfactory approach is to look at the verse in context. We first need to know precisely what Paul means with the word *tongues*. Do we interpret tongues as languages foreign to the Corinthians and thus in the same category as the As-

---

61. *Phillips* substituted these words and says, "That means that 'tongues' are a sign of God's power, not for those who are unbelievers but to those who already believe."

62. B. C. Johanson, "Tongues, a Sign for Unbelievers?: A Structural and Exegetical Study of 1 Corin-thians 14, 20–25," *NTS* 25 (1979): 180–203.

63. Carson, *Showing the Spirit*, p. 55. Scholars affirm these quotations in I Cor.: 6:12, 13; 7:1; 8:1, 4, 5–6, 8; 11:2. But 14:22 is lacking. John C. Hurd, Jr., *The Origin of I Corinthians* (Macon, Ga.: Mercer University Press, 1983), p. 68.

syrian language, which was foreign to Isaiah's contemporaries?[64] According to this view, as God addressed the people of Israel through the Assyrians, who spoke a foreign tongue, so to demonstrate his presence he confronted the unbelievers through the Corinthians who spoke in a tongue (see also v. 25, "God is truly among you"). We must admit, however, that tongue-speaking tended to alienate rather than attract unbelievers. Not tongues but prophecy draws unbelievers to God; Paul will once again show the benefit of prophecy over against the barrier of tongue-speaking (vv. 23–25).

The second part of verse 22 states that "prophecy is not for unbelievers but for believers." If we add the word *sign* (i.e., prophecy is a sign) to give balance to both parts of the verse, we begin to understand Paul's thoughts in this verse, and the argument in verses 23–25. The sign of tongue-speaking serves as God's judgment on unbelievers and the sign of prophecy as God's benediction on his covenant people.[65] Prophecy, the proclamation and teaching of revelation, both edifies believers and calls unbelievers to repentance and a saving faith in Christ. Uninterpreted tongue-speaking can never be an evangelistic aid, but prophecy serves as an effective instrument to bring people to conversion.

Of how much value, then, is tongue-speaking in comparison with the gift of prophecy?[66] Prophecy fills a valuable role in the preaching and teaching ministry of the church, but speaking in tongues without interpretation fails to edify the church. In brief, Paul encourages prophecy so that through its intelligible message an unbeliever is convicted of sin and comes to faith in Christ. For the unbeliever whose heart is hardened and who rejects the gospel, tongue-speaking and prophesying are signs of judgment. This unbeliever is under the same judgment as the unbelieving Jew in the days of Isaiah.

23. So if the whole church comes together in one place and everyone speaks in tongues, and the novices or unbelievers enter, will they not say that you are out of your mind?

a. *A supposition.* "So if the whole church comes together in one place and everyone speaks in tongues." Paul illustrates his point concerning tongue-speaking by resorting to an overstatement. He realizes that the Corinthian believers meet in house churches for worship services and the observance of the sacraments. But now he slightly exaggerates by saying that the whole church should come together in one place (compare 11:20). This could take place when all the house churches would meet outdoors at a given location.[67] Paul continues his exaggeration by alluding to the possibility that *everyone* present in this broad assembly

---

64. Edgar, *Miraculous Gifts*, p. 147; Thomas, *Understanding Spiritual Gifts*, p. 142.

65. Turner, "Spiritual Gifts," p. 21; Grudem, *Prophecy in the New Testament*, pp. 174–76, and his "1 Corinthians 14:20–25: Prophecy and Tongues as Signs of God's Attitude," *WTJ* 41 (1979): 381–96.

66. Dunn, *Jesus and the Spirit*, p. 232. See also J. P. M. Sweet, "A Sign for Unbelievers: Paul's Attitude to Glossolalia," *NTS* 13 (1966–67): 240–57; P. Roberts, "A Sign—Christian or Pagan?" *ExpT* 90 (1979): 199–203.

67. Compare C. K. Barrett, *A Commentary on the First Epistle to the Corinthians*, Harper's New Testament Commentaries series (New York and Evanston: Harper and Row, 1968), p. 326.

would speak in tongues. To make his point, he also says nothing about the interpretation of tongues.

b. *An observation.* "And the novices or unbelievers enter, will they not say that you are out of your mind?" What kind of a witness would such a noisy gathering of Christians be to those who do not belong to the church? Unbelievers would ridicule the believers and accuse them of losing their minds. In fact, at Pentecost the unbelievers in Jerusalem derided the apostles for being drunk when they spoke different languages (Acts 2:13–15). If such simultaneous tongue-speaking should occur in Corinth, the local church would become the laughingstock of the world.

The Greek term *idiōtēs,* translated "uninformed," also appeared in verse 16 (see the commentary). But here and in the next verse (v. 24) we prefer the meaning *novices,* which because of the context differ from the translation in verse 16. Because Paul places this term next to the word *unbelievers,* he leaves the impression that a novice is an uninitiated non-Christian who attends the worship services from time to time. In a sense, in this verse and the next the two terms mean the same thing. The translation *unbelieving novices* is descriptive and to the point.[68]

24. But if all prophesy and a certain unbeliever or novice enters, he is convicted by all and judged by all.

a. "But if all prophesy." The second illustration that Paul offers also depicts a hypothetical scene. He visualizes a worship service in which all the believers prophecy, most likely in sequence to avoid dissonance (see v. 29). Should this ever become reality, the service itself would continue for an interminable period.

b. "And a certain unbeliever or novice enters." Worship services should be open to the public, for Jesus himself said that he always taught openly to everyone and said nothing in secret (John 18:20). The preaching of the Word in the vernacular is also for any unbeliever or novice who wishes to attend. In this verse, the two terms *unbeliever* and *novice* refer to the same person (v. 23).

c. "He is convicted by all and judged by all." Paul borrows two verbs, *convict* and *judge,* from the judicial system. Although he does not specify, we are confident that the verb *to convict* in this verse refers to being convicted by the Word of God and not by human messages. The Holy Spirit through the Scriptures brings people to repentance and to a saving knowledge of the Lord (John 16:8–9). The Word of God, proclaimed by those Corinthians who prophesy, exposes sin in the life of a sinner and makes all things visible to him (compare Eph. 5:13). From the context it is clear that when the Corinthians prophesy they are far more effective in leading people to a saving knowledge of Christ than if they speak in tongues.[69]

---

68. Otto Flender, *NIDNTT,* vol. 2, pp. 456–57; Heinrich Schlier, *TDNT,* vol. 3, p. 217; Barrett, *First Corinthians,* pp. 324–25.

69. See Hoekema, *Tongues and Spirit-Baptism,* p. 94.

Moreover, the believers are given the task of judging all things in the light of the Scriptures (see 2:15). They are to make diligent inquiry in respect to a person who has received the light of the gospel, has accepted Christ Jesus in faith, has renounced his or her former life of sin, and now desires to be a member of the church. Christians cannot accept unbelievers who reject the gospel with hardened heart and blinded mind, for such persons are like the Jews who in unbelief mocked the prophetic word of Isaiah (Isa. 28:11). Hence, the prophet Isaiah taught that many of his contemporaries were unbelievers for whom his message proved to be unproductive.[70]

25. The hidden things of his heart become evident, and thus falling on his face he will worship God, declaring,

"God is truly among you."

a. "The hidden things of his heart become evident." Convicting someone of sin is the work of the Lord. As Paul has written earlier in this epistle, "The Lord . . . will bring to light the hidden things of darkness and will reveal the purposes of the hearts" (4:5). By means of his Word and Spirit, the Lord illumines a person's life, so that everything is open to view. For instance, Paul was converted when Jesus spoke to him; he accepted Jesus' word, received the Holy Spirit, and began to preach in the local synagogues (Acts 9:4–6, 17, 20). The things that Paul had never before considered to be true were now clear to him. Immediately he preached the truth that Jesus is the Son of God.

b. "And thus falling on his face he will worship God." Here is a picture of complete submission to God Almighty: a prostrate sinner lying facedown before his God. This means that he now repudiates all other gods and acknowledges only Jesus as his sovereign Lord. Prostrate posture also depicts a person's unworthiness when God himself is present (see I Kings 18:39).

c. "Declaring, 'God is truly among you.'" Once more Paul turns to the Old Testament Scriptures and quotes from the prophecy of Isaiah (Isa. 45:14; see also Zech. 8:23). The person who is convicted of sin, has turned in faith to God, and lies flat on the ground exclaims: "God is truly among you." These words are an acknowledgment that the power of God is at work in the hearts of sinners. Just as the Egyptians in Isaiah's day recognized God's presence among the people of Israel, so the unbeliever who listens to those Corinthians preach the gospel confesses that God is with them. And joining their company, he with them can say "Immanuel" (God is with us).

Additional Comments on 14:22–25

Paul contrasts the effect of tongue-speaking and prophesying. The first one causes the unbeliever to say that the Christians are out of their minds; the second one causes him to repent and acknowledge that God is in the midst of the believers.

---

70. Calvin, *I Corinthians*, p. 299.

Paul once again stresses the difference between tongue-speaking and prophecy: "He who speaks in a tongue edifies himself. He who prophesies edifies the church. . . . And greater is the one who prophesies than the one who speaks in a tongue, unless he interprets, so that the church may be edified" (vv. 4, 5b). While Paul encourages prophecy, he specifies that tongue-speaking must edify fellow Christians (vv. 5, 12), be interpreted (vv. 5, 27), and take place in a decent and orderly way (v. 40).

Practical Considerations in 14:24–25

Not the prophetic word of man but the prophetic Word of God brings about repentance and conversion. This was true for God's people in both the Old and New Testament eras, as is evident from two illustrations. First, after David committed adultery with Bathsheba and had her husband Uriah killed, God sent the prophet Nathan to David with the ringing message: "You are the man!" (II Sam. 12:7). David repented of his sin and offered to God a broken and contrite heart (Ps. 51:17).

Next, Jesus confronted Paul on the road to Damascus and called him by name: "Saul, Saul, why do you persecute me?" (Acts 9:4). When Jesus identified himself to Paul lying prostrate before him, Paul acknowledged him as Lord. Jesus convicted Paul by telling him that he was persecuting not merely Christians but Jesus himself. Because of this encounter, Paul recognized Jesus' divinity and repented. Soon afterward in local synagogues, Paul proclaimed Jesus as the Son of God.

In today's confused world, faithful preaching of the Word is the indispensable prerequisite for providing competent direction. It is God's Word that convicts people of sin, brings them to repentance, and leads them to a saving knowledge of Christ. Therefore, preachers and teachers of the Scriptures must declare God's full revelation in Christ. They must boldly proclaim the doctrines of heaven and hell, forgiveness and condemnation, sin and salvation. And wherever the Scriptures are faithfully preached, worshipers can sincerely say: God is truly among us.

Greek Words, Phrases, and Constructions in 14:20–22

Verse 20

μὴ παιδία γίνεσθε—the present imperative preceded by the negative particle μή indicates that the Corinthians indeed were childish in their behavior: "stop being children." ταῖς φρεσίν—"your minds." With τῇ κακίᾳ (evil), both nouns are datives of reference. The definite article with the second noun is attracted to the construction of the first noun.

Verses 21–22

ἑτέρων—see also the compound ἑτερογλώσσαις (strange tongues). This adjective expresses a difference from that which is normal. Some manuscripts have the dative plural ἑτέροις modifying χείλεσιν (other lips, KJV, NKJV). However, the preferred reading is "lips of foreigners" to avoid the repetitious reading *other tongues and other lips.*

εἰς—with the accusative *sign,* the preposition expresses purpose or intention: "for a sign."

ὥστε—this is an inferential particle that means "and so, accordingly."[71]

---

71. Moule, *Idiom-Book,* p. 144.

26 What then is the result, brothers? When you come together, each one has a psalm, has a teaching, has a revelation, has a tongue, has an interpretation. Let all things be for edification. 27 If anyone speaks in a tongue, let it be by two or at the most three and each in turn, and let one interpret. 28 But if there is no interpreter, let him be silent in the church and let him speak to himself and to God.

29 And let two or three prophets speak and let the others pass judgment. 30 But if a revelation comes to another who is seated, let the first one be silent. 31 For you can all prophesy one by one so that all may learn and all may be encouraged. 32 And the spirits of prophets are subject to the prophets. 33 For God is a God not of disorder but of peace.

As in all the churches of the saints, 34 let the women keep silent in the churches. For they are not permitted to speak, but let them be submissive, just as the Law says. 35 And if they wish to learn something, let them ask their husbands at home. For it is disgraceful for a woman to speak in church.

36 Or did the word of God originate with you or has it come to you only? 37 If anyone thinks himself to be a prophet or spiritual, let him know that the things which I write to you are a command of the Lord. 38 If anyone disregards [it], he is disregarded [by God].

39 So, my brothers, eagerly desire to prophesy and do not forbid speaking in tongues. 40 But let all things be done decently and in order.

---

6. Orderly Conduct
14:26–40

The worship services of the Corinthian community were far from orderly. Paul already gave the church instructions on celebrating the Lord's Supper (11:17–34) and using spiritual gifts for the edification of fellow church members (14:5, 12). Now he writes additional directions on orderly speaking during the worship services in the Corinthian church. He has to correct people who prize individualism and neglect orderliness at worship.

a. Edification
14:26–28

26. What then is the result, brothers? When you come together, each one has a psalm, has a teaching, has a revelation, has a tongue, has an interpretation. Let all things be for edification.

a. *Question.* The Greek text of the first sentence is short because it lacks a predicate, which we supply in parentheses: "What then is (the result), brothers?" (see v. 15a). The answer to this question is that if disorder stands in the way of hearing and believing, the Corinthian worship services fail to edify. Once more, therefore, Paul emphasizes his familiar theme of edification: if there is chaos at worship, worshipers receive no spiritual benefits.

Whenever Paul touches a sensitive topic that affects the Corinthians personally, he usually addresses them as brothers (see vv. 6, 20, 26, 39) and this verse is no exception. He corrects their disorderly behavior in the church services, where they thoughtlessly promote their individualism and neglect the other members.

b. *Orderliness.* "When you come together, each one has a psalm, has a teaching, has a revelation, has a tongue, has an interpretation." Paul depicts worship that involves many members of the congregation: the one sings a psalm, the other teaches, still another shares a revelation, and the last-mentioned persons speak and interpret a tongue. Paul does not indicate that this list is exhaustive or that he tabulates a typical order of worship. Rather, he mentions some parts of the service at random.[72] For instance, he fails to mention prayer and the reading of the Scriptures, although these elements may be included in the gifts that are listed.

Already Paul had mentioned the singing of a psalm or a hymn (v. 15), a common part of the services in Jewish synagogues and Christian churches. The singing might be either accompanied or unaccompanied by an instrument. In addition, he listed teaching and revelation in the context of knowledge and prophecy (v. 6). We presume that teaching and revelation are related to the exposition of the Word. And last, one of Paul's explicit orders has been that speaking in a tongue in public must always be interpreted; otherwise it lacks value. Everything in the worship service must be done in an orderly manner.

c. *Benefit.* "Let all things be for edification." Every part of the worship service must strengthen the members of the church. That is, when the congregation comes together for worship, the principle of love must be applied and be evident. If this principle is absent, worship itself is worthless in God's sight.

27. If anyone speaks in a tongue, let it be by two or at the most three and each in turn, and let one interpret. 28. But if there is no interpreter, let him be silent in the church and let him speak to himself and to God.

Whenever Paul discusses tongue-speaking, he regulates it in some way or other.[73] Here he is addressing an individual, male or female, and writes the noun *tongue* in the singular. He wants the speaker to pay attention to five constraints.

a. *Numbers.* "Let it be by two or at the most three." Not everyone is permitted to engage in tongue-speaking; only two but no more than three are allowed to speak. With these numbers, Paul denotes that not everyone has received this gift (12:30). Further, he intimates that the restriction applies for any given meeting.

b. *Orderliness.* "And each in turn." Earlier Paul depicted a hypothetical scene in which the whole church spoke in tongues; he pointed out the detriments such action would have (v. 23). Now he wants to preclude any negative effects tongue-speech may have on the evangelistic task of the church. Thus, he regulates the exercise of tongue-speaking to preserve liturgical order at worship.[74] Paul restrains the members of the Corinthian congregation by saying that each may speak in turn: one at a time and no more. Throughout this segment of his discussion, he enforces the rule for orderliness in the church (see v. 33a).

c. *Interpretation.* "And let one interpret." The next restriction has been mentioned earlier but is repeated here. When people speak in a tongue, one of the church members must interpret for the two or three who are permitted to speak

---

72. Fee, *First Corinthians*, p. 690.

73. Refer to Sweet, "A Sign for Unbelievers," p. 254.

74. Consult William Richardson, "Liturgical Order and Glossolalia in 1 Corinthians 14.26c–33a," *NTS* 32 (1986): 144–53.

(compare vv. 5, 13). In the New Testament, the verb *to interpret* and its cognates signify either translating words or conveying the meaning from one language into another.[75] In the Corinthian church, communicating the significance of the spoken words seems to be the case, rather than translating two or three familiar languages in succession.

d. *Silence.* "But if there is no interpreter, let him be silent in the church." In the absence of an interpreter, the tongue-speaker must remain quiet at worship. Paul's remark discloses that the person who has the gift of tongue-speech possesses control of his or her senses. This person has the ability to keep quiet while others successively speak. Note that Paul allows the exercise of uninterpreted tongue-speech in the privacy of one's home.

e. *Devotions.* "And let him speak to himself and to God." The last directive Paul gives the tongue-speaker is to speak privately to oneself and to God. Speaking to God in private has nothing to do with the church at worship. The speaker is engaged in prayer to God and no one may invade the religious privacy of this individual (see the commentary on vv. 2–4).

Greek Words, Phrases, and Constructions in 14:26–28

Verse 26

ἕκαστος—"each one," to which the Western text and the Majority Text add the personal pronoun ὑμῶν (of you). Scholars prefer the deletion of this pronoun.

πρός—with the accusative case of the noun *edification*, this preposition denotes purpose.

Verses 27–28

κατά—this preposition preceding numbers should be understood distributively: "by two or at the most three."

τὸ πλεῖστον—"at the most." Here is a true superlative of the adjective πολύς (much, many) preceded by the definite article τό, for which we supply the noun μέρος (part).

ἑαυτῷ—the reflexive pronoun is used as the dative of advantage.[76]

---

b. Prophets and Revelation
14:29–33a

29. And let two or three prophets speak and let the others pass judgment. 30. But if a revelation comes to another who is seated, let the first one be silent. 31. For you can all prophesy one by one so that all may learn and all may be encouraged.

Minor variations aside, the regulations which Paul writes for the people who prophesy are as sensible as those for tongue-speakers. Note that after Paul repeats the numbers two and three and the command to be silent, he accentuates

---

75. Bauer, p. 194.
76. Blass and Debrunner, *Greek Grammar,* #188.2.

the one more than the other. For the tongue-speakers he requests that one interpreter provide the meaning of what they said, but for prophets he asks the church members to evaluate prophetic utterances. While he tells the tongue-speaker who lacks an interpreter not to speak in church, he encourages its members to prophesy in succession. With respect to tongue-speech Paul does not mention any benefits, but when he refers to prophecy he describes the blessings of instruction and encouragement. The differences between these two spiritual gifts are significant, and Paul is consistent in repeating their dissimilarities. He always places the gift of prophecy at a level that excels the gift of tongue-speaking.

a. *Prophets.* "And let two or three prophets speak." This is the first time Paul writes the noun *prophets* in the current chapter (see 12:28–29; 14:32, 37). In this chapter, he repeatedly writes the cognate verb *prophesy*, which in Greek always appears as a present tense in either the indicative, subjunctive, participle, or infinitive mood (see the commentary on 13:9–10).[77] With the invariable use of the present tense, Paul has in mind more the regular preaching and teaching of the Holy Scriptures than an occasional prophetic statement.

What do the prophets proclaim? Writes Herman Ridderbos: "Prophets are the Spirit-impelled proclaimers of the Word of God to the church, who unfold God's plan of redemption, as well as elucidate and impress upon it the significance of the work of God in Christ in a pastoral and paraenetic sense."[78] And what is the objective of prophecy? Paul teaches that in Corinth prophesying is for edifying, encouraging, and comforting the members of the Christian community (v. 3). The message of the people who prophesy should be in harmony with or come forth out of the revealed Word of God. If a message, either in the form of preaching and teaching or as a spontaneous utterance, conflicts with the teaching of the Scriptures, it does not come from the Lord. The prophet who utters the phrase, "This is what the Lord says," but fails to convey God's Word speaks not for God but for himself. He is fraudulent and misrepresents the Lord. Indeed, false prophets in Old Testament days risked their lives when they uttered falsehood (compare Deut. 13:1–5).

b. *Judgment.* "And let the others pass judgment." Who are those who are asked to pass judgment on the preaching and teaching of the Word? Some commentators think that the rest of the prophets must evaluate prophecy (see v. 32, and 12:10).[79] Others are of the opinion that the listeners, that is, the members of the church, must evaluate and weigh the message that is delivered (compare v. 31).[80] Much can be said for either position, yet the entire context seems to indi-

---

77. I Cor. 11:4, 5; 13:9; 14:1, 3, 4, 5, 24, 31, 39.

78. Herman N. Ridderbos, *Paul: An Outline of His Theology*, trans. John Richard de Witt (Grand Rapids: Eerdmans, 1975), p. 451.

79. E.g., John Albert Bengel, *Bengel's New Testament Commentary*, 2 vols., trans. Charlton T. Lewis and Marvin R. Vincent, 2 vols. (Grand Rapids: Kregel, 1981), vol. 2, p. 250; Kenneth L. Gentry, Jr., *The Charismatic Gift of Prophecy*, 2d ed. (Memphis: Footstool, 1989), p. 69.

80. Carson, *Showing the Spirit*, p. 120; Grudem, *Prophecy in the New Testament*, pp. 73–74.

cate that the members who listen to the prophecies must be the ones to pass judgment on the spoken word. If house churches accommodated at most thirty people, the proportion of prophets in a given congregation would be high. Other members participated in evaluating the messages.

What is the standard by which the listeners judge the words of the speaker? They must evaluate the speaker's message with God's Word. As the Bereans examined the Scriptures every day to see whether Paul's teaching was in harmony with God's revelation (Acts 17:11; see also I Thess. 5:21, *Didache* 11:7 for similar instances), so they are to weigh the words of the prophet.[81] Elsewhere Paul exhorts the believers to let the word of Christ dwell in them richly (Col. 3:16); in teaching and admonishing one another, let the Scriptures serve as the standard.

c. *Revelation.* "But if a revelation comes to another who is seated, let the first one be silent." This sentence is interesting, for it states that a speaker can be interrupted and silenced when someone who is in a sitting position receives a revelation. Paul literally says that "it is revealed to another who is seated," and then gives directions for orderly procedure. But what does he mean with the term *revelation?* J. I. Packer infers that "a prophetic 'revelation' was a God-prompted application of truth that in general terms had been revealed already, rather than a disclosure of divine thoughts and intentions not previously known and not otherwise knowable."[82] The application of God's Word that is revealed to a person seated in the audience cannot be placed on a par with Scripture; it lacks the absolute authority with which God has marked his Word. Yet when a person who receives such a revelation makes it known to fellow believers, they in turn must subject this revelation to the authoritative teachings of the Scriptures. In addition, if a person receives revelation in the form of a prediction, this utterance also must be weighed and evaluated on the basis of God's Word.

d. *Sequence.* "For you can all prophesy one by one." Paul is giving directives about orderly worship; he is not saying that at any worship service everyone has the opportunity to speak. That would fly in the face of Paul's insistence on orderly conduct. With his precept that two or three prophets may address the audience, he intimates that in the course of time every church member will be able to prophesy. God's Spirit not only is in control of prophecy but also gives certain members this particular gift in his proper timing. The Spirit determines when one prophet has had sufficient time and must yield his place to another person.

e. *Benefit.* "So that all may learn and all may be encouraged." Throughout this particular chapter, Paul repeats the concept *to edify,* albeit in different words. Here he says that the person who prophesies must do this so that all may learn "by conversing, inquiring, speaking, listening."[83] And, secondly, he notes that all may receive encouragement from the prophetic word (v. 3).

---

81. Grudem, *Prophecy in the New Testament,* p. 77.
82. Packer, *Keep in Step,* p. 215.
83. Bengel, *New Testament Commentary,* vol. 2, p. 250.

32. And the spirits of prophets are subject to the prophets. 33a. For God is a God not of disorder but of peace.

In Greek the phrase *the spirits of prophets* lacks the definite articles before the nouns (but see Rev. 22:6). In the current text the phrase probably means either "the spiritual gifts" of the prophets or the "manifestations of the Spirit" (see v. 12).[84] The first interpretation harmonizes with Paul's earlier command to "strive eagerly for the spiritual gifts" (v. 1). And the second explanation signifies that no prophet can say that he loses control of himself when he receives a revelation. Every person who prophesies is in full control of his or her senses. No one can say that the Holy Spirit prevails over the prophet's will so that the prophet acts against his own volition. Indeed, says Paul, God is a God not of disorder but of peace. God does not cause confusion, for he expects the prophet to maintain order by controlling himself and others at worship. In the presence of God all worshipers must be at peace with one another.

Practical Considerations in 14:29–33a

When Paul writes that something is revealed to one who is sitting in a worship service, he does not say that God verbally addresses this person. God works through his Spirit in the lives of his people at worship, home, or work; this is a truth to which every believer can testify. The Holy Spirit often instills within us either a firm conviction of God's truth, a vivid impression of reality, or a distinct understanding of a current problem.[85] The Spirit clearly prompts and guides us to speak and act so as to fulfill God's purpose. This divine guidance is revelatory for the individual recipient.[86] In some instances, however, the recipient wisely keeps the information to himself or herself because it is not meant to be proclaimed. At other times, he or she is able to share it with fellow Christians for their edification and the praise of God. Whenever the Spirit of God inspires us to do or to say something, he wants us to promote the cause of Christ. And he desires that we carry out our assignment in harmony with his revealed will.

Greek Words, Phrases, and Constructions in 14:29–31

Verse 29

οἱ ἄλλοι—these two words ("the others") can apply to either the prophets or the members of the congregation. Although the nearness of the adjective ἄλλῳ (v. 30) lends support to the first option, the prophets, the entire context favors the second. See also the commentary on 12:10.

---

84. F. F. Bruce, *1 and 2 Corinthians,* New Century Bible series (London: Oliphants, 1971), pp. 134–35; Dunn, *Jesus and the Spirit,* p. 233.

85. Consult John Murray, *The Collected Writings of John Murray,* 4 vols. (Edinburgh: Banner of Truth, 1976), vol. 1, pp. 186–87.

86. Refer to Wayne A. Grudem, "Prophecy—Yes, But Teaching—No: Paul's Consistent Advocacy of Women's Participation Without Governing Authority," *JETS* 30 (1987): 15–16.

διακρινέτωσαν—this is the present subjunctive (hortatory) of the compound verb δι-ακρίνω (I judge). It signifies the act of judging either the weather by looking at the sky (Matt. 16:3), oneself (I Cor. 11:31), or prophetic words (I Cor. 14:29).[87] Incidentally, the Greek verb *diakrinein* (to pass judgment) does not signify "to interpret [oracles and dreams]."[88]

Verses 30–31

ἐάν—this particle introduces the protasis of a conditional sentence that features probability.

καθ᾽ ἕνα—the preposition has a distributive sense with the numeral *one,* "one by one."[89]

---

c. Orderliness
14:33b–35

33b. As in all the churches of the saints, 34. let the women keep silent in the churches. For they are not permitted to speak, but let them be submissive, just as the Law says. 35. And if they wish to learn something, let them ask their husbands at home. For it is disgraceful for a woman to speak in church.

a. *Textual problems.* Most translators separate verses 33a and 33b because the first part of this verse ("For God is a God not of disorder but of peace") is a complete statement, and to add to it the second part ("As in all the churches of the saints") seems incongruent. In general, translators consider verse 33b ("As in all the churches of the saints") to be the introductory part of the first sentence in verse 34 ("let the women keep silent in the churches"). We admit that the repetition of the phrase *in the churches* detracts from the author's stylistic elegance (v. 34). However, the expression *churches* reflects nuances: the first occurrence ("As in all the churches of the saints") alludes to churches in general and the second ("let the women keep silent in the churches") to worship services. Conversely, verse 33b is not the only place in his epistles where Paul exhibits a lack of exemplary style. We assume that he is concerned not about elegance but rather about providing the churches with rules to bolster unity and harmony (compare 4:17; 7:17; 11:16)—concerns that he has emphasized throughout the epistle.

Some scholars call this segment—a directive about the conduct of women in the church service—a gloss, yet they are unable to find any evidence in Greek manuscripts to support their claim that these verses were added to the text.[90] Thus some versions (e.g., NRSV) place verses 33b–36 in parentheses. A few Western texts transpose verses 34 and 35 following verse 40 (see *Moffatt,* who also includes verse 36 in the transposition).

---

87. Burkhard Gärtner, *NIDNTT,* vol. 1, p. 503.

88. Contra Gerhard Dautzenberg in *EDNT,* vol. 1, p. 306; his translation is refuted by Wayne A. Grudem in "A Response to Gerhard Dautzenberg on 1 Corinthians 12.10," *BibZ* 22 (1978): 253–70.

89. Moule, *Idiom-Book,* p. 60.

90. For instance, Eduard Schweizer, "The Service of Worship. An Exposition of I Corinthians 14," *Interp* 13 (1959): 402–3; Fee, *First Corinthians,* p. 699. Fee asserts that verses 34–35 "were not part of the original text, but were a very early marginal gloss."

To resolve the difficulties with this text, we need to do as we have done with other passages: consider the structure, the larger context, and preeminently the themes or principles Paul has explicated. In verse 29 Paul advised the Corinthians to "let two or three prophets speak and let the others pass judgment"—thus using the verse as a heading for verses 30–33a. In these verses he explains verse 29 and outlines rules of conduct that promote orderly worship. He also specifies how prophecies should be evaluated.[91]

In parallel fashion, and implicitly under the heading of verse 29b,[92] Paul continues with rules of conduct, these relating specifically to women. As verses 30–33a state that others pass judgment on the messages of the prophets, so verses 33b–35 restrain women from passing judgment on men.[93] For this reason, the apostle appeals to the Law.

b. *Command to be silent.* "As in all the churches of the saints, let the women keep silent in the churches." The first occurrence of the word *churches* refers to individual congregations and the second one to their meetings. Paul's command to keep silent cannot be a total ban on speaking in the meetings. This injunction would contradict his earlier statement (11:5), where he spoke of women praying and prophesying at worship. Moreover, we presume that with the men, the women also were singing psalms and hymns in church (14:26). Obviously, Paul is not restricting women from speaking when they worship God. Rather he is saying that they should respect their husbands in accordance with the Law.

c. *Teaching of the Law.* "For they are not permitted to speak, but let them be submissive, just as the Law says." Notice that Paul states the rule on silence three times: "let the women keep silent in the churches" (v. 34a), "they are not permitted to speak" (v. 34b), and "it is disgraceful for a woman to speak in church" (v. 35b). For support on this sensitive issue he appeals to the Law, that is, the Old Testament Scriptures. But what is this teaching of the Law? Here Paul uses the term as a general expression without any reference to a particular Scripture passage.

Earlier in this chapter, however, Paul turned to the Law and quoted from one of the prophets (Isa. 28:11–12 in v. 21). Now he has in mind the account of Genesis 2:18–24 that teaches the creation order in which Adam was created first and then Eve as Adam's helper. From this account, Paul deduces the principle that the wife is subject to her husband as his helper and is accountable to him.

Paul consistently appeals to the creation account of Genesis 2 throughout this epistle. First, in his discussion on sexual immorality (6:16) Paul quotes from Genesis 2:24, "The two shall become one flesh." Next, as he outlines the creation and

91. James B. Hurley, "Man and Woman in 1 Corinthians," Ph.D. diss., Cambridge University, 1973, pp. 71–75; *Man and Woman in Biblical Perspective* (Grand Rapids: Zondervan, 1981), pp. 188–91.
92. Grudem, *Prophecy in the New Testament,* pp. 220–25; D. A. Carson, "'Silent in the Churches': On the Role of Women in 1 Corinthians 14:33b–36," in *Recovering Biblical Manhood and Womanhood: A Response to Evangelical Feminism,* ed. John Piper and Wayne Grudem (Westchester, Ill.: Crossway, 1991), p. 153.
93. James B. Hurley, "Did Paul Require Veils or the Silence of Women? A Consideration of 1 Cor. 11:2–16 and 1 Cor. 14:33b–36," *WTJ* 35 (1973): 217.

the roles of the man and the woman (see 11:8–9) Paul alludes to Genesis 2:18, 21–23. And, last, in the current passage he refers to the role the wife must fulfill with respect to her husband, namely, to be his helper. Especially in spiritual matters, a husband in the home and in church has the responsibility of giving leadership; his wife has the task of assisting him.

The Corinthian women at worship are not told to be silent in respect to praying, prophesying, and singing psalms and hymns. They are, however, forbidden to speak when the prophecies of their husbands are discussed (v. 29). They are asked to observe the creation order recorded in the Law and to honor their husbands. Telling the women three times to be silent, Paul instructs them to respect their husbands at public worship and to reserve their questions for the privacy of the home.

d. *Submission.* "And if they wish to learn something, let them ask their husbands at home." In a conditional sentence that expresses existing customs of the Corinthian women, the emphasis is on the verb *to learn.* Paul is not excluding the women from learning spiritual truths. On the contrary, Mary, the sister of Martha and Lazarus, sat at Jesus' feet and learned from him abiding values (Luke 10:38–42). Similarly, Priscilla had gained spiritual knowledge so that she and her husband Aquila were able to explain the truth of God more adequately to Apollos (Acts 18:26). The women in Corinth are now told to let their spiritual leaders, namely, their husbands, instruct them at home.

e. *Shame.* "For it is disgraceful for a woman to speak in church." This verse teaches a difference between church and home. In the privacy of one's home, the wife may learn from her husband. But in the worship service, a wife who questions her husband about spiritual truths runs the risk of dishonoring him in the presence of the rest of the congregation. To the point, no pastor wishes to be publicly criticized by his wife in a worship service; if she does, she undermines his ministry and is a disgrace to him. Paul wants the women to honor and respect their husbands in harmony with the Scriptures.

Additional Comments on 14:33b–35

The literature on this Scripture passage is voluminous, so that I can only take samples of some prominent views that vary from rejecting the passage to modifying it. These are the views:

a. Some scholars consider this passage to be inauthentic because to them it is an embarrassment to women.[94] But the textual witnesses preclude all claims to inauthenticity.

---

94. E.g., Hans Conzelmann, *1 Corinthians: A Commentary on the First Epistle to the Corinthians,* ed. George W. MacRae, trans. James W. Leitch, Hermeneia: A Critical and Historical Commentary on the Bible (Philadelphia: Fortress, 1975), p. 246. He includes verses 33b and 36. However, these two verses are never included in a possible transposition following verse 40; instead, with verses 34–35 they enjoy the endorsement of all the Greek witnesses. For a rebuttal, see A. Feuillet, "La dignité et le rôle de la femme d'après quelques textes pauliniens: comparaison avec l'Ancien Testament," *NTS* 21 (1975): 157–91.

b. Another view is that Paul's opponents in Corinth had formulated the assertion to have women remain silent, and Paul then reacted to this contention. He refutes his opponents' decree (vv. 33b–35) by asking them two rhetorical questions (v. 36). And at a later date an editor supplied the introductory phrase, "As in all the churches of the saints" (v. 33b).[95] However, this view seriously undermines Pauline authorship and disregards the doctrine of divine inspiration (see the commentary on v. 37). Also, the assumption that verses 34–35 are a lengthy quotation lacks substantiating proof (see the commentary on v. 22).[96]

c. Some scholars contend that there is a contradiction between Paul's command not to allow women to speak and his earlier concession to have them pray and prophesy. They assert that Paul changed his mind after he allowed women to pray and prophesy (11:5). Thus he wrote a corrective injunction (14:33b–35).[97] But Paul's wording in 11:5 is not in the form of a concession; he only states a fact. And in 14:33b–35 he does not impose an absolute ban on speaking but only issues guidelines to promote orderly worship at church.

d. Other writers understand the term *Law* (v. 34b) to be a reference to Genesis 3:16, "Your desire will be for your husband, and he will rule over you"[98] (interpreted as a reference to the woman's sexual attraction to her husband). It is better, however, to think of Genesis 2:21–23 for an earlier allusion to the concept *Law;* a wife honors her husband for his leadership ability as she serves him as helper.[99] Another interpretation is that the word *Law* means Paul gave his own ruling to the Corinthian women.[100] But this explanation conflicts with verse 36, which appeals to the Word of God.

e. The passage (vv. 33b–35) is often approached from a historical and cultural perspective: women and children sat on one side of the aisle and the men on the other side. During the service, women would ask questions of their husbands and thus create a disturbance that detracted from proper worship.[101] Although this explanation has merit, the connection with passing judgment on the prophecies spoken in the assembly should not be overlooked (v. 29).

f. With these few words Paul is not interested in covering every possible situation. Some of the women were married, others were single, while still others were widows. Even though the single women and the widows could not question husbands at home, they might present their questions to the speakers themselves or to other members of their families. With his injunction, Paul wants to avoid embarrassment when a woman fails to

---

95. Robert W. Allison, "Let Women Be Silent in the Churches (1 Cor. 14.33b–36): What Did Paul Really Say, and What Did It Mean?" *JSNT* 32 (1988): 27–60; David W. Odell-Scott, "Let the Women Speak in Church: An Egalitarian Interpretation of 1 Cor. 14:33b–36," *BTB* 13 (1983): 90–93; and "In Defense of an Egalitarian Interpretation of 1 Cor. 14:34–36. A Reply to Murphy-O'Connor's Critique," *BTB* 17 (1987): 100–103; Neal M. Flanagan and Edwina Hunter Snyder, "Did Paul Put Down Women in 1 Cor. 14:34–36?" *BTB* 11 (1981): 10–12.

96. However, see Jerome Murphy-O'Connor, "Interpolations in 1 Corinthians," *CBQ* 48 (1986): 81–94.

97. Hans Lietzmann and Werner Georg Kümmel, *An die Korinther I.II.* Handbuch zum Neuen Testament, vol. 9 (Tübingen: Mohr, 1969), p. 75.

98. E.g., the commentaries of Bengel, p. 250; Godet, p. 739; Grosheide, p. 343; Mare, p. 276; Robertson and Plummer, p. 325.

99. Bruce, *1 and 2 Corinthians*, p. 136.

100. Martin, *The Spirit and the Congregation*, p. 87.

101. In the ancient synagogue, women were in reality forbidden to speak in public. See SB, vol. 3, p. 467.

respect a man who prophesies. This is not to say that a woman cannot use her time and talent in the ministry of the church, but she should do so by honoring those to whom Christ has given authority to rule the church (I Tim. 5:17).

Greek Words, Phrases, and Constructions in 14:34–35

Verse 34

ταῖς γυναῖκες—the definite article with the noun denotes the class of women (see Eph. 5:22). The Majority Text adds ὑμῶν after γυναῖκες, but this may be a scribal addition to harmonize with the phrase *your own husbands* in verse 35. Thus the shorter reading is preferred.

οὐ γὰρ ἐπιτρέπεται—"for it is not permitted." With the dative pronoun αὐταῖς, this present passive verb is translated as active: "they are not permitted." Paul writes the first person singular ἐπιτρέπω in I Timothy 2:12. The verb frequently occurs with the verb *to speak*.

λαλεῖν—the present active infinitive (see also v. 35) describes the act of speaking. The content of speaking is introduced by the verb λέγω in conjugated forms.

Verse 35

μαθεῖν—the aorist infinitive of the verb μανθάνω (I learn) refers to a single action in the course of a worship service. By contrast, Paul uses the present tense μανθανέτω (let her learn) in I Timothy 2:11 for continued action.

ἐν ἐκκλησίᾳ—"in church." The contrast with ἐν οἰκίᾳ (at home) is deliberate and to the point.

---

d. Conclusion
14:36–40

36. Or did the word of God originate with you or has it come to you only? 37. If anyone thinks himself to be a prophet or spiritual, let him know that the things which I write to you are a command of the Lord. 38. If anyone disregards [it], he is disregarded [by God].

a. *Questions.* "Or did the word of God originate with you or has it come to you only?" Some translators include this verse with the preceding paragraph, while others make it part of the following segment. The ones that place it at the head of a new paragraph omit the first word *or*. But in Paul's discourses, the reaction of the readers is often anticipated and can be supplied as an insertion in brackets. Take for example verse 36: "*Or* [if you find it so hard to grant this, then consider:] did the word of God originate with you? Or are you the only people it has reached?"[102]

In verse 36 Paul poses two rhetorical questions that expect a negative reply. He links these questions to his earlier remark, "As in all the churches of the

---

102. Carson, "Silent in the Churches," p. 151; Kenneth N. Taylor supplies the question "You disagree?" at the beginning of verse 36 (TNT).

saints" (v. 33b), and now wants to know whether the Corinthians see themselves as the mother church. Did the church in Corinth give rise to Christ's gospel, that is, the word of God?[103] The answer is, of course not. With the second question, Paul is asking his Corinthian readers if they are the only ones in the world to whom Christ's gospel has come. The same answer holds true: of course not. The gospel originated with Jesus Christ, who commissioned Paul to be the apostle to the Gentiles (see, e.g., Acts 9:15; 22:21; 26:15–18), and the Corinthians are among these Gentiles. Paul has received delegated authority from Christ and thus is able to give commands of the Lord.

b. *Command.* "If anyone thinks himself to be a prophet or spiritual, let him know that the things which I write to you are a command of the Lord." Paul speaks with apostolic authority, which cannot be said of any of the Corinthians who think they are either prophets or spiritual people. The Greek indicates that there were individuals who considered themselves such, but Paul denies them any authoritative status that equals his own.[104] We must understand that the term *prophet* refers not to an official capacity but rather to an ability to prophesy.

The emphasis in this particular verse lies not in the first half but in the second. Here Paul makes it known to his readers that his letter is divinely inspired. The words he writes to the Corinthians are not merely human words but words that have divine authority; they are a command of Jesus Christ, who is speaking through Paul. Hence, the Corinthians have to look beyond Paul and see the Lord Jesus Christ as the speaker.

If the Corinthian readers are spiritually inclined, as many of them believe they are, let them pay close attention to Paul's divinely inspired writings. Those who are filled with the Holy Spirit will demonstrate immediate compliance with the Lord's command. They are the true spiritual people who obey the leading of the Spirit. But others, who place themselves above the apostle, continually voice opposition to Paul's teachings. To them, Paul issues a far-reaching warning.

c. *Neglect.* "If anyone disregards [it], he is disregarded [by God]."[105] The Greek text is short and needs to be supplemented to make the sentence complete. Paul is indicating that there are people who indeed are disregarding his instructions; they are also the ones who pay no attention to God's Word. Therefore, he declares that a person who ignores Paul's teaching will know that God ignores him. Note the resemblance in thought to a saying of Jesus: "But whoever disowns me before men, I will disown him before my Father in heaven" (Matt. 10:33; compare II Tim. 2:12).

---

103. In Scripture, the expression *word of God* occurs numerous times. Here it refers to the gospel of Christ's cross and his resurrection. Berthold Klappert, *NIDNTT*, vol. 3, p. 1110; Gerhard Kittel, *TDNT*, vol. 4, p. 116; Hubert Ritt, *EDNT*, vol. 2, p. 358.

104. Grudem, *Prophecy in the New Testament*, p. 87.

105. Bauer, p. 11. Compare also NCV.

d. *Variations.* For this text, translations usually provide a marginal note in which they show an alternative reading for the second half of verse 38. To illustrate, the New American Standard Bible gives the text as "he is not recognized" (*agnoeitai*) and the note as "let him be ignorant" (*agnoeitō*). By contrast, the New King James Version has the text as "let him be ignorant" and the note as "he is not recognized." The one reading is the indicative (NASB) and the other the imperative (NKJV). And last, some translations have the future tense in the text itself: "he himself will be ignored" (e.g., NIV).

Scholars have difficulty deciding which of these three readings is original, yet they favor the indicative.[106] By choosing either the present or the future indicative, we must explain the passive voice that demands an agent. This agent is not the Corinthian congregation but rather God himself, who in the judgment day ignores anyone who has willfully scorned his Word. This warning is the severest Paul has pronounced thus far in his first epistle to the readers in Corinth.

39. So, my brothers, eagerly desire to prophesy and do not forbid speaking in tongues. 40. But let all things be done decently and in order.

Here are Paul's concluding remarks on this lengthy discourse on prophesying and tongue-speaking. The expression *so* introduces a summary statement that is followed by the words *my brothers.* Notice that after the stern admonition, Paul speaks pastorally by calling the members of the Corinthian church "my brothers," a designation that includes the sisters (compare vv. 6, 20, 26).

Paul writes three clauses in the imperative mood as final remarks on the sensitive topic of prophecy and tongues. First, he repeats verse 1 almost verbatim by saying, "Eagerly desire to prophesy." He uses the present tense for the main verb and the infinitive to indicate continued action. Paul urges the readers to have the constant desire to prophesy according to his directives given in the earlier parts of this chapter (see I Thess. 5:20).

Next, he admonishes the Corinthians not to forbid people to speak in tongues. Paul himself has stated that speaking in tongues is a gift of the Holy Spirit and, accordingly, he cannot prohibit the speaking of tongues. If he were to prohibit anyone, he would be grieving the Spirit of God and extinguishing the Spirit's fire (Eph. 4:30; I Thess. 5:19). He himself possesses this gift (v. 18) and wishes that everyone would have it (v. 5).

Nonetheless, throughout this entire chapter Paul has defined clear limitations for tongue-speaking. He allows tongue-speech, provided the presentation is interpreted, beneficial for the hearers, intelligible, orderly, and given in the context of love. Apparently some of the church members were forbidding others from speaking in tongues, so that Paul now has to rectify the matter.

Thirdly, Paul once more reminds his readers that everything must be done in an appropriate and orderly manner (vv. 26–33; compare 16:14). This last re-

---

106. Bruce M. Metzger, *A Textual Commentary on the Greek New Testament,* 3d corrected ed. (London and New York: United Bible Society, 1975), p. 566.

minder reveals that the opposite was true in the church of Corinth, where impropriety and disorder seemed to be not the exception but the rule.

Greek Words, Phrases, and Constructions in 14:36–39

Verses 36–37

ἤ—a disjunctive particle that means "or." It introduces and adds to rhetorical questions. However, for the sake of style many translators omit this particle. See 6:9, 16, 19; 10:22; II Corinthians 11:7.[107]

μόνους—"only." This adjective in the accusative masculine plural, for the culture of Paul's day, refers to both men and women.

ἐντολή—sustained by a variety of manuscripts, this reading of the word *command* is preferred. A few Western witnesses omit it, but they lack support. The Majority Text has the plural form *commands* (KJV, NKJV), but this reading may be due to a scribal error.

Verses 38–39

ἀγνοεῖται—textual evidence for the present passive indicative of ἀγνοέω (I ignore) is equally strong for the present active imperative ἀγνοείτω (let him be ignorant). Even though the imperative is less forceful than the indicative, "there appears no reason why the indic[ative] should have been altered to the imperat[ive]."[108]

ζηλοῦτε—this present imperative ("be eager") has the articular infinitive τὸ προφη-τεύειν as object. The same grammatical construction is evident in the next clause: "do not forbid speaking in tongues." μὴ κωλύετε actually means that Paul is saying: "you are presently forbidding people to speak in tongues, but now that you have received my regulations, do not discourage people from using the gift of tongue-speaking."

τὸ λαλεῖν—the definite article either was omitted "because of editorial parsimony characteristic of Alexandrian philology or was added to parallel the previous articular infinitive."[109]

Summary of Chapter 14

After writing his letter on love, Paul teaches his readers to follow in the way of love, to strive for spiritual gifts, among which the gift of prophesy is outstanding. Anyone who speaks in a tongue addresses God, but the person who prophesies addresses the people and edifies them.

By using analogies taken from the areas of music and language, Paul illustrates the purpose of tongue-speaking. He mentions the flute, harp, and trumpet and explains their function; and he states that languages are not without meaning. But if spoken words make no sense to the listener, both he and the speaker

---

107. Bauer, p. 342; Thayer, p. 275.
108. Alford, *Alford's Greek Testament*, vol. 2, p. 601. For the opposite view see G. Zuntz, *The Text of the Epistles: A Disquisition upon the Corpus Paulinum* (London: Oxford University Press, 1953), pp. 107–8.
109. Metzger, *Textual Commentary*, p. 567.

remain foreigners to each other. Paul then urges the readers to seek those spiritual gifts that edify the church.

Tongue-speaking should be interpreted so that it may be useful. Christians must pray and sing with full use of their minds, for only in this way can they ensure that their prayer and praise are understood. And understanding allows listeners to say "amen," and to be edified. Paul notes that he would rather speak five words and be understood than ten thousand words that are unintelligible.

Urging the readers to be infants in regard to evil, Paul quotes from the prophecy of Isaiah to show them that the language of the Assyrians was a sign of impending judgment for Israel. In a similar way, tongues are a sign to an unbeliever, but prophesying causes him to be convinced that he is a sinner. Conviction of sin and repentance make him fall down to worship God.

Paul instructs the Corinthians to follow guidelines for orderly worship so that the members of the church are strengthened. Only two or at the most three tongue-speakers may speak, provided that someone interprets. Two or three prophets should speak in turn for instruction and encouragement. Women are told not to ask questions in church but to learn from their husbands at home. Paul appeals to God's Word and reveals that which he writes is the Lord's command. He concludes his discourse by exhorting the Corinthians to be eager to prophesy, not to forbid tongue-speaking, and to do everything in a decent and orderly manner. For God is a God of order and peace.

15

The Resurrection

(15:1–58)

Outline (continued)

15 1 Now, brothers, I make known to you the gospel which I preached to you, which you also received, in which you also stand. 2 By this gospel you are also saved if you hold fast to the word that I preached to you; otherwise you believed in vain. 3 For I delivered to you that which I also received as of first importance: that Christ died for our sins according to the Scriptures, 4 and that he was buried and that he was raised on the third day according to the Scriptures, 5 and that he appeared to Cephas, then to the Twelve. 6 Then he appeared to more than five hundred brothers at one time, most of whom remain until now but some have fallen asleep. 7 After that he appeared to James, then to all the apostles. 8 And last of all he appeared to me also as to one untimely born.

9 For I am the least of the apostles; indeed, I am not fit to be called an apostle, because I persecuted the church of God. 10 But by the grace of God I am what I am, and his grace toward me has not been in vain. However, I labored more than all of them, yet not I, but the grace of God that was with me. 11 Therefore, whether I or they, thus we proclaim and thus you believed.

12 But if Christ is preached, that he has been raised from the dead, how do some among you say that there is no resurrection of the dead? 13 But if there is no resurrection of the dead, not even Christ has been raised. 14 And if Christ has not been raised, then our preaching is vain and also your faith is vain. 15 In addition, we are even found to be false witnesses of God, because we testified in contradiction to God that he raised Christ, whom he did not raise if the dead are not raised. 16 For if the dead are not raised, then neither has Christ been raised. 17 And if Christ has not been raised, your faith is worthless and you are still in your sins. 18 Then also those who have fallen asleep in Christ have perished. 19 If for this life only we have hoped in Christ, we are of all people most to be pitied.

20 But now Christ has been raised from the dead, the firstfruits of those who have fallen asleep. 21 For since by man came death, also by man came the resurrection of the dead. 22 For as in Adam all die, thus also in Christ all shall be made alive. 23 But each in his own order: Christ the firstfruits, then those who belong to Christ at his coming. 24 Then comes the end, when he delivers the kingdom to God the Father, after he has abolished all rule, and all authority and power. 25 For he must rule until he has put all his enemies under his feet. 26 The last enemy that will be abolished is death. 27 For he has put all things under his feet. And when [Scripture] says, "All things are put under him," it is clear that the one who subjected all things to him is excepted. 28 And when all things are subjected to him, then even the Son himself shall be subjected to the one who subjected all things to him, so that God may be all in all.

29 Otherwise what shall they do who are baptized for the dead? If the dead are not raised at all, why then are they baptized in their behalf? 30 And what about us? Why are we in danger every hour? 31 I die every day—yes, indeed, by my boasting about you, brothers, which I have in Christ Jesus our Lord. 32 If according to man I fought with wild animals in Ephesus, what advantage is it to me? If the dead are not raised,

let us eat and drink, for tomorrow we die.

33 Do not be deceived,

Bad company corrupts good habits.

523

34 Come to your senses as you ought and do not sin, for some have no knowledge of God. I say this to put you to shame.

35 But someone will say, "How are the dead raised? And with what kind of body do they come?" 36 You fool! What you sow does not come to life unless it dies. 37 And when you sow, you sow not the body that shall be but a bare kernel, perhaps of wheat or of something else. 38 But God gives it a body just as he wished and to each of the seeds its own body.

39 All flesh is not the same, but there is one flesh of men, another flesh of beasts, another flesh of birds, and another flesh of fish. 40 And there are heavenly bodies and earthly bodies. But the glory of the heavenly bodies is one and the glory of the earthly bodies is another. 41 The glory of the sun is one, the glory of the moon another, and the glory of the stars another. For star differs from star in glory.

42 Thus is also the resurrection of the dead. It is sown in corruption, it is raised in incorruption. 43 It is sown in dishonor, it is raised in glory. It is sown in weakness, it is raised in power. 44 It is sown a physical body, it is raised a spiritual body.

If there is a physical body, there is also a spiritual body. 45 Thus also it is written,

> The first man Adam became a living being,
> the last Adam became a life-giving spirit.

46 However, the spiritual is not first but the physical, then the spiritual. 47 The first man was from the dust of the earth, the second man from heaven. 48 As was the one made of dust, so also are those that are dust; and as is the one heavenly, so also are those that are heavenly. 49 And as we bear the image of the one made of dust, so we shall bear the image of the one who is heavenly.

50 But this I say, brothers, that flesh and blood cannot inherit the kingdom of God, neither shall corruption inherit incorruption. 51 Look, I tell you a mystery: we shall not all fall asleep, but all of us shall be changed 52 in a moment, in the twinkling of an eye, at the last trumpet. For the trumpet shall sound, and the dead shall be raised incorruptible and we shall be changed. 53 For this corruptible must put on incorruption and this mortal must put on immortality. 54 But when this corruptible has put on incorruption and this mortal has put on immortality, then the saying that is written will be realized:

> Death is swallowed up in victory.
> 55 Where, O death, is your victory?
> Where, O death, is your sting?

56 The sting of death is sin, and the power of sin is the law. 57 But thanks be to God, who gives us the victory through our Lord Jesus Christ.

58 So then, my dear brothers, be steadfast, immovable, always abounding in the work of the Lord, knowing that your labor is not in vain in the Lord.

F. The Resurrection
15:1–58

The content of this chapter differs considerably from that of preceding chapters. There Paul wrote about moral, ethical, cultural, and ecclesiastical problems the Corinthians faced. Here he discusses the doctrinal question of the resurrection. This doctrine was a topic of debate in the church of Corinth.

The resurrection of Jesus Christ did not become an articulated doctrine at the time (about A.D. 55) Paul wrote his first epistle to the Corinthians. Far from it. When Peter addressed a multitude of devout Jews on the day of Pentecost, presumably A.D. 30, he already proclaimed Jesus' resurrection (Acts 2:24–36).

Throughout the Book of Acts, we read that the apostles preached the doctrine of the resurrection to both Jews and Gentiles in Jerusalem, Pisidian Antioch, Athens, and Rome. That doctrine was fundamental in apostolic preaching and proved to be basic to the Christian faith (compare, e.g., Acts 17:18). And this doctrine has been and still is the centerpiece of Christianity.

Paul writes that he received and passed on the teaching of Christ's death, burial, and resurrection (v. 3). He implies that at his conversion near Damascus he knew the reality of the resurrection and thus immediately proclaimed the sonship of Jesus Christ in local synagogues (Acts 9:20). Afterward Paul went to Jerusalem and met both Peter and James. Jesus had appeared to both Peter and John between Easter and ascension (see v. 7). These apostles reinforced Paul's knowledge of Jesus' resurrection. In short, the Book of Acts indicates that Paul himself received and passed on the resurrection doctrine after his conversion (see 9:20, 22, 28; 13:30–37; 17:31). He did not wait until he wrote his Corinthian correspondence.

If Paul proclaimed the gospel to the Corinthians when he was with them as their pastor, why did they object to accepting the teaching on the resurrection? Christians of Jewish background accepted the Hebrew doctrine that a person is a unit of body and soul; human existence in the form of a disembodied soul is unthinkable, for body and soul belong together. For Jewish people, the teaching of their physical resurrection meant "the reintegration of the whole person."[1]

In the first century, the Sadducees denied the doctrine of a physical resurrection (Mark 12:18–23; Acts 23:8), yet we cannot prove that they influenced the Jews living in the dispersion. Luke reveals that in Jerusalem a large number of priests converted to the Christian faith (Acts 6:7) and had no relations with the minority party of the Sadducees. We assume, therefore, that in Corinth not the Jewish Christians but some of the Gentile Christians denied the resurrection from the dead (v. 12). Some Corinthian believers, influenced by Greek philosophy, failed to see the importance of a bodily resurrection and were denying its reality (v. 12). Paul knew that he had to counter their denial.

We suspect that Paul did not receive a request by letter (see 7:1, 25; 8:1; 12:1), but that he probably heard a report about Corinthian views on the resurrection of Christ. We infer from the longest chapter in this epistle that for Paul and for the universal church the doctrine of the resurrection is and remains basic.

Paul teaches the doctrine of Christ's resurrection from the Scriptures and numerous eyewitness reports (vv. 1–11). Among the eyewitnesses he mentions the twelve apostles, together with James and himself. He also notes that a group of five hundred believers saw the resurrected Jesus. The testimony of all these witnesses strengthens the readers' faith in Christ.

---

1. Michael Green, *The Empty Cross of Jesus,* The Jesus Library series (Downers Grove: Inter-Varsity, 1984), p. 108.

1. Resurrection of Christ
15:1–8

1. Now, brothers, I make known to you the gospel which I preached to you, which you also received, in which you also stand.

a. "Now, brothers." The word *now* refers more to time than to logic. After a lengthy discourse on propriety in worship, Paul is ready to consider an entirely different topic, namely, the resurrection of the body. He knows that this topic is controversial in the societal setting of ancient Corinth. For this reason, he addresses the readers as brothers, which term in the parlance of that day includes the sisters of the congregation. Paul wants them to know that he is their brother in the Lord.

b. "I make known to you the gospel which I preached to you."[2] The translation of the main verb *to have you know* in this sentence does not imply that Paul is proclaiming a gospel that differs from that of the other apostles.[3] With this verb he conveys that he teaches them once more the gospel which he proclaimed to them in earlier days. Nonetheless, Paul introduces a new element: detailed doctrinal teaching on the physical resurrection of Christ and believers.[4] In his earlier teachings and writings, Paul had already acquainted the believers with the resurrection doctrine (e.g., Acts 13:30; Gal. 1:1). But here in chapter 15, he gives them a comprehensive exposition of this Scriptural doctrine. For this reason he is able to say: "I make known to you the gospel."

On his conversion near Damascus, Paul received the gospel from the Lord Jesus Christ. But later he spent time with Peter and James in Jerusalem; these disciples undoubtedly told him numerous details of Jesus' gospel (Gal. 1:18–19) and equipped him for the ministry. After fourteen years had passed, Paul returned to Jerusalem to confer with the apostles whether his preaching was in harmony with the gospel they proclaimed (Gal. 2:1).

The gospel that Paul preached consisted of the revelation of Jesus Christ, who fulfilled the Old Testament Scriptures. Paul acknowledged that he had not followed Jesus from the time of the Lord's baptism to his ascension (Acts 1:21–22). Yet Paul could say that he was a witness of Jesus' resurrection and thus he had received authority from Christ to proclaim his gospel.

c. "Which you also received, in which you also stand." With these words Paul affirms the Corinthians in their faith. But he subtly reminds them of the responsibility to receive and transmit basic doctrines (compare 11:23; I Thess. 2:13). He expects them not only to accept his gospel but also to proclaim it in Corinth and elsewhere. As Paul received the gospel from Jesus and passed it on to the Corin-

---

2. Compare Gal. 1:11 for similar vocabulary and sentence structure. See also Walter Radl, "Der Sinn Von gnōrizō in 1 Kor 15,1," *BibZ* 28 (1984): 243–45.

3. Consult J. Knox Chamblin, "Revelation and Tradition in the Pauline *Euangelion*," *WTJ* 48 (1986): 1–16.

4. Bauer, p. 163.

thians, so they in turn ought to receive and transmit it to others (see v. 3). He commends them for standing firm in the gospel and accepting it as foundational for their lives.

2. By this gospel you are also saved if you hold fast to the word that I preached to you, otherwise you believed in vain.

Closely connected to verse 1, the first part of verse 2 reveals a climax by which, with his threefold use of the word *also*, Paul emphasizes the gospel:

> which you also received,
> in which you also stand,
> by which you are also saved.

The gospel by itself does not save, but God through the gospel saves a person in Christ.[5] God is the implied agent, as the passive construction reveals. He effects the sinner's salvation. With the present tense of the verb *to save*, Paul indicates that God's saving act is both effective and progressive (compare Rom. 5:9).

Most translators reverse the order of the Greek sentence by placing the clause *if you hold fast* before the clause *to the word that I preached to you*. This is the preferred reading of the text, which then repeats the phrase *the gospel which I preached to you* in verse 1.[6] But what does Paul mean with the term *word*? Perhaps it refers to the content of the gospel he proclaimed. Paul notes that even though the Corinthians are holding fast to Christ's gospel, he wants them to live in accordance with its teachings. If they are merely hearers but not doers of the proclaimed gospel, they have believed in vain. The flow of the verse is that the Corinthians are saved because they have received the gospel; but they must hold on to that gospel and so demonstrate this in their conduct. Otherwise their faith will be hollow and worthless. Faith must exhibit perseverance in the teachings and application of the gospel to be genuinely active. If this is not the case, says Paul, "you have believed in vain."

Doctrinal Considerations in 15:1–2

Can a Christian receive God's good news, take a stand for Jesus Christ, know that he or she is saved, firmly hold to the teachings of the gospel, and yet believe in vain? Will true believers lose their salvation? Certainly not. Then why does Paul write: "Otherwise you believed in vain"?

Because the Greek is clearer than our translations reveal, a careful look at verb tenses is helpful. Note that Paul employs the present tense for the verbs *to be saved* and *to hold fast*.

---

5. F. W. Grosheide, *Commentary on the First Epistle to the Corinthians: The English Text with Introduction, Exposition and Notes*, New International Commentary on the New Testament series (Grand Rapids: Eerdmans, 1953), p. 347.

6. Some versions reflect the Greek word order: "Remember the terms in which I preached the gospel to you—for I assume that you hold it fast and that your conversion was not in vain" (REB; compare GNB).

He commends the Corinthians because they received the gospel and took their stand in it. This is foundational, for what has happened in the past is still valid in the present. Next, Paul says that the Corinthians are saved. Elsewhere he teaches that salvation is a process which, on the one hand, the believers must work out fully, and on the other, God accomplishes by working within them (Phil. 2:12–13). This means that the believers are being saved provided they hold on to the gospel and apply it to their lives. God is at work in the process of salvation and holds on to the believers. He wants them to hold on to him by obeying his Word. Paul writes a conditional clause, "if you hold fast," but he knows that the activity of holding fast is a fact.

Conversely, the people who at one time believed but subsequently refused to hold fast to God's Word provide evidence that they have broken faith with God. Consequently, they consider the gospel to be of no value to them (compare Heb. 4:2). They are the people who have believed in vain and whose temporal faith is to no avail (Matt. 7:22–23; 25:11–12).

Paul's concluding remark, "otherwise you believed in vain," affirms that believers who continue to hold on to Christ and obey God's Word are safe and secure. God will never forsake them, for they belong to him.

---

3. For I delivered to you that which I also received as of first importance: that Christ died for our sins according to the Scriptures, 4. and that he was buried and that he was raised on the third day according to the Scriptures, 5. and that he appeared to Cephas, then to the Twelve.

a. *Tradition.* "For I delivered to you that which I also received as of first importance." Paul states that the gospel is not a teaching he himself has formulated. He indicates that he received it from the Lord (Gal. 1:12) and that he considered the apostles' teaching an authoritative tradition that originated in Jesus Christ. Upon receiving this teaching, he was obliged to pass it on to both Jews and Gentiles (Acts 20:21) and at the same time to serve as its guardian (compare 11:23). The terms *to receive* and *to deliver* are technical terms that appear in both Jewish and Greek contexts.

The gospel that Paul received from Jesus and the apostles appears to be formulated here as a primitive creed used in the confessions of faith by the early Christians and in the preaching and teaching of their churches.[7] This summary is founded on the Scriptures. Paul in three verses twice uses the phrase *according to the Scriptures* to demonstrate that the gospel is rooted in and emerges from the Old Testament. For him, the elementary teachings of this gospel are these four redemptive facts:

1. *that* Christ died for our sins,
   according to the Scriptures;
2. *that* he was buried;

---

7. Jerome Murphy-O'Connor, "Tradition and Redaction in 1 Cor 15:3–7," *CBQ* 43 (1981) 582–89; John Kloppenborg, "An Analysis of the Pre-Pauline Formula 1 Cor 15:3b–5 in Light of Some Recent Literature," *CBQ* 40 (1978): 351–67; Murray J. Harris, *Raised Immortal: Resurrection and Immortality in the New Testament* (Grand Rapids: Eerdmans, 1983), p. 32.

3. *that* he was raised on the third day,
   according to the Scriptures; and
4. *that* he appeared to Cephas, then to the Twelve.

These facts are the most important ones in Paul's gospel presentation.

In verse 3 the translation *at first* instead of "of first importance" is possible. The passage, however, stresses not that Paul was the first person to proclaim the gospel in Corinth. Rather, these four facts epitomize the intrinsic significance of the gospel.

b. *Death.* "That Christ died for our sins according to the Scriptures." Note that Paul uses the name *Christ* and not *Jesus* to point to the official role of the Messiah. With his reference to the Old Testament, Paul points to the prophecy of Isaiah. The prophet relates that the Messiah, God's anointed one, the suffering servant, was pierced for our transgressions and crushed for our iniquities. Isaiah further writes that all our sins were put on the servant, and that he died for the sins of his people (Isa. 53:5–6, 8–9; see also Ps. 22:16; I Peter 3:18).

Jesus fulfilled the messianic prophecies of Psalm 22 and Isaiah 53. When he instituted the Lord's Supper, Jesus gave verbal expression to the doctrine that the Messiah died for the sins of his people. He said, "This is my blood of the covenant, which is poured out for many for the forgiveness of sins" (Matt. 26:28).

The concept *for our sins* occurs elsewhere in Paul's epistles (e.g., Rom. 5:8; 8:32; Gal. 1:4;[8] Eph. 5:2; Titus 2:14). In these passages, the Greek preposition *hyper* (for) expresses the idea of Jesus being both our representative and our substitute.[9] In short, Christ not only represents us before God but also takes our place by dying for our sins on the cross.

The clause *Christ died for our sins* is the doctrinal summary of the atonement. As our substitute, Christ died to appease God and meet the demands of the law (Rom. 3:25–26; 5:9–19).[10] As our advocate, he effected reconciliation and made us righteous before God (II Cor. 5:21; I John 2:1–2). As our mediator, he established a new covenant and accepted us as partners (Luke 22:20; I Cor. 11:25). And as our Savior, he grants us eternal life through faith in him (John 3:16).

When Jesus met the disciples in the upper room on Easter Sunday, he told them that everything had to be fulfilled that was written in the Scriptures about him (Luke 24:45–46). The Old Testament declares that Christ will suffer (Ps. 22; Isa. 53), and that he will rise from the dead on the third day (Ps. 16:9–11; Isa. 53:10–11).

---

8. The Majority Text has the variant reading περί (for). In the New Testament, ὑπέρ is replaced by περί but not the reverse. Berthold Klappert, "Zur Frage des semitischen oder griechischen Urtextes von I. Kor. XV. 3–5," *NTS* 13 (1966–67): 168–73.

9. R. C. Trench, *Synonyms of the New Testament,* ed. Robert G. Hoerber (Grand Rapids: Baker, 1989), pp. 325–26; Murray J. Harris, *NIDNTT,* vol. 3, pp. 1196–97.

10. Herman N. Ridderbos, *Paul: An Outline of His Theology,* trans. John Richard de Witt (Grand Rapids: Eerdmans, 1975), p. 188.

c. *Burial.* "And that he was buried." Apart from the Gospel writers, only Paul mentions Jesus' burial. He notes that Jesus was taken down from the tree and laid in a tomb (Acts 13:29). He identifies the believer's baptism with Christ's burial (Rom. 6:4; Col. 2:12). And in the current text he mentions interment as the consequence of death and as the harbinger of the resurrection. Jesus' burial points "backward to the reality of the death and forward to the character of the resurrection."[11]

d. *Resurrection.* "And that he was raised on the third day according to the Scriptures." Translations fail to do justice to the difference in verb tenses of the Greek text in verses 3 and 4. The Greek uses the past tense to describe a single action in the past for Jesus' death and burial. But for the verb *to be raised* the Greek has the perfect tense to indicate an action that occurred in the past but has lasting relevance for the present (see vv. 12, 13, 14, 16, 17, 20; compare II Tim. 2:8). That is, Jesus was raised from the dead and continues his life in the resurrected state.

The passive voice denotes the implied agent, namely, God. In their speeches and sermons, both Peter and Paul present the active voice with respect to Jesus' resurrection and say that God raised Jesus from the dead (Acts 3:15; 4:10; 5:30; 10:40; 13:30, 37). To both the Jews and the Gentiles, the apostles proclaimed Jesus' death and resurrection as the heart of the good news. Therefore, with respect to the most important facts of the gospel, Michael Green observes, "It is the death and resurrection of Jesus, the empty cross, which lies at the heart of the apostolic Christianity and is God's good news for the world."[12]

The evidence of the empty tomb emphasizes that Jesus' resurrection was physical. The four writers of the Gospels explicitly describe the emptiness of the tomb by relating the appearance of the angels and the presence of the graveclothes (Matt. 28:5–6; Mark 16:5–6; Luke 24:3–4; John 20:6–8). After his resurrection, Jesus' physical body could be touched (John 20:27), could be recognized with difficulty by the disciples (John 20:14–15; 21:4, 7), could come and go through locked doors (John 20:19, 26), and could consume a piece of broiled fish (Luke 24:42–43). On occasion, Jesus ate and drank with his disciples (Acts 1:4; 10:41). Yet his body was also transformed to transcend time and space. We simply do not have answers for questions about Jesus' resurrected body.[13] The Scriptures do not reveal this information.

Jesus was raised from the dead on the third day, writes Paul, according to the Scriptures. Indeed, Jesus himself taught that he would be killed and on the third day be raised (Matt. 16:21). But do the Old Testament Scriptures teach his res-

---

11. R. St. John Parry, *The First Epistle of Paul the Apostle to the Corinthians,* Cambridge Greek Testament for Schools and Colleges (Cambridge: Cambridge University Press, 1937), p. 216.

12. Green, *The Empty Cross,* p. 138.

13. Consult Murray J. Harris, *From Grave to Glory: Resurrection in the New Testament* (Grand Rapids: Zondervan, 1990), pp. 139–46; Stephen T. Davis, "Was Jesus Raised Bodily?" *ChrSchRev* 14 (1985): 140–52; Francis Foulkes, "Some Aspects of St. Paul's Treatment of the Resurrection of Christ in 1 Corinthians XV," *AusBRev* 16 (1968): 15–30.

urrection on the third day? The answer is twofold. There is no specific reference in any one text; yet, a combination of passages provides sufficient evidence of the concept of the resurrection. For example, we read that God will restore Israel on the third day (Hos. 6:2); Jonah was inside the fish for three days and three nights (Jonah 1:17; Matt. 12:40). And Isaiah prophesies the resurrection of the Messiah (Isa. 53:10–12). Gordon D. Fee concludes, "The O[ld] T[estament] as a whole bears witness to the resurrection on the third day. . . . An early tradition saw the combined evidence of Ps[alms] 16:8–11 and 110:1 as bearing witness to the Messiah's resurrection (cf. Acts 2:25–36)."[14]

The early Christians considered Easter Sunday as the third day following the death of Jesus on Good Friday. On that Sunday, the first day of the week, Jesus appeared to the women, Mary Magdalene, the two men of Emmaus, Peter, and the ten disciples in the upper room.[15]

e. *Appearances.* "And that he appeared to Cephas, then to the Twelve." In this verse and the next three, Paul enumerates Jesus' postresurrection appearances. He has in mind the physical presence of the resurrected Lord, not visions of the kind Paul experienced when Jesus spoke to him in Corinth and Jerusalem (Acts 18:9–10; 23:11). Yet Paul lists himself as one to whom Jesus appeared on the way to Damascus. This appearance differed definitively from those of the pre-ascension period.

What does Paul mean with the Greek word *ophthē* (he appeared, he was seen)? During the forty-day period between Easter and ascension, the witnesses saw the Lord but did not always recognize him. There was a *"certain ambiguity* in the appearances"[16] that, however, did not diminish the joy of those who testified to the fact that Jesus was raised from the dead.

The first person Paul mentions is Peter, whom he usually calls Cephas (1:12). This is the Aramaic name for Peter (John 1:42).[17] Did Peter see Jesus? Yes, because on Easter Sunday, the disciples in the upper room told the men of Emmaus, "The Lord has risen and has appeared to Simon" (Luke 24:34). That morning, the angel instructed the women to tell the disciples and Peter to go to Galilee, where Jesus would meet them (Mark 16:7). There Jesus forgave Peter and reinstated him (John 21:15–19). The Book of Acts reveals that immediately after Jesus' ascension Peter became the undisputed leader in the Jerusalem church. For this reason, he is mentioned first in the list of Jesus' appearances, even though the women preceded him as witnesses of the resurrection.

---

14. Gordon D. Fee, *The First Epistle to the Corinthians,* New International Commentary on the New Testament series (Grand Rapids: Eerdmans, 1987), p. 727.

15. Respectively see Mark 16:1–8, 9–11; Luke 24:13–32, 34, 36–43.

16. James D. G. Dunn, *Jesus and the Spirit: A Study of the Religious and Charismatic Experience of Jesus and the First Christians as Reflected in the New Testament* (Philadelphia: Westminster, 1975), p. 123 (his italics).

17. I Cor. 1:12; 3:22; 9:5; 15:5; Gal. 1:18; 2:9, 11, 14. In the Greek, the name *Peter* occurs only in Gal. 2:7, 8. The combination *Simon Peter* or *Simon* is not found in Paul's epistles.

Next, Paul mentions that Jesus appeared to the Twelve, which in the four Gospels and Acts is the common term for the disciples. True, Judas had committed suicide and Thomas refused to meet with his colleagues that first Sunday evening, but these details are not relevant here because Paul uses the term collectively. These men served as Jesus' official representatives and witnesses of his resurrection. Perhaps this is the reason that references to the appearances to the women and the two men of Emmaus are omitted.

6. Then he appeared to more than five hundred brothers at one time, most of whom remain until now but some have fallen asleep.

Because of a change in the structure of the passage, we conclude that the creedal formula ends in verse 5, perhaps after the verb *he appeared*.[18] We are confident that verse 6 was not part of the primitive creed.

Nothing in the Gospels or Acts corroborates the figure of 500 brothers. The nearest number is 120 persons who met to appoint a successor to Judas Iscariot (Acts 1:15). Whether a large group of people—witnesses chosen by God (Acts 10:41)—was present in Galilee cannot be verified.[19] The point of this passage is not the location of the appearance but the number of witnesses who could testify to the resurrection. In a Jewish court of law, the presence of two or three witnesses was mandatory to prove the veracity of an event. By appearing to five hundred believers at one time, Jesus provided overwhelming proof of being alive.

Paul adds that most of the five hundred were still living at the time he writes the epistle. He implies that should some people doubt the fact of Jesus' triumph over the grave, they can consult any of the believers who saw the resurrected Lord. Where these witnesses lived cannot be ascertained but we understand that both Paul and the Corinthians were acquainted with many of them. Paul seems to indicate that skeptics could go to the witnesses and ask them to give their testimony.

The phrase *some have fallen asleep* is a euphemism that the early Christians had adopted as a reference to death. They viewed the natural death of a believer as a sleep from which a person awakes. Thus they used the phrase as an analogy to the resurrection.

7. After that he appeared to James, then to all the apostles. 8. And last of all he appeared to me also as to one untimely born.

a. "After that he appeared to James." We know that half a year before Jesus' death his brothers, including James, still did not believe in him (John 7:5). But immediately after Jesus' ascension, his brothers believed and were with the apostles in the upper room (Acts 1:13–14; compare also I Cor. 9:5). Paul's allusion to James in the context of appearances is possibly due to the prominent position

---

18. Murphy-O'Connor, "Tradition," p. 582.

19. Compare the studies of Peter J. Kearney, "He Appeared to 500 Brothers (1 Cor. XV 6)," *NovT* 22 (1980): 264–84; S. M. Gilmour, "The Christophany to More Than Five Hundred Brethren," *JBL* 80 (1961): 248–52; Eric F. F. Bishop, "The Risen Christ and the Five Hundred Brethren (1 Cor 15, 6)," *CBQ* 18 (1956): 341–44.

James filled in the early Christian community.[20] James listened to Paul when the former persecutor returned to Jerusalem as a believer (Gal. 1:19). James filled Peter's place when the apostle fled Jerusalem after his release from prison (Acts 12:17). Paul considered James, Peter, and John the three pillars of the church (Gal. 2:9); and at the conclusion of his third missionary tour, Paul reported to James and the elders in Jerusalem (Acts 21:18–19). As Paul mentions Peter so he names James, probably because of all the believers these two were known for their leadership abilities.

b. "Then to all the apostles." This clause seems merely to repeat verse 5, which mentions the Twelve, or to conflict with it. Understanding the clause depends on understanding the term *apostle*. In the Gospels of Matthew, Mark, and Luke, the word *apostles* signifies the Twelve (Matt. 10:2; Mark 3:14; Luke 6:13). It had that connotation after Judas Iscariot committed suicide and before Matthias was appointed. By contrast, in Acts Luke uses the term to refer to the Twelve, the initial proclaimers and the guardians of the gospel, and to describe Paul and Barnabas (Acts 14:14). The church of Antioch commissioned Paul and Barnabas to take the gospel to the Gentiles; hence, these two men are called apostles, in the sense of preachers of the gospel. Andronicus and Junias, according to Paul, were outstanding among the apostles (Rom. 16:7).

In the earliest, most specific usage, an apostle was both a witness of Jesus' resurrection and appointed by Jesus himself (Acts 1:21–26). We have no information that the persons whom Luke and Paul mention met these qualifications. Accordingly, we would be incorrect in applying Luke's and Paul's usage in this text. We conclude, then, that the expression *all the apostles* is synonymous with "the Twelve" (v. 5). The mention of the Twelve refers to Jesus' Easter appearance and that of a week later (John 20:19, 26). The reference to the apostles is to Jesus' ascension appearance (Acts 1:6–11).[21] The references together highlight the first and the last days of Jesus' physical appearances.

c. "And last of all he appeared to me also." What is the meaning of the expression *last of all?* It means that Paul is last in line of all the appearances. He takes last place because of his sudden conversion experience that occurred years after Jesus' ascension.

Paul alludes to his conversion experience on the way to Damascus and calls the encounter with Jesus a vision from heaven (Acts 26:19). This encounter was not a hallucination but a genuine revelation of the resurrected Lord. Notice that Paul uses the verb *he appeared* once more, but now specifically for himself. He wants to indicate that he also belongs to that special group of people who saw Jesus. Paul never followed the Lord from the day of Jesus' baptism to that of his

---

20. For the account of Jesus' appearance to James in the apocryphal Gospel of the Hebrews (Jerome *De Viris Illustr.* 2), see Edgar Hennecke, Wilhelm Schneemelcher, and R. McL. Wilson, *New Testament Apocrypha*, 2 vols. (Philadelphia: Westminster, 1963–64), vol. 1, p. 165.

21. Consult Frederic Louis Godet, *Commentary on First Corinthians* (1886; reprint ed., Grand Rapids: Kregel, 1977), pp. 764–65.

ascension. Nonetheless he saw Jesus in a vision as clearly as the apostles did during the forty-day period between Easter and ascension. He definitely is the last apostle whom Jesus called.[22] For that reason Paul could write, "to me also."

d. "As to one untimely born." The choice of words is unusual, for the Greek term *to ektrōma* occurs only once in the New Testament.[23] Negatively, it can mean an untimely stillbirth or an aborted fetus. But note that Paul applies the term to himself as an illustration; he writes the word *as*, which is similar to "for example." I do not think that the example has anything to do with physical looks or spiritual immaturity. Positively, therefore, the immediate context speaks of apostleship. God had appointed Paul from his mother's womb to be an apostle (Gal. 1:15), but the appointment was frustrated when Paul persecuted the church[24] and was delayed until the time of his conversion.

Paul had neither followed the Lord nor seen the empty tomb on Easter Sunday. Yet Paul could claim that he had personally seen the risen Christ (9:1), who appointed him to be an apostle to the Gentiles.[25] Jesus discounted a period of discipleship for Paul, overlooked Paul's record as persecutor of the church, and made his conversion the starting point of his apostleship. His appointment is abnormal, but so is Christ's appearance to Paul near Damascus.

We do not have to assume that Paul purposely took a contemptuous term that his opponents may have used to describe him. Rather, the context applies the words *one untimely born* to Paul to effect a contrast between himself and the others to whom Jesus appeared.[26] The term that Paul uses to describe himself is unrefined, but in the succeeding context he explains the intent.

Doctrinal Considerations in 15:3–8

A few lines full of theological significance summarize the truth of Christ's gospel. They relate to Jesus' death, burial, and resurrection and as such present the good news of salvation.

Agnostics and atheists have no problem accepting Jesus' death and burial; they see the inevitability of death. Because Jesus was condemned in a Roman court, his death on a wooden cross was the unavoidable penalty a misguided revolutionary had to pay.

To say that Jesus rose from the grave and thus conquered death is preposterous to the modern mind. No one has ever returned from the grave, so to unbelievers the story of Jesus' resurrection must be a fabrication of his distraught followers who thought that he was still with them.

---

22. Refer to P. R. Jones, "1 Corinthians 15:8: Paul the Last Apostle," *TynB* 36 (1985): 3–34.

23. The term appears three times in the LXX (Num. 12:12; Job 3:16; Eccl. 6:3).

24. G. W. E. Nickelsburg, "An *ektrōma*, Though Appointed from the Womb: Paul's Apostolic Self-Description in 1 Corinthians 15 and Galatians 1," *HTR* 79 (1986): 198–205.

25. Acts 9:15; Rom. 11:13; 15:15–16; Gal. 1:16; 2:7–8. Consult Colin Brown, *NIDNTT*, vol. 1, pp. 183–84.

26. Compare Peter von der Osten-Sacken, *EDNT*, vol. 1, p. 423; Johannes Schneider, *TDNT*, vol. 2, p. 466.

Yet the doctrinal truth of the resurrection is the teaching of the four Gospels, the Book of Acts, the Epistles, and the Revelation. Paul states unequivocally that Jesus was raised on the third day according to the Old Testament Scriptures. For him, the resurrection is an undeniable truth, which entails that everyone who believes in Christ will also be raised from the dead. Christ conquered death not for himself alone but for his people.

Greek Words, Phrases, and Constructions in 15:2–8

Verse 2

τίνι λόγῳ—here is an abbreviated sentence structure that should read as τούτῳ τῷ λόγῳ, ᾧ. The pronoun τίς takes the place of ὅστις (whatever).[27] The sentence reads: "If you hold to this word, which I proclaim to you."

εἰ—this particle is part of the protasis of a conditional sentence and indicates that the clause expresses a fact.

ἐκτὸς εἰ μή—the combination of these three words reveals redundancy; it serves as an idiomatic expression that signifies "unless, except."

εἰκῆ ἐπιστεύσατε—here is a combination of adverb and verb in the aorist tense. The adverb is used as a dative of manner and conveys the sense "without due consideration, in a haphazard manner."[28] The aorist tense denotes action in the past.

Verses 3–4

ἐν πρώτοις—the adjective in the plural can be either masculine or neuter. Of the two, the neuter is preferred: "among the first things," that is, the things of primary importance.

ὑπέρ—where this preposition appears in the New Testament context of suffering and dying, it usually refers to Christ's death. Christ died for, that is, in behalf of, his people. Compare John 11:50–52.

ἐγήγερται—the perfect passive tense of the verb ἐγείρω (I raise) expresses an action that occurred in the past but has abiding value for the present. This perfect tense is unique because it follows the single occurrence of the past tense in the two verbs *he died* and *he was buried.*

Verse 5

δώδεκα—"the Twelve" is a word that applies to the immediate circle of Jesus' disciples. The term *eleven* applies appropriately to the group of disciples between Easter and ascension (Matt. 28:16; Mark 16:14; Luke 24:9, 33; Acts 1:26).

Verses 6–7

ἐκοιμήθησαν—the aorist passive of the verb κοιμάομαι (I fall asleep) connotes the falling asleep of some believers at various times. The verb is used euphemistically to describe death.

πᾶσιν—because this adjective follows the noun *apostles*, not the adjective but the noun receives the emphasis. Paul is saying, "to the apostles, indeed to all the apostles." In a

---

27. Grosheide, *First Corinthians*, p. 348 n. 2.
28. Bauer, p. 222.

sense, James cannot be included because he never left Jerusalem and thus he was not a missionary sent out to proclaim the gospel.[29]

Verse 8

ὡσπερεὶ τῷ ἐκτρώματι—the first word actually means "so to speak." It is a combination of ὥσπερ (as) and εἰ (if): "as it were." The noun ἔκτρωμα (untimely birth) derives from the verb ἐκτιτρώσκω (I cause an abortion). It refers to an abnormality in life that Paul describes with the definite article—that is, he refers to himself. Of all the apostles (John excepted, see Rev. 1:12–20), he had the privilege of seeing the Lord after the ascension.[30]

---

2. The Apostolicity of Paul
15:9–11

The word choice in the preceding verse (v. 8) forces Paul to present a fuller explanation of his apostolate. The churches questioned whether Paul was a legitimate apostle. They knew that he had never followed Jesus, but instead had tried to destroy the church through severe persecutions. Yet Jesus called him to proclaim the gospel to both the Jews and the Gentiles.

9. For I am the least of the apostles; indeed, I am not fit to be called an apostle, because I persecuted the church of God.

The word *for* prefaces an explanation of the imagery Paul presented: the untimely birth of his apostleship. He is purposely humble and knows that he did not belong to the circle of the Twelve, who met the requirements for apostolicity (Acts 1:21–22). Barnabas introduced him to the apostles and told them that Jesus had called him on the way to Damascus and that Paul had fearlessly preached in the name of Jesus (Acts 9:27). The apostles had accepted Paul, but he remained subordinate to them. After fourteen years, he returned to Jerusalem to see if the gospel he preached was in harmony with the one the apostles proclaimed (Gal. 2:1–2).

The apostles recognized his special ministry to the Gentiles and later placed Paul on a footing equal with them (Gal. 2:8–9). Although Paul knew the Scriptures and theology (Acts 5:34–39; 22:3), he lacked the teaching that the apostles had received from Jesus (Acts 4:13). Appropriately, he presents himself as the least among the apostles (compare Eph. 3:8; I Tim. 1:15).

In addition, Paul asserts that he is not worthy of the name *apostle* and states the reason: he persecuted the church of God. Near Damascus, Jesus asked him, "Saul, Saul, why do you persecute me?" (Acts 9:4; 22:7; 26:14). From that moment, Paul knew that he had persecuted Jesus himself. For him, the realization

---

29. Friedrich Blass and Albert Debrunner, *A Greek Grammar of the New Testament and Other Early Christian Literature*, trans. and rev. Robert Funk (Chicago: University of Chicago Press, 1961), #275.5.
30. A. T. Robertson, *A Grammar of the Greek New Testament in the Light of Historical Research* (Nashville: Broadman, 1934), p. 757.

of this crime could not be erased from his memory. He refers repeatedly to his life as a persecutor (Acts 26:9; Gal. 1:13; I Tim. 1:12–14).

The expression *church of God* (10:32) should not be limited to the Jerusalem church where Paul vented his rage against the Christians. He sought to destroy the churches in Judea and asked for letters from the high priest to do the same in Damascus (Acts 9:2; 22:5) and other foreign cities (Acts 26:11). The expression, then, denotes the universal church of that day.

10. But by the grace of God I am what I am, and his grace toward me has not been in vain. However, I labored more than all of them, yet not I, but the grace of God that was with me.

a. "But by the grace of God I am what I am." When Paul reviews the course of his life, from his student days in Jerusalem to his actions as persecutor of the church and as apostle to the Gentiles, he exclaims that by God's grace he is what he is. The grace of God is power that flows from God to the apostles.[31] For instance, Paul and Barnabas experience divine grace when they travel to Cyprus and Asia Minor on their first missionary journey. They are supported in prayer by their commissioning church in Antioch that commends them to the grace of God (Acts 14:26). God's grace keeps them safe during their travels so that they are able to return to Antioch and report what God has done through them.

Paul sees the grace of God operative throughout his life from birth (Gal. 1:15) to his career as an apostle of Jesus Christ (Eph. 3:7–8). Freely he acknowledges that his accomplishments are due to God's grace. Note that he writes "I am what I am," not "I am who I am." Paul is interested in looking at himself not as a person but as an instrument in God's hand to further the cause of the gospel (compare Acts 21:19).

b. "And his grace toward me has not been in vain." Paul utters this statement of thanksgiving to God because God has extended grace to him. Three times in this verse Paul writes the term *grace;* he lives, travels, and works by God's grace. We are not aware of the work the other apostles performed, because the New Testament fails to reveal this information. But if we consider the distances Paul traveled to proclaim the gospel, the churches he was able to establish, and the care he expended on them, we stand amazed at the yeoman's work he performed in the relatively short span of two decades.

The Greek expression *kenē*, which I have translated "in vain" signifies "without effect," that is, "without reaching its goal."[32] By relating that God's grace to him was not in vain, Paul is stating positively that it bore extraordinary results. He is specific in this particular verse when he twice declares that God's grace was directed to him—"his grace toward me" and "the grace of God was with me." Paul knew that God blessed his labors.

c. "However, I labored more than all of them." The adversative *however* goes back to Paul's remark about being the least of the apostles. His record of suffer-

31. Hans-Helmut Esser, *NIDNTT*, vol. 2, 119.
32. Bauer, p. 427.

ing for the sake of Christ is impressive by anyone's standards.[33] While in Ephesus, he toiled as a tentmaker to support himself financially (Acts 20:34). In the rented hall of Tyrannus he daily instructed his students (Acts 19:9). And the remaining time was spent in preaching and teaching publicly from house to house (Acts 20:20). Moreover, he wrote letters to the members of the church in Corinth and visited them, too (5:9; II Cor. 2:1–4).

We have a collection of thirteen epistles of Paul, so that in respect to literary activities Paul excels the other letter writers of the New Testament. Paul had received the training to write letters and he fearlessly preached the gospel to Jew and Gentile. Indeed he was God's chosen instrument to do this work. Yet the clause "I labored more than all of [the apostles]" should not be understood to mean the combined labors of the Twelve, but the work of any one of these apostles.

d. "Yet not I, but the grace of God that was with me." Let no one think that Paul ever credits himself for the work he has performed. He shuns self-glorification but expresses gratitude to God; he glories in his Lord and Savior. Being far from idle in his calling, Paul presents the results of his labors to God. He humbly acknowledges that he has been able to accomplish all his achievements only by God's grace.

11. Therefore, whether I or they, thus we proclaim and thus you believed.

The adverb *therefore* not only summarizes the preceding discourse but also forms a link with verse 8. The intervening verses (vv. 9–10) are a short digression in which Paul explains his status with respect to the apostles. Paul stresses the power of God's grace in his life and ministry, not for the purpose of elevating himself above the other apostles but to thank God for his mercy and love.

With this last sentence, Paul indicates that he is not interested in persons but in the cause and effect of the gospel message. Paul desires nothing less than that he, the apostles, or anyone else proclaims the good news of Jesus' death, burial, and resurrection. The basis of Christianity is the doctrine of the resurrection; without it the Christian religion ceases to exist. Paul and his associates preached the gospel in Corinth with the result that the people there believed in Jesus Christ.

Greek Words, Phrases, and Constructions in 15:9–10

ἐλάχιστος—this is a true superlative of the adjective μικρός (small, little) and means "the least."

ὅς—the relative pronoun in the masculine nominative case obstructs smooth English in a literal translation. Modern versions render it "indeed."

εἰς ἐμέ and σὺν ἐμοί—notice the differing prepositions that Paul uses: εἰς denotes "toward," "into," and "in me"; σύν means "together with me." The first refers to Paul's conversion experience, the second to God's grace that surrounds him in his ministry.

ὅ—the deliberate choice of the neuter relative pronoun instead of the masculine ὅς stresses the thing, not the person: "*what* I am" instead of "*who* I am."

---

33. See II Cor. 4:8–11; 6:4–10; 11:23–29.

3. Resurrection of the Dead
15:12–34

From his summary of the gospel (vv. 3–5), Paul selects the doctrine of the resurrection for further discussion.[34] Positively, he affirms that Christ has been raised from the dead and follows this up with a query why some people deny this historical and redemptive fact. Negatively, he examines the results of repudiating this doctrine: that the apostles' preaching and the believers' faith are empty and powerless. Without proclaiming the doctrine of the resurrection, preachers utter falsehoods, people remain in sin, believers who have died in Christ are lost, and Christians are to be pitied. Hence, when opponents to the Christian faith attack and undermine the tenet of the resurrection, they seek to destroy Christianity's foundation. Should they succeed in their assault, the church founded on Jesus Christ would disintegrate and eventually cease to exist. In short, the resurrection doctrine is basic to the Christian faith.

a. Logical Argument
15:12–19

12. But if Christ is preached, that he has been raised from the dead, how do some among you say that there is no resurrection of the dead?

a. "But if Christ is preached, that he has been raised from the dead." The first part of this conditional sentence states a fact. That is, Christ's gospel is being proclaimed in Corinth and elsewhere. The word *Christ* obviously represents the gospel that originated with him and that his followers continue to proclaim.

To prove the veracity of Jesus' resurrection (vv. 5–8), Paul has listed Jesus' numerous appearances after he rose from the dead and before he ascended to heaven. The perfect tense in Greek of the verb *to raise* indicates that Christ's resurrection, which happened in the past, has lasting significance for the present. By conquering death Jesus Christ never has to face death again. The phrase *from the dead* means that Jesus has been raised by God the Father from death. To be precise, the Greek text has the plural word *dead*, which must be understood in a general sense. If then God raised Jesus from the dead, he will also raise believers from death at the end of time (6:14). Paul intimates that everyone who believes in Jesus shares in his resurrection (15:20–23).

b. "How do some among you say that there is no resurrection of the dead?" Paul has stated that Christ has been raised from the dead. Now he asks why some Corinthians deny the doctrine of the resurrection. They did not reject this doc-

---

34. Literature on this topic is prolific. Selected publications are Kathryn W. Trim, "Paul: Life after Death. An Analysis of 1 Corinthians 15," *Crux* 14 (1978): 129–50; Robert Sloan, "Resurrection in I Corinthians," *SWJourTh* 26 (1983): 69–91; A. J. M. Wedderburn, *Baptism and Resurrection: Studies in Pauline Theology against Its Graeco-Roman Background*, WUNT 44 (Tübingen: Mohr-Siebeck, 1987); M. C. de Boer, *The Defeat of Death: Apocalyptic Eschatology in 1 Corinthians 15 and Romans 5*, JSNT Supplement Series 22 (Sheffield: JSOT, 1988); Norman L. Geisler, "The Significance of Christ's Physical Resurrection," *BS* 146 (1989): 148–70.

trine but reinterpreted it by saying that Christ's resurrection was spiritual. They taught that with Christ they were also raised from the dead at the time of their baptism. Thus for them the resurrection had already taken place and had only passing significance. They did not accept it as a tenet of the Christian faith and, therefore, were in danger of separating themselves from the church.

Elsewhere, Paul writes that because Hymenaeus had shipwrecked his faith, Paul handed him over to Satan (I Tim. 1:19–20). With Philetus, Hymenaeus denied the doctrine of a bodily resurrection and destroyed the faith of some believers (II Tim. 2:17–18).[35] We are not sure how many people in Corinth questioned this doctrine, what influence they exerted in the church, or who they were. In view of the lengthy discourse on this particular doctrine, we assume that these Corinthians were influential.[36]

Influenced by Greek philosophy, these church members argued that the soul (which is immortal) returns to God who gave it (Eccl. 12:7) but that the body is mortal and at death descends into the grave. The soul, they believed, is raised to be with God and enjoys eternal life but the body is annihilated. This is a truncated view of the resurrection, for God created Adam with body and soul as a complete human being. The soul and the body are God's creation and share in Christ's resurrection. Christ rose physically from the dead, as Paul proves with his list of Jesus' appearances (vv. 5–8). Over against the Greek philosophical view of some Corinthians, in chapter 15 Paul develops a scriptural perspective. In the next verse, he presents an argument that shows both contrast and logic.

13. But if there is no resurrection of the dead, not even Christ has been raised.

Placing verses 12 and 13 in parallel columns, we observe that Paul contrasts his thoughts:

	Verse 12	*Verse 13*
	But if Christ is preached,	But if there is
	that he has been raised	no resurrection
	from the dead,	of the dead,
how do some among you say		
	that there is	not even Christ
	no resurrection	has been raised.
	of the dead?	

With irrefutable logic, Paul counters the Corinthians' erroneous view that God raises the soul but not the body. If some people hold to a spiritual resurrection of the soul and deny a bodily resurrection, then the inevitable conclusion must be

---

35. Refer to George W. Knight III, *The Pastoral Epistles: A Commentary on the Greek Text*, New International Greek Testament Commentary series (Grand Rapids: Eerdmans; Carlisle: Paternoster, 1992), pp. 109–12, 413–14; J. N. Vorster, "Resurrection Faith in 1 Corinthians 15," *Neotest* 23 (1989): 287–307.

36. Consult Harris, *Raised Immortal*, p. 15; *From Grave to Glory*, p. 190; R. A. Horsley, "'How can some of you say that there is no resurrection of the dead?' Spiritual Elitism in Corinth," *NovT* 20 (1978): 203–31.

that Christ's body is still in the tomb and his redemptive work fruitless. Indeed, Jesus did not come to earth, die on the cross, and rise from the dead for himself but for those whom he redeems.[37] A gospel without the tenet of the resurrection has no message of redemption.

With the double negative in the two parts of this verse, Paul writes a conditional sentence that is contrary to reality. The clause *if there is no resurrection of the dead* contrasts the fact that there is a resurrection. But if the critics deny this fact, then Paul draws for them the inescapable conclusion that Christ's physical body did not rise from the grave either.

14. And if Christ has not been raised, then our preaching is vain and also your faith is vain.

a. "And if Christ has not been raised." Paul continues writing a conditional sentence that contrasts incorrect teaching with reality. Paul states that to deny Christ's resurrection is to go against all the pertinent evidence that was available in the early church. Hundreds of people in Paul's day could testify to the resurrection because they had personally seen their glorified Lord. The apostles aside, about five hundred people saw the living Lord between Easter and ascension (vv. 5–8). Paul could tell the Corinthians to consult these eyewitnesses. Even he himself had seen Jesus near Damascus, and for that reason proclaimed the message of his risen Lord.

b. "Then our preaching is vain and also your faith is vain." The logic of Paul's discourse is compelling. If Christ is still in the tomb outside Jerusalem, he argues, then the content of my preaching is nothing but empty words and I with all the other apostles and preachers am a charlatan. More, the faith of all those who listen to Paul and his companions is vain. Both he and his listeners would be ill served if they would have to believe a lie and perpetuate it.

Doctrinal Considerations in 15:14

The Roman soldier who pierced Jesus' side and saw blood and water gush forth knew that Jesus had died. Jesus' broken body was beyond restoration and had to be buried. Thus, from a medical point of view the resurrection of Jesus' body is unthinkable, for nobody has ever returned from the grave. Some theologians have tried to meet this medical objection by giving a modern interpretation to the word *resurrection*. They explain the term spiritually and say that the resurrection is not an objective event of Jesus coming forth from the tomb outside Jerusalem. They say that no one was present to witness Jesus leaving the burial place, for the guards became like dead men (Matt. 28:2–4). And they conclude that the story of his resurrection, which cannot be verified by observation, is not part of history.

These theologians interpret the resurrection as a subjective experience that occurs in the hearts of believers. They allege that when believers listen to and obey the Word of

---

37. Compare John Calvin, *The First Epistle of Paul the Apostle to the Corinthians*, Calvin's Commentaries series, trans. John W. Fraser (reprint ed.; Grand Rapids: Eerdmans, 1976), p. 318.

God, the resurrection takes place in their hearts.[38] We admit that this spiritual interpretation is ingenious, for it dispels all the objections raised by medical scientists and empirical historians. Whenever preachers proclaim this spiritual resurrection message, no critic voices objections.

The truth of the matter, however, is that this message has identified the doctrine of the resurrection with a description of a believer's conversion experience. This spiritual interpretation has no bearing at all on the physical resurrection of Jesus and on that of all his followers. In reality, it has nothing in common with the doctrine expressed in the Apostles' Creed: "I believe in the resurrection of the body."

Critics of the resurrection doctrine demand evidential proof from eyewitnesses that Jesus rose physically from the dead and left the tomb. They assert that because the New Testament Scriptures fail to provide such observable proof, the Christian faith is dubious. One of them even suggests the possibility that archaeologists in Jerusalem would unearth a letter written by Caiaphas addressed to Pontius Pilate. This letter, then, would reveal a detailed plan to move Jesus' body from the tomb and place it in an undisclosed location.[39] Would the Christian faith be seriously damaged by such a letter and lose its credibility?

The answer is absolutely not. Consider the difference in the respective points of departure of believers and unbelievers. Christians accept the teachings of Scripture in faith, but the unbeliever rejects them. Christians believe the doctrine of Christ's resurrection, but the unbeliever denies it. Sufficient for Christians, but insufficient for unbelievers, is the testimony of the apostles who were eyewitnesses of their Master's resurrection (Acts 1:22; 3:15). Scripture hints that at the time of Jesus' ascension many people met the requirement for apostleship because they were eyewitnesses of the resurrection. And Scripture teaches that by the testimony of two or three witnesses truth is established (Deut. 19:15).

If Pilate had moved Jesus' body to a secret place, the resurrection doctrine would in fact rest on the fraudulent testimony of apostles and numerous believers. Then Christ would be an imposter, his apostles deceivers, and the church a sham. Instead Christ himself is the truth and so is God's Word (John 14:6; 17:17).

---

15. In addition, we are even found to be false witnesses of God, because we testified in contradiction to God that he raised Christ, whom he did not raise if the dead are not raised.

a. "In addition, we are even found to be false witnesses of God." Paul is by no means finished with his logical analysis. He has much more to say, for he emphatically points out that should Christ's resurrection be falsehood, Paul and his associates would be exposed as "impostors of the worst kind."[40] They would be branded as false witnesses who were spreading lies to gullible people and deceiving them. Not only that, they would testify falsely of God and thus stand guilty before God himself.

---

38. Willi Marxsen, *The Resurrection of Jesus of Nazareth* (Philadelphia: Fortress; London: SCM, 1970).

39. Donald W. Viney, "Grave Doubts About the Resurrection," *Encounter* 50 (1989): 127. See the contrast in William L. Craig, *Assessing the New Testament Evidence for the Historicity of the Resurrection of Jesus*, Studies in the Bible and Early Christianity 16 (Lewiston, N.Y.; Queenston, Ont.; and Lampeter, UK: Mellen, 1989), p. 396; Gary R. Habermas, "Jesus' Resurrection and Contemporary Criticism: An Apologetic (Part II)," *CrisTheolRev* 4 (1990): 373–85.

40. Godet, *First Corinthians*, p. 773.

The phrase *false witnesses of God* can be taken either objectively or subjectively. It can mean objectively that Paul and his co-workers were giving a false report of what God had done in Christ. And subjectively it can signify that they were sent forth by God himself to preach and practice deceit. Of the two interpretations, only the first one is acceptable: God does not commission people to represent him deceitfully. The above-mentioned phrase, then, has an objective connotation and implies that if Christ's resurrection is a falsehood, those who proclaim it as a tenet of faith are liars. These people must stand before God's tribunal as impostors. They are in the same category as the false prophets of the Old Testament era (Deut. 18:20–22) and the false apostles of the New Testament era (I John 5:10; II John 10).

b. "Because we testified in contradiction to God that he raised Christ." The concept *speaking against someone* is legal terminology. It is used when a witness swears an oath to affirm the truth of his testimony.[41] Truth is at stake, because either God raised Jesus from the dead or, if the resurrection did not take place, Paul and all his associates preach a lie and speak against God. But why would they promulgate deception, be willing to suffer and die for it, and acknowledge that they must face the God of truth?

c. "Whom he did not raise if the dead are not raised." In translation, the last segment of verse 15 repeats the wording of verse 13. The resurrection of Jesus Christ is inseparably linked to the resurrection of the dead. This truth comforts the believer whose hope is built on Christ. How does this truth comfort the Christian? A sixteenth-century catechism replies:

> Not only my soul
> will be taken immediately after this life
>   to Christ its head,
> but even my very flesh,
>   raised by the power of Christ,
> will be reunited with my soul
> and made like Christ's glorious body.[42]

16. For if the dead are not raised, then neither has Christ been raised.

This verse also repeats verse 13 (see v. 14). The reiteration serves to alert the readers to the consequences of denying the doctrine of Jesus' resurrection. Those who deny this doctrine implicitly label God a liar and the apostles false witnesses. But these people ought to realize that they will have to appear before God's judgment throne to give an account of what they have said.

17. And if Christ has not been raised, your faith is worthless and you are still in your sins.

Verse 17 is a continuation of the preceding verse. Paul extends his compelling

---

41. Consult Robertson, *Grammar*, p. 607.
42. Heidelberg Catechism, answer 57.

logic to have the readers view the effect of a denial of the resurrection. Step by step he reveals to them the spiritual implications of this denial.

Paul addresses the Corinthians with the use of the second person plural *you.* He says, "if you deny Christ's resurrection, then you should realize that your faith is worthless" (compare v. 2). In verse 14 Paul uses the adjective *useless,* but here "worthless." The difference is that the Greek adjective *kenē*, translated "useless," expresses emptiness and the Greek adjective *mataia*, translated "worthless," connotes aimlessness.[43]

What are the ramifications of a worthless faith? For one thing, if Christ is not raised from the grave, he is dead; a dead Christ is unable to justify believers; and unjustified believers remain in their sins. We draw the inevitable conclusion that the justification of believers rests squarely on the resurrection of Jesus Christ.[44] Without the risen Christ there is no justification, without justification there is no living faith, and without living faith there is no forgiveness of sin. Paul confronts the Corinthians who reject Christ's resurrection and in effect tells them: "If you remain in your sins, your faith is worthless, you show no sign that you belong to God's sanctified people, and you are not saved."

Yet, Paul had written that the Corinthians were sanctified in Christ Jesus, would be kept strong to the end, and were called into God's fellowship (1:2, 8, 9). More than that, Paul had told them that they were washed, sanctified, and justified in the name of Jesus through the Spirit of God (6:11). Their sins were forgiven; they were made holy and righteous in Christ Jesus. Paul does not contradict himself in this letter; rather, he wants the Corinthians to understand his logic and see the error of their way. They must grasp the effect that denying Jesus' resurrection has on their spiritual lives and therefore they must come to repentance. Paul wants them to possess the assurance that they have been redeemed by Jesus Christ, who died and rose from the grave on their behalf. He wants them to know that on the basis of Jesus' resurrection they have been justified and sanctified.

18. Then also those who have fallen asleep in Christ have perished.

Paul arrives at the conclusion of his logical argument and introduces it with the Greek expression *ara*, which in this verse means "as a result." He asks his readers to reflect on a point that relates to a past generation of believers. He refers to those who have fallen asleep, which is a New Testament euphemism commonly used for those who have died.[45] (In English, we circumscribe the word *death* with the euphemism *he passed away.*) The New Testament euphemism relates not to sleep of the soul but to a physical body waiting in a grave for the day

---

43. Trench, *Synonyms of the New Testament*, pp. 191–92.

44. Richard B. Gaffin, Jr., *The Centrality of the Resurrection: A Study in Paul's Soteriology* (Grand Rapids: Baker, 1978), p. 124; Hans Conzelmann, *1 Corinthians: A Commentary on the First Epistle to the Corinthians*, ed. George W. MacRae, trans. James W. Leitch, Hermeneia: A Critical and Historical Commentary on the Bible (Philadelphia: Fortress, 1975), p. 266.

45. See the Greek of Matt. 27:52; John 11:11–12; Acts 7:60; 13:36; I Cor. 7:39; 11:30; 15:6, 18, 20, 51; I Thess. 4:13–15; II Peter 3:4.

of resurrection. In the current text, however, the expression *fallen asleep in Christ* applies to Christians who at the time of death believed that they would enter heaven to be eternally with Christ. The Corinthians believed that the separation of body and soul would come to an end when Jesus returns (I Thess. 4:16).

If a person denies the resurrection, Paul informs his readers, the logical implication is that those who have died in Christ are lost. If Christ has not risen from the dead, then God condemns people to everlasting punishment because of their sins; they never enter heaven to be in God's presence; and, last, their bodies remain forever in the grave. Cut off from the living God, they have perished. If the Corinthians who deny the resurrection doctrine say that those who have died are with Jesus, then they contradict themselves. A denial of the resurrection would mean that all have perished, including Jesus.

The Corinthians, however, believe that their loved ones have died in Christ. Paul forces them to see the fallacy of their thinking. They must realize that if believers died in Christ, Christ himself welcomes them into heaven. Hence, Jesus Christ has risen from the dead and is alive. Death is unable to break the bond that exists between Christ and believers throughout this earthly life.[46] That bond continues into the life hereafter and lasts eternally (compare Rom. 6:11).

19. If for this life only we have hoped in Christ, we are of all people most to be pitied.

The wording of this verse gives rise to interpretations that arise from the place and significance of the adverb *only*. Note the following observations:

First, the Greek text has the word *only* at the end of the first clause and links it to the verb construction *we have hoped*. The New American Bible reflects this link: "If we have only hoped in Christ in this life, we are of all men most to be pitied." This reading makes Paul say that the Corinthians have been wrong in placing their hope only in Christ. He certainly is not indicating that believers should put their trust in human beings, too (see Ps. 146:3). Nor does he intimate that Christians ought to fix their attention on Jesus (Heb. 12:2) for the life hereafter and show a total disregard for the present. What, then, is Paul stressing in this concluding verse of this part of the discussion? This becomes plain in the second interpretation.

If we place the adverb *only* after "for this life" and before "we have hoped in Christ," the adverb controls the entire first clause.[47] Then the reading decisively limits our relationship with Jesus Christ to this earthly life and puts him on a horizontal instead of a vertical level. Consequently our relationship with Christ ceases when death ends our physical life, and we have no hope of resurrection.

---

46. Ridderbos, *Paul*, p. 506.

47. C. K. Barrett, *A Commentary on the First Epistle to the Corinthians*, Harper's New Testament Commentaries series (New York and Evanston: Harper and Row, 1968), p. 350; Leon Morris, *The First Epistle of Paul to the Corinthians*, rev. ed., Tyndale New Testament Commentaries series (Leicester: Inter-Varsity; Grand Rapids: Eerdmans, 1987), p. 208.

Paul stresses the verb *to hope* with a Greek construction of a perfect participle that perhaps can best be translated "we have been hoping." The perfect tense describes an action that took place in the past and continues to the present. From the time of conversion to that of death, the Corinthians who died had been living on the basis of hope.[48] When they died, that hope did not became reality but turned into disillusionment. Paul states that when hope is dashed, believers are deluded and are the most pitiable of all people. Unbelievers live without hope and thus seek to get as much out of the present life as possible. The believers hope for the restoration of all things in the life to come. If their hope vanishes at the time of death, they are to be pitied more than anyone.[49]

Greek Words, Phrases, and Constructions in 15:12–19

Verses 12–14

ἐκ νεκρῶν—"from the dead." Without the definite article νεκροί means the dead in general; with the article it means Christians who have died.[50]

ἐν ὑμῖν τινες—the preposition ἐν conveys a partitive sense: "some of you."

εἰ—the conditional sentences in verses 13–18 are of the contrary-to-fact type. In succession, the conditional sentences develop logical reasoning in Paul's presentation.[51]

ἐγήγερται—see the entry at verse 4.

κενόν—"empty." The position of this adjective denotes emphasis: "Then empty is our preaching, and empty is your faith."

ὑμῶν—some major Greek manuscripts have the reading ἡμῶν, but the context demands "your faith" to counterbalance "our preaching."[52]

Verse 15

κατά—with the genitive τοῦ θεοῦ, this preposition conveys the idea *against God.*

εἴπερ—in this compound, the particle -περ places urgent stress on the particle εἰ (if) that introduces the conditional clause: "if, as they say, it is true that. . . ."[53]

ἐγείρονται—Paul writes the present tense in the passive to explain that the implied agent is God who raises the dead.

Verses 18–19

κοιμηθέντες—the aorist passive participle from κοιμάω (I fall asleep, die, pass away) denotes simultaneous action with the main verb *to perish.*

---

48. Compare Geerhardus Vos, *The Pauline Eschatology* (1930; reprint ed., Phillipsburg, N.J.: Presbyterian and Reformed, 1986), p. 31.

49. The pseudepigraphal book II Bar. 21:13 reflects similar pessimism: "For if only this life exists which everyone possesses here, nothing could be more bitter than this." James H. Charlesworth, ed., *The Old Testament Pseudepigrapha*, 2 vols. (Garden City, N.Y.: Doubleday, 1983), vol. 1, p. 628.

50. Joachim Jeremias, "'Flesh and Blood cannot inherit the Kingdom of God' (1 Cor. XV. 50)," *NTS* 2 (1955–56): 155–56; Blass and Debrunner, *Greek Grammar*, #254.2.

51. Blass and Debrunner, *Greek Grammar*, #372.2b.

52. Bruce M. Metzger, *A Textual Commentary on the Greek New Testament*, 3d corrected ed. (London and New York: United Bible Societies, 1975), pp. 567–68.

53. Blass and Debrunner, *Greek Grammar*, #454.2.

μόνον—"only." Nigel Turner observes: "In this sentence the adverb *monon* occurs, not after the words 'in this life,' but after the verb, indeed after the whole sentence. There is no contrast intended between having faith while we are in this world and having it in some other. The contrast is rather between having faith *only* and having faith supported by the reality of Christ's present risen life."[54]

ἐλεεινότεροι the comparative adjective of ἐλεεινός (pitiable) serves as a superlative: "most miserable."

---

b. Reality of the Resurrection
15:20–28

(1) In Adam and in Christ
15:20–22

20. But now Christ has been raised from the dead, the firstfruits of those who have fallen asleep.

a. "But now." The first two words in this text are important. The first one is the adversative *but* that changes the discourse from a series of negative statements on the resurrection (vv. 12–19) to a positive testimony on Christ raised from the dead. After writing seven conditional statements to demonstrate the effect of denying the resurrection, Paul turns from the contrary teaching of some Corinthians to the consistent doctrine of the Christian church: the tenet of Christ's resurrection.

The second word *now* can indicate a temporal reference, a logical conclusion or, in this verse, both. For Paul, the raising of Christ from the dead was a historical fact with far-reaching and lasting implications; Christ Jesus has been raised by God the Father to effect the restoration of all his people. Conversely, the adverb *now* signals the logical conclusion of Paul's lengthy discussion on the denial of the resurrection that some Corinthians championed.[55]

b. "Christ has been raised from the dead." This brief testimony sketches an incontrovertible fact that is rooted in history and is basic to the Christian faith: Christ arose. The evidence Paul has marshaled in the earlier part of this chapter is sufficient for believers, namely, the empty tomb and the appearances (see vv. 3–8). Granted that unbelievers continue to scoff, Christians do not need further proof for this historic truth that in their minds is irrefutable (see Acts 3:15; 26:23).

Paul repeats the words he wrote in verse 12. There he put the statement "If Christ has been raised from the dead" in conditional form, but here he phrases it as a declaration that relates a historical fact. There he raised the theological question that some Corinthians denied this fact, while he himself attested its truth.[56] Here he reiterates positively the truth of the resurrection; he knows that

---

54. Nigel Turner, *Grammatical Insights into the New Testament* (Edinburgh: Clark, 1965), pp. 113–14.
55. Bauer translates the Greek words *nuni de* "but, as a matter of fact" (p. 546).
56. Jan Lambrecht, "Paul's Christological Use of Scripture in 1 Cor. 15.20–28," *NTS* 28 (1982): 503.

only some of the Corinthians deny Christ's resurrection. Perhaps the readers have not understood the implications of this redemptive doctrine, but after Paul's expansive discourse on the subject they should now be able to realize the profound importance of this teaching.

The question remains whether Paul now excludes those who deny Christ's resurrection or addresses all the Corinthians. Is he continuing his discourse directed against those who reject this teaching or is Paul now speaking only to those who accept it?[57] There is no indication in the current section (vv. 20–28) that Paul excludes anyone. In effect, after thoroughly discussing the negative consequences of denying the resurrection, Paul invites all his readers to examine the positive aspects of confessing this doctrine.

c. "The firstfruits of those who have fallen asleep." This clause is a pithy statement of only three words in the Greek text, yet it is filled with meaning. Paul assumes that his readers are acquainted with the Old Testament teachings on the firstfruits. These were the earliest gathered fruits that the people offered to God in recognition of his faithfulness for providing crops in due season. Moses instructed the Israelites to offer, before the Lord on the day after the Sabbath following the Passover feast, a sheaf of the first grain that was harvested (Lev. 23:9–11). Exactly seven weeks later, they were to present an offering of new grain to the Lord (Lev. 23:15–17; see also Deut. 26:1–11). In a later century, Israel was called the firstfruits (Jer. 2:3). Paul applied this word to the first converts in western Asia Minor and in southern Greece respectively (Rom. 16:5; I Cor. 16:15, NASB). And the 144,000 redeemed from the earth are offered as firstfruits to God (Rev. 14:3; compare James 1:18).[58]

The term *firstfruits* signals that the first sheaf of the forthcoming grain harvest will be followed by the rest of the sheaves. Christ, the firstfruits raised from the dead, is the guarantee for all those who belong to him that they also will share in his resurrection. Paul describes the people who belong to Christ as those who have fallen asleep. He is not mentioning Jesus' resurrection with reference to either the temporal or the religious aspect of the Jewish Passover. He means that Christ's resurrection is a down payment for his people (v. 23) or their guarantee (II Cor. 1:22). Christ is not the firstfruits of those who have been raised but of those who have died.[59] In fact, no human being has been raised physically from the dead. The sons of both the widow of Zarephath and the Shunammite died in later years; so did the daughter of Jairus, the young man of Nain, and Lazarus. Only Christ has conquered death and is risen from the dead. All others must wait for their bodily resurrection until the appointed time.[60]

---

57. For a discussion, see William Dykstra, "I Corinthians 15:20–28, An Essential Part of Paul's Argument Against Those Who Deny the Resurrection," *CTJ* 4 (1969): 195–211.

58. Compare also Rom. 8:23; II Thess. 2:13, NRSV.

59. Conzelmann, *1 Corinthians*, p. 268.

60. Ralph P. Martin, *The Spirit and the Congregation: Studies in 1 Corinthians 12–15* (Grand Rapids: Eerdmans, 1984), p. 110.

21. For since by man came death, also by man came the resurrection of the dead. 22. For as in Adam all die, thus also in Christ all shall be made alive.

We note the following points:

a. *Parallels.* Paul reveals typical Semitic parallelism in these two verses, in which he connects man and death in the first clause and man and the resurrection of the dead in the second. He compares Adam with Christ and notes that death came through Adam but life comes through Christ. The clauses reinforce one another, and the second one is longer than the first in each verse.

For since	also
by man came	by man came
death	the resurrection of the dead
For as	thus also
in Adam all	in Christ all
die	shall be made alive

b. *Allusion.* The two words *for since* express cause; they form the link between the preceding verse (v. 20) and this passage. The words explain the entrance of death into the world.

Paul alludes to the Old Testament Scriptures and in particular to Genesis 3:17–19, which relates that because of sin Adam and Eve and their progeny became subject to death. The Greek has the preposition *dia* (by) to show that man is the agent responsible for death. As Augustine put it,

> Before the fall, Adam was able to sin or not to sin;
> after the fall, he was not able not to sin.

This means that in his purity Adam had the ability not to sin and through his obedience to receive immortality. But through his disobedience, he and the human race received the penalty of death (Gen. 2:17; 3:19). Christ lived obediently without sin and conquered death for the benefit of all his people.

In the Greek of verse 21, Paul omits not only the verbs but also all the definite articles to stress the abstract quality of the nouns *man, death, resurrection,* and *dead.* He emphasizes that death entered the world because of sin committed by man. And death, having been caused by a human being, can be made ineffective only by a human being (compare Rom. 5:12, 18). The corollary of death is the resurrection from the dead, which has been accomplished by Christ, who triumphed over death. He is able to set free from the grip of death those who belong to him.

c. *Meaning.* The concept of resurrection centers on Jesus Christ, who as both God and man has conquered death and has risen victoriously from the grave. Although Christ's resurrection has already taken place, that of his people must wait.

Paul placed the preposition *in* before the name *Adam* and the name *Christ.* Thereby he indicates that Adam is the head of the human race and Christ the head of God's people. In the Greek text, he placed a definite article before each name to confirm that they represent historical persons.[61] His statement, "as in Adam all die, thus also in Christ all shall be made alive," has the present tense in the first clause and the future tense in the second. The present tense indicates the recurring reality of death, and the future reveals the definite promise of the resurrection.

The adjective *all* should not be interpreted to mean that Paul teaches universal salvation. Far from it. The meaning of verse 22 is that as all those who by nature have their origin in Adam die, so all those who by faith are incorporated in Christ shall be made alive.[62] Whereas all people face death because of Adam's sin, only those who are in Christ receive life because of his resurrection. The New Testament teaches that the verb *to give life* refers only to believers and not to unbelievers.[63] Paul elucidates the rising from the dead of Christ and his people but not that of pagans.

Will there be a general resurrection? Yes, believers will be raised to everlasting life but unbelievers to shame and everlasting contempt (Dan. 12:2). And Jesus said: "Those who have done good will rise to live, and those who have done evil will rise to be condemned" (John 5:29).

Greek Words, Phrases, and Constructions in 15:20–22

Verse 20

ἀπαρχή—without the definite article, the noun *firstfruits* expresses the quality of Christ's resurrected life.

τῶν κεκοιμημένων—this is the perfect passive participle of the verb κοιμάω (I fall asleep). With the definite article it relates to all those who have died believing in Christ and whose bodies are awaiting the day of resurrection (compare v. 18).

Verses 21–22

ἐπειδὴ γάρ—"for since" (see 1:21). The conjunction γάρ links verse 21 to the preceding passage.

ἀνάστασις—this noun, "resurrection," derives from the verb ἀνίστημι (I stand up), not from ἐγείρω (I arise). "Closer study shows that *egeirō*, especially in the pass[ive], is used predominantly for what happened at Easter, [that is,] the wakening of the Crucified to life, while *anhistēmi* and *anastasis* refer more especially to the recall to life of people during the earthly ministry of Jesus and to the eschatological and universal resurrection."[64]

πάντες—the adjective occurs twice following the names of Adam and Christ respectively. The prepositional phrases *in Adam* and *in Christ* limit the scope of the adjective, so that all in Adam face death and all in Christ receive life through him. The preposition ἐν means "in the sphere of."

---

61. Archibald Robertson and Alfred Plummer, *A Critical and Exegetical Commentary on the First Epistle of St. Paul to the Corinthians*, International Critical Commentary, 2d ed. (1911; reprint ed., Edinburgh: Clark, 1975), p. 352.
62. Ridderbos, *Paul*, pp. 340–41; Vos, *Pauline Eschatology*, pp. 240–41.
63. E.g., John 5:21; 6:63; Rom. 4:17; 8:11; I Cor. 15:45.
64. Lothar Coenen, *NIDNTT*, vol. 3, p. 276.

ζωοποιηθήσονται—"shall be made alive." This future passive reveals that Christ is the agent in the resurrection of the believers and that the event will occur in the future.

---

(2) The Coming of the Lord
15:23–28

23. But each in his own order: Christ the firstfruits, then those who belong to Christ at his coming. 24. Then comes the end, when he delivers the kingdom to God the Father, after he has abolished all rule, and all authority and power.

a. "But each in his own order: Christ the firstfruits." The first word *but* in this sentence is a mild form of the adversative. It explains the sequence of those people who are made alive in Christ. Paul also uses the Greek term *tagma*, which in other places relates to companies of soldiers; here, it is devoid of any connection with the military. It means first "rank" and next "order": Christ is the firstborn from among those raised from the dead and has supremacy (Col. 1:18); he is also the first in sequence. After Christ has been raised, then those who belong to him will receive a glorified body.[65] Once again, Paul calls Christ the firstfruits (v. 20) to highlight the fact that the full harvest will ensue in due time. Christ the first in the resurrection will be followed by countless multitudes who belong to him.

b. "Then those who belong to Christ at his coming." Paul mentions two categories: Christ and his people. Christ is alone in the first classification and all the believers are in the second one. The resurrection of his people takes place in two stages: first the dead in Christ will rise from their graves, and then the believers who are alive will be transformed (I Thess. 4:16–17). But notice that Paul says nothing about a resurrection of unbelievers, even though both the Old and New Testaments relate that these people will be raised to shame and everlasting contempt (Dan. 12:2; John 5:29).

In a succeeding context, Paul reveals that when Christ returns believers will be transformed. "We shall not all of us fall asleep, but all of us shall be changed in a moment, in the twinkling of an eye, at the last trumpet. For the trumpet shall sound, and the dead shall be raised incorruptible and we shall be changed" (vv. 51–52). In brief, because Christ has been raised, all his people who are dead or alive at his coming will be raised and glorified.

c. "Then comes the end." The first clause of the Greek text lacks a verb; one must be supplied to complete the thought. This supplied verb can be either "comes" or "will come." The end will occur after the resurrection of the people whom Christ redeemed.[66]

---

65. "The primary issue in 1 C[orinthians] 15 is the resurrection of Christians, who receive a new corporeality." Gerhard Delling, *TDNT*, vol. 8, p. 32.

66. For millennial studies, consult Hans-Alwin Wilcke, *Das Problem eines messianischen Zwischenreichs bei Paulus*, ATANT 51 (Zürich and Stuttgart: Zwingli Verlag, 1967); Wilber B. Wallis, "The Problem of an Intermediate Kingdom in 1 Corinthians 15:20–28," *JETS* 18 (1975): 229–42; C. E. Hill, "Paul's Understanding of Christ's Kingdom in 1 Corinthians 15:20–28," *NovT* 30 (1988): 297–320.

With the word *then* Paul introduces not the resurrection of a third group but simply the end. In other words, this adverb does not necessarily suggest an interlude between the resurrection of the believers and the end of time. Because of its brevity, the clause *then comes the end* does not appear to support the teaching of an intermediate kingdom before the consummation of the age. Rather, it signifies that "after all this has happened, will the end or the consummation of Christ's Messianic work come."[67] The words *the end* suggest not only "last in sequence" but also the conclusion of Christ's redemptive work for his people.[68]

In the apocryphal book II Esdras, the clause *then comes the end* has a parallel that speaks about resurrection and judgment. "The earth will give up those who sleep in it. . . . The Most High will be seen on the judgement-seat, and *there will be an end* of all pity and patience" (7:32–33, REB; italics added). The term *end* means the consummation of time. Because the expression stands by itself, we understand it in an absolute sense. Paul writes a few ensuing clauses to inform his readers about Christ's work in the end: handing over the kingdom to the Father; abolishing all rule, authority, and power; destroying death; and subjecting himself to God that he may be all in all.

d. "When he delivers the kingdom to God the Father, after he has abolished all rule, and all authority and power." This is the word order of the Greek text, but the meaning of the text demands a reversal of these two clauses. Christ must first abolish his enemies before he hands over the kingdom to his Father.

The Greek verb *katargeō*, which is translated "I abolish," conveys the idea of making ruling powers ineffective, that is, by terminating and setting them aside.[69] Paul enumerates three categories: all rule, all authority, and power. These expressions were often used by the Jews to designate the demons. Where they occur in Paul's epistles, the context must determine if the text refers to demonic powers.[70] After the resurrection of the believers, Christ will abolish these spiritual forces of evil (Eph. 6:12). He will destroy the power of all rule, all authority, and power in heavenly places and will do so in a single action. After he accomplishes that feat, he hands the kingdom to his Father and this marks the end.

God entrusted the kingdom to Christ for the period lasting from his first coming to his second coming. When Jesus said, "All authority in heaven and on earth has been given to me" (Matt. 28:18), he uttered his enthronement speech. At the end of time, Christ will deliver the kingdom to God the Father when he has destroyed all the hostile spiritual forces. Thus Christ's kingdom lasts from his own resurrection to that of the resurrection of all believers; afterward there will be the destruction of all pernicious powers.

67. Anthony A. Hoekema, *The Bible and the Future* (Grand Rapids: Eerdmans, 1979), p. 184; Ridderbos, *Paul*, pp. 557–58.

68. Martin, *The Spirit and the Congregation*, p. 117.

69. Bauer, p. 417.

70. Rom. 8:38; Eph. 1:21; 3:10; 6:12; Col. 1:16; 2:10, 15. Walter Grundmann writes, "The term *dynameis* is designed to express the power of angelic and demonic forces," *TDNT*, vol. 2, p. 295; Werner Foerster, *TDNT*, vol. 2, p. 573; Conzelmann, *1 Corinthians*, p. 272.

25. For he must rule until he has put all his enemies under his feet.

Paul continues to explain the significance and the time span of Christ's rule with the conjunction *for*. He advances the concept of divine necessity by saying not that Christ rules but that he must rule. He implies that God the Father has given his Son the mandate both to reign and to complete the divine plan of redemption.

Throughout his correspondence with the Corinthians, Paul bases his teachings on the Scriptures. Here he alludes to one of the psalms that speaks of Christ's kingship:

> The LORD says to my Lord:
> "Sit at my right hand
> until I make your enemies
> a footstool for your feet."
> [Ps. 110:1; Matt. 22:44]

The allusion displays Paul's freedom in adapting the Scriptures. David, the psalmist, portrays God as the speaker who addresses his Son and reveals that God will subjugate the enemies to be a footstool for his Son's feet. But Paul rewrites the Old Testament text to give it a christological emphasis and have Christ overpower all his enemies. This passage should not be interpreted to stress the work of either God or Christ. The context shows that both God and Christ function alternatively as subjects of the verbs in verses 20–28.[71]

Christ's universal reign begins when he rises victoriously from the grave in his state of exaltation and ends when he effectively eliminates the power of all his spiritual enemies. These enemies are all the spiritual forces that have rule, authority, and power (v. 24). Peter writes that at Christ's ascension, the "angels, authorities and powers [were placed] in submission to him" (I Peter 3:22). During Christ's reign they continue to exercise their demonic influence until he abolishes their powers at the end of time.

When Christ destroys the last enemy, namely, death, he has already delivered his kingdom to God the Father. Consequently, the services of angels to believers have come to an end, for God's people will have received full salvation (see Heb. 1:14). During the time of Christ's kingdom, the process of conquest continues until it finally enters the settled permanent state of God's kingdom.

26. The last enemy that will be abolished is death.

Among the hostile forces is the power of death. For the human race, this force has continued to rule from the time of Adam's sin (see Gen. 2:17; 3:17, 19) until the present. We view death as a power that is foreign to the human race; it became triumphant over humanity when Satan induced man to sin. Adam's disobedience resulted in the death of himself, his wife, and all his descendants. But Jesus conquered death through his resurrection and will abolish it in the consummation.

---

71. Fee, *First Corinthians*, p. 755 n. 44.

The adjective *last* describes death and should be interpreted to mean that death is the last foe among the demonic forces that exercise rule, authority, and power over humanity (v. 24). This domination, however, is abolished when all Christ's people have been raised from the dead and are glorified.

Paul writes the verb *to abolish* in the passive voice and intimates that God is the agent who will terminate the power of this destructive force. God brought Jesus back to life and has given his followers the assurance that they also will be raised from the dead. If there is no resurrection, death continues to sway its power. But if there is a resurrection of all the believers, the power of death ends once for all.

Those Corinthians who denied the resurrection also failed to realize Christ's triumph over death, for he holds the keys of death and the grave (Rev. 1:18). According to the apostle John, both death and Hades will be thrown into the lake of fire which is the second death (Rev. 20:14). In the renewal of heaven and earth, death will be no more (Rev. 21:4).

Scholars note an attractive symmetrical structure in verses 24–28 (see the illustration below). Verse 26 (E) is at the center. Verse 25 (D) corresponds with verse 27 (D'), verse 24 (C) with verse 27 (C'), verse 24 (B) with verse 28 (B'), and verse 24 (A) with verse 28 (A').[72] The verses that show parallels reinforce each other and reiterate their meaning.

In verse 25, Paul alludes to Psalm 110:1 with its message of the subjection of all Christ's enemies under his feet. In verse 27, he broadens this message to include everything (in similar wording taken from Ps. 8:7). Further, the phrase *then comes the end* in verse 24 signifies that God is all in all as supreme ruler in this universe (v. 28).

    (A) 24. Then comes the end,

        (B) when he delivers the kingdom to God the Father,

            (C) after he has abolished all rule, and all authority and power.

                (D) 25. For he must rule until he has put all his enemies under his feet.

                    (E) 26. The last enemy that will be abolished is death.

                (D')27. For he has put all things under his feet.

            (C')And when he says, "All things are put under him," it is clear that the one who subjected all things to him is excepted.

        (B') 28. And when all things are subjected to him, then even the Son himself shall be subjected to the one who subjected all things to him

    (A') so that God may be all in all.

---

72. See the variations in and the discussions of Wallis, "Intermediate Kingdom," pp. 229–42; Hill, "Christ's Kingdom," pp. 297–320; and Jan Lambrecht, "Structure and Line of Thought in 1 Cor. 15:23–28," *NovT* 32 (1990): 143–51.

27. For he has put all things under his feet. And when [Scripture] says, "All things are put under him," it is clear that the one who subjected all things to him is excepted.

a. "For he has put all things under his feet." This is a direct quotation from Psalm 8, where David sings of man's purity prior to the fall. God clothed Adam with glory and honor and made him ruler over his creation. He made everything subject to the man to whom he had given authority. Thus, Adam gave names to all the animals and they obeyed him without fear (Gen. 2:20).

With the conjunction *for*, Paul shows that God, who will destroy the power of death, allowed death to enter human life near the beginning of history. The subject of the psalm quotation is God himself, and the purpose of the psalm is to reveal Adam's sinlessness before the fall. The stark reality of sin has undermined man's authority, so that the writer of the epistle to the Hebrews observed, "Yet at present we do not see everything subject to him. But we see Jesus, who was made a little lower than the angels, now crowned with glory and honor" (2:8–9). Jesus as the second Adam is the firstfruits of a creation that is restored through his mediatorial work. Hence, like the writer of Hebrews, Paul has in mind not God's people, who are not yet fully restored, but Jesus Christ whom God through suffering has perfected (Heb. 2:10). God subjected all things, including death, to his Son Jesus Christ.

b. "And when [Scripture] says, 'All things are put under him.'" God has placed everything under Christ's feet (Eph. 1:22), and left nothing that is not subject to him. Psalm 8 speaks of only the flocks and herds, birds and fish, and the stars. But the words *all things* comprise everything that belongs to this universe. All the good things in this world bring honor to Jesus Christ, and all the evil things terminate when he abolishes their power and influence. Finally, death is the last evil power that loses its relentless grip on the human race at Christ's resurrection; at the resurrection of all believers it will be completely powerless.

c. "It is clear that the one who subjected all things to him is excepted." God has given everything to his Son through whom he created the universe (John 1:3; Col. 1:16; Heb. 1:2). All things in this creation are subject to the Creator himself. Therefore it stands to reason that the uncreated God the Father, who commissioned his Son to form the universe, should not be in subjection to Christ. During the time that precedes the resurrection of the saints, Jesus serves his people as a mediator who intercedes for them (Rom. 8:34) and prepares a place for them (John 14:3). When all things are eventually subject to Christ, then he delivers the kingdom to God the Father. This marks the completion of his mediatorial work.

28. And when all things are subjected to him, then even the Son himself shall be subjected to the one who subjected all things to him, so that God may be all in all.

This is Paul's conclusion to the doctrine of the Lord's return (vv. 23–28). The first part of the conclusion parallels the second segment of verse 24, where he writes that Christ submits the kingdom to God the Father. In the current verse, Paul uses a different verb to express the same idea. The verb *to subject* occurs here three times in three different Greek forms.

a. "And when all things are subjected to him." Christ Jesus fills the role of the second Adam and serves as God's appointed ruler in this universe. Jesus' disciples were amazed that even the wind and the waves of the Galilean lake obeyed him (Matt. 8:27). The demons submitted to him when he exorcised them (see, e.g., Matt. 8:28–34), and Satan himself fell from heaven (Luke 10:18). Christ is the sovereign ruler in heaven and on earth. When every hostile power, including death, has become a footstool for his feet, the time has come for the Son to submit the kingdom to his Father (v. 24).

b. "Then even the Son himself shall be subjected to the one who subjected all things to him." God has made everything in heaven and on earth subject to Jesus Christ his Son. Consequently, God is completely in control and has delegated responsibility to his Son. The Son proceeds eternally from God the Father (Ps. 2:7) and confesses that he can do nothing by himself and can do only those things which he sees the Father doing (John 5:19).

But how can the Son be both subject and equal to the Father? Charles Hodge observes, "In one sense he is subject, in another sense he is equal. The son of a king may be the equal of his father in every attribute of his nature, though officially inferior. So the eternal Son of God may be coequal with the Father, though officially subordinate."[73] This means that in his office as redeemer and mediator Christ is subject to God the Father. When he has completed the task God assigned to him, he delivers the kingdom to God.

c. "So that God may be all in all." In a sense, this last clause is similar in meaning to that of the phrase *then comes the end* (v. 24). When the Son delivers the kingdom to God, then the end has come; then the only sovereign ruler is God himself. He commissioned his Son and gave him authority, which God receives back when the Son completes his work. God, then, is the ultimate sovereign.

Elsewhere Paul concludes a beautiful doxology by describing God's sovereignty in these words: "For from him and through him and to him are all things. To him be the glory forever! Amen" (Rom. 11:36). The expression *all things* is comprehensive and includes everything without exception. That which is evil will have been abolished forever and that which is pure reflects God's glory.

The clause *so that God may be all in all* echoes a familiar theological theme in the Scriptures that is articulated well by one of the minor prophets:

> The LORD will be king over the whole earth. On that day there will be one LORD, and his name the only name. [Zech. 14:9; see Deut. 6:4; Isa. 43:11]

---

73. Charles Hodge, *An Exposition of the First Epistle to the Corinthians* (1857; Grand Rapids: Eerdmans, 1965), pp. 333–34.

Doctrinal Considerations in 15:23–28

Christ's mediatorial work comes to an end when he hands over the kingdom to God the Father. When his people eventually rise from the dead and are glorified, he no longer is their mediator, for his redemptive task is finished. Sin will be blotted out, Satan with his hordes powerless and consigned to hell, and death destroyed. Then Christ, who with his glorified body brought earth to heaven, will bring heaven to earth at the renewal of all things.

The work of redemption is broader than saving the souls of God's people. Their bodies are also redeemed and will be raised or, if they are alive at the last day, will be transformed. Through Christ, this earth with everything in it has been created, has been redeemed, and in the end with the heavens will be renewed. Indeed, this entire universe will be completely restored, so that God may be all in all.

At Jesus' return the resurrection of all believers, the general judgment, and the renewal of heaven and earth will occur. Because these events take place "on the threshold of eternity," consideration of an exact chronology should not be pressed.[74] The events transpire when Christ's mediatorial work is being completed, for his reign terminates when he delivers the kingdom to his Father.

When the kingdom is transferred from the Son to the Father, this does not mean that Christ is no longer his Son. He continues to be God's eternal Son. When the Son subjects himself to the Father, this does not imply that he no longer exercises power. He continues to sit on his throne but now with those who belong to him. He does not abdicate his throne but invites his people to sit with him as judges.[75] Jesus is a brother to all those whom he has redeemed (Ps. 22:22; Heb. 2:12) but will always have supremacy (Col. 1:18).

Greek Words, Phrases, and Constructions in 15:23–28

Verses 23–24

εἶτα τὸ τέλος—"Since in enumerations εἶτα of[ten] serves to put things in juxtaposition without reference to chronological sequence, it becomes in general a transition-word *furthermore, then, next.*"[76] The Greek τὸ τέλος can mean "the rest" of those who have not risen from the dead, "at last," or "the final consummation" of all things. Scholars prefer the third interpretation, which presents the phrase as a noun.[77]

καταργήσῃ—this is the aorist (single action) of the compound verb καταργέω (I abolish, destroy), which has the perfective meaning of doing something thoroughly.

Verses 25–26

δεῖ . . . βασιλεύειν—the infinitive *to rule* is in the present tense preceded by the auxiliary verb δεῖ (he must). This verb expresses compulsion and duty, for God sent forth the Son to fulfill his plan of redemption.

74. Raymond O. Zorn, *Church and Kingdom* (Philadelphia: Presbyterian and Reformed, 1962), p. 134.
75. Matt. 19:28; Luke 22:30; Rev. 3:21; 4:4; 20:4.
76. Bauer, p. 234.
77. Consult Barrett, *First Corinthians*, p. 356.

θῇ—Paul changes the original wording θῶ (I place; Ps. 110:1), in which God is the agent, to the third person singular with Christ as subject.

καταργεῖται—here the present tense of this verb has a future connotation, "will abolish" (compare v. 24).

Verses 27–28

πάντα—the context of Psalm 8 alludes to the universe, while πάντας in verse 25 refers to Christ's enemies.

At this point in the discourse, Paul wishes to make additional comments about the resurrection of the dead. He implies that especially those Corinthians who reject this doctrine must hear further considerations. Paul presents arguments that touch on baptism for the dead, physical danger, laxity, and corruption of character. Unfortunately, details for these arguments are sparse. With a modern analogy, we could say that these verses, when they were written, had some explanatory footnotes that are no longer extant. These footnotes probably were in the form of oral explanations given when Paul arrived in Corinth (11:34). We do not have the necessary information and consequently we must resort to guesswork to explain the text.

c. Arguments Regarding the Resurrection
15:29–31

29. Otherwise what shall they do who are baptized for the dead? If the dead are not raised at all, why then are they baptized in their behalf?

Paul now addresses the practice of those people who are being baptized for the dead. He confronts only those few people who observed this practice, for he uses the pronoun *they* and not *you* in this text. We assume that Paul vigorously denounced such actions; there is no evidence that churches in the apostolic era ever practiced baptism for the dead.

In the third century, Tertullian comments on this verse and remarks that Paul disapproved of the practice of being baptized for the dead. One hundred years later, Chrysostom described a bizarre procedure of some Marcionite dissenters who baptized a person who had suddenly died without the sign of baptism. He, too, voiced his disapproval and even declared the Marcionite practice superstitious.[78]

Throughout the centuries, explanations for verse 29 have been numerous and varied; many of them concern the phrases *baptized for the dead* and *baptized in their behalf.* In spite of all the exegesis, a satisfactory solution appears to be elusive. I am not presenting a résumé of every possible suggestion; instead I mention several attempts to clarify the text.

---

78. Chrysostom *Homily 40.1 on 1 Corinthians*; Tertullian *Against Marcion* 5.10, and *Resurrection of the Flesh* 48.

1. Living members of the church were baptized vicariously for those believers who had died but had not received the sacrament of baptism. But what is the point of this practice, when believers at death are immediately glorified in the presence of the Lord? What will they gain by being baptized by proxy?

2. The Greek preposition *hyper* (for) in the phrase *for the dead* is interpreted to mean "*above* the graves of the dead." This explanation and the one that takes the preposition *hyper* to signify "*for the sake of* the dead" both refer to representative baptisms. However, the practice of "vicarious baptism requires us to think of the Corinthians' faith in baptism as magical at worse[sic] or mechanical at best."[79]

3. Unbelievers sympathetic toward Christians who had died requested baptism on behalf of the dead and then expected to be in their company at the resurrection.[80] The question remains whether these baptismal candidates expressed faith in Jesus Christ.

4. The phrase *baptized for the dead* echoes a similar phrase, "praying for the dead" (see II Macc. 12:40).[81] But the teachings of Christ and the apostles never include uttering prayers for the dead. The echo aside, these two phrases have nothing in common.

5. The literal interpretation of the word *baptized* is replaced by a metaphor. For example, Jesus asked James and John if they could drink the cup that he had to drink or be baptized with the baptism that he would be baptized with (Mark 10:38; see also Luke 12:50). Jesus used the concept *baptism* as a metaphor for his imminent suffering and death on the cross. Is Paul by analogy conveying a symbolic meaning of the text so that the expression *the dead* signifies death? The text then should read "being baptized by experiencing death." Without disparaging the significance of a martyr's death, I think that this interpretation veers away from the message of the text.

6. Catechumens who were at the point of death asked for baptism. They had already accepted Christ in faith but because of disease or accident felt the nearness of death and requested baptism.[82] The problem is that this interpretation of the Greek preposition *hyper* is contrived.

7. As a last resort, conjectures are suggested. One hypothesis is to emend the last part of verse 29 to read "they are baptized in *our* behalf" instead of "they are baptized in *their* behalf" (italics added). The use of the first person plural creates a parallel between verse 29 and verse 30, "Why are we also in danger every hour?"

---

79. Martin, *The Spirit and the Congregation*, p. 119. Jerome Murphy-O'Connor, however, suggests the phrase *those baptized for the dead* to be a Corinthian taunt directed at Paul's apostolic suffering (vv. 31–32). See his "'Baptized for the Dead' (1 Cor., XV, 29) A Corinthian Slogan?" *RB* 88 (1981): 532–43.

80. Robertson and Plummer, *First Corinthians*, pp. 359–60; Maria Raeder, "Vikariatstaufe in I Kor. 15:29?" *ZNW* 46 (1956): 258–60; Jeremias, "Flesh and Blood," pp. 155–56; J. K. Howard, "Baptism for the Dead: A Study of 1 Corinthians 15:29," *EvQ* 37 (1965): 137–41.

81. Consult the literature provided by Ethelbert Stauffer, *New Testament Theology* (London: SCM, 1955), p. 299 n. 544.

82. Calvin, *I Corinthians*, p. 330.

Another hypothesis is to find a Greek verb similar to that of *to do*: "what shall they do." The proposal is made that the Greek verb *to believe* ("what shall they believe") was the original text and eventually was changed to the verb *to do*.[83]

Conjectures, however, are highly subjective and should be regarded as nothing more than suggestions. Indeed, we would be better off to admit that the text is unclear and noncommunicative than to accept a superficial hypothesis.

Let us now return to the text itself and examine its individual sentences and clauses.

a. "*Otherwise what shall they do who are baptized for the dead?*" The word *otherwise* calls attention to the preceding segment (vv. 20–28) that speaks about the implications of the resurrection of Christ for the believers. If this resurrection were not so, Paul argues, what comments do those people have who are being baptized for the dead? Their willingness to be baptized is utterly pointless if the dead do not rise from their graves. The present tense of the Greek participle *being baptized* indicates that the baptismal candidates are active participants. They are baptized for a group called "the dead." The general rule is that without the definite article in Greek, the expression *the dead* signifies the dead in general. With the definite article, the term means Christians who have died.[84] Conclusively, Paul thinks of those believers who await the day of resurrection.

b. "*If the dead are not raised at all, why then are they baptized in their behalf?*" The first clause lists a condition that is contrary to fact, for in the preceding verses Paul has proved the veracity of the resurrection. In other words, he tells his readers that some of them may deny the resurrection, yet God's people will rise from the dead. For the sake of argument, Paul states this fact as untrue. He wants the deniers to answer the question why people are baptized for the dead. The two sentences of this verse display parallelism to stress the issue that the practice of being baptized for the dead is pointless when the dead do not rise from the grave.

What is the meaning of this verse? Even though many scholars suggest a literal interpretation as a vicarious baptism, the objections are formidable. In all humility I confess that the sense of this text escapes me; verse 29 remains a mystery.

30. And what about us? Why are we in danger hour by hour?

Paul continues with an additional comment in question form. His query concerns himself and his companions—not the Corinthians—who diligently do their work for the Lord. This work entails untold dangers. In Acts, Luke reports many of the perils Paul encountered on his missionary journeys and in Jerusalem. Paul also lists still more dangers he and his co-workers have had to endure for the sake of the gospel: hunger, thirst, exposure, physical attack, verbal abuse,

---

83. Jean Héring writes, "We should like to think that the Apostle dictated '*pisteuousin*' = 'what do they *believe* who are baptized for the dead', a verb which might easily have been corrupted to '*poiēsousin*'." See *The First Epistle of Saint Paul to the Corinthians*, trans. A. W. Heathcote and P. J. Allcock (London: Epworth, 1962), p. 171.

84. Jeremias, "Flesh and Blood," pp. 155–56.

and persecution (4:9–13). He describes what he has had to suffer in Ephesus without mentioning periods of discouragement and depression. His next letter contains catalogs of perils and adversities his associates and he have borne (II Cor. 4:8–11; 11:23–29).

Why would Paul endure imprisonment, severe flogging, beating, stoning, and repeated exposures to death? If there is no hope for the renewal of life through the resurrection of Christ, why would Paul risk his life again and again? He freely admits, "We are fools because of Christ" (4:10). He toiled harder than anyone else for the hope of the resurrection.

31. I die every day—yes, indeed, by my boasting about you, brothers, which I have in Christ Jesus our Lord.

The first clause of this passage belongs to the preceding verse (v. 30), where Paul spoke of facing dangers on a daily basis. Now he writes that he is dying day by day. However, he fails to explain what he has in mind. We presume that the clause reflects the dangerous circumstances Paul daily experiences in Ephesus.

The flow of thought breaks abruptly as Paul switches from his remarks about facing danger and death to his boasting about the Corinthians. He anticipates that the Corinthians will question his sincerity because they are not acquainted with Paul's conditions in Ephesus. When Paul was with them in Corinth he experienced stiff opposition but not mortal danger. Thus, to assure his readers that his comments are true, he first addresses them as his spiritual brothers and, by implication, sisters. Next, in the Greek he swears to the veracity of his remarks by saying that they are just as true as his boasting about them is true. And he makes his boast in Christ Jesus the Lord. Paul often reproved the Corinthians, yet he always boasted of their faith in Jesus Christ.[85]

32. If according to man I fought with wild animals in Ephesus, what advantage is it to me? If the dead are not raised,

let us eat and drink, for tomorrow we die.

Paul spent three years in Ephesus during his third missionary journey, but the only account of this interval is what Luke reports in Acts 19:1–20:1. We note that the encounters in Ephesus were perilous. Whatever the hazard may have been, Paul relates that God raised him from the dead, as it were (see II Cor. 1:8–10).

a. "If according to man I fought with wild animals in Ephesus." Is this statement to be taken literally or figuratively? We cannot imagine that Paul would have survived attacks by some ferocious beasts in an arena at Ephesus. True, Paul related that he was delivered from the lion's mouth (II Tim. 4:17), but Roman law would restrict local authorities from throwing Paul, a Roman citizen, to the lions. If he had been cast to the lions, it would have been proof that he had lost his Roman citizenship.[86] But when he was imprisoned in Caesarea, he appealed to Caesar on the basis of that citizenship (Acts 25:11).

85. See II Cor. 7:4, 14; 8:24; 9:3–4.
86. Abraham J. Malherbe, "The Beasts at Ephesus," *JBL* 87 (1968): 71–80.

Note these points: First, there is eloquent support for understanding this clause figuratively. It comes from an early Christian source, Ignatius. As a martyr on his way to Rome he writes, "From Syria to Rome I am fighting with wild beasts, by land and sea, by night and day, bound to 'ten leopards' (that is, a company of soldiers)."[87]

Next, if Paul had faced wild beasts in the arena of Ephesus, we would have expected to see this event listed in his catalog of sufferings (II Cor. 11:23–29). It is absent. We realize that an argument from silence does not prove much, yet we cannot envision that Paul would include an event that should be understood figuratively.

Third, Paul mentions the exact location where the encounter took place, namely, Ephesus. Luke portrays the danger Paul faced there during the riot instigated by Demetrius and his associates. These people behaved like wild beasts (Acts 19:23–41).

And last, although the phrase *according to man* can be explained in various ways, we assume that it conveys the sense of Paul engaged in a fight with human beings, not with wild beasts. In their opposition to God and his Word, these people attempted to cause Paul bodily harm. We admit, however, that in this context the phrase remains obscure.

b. "What advantage is it to me?" Paul is asking that if he has suffered both physical and verbal abuse for the sake of Christ, what good is it to him without the certainty of the resurrection? The remark *to me* is highly personal because Paul is reflecting on his own life in the ministry of Jesus Christ.

c. "If the dead are not raised, let us eat and drink, for tomorrow we die." This sentence features a condition that is contrary to reality. Paul says, "If the dead are not raised," but he implies that they are raised. For the sake of the argument, therefore, he introduces this contrary-to-fact statement. He adds a literal quote taken from Isaiah 22:13 to conclude the conditional sentence: "Let us eat and drink, for tomorrow we die." Paul thinks of the lighthearted attitude of the people in Jerusalem when a foreign army began to devastate their country. Instead of seeking strength from the Lord in prayer, they indulged in revelry by slaughtering cattle, eating meat, and drinking wine. Instead of mourning for their sins, they purposely turned away from God and uttered the above-mentioned proverb.

Jesus evokes an echo of this proverb in the parable of the rich fool who builds bigger barns to store a bumper crop. The fool says, "Take life easy; eat, drink and be merry." But God says, "You fool! This very night your life will be demanded from you" (Luke 12:19–20).

Paul portrays people who have decided there is no resurrection, so they choose to live apart from God. He anticipates that the Christians in Corinth will immediately see the folly of not believing the doctrine of the resurrection. If they reject this doctrine, they will have to bear the consequences.

---

87. Ignatius *Romans* 5.1 (LCL).

33. Do not be deceived,

bad company corrupts good habits.

This is the second time that Paul warns the Corinthians not to be deceived by members of their own society (6:9).[88] The first time he admonished them not to adopt the lifestyles of immoral people, for such people will not inherit the kingdom of God. Now he warns them not to accept a deviant doctrine that denies the resurrection. Paul realizes the ease with which people accept perverted principles and lifestyles as normative. Without any reflection on the issues at stake, they go astray by adopting wrong beliefs and behavior. For this reason, Paul quotes a proverb from the work *Thais* of the Greek poet Menander: "Bad company corrupts good habits." No doubt the proverb was well known among Greek-speaking people in Greece and elsewhere.[89]

The epigram is to the point because the Greek has the word *homiliai,* which can mean both "company" and "speech." (From this word we derive our expression *homily.*) When we associate with or take delight in bad company, we run the risk of adopting profane and filthy language that corrupts our reputable character. Our speech reveals our inner self; it can either enhance or diminish our reputation.

Why does Paul quote this proverb while discussing the merit of Christ's resurrection? Presumably, those who deny the doctrine of the resurrection scoff at this teaching (compare II Peter 3:3–4). Their influence in the Corinthian church is deadly when allowed to continue without correction. Here Paul envisions the segment in the church that repudiates the teaching that Christ rose from the dead (v. 12; see also 6:12–14). These spiritually myopic people considered only their physical existence, which in their opinion would end in death. Hence, their moral outlook on life declined and influenced the rest of the Corinthian believers.

34. Come to your senses as you ought and do not sin, for some have no knowledge of God. I say this to put you to shame.

a. "Come to your senses as you ought."[90] Paul addresses all the members of the Corinthian church and alerts them to the spiritual dangers that surround them. The warning is timely and urgent: "Come to your senses right now because you are in a daze." The meaning of the Greek verb *eknēphō* (I become sober) suggests that the people in Corinth were unable to think clearly about matters pertaining to life and death. Consequently, they were in danger of losing their moral integrity.[91] Paul roused them from their lethargy and alerted them to clear thinking concerning the resurrection. He tells them to wake up once for all, for this is what they ought to do.

---

88. Gal. 6:7; James 1:16; and see I Cor. 3:18.
89. Refer to Conzelmann, *1 Corinthians,* p. 278 n. 139.
90. Bauer, p. 243.
91. Consult Otto Bauernfeind, *TDNT,* vol. 4, p. 941; Philip J. Budd, *NIDNTT,* vol. 1, p. 515.

b. "And do not sin." The Greek verb *hamartanō* (I sin) is the present tense in the imperative mood. Paul commands his readers to stop sinning. What are they doing that causes him to issue this stern command? They have to return to being right with God about the doctrine of the resurrection. In case they continue to doubt this teaching, they are placing themselves in a profound spiritual crisis. If they doubt this basic tenet of the faith, they begin to abandon God by choosing to live in ignorance.

c. "For some have no knowledge of God." Paul explains the reason for calling the Corinthians out of their stupor: they lack knowledge of God. Some of the Corinthians who deny the fundamental teaching of the resurrection have no knowledge of a personal God (v. 12; compare also Matt. 22:29). They have a general concept of a divine Being but have no communication with the living God. They are no different from the heathen who revel in passionate lust and live in ignorance of God (I Thess. 4:5; Wis. 13:1).

d. "I say this to put you to shame." Paul challenges the members of the Corinthian congregation to consider the meaning of the resurrection, to recognize false teaching, and to live holy lives. He warns them not to emulate the false teachers and become ignorant in doctrine and knowledge of God. Paul appeals to them to desist following those who lead them astray and upset their faith in God.[92]

Instead of being followers, the Corinthians should be leaders in the church of Jesus Christ. They must know that ignorance of God and his Word is a shame to anyone who bears the name *Christian*. Therefore, Paul shames his readers in the hope of seeing a complete reversal of their lethargy. He expects that a correct understanding of the resurrection and its meaning will cause them to abandon bad company and to strive for reputable qualities that God approves.

Greek Words, Phrases, and Constructions in 15:29–34

Verse 29

ἐπεὶ τί—this combination denotes contrast and introduces a rhetorical question: "Otherwise what shall they do?"

εἰ . . . οὐκ—because the negative particle is οὐκ and not μή, the translation of the protasis of the conditional sentence is not "unless" but "if . . . not."

τί καί—the question Paul raises is, "For what reason are they still being baptized?"[93]

Verses 30–31

πᾶσαν ὥραν—the accusative is as much extension as adverbial and conveys the meaning "constantly."[94]

---

92. Refer to Homer A. Kent, "A Fresh Look at 1 Corinthians 15:34: An Appeal for Evangelism or a Call to Purity," *GThJ* 4 (1983): 3–14; for an emphasis on evangelism see Robert G. Gromacki, *Called to Be Saints: An Exposition of I Corinthians* (Grand Rapids: Baker, 1977), p. 192.

93. Blass and Debrunner, *Greek Grammar*, #442.14.

94. Robertson, *Grammar*, p. 470.

νή—"truly, yes." This particle expressing strong affirmation occurs only here in the New Testament. It precedes the accusative case of a person or thing by which one swears, which is τὴν ὑμετέραν καύχησιν (your boast). The possessive pronoun, however, is objective: "my boasting about you," not subjective: "your boasting about me." The variant ἡμετέραν (our) perhaps resulted from misunderstanding the objective genitive and the close connection with the first person singular "I have."[95]

Verses 32–33

εἰ—the first instance introduces a simple-fact conditional clause that conveys reality. The second instance is a condition that is not true to fact.

ἀποθνῄσκομεν—this present indicative serves as a futuristic present, "we shall die" (compare v. 26).[96]

μὴ πλάνασθε—the present imperative preceded by the negative particle μή reveals that the readers were indeed wandering from the truth. Paul's stern command, "Do not be led astray any longer," calls them back to reality.

Verse 34

ἐκνήψατε—this verb in the aorist imperative is a compound that conveys an intensive idea: "Become completely sober." The aorist is ingressive.

μὴ ἁμαρτάνετε—"stop sinning." The command in the present shows that the people continued to sin because they had become ignorant.

ἀγνωσίαν ... ἔχουσιν—"they possess ignorance." This is a contradiction of sorts—they possess nothing. The Corinthians are unable to call ignorance bliss, for Paul puts them to shame for their lack of knowledge.

---

4. Parallels to the Resurrection Body
15:35–44a

Believers frequently ask questions concerning the raising of their bodies in the life hereafter. They want to know what kind of bodies they will have, and thus they search the Scriptures for answers. The Bible teaches us about creation, the fall into sin, redemption, and restoration. It reveals some basic points about the renewal of all things, but it fails to answer all the questions that linger. In Paul's day, Christians were asking him to give them additional details about the resurrection and Christ's return (I Thess. 4:13–18).

A Corinthian inquirer could ask questions about the nature of the resurrection. Paul begins his answers to this query by resorting to examples taken from God's creation: the procreation of plants; the physical differences in human beings, animals, birds, and fish; and the splendor of this earth that varies from the splendor of the sun, moon, and stars. That is, Paul directs the attention of the inquirer to the diversity we are able to observe in creation. With his answers, he de-

---

95. Consult D. S. Deer, "Whose Pride/Rejoicing/Glory(ing) in I Corinthians 15. 31?" *BibTr* 38 (1987): 126–28; Metzger, *Textual Commentary*, p. 568.
96. C. F. D. Moule, *An Idiom-Book of New Testament Greek*, 2d ed. (Cambridge: Cambridge University Press, 1960), p. 7.

lineates the heart of the resurrection doctrine by clarifying the mode in which this redemptive event takes place.

a. Life Out of Death
15:35–38

35. But someone will say, "How are the dead raised? And with what kind of body do they come?"

The first word in this verse is the adversative *but*, which introduces a contrast to the preceding text. This word implies that Paul anticipated questions from the audience and that he himself formulated and answered them. We deduce from Paul's sharp retort ("You fool!" [v. 36] that these queries had already been posed at one time or another by those Corinthians who repudiated the doctrine of the resurrection. Moreover, they had uttered their queries derisively.[97]

Paul first fields the two questions on the manner and the form of the resurrected body and then responds to them. He answers the query on the mode of the resurrection in verse 36 and he explains the form of our renewed bodies in the next few verses. The two questions reinforce each other, as the parallel columns clearly show:

how are	with what
the dead	kind of body
raised	do they come

The first line lists the interrogatives *how* and *what*; in the second line the expression *the dead* evokes questions about the *kind of body* a deceased person will have; and the third line features the synonyms *raised* and *come*.

Let us take a closer look at these two questions. Those who deny the resurrection actually ask, "Is it possible for the dead to be raised?" They doubt that a dead body can be raised at all. Indeed, they do not believe that a decaying body that is either buried or burned is capable of bringing forth a new body.[98] They question whether a resurrected body will be exactly the same as the body that died, for if it is not the same, how can one speak of a resurrection?

Greek philosophers taught the immortality of the soul but denied the immortality of the body. Paul was scorned by Epicurean and Stoic philosophers in Athens when at the end of his Areopagus address he mentioned the resurrection from the dead (Acts 17:31–32). Conversely, Jewish rabbis believed that God created man as a unit of body and spirit. At death the spirit returns to God who gave it and the body returns to the dust of the earth (Eccl. 12:7). And at the resurrection, the dead will rise with the same body that perished.[99]

---

97. Consult Gaffin, *Centrality of the Resurrection*, p. 78.
98. Robertson and Plummer, *First Corinthians*, p. 366; Ronald J. Sider, "The Pauline Conception of the Resurrection Body in I Corinthians XV. 35–54," *NTS* 21 (1975): 428–39.
99. SB, vol. 3, p. 474; II Bar. 50.1–51.10, in *The Old Testament Pseudepigrapha*, Charlesworth, ed., vol. 1, pp. 637–38.

But those Corinthians who were influenced by Greek philosophy repudiated the teachings on the resurrection. They told Paul that raising a person from the dead was impossible. They refused to listen to the message of the Old Testament Scriptures, the account of Jesus' resurrection, and the promise that believers in Christ will rise from the dead. Last, they rejected the thought of continuity, for they saw only the dissolution of the physical body when death occurred.

36. You fool! What you sow does not come to life unless it dies.

No wonder, then, that Paul vented his disgust with the words *you fool!* He writes the singular form in harmony with the question that one of his opponents uttered, but he addresses the outburst to everyone who denies the resurrection. Fools fail to think even when all the facts are self-evident and plain. They despise wisdom, distort the truth, and display indifference to God and his revelation. On the other hand, people who fear God depend on him for the gift of wisdom.

Paul alludes to the world of plants, a world that provides vivid illustrations of the continuity of life. He confronts the foolish person who denies the resurrection account; he points to something this person does from time to time: sowing seed. When someone plants a seed in fertile soil that has sufficient moisture and warm temperature, it germinates. The germination process causes the seed to disintegrate. That dying seed gives birth to new life in the form of a developing plant that eventually matures and produces seed (see John 12:24). Notice that we sow the seed but are unable to bring about germination and new life. That is God's work.

This illustration of a seed is apt; it applies to the human body that at death descends into the grave. The body disintegrates and in the course of time disappears completely. The analogy does not include a specific period of time, for that is not germane to the issue. The point is that life comes forth out of death. No human being on earth is able to bring forth new life out of the body that has returned to the dust of the ground. Only God through Christ can reassemble the dust particles of the human body to call it forth in glorified form and newness of life.

Modern English translations use the active voice in this verse: "What you sow does not come to life." But the Greek text has the passive voice of the verb *to come to life,* which an older version (KJV) translates accurately: "is quickened." The passive voice conveys the sense that God alone is the agent who creates life and that human beings can only watch this miracle occur.[100] Life comes from God who is its source.

37. And when you sow, you sow not the body that shall be but a bare kernel, perhaps of wheat or of something else.

A scoffer could argue that no one has ever seen a new body come forth out of a grave. He could state that new birth takes place when the next generation

---

100. Two versions have the passive voice: NJB, "it is given new life"; and *Cassirer,* "[seed] has no life given to it."

makes its debut. In other words, Paul should revise his analogy and compare new plant life with new human life.

Paul takes a different approach to the process of sowing and growing. He notes that the seed that is sown is only a bare kernel either of wheat or of other plants. That seed has a specific form and substance; it is round or oval and it is hard and dry. He tells his reader that what is sown, germinates and develops into a plant. Yet in form the plant is entirely different from the dry seed that was sown. That plant continues to develop and is incomparably more beautiful than the kernel.

Paul's reply to his opponent reveals a contrast of the bare kernel with the growing plant. "And when you sow, you sow not the body that shall be but a bare kernel, perhaps of wheat or of something else." No one in his right mind plants a seed with the expectation of immediately receiving a new seed in return. Paul places the emphasis in this verse on the act of sowing that eventuates in the growing of a plant. Ralph P. Martin puts the truth of Paul's statement in an epigram: "In the world of nature, which is God's world, what is *sown* is not identical with what is *grown*, though it is related to it."[101]

The question of continuity and discontinuity is relevant. Plants and trees, fish and fowl, wild animals and livestock always show continuity in reproduction. Nevertheless, there is also a sense of discontinuity when a kernel germinates and develops into a plant. A seed brings forth its own kind of plant, which in turn produces the same kind of seed. The details should not be pressed, however, for the plant procreates the seed that was sown. In this text, Paul is not yet ready to comment on the difference between the perishable body and the imperishable body, the mortal and the immortal state of a human being. He will do so in a few succeeding verses (vv. 42, 52–54). For the moment, he emphasizes the truth that out of the dying seed new life springs forth.

Jesus' physical body was placed in the tomb, but on the third day he arose in a glorified body that showed continuity—his followers recognized him. Yet it was also completely different, for it was no longer subject to time and space. Jesus' body could enter and leave a room while the doors were shut (John 20:19, 26; Luke 24:31). The newness of his body reveals a dimension we in our present state fail to comprehend.

38. But God gives it a body just as he wished and to each of the seeds its own body.

Paul does not elaborate on the human body that will be raised from the dead. Instead he teaches that it is God who provides future bodies for every seed that is sown in his creation. Notice that Paul writes "just as [God] wished" in the past tense as an allusion to the creation account. God placed his will on his creation so that every plant should procreate its own kind (Gen. 1:11–12). Thus, according to his will God gives to every seed that is sown its own body. Paul stresses that God works out his plan of creation in harmony with his will, and that will encom-

---

101. Martin, *The Spirit and the Congregation*, pp. 133–34 (italics are his).

passes the human body that is raised from the dead. We know that God is in control and thus we await the day of resurrection to receive new bodies.

Doctrinal Considerations in 15:35–38

Christians believe that their bodies will be raised from the dead when Jesus returns. They know that Scripture tells them that their own bodies will be transformed and glorified; they will not receive completely different bodies.

Yet questions concerning the resurrection are numerous and varied. Here are a few: Will an elderly person whose body was ravaged by an incurable disease be raised as a youth? Will an infant who died because of accident or ailment be like an adult? Will we not only recognize our loved ones but also know the saints of other eras? Will there be a continual tie with family members? We are unable to answer these questions and wisely refrain from speculation. Where the Scriptures are silent we also are silent.

The Scriptures reveal that Jesus' disciples recognized him and saw the scars in his hands and side (John 20:27). Further, Jesus taught that at the resurrection marriage will cease, for everyone will be like the angels in heaven (Matt. 22:30).

At the transformation the characteristic features of an individual will be evident. To illustrate, an infant shows certain features that remain the same throughout his or her life. As distinct changes take place throughout childhood, adolescence, adulthood, and old age, these features display continuity. The glorification of our bodies, however, provides a new dimension that marks a measure of discontinuity. Both the resurrection of the body and the immortality of the soul prove the continued extension of our human existence. We have the assurance in Jesus Christ whose resurrection is the deposit that guarantees the resurrection of all his followers.

Greek Words, Phrases, and Constructions in 15:35–38

Verses 35–36

ποίῳ—this interrogative pronoun has its own qualitative sense, "with what kind."

ἄφρων—an adjective composed of the privative ἀ (un-) and the verb φρονέω (I think).

σύ—the second person pronoun is emphatic as it follows the expletive *fool* and precedes the subordinate clause to which it belongs.

Verses 37–38

γενησόμενον—the future middle participle of γίνομαι (I am, become) is ingressive, "the body that shall be."

γυμνόν—"naked." This adjective describes the plain form of a kernel (of wheat) and does not describe the human body (compare its use in 14:10).

εἰ τύχοι—this is a brief parenthetical phrase, "if it so happens" or "perhaps." The verb is in the optative mood.

ἑκάστῳ . . . ἴδιον—"each . . . its own distinctive body." Paul expresses the law that God had placed in creation with the words *according to its kind* (see, e.g., Gen. 1:24).

---

b. Species, Stars, and Planets
15:39–41

39. All flesh is not the same, but there is one flesh of men, another flesh of beasts, another flesh of birds, and another flesh of fish.

From the first analogy—that life comes forth out of death—Paul moves to the second, the dissimilarity of flesh. He writes about the physical substance of living creatures, that is, the flesh of human beings, beasts, birds, and fish. (Incidentally, notice that this order is reversed in the creation account, Gen. 1:20–27.) There is no question that the physiology of all these creatures differs considerably. The flesh of a human being varies from that of cattle, fowl, or fish, for God has created each one unlike the other. In God's creation, we find an overwhelming variation that is complimentary through its nonconformity.

What is Paul trying to say with this second analogy? It should be understood as a follow-up of the last part of the preceding verse (v. 38): "God gives . . . to each of the seeds its own body." Just as there is immeasurable diversity in the plant world, so there is infinite dissimilarity in the world of man, animal, bird, and fish. God has placed human beings above all the other creaturely categories that Paul has listed here in descending order. May we not expect, then, that God is able to give both men and women transformed and glorified bodies? Did he not appoint Adam to be the head of his creation? And did he not crown him with glory and honor? All these rhetorical questions deserve a positive reply.

40. And there are heavenly bodies and earthly bodies. But the glory of the heavenly bodies is one and the glory of the earthly bodies is another. 41. The glory of the sun is one, the glory of the moon another, and the glory of the stars another. For star differs from star in glory.

In this third analogy, Paul discerns the heavenly luminaries, the sun, moon, and stars. Comparing these heavenly spheres with the creatures that inhabit the earth, he observes tremendous differences. The first sentence in his text is factual and self-evident: "And there are heavenly bodies and earthly bodies." It contrasts the magnitude of heavenly objects and the minuscule size of earthly things.

Some scholars reject this interpretation in favor of a literal translation of the word *body* and refer it only to physical substances of flesh and blood. But in Greek, as in English, the word can refer to objects including water, snow, and hail. The Greeks even called the world a body, so that the use of this term is not at all out of place when it alludes to the celestial bodies.[102]

The context of verses 40 and 41 demonstrates that Paul is talking about celestial spheres and not about angelic bodies that are invisible to the human eye. The point of this analogy is not the magnitude or minuteness of certain objects but the splendor each one exhibits. In translation, the expression *glory* occurs six times (five times in the Greek text).

---

102. Eduard Schweizer, *TDNT*, vol. 7, pp. 1035–41.

The next line in verse 40 is also factual: "But the glory of the heavenly bodies is one and the glory of the earthly bodies is another." The brilliance of the celestial luminaries is awe-inspiring, yet the majesty of the mountains and the forests cannot be underestimated. Each has a luster of its own.

Similarly, the intense radiance of the sun cannot be compared with the soft glow of the moon's reflected light. As the one planet or star differs from another in heavenly brilliance and magnitude, none is without significance. God created all of them with various degrees of grandeur. There is not one of them alike, for each radiates or reflects its own glow. In conclusion, we ask: If God has encircled the celestial luminaries with indescribable glory, will he not be able to clothe human beings with transformed and glorified bodies? To ask the question is to answer it.

Greek Words, Phrases, and Constructions in 15:39–41

Verse 39

οὐ πᾶσα σάρξ—the negative particle οὐ may negate either the second part of the clause ("all flesh is not the same") or only the adjective πᾶσα (not all). The first choice can be translated, "Not every kind of flesh is the same."

κτηνῶν . . . πτηνῶν—Paul resorts to alliteration. The first noun derives from the verb κτάομαι (I acquire) and signifies livestock, not wild animals. The second word is a substantivized adjective πτηνός (feathered, winged) that serves as a synonym of πετεινόν (bird).

Verses 40–41

καὶ σώματα—the verb ἐστίν must be supplied: "There are bodies."

ἑτέρα μέν . . . ἑτέρα δέ—the adjectives with the particles are used to express contrast: "the one . . . the other." The same is true for the combination ἄλλη μέν . . . ἄλλη δέ (v. 39), which denotes the concept *different*.[103]

ἀστέρος—"star"; the genitive case is governed by the verb διάφερει (differs).

---

c. Sown and Raised
15:42–44a

42. Thus is also the resurrection of the dead. It is sown in corruption, it is raised in incorruption. 43. It is sown in dishonor, it is raised in glory. It is sown in weakness, it is raised in power. 44a. It is sown a physical body, it is raised a spiritual body.

a. *Text.* We have made a paragraph division in the middle of verse 44; the second part of this verse forms the introductory sentence to the succeeding section. Other translations have a break at the end of that verse.[104]

---

103. Robertson, *Grammar*, pp. 748–49.
104. One translation makes verse 44b part of verse 45 (NAB).

After the first sentence in verse 42, Paul composes four lines of recurring verbs and contrasting nouns. Placed in parallel columns, we note that the first three lines feature the preposition *in*. The last line repeats the noun *body* but qualifies it with the adjectives *physical* and *spiritual* respectively. The nouns in the first three lines in the first column reflect a descending order. The nouns of these lines in the second column reveal an ascending order.

It is sown in corruption,	it is raised in incorruption.
It is sown in dishonor,	it is raised in glory.
It is sown in weakness,	it is raised in power.
It is sown a physical body,	it is raised a spiritual body.

b. *Explanation.* "Thus is also the resurrection of the dead." This sentence functions as a bridge between the preceding and succeeding verses. With the word *thus*, the sentence is a comparison, yet this comparison should not be pushed to the limit. In general, the first three lines of verses 42b–43 are a further explication of the seed that is sown and the plant that arises from it (vv. 36–38). The last line (v. 44a) relates to the picture of earthly and heavenly bodies (vv. 40–41).

"It is sown in corruption, it is raised in incorruption." Paul writes that the whole creation has been subjected to futility. Because of man's sin and God's subsequent curse it is in bondage of decay (refer to Rom. 8:19–21). This world tainted by corruption will not be annihilated at the consummation but renewed. Then it will be restored in incorruption. In this life, the physical bodies of believers endure the ravages of corruption, but at the resurrection these bodies will be raised in incorruption (see vv. 50–53). The dissolution of the human body when committed to the grave is the ultimate humiliation for humans who were crowned with glory and honor to rule God's creation (Ps. 8:5b; Heb. 2:7b, 9). They will receive that exalted rank again when they are raised to newness of life. Paul writes that Christ Jesus will transform our humiliated bodies to conform them to his glorious body (Phil. 3:21).[105]

"It is sown in dishonor, it is raised in glory." Although the people who attend funeral services pay due respect to the dead, the fact remains that death robs a person of all dignity. At burial we commit a lifeless body to the dust of the earth. Burials are vivid and constant reminders of the curse of death God pronounced upon Adam and Eve and their descendants: "You return to the ground, since from it you were taken; for dust you are and to dust you will return" (Gen. 3:19). But through Jesus' resurrection death has been conquered, for he lives and we shall live with him.

We still face the effect of death, even though we know that its power has been abrogated. Our bodies will return to dust but at the end of time will rise from the dead. The resurrection of the dead, then, is similar to a disintegrating seed that

---

105. Compare Calvin, *I Corinthians*, p. 337.

gives life to a plant. But note that in the act of sowing, burial of the seed precedes its death. When humans die, death precedes burial.[106]

What is meant by the word *sown?* The resemblance of a seed to a body is striking. A seed has life, but when sown loses its life to give birth to a plant. A believer in Christ has received eternal life already in this present age (see John 17:3; I John 5:11–13). When death occurs and the body descends into the grave, the principle of eternal life remains valid. By retaining the correlation of seed and body, we assert that burial is a figurative sowing in anticipation of the future harvest at the time of the resurrection. The promise stands that we shall receive glorified bodies reunited with glorified souls (v. 49; Rom. 8:29; Col. 3:4). Thus the fullness of eternal life comes when the body is renewed and reunited with the soul in glory.

"It is sown in weakness, it is raised in power." When death separates the soul from the body, the remains are completely powerless. The corpse is a mere shell of the departed soul. But when the body comes back to life in glory and is reunited with the soul, it demonstrates power that is unimaginable.

"It is sown a physical body, it is raised a spiritual body." This line differs from the preceding three lines; it contrasts the physical and spiritual aspects of the body. In a sense, the line is a summary statement of the preceding verse and an introduction to the next paragraph.

The contrast of the physical body with the spiritual body is profound, for it alludes to the changed and glorified body of Jesus. While on earth, Jesus was bound by time and space. True, he performed miracles including walking on water, but his physical body was subject to human weaknesses (Heb. 4:15). He needed food, drink, and sleep; he suffered indescribable verbal and physical abuse; his body succumbed to death and was placed in a tomb. But when he arose from the grave, his body had changed and was no longer limited by the laws of time and space. Locked doors did not prevent Jesus from entering the room where the disciples were staying in Jerusalem (John 20:19, 26). During ten appearances he was with his followers for short periods. But Scripture fails to reveal where Jesus was the rest of the time before his ascension. After his death, his earthly citizenship had terminated and he had become a heavenly inhabitant (Phil. 3:20).

The disciples recognized Jesus' glorified body; therefore we know that he indeed has his own physical body now in heaven. We, too, will have our own bodies at the time of the resurrection. Paul identifies the renewed body as spiritual, which means that it is not immaterial but assumes a different dimension.

Our resurrected body, says Paul, will be spiritual. But what does he convey with the word *spiritual?* He intimates that our physical bodies are guided by our souls, and he describes our bodies raised from the dead as being completely Spirit-filled and Spirit-governed. Granted that our physical bodies serve us in this present life, they need spiritual characteristics for the coming age. The resurrect-

---

106. Consult Robertson and Plummer, *First Corinthians*, p. 380.

ed body will be completely filled with the Spirit of glory. This glorified body is not immaterial but rather has spiritual aspects that lift it to a supernatural level.[107]

Conclusively, in verse 44a we discover a distinct emphasis on the continuity of the body in this life and the hereafter. But there is also a measure of discontinuity in view of the spiritual transformation of the body when the body is raised from the dead.

Greek Words, Phrases, and Constructions in 15:44a

ψυχικόν—an adjective from the noun ψυχή (soul, life) that because of its -ικόν ending denotes appearance and characteristics. It describes "the life of the natural world and whatever belongs to it, in contrast to the supernatural world, which is characterized by πνεῦμα (spirit)."[108] Notice that Paul deliberately chooses this adjective instead of φυσικός (natural, in accordance with nature) to relate it to the noun ψυχή (soul) in the next verse (v. 45).

πνευματικόν—the physical body is contrasted to the spiritual body; the first one has natural qualities and the second has supernatural characteristics.

---

5. Physical and Spiritual Bodies
15:44b–49

44b. If there is a physical body, there is also a spiritual body. 45. Thus also it is written,

The first man Adam became a living being,
the last Adam became a life-giving spirit.

In the second half of verse 44, Paul repeats the nouns in the first half. The sentence structure of the second part differs, for it has an introduction, a conditional sentence that expresses a simple fact. Paul states the obvious truth that every one of us has a physical body. Taking this simple fact, he asserts that we also have a spiritual body.

When God created Adam and Eve, they had sinless physical bodies. After the fall into sin, their bodies were not fit for the Holy Spirit to fill them permanently. When Christ redeems his people, their bodies become temples of the Spirit (6:19). But sin grieves the Spirit of God and even extinguishes the Spirit's fire (Eph. 4:30; I Thess. 5:19). Also, the physical body is marred by corruption, dishonor, and weakness. But the spiritual body is delivered from and characterized by incorruption, glory, and power (see vv. 42, 43).[109] With the adjective *spiritual,*

---

107. From the numerous studies on this subject, I refer to John A. Schep, *The Nature of the Resurrection Body* (Grand Rapids: Eerdmans, 1964), pp. 220–27; Richard A. Muller, *ISBE*, vol. 4, pp. 145–50; Harris, *Raised Immortal,* pp. 118–19, 133; Harris, *From Grave to Glory,* pp. 191–98; Gaffin, *Centrality of the Resurrection,* pp. 68–70; Vos, *Pauline Eschatology,* pp. 183–85.

108. Bauer, p. 894.

109. Vos, *Pauline Eschatology,* pp. 166–67.

Paul does not convey the thought of an ethereal or an immaterial body; rather he intimates that the Holy Spirit is thoroughly filling and governing this glorified body.

After writing that a person has a physical and a spiritual body, Paul proves his teaching from the Scriptures of the Old Testament. He follows Jesus' example of instructing the people from the Word of God (compare Luke 24:25–27, 44). The formula Paul employs differs from the usual "as it is written" (see, e.g., 10:7). Using a slightly different model, he compares what he has said with the revealed Word.

a. "Thus also it is written, 'The first man Adam became a living being.'" The quotation is from the account of God creating Adam from the dust of the earth: "and the man became a living being" (Gen. 2:7). Paul expands this text by adding the adjective *first* and the name *Adam*. In fact, he gives an interpretation and an application of this particular text by stating the parallel of Adam and Christ.[110] He compares Adam to Christ with the use of a hermeneutical rule that is commonly employed by the Jewish writers of the New Testament; it is the rule of going from the lesser to the greater (for a striking example, see Heb. 9:13–14).

In an earlier passage (vv. 21–22), Paul already had paralleled Adam and Christ; now he continues the analogy. Adam is the first human who through God's creative power became a living being, literally, a living soul. Adam is the head of the human race. Made in the image of God, Adam passed on to his offspring both physical qualities and moral attributes. But Adam did not receive the gift of immortality, because God wanted to test him in a probationary period (Gen. 2:17). Adam failed and through him sin entered the world and with sin came death (Rom. 5:12). Angels drove Adam from the Garden of Eden to prevent him from eating the fruit of the tree of life and living forever (Gen. 3:22–24). However, that which was lacking in Adam is now perfected in Christ. By conquering death, the second Adam achieved immortality.

b. "The last Adam became a life-giving spirit." For this clause that parallels the preceding one, Paul is unable to turn to the Old Testament Scriptures. He has to rely on his insight into Christ's redemptive work and formulate the correct parallel. He calls Christ the last Adam as a reflection on a parallel to and contrast with the first Adam. By writing the word *last*, Paul notes that Christ is the complete fulfillment of the first Adam.

The verb associated with both Adam and Christ is "became." That is, when God created Adam, he became a living being; and when Christ entered the world in human form, he became the one through whom God gives eternal life to every believer (John 3:16; 17:3; I John 4:11–12). Christ suffered death, but conquered it. When he arose from the grave, he received the authority to grant the gift of immortality to his people.

---

110. Refer to James D. G. Dunn, "I Corinthians 15:45—last Adam, life-giving spirit," in *Christ and Spirit in the New Testament*, ed. Barnabas Lindars and Stephen S. Smalley (Cambridge: Cambridge University Press, 1973), p. 130.

The clause "the last Adam became a life-giving spirit" refers to Christ's resurrection from the dead. When he defeated death, he obtained a transformed human body that is spiritual. When he rose from the dead, the Holy Spirit became the Spirit of Christ (see II Cor. 3:17). And the Spirit granted Christ the power to give life to his followers and to make their physical bodies like his own.[111] Before his death, Jesus raised people from the dead (the daughter of Jairus, the young man of Nain, and Lazarus), but their physical bodies remained mortal. After his resurrection, immortality for his people became a certainty.

Although Christ grants us eternal life now only in principle, immortality will be fully realized in body and soul at the time of the consummation. Although death overshadows the present era, the dawn of eternal life announces the new day of the future.[112]

The contrast in verse 45 is between Adam's soul and Christ's spirit. This does not mean that Adam did not have a spirit; that Christ lacked a soul; or that a person consists of body, soul, and spirit. These questions are irrelevant to Paul's discussion. Paul stresses the fact that Christ through the Holy Spirit gives life. In another context he writes,

And if the Spirit of him who raised Jesus from the dead is living in you, he who raised Christ from the dead will also give life to your mortal bodies through his Spirit, who lives in you. [Rom. 8:11]

Jesus testifies that the Spirit gives life to his people (John 6:63; compare 7:37–39). The emphasis in the current text is not on quickening a person's spiritual life but on resurrecting the physical body. Just as Jesus' body was transformed at his resurrection, so his followers will experience a physical transformation at Christ's return and receive from him a body that is completely controlled by the Holy Spirit. All the believers will have a spiritual body that is akin to the body of Christ (Phil. 3:20–21).

46. However, the spiritual is not first but the physical, then the spiritual.

After Paul's reference to the Scriptures, he returns to the wording of verse 44, where he used the word *body*. Now he omits the word but implies it. This means that verse 45 with its quotation from an Old Testament Scripture passage should be understood as a parenthetical comment.

The adversative *however* is rendered by some translators as *observe* in the imperative.[113] In other words, Paul is calling attention to the sequence in which God brought into being the physical and spiritual bodies. He is not saying that Adam and Christ represent two timeless modes of existence that are opposed to each other. Rather, Paul considers the first and the last Adam in terms of Christ redeeming the believing members of Adam's race in the course of history. We ob-

---

111. Refer to II Cor. 4:14; Col. 1:18; Rev. 1:5.
112. Compare Vorster, "Resurrection Faith," p. 303.
113. See NEB, REB, *Cassirer*.

serve, therefore, that believers will bear the image of Christ, just as they bear the image of Adam (see v. 49).[114] Both Adam and Christ are representative heads: Adam is the head of the human race, and Christ is the head of his redeemed people. Believers receive their physical body through Adam and their spiritual bodies through their resurrected Lord and Savior.

Why does Paul stress the sequence of physical and spiritual bodies? Some scholars contend that he opposed the teaching of his countryman Philo, who wrote that God first created the ideal heavenly man (Gen. 1:26) and then made the physical man from the dust of the earth (Gen. 2:7).[115] Others dispute this suggestion and think that Paul is opposing those Corinthians who denied Paul's resurrection teaching (v. 12) by spiritualizing it.[116] We agree. By mentioning the physical and spiritual bodies of Adam and Christ, Paul presents the record in historical perspective.

47. The first man was from the dust of the earth, the second man from heaven.

Once again Paul alludes to the creation record (Gen. 2:7b); to be precise, to God creating Adam from the dust of the earth (Gen. 2:7a). Paul presents a brief verse in which he contrasts Adam, who came from the dust of the earth, with Christ, who came from heaven. This verse follows the wording of the Old Testament text: "The LORD God formed the man from the dust of the ground" (Gen. 2:7a). But notice that Paul uses the Greek adjective *choikos* (made of the earth or dust, earthy) to describe Adam.[117] For the creation of Adam, God gathered particles of dust from the earth. Adam did not descend from a primate transformed into a human; he is God's unique creation.

The parallel structure in this verse is decidedly incomplete, for the second half lacks a counterpart to the phrase *made from the dust.* Whereas Adam is made of dust from the earth, Christ is from heaven. Some Greek manuscripts have added the words *the Lord* to the text: "and the second man is the Lord from heaven" (KJV, NKJV). Another early manuscript (P[46]) has the reading "the second man is spiritual from heaven." The shorter reading is preferred, however, in view of the usual tendency of ancient scribes to clarify the text by adding a word or two.

Paul wants to stress the contrast of origins between Adam and Christ: the one is from the earth while the other is from heaven. He is not referring to the preexisting Christ whose creational work is recorded elsewhere (John 1:1; Col. 1:15–18; Heb. 1:2). No, he has in mind Jesus coming from heaven to earth and assuming flesh and blood to share in our humanity (Heb. 2:14). We gave Jesus a physical body, so to speak, and from him we receive glorification.

Adam came from the dust upward and Christ came from heavenly glory downward (compare Phil. 2:6–8). When Jesus was conceived and born, he, like all other descendants of Adam, had a human body. In fact, his body was mortal.

---

114. Ridderbos, *Paul,* p. 543.

115. Philo *Opif. Mundi* 134; *Leg. alleg.* 1.31.

116. Consult Fee, *First Corinthians,* p. 791.

117. Bauer, p. 883.

And when Adam is raised on the day of resurrection, he with all other believers will receive a glorified body like that of Jesus.

However, Paul is not merely contrasting the body of Adam with the body of Jesus. He writes the word *man* for both Adam and Jesus. That expression encompasses the total humanness of these two persons as they individually represent their own respective physical and spiritual offspring: Adam represents the human race and Christ the redeemed.

48. As was the one made of dust, so also are those that are dust; and as is the one heavenly, so also are those that are heavenly.

Paul stresses the fact that Adam and all his descendants have their origin in the dust of the earth. All of us are of this earth and belong to it. Adam is the pattern and his offspring are copies. We do not have to ask about the color of the father of the human race, for that question is irrelevant. The first part of this verse conveys only the origin of the entire human race: we are of the earth, earthy.

The contrast lies in the second half of this verse (compare John 3:13, 31). Christ Jesus has his origin in heaven, and he confers on all his people heavenly glory. It is true that God's people in this life already have received in principle this heavenly glory (II Cor. 3:18). They already enjoy a foretaste by means of their spiritual rebirth; because of the indwelling power of the Holy Spirit and God's enlightening revelation, they reflect divine glory in their daily lives. But this is not the point of the text. This verse teaches that at the resurrection all the redeemed will fully partake of the heavenly glory that belongs to Christ.

49. And as we bear the image of the one made of dust, so we shall bear the image of the one who is heavenly.

Paul is not quite finished with his discourse on the parallel between Adam and Christ; with the conjunction *and* he links the content of this verse to the preceding context. The key word in this passage is *image*, which occurs twice. Throughout the history of the human race, all Adam's descendants have borne and continue to bear his image. To illustrate, Seth was born when Adam had lived 130 years; he was born in Adam's likeness and image (Gen. 5:3). That image, says Paul, belongs to a human being made of dust particles; the word choice underscores the frailty that he and every one of his offspring possess.

Paul repeats the word *image* in the second line of this verse: "we shall bear the image of the one who is heavenly." He is not alluding to the preexistent Christ but to the exalted Lord, who ascended to heaven in his glorified body. Through his resurrection, Christ gives us the promise that we shall bear his likeness (Phil. 3:21), his image, to which we shall be conformed "not only as a likeness in appearance or shape, but in mode of existence" (see Rom. 8:29).[118]

Usually children not only bear the external image of their parents but also they reveal the talents, traits, and characteristics of their father or mother. We as God's children will bear the image of his Son in the fullest sense of the word. We

118. Ridderbos, *Paul*, p. 545.

shall be like him in body and soul with this exception: Jesus will have the preeminence among his people (Col. 1:18).

The tense of the verb *to bear* is the future and not the present. Therefore, it points to the impending resurrection of the body. Paul is not exhorting his readers to lead holy lives in conformity to the pattern Christ has set. Throughout this passage Paul has presented instruction; he has not exhorted his readers. Hence, the context demands not an exhortation ("let us bear the image") but doctrine ("we shall bear the image").[119]

Doctrinal Considerations in 15:44–49

Jesus Christ as the second Adam partook of the humanity that we have inherited from the first Adam. Jesus' physical body was subject to death, but was raised from the dead in glorified form. After forty days he ascended to heaven in human form and took his place at the right hand of God the Father.

At times Christians on their deathbed reveal a glimpse of heaven to their loved ones. Some even mention that they see Jesus welcoming them; they describe Jesus as a man whose hands show the nail marks he received on the cross. This should not be a surprise; the Scriptures report that Stephen looked up to heaven and "saw the glory of God, and Jesus standing at the right hand of God" (Acts 7:55). Stephen identified Jesus as the Son of Man, which in itself is unusual. Throughout the New Testament, no one calls Jesus by that name; the Evangelists note that only Jesus uses it to refer to himself. But Stephen notes that Jesus in the form of a man fulfilled the messianic prophecies and after completing his earthly mission returned in human form to heaven. Jesus sits or stands physically next to God the Father. The fact that his body is in heaven is our assurance that we too shall be like him and with him eternally.

Greek Words, Phrases, and Constructions in 15:45–49

Verse 45

εἰς—the preposition follows the verb ἐγένετο (he became) and signifies *"resulting in"* a living being (compare Rom. 10:10).[120]

ἔσχατος—the "last," which is also Jesus' self-designation when he appeared to John on the island of Patmos (Rev. 1:17; 2:8; 22:13). Here it is the equivalent of δεύτερος (second, v. 47). There are no more.

Verses 47–48

ἐκ γῆς—"from the earth." The specific quality of the earth is contrasted with heavenly origin, ἐξ οὐρανοῦ (from heaven).

---

119. Translators and commentators prefer the future tense to the aorist subjunctive. Among the exceptions are G. G. Findlay, *St. Paul's First Epistle to the Corinthians*, in vol. 3 of *The Expositor's Greek Testament*, ed. W. Robertson Nicoll, 5 vols. (1910; reprint ed., Grand Rapids: Eerdmans, 1961), p. 939, and Fee, *First Corinthians*, p. 795.

120. Moule, *Idiom-Book*, pp. 70, 204.

χοϊκός—this is an adjective derived from the noun χοῦς (dust); the ending -ικος indicates having the characteristics of dust. The adjective appears four times in three verses (vv. 47, 48 [twice], and 49). Paul stresses the earthy origin of the human race.

οἷος . . . τοιοῦτος—a comparison in which the first correlative means "of what sort" and the second denotes quality, "of such a kind, such as this."[121]

Verse 49

ἐφορέσαμεν—the aorist of the verb φορέω (I bear; I wear) is translated in the perfect tense. Even though the better manuscripts support the aorist subjunctive φορέσωμεν (let us bear), the context calls not for the hortatory subjunctive but for the future indicative. And last, some translations have the verb *to wear* (GNB, NEB, REB, *Cassirer*) but the verb *to bear* is preferred.

---

6. Immortality and Victory
15:50–57

This lengthy chapter is finally coming to a conclusion. Paul begins a new paragraph to relate how believers will receive their new spiritual bodies. His finale is one of triumph because with it Paul fully answers the question raised by his opponent, "How are the dead raised? And with what kind of body do they come?" (v. 35). He teaches that our mortal bodies will be not revived but transformed to live imperishably and eternally. Jesus Christ is the victor over sin and death, and we share that victory with him.

a. Transformation
15:50–53

50. But this I say, brothers, that flesh and blood cannot inherit the kingdom of God, neither shall corruption inherit incorruption.

a. "But this I say, brothers." The first person singular *I* and the vocative *brothers*, which as elsewhere includes the sisters, are personal. The clause itself differs only in stress from an identical address (7:29). Paul speaks assertively. He is intent on proceeding from an earlier section in which he explained what our bodies are and will be (vv. 42–49) to a discussion about how our bodies will be transformed. And with the address *brothers* he speaks pastorally to stimulate his readers' interest in the formation of their future bodies.

b. "That flesh and blood cannot inherit the kingdom of God." Paul uses the expression *flesh and blood* to designate the corruptible body of everyone who is human. He teaches that the physical part of man must perish to be renewed and transformed into a glorified body.[122] The expression as such is a figure of speech for the physical body. It is a Semitic phrase that occurs repeatedly in rabbinic sources to denote the utter frailty and mortality of a human being. As such it is

---

121. Bauer, pp. 562, 821.
122. Compare Hans Seebass, *NIDNTT*, vol. 1, p. 675; Eduard Schweizer, *TDNT*, vol. 7, p. 129. Consult also Sider, "Resurrection Body," pp. 428–39.

considered to be singular; that is, it is followed in the Greek by a verb in the singular. Moreover, the Greek text of the Old Testament (the Septuagint) and the New Testament frequently have either "flesh and blood" or the reverse order.[123]

What is the meaning of the phrase *flesh and blood* in connection with inheriting God's kingdom? If we should understand the phrase literally, Paul would be saying that no human inherits the kingdom. But this is not the case, for believers have the promise that they are heirs and co-heirs with Christ (Rom. 8:17). Paul is saying that the mortal body in its existing state cannot enter God's presence. Only at the transformation, when God fulfills his promise to all the saints, will the redeemed inherit the kingdom of God. The concept *inherit*, then, is synonymous with the resurrection of the dead.

This is the last time Paul mentions the phrase *kingdom of God* in this epistle. (Earlier Paul had written that the ungodly will not inherit the kingdom of God; he mentioned, among others, sexually immoral people, thieves, slanderers, and swindlers [6:9–10].) The phrase relates to the final stage in which God's kingdom is set free from powers that now reign. These powers must all submit to Jesus Christ, who at the time of the consummation delivers the kingdom to God the Father (v. 24).

c. "Neither shall corruption inherit incorruption." The second half of verse 50 parallels the first part. We observe that Paul repeats parts of his earlier statement, "[The body] is sown in corruption, it is raised in incorruption" (v. 42). That which is sinful and corrupt cannot enter the presence of God and obtain that which is incorrupt. When that which is corrupt has been changed to a state of incorruption, we can speak of laying claim to the inheritance God offers to us. If we understand the two lines in this verse as a synonymous parallel, then we see that the terms *flesh and blood* and *corrupt* are identical in meaning.[124] And the expressions *kingdom of God* and *incorruption* point to the end of time when Christ delivers to God the kingdom inhabited by citizens who share his incorruption (see vv. 24–28).

51. Look, I tell you a mystery: we shall not all fall asleep, but all of us shall be changed 52. in a moment, in the twinkling of an eye, at the last trumpet. For the trumpet shall sound, and the dead shall be raised incorruptible and we shall be changed.

a. "Look, I tell you a mystery." The writers of the New Testament in the Gospels, Acts, Epistles, and Revelation write the expression *look* repeatedly as an idiom of Semitic speech. But surprisingly, in his epistles Paul only occasionally uses the word; indeed, it appears once in this epistle.[125] He answers an anticipated

---

123. See the Greek text of Sir. 14:18; 17:31; Matt. 16:17; I Cor. 15:50; Gal. 1:16; Eph. 6:12; Heb. 2:14. Refer to Jeremias, "'Flesh and Blood,'" pp. 151–59. And see the objections raised by Ridderbos, *Paul*, p. 546.

124. Refer to John Gillman, "Transformation in 1 Cor 15, 50–53," *EphThL* 58 (1982): 309–33; Kôshi Usami, "'How are the dead raised?' (1 Cor. 15, 35–58)," *Bib* 57 (1976): 489–90; Günther Harder, *TDNT*, vol. 9, pp. 103–5.

125. For the other Pauline epistles see the Greek of II Cor. 5:17; 6:2, 9; 7:11; 12:14; Gal. 1:20.

question: How will the believer be changed to inherit God's kingdom? Thus he tells his readers a mystery, which is a revelation from God through Paul about the future transformation of the believers.[126] In a similar context about the end times, Paul alludes to this revelation as a word of the Lord (I Thess. 4:15).

b. "We shall not all fall asleep, but all of us shall be changed." Paul speaks euphemistically about death when he writes "fall asleep" (see vv. 6, 18, 20). He means to say that some believers will not have to face death; not everyone will die a physical death. Those who live to the end will be changed at Christ's return and so will all those who have died in the Lord.

The language in this second part of verse 51 includes Paul himself, yet no one should make the text say more than it intends to reveal. Instead, the pronoun *we* should be understood as a general remark to include all believers. Among them are those who will physically see the return of Christ on the clouds of heaven (I Thess. 4:15–17). Paul reveals that "all of us shall be changed," including those who are alive at Christ's coming. The change he has in mind is the complete alteration of the believer's physical state, an alteration that will take place in the twinkling of an eye.

c. "In a moment, in the twinkling of an eye, at the last trumpet." The Greek term Paul uses for "moment" is *atomos,* from which we have the derivative *atom.* The word refers to something so small that it cannot be divided any more. Here *atomos* applies to time. The phrase *in the twinkling of an eye* is appositional; it represents a momentary wink of the eyelid. (Our equivalent is "in a split second," which commonly signifies the shortest possible moment.) In such a brief moment the miracle of transformation will occur both for those who rise from the dead and for those who are alive.[127]

Paul indicates that the last trumpet will sound to announce the occurrence of the resurrection. This trumpet blast is the final one in the history of redemption. Other New Testament passages that speak of Christ's return have the wording *a loud trumpet call* (Matt. 24:31) and *the trumpet call of God* (I Thess. 4:16). The Old and New Testaments, the Apocrypha, and rabbinic writings refer to the blowing of the trumpet to announce imminent divine revelation, the judgment day, and the resurrection.[128]

d. "For the trumpet shall sound, and the dead shall be raised incorruptible and we shall be changed." Within the shortest time possible, the general resurrection and transformation will take place. When the trumpet blast sounds, not a single one of God's people will be neglected. The dead will rise in an incorruptible state, and those who are alive at Christ's coming will be transformed.

---

126. Compare the usage of "mystery" in 2:7; 4:1; 13:2; 14:2.

127. G. M. M. Pelser, "Resurrection and eschatology in Paul's letters," *Neotest* 20 (1986): 37–46; Donald Guthrie, "Transformation and the Parousia," *VoxEv* 14 (1984): 39–51.

128. See, e.g., Exod. 19:16; Rev. 4:1; 8:2–9:14; II Esd. 6:23, and rabbinic references in SB, vol. 3, p. 481; Gerhard Friedrich, *TDNT,* vol. 7, p. 84.

Paul is not at all restrictive when he writes "we shall be changed," for earlier he wrote the adjective *all* in the clause "all of us shall be changed" (v. 51).[129] Thus once again he uses the personal pronoun *we* in a broader sense. He includes himself with all the believers, those in their graves and those who are living.

In typical Semitic style, Paul writes the passive voice without stating who the agent is at the time of the resurrection. He avoids using God's name, yet God himself is the agent who will raise the dead and transform instantaneously all those who are alive at Christ's coming.

Paul is not saying that Christ's return will happen during his lifetime. Like every one of us, Paul looked forward eagerly to the end. From God's revelation we learn that although Christ's coming is imminent, no one except God the Father knows the day or hour of this event (Matt. 24:36). Indeed Jesus told the apostles that it was not for them to know the times and seasons the Father has determined (Acts 1:7). Paul is not saying anything definite about Christ's return. Yet he, like any of us today, would express the desire to be alive when that joyous occasion comes.[130]

53. For this corruptible must put on incorruption and this mortal must put on immortality.

The verse has two parallel parts that mutually support each other:

this corruptible	and this mortal
must put on	must put on
incorruption	immortality

Note, first, the two demonstrative pronouns *this* that specify the corruptible and mortal frame of man. Next, the Greek word *phtharton* means that which is subject to decay or destruction applied to mortal man.[131] Third, the verb *must* denotes divine necessity and is auxiliary to the main verb *put on*. In the Greek, it can be understood in the passive voice and implies that God is the agent. In other words, individual believers must be clothed by God with incorruption and immortality. They cannot dress themselves with these qualities but must wait for God to do this for them. And last, the verb *to put on* refers figuratively to being clothed (compare II Cor. 5:4).

This text conveys not only the message of transformation of believers but also a measure of discontinuity with the past. The physical existence of past and present believers is characterized by corruption and mortality. Yet continuity is also the clear message of this verse, because it is the earthly body that will be clothed with incorruption and immortality.[132]

---

129. Consult A. C. Perriman, "Paul and the Parousia: 1 Corinthians 15.50–57 and 2 Corinthians 5.1–5," *NTS* 35 (1989): 512–21; John Gillman, "A Thematic Comparison: 1 Cor 15:50–57 and 2 Cor 5:1–5," *JBL* 107 (1988): 439–54.

130. Compare R. C. H. Lenski, *The Interpretation of St. Paul's First and Second Epistle to the Corinthians* (1935; Columbus: Wartburg, 1946), p. 737.

131. Bauer, p. 857.

132. Consult Gillman, "Transformation," pp. 331–32.

Greek Words, Phrases, and Constructions in 15:50–53

Verses 50–51

δύναται—the singular verb has a compound subject, "flesh and blood." But Paul seems to have in mind only the first subject.[133]

πάντες οὐ κοιμηθησόμεθα—the negative precedes the verb, but it negates the adjective *all*. Taken literally, this would mean that Paul would not die but see Christ's return. But because Paul died, scribes transferred the negative to the next clause: "We shall all fall asleep, but not all of us shall be changed." Still other texts omit the negative in both clauses. These are attempts to modify the text. The preferred reading is the one adopted by most translators.

Verses 52–53

ῥιπῇ—the traditional (and correct) reading of the text is "in the twinkling [of an eye]" instead of ῥοπῇ (in a moment).[134]

τοῦτο—note the emphatic position of the demonstrative pronoun that occurs four times in this and the next verse.

---

b. Celebration
15:54–57

54. But when this corruptible has put on incorruption and this mortal has put on immortality, then the saying that is written will be realized:

> **Death is swallowed up in victory.**
> **55. Where, O death, is your victory?**
> **Where, O death, is your sting?**

Verse 54a is a continuation and a verbal repetition of verse 53. By adding two time references, *when* and *then*, and changing the tense of the verb *to put on* to the past, Paul speaks as if a future event has already occurred. To be precise, the fulfillment of Paul's words took place when Jesus rose from the dead. And with that resurrection, all believers know that also they will rise from the grave. This text is a vivid illustration of the constant tension in the New Testament of the *now* and the *not yet*. Through Jesus Christ, we acknowledge the reality of the resurrection, and through his promise to us we shall appropriate it at the consummation.

For the last time in this epistle, Paul quotes prophetic passages from the Old Testament Scriptures (Isa. 25:8; Hos. 13:14). He puts the fulfillment of the first prophecy in the future with these introductory words, "Then the saying that is written will be realized." He quotes from the prophecy of Isaiah, but follows neither the Hebrew text nor the Septuagint. This is the translation of the Hebrew Scriptures: "He will swallow up death forever" (Isa. 25:8). And the Greek translation reads, "Death forcefully has swallowed [them] up." According to the He-

---

133. Robertson, *Grammar*, p. 405.

134. G. Zuntz, *The Text of the Epistles: A Disquisition upon the Corpus Paulinum* (London: Oxford University Press, 1953), pp. 37–39.

brew text, the subject is God and death the object. But notice that Paul makes death the subject with the verb *to swallow up* in the passive. He adopts the Semitic style of writing the passive to circumvent the use of the divine name; he implies that God has eliminated death, that is, the power of death (refer to Heb. 2:14). And last, Paul changes the Hebrew translation *forever* to "in victory." His wording accords with readings in other Greek translations of the Hebrew text.[135]

"Death is swallowed up in victory." Looking back at Jesus' triumph over death and forward to the resurrection of all believers, Paul bursts out in jubilation. He understands the demise of life's mortal enemy: death. Even though death continues to wield power as Christ's last enemy (v. 26), Paul knows that God will destroy it. Death's days are numbered.

Paul taunts death and asks mockingly: "Where, O death, is your victory? Where, O death, is your sting?" He borrows this second prophecy from Hosea, who writes that God will ransom the children of Israel from the grave and will deliver them from death. The prophet queries, "Where, O death, are your plagues? Where, O grave, is your destruction?" (Hos. 13:14). The Greek translation reads: "Where, O death, is your penalty? Where, O grave, is your sting?" Paul has changed the word *penalty* into "victory" to suit the flow of his presentation. And in the second question he has substituted the word *death* for "grave," which in the Septuagint is Hades. But Paul never uses Hades in all his epistles. Perhaps he feared being misunderstood by those Greek readers who were acquainted with ancient mythology in which Hades was a Greek god and the underworld was called "the house of Hades." This word, then, could not be part of Paul's vocabulary.[136]

A last comment on this verse. When Jesus stopped Paul on the way to Damascus, he said that it was hard for Paul to kick against the goads (Acts 26:14). Paul had to cope with the scars of these goads the rest of his life. Now Paul sees that death no longer has a goad and is, in a sense, powerless. Other scholars refer to the word *sting* as that of a scorpion. Both a goad and a sting strike fear into the heart of man. But those who are in Christ do not fear death with its goad or sting, for they know that Jesus indeed has conquered death. Therefore, Paul can boldly say:

56. The sting of death is sin, and the power of sin is the law.

In a single verse Paul expresses the doctrine of sin, the law, and death.[137]

---

135. The translations of Aquila and Theodotion. SB, vol. 3, p. 481; Rodolphe Morissette, "Un midrash sur la Mort (*1 Cor., XV, 54c à 57*)," *RB* 79 (1972): 169. Without vowel pointing, the Hebrew word *nṣḥ* can mean either "forever" or "be victorious."

136. Both the KJV and *Phillips* have "grave"; the NKJV has "Hades." Metzger comments, "The reading *Hades* is . . . an assimilation to the Septuagint." See *Textual Commentary*, p. 570.

137. Some scholars are of the opinion that this verse is a gloss that has been added to the manuscript. They affirm that the apostle could have added the gloss at a later date, but contend that because of its brevity, the verse is out of place in this paragraph. See, e.g., Friedrich Wilhelm Horn, "1 Korinther 15,56—ein exegetischer Stachel," *ZNW* 82 (1991): 88–105.

But there is no proof that Paul could not have written it in this context as a summary of his own theology. He wrote this verse two years before he composed his letter to the Romans, a letter in which he fully explained the relation sin has to the law, and sin and the law to death (e.g., Rom. 6:23; 7:9–11, 13).

What is this sting of death? Paul answers: sin. And what is the power of sin? Paul says: the law. So, what is the relation of sin, the law, and death? Sin is the cause of death, and knowledge of sin comes through the law. In brief, the law has a causative function.[138] It brings to light sin committed against God. It gives sin its power, that without the law is dead (Rom. 7:8). The law, which is good, arouses sinful passions (Rom. 7:5), and as such empowers sin. The law convicts and condemns the sinner to death. Thus the law is an instrument of death because the sinner is unable to fulfill its demands. John Calvin observes, "Death has no other weapon except sin, with which to wound us, since death comes from the wrath of God. But God is angry only with our sins; do away with sin then, and death will not be able to harm us any more. . . . It is the *Law* of God that gives that sting its deadly power."[139]

Is there no hope? Yes, in response to Paul's cry, "Who will rescue me from this body of death," he answers, "Thanks be to God—through Jesus Christ our Lord!" (Rom. 7:24b–25). Paul proclaims the good news that Jesus Christ has fulfilled the law for his people.

57. But thanks be to God, who gives us the victory through our Lord Jesus Christ.

Paul's jubilation is an appropriate climax to his lengthy discourse on the resurrection. In this climax he expresses his gratitude to God for the victory obtained through Jesus Christ. The key word in this verse is the term *victory*, which echoes the Old Testament quotations in the previous verses (vv. 54–55).

What is this victory? Jesus died because of our sins and conquered death for us by rising from the grave. Through his death, he set us free from the bondage of sin and declared us righteous before God. On the basis of his resurrection and glorification, we look forward to being like him. By faith in Christ, we share his victory over Satan, death, hell, and the grave (compare I John 5:4). Conclusively, our risen Lord triumphantly holds the keys of death and Hades (Rev. 1:18).

While serving Christ, Paul repeatedly faced death. Even though he knows that death is still a powerful force on earth, he is absolutely certain that Jesus Christ has conquered death. Hence, he writes "God . . . gives us the victory." Paul uses the present tense; that is, God keeps on giving us the victory in Christ. We may appropriate Jesus' triumph and rejoice in the riches of salvation that are ours.

Paul clearly states that God gives us the victory through our Lord Jesus Christ. He notes first the work that Christ performed to set us free; next, he identifies Jesus as our Lord. We acknowledge him as our Lord and in gratitude serve him without distraction by doing his will. Christ is our victorious Lord and we are his grateful servants.

138. J. A. D. Weima, "The Function of the Law in Relation to Sin: An Evaluation of the View of H. Räisänen," *NovT* 32 (1990): 219–35; Stephen Westerholm, *Israel's Law and the Church's Faith: Paul and His Recent Interpreters* (Grand Rapids: Eerdmans, 1988), p. 99; Frank Thielman, "The Coherence of Paul's View of the Law: The Evidence of First Corinthians," *NTS* 38 (1992): 235–53.
139. Calvin, *I Corinthians*, p. 346.

Greek Words, Phrases, and Constructions in 15:54–57

Verses 54–55

γενήσεται—the future of the verb γίνομαι (I become, am) conveys the meaning *will be realized.*

κατεπόθη—the aorist passive of the compound verb καταπίνω (I drink down, swallow) shows direction.

νῖκος—the neuter noun is a late form of νίκη (victory).

Verses 56–57

Notice that in verse 56 every noun has a definite article. The verb *to be* must be supplied.

τῷ δὲ θεῷ—the adversative is the strong *but* (see v. 20). The definite article and noun are first in the sentence for emphasis.

χάρις—in the present context, the word means "thanks" but has the implied message that we share Christ's victory through grace.

τῷ διδόντι—the present participle describes action that takes place at the same time as that of the implied verb *to be.*

---

7. An Exhortation
15:58

58. So then, my dear brothers, be steadfast, immovable, always abounding in the work of the Lord, knowing that your labor is not in vain in the Lord.

The exhortation has little to do with the immediately preceding verses on the victory the believers share with Jesus Christ. It is an entreaty that arises from the entire chapter if not the whole epistle. The last instructions and final greetings aside, Paul has come to the end of his epistle and now admonishes his readers to do the work of the Lord.

a. "So then, my dear brothers." The first two words introduce a concluding statement. Paul frequently uses this expression in his epistles. For the last time in this letter he addresses the recipients in a personal manner by calling them "dear brothers [and sisters]." At two other places, Paul addresses the readers as "my dear children" (4:14) and "my dear friends" (10:14). Each time he speaks to the Corinthians as a father to his children. He remains the spiritual father of the Corinthians, who through the preaching of the gospel are his offspring (4:15). Paul is their pastor who loves them despite the numerous difficulties in the church.

b. "Be steadfast, immovable." Paul commends the believers for their steadfastness and exhorts them to continue their dedication to the Lord (compare Col. 1:23). Amid the onslaught of diverse teaching in a pagan culture, he urges them to remain firm in the Lord and not to waver. Paul tells the Corinthians to be immovable. This last word is a compound that signifies an inability to move from their spiritual moorings. Paul is not talking about retaining the status quo in the church. He wants the people to grow in their love for the Lord and to communicate this in their deeds.

c. "Always abounding in the work of the Lord." After telling his readers not to be moved in any way, Paul encourages them to excel in the Lord's work. To express constancy and emphasis he adds the word *always* which, in the original, he places last in the clause for emphasis. What is the work of the Lord? The work entails preaching and teaching Christ's gospel, applying the contents of Scripture to our lives, edifying one another, and loving our neighbor as ourselves (compare 16:10). It consists of an earnest desire to keep God's commandments and to do so out of gratitude for our salvation provided through his Son. As his love extends to us without measure, so our selfless deeds are done for him without measure.

d. "Knowing that your labor is not in vain in the Lord." The faithful Corinthians have a sure knowledge that the deeds done out of love and thankfulness to God will not be forgotten (see Heb. 6:10). The word *labor* is often used by Paul in a missionary setting and means working with his own hands for his own support (4:12) "and for activity in the Christian community as a whole."[140] Such labor given freely in service to the Lord is never in vain because the Lord himself blesses his servants (Matt. 19:29).

Summary of Chapter 15

This chapter is doctrinal, lengthy, and conclusive. Paul begins by reminding his readers of the gospel he proclaimed to them. He summarizes its content by mentioning Christ's birth, death, burial, resurrection, and appearances. He notes that he delivered to them this gospel that is in harmony with the Scriptures. He enumerates Jesus' appearances to Peter, the Twelve, the five hundred brothers, James, and Paul himself. Paul does not deem himself worthy to be called an apostle, but he says that by the grace of God he is.

Some Corinthians questioned the doctrine of the resurrection. Paul equates the resurrection of the dead with that of Christ and asserts that if the one is not true, neither is the other. If Christ is not raised, then the preaching of the apostles is useless and so is the faith of the Corinthians. If this is so, then the Corinthians are still in their sin and are objects of pity.

With certainty Paul proclaims the resurrection of Christ. He notes that death came through Adam but life through Christ. He reveals the resurrection in two stages: first Christ, next those who belong to him. Then comes the end, when Christ will deliver the kingdom to God the Father. All his enemies will be destroyed, including death. When the Son has delivered everything to the Father, then he himself is subject to God so that God may be all in all. Paul concludes this part of the chapter by asking questions concerning baptism for the dead and the significance of fighting wild beasts in Ephesus. He calls the readers back to correct thinking; he urges them to stop sinning, and not to be ignorant of God.

---

140. Herbert Fendrich, *EDNT*, vol. 2, p. 307.

With a number of examples taken from the natural world, Paul explains the means and the manner of the resurrection from the dead. He writes about seeds and plants; the flesh of animals, birds, and fish; the splendor of the sun, moon, and stars. He teaches that the dead will rise with the bodies they had on earth, except that they are raised imperishable in glory as spiritual beings. Paul reveals that as Adam passed on his earthly body to his descendants, so Christ is passing on his heavenly body to believers.

Paul declares that at the return of Christ, the transformation of the believers will occur in a flash with the sounding of the last trumpet. Then the dead come back to life and those who are in Christ will be changed. They will be imperishable and immortal. Paul taunts death by quoting from the prophecies of Isaiah and Hosea and expresses thanks to God for the victory through Jesus Christ. He exhorts the readers to be steadfast and stable in their work for the Lord, work that will not be in vain.

16

Collection for God's People

(16:1–4)

and
Conclusion

(16:5–24)

Outline (continued)

16 1 Now concerning the collection for the saints, just as I directed the churches of Galatia, so you do also. 2 On the first day of the week, let each one of you put aside something and store it up as he may prosper, so that when I come collections will not have to be made. 3 And when I come, I will send those men whom you approve with letters [of recommendation] to take your gift to Jerusalem. 4 And if it is fitting that I go, they will go with me.

G. Collection for God's People
16:1–4

The epistle as such has come to an end except for some final directions, exhortations, and greetings. Paul reveals that he plans to travel to Jerusalem to alleviate the poverty of the saints in that city (Acts 19:21; 24:17; II Cor. 8–9). He wants to collect monetary gifts from the believers in Corinth, just as he is doing in all the Gentile churches. Paul's underlying purpose for these collections is to promote unity in the churches of Jewish and Gentile backgrounds. His objective is to break down any animosity that continues to separate Jewish Christians from Gentile Christians.

1. Now concerning the collection for the saints, just as I directed the churches of Galatia, so you do also.

The first two words, "now concerning," are Paul's reply to a question included in the Corinthian letter addressed to him (7:1). With these two words as an introduction, Paul also answers questions regarding marriage, meat offered to idols, spiritual gifts, the collection for the poor in Jerusalem, and Apollos (7:1, 25; 8:1; 12:1; 16:1, 12).

The Jerusalem church oversaw the churches that Paul founded (Acts 15:4; 18:22; 21:17–19). Yet we have no scriptural evidence that this church levied taxes on Gentile Christians, just as the Jerusalem priests compelled the Jews in Israel and in dispersion to pay the annual temple tax. Rather, Paul taught Gentile believers that they should joyfully share material blessings with the Jerusalem Christians, because the Jerusalem saints had shared with them spiritual blessings (Rom. 15:26–27). They should know that they were indebted to the church in Jerusalem.[1] Paul wanted them to be cheerful givers who without reluctance or

---

1. Murray J. Harris, *NIDNTT*, vol. 3, p. 752; Gerhard Kittel, *TDNT*, vol. 4, pp. 282–83; Keith F. Nickle, *The Collection: A Study in Paul's Strategy*, SBT 48 (London: SCM; Naperville, Ill.: Allenson, 1966); Dieter Georgi, *Die Geschichte der Kollecte des Paulus für Jerusalem* (Hamburg: Reich, 1965).

compulsion generously gave their gifts to support the poor (II Cor. 9:7). The church is obliged to take care of its own people and of others who are needy (James 2:15–16; I John 3:17).

After the early years of Christianity, during which there were no poor among the Christians (Acts 4:34), the Jerusalem church had experienced hard times. The great persecution following the death of Stephen had driven most of the church members away from that city (Acts 8:1b). Without possessions and businesses, these refugees had joined the ranks of the poor (James 2:6; 5:1–6); the believers who stayed in Jerusalem, along with those who returned, faced difficult economic times. Less than a decade later they endured a protracted period of severe famine (Acts 11:28). And in later years they experienced economic adversities, for Paul writes that there were poor people among the saints in Jerusalem (Rom. 15:26; nevertheless, some Christians there seemed to be prospering).

Paul was eager to lend aid to the poor as he had promised to do when James, Peter, and John extended to him "the right hand of fellowship" (Gal. 2:9–10). Indeed, he and Barnabas had delivered famine relief from the church in Antioch to the Christians in Judea (Acts 11:29–30). Thus, we suggest that Paul had mentioned to the Corinthians by either Timothy, Titus, or letter the matter of taking care of the economically poor believers in Jerusalem. The definite article in the expression *the collection* actually means "the well-known collection." In their letter to him they had asked details on how to proceed in gathering the money.[2]

Just as he urged the Galatian believers to do good to all people but especially to fellow believers (Gal. 6:10), so he told the Corinthians to collect money for the poor in Jerusalem. The churches of Galatia are those that Paul and Barnabas founded during the first missionary journey: Pisidian Antioch, Iconium, Lystra, and Derbe (Acts 13–14). Also, Luke mentions that Gaius of Derbe and Timothy of Lystra accompanied him to Jerusalem with the monetary gift (Acts 16:1; 20:4; 24:17).[3] As representatives of their churches, they safeguarded the money that was sent to the poor in Jerusalem.

Paul tells the Corinthians to follow the instructions he had given the churches in Galatia. With apostolic authority he orders the believers to care for the poverty-stricken saints in Jerusalem.

2. On the first day of the week, let each one of you put aside something and store it up as he may prosper, so that when I come collections will not have to be made.

a. "On the first day of the week." This is the customary Jewish wording for what we today call Sunday (Matt. 28:1 and parallels; Acts 20:7; see also Rev. 1:10). In

---

2. Gerd Luedemann, *Paul, Apostle to the Gentiles: Studies in Chronology*, trans. F. Stanley Jones (Philadelphia: Fortress, 1984), p. 81; John C. Hurd, Jr., *The Origin of I Corinthians* (Macon, Ga.: Mercer University Press, 1983), p. 233.

3. C. K. Barrett suggests churches in northern Galatia. See *A Commentary on the First Epistle to the Corinthians*, Harper's New Testament Commentaries series (New York and Evanston: Harper and Row, 1968), p. 386.

the evening of the first day of the week, Christians gathered for the breaking of bread, that is, the Lord's Supper (Acts 20:7). Early Christians commemorated the first day of the week as the day of Jesus' resurrection.[4] And they chose that day for worship and fellowship.

b. "Let each one of you put aside something and store it up as he may prosper." Paul teaches the Corinthians the commendable habit of continued giving to the Lord. He uses the present tense of the verb *to put aside* to indicate that every believer must do so regularly. Paul fails to say where the "something" should be stored, but he implies that the individual believer should store these gifts "by himself" until Paul arrived to collect them.

True, the Corinthian church had administrators (12:28), and deacons were charged with administering funds and caring for the poor (Acts 6:1–6; compare Phil. 1:1; I Tim. 3:8–13). Undoubtedly, they gathered donations from the Christians to carry out their ministry to the needy. But the wording of the text seems to suggest that gifts for the Jerusalem Christians were kept by the individual at home. Paul tells the Corinthian believers to give on the first day of the week but he does not stipulate that their gifts be collected by church officials.[5] The money was not for local needs, to be distributed by the deacons. It was a special gift set aside by the individual for the Jerusalem saints.

How much ought the Corinthian believer to give? The word *tithe* does not occur. Instead Paul lays down the clear principle that a believer should give in relation to the prosperity he or she receives from the Lord. In the Greek, the verb *to prosper* means "to be led along a good road."[6] The agent for this prosperity is the Lord, to whom believers gratefully ought to donate their gifts.

c. "So that when I come collections will not have to be made." This is the second time that Paul notifies the Corinthians of his forthcoming visit (4:18–21). The first indication was to rebuke them; now he says that he will come to ascertain that the Corinthians have indeed made collections. By giving them adequate instructions, he avoids pressuring the Christians to give money hastily. He desires to do all things properly.

3. And when I come, I will send those men, whom you approve, with letters [of recommendation] to take your gift to Jerusalem.

In harmony with a discussion on his personal income (9:7–18), Paul avoids involving himself in collecting the money and taking it to Jerusalem. He wants the Corinthian church to select and approve men for this task. Men from Macedo-

---

4. Max Turner, "The Sabbath, Sunday, and the Law in Luke/Acts," in *From Sabbath to Lord's Day: A Biblical, Historical, and Theological Investigation*, ed. D. A. Carson (Grand Rapids: Zondervan, 1982), p. 137.

5. Among others, see Samuele Bacchiocchi, *From Sabbath to Sunday: A Historical Investigation of the Rise of Sunday Observance in Early Christianity* (Rome: Pontifical Gregorian University Press, 1977), pp. 93–95; Willy Rordorf, *Sunday: The History of the Day of Rest and Worship in the Earliest Centuries of the Christian Church*, trans. A. A. K. Graham (London: SCM; Philadelphia: Westminster, 1968), pp. 193–94.

6. Bauer, p. 323.

nia and Asia Minor also were appointed to carry the gift to the saints in Jerusalem. Thus Paul could never be accused of enhancing his own assets.

No representatives from Corinth are listed as accompanying Paul to Jerusalem (Acts 20:4). Who was the brother chosen by the churches to travel with Paul and his company to deliver the gift (II Cor. 8:18–19)? This person had earned the trust of the Corinthians, but whether he was either Barnabas, Luke, or another apostolic helper we shall never know.[7]

Translators are divided regarding the identity of the letters' author. Did Paul write the letters of recommendation for the men approved by the Corinthians?[8] Or did the church in Corinth compose these letters?[9] In view of Paul's apostolic authority, knowledge of the leaders in Jerusalem, and desire for ecclesiastical unity, I suggest that Paul wrote the letters recommending these Gentile Christians from Greece to the Jewish Christians in Judea. In Paul's day, people who were sent on missions often carried credentials. These credentials were written by the sending agent or agency that recommended the carrier (Acts 9:2; 15:23; 22:5; Rom. 16:1; II Cor. 3:1–3).

The term Paul uses for gift is the Greek word *charis*, which in this verse denotes a charitable donation as an expression of goodwill. It is the gracious gift of Christians in Corinth to those in Jerusalem.

4. And if it is fitting that I go, they will go with me.

This verse reveals a measure of hesitation on Paul's part. He wanted to be in charge of sending the bearers of the collection and thus wrote letters to introduce the men to the leaders in Jerusalem. On the other hand, Paul refused to be responsible for collecting, safeguarding, and delivering the amount. His objective was to be above reproach and suspicion and to be approved by both God and man (II Cor. 8:20–21).

Paul is asking the church members whether they deem it proper that he should travel with their representatives. He himself had decided to go to Jerusalem after he had visited the churches in Macedonia and Greece (Acts 19:21), but he wished to obtain the church's confirmation.

Practical Considerations in 16:1–2

One of the elements of worship is giving gifts to God in thankful response to his numerous blessings. We worship God regularly on Sunday and even on set and special days during the week. We come to church for worship because God wants to meet us and speak to us from his Word. We sing his praises, confess our sins, express thanks for answered prayer, and present our petitions. We demonstrate our love to him not only by doing his will but also by offering our gifts.

Paul teaches the Corinthians to set aside their gifts on the first day of the week and to do so regularly, a teaching that reflects God's provisions for his people. God provides dai-

---

7. Refer to Ralph P. Martin, *2 Corinthians*, WBC 40 (Waco: Word, 1986), pp. 274–75.

8. GNB, NAB, NASB, NEB, NIV, NJB, REB, SEB, *Phillips.*

9. JB, KJV, MLB, NKJV, RSV, NRSV.

ly the needs of the believers, and he instructs them to pray for their daily bread (Matt. 6:11; Luke 11:3). As God taught the people of Israel to honor him with their wealth and the firstfruits of all their crops (Prov. 3:9), so he teaches the New Testament people to honor him by giving liberally (Luke 6:38; 21:1–4). God gives faithfully in answer to the prayers of his people (I John 5:14–15). Similarly, his people should regularly offer their gifts to him as their act of worship.

Greek Words, Phrases, and Constructions in 16:1–4

Verses 1–2

τῆς λογείας τῆς—a collection for the poor. Note that Paul uses the article twice to specify the particular gift for the Jerusalem saints.

κατά—the preposition is used distributively, in the sense of every first day of the week.

παρ᾽ ἑαυτῷ—"alongside of himself." This literal translation indicates that the giver kept the gift in his home.

Verses 3–4

δι᾽ ἐπιστολῶν—the preposition διά followed by the genitive case denotes the manner by which Paul sends the emissaries. The noun *letters* may be an idiomatic plural for "a letter."[10]

τοῦ κἀμὲ πορεύεσθαι—the articular infinitive serves as subject of the verb *to be.*[11] The genitive appears to be influenced by the adjective ἄξιον (fitting) and the personal pronoun ἐμέ in contracted form is the subject of the infinitive.

---

5 I shall come to you after I go through Macedonia. I am going through Macedonia, 6 and perhaps shall stay with you for some time or even spend the winter, so that you may send me on my way, wherever I may go. 7 For I do not wish to see you now in passing, for I hope to remain with you for some time if the Lord permits. 8 But I shall remain in Ephesus until Pentecost. 9 For a wide door for effective service has been opened to me, and there are many adversaries.

10 Now if Timothy comes, see that he does not have to be afraid when he is among you, for he is doing the work of the Lord, just as I also do. 11 Let no one therefore despise him. Send him on his way in peace, so that he may come to me. For I am expecting him with the brothers.

12 Now concerning our brother Apollos, I encouraged him greatly to come to you with the brothers. And indeed he was unwilling to come now. But he will come when he has an opportunity.

13 Be on the alert, stand firm in the faith, be men of courage, be strong. 14 Let everything you do be done with love.

15 And I appeal to you, brothers. You know the household of Stephanas, that they were the firstfruits of Achaia and they have given themselves to the ministry of the saints. 16 Now I urge you, brothers, to submit to such men and to everyone who works and toils with us. 17 And I rejoice over the coming of Stephanas, Fortunatus, and Achaicus, because they supplied what was lacking from you. 18 For they refreshed my spirit and yours. Therefore acknowledge such men.

---

10. C. F. D. Moule, *An Idiom-Book of New Testament Greek*, 2d ed. (Cambridge: Cambridge University Press, 1960), p. 57.

11. Compare A. T. Robertson, *A Grammar of the Greek New Testament in the Light of Historical Research* (Nashville: Broadman, 1934), p. 1061.

19 The churches in the province of Asia greet you. Aquila and Priscilla heartily greet you in the Lord with the church that meets in their house. 20 All the brothers greet you. Greet one another with a holy kiss.

21 I, Paul, write this greeting in my own hand. 22 If anyone does not love the Lord, let him be accursed. Maranatha! 23 The grace of our Lord Jesus be with you. 24 My love be with you all in Christ Jesus. Amen.

IV. Conclusion
16:5–24

A. Paul's Requests
16:5–12

In the next two paragraphs Paul relates his travel plans, the forthcoming visit of Timothy to Corinth, and the reception of Apollos. The allusion to two time references—spending the winter in Corinth and staying in Ephesus until Pentecost—leaves the impression that he wrote this epistle possibly a month or two earlier.[12] Effective evangelistic work kept Paul in Ephesus for some time.

Timothy needed a word of commendation to the Corinthians. Due to his youth and timid personality, Timothy had been adversely received at an earlier visit (compare Acts 18:5). Apollos also had his own reasons for being unwilling to return to Corinth. Paul's remarks are cryptic and open to conjecture.

1. Paul's Travel Plans
16:5–9

5. I shall come to you after I go through Macedonia. I am going through Macedonia, 6. and perhaps shall stay with you for some time or even spend the winter, so that you may send me on my way, wherever I may go.

a. "I shall come to you after I go through Macedonia." According to Luke, Paul planned to travel via Macedonia to Corinth and from there to Jerusalem (Acts 19:21). Indeed, he visited the churches in Macedonia and eventually arrived in Corinth, where he stayed for three months (Acts 20:1–3a). The time spent there was undoubtedly during the winter months, when sea travel was impossible.

After he had composed this epistle and sent it to the church in Corinth, Paul decided to cross the Aegean Sea for a double visit. First he would spend some time with the Corinthians, although he would not yet make arrangements for the collection. Then he would travel on foot to Macedonia to visit the churches. Afterward he would return to Corinth and depart for Judea (II Cor. 1:15–16). But because his brief visit to Corinth proved to be painful, he changed his mind. He returned to Ephesus without visiting the churches in Macedonia (II Cor. 2:1).[13]

---

12. On the basis of 5:7 and 15:20, some commentators suggest that Paul wrote this epistle at Easter. Whether he composed the letter before or after Easter is inconsequential. For a discussion on the chronology of Paul's stay in Ephesus and Corinth consult the Introduction.

13. Consult Gordon D. Fee, "ΧΑΡΙΣ in II Corinthians 1.15: Apostolic Parousia and Paul-Corinth Chronology," *NTS* 24 (1977–78): 533–38.

b. "I am going through Macedonia, and perhaps shall stay with you for some time or even spend the winter." Ever since his departure from Philippi, Thessalonica, and Berea on his second missionary journey, Paul had been unable to return to the Macedonian churches for many years. He told the church in Thessalonica that his plan to visit was blocked by Satan (I Thess. 2:18). Even though Timothy, Silas, and Erastus had visited and served the churches in Macedonia (Acts 18:5; 19:22), Paul had only sent them letters (I and II Thess.). He had not been able to see them personally. His plan to travel through Macedonia meant that he wanted to spend time with the believers in the various churches.

After ministering to the Macedonians and receiving their gifts for the poor who were in Jerusalem (compare II Cor. 8:1–7), Paul planned to travel to Corinth to stay with the believers there for a considerable period. He foresaw that he would be in Corinth until spring, as inclement weather made sea travel impossible during the winter. In short, Luke relates that he stayed in Greece three months (Acts 20:3).

c. "So that you may send me on my way, wherever I may go." Paul's travel plans were indefinite, for he left open the possibility of preaching the gospel in other regions (e.g., Illyricum [present-day Albania and the former Yugoslavia] and Spain [Rom. 15:19, 24, 28]). He considered his visit to Jerusalem obligatory, for he wanted to report on the progress of the Gentile churches (Acts 21:18–19) before he would set out for new fields of labor.[14] Thus he waited for God to lead him in making his plans.

Traveling missionaries received food, beverages, lodging, and financial aid from the Christian churches (see v. 11; Rom. 15:24; II Cor. 1:16; Titus 3:13; III John 6). Not the pagans but the Christians are obliged to supply the missionaries' physical needs and to send them on their way. Paul himself, however, had told the Corinthians that he would offer the gospel free of charge and not request financial remuneration (9:17–18).

7. For I do not wish to see you now in passing, for I hope to remain with you for some time if the Lord permits.

Paul informs the readers that he has no intention of paying them a brief visit. He desires to spend some time with them to renew the ties he had formed when he founded the church. He wanted to express his love for them and knew that they, in turn, would reciprocate.

We have no reason to believe that at an earlier occasion Paul had briefly visited the Corinthians. The term *now* points not to the past but to the present and the future. Paul reveals his plan to remain with the church in Corinth after a lengthy absence. The numerous moral and spiritual problems of its members compel him to think of spending considerable time with them. Paul needs a sea-

---

14. Grosheide is of the opinion that Paul wrote I Cor. before he had decided to travel to Jerusalem (Acts 19:21–22) or that he had not yet fully determined his plans. *Commentary on the First Epistle to the Corinthians: The English Text with Introduction, Exposition and Notes*, New International Commentary on the New Testament series (Grand Rapids: Eerdmans, 1953), p. 399 n. 4.

son during which he can remove the inconsistencies currently present in the Corinthian congregation.

God's people ought to know that their time is in God's hands. They should place their lives in submission to God's will. New Testament saints set the example of living in harmony with the Lord's will.[15]

8. But I shall remain in Ephesus until Pentecost. 9. For a wide door for effective service has been opened to me, and there are many adversaries.

Here is a definite reference to time, Pentecost, without any indication regarding the year. For the Jews, Pentecost was the feast of the harvest celebrated seven weeks after Passover (Lev. 23:9–16). This would be in the second part of May or the first half of June. The Christians commemorated the outpouring of the Holy Spirit in Jerusalem (Acts 2:1–4). Exactly a year later, Paul traveled to Jerusalem and arrived in time for Pentecost (Acts 20:16).

Paul writes that he has work to do in Ephesus; he has numerous evangelistic opportunities in that city. He uses a figurative expression, "a wide door for effective service." Elsewhere he employs similar language: "The Lord had opened a door for [him in Troas]" (II Cor. 2:12; see also Col. 4:3). We are unable to say when this took place, for the uproar in Ephesus that Demetrius and his guild instigated may have occurred after Paul composed his letter (Acts 19:23–41). Paul lectured in the hall of Tyrannus, taught both publicly and from house to house, and called to repentance both Jews and Greeks in Ephesus and in the province of Asia (Acts 19:9–10; 20:20–21).

The adjective *effective* is balanced by the noun *adversaries*. Here are the two sides of the proverbial coin. Paul's service in the church and the community is effective and gains many converts, but the presence of numerous enemies keeps him on guard and prevents him from being overly confident. Among his opponents are the silversmiths whose livelihood is in jeopardy as people turn from the worship of dead idols to the service of the living Christ. In addition, some Jews maliciously opposed Paul and aligned themselves with the Gentiles and their attack (Acts 19:9, 33–34). Paul refrains from providing details, but the sketch itself is sufficiently clear. Satan threw his might and power against Paul's work and associates, and the church in Ephesus (compare Phil. 1:28).

Greek Words, Phrases, and Constructions in 16:5–9

Verses 5–6

διέρχομαι—although the tense of this verb ("I go through") is present, it has a future connotation.

πρός—this preposition followed by the accusative denotes position and means "with."

τύχον—"perhaps." The aorist participle in the neuter accusative functions as an adverb expressing manner.

---

15. Paul in Acts 18:21, Rom. 1:10, 15:32, and I Cor. 4:19; the writer of Hebrews in 6:3; and James in 4:13–15.

παραμενῶ—the future tense of the compound ("I shall stay") is identical in meaning to καταμενῶ. Of the two verbs, the first one is preferred.

Verses 8–9

τῆς πεντηκοστῆς—"Pentecost." This is an abbreviation of the full form, "the day of Pentecost" (Acts 2:1; 20:16).

ἀνέῳγεν—the second perfect intransitive of the verb ἀνοίγω (I open). The perfect shows lasting effect (compare II Cor. 6:11; John 1:51).

---

2. Timothy's Arrival
16:10–11

10. Now if Timothy comes, see that he does not have to be afraid when he is among you, for he is doing the work of the Lord, just as I also do.

a. "Now if Timothy comes." This is the second time in this epistle that Paul mentions Timothy (4:17). He sent Timothy to the Corinthians, probably through Macedonia (Acts 19:22), and is uncertain of the time of Timothy's arrival. Hence, Paul writes a conditional clause in which the particle *if* relates to Timothy's eventual arrival.

Paul does not indicate who delivered this letter to the Corinthian church. Certainly Timothy was not the carrier, for then we would have expected his name to be in the greetings of this epistle (1:1). Also, because Paul's first epistle does not say that Timothy returned with a report of his visit to the Corinthians, we infer that this letter arrived in Corinth before Timothy's visit. By the time Paul wrote his second letter, Timothy had returned (II Cor. 1:1). We conclude that Paul sent him only once to Corinth (4:17; 16:10) and that he is now unsure about the exact time of Timothy's arrival. Timothy's journey to the Macedonian churches necessitated land travel while Paul's epistle was sent by ship to Corinth.[16]

b. "See that he does not have to be afraid when he is among you." Paul writes an imperative to the Corinthians: he instructs them to receive Timothy courteously and respectfully. We assume that Timothy's age had something to do with his relation to the church in Corinth (see I Tim. 4:12). Venturing a guess, we judge Timothy to be in his twenties at the time Paul writes this letter. His youth may have hindered him from exercising authority in the Corinthian community. Moreover, the church in Corinth may have considered him to be not the chief spokesman but Paul's deputy, that is, a person who is second in command. And last, some members had expressed their differences with Paul; they would now not have to face the apostle but could express their arrogance without impunity in the presence of his representative (compare 4:18).

In his pastoral epistles, Paul reveals that Timothy was not enjoying robust health (I Tim. 5:23), was timid (II Tim. 1:7), and had to be taught how to instruct

---

16. Luedemann, *Paul, Apostle to the Gentiles*, p. 93.

groups of people and how to control his own inclinations (I Tim. 5).[17] By all appearances, Timothy was not an imposing figure but someone who might be abused verbally in the Corinthian church. For this reason, Paul instructs the readers to accept Timothy so that he does not have to be afraid in their midst.

c. "For he is doing the work of the Lord, just as I also do." The reason for making Timothy feel at ease is the labor he performs. He is doing the work of the Lord that Paul himself performs (see 15:58). In other words, Paul ascribes equal authority to Timothy because of his work on behalf of Christ. Paul does not place himself above his co-workers, even though he is an apostle and they are apostolic helpers. He intimates that the readers should respect Timothy because of his calling and should accept him as they would Paul. Elsewhere Paul teaches that especially those persons whose work is preaching and teaching the gospel are worthy of double honor (I Tim. 5:17).[18] The Corinthians, then, must receive Timothy for the sake of his work in the Lord.

11. Let no one therefore despise him. Send him on his way in peace, so that he may come to me. For I am expecting him with the brothers.

a. "Let no one therefore despise him." On account of Timothy's spiritual work, no one in the Corinthian community ought to reject him and treat him with contempt. He is a servant of the Lord, so that rejection of the servant is the same as rejection of his Sender. Paul is not saying that the Corinthians have been doing this in the past, but he cautions them about the possibility of despising Timothy.

b. "Send him on his way in peace, so that he may come to me." The New Testament provides no information about Timothy's arrival and reception in Corinth. Paul writes clearly about Titus, whose report concerning the Corinthian visit he anxiously awaited.[19] But he reveals nothing about Timothy's work in Corinth. This does not mean that Timothy fulfilled a minor role in the ministry of the Word. On the contrary, many churches regarded Timothy as a faithful co-worker with Paul. His name occurs with that of Paul in the greetings to the churches in Corinth, Philippi, Colosse, and Thessalonica.[20]

Paul instructs the Corinthians to aid Timothy in his travels by providing him with the basic necessities of life (food, drink, lodging, and money). Above all, he wants them to bid Timothy farewell in peace. He desires spiritual tranquility within the Corinthian church reflected by the manner in which they send Timothy on his return trip. And Paul would receive a first-hand report from his colleague in the ministry.

c. "For I am expecting him with the brothers." The repetition of the first person singular personal pronoun ("to me" and "I am expecting him") confirms that Paul is vitally interested in Timothy's mission. The Corinthians should un-

---

17. Consult Gerald F. Hawthorne, *ISBE*, vol. 4, pp. 857–58.

18. Refer to William Hendriksen, *Exposition of the Pastoral Epistles*, New Testament Commentary series (Grand Rapids: Baker, 1965), pp. 179–81.

19. II Cor. 2:13; 7:6, 13–15; 8:6, 16–17, 23; 12:18.

20. Respectively, II Cor. 1:1; Phil. 1:1; Col. 1:1; I Thess. 1:1; II Thess. 1:1.

derstand that meeting with Timothy is the same as meeting Paul himself. If they repudiate him, they will have to meet Paul eventually.

The noun *brothers* can be construed with either the pronoun *I* or *him*. It can mean that Paul with the brothers in Ephesus expects Timothy to come.[21] Or it can mean that Paul expects Timothy to come to him with travel companions.[22] Which of the two interpretations is preferred? Timothy did not travel alone to Macedonia but was accompanied by Erastus, a resident of Corinth (Acts 19:22; Rom. 16:23b). It is possible that Erastus together with other travel companions escorted Timothy on his return. On the other hand, the three Corinthian delegates (Stephanas, Fortunatus, and Achaicus [v. 17]) may have awaited Timothy's return. Yet why would these three men have to wait for Timothy to return to Ephesus after they had communicated their messages to Paul? We conclude that certainty is lacking for either interpretation. Like other dilemmas in Paul's epistles, this problem remains unresolved.

Greek Words, Phrases, and Constructions in 16:10–11

ἐάν—this particle followed by the verb ἔλθῃ (he comes) in the subjunctive expresses uncertainty regarding Timothy's arrival time.

πρός—see the comment at verse 6.

ἐξουθενήσῃ—"let no one despise him." Here is a rare occurrence of the hortatory subjunctive in the third person singular.[23]

---

3. Apollos's Reluctance
16:12

12. Now concerning our brother Apollos, I encouraged him greatly to come to you with the brothers. And indeed he was unwilling to come now. But he will come when he has an opportunity.

The last request in this series of three is asking Paul's co-worker Apollos to go to Corinth to serve the church. Apollos was the learned orator from Alexandria who had been commissioned by the Ephesians to minister to the spiritual needs of the Corinthians (Acts 18:24–28; 19:1). Because he was a skilled orator, Apollos was appreciated and had numerous friends in Corinth. In fact, the Corinthians had formed an Apollos party—which Apollos, like Paul, repudiated (1:12; 3:4–6, 22).

One wonders who was pastor of the church in Corinth or whether the pastorate was vacant. Is the church asking Apollos to come for a brief visit or to be the pastor for an extended period? The invitation is the last item in their letter addressed to Paul, as is evident from the first two words in this verse ("now con-

---

21. KJV, NKJV, JB, NJB, *Cassirer.*

22. GNB, NAB, NCV, NIV, SEB, *Phillips.*

23. Moule, *Idiom-Book,* p. 22.

cerning"; see 7:1, 25; 8:1; 12:1; 16:1). The Corinthians relay the invitation via Paul and ask him to intervene on their behalf. Paul had never considered Apollos to be a competitor but always a faithful fellow worker. Therefore, Paul does not hesitate to persuade Apollos to go and visit the Corinthians. He calls him "our brother" and notes that he has greatly encouraged Apollos to accompany the brothers, that is, the three delegates from Corinth, on their homeward journey (v. 17).

We do not know the reason for Apollos's reluctance to go to Corinth. We surmise that he was fully aware of the many problems and divisions in the life of the church. He knew that Paul both planned to visit Corinth and was instructing the congregation by correspondence. And last, he did not wish to interfere with the work Paul was doing.

Apollos is the person who has to answer the call to visit the Corinthian church. He makes it known that he is unwilling to go at the moment, but at the right time in the future he will travel to Corinth. The past tense of the verb in the sentence ("and indeed he was unwilling to come now") shows that Apollos is no longer in Paul's presence at the time this verse was written. Apollos had decided not to go now but was willing to visit Corinth at another time.

Greek Words, Phrases, and Constructions in 16:12

πολλά—the adjective is pressed into service as an adverb meaning "greatly" or "strongly."

πάντως οὐκ—an emphatic combination signifying "not at all" or "wholly not."

θέλημα—this noun stands by itself without qualifiers and therefore appears to refer not to the will of God but to the will of Apollos.[24]

B. Exhortations and Greetings
16:13–24

A number of exhortations and references to certain Corinthians are part of the conclusion to this chapter. The last few verses (vv. 19–21) consist, first, of final greetings from churches and individuals; Paul writes his greeting in his own hand. Next, Paul censures those who do not love the Lord. Praying for the return of Jesus Christ, he commends the readers to the grace of the Lord Jesus.

1. Final Admonitions
16:13–18

13. Be on the alert, stand firm in the faith, be men of courage, be strong. 14. Let everything you do be done with love.

---

24. Meinrad Limbeck, *EDNT*, vol. 2, p. 137. However, Gottlob Schrenk (*TDNT*, vol. 3, p. 59) understands it as the will of God.

Like a general in the army of the Lord, Paul gives short orders in rapid succession and expects his people to put his commands into practice. He is confident that they are already obeying these directives, but he exhorts the readers to persevere.

a. "Be on the alert." The first command is to be vigilant, especially with a view toward Christ's return (see v. 22). These words occur frequently in the eschatological passages of the New Testament.[25] They imply that God's people should remain watchful and fully alert to thwart the spiritual forces of darkness.

b. "Stand firm in the faith." Paul issues a second order, which is similar in meaning to his concluding exhortation of the preceding chapter, "Be steadfast" (15:58). He adds the prepositional phrase *in the faith* to indicate the immovability of the believer with respect to trusting God—subjective faith. As a soldier firmly defends the interests of his nation, so the Christian stands firm in relation to the teachings of God's Word—objective faith. Paul's directive to stand firm, with or without modifiers, appears repeatedly in his epistles.[26]

c. "Be men of courage." The Greek verb *andrizesthe* in the imperative plural means "acquit yourselves like men." This is the only place in the New Testament where the verb appears, yet the sense is sufficiently clear. No soldier in the army of Jesus Christ may be fainthearted; in his presence, there is no place for cowards and weaklings.

d. "Be strong." In a series of four commands, this last imperative is synonymous with the preceding one. In the passive voice, the verb means to be made strong through experiences that God prepares for the believer (see Ps. 31:24; Eph. 6:10).

e. "Let everything you do be done with love." This is an echo of Paul's remark in an earlier chapter on the use of spiritual gifts: "But let all things be done decently and in order" (14:40). Paul is not interested in aggressive force without the virtue of love. He shows the church of Jesus Christ "an even more excellent way," namely, to follow the path of Christian love (12:31; 13; 14:1). A militant church battles sin but loves the sinner.

> Like a mighty army,
> Moves the Church of God . . .
> One in hope and doctrine,
> One in charity.
>
> —Sabine Baring-Gould

15. And I appeal to you, brothers. You know the household of Stephanas, that they were the firstfruits of Achaia and they have given themselves to the ministry of the saints.

---

25. E.g., see Matt. 24:42; 25:13; Mark 13:35, 37; I Thess. 5:6; Rev. 3:3; 16:15. See also Albrecht Oepke, *TDNT*, vol. 2, p. 338.

26. Gal. 5:1; Phil. 1:27; 4:1; I Thess. 3:8; II Thess. 2:15. Consult Walter Grundmann, *TDNT*, vol. 7, p. 639; Michael Wolter, *EDNT*, vol. 2, p. 207.

a. "And I appeal to you, brothers." After a series of commands, Paul now issues an appeal addressed to the brothers and sisters in the Corinthian church. Apparently they failed to respect the office bearers who worked diligently in their local congregation to advance the cause of Christ. A weakness in that church seems to have been a disregard for the authority invested in their spiritual leaders.

b. "You know the household of Stephanas, that they were the firstfruits of Achaia." Paul states the fact that the Corinthians are fully acquainted with the household of Stephanas. At the beginning of this epistle, he already mentioned Stephanas and his household. Paul baptized him and all those who belonged to his family (1:16). Indeed he included Stephanas, as an afterthought, with those whom Paul himself had baptized. Granted that at Athens, Dionysius, Damaris, and others became believers (Acts 17:34), here is the first indication of a person and his entire family being baptized.

Paul calls Stephanas and his household the firstfruits, which in Old Testament times was a harvest term used when the first ears of grain were reaped (Lev. 23:9–11, 15–17; Deut. 26:1–11). In Paul's vocabulary, the expression *firstfruits* has a spiritual meaning: Christ is the reaper who presents a new harvest of his people to God the Father. For Paul, the household of Stephanas in Corinth and Epenetus in the province of Asia (Rom. 16:5) are the firstfruits of Gentile missions.[27] After the firstfruits are gathered, the real harvest is imminent.

c. "They have given themselves to the ministry of the saints." From the outset, Stephanas and his family took upon themselves the task of ministering to the spiritual needs of those Corinthians who became Christians. Their work was to serve God's people (see 12:5). They volunteered their services and, blessed with organizational talent, did the arduous work that developing a church requires. As is often the case, some people in the congregation did not always appreciate these labors and repudiated the members of Stephanas's household. One of the complaints could have been that these members had never been officially appointed to serve the church but had appointed themselves. Jealousy and rivalry were undermining the spiritual welfare of the membership. Paul, however, has a high view of church membership and calls the believers "saints." He implies that even those who are critical of the church's servants are called saints (compare 1:2).

The sentence structure in the Greek is awkward, as translations that follow the word order of the original text reflect.[28] Paul begins verse 15 with an exhortation, "I appeal to you, brothers," which he interrupts with an explanatory note about the household of Stephanas. After writing this note, he applies the entreaty to the content of verse 16. For the sake of a smooth translation, I have repeated the exhortation in slightly altered form.

16. Now I urge you, brothers, to submit to such men and to everyone who works and toils with us.

---

27. Refer to Robert Murray, "New Wine in Old Wineskins XII. Firstfruits," *ExpT* 86 (1974–75): 164–68.

28. E.g., see KJV, NKJV, NASB.

Paul implores the members of the Corinthian church to submit to their leaders and to do so out of love for one another and without compulsion. Notice that he addresses the readers as brothers (and sisters) to show his tender love for them. He realizes that in a developing community, tensions are unavoidable. But these tensions should be alleviated and eliminated in the context of Christian love.

A literal translation shows emphasis: "that you also be in subjection to such men" (NASB). Paul wants the readers to realize that they themselves must be in submission to their leaders. As the younger men must submit themselves to the authority of their elders (I Peter 5:5), so Christians willingly must submit to one another (Eph. 5:21).[29] They should renounce their own preferences and in humility and love regard others better than themselves (Phil. 2:3). Thus, Paul urges the Corinthians to be in subjection to their leaders who diligently serve the members of the Christian community. The writer of the epistle to the Hebrews also urges his readers to obey their leaders and to submit to their authority (13:17).[30]

The people who should be respected are the leaders from the family of Stephanas. But Paul broadens the circle by including "everyone who works and toils with us." This means that the apostles, their helpers, and all other church workers should be accorded proper respect (I Tim. 5:17). Paul is not merely writing synonyms when he mentions the verbs *to work* and *to toil*. There is a distinct difference between working and toiling. The former signifies being productive; the latter connotes working hard and long in the interest of attaining a goal.

When church members honor the hardworking servants in the church, they themselves will follow their example. A church with willing workers proves to be a powerhouse that illumines and benefits the entire community in which it is located. Let every Christian adopt the old adage that still speaks volumes:

> Only one life, 't will soon be past;
> Only what is done for Christ will last.

17. And I rejoice over the coming of Stephanas, Fortunatus, and Achaicus, because they supplied what was lacking from you. 18. For they refreshed my spirit and yours. Therefore acknowledge such men.

a. "And I rejoice over the coming of Stephanas, Fortunatus, and Achaicus." The arrival and the presence of three Corinthian church leaders proved to be a tremendous source of joy for Paul. These three had given him the letter from the Corinthians and had acquainted Paul with the spiritual condition and the problems of their church.

---

29. Gerhard Delling, *TDNT*, vol. 8, pp. 44–45.

30. The author of Hebrews writes the Greek verb *hypeikō* (I give way, submit), a synonym of *hypotassō* (I submit).

This is now the third time that Paul mentions the name *Stephanas* (1:16; 16:15, 17), which in Greek means "the one who bears a crown." Stephanas was the most influential of the three men, for he had a household. Whether his two companions belonged to this household is a conjecture. Both men could have been slaves. We know next to nothing about them because their names occur only once in the New Testament. The name *Fortunatus* is a Latin term that signifies "the blessed one." And *Achaicus* simply means "the one from the province of Achaia."

These three men were not the members of Chloe's household (1:11) who came to Paul with an oral report on the divisions in the church. Stephanas and his two friends were well-known leaders who acquainted Paul with the spiritual life of the congregation. The oral report of Chloe's people was unofficial; that of the three-man delegation was official. The church commissioned Stephanas, Fortunatus, and Achaicus to carry their letter and to answer any questions Paul might raise. Further, Paul was unhappy with the report of Chloe's people but rejoiced in the arrival and presence of the Corinthian delegation. He mentions the brothers in verse 12 and identifies them by name in verse 17. He shows that a special bond existed between himself and the Corinthian trio.

b. "Because they supplied what was lacking from you." The personal pronoun *you* is open to two interpretations. Objectively, it can signify that the three church workers filled the void created by Paul's absence from Corinth; and subjectively it can signify that Paul had a longing to see the Corinthian believers, a longing that the three delegates by their presence tried to fill.[31] In addition, we presume that Paul inquired about the members of the Corinthian church and, after reading their letter, asked further questions. The better of the two choices, then, is the subjective interpretation.

c. "For they refreshed my spirit and yours." Why does Paul rejoice? Because Stephanas, Fortunatus, and Achaicus were able to renew Paul's spirit with good reports about the church (compare II Cor. 7:13). They encouraged him with positive accounts that counterbalanced the negative report he had received from the members of Chloe's household. They experienced Paul's love for them; and they, in turn, demonstrated their affection for him. They not only refreshed Paul's soul; upon their return to Corinth, they would be able to inform the church about Paul's love for them. Their visit with Paul would be a blessing to them. Besides, they would be able to deliver Paul's letter and answer questions Corinthians might raise.

d. "Therefore acknowledge such men." This is the last command Paul has for the Corinthians. When the trio returns to Corinth from their visit with Paul, they need to be warmly received in the community and duly recognized as leaders. The words *such men* go beyond the Corinthian trio and include all the people who unfailingly give of their time and talent to the well-being of Christ's church.

---

31. Compare Bauer, p. 836.

Greek Words, Phrases, and Constructions in 16:15–18

Verses 15–16

ἀπαρχή—"firstfruits." Although the word is in the singular, it has a plural connotation that is evident in the verb and reflexive pronoun ἔταξαν ἑαυτούς (they appointed themselves). Also note a possible play on words in this verb and the compound ὑποτάσσησθε (you submit yourselves).

Verses 17–18

ὑμέτερον—this possessive pronoun in the neuter singular is replaced by the second person plural ὑμῶν, as in the reading of the Majority Text.[32] The possessive pronoun is the more original, yet in translation the matter is inconsequential.

τοιούτους—this correlative adjective in the plural denotes quality, "of such a kind."

---

2. Final Greetings
16:19–24

In this last segment of the epistle, the concept *greet* occurs five times. First, there are the greetings of churches in the province of Asia; they are followed by those of the missionary couple Aquila and Priscilla with their house church. Then there are the compliments from all the brothers, succeeded by the manner of greeting one another, and last, Paul's best wishes in his own handwriting.

The last three verses (vv. 22–24) constitute the benediction. It includes a curse on all those who do not love the Lord, a petition for the Lord's return, and the customary wish for the Lord's grace. As a last remark, Paul assures the readers of his love for them in Christ Jesus.

19. The churches in the province of Asia greet you. Aquila and Priscilla heartily greet you in the Lord with the church that meets in their house.

a. "The churches in the province of Asia greet you." Almost the entire western part of Asia Minor was known as the Roman province of Asia during the first few centuries of the Christian era. Jewish people living in the major cities of that province were among the first to hear the gospel, especially in Ephesus. Paul came to Ephesus on his way to Syria and taught in the local synagogue, where he was well received. At the request of the Jews, he promised to return to them (Acts 18:18–21). When Paul arrived in Ephesus for the second time, he at first spoke in the local synagogue for three months and then taught in the lecture hall of Tyrannus for two years. The effect was that "all the Jews and the Greeks who lived in the province of Asia heard the word of the Lord" (Acts 19:10). Students of Paul became pastors who founded churches in the western part of Asia Minor. Among these pastors were Epaphras, who labored faithfully in Colosse, Laodi-

---

32. Compare Friedrich Blass and Albert Debrunner, *A Greek Grammar of the New Testament and Other Early Christian Literature,* trans. and rev. Robert Funk (Chicago: University of Chicago Press, 1961), #285.1.

cea, and Hierapolis (Col. 4:12–13); Tychicus, who was a faithful minister and fellow servant of Paul in Colosse and Ephesus (Acts 20:4; Col. 4:7; Eph. 6:21); Philemon and Archippus, who were fellow workers in Colosse (Philem. 1–2); and Trophimus, who was an Ephesian (Acts 20:4; 21:29). The church at Ephesus occupied first place among the seven churches in the province of Asia (Rev. 1:11; 2:1–7). From Ephesus, Christianity spread throughout the province, so that at the time Paul composed his first epistle to the Corinthians many churches had been formed.

Paul conveys the greetings of the churches in the province of Asia and thus stresses both the unity and the universality of Christ's church. These ecumenical greetings conveyed the thought of peace and love. Also, a greeting expressed by Christians "strengthens the bond of fellowship with those who are engaged in the same task and who serve the same Lord."[33]

b. "Aquila and Priscilla heartily greet you in the Lord." Aquila was born and raised in Pontus, a province in the northern part of Asia Minor. He was of Jewish descent and had settled in Rome with his wife, Priscilla. Both were expelled from the imperial city by edict of Emperor Claudius about A.D. 49 and moved to Corinth, where they practiced their tentmaking trade (Acts 18:2–3). When Paul arrived in Corinth, they provided lodging for him and became active participants in his missionary endeavors. With him they traveled to Ephesus, where they explained to Apollos the way of God more clearly (Acts 18:26). They opened their home to fellow believers and founded a church. Priscilla, abbreviated as Prisca, was a talented teacher whom Paul at times mentions before her husband. Aquila and Priscilla left Ephesus, took up residence in Rome for a while, and then returned to Ephesus. Paul mentions their names in his greetings (Rom. 16:3; II Tim. 4:19).

c. "With the church that meets in their house." House churches were common in apostolic times. Aquila and Priscilla founded house churches in Ephesus and in Rome (Rom. 16:5); Nympha had a church in her home (Col. 4:15); and Philemon opened his home to church gatherings (Philem. 2). House churches did not exist as individual groups separate from the local church; the local church in the first century met in the homes of private parties.[34]

20. All the brothers greet you. Greet one another with a holy kiss.

The first part of this verse appears to be redundant. Paul had already sent the greetings of the churches and of Aquila and Priscilla and their house church; now he conveys the greetings of all the brothers and sisters. The greeting of the Ephesian church members included a warm embracing of the Corinthian believers. Furthermore, their gesture of affection must be expressed with a holy kiss, which in Paul's times and culture was customary and expected.[35] With the de-

---

33. Hans Windisch, *TDNT*, vol. 1, p. 501.

34. Marlis Gielen, "Zur Interpretation der paulinischen Formel *hē kat' oikon ekklēsia*," *ZNW* 77 (1986): 109–25.

35. See also Rom. 16:16; II Cor. 13:12; I Thess. 5:26; compare I Peter 5:14.

scriptive adjective *holy,* Paul prevents any misunderstanding. In addition to a mutual embrace, the act of kissing included a touching of the cheeks probably on the left and on the right and possibly a touching of the lips to the other person's cheek.[36]

21. I, Paul, write this greeting in my own hand.

Writing letters was frequently done by scribes at the request of individuals who dictated the message. At times, scribes identified themselves (Tertius in Rom. 16:22) or were mentioned by name (Silas in I Peter 5:12). We are not sure whether Paul employed a scribe to write the current epistle, but we do know that the phrase *greeting in my own hand* means that this is a genuine letter from the author. Paul tells the Thessalonians that the greeting in his own hand is the characteristic mark in all his letters (II Thess. 3:17; see Gal. 6:11; Col. 4:18; Philem. 19). The recipients in Corinth knew Paul's style of writing and recognized his penmanship.[37]

22. If anyone does not love the Lord, let him be accursed. Maranatha!

a. *Curse.* Not all the recipients of this epistle love the Lord Jesus, as is evident from a number of passages where Paul reproaches those who deliberately undermined the church.[38] With the use of a conditional clause, he notes that there are indeed people in the church who have no affection for Christ. Paul does not write the Greek word *agapaō,* which denotes a genuine spiritual love and which he uses everywhere in his epistles. Except for Titus 3:15, this is the only place where Paul chooses the verb *phileō;* it signifies affection.

Paul utters a formula that curses anyone who opposes the Lord Jesus, much as he invokes a curse on preachers who proclaim not Christ's gospel: "As we have said before, so I say again now, if any man is preaching to you a gospel contrary to that which you received, let him be accursed" (Gal. 1:9, NASB).

b. *Call.* "Maranatha." This is an Aramaic expression that can be translated either as an imperative, "Our Lord, come!" or as a perfect indicative, "Our Lord has come." In view of the similar petition in Revelation 22:20, "Come, Lord Jesus," the imperative is preferred.[39]

The use of an Aramaic word in the Greek community of Corinth is intriguing but not unusual. The writers of the New Testament were not averse to Aramaic terms. The Christians adopted a Jewish vocabulary that included the words *Abba* (Rom. 8:15: Gal. 4:6), *Amen* (14:16; 16:24; II Cor. 1:20), *Halleluiah* (Rev. 19:1, 3, 4, 6), *Hosanna* (Matt. 21:9, 15; Mark 11:9–10; John 12:13), and *Maranatha.*

What is Paul's purpose for calling on the Lord Jesus to return? Some scholars regard the verse as a formula that was part of the liturgy for celebrating the Lord's Supper.[40] There are similarities but not to the extent that in this passage

---

36. John Ellington, "Kissing in the Bible: Form and Meaning," *BibTr* 41 (1990): 409–16.

37. John Nijenhuis, "The Greeting in My Own Hand—*Paul*," *BibToday* 19 (1981): 255–58.

38. Compare, e.g., 4:18–19; 5:13; 6:9–10; 12:3; 14:36–38; 15:12.

39. J. A. Emerton, "*MARANATHA and EPHPHATHA,*" *JTS* 18 (1967): 427–31.

40. Fee, *First Corinthians,* p. 834 n. 6.

Paul refers to a communion celebration. True, the early church recognized the very presence of Jesus at communion and earnestly prayed for the physical return of the Lord in their midst: Come, Lord Jesus! (*Didache* 10:6). But in the current text, Paul adds the word *Maranatha* to a curse formula. This means that he implores the Lord to come as Judge to mete out punishment. He prays that the Lord will come quickly and remove those people who do not love him.[41]

23. The grace of our Lord Jesus be with you. 24. My love be with you all in Christ Jesus. Amen.

The conclusion to this epistle is the usual benediction recorded in many epistles. Paul prays that the Lord Jesus may extend his forgiving grace and his spiritual presence to all the recipients of this letter. His is a prayer for the physical and spiritual well-being of God's people.

The last sentence in this epistle expresses Paul's personal love for all the Corinthians who are in Christ Jesus. He wants them to know that his love for them is truly spiritual in the Lord. He calls judgment on those who refuse to love the Lord, but for Jesus' followers he has genuine love.

Doctrinal Considerations in 16:22

Churches sometimes look for a unique name to identify themselves. They choose the word *Maranatha* and want to be known as a church that prays for and anticipates the imminent return of Jesus Christ. But in the universal church, every sincere Christian longs for the day of the Lord and prays fervently for his return. Peter instructs his readers that they must "look forward to the day of God and speed its coming" (II Peter 3:12). He means that all believers must hasten that day by proclaiming and teaching Christ's gospel to all the inhabitants and the nations of the world. Peter himself addressed a multitude and told the people to repent so that God may send the Christ (Acts 3:19–21). When men, women, and children throughout the world repent and turn to Christ, they will hasten his return.

The prayer "Amen. Come, Lord Jesus" (Rev. 22:20) is a response to Jesus' promise, "Yes, I am coming soon." Both the Holy Spirit and the bride, that is, the church, are earnestly praying for the coming of Jesus Christ. The bride longs for the coming of the bridegroom to be together eternally in joyful celebration.

Greek Words, Phrases, and Constructions in 16:19–22

Verse 19

ἀσπάζεται—the subject of the verb *to greet* is a compound plural followed by the singular verb form. Although the Majority Text features the verb in the plural, the more difficult reading is preferred.

---

41. C. F. D. Moule, "A Reconsideration of the Context of *Maranatha*," *NTS* 6 (1960): 307–10; Oscar Cullmann, *Early Christian Worship*, SBT, 1st series 10 (London: SCM, 1953), pp. 13–14; J. J. Hughes, "Maranatha," *ISBE*, vol. 3, p. 243. Compare W. F. Albright and C. S. Mann, "Two Texts in I Corinthians," *NTS* 16 (1970): 271–76.

Πρίσκα—the variant reading Πρίσκιλλα is adopted by the Textus Receptus on the basis of numerous manuscripts. Luke writes the full form (Acts 18:2, 18, 26), but Paul prefers the diminutive Πρίσκα in three of his epistles (Rom. 16:3; I Cor. 16:19; II Tim. 4:19).[42]

Verses 21–22

Παύλου—the proper noun stands in apposition to the possessive pronoun and noun ἐμῇ χειρί (my own hand).

ἤτω ἀνάθεμα—the present imperative from the verb εἰμι (I am) is used as an optative of wish. With the noun, it pronounces a prayer for damnation on those who separate from Christ.

Μαραναθά—it is a transliterated word from the Aramaic and is preferably interpreted as an imperative.

Summary of Chapter 16

At an earlier occasion, Paul had instructed the Galatian churches to gather a monetary collection for the support of the poverty-stricken saints in Jerusalem. Now he tells the Corinthian believers to do likewise. He charges them to set aside money regularly on the first day of the week, so that when Paul arrives in Corinth no collections will have to be made. He will write letters of introduction for the men who will carry the gift to Jerusalem, and he himself may accompany them if it is advisable.

Paul reveals his travel plans: he wants to travel through Macedonia and upon arriving in Corinth spend the winter there. At present, he will stay in Ephesus until Pentecost; he writes that a door of evangelistic opportunity has opened. Timothy is expected to arrive in Corinth, and Paul asks the Corinthians to receive him warmly because of his work. He advises the readers to send Timothy on his way. Apollos, who was invited to visit Corinth, expressed unwillingness to go, yet Paul encourages him to accept the invitation. Apollos says that he will do so when the opportunity arises.

The name of Stephanas is mentioned with respect to his household, conversion, and service to the saints. Paul exhorts the readers to submit to such leaders. The visit of Stephanas, Fortunatus, and Achaicus makes him happy, for they have refreshed Paul's spirit.

The chapter ends with greetings from the churches in the province of Asia, Aquila and Priscilla with their house church, and all the believers. Paul sends his greetings by signing the epistle. All those who do not love the Lord are placed under a curse. Paul commends the readers to the grace of the Lord Jesus and extends to them his love in Christ Jesus.

---

42. Consult Bruce M. Metzger, *A Textual Commentary on the Greek New Testament*, 3d corrected ed. (London and New York: United Bible Societies, 1975), p. 570.

Select Bibliography[*]

Commentaries

Alford, Henry. *Alford's Greek Testament: An Exegetical and Critical Commentary.* 7th ed. 4 vols. 1887. Grand Rapids: Guardian, 1976.

Allo, P. E.-B. *Saint Paul Premiére Épitre aux Corinthiens.* Études Biblique. 2d ed. Paris: Gabalda, 1934.

Barclay, William. *The Letters to the Corinthians.* The Daily Study Bible. 2d ed. Philadelphia: Westminster, 1956.

Barrett, C. K. *A Commentary on the First Epistle to the Corinthians.* Harper's New Testament Commentaries series. New York and Evanston: Harper and Row, 1968.

Bengel, John Albert. *Bengel's New Testament Commentary.* Translated by Charlton T. Lewis and Marvin R. Vincent. 2 vols. Grand Rapids: Kregel, 1981.

Brown, Raymond E., et al., ed. *The New Jerome Biblical Commentary.* Englewood Cliffs, N.J.: Prentice Hall, 1990.

Bruce, F. F. *1 and 2 Corinthians.* New Century Bible series. London: Oliphants, 1971.

Calvin, John. *The First Epistle of Paul the Apostle to the Corinthians.* Calvin's Commentaries series. Translated by John W. Fraser. Reprint ed. Grand Rapids: Eerdmans, 1976.

Carson, D. A. *Matthew,* in vol. 8 of *The Expositor's Bible Commentary,* edited by Frank E. Gaebelein. 12 vols. Grand Rapids: Zondervan, 1984.

Conzelmann, Hans. *1 Corinthians: A Commentary on the First Epistle to the Corinthians.* Edited by George W. MacRae. Translated by James W. Leitch. Hermeneia: A Critical and Historical Commentary on the Bible. Philadelphia: Fortress, 1975.

Craig, Clarence T. *The First Epistle to the Corinthians.* Vol. 10 in *The Interpreter's Bible.* New York: Abingdon, 1953.

Fascher, Erich. *Der erste Brief des Paulus an die Korinther.* Erster Teil. Theologischer Handkommentar zum Neuen Testament. 3 Aufl. Berlin: Evangelische Verlagsanstaldt, 1984.

Fee, Gordon D. *The First Epistle to the Corinthians.* New International Commentary on the New Testament series. Grand Rapids: Eerdmans, 1987.

---

[*]Consult the Index of Authors and the footnotes for references to the numerous books and articles considered in the commentary.

Select Bibliography

Findlay, G. G. *St. Paul's First Epistle to the Corinthians*. Vol. 3 of *The Expositor's Greek Testament*. Edited by W. Robertson Nicoll. 1910. Grand Rapids: Eerdmans, 1961.

Godet, Frederic Louis. *Commentary on First Corinthians*. 1886. Grand Rapids: Kregel, 1977.

Gromacki, R. G. *Called to Be Saints: An Exposition of I Corinthians*. Grand Rapids: Baker, 1977.

Grosheide, F. W. *Commentary on the First Epistle to the Corinthians: The English Text with Introduction, Exposition and Notes*. New International Commentary on the New Testament series. Grand Rapids: Eerdmans, 1953.

———. *De Eerste Brief van den Apostel Paulus aan de Kerk te Korinthe*. Kommentaar op het Nieuwe Testament series. Amsterdam: Van Bottenburg, 1932.

Harrisville, Roy A. *I Corinthians*. Augsburg Commentary on the New Testament series. Minneapolis: Augsburg, 1987.

Hendriksen, William. *Exposition of the Pastoral Epistles*. New Testament Commentary series. Grand Rapids: Baker, 1965.

———. *Exposition of I and II Thessalonians*. New Testament Commentary series. Grand Rapids: Baker, 1955.

———. *Exposition of the Gospel according to Luke*. New Testament Commentary series. Grand Rapids: Baker, 1978.

Héring, Jean. *The First Epistle of Saint Paul to the Corinthians*. Translated by A. W. Heathcote and P. J. Allcock. London: Epworth, 1962.

Hodge, Charles. *An Exposition of the First Epistle to the Corinthians*. 1857. Grand Rapids: Eerdmans, 1965.

Holladay, Carl. *The First Letter of Paul to the Corinthians*. The Living Word Commentary. Austin: Sweet, 1979.

Kilgallen, John J. *First Corinthians. An Introduction and Study Guide*. New York and Mahweh, N.J.: Paulist, 1987.

Kistemaker, Simon J. *Exposition of the Acts of the Apostles*. New Testament Commentary series. Grand Rapids: Baker, 1990.

Knight, George W., III. *The Pastoral Epistles: A Commentary on the Greek Text*. The New International Greek Testament Commentary series. Grand Rapids: Eerdmans; Carlisle: Paternoster, 1992.

Lang, F. *Die Briefe an die Korinther*. Das Neue Testament Deutsch series 7. Göttingen: Vandenhoeck und Ruprecht, 1986.

Lenski, R. C. H. *The Interpretation of St. Paul's First and Second Epistle to the Corinthians*. 1935. Columbus: Wartburg, 1946.

Lietzmann, Hans. *An die Korinther I, II*. Handbuch zum Neuen Testament. Edited by Werner Georg Kümmel. Tübingen: Mohr, 1969.

Lightfoot, J. B. *Notes on the Epistle of St. Paul from Unpublished Commentaries*. 1895. Grand Rapids: Zondervan, 1957.

MacArthur, John, Jr. *1 Corinthians*. The MacArthur New Testament Commentary series. Chicago: Moody, 1984.

Mare, W. Harold. *1 Corinthians*, in vol. 10 of *The Expositor's Bible Commentary*, edited by Frank E. Gaebelein. 12 vols. Grand Rapids: Zondervan, 1976.

Moffatt, James. *The First Epistle of Paul to the Corinthians*. The Moffatt New Testament Commentary. London: Hodder and Stoughton, 1938.

Morris, Leon. *1 Corinthians*. The Tyndale New Testament Commentaries series. Rev. ed. Leicester: Inter-Varsity; Grand Rapids: Eerdmans, 1987.

616

Select Bibliography

Murphy-O'Connor, Jerome. *1 Corinthians*. New Testament Message series. Wilmington, Del.: Glazier, 1979.

———. "The First Letter to the Corinthians." In *The New Jerome Biblical Commentary*. Englewood Cliffs, N.J.: Prentice Hall, 1990.

Orr, W. F., and J. A. Walther. *I Corinthians*. The Anchor Bible. Vol. 32. Garden City, N.Y.: Doubleday, 1976.

Parry, R. St. John. *The First Epistle of Paul the Apostle to the Corinthians*. Cambridge Greek Testament for Schools and Colleges. Cambridge: Cambridge University Press, 1937.

Prior, David. *The Message of 1 Corinthians: Life in the Local Church*. The Bible Speaks Today series. Leicester and Downers Grove: Inter-Varsity, 1985.

Robertson, Archibald, and Alfred Plummer. *A Critical and Exegetical Commentary on the First Epistle of St. Paul to the Corinthians*. International Critical Commentary series. 2d ed. 1911. Edinburgh: Clark, 1975.

Ruef, John. *Paul's First Letter to Corinth*. Westminster Pelican Commentaries. London: SCM; Philadelphia: Westminster, 1977.

Schlatter, Adolf. *Die Korintherbriefe*. Stuttgart: Calwer Verlag, 1962.

Snyder, Graydon F. *First Corinthians: A Faith Community Commentary*. Macon, Ga.: Mercer University Press, 1992.

Thrall, Margaret E. *The First and Second Letters of Paul to the Corinthians*. Cambridge: Cambridge University Press, 1965.

VanGemeren, Willem A. *Psalms*, in vol. 5 of *The Expositor's Bible Commentary*, edited by Frank E. Gaebelein. 12 vols. Grand Rapids: Zondervan, 1991.

Wendland, H. D. *Die Briefe an die Korinther*. Das Neue Testament Deutsch. Göttingen: Vandenhoeck und Ruprecht, 1968.

Wilson, Geoffrey B. *I Corinthians: A Digest of Reformed Comment*. London: Banner of Truth Trust, 1971.

Wolff, Christian. *Der erste Brief des Paulus an die Korinther*. Zweiter Teil. Theologischer Handkommentar zum Neuen Testament. 2 Aufl. Berlin: Evangelische Verlagsanstalt, 1982.

Studies

Aune, David E. *Prophecy in Early Christianity and the Ancient Mediterranean World*. Grand Rapids: Eerdmans, 1983.

Bacchiocchi, Samuele. *From Sabbath to Sunday: A Historical Investigation of the Rise of Sunday Observance in Early Christianity*. Rome: Pontifical Gregorian University Press, 1977.

Baird, William. *The Corinthian Church, A Biblical Approach to Urban Culture*. New York: Abingdon, 1964.

Barrett, C. K. "Cephas and Corinth," in *Abraham unser Vater: Juden und Christen im Gespräch über die Bibel, Festschrift für Otto Michel zum 60*, edited by Otto Betz, Martin Hengel, and Paul Schmidt. Leiden: Brill, 1963.

———. *Essays on Paul*. Philadelphia: Westminster, 1982.

Bartchy, S. Scott. *ΜΑΛΛΟΝ ΧΡΗΣΑΙ: First-Century Slavery and the Interpretation of 1 Corinthians 7:21*. SBL Dissertation Series 11. Missoula, Mont.: SBL, 1973.

Beare, Frank W. "Speaking with Tongues: A Critical Survey of the New Testament and Evidence." In *Speaking in Tongues: A Guide to Research on Glossolalia*, edited by Watson E. Mills. Grand Rapids: Eerdmans, 1986. Reprinted in *JBL* 83 (1964): 229–46.

Beasley-Murray, G. R. *Baptism in the New Testament*. Grand Rapids: Eerdmans, 1962.

Select Bibliography

Bittlinger, Arnold. *Gifts and Graces: A Commentary on 1 Corinthians 12–14.* Translated by Herbert Klassen and Michael Harper. Grand Rapids: Eerdmans, 1967.

Black, Matthew. *The Scrolls and Christian Origins: Studies in the Jewish Background of the New Testament.* New York: Scribner, 1961.

Burdick, Donald W. "οἶδα and γινώσκω in the Pauline Epistles." In *New Dimensions in New Testament Study*, edited by Richard N. Longenecker and Merrill C. Tenney. Grand Rapids: Zondervan, 1974.

Campolo, Tony. *How to Be Pentecostal without Speaking in Tongues.* Dallas: Word, 1991.

Carr, Wesley. *Angels and Principalities.* Cambridge: Cambridge University Press, 1981.

Carson, D. A. *The Cross and Christian Ministry.* Grand Rapids: Baker, 1993.

————. *Showing the Spirit: A Theological Exposition of 1 Corinthians 12–14.* Grand Rapids: Baker, 1987.

————. "'Silent in the Churches': On the Role of Women in 1 Corinthians 14:33b–36." In *Recovering Biblical Manhood and Womanhood: A Response to Evangelical Feminism*, edited by John Piper and Wayne Grudem. Westchester, Ill.: Crossway, 1991.

Chenderlin, Fritz. *"Do This as My Memorial." The Semantic and Conceptual Background and Value of Anamnēsis in 1 Corinthians 11:24–25.* Analecta Biblica 99. Rome: Biblical Institute Press, 1982.

Chevallier, Max-Alain. *Esprit de Dieu, Paroles d'Hommes.* Neuchâtel: Delachaux, 1966.

Craig, William L. *Assessing the New Testament Evidence for the Historicity of the Resurrection of Jesus.* Studies in the Bible and Early Christianity 16. Lewiston, N.Y.; Queenston, Ont.; Lampeter, U.K.: Mellen, 1989.

Currie, Stuart D. "Koinonia in Christian Literature to 200 A.D." Ph.D. diss., Emory University, 1962.

Davidson, Richard M. *Typology in Scripture: A Study of Hermeneutical ΤΥΠΟΣ Structures.* Andrews University Seminary Doctoral Dissertation series, vol. 2. Berrien Springs, Mich.: Andrews University Press, 1981.

Davis, James A. *Wisdom and Spirit: An Investigation of 1 Corinthians 1.18–3.20 Against the Background of Jewish Sapiential Traditions in the Greco-Roman Period.* Lanham, Md.: University Press of America, 1984.

de Boer, M. C. *The Defeat of Death: Apocalyptic Eschatology in 1 Corinthians 15 and Romans 5.* JSNT Supplement Series 22. Sheffield: JSOT, 1988.

De Boer, Willis P. *The Imitation of Paul: An Exegetical Study.* Kampen: Kok, 1962.

Deissmann, Adolf. *Bible Studies.* Reprint ed. Winona Lake, Ind.: Alpha, 1979.

Derrett, J. D. M. *Law in the New Testament.* London: Darton, Longman and Todd, 1970.

Dodd, C. H. "The Primitive Catechism and the Sayings of Jesus." In *New Testament Essays: Studies in Memory of Thomas Walter Manson*, edited by A. J. B. Higgins. Manchester: Manchester University Press, 1959.

Dungan, David L. *The Sayings of Jesus in the Churches of Paul: The Use of the Synoptic Tradition in the Regulation of Early Church Life.* Philadelphia: Fortress, 1971.

Dunn, James D. G. *Baptism in the Holy Spirit.* SBT second series 15. London: SCM, 1970.

————. "I Corinthians 15:45—last Adam, life-giving spirit." In *Christ and Spirit in the New Testament*, edited by Barnabas Lindars and Stephen S. Smalley. Cambridge: Cambridge University Press, 1973.

————. *Jesus and the Spirit: A Study of the Religious and Charismatic Experience of Jesus and the First Christians as Reflected in the New Testament.* Philadelphia: Westminster, 1975.

Edgar, Thomas R. *Miraculous Gifts: Are They for Today?* Neptune, N.J.: Loizeaux, 1983.

————. *Understanding Spiritual Gifts: The Christian's Special Gifts in the Light of 1 Corinthians 12–14.* Chicago: Moody, 1984.

Ellis, E. Earle. "How the New Testament Uses the Old." In *New Testament Interpretation: Essays on Principles and Methods*, edited by I. Howard Marshall. Grand Rapids: Eerdmans; Exeter: Paternoster, 1977.

————. *Paul's Use of the Old Testament.* Grand Rapids: Eerdmans, 1957.

————. *Prophecy and Hermeneutic in Early Christianity: New Testament Essays.* Grand Rapids: Eerdmans, 1978.

Fee, Gordon D. "Toward a Theology of I Corinthians." In *Society of Biblical Literature 1989 Seminar Papers*, edited by David J. Lull. Atlanta: Scholars, 1989.

Fine, John V. A. *The Ancient Greeks: A Critical History.* Cambridge, Mass., and London: Harvard University Press, 1983.

Furnish, Victor Paul. "Theology in I Corinthians: Initial Soundings." In *Society of Biblical Literature 1989 Seminar Papers*, edited by David J. Lull. Atlanta: Scholars, 1989.

Gaffin, Richard B., Jr. *The Centrality of the Resurrection: A Study in Paul's Soteriology.* Grand Rapids: Baker, 1978.

————. *Perspectives on Pentecost: New Testament Teaching on the Gifts of the Holy Spirit.* Phillipsburg, N.J.: Presbyterian and Reformed, 1979.

————. *Resurrection and Redemption: A Study in Pauline Soteriology.* Philadelphia: Westminster Student Service, 1969.

Gardner, Paul D. "The Gifts of God and the Authentication of a Christian." Ph.D. dissertation, Cambridge University, 1989.

Gasque, W. Ward, and Ralph P. Martin, eds. *Apostolic History and the Gospel.* Grand Rapids: Eerdmans, 1970.

Gentry, Kenneth L., Jr. *The Charismatic Gift of Prophecy.* 2d ed. Memphis: Footstool, 1989.

Georgi, Dieter. *Die Geschichte der Kollecte des Paulus für Jerusalem.* ThF 38. Hamburg: Reich, 1965.

Ginn, Richard J. *The Present and the Past: A Study of Anamnesis.* Allison Park, Penn.: Pickwick Publications, 1989.

Glen, J. Stanley. *Pastoral Problems in First Corinthians.* London: Epworth, 1964.

Green, Michael. *The Empty Cross of Jesus.* The Jesus Library series. Downers Grove: InterVarsity, 1984.

Gross, Edward N. *Miracles, Demons, and Spiritual Warfare: An Urgent Call for Discernment.* Grand Rapids: Baker, 1990.

Grudem, Wayne. *The Gift of Prophecy in 1 Corinthians.* Washington, D.C.: University Press of America, 1982.

————. *The Gift of Prophecy in the New Testament and Today.* Westchester, Ill.: Crossway, 1988.

Gundry, Robert H. *Sōma in Biblical Theology: With Emphasis on Pauline Anthropology.* 1976. Grand Rapids: Zondervan, Academie Books, 1987.

Hall, Barbara. "All Things to All People: A Study of 1 Corinthians 9:19–23." In *The Conversation Continues: Studies in Paul and John. In Honor of J. Louis Martyn*, edited by Robert T. Fortna and Beverly R. Gaventa. Nashville: Abingdon, 1990.

Harris, Murray J. *From Grave to Glory: Resurrection in the New Testament.* Grand Rapids: Zondervan, 1990.

————. *Raised Immortal: Resurrection and Immortality in the New Testament.* Grand Rapids: Eerdmans, 1983.

Select Bibliography

Hasel, Gerhard F. *Speaking in Tongues: Biblical Speaking in Tongues and Contemporary Glosso-lalia.* Berrien Springs, Mich.: Adventist Theological Society Publications, 1991.

Heinemann, Joseph. *Prayer in the Talmud: Forms and Patterns.* Studia Judaica, edited by E. L. Ehrlich, vol 9. Berlin and New York: Walter de Gruyter, 1977.

Hierzenberger, Gottfried. *Weltbewertung bei Paulus nach 1 Kor 7,29–31.* Düsseldorf: Patmos, 1966.

Hill, David. "Christian Prophets as Teachers or Instructors in the Church." In *Prophetic Vocation in the New Testament and Today,* edited by J. Panagopoulos. *Supplements to Novum Testamentum,* vol. 45. Leiden: Brill, 1977.

Hodge, Charles. *An Exposition of the First Epistle to the Corinthians.* 1857. Grand Rapids: Eerdmans, 1965.

Hoekema, Anthony A. *The Bible and the Future.* Grand Rapids: Eerdmans, 1979.

————. *Five Views on Sanctification.* Grand Rapids: Zondervan, Academie Books, 1987.

————. *Saved by Grace.* Grand Rapids: Eerdmans; Exeter: Paternoster, 1989.

————. *Tongues and Spirit-Baptism: A Biblical and Theological Evaluation.* Reprint ed. Grand Rapids: Baker, 1981.

Hoerber, Robert G. *Studies in the New Testament.* Cleveland: Biblion, 1991.

Hurd, John C., Jr. *The Origin of I Corinthians.* Macon, Ga.: Mercer University Press, 1983.

Hurley, James B. *Man and Woman in Biblical Perspective.* Grand Rapids: Zondervan. 1981.

————. "Man and Woman in 1 Corinthians." Ph.D. dissertation, Cambridge University, 1973.

Jeremias, Joachim. *The Eucharistic Words of Jesus.* Translated by Norman Perrin from the German 3d rev. ed. New York: Charles Scribner's Sons, 1966.

————. "'Flesh and Blood Cannot Inherit the Kingdom of God' (I Cor. XV.50)." In *Abba.* Göttingen: Vandenhoeck und Ruprecht, 1966.

Jewett, Robert. *A Chronology of Paul's Life.* Philadelphia: Fortress, 1979.

Jones, David L. "Luke's Unique Interest in Historical Chronology." In *Society of Biblical Literature 1989 Seminar Papers,* edited by David J. Lull. Atlanta: Scholars, 1989.

Kistemaker, Simon J. *The Parables of Jesus.* Grand Rapids: Baker, 1980.

Kloosterman, Nelson D. *Scandalum Infirmorum et Communio Sanctorum: The Relation between Christian Liberty and Neighbor Love in the Church.* Neerlandia, Alberta: Inheritance Publications, 1991.

Knight, George W., III. *Prophecy in the New Testament.* Dallas: Presbyterian Heritage, 1988.

Kuiper, R. B. *The Glorious Body of Christ.* Grand Rapids: Eerdmans, n.d.

Lehmann, Helmut T., ed. *Luther's Works.* 55 vols. *Career of the Reformer: I,* vol. 31. Philadelphia: Muhlenberg, 1957.

Léon-Dufour, Xavier. *Sharing the Eucharistic Bread: The Witness of the New Testament.* Translated by Matthew J. O'Connell. New York and Mahwah, N.J.: Paulist, 1982.

Luck, William F. *Divorce and Remarriage: Recovering the Biblical View.* San Francisco: Harper and Row, 1987.

Luedemann, Gerd. *Paul, Apostle to the Gentiles: Studies in Chronology.* Translated by F. Stanley Jones. Philadelphia: Fortress, 1984.

MacArthur, John, Jr. *Charismatic Chaos.* Grand Rapids: Zondervan, 1992.

MacDonald, William G. "The Place of Glossolalia in Neo-Pentecostalism." In *Speaking in Tongues: Let's Talk about It,* edited by Watson E. Mills. Waco: Word, 1973.

Malherbe, Abraham J. *Social Aspects of Early Christianity.* 2d enl. ed. Philadelphia: Fortress, 1983.

Marshall, I. Howard. *Last Supper and Lord's Supper.* Grand Rapids: Eerdmans, 1980.

Martin, Ralph P. *New Testament Foundations: A Guide for Christian Students.* 2 vols. Grand Rapids: Eerdmans, 1975–78.

———. *2 Corinthians.* Word Biblical Commentary series 40. Waco: Word, 1986.

———. *The Spirit and the Congregation: Studies in 1 Corinthians 12–15.* Grand Rapids: Eerdmans, 1984.

———. *The Worship of God: Some Theological, Pastoral, and Practical Reflections.* Grand Rapids: Eerdmans, 1982.

Marxsen, Willi. *The Resurrection of Jesus of Nazareth.* Philadelphia: Fortress; London: SCM, 1970.

Morris, Leon. *New Testament Theology.* Grand Rapids: Zondervan, Academie Books, 1986.

Murphy-O'Connor, Jerome. *St. Paul's Corinth: Texts and Archaeology.* Good New Studies, vol 6. Wilmington, Del.: Glazier, 1983.

Murray, John. *The Collected Writings of John Murray.* 4 vols. Edinburgh: Banner of Truth, 1976.

Neuer, Werner. *Man and Woman in Christian Perspective.* Translated by Gordon J. Wenham. Westchester, Ill.: Crossway, 1991.

Nickle, Keith F. *The Collection: A Study in Paul's Strategy.* SBT 48. London: SCM; Naperville, Ill.: Allenson, 1966.

O'Brien, Peter T. *Introductory Thanksgivings in the Letters of Paul.* Leiden: Brill, 1977.

Ogg, George. *The Chronology of the Life of Paul.* Epworth: London, 1968.

———. *The Odyssey of Paul.* Old Tappan, N.J.: Revell, 1968.

Oostendorp, Derk W. *Another Jesus: A Gospel of Jewish-Christian Superiority in II Corinthians.* Kampen: Kok, 1967.

Orosius, Paulus. *The Seven Books of History Against the Pagans.* Fathers of the Church series. Translated by Roy J. Deferrari. Washington, D.C.: Catholic University Press, 1964.

Osburn, Carroll D. "The Text of I Corinthians 10:9." In *New Testament Textual Criticism, Its Significance for Exegesis. Essays in Honour of Bruce M. Metzger,* edited by Eldon J. Epp and Gordon D. Fee. Oxford: Clarendon, 1981.

Packer, J. I. *Keep in Step with the Spirit.* Old Tappan, N.J.: Revell, 1984.

Pearson, B. A. *The Pneumatikos-Psychikos Terminology in I Corinthians, A Study in the Theology of the Corinthian Opponents of Paul and Its Relation to Gnosticism.* SBL Dissertation Series 12. Missoula, Mont.: SBL, 1973.

Pierce, Claude A. *Conscience in the New Testament.* London: SCM, 1955.

Plank, K. A. *Paul and the Irony of Affliction.* SBL Semeia Studies. Atlanta: Scholars, 1987.

Ramsay, W. M. *The Letters to the Seven Churches of Asia and Their Place in the Plan of the Apocalypse.* New York: Hodder and Stoughton, n.d.

Reisinger, Ernest C. *What Should We Think of "the Carnal Christian"?* Edinburgh: Banner of Truth Trust, 1978.

Ridderbos, Herman N. *Paul: An Outline of His Theology.* Translated by John Richard de Witt. Grand Rapids: Eerdmans, 1975.

Rordorf, Willy. "The *Didache.*" In *The Eucharist of the Early Christians.* Translated by Matthew J. O'Connell. New York. Pueblo, 1978.

———. *Sunday: The History of the Day of Rest and Worship in the Earliest Centuries of the Christian Church.* Translated by A. A. K. Graham. London: SCM; Philadelphia: Westminster, 1968.

Ryle, J. C. *Holiness: Its Nature, Hindrances, Difficulties, and Roots.* Reprint ed. London: Clarke, 1956.

Schep, John A. *The Nature of the Resurrection Body.* Grand Rapids: Eerdmans, 1964.

Schmithals, Walter. *Gnosticism in Corinth: An Investigation of the Letters to the Corinthians.* Translated by John E. Steeley. New York: Abingdon, 1971.

Schreiner, Thomas R. "Head Coverings, Prophecies and the Trinity." In *Recovering Biblical Manhood and Womanhood: A Response to Evangelical Feminism,* edited by John Piper and Wayne Grudem. Westchester, Ill.: Crossway, 1991.

Smallwood, E. M. *The Jews under Roman Rule.* Leiden: Brill, 1976.

Sweetman, Leonard, Jr. "The Gifts of the Spirit: A Study of Calvin's Comments on I Corinthians 12:8–10; 28; Romans 12:6–8; Ephesians 4:11." In *Exploring the Heritage of John Calvin,* edited by David E. Holwerda. Grand Rapids: Baker, 1976.

Theissen, Gerd. *The Social Setting of Pauline Christianity: Essays on Corinth.* Edited and translated by John H. Schütz. Philadelphia: Fortress, 1982.

Thomas, Robert L. *Understanding Spiritual Gifts: The Christian's Special Gifts in the Light of 1 Corinthians 12–14.* Chicago: Moody, 1978.

Turner, Max. "The Sabbath, Sunday, and the Law in Luke/Acts." In *From Sabbath to Lord's Day: A Biblical, Historical, and Theological Investigation,* edited by D. A. Carson. Grand Rapids: Zondervan, 1982.

VanGemeren, Willem A. *Interpreting the Prophetic Word.* Grand Rapids: Zondervan, Academie Books, 1990.

Vischer, Lukas. *Die Auslegungsgeschichte von I. Kor.6, 1–11, Rechtsverzicht und Schlichtung.* Beiträge zur Geschichte der Neutestamentlichen Exegese series. Tübingen: Mohr [Siebeck], 1955.

Vos, Geerhardus. *The Pauline Eschatology.* 1930. Phillipsburg, N.J.: Presbyterian and Reformed, 1986.

Warfield, B. B. *Counterfeit Miracles.* Reprint ed. Edinburgh: Banner of Truth, 1986.

Wedderburn, A. J. M. *Baptism and Resurrection: Studies in Pauline Theology against Its Graeco-Roman Background.* WUNT 44. Tübingen: Mohr-Siebeck, 1987.

Westerholm, Stephen. *Israel's Law and the Church's Faith: Paul and His Recent Interpreters.* Grand Rapids: Eerdmans, 1988.

Wilcke, Hans-Alwin, *Das Problem eines messianischen Zwischenreichs bei Paulus.* ATANT 51. Zürich und Stuttgart: Zwingli Verlag, 1967.

Wilckens, U. *Weisheit und Torheit.* Tübingen: Mohr-Siebeck, 1959.

Williams, J. Rodman. *The Pentecostal Reality.* Plainfield, N.J.: Logos International, 1972.

Willis, Wendell Lee. *Idol Meat in Corinth, The Pauline Argument in 1 Corinthians 8 and 10.* SBL Dissertation Series 68. Chico, Calif.: Scholars, 1981.

Winter, Bruce W. "Are Philo and Paul Among the Sophists? A Hellenistic Jewish and a Christian Response to a First Century Movement." Ph.D. dissertation, Macquarie University, 1988.

Wischmeyer, Oda. *Der Höchste Weg. Das 13 Kapitel des 1. Korintherbriefes.* Gütersloh: Gütersloher Verlagshaus Gerd Mohn, 1981.

Yarbrough, O. Larry. *Not Like the Gentiles: Marriage Rules in the Letters of Paul.* SBL Dissertation Series 80. Atlanta: Scholars, 1985.

Zorn, Raymond O. *Church and Kingdom.* Philadelphia: Presbyterian and Reformed, 1962.

Zuntz, G. *The Text of the Epistles: A Disquisition upon the Corpus Paulinum.* London: Oxford University Press, 1953.

Select Bibliography

Tools

Aland, Kurt, and Barbara Aland. *The Text of the New Testament.* Translated by Erroll F. Rhodes. Grand Rapids: Eerdmans; Leiden: Brill, 1987.

Balz, Horst, and Gerhard Schneider, eds. *Exegetical Dictionary of the New Testament.* 3 vols. Grand Rapids: Eerdmans, 1990–93.

Bauer, Walter. *A Greek-English Lexicon of the New Testament and Other Early Christian Literature.* 2d rev. and augmented ed. by F. Wilbur Gingrich and Frederick W. Danker from Walter Bauer's fourth ed. Chicago and London: University of Chicago Press, 1979.

Blass, Friedrich, and Albert Debrunner. *A Greek Grammar of the New Testament and Other Early Christian Literature.* Translated and revised by Robert Funk. Chicago: University of Chicago Press, 1961.

Bromiley, Geoffrey W., ed. *The International Standard Bible Encyclopedia.* 4 vols. Rev. ed. Grand Rapids: Eerdmans, 1979–88.

Brown, Colin, ed. *New International Dictionary of New Testament Theology.* 3 vols. Grand Rapids: Zondervan; Exeter: Paternoster, 1975–78.

Burton, E. D. *Moods and Tenses of New Testament Greek.* Edinburgh: Clark, 1898.

Calvin, John. *Institutes of the Christian Religion.* Translated by Henry Beveridge. 8th American ed. 2 vols. Grand Rapids: Eerdmans, 1949.

Charlesworth, James H., ed. *The Old Testament Pseudepigrapha.* 2 vols. Garden City, N.Y.: Doubleday, 1983.

Dana, H. E., and Julius R. Mantey. *A Manual Grammar of the Greek New Testament.* 1927. New York: Macmillan, 1967.

Elwell, Walter A., ed. *Evangelical Dictionary of Theology.* Grand Rapids: Baker, 1984.

———, ed. *Baker Encyclopedia of the Bible.* 2 vols. Grand Rapids: Baker, 1988.

Epstein, Isidore, ed. *The Babylonian Talmud:* Seder Nezikin, 4 vols. London: Soncino, 1935.

Eusebius. *Ecclesiastical History.* Translated by Kirsopp Lake and J. E. L. Oulton. 2 vols. Loeb Classical Library series. Cambridge: Harvard University Press, 1980.

Farstad, Arthur R., and Zane C. Hodges. *The Greek New Testament According to the Majority Text.* Nashville: Nelson, 1982.

Funk, Robert W. *Language, Hermeneutic, and Word of God: The Problem of Language in the New Testament and Contemporary Theology.* New York, Evanston, and London: Harper and Row, 1966.

Goold, E. P., ed. *The Apostolic Fathers.* Translated by Kirsopp Lake. 2 vols. Loeb Classical Library series. Cambridge: Harvard University Press; London: Heinemann, 1976.

Guthrie, Donald. *New Testament Theology.* Downers Grove: Inter-Varsity, 1981.

———. *New Testament Introduction.* 3d ed. Downers Grove: Inter-Varsity, 1971.

Hanna, Robert. *A Grammatical Aid to the Greek New Testament.* Grand Rapids: Baker, 1983.

Hennecke, Edgar. *New Testament Apocrypha.* Edited by Wilhelm Schneemelcher. Translated by R. McL. Wilson. 2 vols. Philadelphia: Westminster, 1963–64.

Henry, Carl F. H., ed. *Baker's Dictionary of Christian Ethics.* Grand Rapids: Baker, 1973.

Josephus, Flavius. *Antiquities.* Loeb Classical Library series. London: Heinemann; New York: Putnam, 1966–76.

———. *Life* and *Against Apion.* Loeb Classical Library series. London: Heinemann; New York: Putnam, 1966–76.

———. *Wars of the Jews.* Loeb Classical Library series. London: Heinemann; New York: Putnam, 1966–76.

Select Bibliography

Kittel, Gerhard, and Gerhard Friedrich, eds. *Theological Dictionary of the New Testament.* Translated by Geoffrey W. Bromiley. 10 vols. Grand Rapids: Eerdmans, 1964–76.

Ladd, George E. *A Theology of the New Testament.* Grand Rapids: Eerdmans, 1974.

Metzger, Bruce M. *A Textual Commentary on the Greek New Testament.* 3d corrected ed. London and New York: United Bible Societies, 1975.

Morris, Leon. *New Testament Theology.* Grand Rapids: Zondervan, Academie Books, 1986.

Moule, C. F. D. *An Idiom-Book of New Testament Greek.* 2d ed. Cambridge: Cambridge University Press, 1960.

Moulton, James Hope, and Wilbert Francis Howard. *A Grammar of New Testament Greek.* Vol. 2, *Accidence and Word-Formation.* Edinburgh: Clark, 1929.

Nestle, E., and Kurt Aland. *Novum Testamentum Graece.* 26th ed. Stuttgart: Deutsche Bibelstiftung, 1981.

Roberts, Alexander, and James Donaldson, eds. *The Ante-Nicene Fathers.* Translations of Writings of the Fathers down to A.D. 325. 14 vols. Grand Rapids: Eerdmans, 1899–1900.

Robertson, A. T. *A Grammar of the Greek New Testament in the Light of Historical Research.* Nashville: Broadman, 1934.

Roth, Cecil, ed. *Encyclopedia Judaica.* 16 vols. New York: Macmillan, 1972.

Stauffer, Ethelbert. *New Testament Theology.* London: SCM, 1955.

Strack, H. L., and P. Billerbeck. *Kommentar zum Neuen Testament aus Talmud und Midrasch.* 5 vols. Munich: Beck, 1922–28.

Tenney, Merrill C., ed. *The Zondervan Pictorial Encyclopedia of the Bible.* 5 vols. Grand Rapids: Zondervan, 1975.

Thayer, Joseph H. *A Greek-English Lexicon of the New Testament.* New York, Cincinnati, and Chicago: American Book Co., 1889.

Trench, R. C. *Synonyms of the New Testament.* Edited by Robert G. Hoerber. Grand Rapids: Baker, 1989.

————. *A Grammar of New Testament Greek.* Vol 3. Edinburgh: Clark, 1963.

Turner, Nigel. *Grammatical Insights into the New Testament.* Edinburgh: Clark, 1965.

Index of Authors

Index of Scripture

Index of Scripture

Index of Scripture

9:11—38
10:1—44
10:1–11—285
10:5—39 n. 18
10:7—47
10:9–10—148
10:10—15, 47, 74,
168, 284
10:12—90
10:15—337
10:17—63 n. 78, 65
10:18—391
11:1—130
11:3—123 n. 57
11:6—15, 39 n. 18, 47
11:7—302, 518
11:9—295
11:10—300
11:12—63 n. 78
11:14—425
11:18—63 n. 78
11:19—139
11:23–25—314
11:23–27—140
11:23–28—74, 288
11:23–29—456, 538n,
561, 562
12:1—484
12:1–6—496
12:2–4—480
12:4—453
12:5—140
12:7—74, 161, 484
12:9—60, 140, 423,
436
12:10—140, 456
12:11–21—285
12:12—424
12:13—295 n. 26,
384 n. 53
12:14—299,
581 n. 125
12:20—46 n. 38, 102
13:1—6
13:1–10—285
13:4—49 n. 45, 60,
140, 196
13:5–6—401
13:5–7—316
13:7—391
13:12—610 n. 35
13:14—344
15:24—17

Galatians

1:1—34, 34 n. 3, 285,
414, 526
1:2—384 n. 53
1:3—36 n. 10
1:4—529
1:6–7—285
1:9—611
1:10—301
1:11—526 n. 2
1:12—285, 528
1:13—537
1:14—487
1:15—34, 534, 537
1:15–16—285, 302
1:16—51, 534 n. 25,
581 n. 123
1:18—9 n. 19, 47, 393,
531 n. 17
1:18–19—8, 220, 526
1:19—533
1:20—581 n. 125
1:21—8
1:22—64 n. 79,
384 n. 53
1:22–23—285
2:1—9, 526
2:1–2—536
2:1–13—289
2:2—313 n. 74, 484
2:4—306
2:7—47, 531 n. 17
2:7–8—534 n. 25
2:7–9—306
2:8—47, 531 n. 17
2:8–9—536
2:9—47, 109,
531 n. 17, 533
2:9–10—594
2:11—47, 531 n. 17
2:11–14—262, 276,
307
2:11–16—284
2:14—47, 531 n. 17
2:16—131
2:19–20—122 n. 55
3:1—49 n. 45
3:13—59
3:15—489
3:27—323, 431
3:27–28—431
3:28—231 n. 57, 310,
369, 375, 376, 379
3:29—123
4:6—89, 611

4:6–7—203
4:9—264
4:12—145
4:13–14—74
4:15—74
4:17—138
4:19—144
4:21–31—326
4:24—326
5:1—235, 306, 337,
605 n. 26
5:1–6—371
5:2—231
5:5—40
5:5–6—470 n. 53
5:6—64 n. 79,
231 n. 57
5:7—313 n. 74
5:9—164
5:10—285
5:11—59, 61
5:13—273, 305, 306,
357, 436
5:15—66 n. 86
5:19–21—149
5:20—46 n. 38, 102,
169, 170 n. 33
5:21—149 n. 53
5:22—458
5:22–23—431, 446
5:24—49 n. 45
6:2—308
6:3—136, 263
6:6—298
6:7—119 n. 47,
188 n. 26, 563 n. 88
6:10—594
6:11—74, 611
6:14—49 n. 45, 73,
300
6:15—231 n. 57

Ephesians

1:1—34 nn. 3–4
1:2—36 n. 10, 268n
1:5–6—471
1:7—38
1:13—64 n. 79
1:18—65
1:21—552 n. 70
1:22—366 n. 11, 367,
555
1:22–23—159, 429
1:23—440
2:1—92

2:3—228
2:4—38
2:5—54
2:8—54
2:8–9—188
2:11–13—103 n. 10
2:19–22—108
2:20—109, 110, 442,
479
2:21—116, 116 n. 44
2:22—109
3:2—109
3:3—82
3:4—129 n. 4
3:5—442, 484
3:7—105
3:7–8—109, 537
3:8—38, 130, 536
3:8–9—302
3:10—552 n. 70
3:17–19—82
4:1—61
4:2–5—470 n. 53
4:8—418
4:11—424, 441, 442,
443, 479
4:12—420
4:13—80 n. 15,
467 n. 45
4:15—366, 366 n. 11,
367
4:21—285
4:26—460
4:29—109
4:30—117, 161, 202,
517, 574
5:2—529
5:3–5—245
5:5—17 n. 33, 149,
149 n. 53, 169, 170
5:11—132, 214
5:13—502
5:14—494n
5:19—492
5:20—37 n. 14
5:21—607
5:21–33—200
5:22—216, 249, 515
5:22–23—367
5:22–33—209
5:23—212, 323, 342,
366, 366 n. 11, 367
5:24—216
5:27—35, 117
5:28—216